W9-DIT-554

CRITICAL SURVEY
OF
LONG FICTION

CRITICAL SURVEY
OF
LONG FICTION

English Language Series

REVISED EDITION

Say-Wau

7

Edited by
FRANK N. MAGILL

SALEM PRESS

Pasadena, California   Englewood Cliffs, New Jersey

REF
PR
821
.C7
1991
v. 7

Copyright © 1991 by SALEM PRESS, INC.
All rights in this book are reserved. No part of this work
may be used or reproduced in any manner whatsoever or
transmitted in any form or by any means, electronic or
mechanical, including photocopy, recording, or any information storage and retrieval system, without written
permission from the copyright owner except in the case
of brief quotations embodied in critical articles and reviews. For information address the publisher, Salem
Press, Inc., P. O. Box 50062, Pasadena, California 91105.

∞ The paper used in these volumes conforms to the
American National Standard for Permanence of Paper
for Printed Library Materials, Z39.48-1984.

Library of Congress Cataloging-in-Publication Data
Critical survey of long fiction. English language series/
  edited by Frank N. Magill. — Rev. ed.
     p.   cm.
  Includes bibliographical references and index.
    1. English fiction—Dictionaries. 2. American
fiction—Dictionaries. 3. English fiction—
Bio-bibliography. 4. American fiction—
Bio-bibliography. 5. Novelists, English—
Biography—Dictionaries. 6. Novelists, American—
Biography—Dictionaries.
I. Magill, Frank Northen, 1907-
PR821.C7   1991
823.009′03—dc20   91-19694
ISBN 0-89356-832-5 (volume 7)   CIP

PRINTED IN THE UNITED STATES OF AMERICA

LIST OF AUTHORS IN VOLUME 7

CRITICAL SURVEY
OF
LONG FICTION

DOROTHY L. SAYERS

Born: Oxford, England; June 13, 1893
Died: Witham, England; December 17, 1957

Principal long fiction

Whose Body?, 1923; *Clouds of Witness*, 1926; *Unnatural Death*, 1927 (also as *The Dawson Pedigree*); *Lord Peter Views the Body*, 1928; *The Unpleasantness at the Bellona Club*, 1928; *The Documents in the Case*, 1930 (with Robert Eustace); *Strong Poison*, 1930; *The Five Red Herrings*, 1931 (also known as *Suspicious Characters*); *The Floating Admiral*, 1931 (with others); *Have His Carcase*, 1932; *Ask a Policeman*, 1933 (with others); *Murder Must Advertise*, 1933; *The Nine Tailors*, 1934; *Gaudy Night*, 1935; *Six Against the Yard*, 1936 (with others; also as *Six Against Scotland Yard*); *Busman's Honeymoon*, 1937; *Double Death: A Murder Story*, 1939 (with others); *The Scoop, and Behind the Scenes*, 1983 (with others); *Crime on the Coast, and No Flowers by Request*, 1984 (with others).

Other literary forms

In addition to the twelve detective novels that brought her fame, Dorothy L. Sayers wrote short stories, poetry, essays, and plays, and distinguished herself as a translator and scholar of medieval French and Italian literature. Although she began her career as a poet, with Basil Blackwell bringing out collections of her verse in 1916 and 1918, Sayers primarily wrote fiction from 1920 until the late 1930's, after which she focused on radio and stage plays and a verse translation of Dante. She also edited a landmark anthology of detective fiction, *Great Short Stories of Detection, Mystery, and Horror* (1928-1934).

Outside of her fiction, the essence of Sayers' mind and art can be found in *The Mind of the Maker* (1941), a treatise on aesthetics that is one of the most illuminating inquiries into the creative process ever written; in her essays on Dante; and in two religious dramas, *The Zeal of Thy House* (1937), a verse play written for the Canterbury Festival that dramatizes Sayers' attitude toward work, and *The Man Born to Be King*, a monumental series of radio plays first broadcast amidst controversy in 1941-1942, which takes up what Sayers regarded as the most exciting of mysteries: the drama of Christ's life and death, the drama in which God is both victim and hero. Of her many essays, the 1946 collection *Unpopular Opinions* and the 1947 *Creed or Chaos?* provide a good sampling of the acumen, wit, and originality with which Sayers attacked a variety of subjects, including religion, feminism, and learning.

In 1972, James Sandoe edited *Lord Peter*, a collection of all the Wimsey stories. Two other collections, both published during Sayers' lifetime (*Hangman's Holiday*, 1933, and *In the Teeth of the Evidence*, 1939), include non-

Wimsey stories. At her death, Sayers left unfinished her translation of Dante's *Cantica III: Paradise*, which was completed by her friend and colleague Barbara Reynolds and published posthumously in 1962 as the final volume in the Penguin Classics edition of Dante that Sayers had begun in 1944. An unpublished fragment of an additional novel, called *Thrones, Dominations* and apparently abandoned by Sayers in the 1940's, was also left unfinished, as was her projected critical/biographical study of Wilkie Collins. This last fragment was published in 1977. From 1973-1977, the British Broadcasting Corporation (BBC) produced excellent adaptations of five of the Wimsey novels for television, thus creating a new audience for Sayers' work.

Achievements

One of the chief pleasures for readers of Dorothy Sayers is the companionship of one of fiction's great creations, Lord Peter Wimsey, that extraordinarily English gentleman, cosmopolite, detective/scholar. Although the Wimsey novels were created primarily to make money, his characterization demonstrates that his creator was a serious, skillful writer. As the novels follow Wimsey elegantly through murder, mayhem, and madness, he grows from an enchanting caricature into a fully realized human being. The solver of mysteries thus becomes increasingly enigmatic himself. Wimsey's growth parallels Sayers' artistic development, which is appropriate, since she announced that her books were to be more like mainstream novels than the cardboard world of ordinary detective fiction.

Lord Peter is something of a descendant of P. G. Wodehouse's Bertie Wooster, and at times he emulates Conan Doyle's Sherlock Holmes, but in Wimsey, Sayers essentially created an original. Sayers' novels integrate elements of earlier detective fiction—especially the grasp of psychological torment typified by Joseph Sheridan Le Fanu and the fine delineation of manners exemplified in Wilkie Collins—with subjects one would expect from a medieval scholar: virtue, corruption, justice, punishment, suffering, redemption, time, and death. The hallmarks of her art—erudition, wit, precision, and moral passion—provoke admiration in some readers and dislike in others.

Sayers' novels are filled with wordplay that irritates those who cannot decipher it and delights those who can. Her names are wonderful puns (Wimsey, Vane, Freke, de Vine, Snoot, Venables), her dialogue is embedded with literary allusions and double entendres in English, French, and Latin, and her plots are spun from biblical texts and English poetry. Reading a Sayers novel, then, is both a formidable challenge and an endless reward. Hers are among the few detective novels that not only bear rereading, but actually demand it, and Sayers enjoys a readership spanning several generations. To know Sayers' novels is to know her time and place as well as this brilliant, eccentric, and ebullient artist could make them known. Because of her exquisite language, her skill at delineating character, and her fundamentally serious mind, Sayers' detective fiction also largely transcends the limits of its time and genre. Certainly this is true of novels such as *Strong Poison*, *The Nine Tailors*, *Gaudy Night*, and *Busman's Honeymoon*, books which did much toward making the detective novel part of serious English fiction.

Biography

Dorothy Leigh Sayers was born on June 13, 1893, in the Choir House of Christ Church College, Oxford, where her father, the Reverend Henry Sayers, was Headmaster. Mr. Sayers' family came from County Tipperary, Ireland; his wife, the former Helen Mary Leigh, was a member of the old landed English family that also produced Percival Leigh, a noted contributor to the humor magazine, *Punch*. Sayers' biographer, James Brabazon, postulates that her preference for the Leigh side of the family caused her to insist upon including her middle initial in her name; whatever the reason, the writer wished to be known as Dorothy L. Sayers.

When Sayers was four, her father left Oxford to accept the living of Bluntisham-cum-Earith in Huntingdonshire, on the southern edge of the Fens, those bleak expanses of drained marshland in eastern England. The contrast between Oxford and the rectory at Bluntisham was great, especially as the new home isolated the family and its only child. Sayers' fine education in Latin, English, French, history, and mathematics was conducted at the rectory until she was almost sixteen, when she was sent to study at the Godolphin School, Salisbury, where she seems to have been quite unhappy. Several of her happiest years followed this experience, however, when she won the Gilchrist Scholarship in Modern Languages and went up to Somerville College, Oxford, in 1912. At Somerville, Sayers enjoyed the congenial company of other extraordinary women and men and made some lasting friends, including Muriel St. Clare Byrne. Although women were not granted Oxford degrees during Sayers' time at Somerville, the University's statutes were changed in 1920, and Sayers was among the first group of women to receive Oxford degrees in that year (she had taken first honors in her examination in 1915).

Following her undergraduate days, Sayers did various kinds of work for several years: first, as poetry editor for Blackwell's in Oxford from 1916 to 1918, then as a schoolmistress in France in 1919, and finally in London, where she worked as a free-lance editor and as an advertising copywriter for Benson's, England's largest advertising agency. At Benson's, Sayers helped create "The Mustard Club," a phenomenally successful campaign for Colman's mustard. Around 1920, when Sayers' mind was focused not only upon finding suitable employment but also upon surviving economically, the character of Lord Peter Wimsey was miraculously born, and Sayers' first novel, *Whose Body?*, introduced him to the world in 1923.

These early years in London were scarred by two bitterly disappointing love affairs, one of which left Sayers with a child, born in 1924. The novelist married Oswald Atherton Fleming, a Scottish journalist, in 1926, and shortly thereafter assumed financial responsibility for him as he became ill and ceased working several years after their marriage. Perhaps these pressures encouraged Sayers to keep turning out the increasingly successful Wimsey novels.

By the end of the 1930's, however, Sayers was in a position to "finish Lord Peter off" by marrying him to Harriet Vane, the detective novelist who first appeared in *Strong Poison* and who, like Wimsey, reflected part of Sayers' personality. After the Wimsey novels, Sayers was free to do the kind of writing she had always wanted to do: manifestly serious work such as religious dramas and a translation of Dante that would occupy most of her time from 1944 to 1957. While working on these demanding projects and writing incisive essays on a wide range of issues, Sayers also became something of a public figure, playing the role of social critic and Christian apologist with great brilliance and panache.

On December 17, 1957, Sayers died of an apparent stroke while alone in the house that she had shared with Fleming from 1928 until his death in 1950. Although she left an unpublished autobiographical fragment, "My Edwardian Childhood," much of Sayers' life is reflected in her novels, which depict the Oxford of her college days (*Gaudy Night*), the Fen wastes of her girlhood (*The Nine Tailors*), and the excitement and confusion of the London she knew as a young writer (*Murder Must Advertise*). Excellent though much of her other work is, Sayers will probably be remembered primarily for her novels.

Analysis

If one should wish to know England as it was between the two world wars—how it was in its customs, among its different classes and in its different regions, how it regarded itself and the world, what weaknesses festered, what strengths endured—there is no better place to learn its soul or to revel in its singular delights and peccadilloes than in the novels of Dorothy L. Sayers. When Harriet Vane marries Peter Wimsey in *Busman's Honeymoon*, she happily realizes that she has "married England," revealing that Sayers herself recognized the symbolic import of her hero. As a survivor of World War I, a war that decimated a generation of young Englishmen and left their society reeling, Wimsey represents England's fragile link with a glorious past and its tenuous hold on the difficult present. His bouts of "nerves" and persistent nightmares dramatize the lasting effects of this "War to End All Wars," while his noble attempts at making a meaningful life represent the difficult task of re-creating life from the rubble.

Sayers' England encompasses tiny villages unchanged for centuries (*Busman's Honeymoon*), the golden-spired colleges of Oxford (*Gaudy Night*), the "gloom and gleam" of London (*Murder Must Advertise*), the deceptive calm of the southern seacoast (*Have His Carcase*), the brooding Fens (*The Nine*

Tailors), and the primitive north counties (*Clouds of Witness*). The novelist ranges throughout this varied landscape with some constants: accompanied by his indefatigable "man," Bunter (who is Jeeves transformed), Lord Peter reasons his way through all but one mystery (he is absent from *The Documents in the Case*). Through Wimsey's well-wrought consciousness, Sayers maintains a certain *Weltanschauung* that seems a peculiar blend of mathematical rigor and lush, witty, insightful language.

Carolyn Heilbrun's praise for Sayers' special blend of "murder and manners" points out to an understanding of both the novelist's appeal and her place in English fiction: Sayers is an inheritor not only of the more literary branch of detective fiction, but also of the older comedy-of-manners tradition. She can reveal a character, time, or place in a bit of dialogue or one remark. From a brief sentence, for example, the reader knows the Duchess of Denver: "She was a long-necked, long-backed woman, who disciplined herself and her children." A short speech summarizes all *The Unpleasantness at the Bellona Club*, revealing not only a character but also the values and condition of his world:

> Look at all the disturbance there has been lately. Police and reporters—and then Penberthy blowing his brains out in the library. And the coal's all slate. . . . These things never happened before the War—and great heavens! William! Look at this wine! . . . Corked? Yes, I should think it *was* corked! My God! I don't know what's come to this club!

The character upon whom Sayers lavishes most of her considerable talent is Lord Peter. Although it is possible, as some of her critics have said, that Sayers created Wimsey, the perfect mate for an intellectual woman, because actual men had disappointed her, the psychobiographical approach can explain only part of her novels' motivation or meaning. In Wimsey, Sayers dramatizes some significant human problems, including the predicament of the "Lost Generation," the necessity of every person's having a "proper job," and the imperative synthesis of forces that are often perceived as opposites, but which are really complementary: intellect and emotion, good and evil, male and female. When viewed in these terms, Sayers' fictional world fits naturally into the entire cosmos of her creation, because it deals with some of the very subjects she addressed in other, more patently serious forms.

It is appropriate to speak of all Sayers' work as one, for, as she concludes in *The Mind of the Maker*, "the sum of all the work is related to the mind [of the artist] itself, which made it, controls it, and relates it to its own creative personality." From beginning to end, Sayers' work investigates the possibility of creative action; for her the creative act consists of establishing equilibrium among competing powers, of drawing together disparate, even warring elements. Of course, since she writes detective novels, Sayers focuses upon the opposite of creative action in the crimes of her villains, crimes that destroy life, property, sanity, peace. Wimsey, who solves the mysteries and thereby makes a life from destruction, is the creative actor.

The Mind of the Maker argues that there is a discoverable moral law, higher than any other, that governs the universe. In a way, Sayers' novels attempt to discover or reveal this universal moral law, which in its most superficial form is reflected in civil codes. This process of moral discovery, however, becomes increasingly complex and ambiguous; if Sayers' subjects are constant, her understanding of them deepens as her art matures. Since Sayers' artistic maturation parallels her hero's development, a comparison of how Wimsey functions in the early and late novels will elucidate both the consistency and the change that mark Sayers' fiction.

The most striking quality of *Whose Body?* as a first novel is the deftness with which it presents Sayers' hero and his world. In its opening pages, the reader gets to know Lord Peter Wimsey, the dashing man-about-town and collector of rare books (which, amazingly, he seems to read). Keen of mind and quick of tongue, like an exotic bird chirping in a formal English garden that, perhaps, conceals a jolly corpse or two, he is a remarkable personage at birth. Wimsey is also quite marvelously a wealthy man who knows how to spend both his time and his money; his elegant apartment's only acknowledged lack is a harpsichord for his accomplished renditions of Domenico Scarlatti. The product of an older England marked by civility, restraint, and order, Wimsey is accompanied in his first tale by two challengers to his wits and position: his valet, Bunter, and the middle-class Inspector Parker of Scotland Yard, who will make sure that Wimsey never nods during fourteen years of fictional sleuthing. Even his mother, the delightfully balmy Duchess of Denver, is introduced here, and the reader quickly guesses from their relationship that Sayers is interested in how men and women coexist in this world. The Dowager Duchess and her son are as different in appearance as they are similar in character, the narrator remarks, thus signaling that the superficial differences between men and women often conceal more important similarities. Wimsey and his entourage enter the world nearly complete, and their creator has a firm grasp of character, dialogue, and the mystery plot from the beginning of her career.

The theme of *Whose Body?* plants the seeds of one of Sayers' ever-flourishing ideas. Her first and perhaps most horrid villain, Sir Julian Freke, suffers from one of the great problems facing modern man: the disassociation from mind and heart that often renders "civilized" people incapable of moral behavior. The great surgeon Freke, who is aptly named because he is a freakish half-human, denies the importance of intangibles such as the conscience, which he considers akin to the vermiform appendix. With this perfectly criminal attitude, Freke coolly kills and dissects an old competitor, ironically from one of the oldest, least rational of motives, jealousy and revenge. Freke therefore demonstrates Sayers' point: that man, as a creature of both intellect and passion, must struggle to understand and balance both if moral action is to be possible. Freke, the dissector of life, destroys; the destruction he causes awaits the truly healing powers of a creative mind.

The somewhat surprising link between moral action and detective work is suggested by Wimsey, who observes that anyone can get away with murder by keeping people from "associatin' their ideas," adding that people usually do not connect the parts of their experience. The good detective, however, must study the fragments of human life and synthesize the relevant data. This synthesis, the product of imagination and feeling as well as reason, reveals not only "who did it," but how, and why. Thus, according to Sayers' own definitions, her detective pursues moral action in his very sleuthing, not only in its final effects of punishment for the criminal and retribution for society. Wimsey's detective method typifies this creative synthesis by incorporating different aspects of a rich experience: poetry, science, history, psychology, haberdashery, weather reports. When Wimsey finally realizes that Freke is the murderer, he remembers "not one thing, nor another thing, nor a logical succession of things, but everything—the whole thing, perfect and complete . . . as if he stood outside the world and saw it suspended in infinitely dimensional space." In this moment, Wimsey is not merely a successful detective, he is a creator, his mind flashing with godlike insight into human life. The story has moved, therefore, from destruction to creation because disparate aspects of life have been drawn together.

Freke's failure as a human being is exemplified in his failure as a physician, just as Wimsey's successful life is instanced in the skillful performance of his "job," his compulsive "hobby of sleuthing." More than a hobby, detection is actually Wimsey's "proper job." In a crucial discussion with Inspector Parker, Wimsey admits to feeling guilty about doing detective work for fun, but the perceptive Parker warns him that, as a basically responsible person for whom life is really more than a game, he will eventually have to come to terms with the seriousness of his actions. What is clear to the reader at this point is that Wimsey, an English aristocrat displaced by social change and scarred by World War I, is at least carving out a life that is socially useful while it is personally gratifying. He is not simply feeding the Duke of Denver's peacocks.

If Wimsey seems almost too perfect in the early novels, Sayers redeems him from that state by slowly revealing the finite, flawed, and very human man within the sparkling exterior. To make this revelation, she has to create a woman capable of challenging him, which she does in the character of Harriet Vane. By the time he appears in *The Nine Tailors*, Wimsey is less of a god and more of a human being. After all, the great lover has been humiliatingly unsuccessful in wooing Harriet Vane, whom he saved from the hangman four years earlier in *Strong Poison*. The beginning of *The Nine Tailors* finds Wimsey, the super-sleuth, wandering about the Fens, that bleak terrain of Sayers' childhood, muttering about the misery of having one's car break down on a wintery evening and dreaming of hot muffins. When offered shelter at the rectory of Fenchurch St. Paul, the great connoisseur of haute cuisine is delighted with tea and oxtail stew. The greatest change in Wimsey's character and in Sayers' fiction, however, is evidenced in the novel's richer, more subtle structure, and in its newly complex view of crime and punishment, of good and evil.

Indicative of Sayers' increasing subtlety, *The Nine Tailors* is as much a metaphysical meditation on time and change as it is a murder mystery; there is not even a corpse until Part II. In place of Lord Peter's jolly but rather macabre singing of "We insist upon a [dead] body in a bath" (in *Whose Body?*), *The Nine Tailors* resonates with the sound of church bells and an explication of campanology (bell or change-ringing). The bells at Fenchurch St. Paul, which are rung for both weddings and funerals, seem ambiguously to stand for both life and death, good and evil. The whole question of good versus evil is quite complicted here, for unlike the wholly innocent victim of the cold-blooded murder in *Whose Body?*, the man killed here is probably the worst person in the book, and he is accidentally killed by the ringing of holy bells. Locked in the church's bell chamber as a precaution by someone who knows of his criminal past, Geoffrey Deacon is killed by the intense sound of the bells, and ultimately by the hands of every man who unwittingly pulls a bell rope that New Year's Eve. This group includes Wimsey, who just happens to be there because of several coincidences.

Although Deacon perhaps deserves to die, not only for his jewel robbery but also because of a generally dishonorable life, his death forces Wimsey to reexamine himself and his motives. In ringing the changes, Wimsey thought he was simply following a set of mathematical permutations to a neat conclusion; in reality, he was taking a man's life. This greatly sobers the old puzzle-solver, who has always had some qualms about attacking life as a game. Indeed, Wimsey's role in Deacon's death is but an exaggerated version of the detective's role in any mystery: he causes the villain or criminal to come to justice, which usually means death. Wimsey cannot ignore the consequences of his actions in *The Nine Tailors*, because they are direct, obvious, and significant in human terms. He voices his concern about the morality of all his "meddling" to the rector, who assures him that everyone must "follow the truth," on the assumption that this path will lead invariably if somewhat indirectly to God, who has "all the facts" in the great case of life. Thus, it is impossible to be too curious, to probe too far, to ask too many questions, even though some answers or consequences may be painful.

In this great novel, Wimsey actually experiences the central Christian paradox, that of good coming from evil or of the two being inextricably linked. The mystery is over when he realizes, in a grisly pun, that Deacon's killers are already hanged, since they are the very bells in the church's tower. As one of the inscriptions on this ancient church says, the nine tailors, or the nine peals, "make a man," suggesting that the bells not only signify a man when they toll his passing, but also stand as timeless, disinterested judges of human behavior. The dead man, Deacon, mocked honorable work in his thievery, and thus began the cycle of destruction that ends in his own death, a death which ironically leads to Wimsey's discovery or creative act. From evil thus confronted and comprehended, good may grow. Mr. Venables, the rector, wittily pricks Wimsey with the irony that "there's always something that lies behind a mystery . . . a solution of some kind." For Wimsey, as for Sayers, even the solution to a mystery leads to further mysteries; the answer to the mystery of Deacon's death leads to a more subtle inquiry into one of the essential mysteries of life: how to determine responsibility or meaning for human action. In this paradoxical world, victims may be villians and right action is often based in error, chance, or even transgression.

Wimsey leaves this complex novel with greater insight into himself and the ambiguous nature of life; he is, therefore, finally ready to come to terms with the greatest mystery of his life, Harriet Vane, who is also about ready to accept his inquiry. In *Gaudy Night*, Wimsey reaches his fulfillment, a fulfillment that is expressed in terms of resolving the conflict between man and woman, between intellect and emotion, and between good and evil. In fact, Wimsey's fulfillment represents the culmination of Sayers' search for a resolution of these forces. The novel's subject is also one of Sayers' oldest: the moral imperative for every person to do good work that is well done, and the terrible consequences of not doing so. All of these ideas come into play in this subtle novel, which is on one level the mystery of the "Shrewsbury Poison Pen" and on another, more important one, an unusual and profound love story. Reflecting the subtlety and delicacy with which Sayers spins her tale, there is not even a death in this book; the psychological violence caused by the Poison Pen is alarming, but here evil is banal, and all the more powerful for being so.

Gaudy Night takes place at Oxford, which held happy memories for Sayers as the place of her birth and formal education, and the entire novel is a paean to that golden-spired city. Harriet Vane goes to Oxford to attend the Shrewsbury Gaudy, an annual spring homecoming celebration, where she has the opportunity to judge her old classmates and teachers in terms of how well they, as women, have been able to live meaningful lives. Shrewsbury is obviously a fictional version of Somerville, Sayers' college, and just as clearly Vane, a famous detective novelist who is wrestling with the question of "woman's work" and with the problem of rendering reality in fiction, is to some extent Sayers, the self-conscious artist. Having been pursued by Wimsey for five frustrating years, Vane finally accepts him at the end of *Gaudy Night*. She accepts him because the experiences in this book teach her three interrelated things: that Wimsey, as an extraordinary man, will not prevent her from doing her "proper job," a consequence she feared from any relationship with a man; that men and women can live together and not destroy each other, but create a good life; and therefore, that there can be an alliance between the "intellect and the flesh." Vane's discoveries in this novel thus signal the solution of problems that had preoccupied Sayers throughout her career.

Vane learns all of these things through Wimsey's unraveling of the mystery of the Poisen Pen, who is a woman frightfully flawed because she has never been able to strike a balance between the intellect and the flesh, and therefore has never done her proper job. Annie Wilson, the Poison Pen who creates so much confusion and instills so much fear in the intellectual women of Shrewsbury, is the victim of sentimentality and a radically disassociated sensibility; she hates all learning because her dead husband was punished long ago for academic dishonesty. Ironically, Harriet Vane suffers from the same problem, but in its other manifestation; she begins the novel capable of trusting only the intellect, and fears any bonds of the flesh or heart. When she finally sees that neither the sentimentality of Annie nor the hyperintellectualism of Shrewsbury can solve the "problem of life," Harriet realizes that it is only through balancing intellect and passion that creative or truly human action is possible.

Wimsey, who solves the mystery because he is able to bring these forces into equilibrium and to acknowledge the potency of both, is rendered acceptable to Vane because of this ability. Her new willingness to admit her feelings reveals to her what Sayers' readers had known for a long time: she loves Wimsey. The man she loves has changed, too. He is no longer an unattainable paragon who sees good and evil as discrete and life as a game, but a middle-aged man who fears rejection and death, who is idiotically vain about his hands, and who, to Harriet's surprise, looks as vulnerable as anyone else when he falls asleep: the man behind the monocle. All of this does not argue that Wimsey is less extraordinary than he was; in fact, perhaps what is most extraordinary about him now is that he seems a real person—flawed, finite, vulnerable—who is yet capable of that rare thing, creative action. Indeed, his very life seems a work of art.

Wimsey and Vane finally embark upon marriage, that most mundane and mysterious of journeys, in *Busman's Honeymoon*, the final novel that Sayers aptly called a "love story with detective interruptions": the detective novelist had moved that far from the formula. In the closing scene of this last novel, Wimsey admits that his new wife is "his corner," the place where he can hide from a hostile, confusing world and shed tears for the murderer whose execution he caused. This is not the Wimsey who blithely dashed about in the early novels, treating criminals as fair game in an intellectual hunting expedition, but it is the man he could have become after fourteen years of living, suffering, and reflecting. Indeed, it was a masterful stroke for Sayers to create Harriet Vane, a woman who could match Wimsey's wits and passions, because through her and through his loving her, the reader can learn the most intimate facts of this once-distant hero. If a man is to cry in front of anyone, that witness should most likely be his wife, especially if she is an extraordinary person who understands his tears. The early Wimsey may have been the kind of man that an intellectual woman would imagine for a mate, but the mature Wimsey is one with whom she could actually live. The fragment of a later novel called *Thrones, Dominations* indicates that the Wimsey-Vane marriage was just this workable.

Finally, the marriage of Wimsey and Vane symbolizes the paradoxical and joyful truth of good coming out of evil, for if Harriet had not been falsely accused of murder, they would never have met. She quiets Wimsey in one of his familiar periods of painful self-scrutiny about his "meddling" by reminding him that, if he had never meddled, she would probably be dead. The point seems clear: that human action has consequences, many of which are unforeseen and some painful, but all necessary for life. It is not difficult to imagine a novelist with this vision moving on shortly to the drama of Christ's crucifixion and resurrection, nor even the next step, her study and translation of that great narrative of good and evil, desire and fulfillment, mortality and eternity, Dante's *The Divine Comedy* (c. 1320). Indeed, all of Sayers' work is of a piece, creating that massive unity in diversity by which she defined true art.

Catherine Kenney

Other major works

SHORT FICTION: *Hangman's Holiday*, 1933; *In the Teeth of the Evidence and Other Stories*, 1939; *Lord Peter*, 1972 (James Sandoe, editor); *Striding Folly*, 1972.

PLAYS: *Busman's Honeymoon*, 1937 (with Muriel St. Clare Byrne); *The Zeal of Thy House*, 1937; *The Devil to Pay, Being the Famous Play of John Faustus*, 1939; *Love All*, 1940; *The Man Born to Be King: A Play-Cycle on the Life of Our Lord and Saviour Jesus Christ*, 1941-1942; *The Just Vengeance*, 1946; *The Emperor Constantine*, 1951 (revised as *Christ's Emperor*, 1952).

POETRY: *Op I*, 1916; *Catholic Tales and Christian Songs*, 1918; *Lord, I Thank Thee—*, 1943; *The Story of Adam and Christ*, 1955.

NONFICTION: *Papers Relating to the Family of Wimsey*, 1936; *An Account of Lord Mortimer Wimsey, the Hermit of the Wash*, 1937; *The Greatest Drama Ever Staged*, 1938; *Strong Meat*, 1939; *Begin Here: A War-Time Essay*, 1940; *Creed or Chaos?*, 1940; *The Mysterious English*, 1941; *The Mind of the Maker*, 1941; *Why Work?*, 1942; *The Other Six Deadly Sins*, 1943; *Unpopular Opinions*, 1946; *Making Sense of the Universe*, 1946; *Creed or Chaos? and Other Essays in Popular Theology*, 1947; *The Lost Tools of Learning*, 1948; *The Days of Christ's Coming*, 1953, revised 1960; *Introductory Papers on*

Dante, 1957; *The Story of Easter*, 1955; *The Story of Noah's Ark*, 1955; *Further Papers on Dante*, 1957; *The Poetry of Search and the Poetry of Statement, and Other Posthumous Essays on Literature, Religion, and Language*, 1963; *Christian Letters to a Post-Christian World*, 1969; *Are Women Human?*, 1971; *A Matter of Eternity*, 1973; *Wilkie Collins: A Critical and Biographical Study*, 1977 (edited by E. R. Gregory).

CHILDREN'S LITERATURE: *Even the Parrot: Exemplary Conversations for Enlightened Children*, 1944.

TRANSLATIONS: *Tristan in Brittany*, 1929 (by Thomas the Troubadour); *The Heart of Stone, Being the Four Canzoni of the "Pietra" Group*, 1946 (by Dante); *The Comedy of Dante Alighieri the Florentine*, 1949-1962 (Cantica III with Barbara Reynolds); *The Song of Roland*, 1957.

EDITED TEXTS: *Oxford Poetry 1917*, 1918 (with Wilfred R. Childe and Thomas W. Earp); *Oxford Poetry 1918*, 1918 (with Earp and E. F. A. Geach); *Oxford Poetry 1919*, 1919 (with Earp and Siegfried Sassoon); *Great Short Stories of Detection, Mystery, and Horror*, 1928-1934 (also as *The Omnibus of Crime*); *Tales of Detection*, 1936.

Bibliography

Brabazon, James. *Dorothy L. Sayers: A Biography*. New York: Charles Scribner's Sons, 1981. The "authorized" biography based upon Sayers' private papers, containing an introduction by her only son, Anthony Fleming. Brabazon shows that Sayers' real desire was to be remembered as an author of poetry and religious dramas and as a translator of Dante.

Dale, Alzina Stone. *Maker and Craftsman: The Study of Dorothy L. Sayers*. Grand Rapids, Mich.: Wm. B. Eerdmans, 1978. Written in a popular style for a general audience, this brief (158-page) biography is a good starting place for further study of Sayers as both a mystery writer and a scholar. Illustrated.

Gaillard, Dawson. *Dorothy L. Sayers*. New York: Frederick Ungar, 1981. In a brief 123 pages, Dawson tries to establish a link between Sayers' detective fiction and her other literary works. One chapter is devoted to her short stories, four to her mystery novels, and a sixth to a summary of Sayers' literary virtues.

Hall, Trevor H. *Dorothy L. Sayers: Nine Literary Studies*. Hamden, Conn.: Archon Books, 1980. In nine critical essays, Hall discusses the connection between Sayers' creation, Lord Peter Wimsey, and Arthur Conan Doyle's creation, Sherlock Holmes. Hall also speculates in some detail on the influence of Sayers' husband, Atherton Fleming, on her writing.

Scott-Giles, Charles Wilfrid. *The Wimsey Family: A Fragmentary History from Correspondence with Dorothy Sayers*. New York: Harper & Row, 1977. Scott-Giles, an expert on heraldry, creates a family history and biography for Sayers' most memorable creation, Lord Peter Wimsey. Illustrations include the Wimsey family coat of arms, designed by Sayers.

Youngberg, Ruth Tanis. *Dorothy L. Sayers: A Reference Guide*. Boston: G. K. Hall, 1982. An extensive guide to 942 English-language reviews, articles, books, introductions, and addresses published between 1917 and 1981. The annotations are designed to provide information, rather than criticism, to allow the reader to evaluate the particular item's usefulness.

SIR WALTER SCOTT

Born: Edinburgh, Scotland; August 15, 1771
Died: Abbotsford, Scotland; September 21, 1832

Principal long fiction

Waverley: Or, 'Tis Sixty Years Since, 1814; *Guy Mannering*, 1815; *The Antiquary*, 1816; *The Black Dwarf*, 1816; *Old Mortality*, 1816; *Rob Roy*, 1817; *The Heart of Midlothian*, 1818; *The Bride of Lammermoor*, 1819; *A Legend of Montrose*, 1819; *Ivanhoe*, 1819; *The Monastery*, 1820; *The Abbot*, 1820; *Kenilworth*, 1821; *The Pirate*, 1821; *The Fortunes of Nigel*, 1822; *Peveril of the Peak*, 1823; *Quentin Durward*, 1823; *St. Ronan's Well*, 1823; *Redgauntlet*, 1824; *The Betrothed*, 1825; *The Talisman*, 1825; *Woodstock*, 1826; *The Fair Maid of Perth*, 1828; *Anne of Geierstein*, 1829; *Count Robert of Paris*, 1831; *Castle Dangerous*, 1831; *The Siege of Malta*, 1976.

Other literary forms

Sir Walter Scott's first published work was a translation of two ballads by Gottfried August Bürger, which appeared anonymously in 1796. In 1799, he published a translation of Johann Wolfgang von Goethe's drama *Goetz von Berlichingen*. In 1802, the first two volumes of *Minstrelsy of the Scottish Border* appeared, followed by the third volume in 1803. This was a collection of popular ballads, annotated and often emended and "improved" with a freedom no modern editor woud allow himself. A fascination with his country's past, formed in his early years and lasting all his life, led him to preserve these ballads, the products of a folk culture that was disappearing. In 1805 came *The Lay of the Last Minstrel*, the first of the series of long narrative poems that made Scott the most widely read poet of the day. It was followed by *Marmion: A Tale of Flodden Field* (1808). *The Lady of the Lake* (1810) brought him to the height of his popularity as a poet. The later poems were less successful and he was gradually eclipsed by Lord Byron. In 1813, he completed the manuscript of a novel he had laid aside in 1805. This was *Waverley*, which appeared anonymously in 1814. (Scott did not publicly admit authorship of his novels until 1827.) It created a sensation and launched him on the series that remained his chief occupation until the end of his life. Other important works were his editions of Dryden (1808) and of Swift (1814), a series of lives of the English novelists completed in 1824, and *The Life of Napoleon Buonaparte*, begun in 1825 and published in nine volumes in 1827. *Chronicles of the Canongate* (1827) is composed of three short stories: "The Highland Widow," "The Two Drovers," and "The Surgeon's Daughter."

Achievements

The central achievement of Scott's busy career is the series of novels that is conventionally designated by the title of the first of them. The sheer bulk of the Waverley novels is in itself impressive, as is the range of the settings they present. For example, *Ivanhoe* is set in twelfth century England, *The Talisman* in the Holy Land of the Third Crusade, *Quentin Durward* in fifteenth century France, *The Abbot* in the Scotland of Queen Mary, *Kenilworth* in the reign of Elizabeth, and *The Fortunes of Nigel* in that of James I. In spite of his wide reading, tenacious memory, and active imagination, Scott was not able to deal convincingly with so many different periods. Moreover, he worked rapidly and sometimes carelessly, under the pressures of financial necessity and, in later years, failing health. Some of the novels are tedious and wooden, mechanical in their plots and stilted in their dialogue. Scott himself was aware of their flaws and he sometimes spoke and wrote slightingly of them.

Yet most readers find that even the weaker novels have good things in them, and the best of them have a narrative sweep and a dramatic vividness that render their flaws unimportant. The best of them, by common consent, are those set in Scotland as far back as the latter part of the reign of Charles II. When he attempted to go further back, he was less successful, but in such novels as the four discussed below—*Waverley, Old Mortality, Rob Roy*, and *The Heart of the Midlothian*—Scott's sense of history is strong. They are among the most impressive treatments of his great theme, the conflict between the old and the new, between Jacobite and Hanoverian, between the heroic, traditional, feudal values of the Tory Highlands and the progressive commercial interests of the Whig Lowlands, between stability and change. Though some of the other novels offer historical conflict of a comparable kind (*Ivanhoe* and *Quentin Durward*, for example), the Scottish novels present the conflict with particular insight and force and convey a strong sense of the good on both sides of it. Scott values the dying heroic tradition even as he recognizes the benefits that change brings. Earlier writers had mined the past to satisfy a market for the exotic, the strange, or the merely quaint. Scott saw the past in significant relation to the present and created characters clearly shaped by the social, economic, religious, and political forces of their time, thus providing his readers with the first fictions that can properly be called historical novels.

Biography

An important factor in the vividness of the Scottish novels was the strong oral tradition to which Sir Walter Scott had access from his early childhood. After a bout with polio in his second year, he was sent away from Edinburgh to his paternal grandfather's house at Sandyknowe in the Border country, in the hope that the climate would improve his health. It did, and though he remained lame for the rest of his life, his boyhood was an active one. In this region from which his ancestors had sprung, he heard stories of Border raids, Jacobite risings, and religious struggles from people for whom the past sur-

vived in a living tradition. Throughout his life he added to his fund of anec-
dotes, and his notes to the novels show how very often incidents in them are
founded on actual events which he had learned about from the participants
themselves or from their more immediate descendants.

Scott's father was a lawyer, and in 1786, having attended Edinburgh High
School and Edinburgh University, Scott became an apprentice in his father's
office. In 1792, he was admitted to the bar, and all his life he combined legal
and literary activities. After losing his first love, Williamina Belsches, to a
banker, he married Charlotte Carpenter in 1798. In 1805, he entered into a
secret partnership with the printer James Ballantyne, and four years later
they formed a publishing firm. This firm ran into financial difficulties, and in
1813, Scott escaped ruin only through the intervention of another publisher,
Archibald Constable. Scott continued to overextend himself. In 1811, he had
bought a farm on the Tweed at a place he named Abbotsford, and in the
years that followed he wrote furiously to provide funds for building a splendid
house and buying additional land. His ambition was to live the life of a laird.
In 1826, the financial collapse of Constable and Ballantyne ruined Scott. In
his last years, he worked tirelessly to pay his creditors. The effort told on his
health, and he died in 1832, at the age of sixty-one. The debts were finally
cleared after his death by the sale of his copyrights.

Analysis

Waverley displays, at the start of Sir Walter Scott's career as a novelist,
many of the features that were to prove typical of his best work. In the Jacobite
rebellion of 1745, he saw an instance of the conflict between the older feudal
and chivalric order, strongly colored with heroic and "romantic" elements,
and the newer order of more practical and realistic concerns which had already
begun to supplant it. His focus is not on the great public figures whose fates
are at stake, and this too is typical. The Pretender, Prince Charles Edward,
is not introduced until the novel is more than half over, and most of the major
events of this phase of his career are only alluded to, not presented directly.
He is shown almost exclusively in his dealings with the fictional character for
whom the novel is named, and largely through his eyes.

Edward Waverley, like so many of Scott's heroes, is a predominantly passive
character who finds himself caught between opposing forces and "wavering"
between his loyalty to the House of Hanover, and the attractions of the Stuart
cause. Though his father occupies a post in the Whig ministry, he has been
reared by his uncle Sir Everard, a Tory who had supported the earlier Jacobite
rebellion of 1715, though not so actively as to incur reprisals when it was put
down. His father's connections procure Edward a commission in King
George's army, and he is posted to Scotland. Shortly after arriving, he makes
an extended visit to his uncle's Jacobite friend, the Baron of Bradwardine,
and his daughter Rose. When a Highland raider, Donald Bean Lean, steals

several of the Baron's cows, Waverley goes into the Highlands in the company of a follower of Fergus MacIvor, a chieftain who has the influence to secure the return of the cows. Waverley is impressed by Fergus and infatuated with his sister Flora. They are both confirmed Jacobites preparing to declare for the Pretender upon his arrival in Scotland.

As a result of Waverley's protracted absence and of a mutiny among the small band of men from his family estate who had followed him into the army, Waverley is declared absent without leave and superseded in his office. By coincidence, his father also loses his government position. Waverley's resentment at this twofold insult to his family by the Hanoverian government is heightened when, on a journey to Edinburgh to clear himself, he is arrested. Rescued by Donald Bean Lean, he is later brought to Edinburgh (now in the hands of the Jacobites), meets the Pretender, and is won over to his cause. He takes part in the Jacobite victory at Preston, but is separated from Fergus' troop in a skirmish at Clifton, in which Fergus is captured. After a period in hiding, Waverley is pardoned, through the good offices of Colonel Talbot, whom he had saved from death and taken prisoner at Preston. Fergus is executed for treason.

Objections to *Waverley* usually center on the character of the hero, whom Scott himself called "a sneaking piece of imbecility." Certainly it is possible to be impatient with his lack of self-awareness, and the frequency with which he is acted upon rather than acting puts him often in a less than heroic light. Waverley, however, is not intended to be a romantic hero, and his suscep- tibility to external influence is necessary to enable Scott to show within a single character the conflict between the two forces that compose the novel's theme. For most of the book, Scott's view of the hero is ironic, emphasizing his failings. There is, for example, his vanity. One of the things that reconciles his Jacobite Aunt Rachel to his serving in the Hanoverian army is the fact that he is becoming infatuated with a local girl. Scott mocks Waverley's feel- ings, first by giving their object the inelegant name of Cecilia Stubbs, and then by telling the reader that on Waverley's last Sunday at the parish church he is too preoccupied with his own dashing appearance in his new uniform to notice the care with which Miss Stubbs has arrayed herself. The complement of this detail occurs later in the novel when Waverley, having joined the Jacobites, puts on Highland dress for the first time, and one of Fergus' fol- lowers remarks that he is "majoring yonder afore the muckle pier-glass." More seriously, the memory of "the inferior figure which he had made among the officers of his regiment," resulting from his inability to keep his mind on detail and routine, contributes to his decision to change sides.

In addition to exposing his vanity, Scott often undercuts Waverley's roman- tic view of experience. On finding himself for the first time in the Highlands, he muses over "the full romance of his situation." It occurs to him that "the only circumstance which assorted ill with the rest, was the cause of his journey—the Baron's milk cows! this degrading incident he kept in the background." If, instead of deploring Waverley's inadequacy as a romantic hero, one attends to the irony with which Scott undercuts his fascination with romance and heroism, one will be better prepared for the author's reluctant dismissal of heroic virtues at the end of the novel. Waverley's character is perfectly appropriate to one who will survive into the new age, an age in which the dashing but destructive energies of Fergus have no place.

The real problem with the character is not his passivity or his ordinariness, but Scott's occasional failure to dramatize certain features of his personality, as opposed to merely making assertions about them. On two occasions he is credited with remarkable conversational powers, but no sample of them is given. During Waverley's period in hiding, Scott declares, "he acquired a more complete mastery of a spirit tamed by adversity, than his former experience had given him," but there is no demonstration of this "mastery." These flaws, however, hardly justify dismissing the characterization as a failure. The eagerness of Waverley's response to the new scenes and experiences he encounters, the growth of his resentment against the established government and his conversion to Jacobitism, his delayed recognition of his love for Rose, the cooling of his regard for Fergus as he comes to see the chieftain's selfishness and then the reawakening of that regard when Fergus is in danger—all these phases of his development are convincingly presented. Moreover, there are a few scenes where he shows real firmness (for example, his confrontation with Fergus when he has been shot at by one of Fergus' men), and several where he displays active generosity.

This said, one may concede that Waverley remains a rather slender figure to carry the weight of a novel of this length. He does not have to, however, for Scott surrounds him with a number of vivid characters from a wide range of classes and backgrounds. It is chiefly through their speech that he makes his characters live. The dialogue is not consistently successful: the bright small talk between Fergus and Flora can be downright dreadful, and some of the language of the other upper-class characters is stiff. The speech of most of the secondary characters, however, is convincing, and the dialect writing is particularly effective. Scott's most important contribution here is the achievement of a wide variety of tones in dialect speech. Before Scott, dialect was almost exclusively a comic device, but he was able to write dialect in different keys all the way up to the tragic. The best evidence of this is the scene in which Fergus and his follower Evan Dhu Maccombich are condemned to death. When Evan Dhu offers his life and the lives of five others in exchange for his chieftain's freedom, volunteering to go and fetch the five others himself, laughter breaks out in the courtroom. In a speech that loses nothing in dignity by being couched in dialect, Evan Dhu rebukes the audience and then proudly rejects the judge's invitation to plead for grace, preferring to share his chieftain's fate.

Fergus is perhaps the most interesting of the major characters. He possesses throughout the capacity to surprise the reader. Scott prepares the reader carefully for his first appearance. Waverley first hears of him in Chapter 15 as an extorter of blackmail or protection money and is surprised to learn that he is nevertheless considered a gentleman. When he is introduced several chapters later, the reader discovers that this feudal leader of a troop of half-savage Highlandmen is a polished and literate individual with a very good French education. He is clearly fond of his sister, and yet quite prepared to exploit her as bait to draw Waverley into the Jacobite ranks. In the early part of the novel, the emphasis is on his courage, his hospitality, and his ability to inspire loyalty, and he is for the most part an attractive figure.

Gradually, however, both Waverley and the reader come to view him more critically. It grows increasingly clear that his commitment to the Jacobite cause is founded on self-interest. On learning that Prince Charles Edward is encouraging Bradwardine to leave his estate to Rose instead of to a distant male relative, he attempts to make the Prince promote his marriage to Rose. When the Prince refuses, he is furious, later saying that he could at that moment have sold himself to the devil or King George, "whichever offered the dearest revenge" (chap. 53). Yet as the Jacobite fortunes ebb, his generosity returns, and for the first time he attempts to use his influence over Waverley for the latter's good, telling him there is no dishonor in his extricating himself from the now certain wreck of their cause and urging him to marry Rose: "She loves you, and I believe you love her, though, perhaps, you have not found it out, for you are not celebrated for knowing your own mind very pointedly." He refuses to allow Waverley to witness his execution, and, by a generous deception regarding the hour at which it is to take place, he spares his sister the pain of a final interview. As he strides out of his cell, it is he who is supporting Waverley.

Throughout the novel, the portrait of Fergus is sharpened by a number of contrasts, explicit and implicit, between him and other characters. The contrast with Waverley is obviously central. There is also a contrast between him and his sister. While Fergus' Jacobitism is tinged with self-interest and he sometimes resorts to duplicity to advance the cause, Flora's devotion to the Stuarts is absolutely pure. She cannot reconcile herself to her brother's dealing with a thief of Donald Bean Lean's stripe even in the interest of the cause, and she resists his wish that she encourage Waverley's infatuation with her in order to win him to their side. Fergus' preoccupation with the more practical aspects of the campaign is set against Bradwardine's comically pedantic concern with form and ceremony in the question of whether and how to exercise his hereditary privilege of drawing off the king's boots. Yet Bradwardine's old-fashioned loyalty lacks all taint of self-interest, and, though he has been largely a comic figure, he behaves after the failure of the rebellion with a gallant fortitude comparable to that of Fergus. In the latter part of the novel, a new character enters to serve as Fergus' complete antithesis. Colonel Talbot, who supplants him in guiding Waverley's fate, differs from Fergus on practically every count—political affiliation, disinterested generosity, attitude toward women, and even age.

Several other characters are paired in contrast. Flora's strength of character, heroic bent, intellectual accomplishments, and striking beauty are repeatedly contrasted with the less remarkable gifts of the placid and domestic Rose. Sir Everard Waverley and his brother Richard are opposite numbers in all respects. When Waverley is arrested on his way to Edinburgh, Melville and Morton, the magistrate and the clergyman who hear his defense, take differing views of his case. One of Fergus' henchmen, Callum Beg, commits a crime for his master when he attempts to shoot Waverley, while Humphry Houghton, one of Waverley's followers, involves himself in a conspiracy and mutiny. Both are carrying out what they mistakenly believe to be their masters' wishes, and they receive differing treatment for their actions.

This network of contrasts contributes much to the unity of a novel that is sometimes criticized as loosely structured. Scott's General Preface to the 1829 edition of the whole series lends credence to this charge: "The tale of Waverley was put together with so little care, that I cannot boast of having sketched any distinct plan of the work. The whole adventures of Waverley, in his movements up and down the country with the Highland cateran Bean Lean, are managed without much skill." Whatever Scott meant by this, it cannot really be said that the book is loosely plotted. A glance at the retrospective explanations contained in Chapters 31 and 65 will remind any reader of the great number of details that at first looked unimportant but that turn out to be essential to the mechanics of the plot. Such after-the-fact explanations may be technically awkward, and they may lay Scott open to the charge of unnecessary mystification in the episodes leading up to them, but they certainly evidence some careful planning.

It is rather for excessive reliance on coincidence that the plot can be criticized. The retrospective explanations just mentioned make some of these appear less unreasonable and incredible, but there are still a great many of them, and this is true of all Scott's novels. Also, the pace of the narrative is at times uncertain. Although the opening chapters describing Waverley's education are important to an understanding of the character, they make an undeniably slow beginning, and some of the set pieces retard the narrative flow.

In spite of its flaws, however, the novel is sustained by its central theme of the process of historical change and by Scott's ability to do justice to both sides in the conflict. Part of him responded strongly to the gallant romance of the Jacobite and to the love of tradition behind it. At the same time, he realized that the world had passed all that by. As Waverley himself points out, there have been four monarchs since James II was deposed, and the divine right absolutism for which the Stuarts stood would have sorted ill with the political and economic realities of the mid-eighteenth century. So Fergus is executed, his head is stuck up over the Scotch gate, and the Edinburgh youth whom Waverley has engaged as a valet comments, "It's a great pity of Evan Dhu, who was a very weel-meaning, good-natured man, to be a Hielandman; and indeed so was [Fergus MacIvor] too, for that matter, when he wasna in ane o' his tirrivies [tantrums]." In a snatch of dialogue, the heroic perspective is replaced by one more down-to-earth and commonplace. The threat to the prevailing order that the rebellion represented is already diminishing in importance in the popular view. To the common man secure in the established order, the energies that burned in Fergus amount to no more than "tirrivies."

Old Mortality deals with an earlier rebellion, one in which the issue is religious. Charles II had won the support of the Scottish Presbyterians by subscribing to the Solemn League and Covenant, which provided for the establishment of Presbyterianism as the state religion in Scotland and in England and Ireland as well. After the Restoration, however, Charles sought to impose episcopacy on Scotland, and the Covenanters were persecuted for their resistance to the bishops. In 1679, the assassination of the Archbishop of St. Andrews by a small party of Covenanters led by John Balfour of Burley sparked a gathering of insurgents who managed at Drumclog to defeat the Cavalier forces under John Graham of Claverhouse that were sent against them. A few weeks later, however, the Covenanters, divided by moderate and extremist factions, were routed at Bothwell Bridge by an army commanded by the Duke of Monmouth. The novel's title is the nickname of an old man who travels through Scotland refurbishing the markers on the graves of the martyred Covenanters.

Out of these events, Scott built one of his starkest and swiftest plots. Once again he portrays a hero caught between conflicting forces. Just after the Archbishop's murder, Henry Morton gives shelter to Burley because Burley and his father had been comrades-in-arms and Burley had saved the elder Morton's life. Henry Morton's moderate principles lead him to condemn the murder, but he also deplores the oppression that provoked it, and Burley hopes that he will eventually take up arms with the Covenanters. Morton is, however, drawn to the Cavalier side by his love for Edith Bellenden (one of Scott's more pallid heroines) and by his friendship for her granduncle.

Morton receives some firsthand experience of the oppressive measures of the Cavaliers when he is arrested for harboring the fugitive Burley and is brought before Claverhouse. This figure is Burley's opposite number, rather as Talbot is Fergus MacIvor's in *Waverley*, except that Talbot is wholly admirable while Claverhouse is a more complex character. Like Burley, Claverhouse sees in Morton qualities of courage and leadership that could be valuable to the rebels. He is about to have him executed when one of his subordinates, Lord Evandale, intervenes. Evandale is a suitor of Edith, and at her request he generously asks Claverhouse to spare his rival's life. Morton is carried along as a prisoner with Claverhouse's troops, and when they are defeated by the Covenanters at Drumclog, he is set free. Under Burley's auspices, he is given a high post in the rebel army.

In this phase of the novel, Morton shows himself a much more active hero than Waverley. He quickly repays his debt to Evandale by saving his life in the rout of the loyalist forces, and he does so again in a later chapter, when Evandale has become Burley's prisoner. He plays a prominent part in the Covenanters' attempts to take Glasgow. He draws up a statement of the rebels' grievances and presents it to Monmouth just before the battle of Bothwell Bridge, and even though the Covenanters obstinately refuse the terms he secures, he does not defect but instead fights heroically in the battle that ensues.

In spite of the vigor with which Morton fulfills his commitment to the Presbyterians, they distrust him, and Scott sharply dramatizes their ignorance, factiousness, bigotry, and cruelty. He also exposes the unscrupulous streak in Burley's enthusiasm. This zealot is convinced that the most barbaric cruelties and the rankest deceptions are justified by his cause. He is surrounded by a gallery of fanatics, of whom the most horrifying is the insane preacher Habbakuk Mucklewrath. In flight after the defeat at Bothwell Bridge, Morton and his servant Cuddie stumble upon a group of Covenanting leaders in an isolated farmhouse at Drumshinnel. They have been praying for guidance, and the arrival of Morton, whom they irrationally regard as the cause of their defeat, convinces them that God has sent him to them as a sacrifice. They conduct a kind of trial, though the verdict of death is never in doubt. It is the Sabbath, however, and they are unwilling to execute him before midnight. Eventually, Mucklewrath jumps up to put the clock ahead, crying, "As the sun went back on the dial ten degrees for intimating the recovery of holy Hezekiah, so shall it now go forward, that the wicked may be taken away from among the people, and the Covenant established in its purity."

This display of the Covenanters' fanaticism is the complement of the earlier trial before Claverhouse, in which Morton was threatened with the arbitrary cruelty of the Cavalier side. Ironically, it is Claverhouse who now arrives to save Morton. (He has been led to the farmhouse by Cuddie, who had been allowed to escape.) Most of the Covenanters are slaughtered. Riding back to Edinburgh in the custody of his rescuers, Morton is divided between horror at Claverhouse's habitual cold indifference to bloodshed and admiration for his urbanity and his valor. Claverhouse admits that he is as much a fanatic as Burley but adds, "There is a difference, I trust, between the blood of learned and reverend prelates and scholars, of gallant soldiers and noble gentlemen, and the red puddle that stagnates in the veins of psalm-singing mechanics, crack-brained demagogues, and sullen boors." Scott counters this assessment in the very next chapter by showing the fortitude of one of the Covenanting leaders, Ephraim MacBriar, as he is brutally tortured and then condemned to death. The reader may also recall that it was prolonged imprisonment by the Cavaliers that drove Mucklewrath insane. As in *Waverley*, Scott sees both sides objectively.

Morton is sentenced to exile, and there is a gap of ten years in the narrative. In 1689, when the Glorious Revolution has put William and Mary on the throne, Morton is free to return to Scotland. Edith is on the point, finally, of accepting marriage to Evandale. Claverhouse, loyal to the Stuarts, is now ironically a rebel in his turn. He is killed in the battle of Killecrankie, but his army is victorious. He had once said to Morton, "When I think of death . . . as a thing worth thinking of, it is in the hope of pressing one day some well-fought and hard-won field of battle, and dying with the shout of victory in my ear—*that* would be worth dying for, and more, it would be worth having lived for!" The rather too crowded closing pages describe the deaths of Burley and Lord Evandale.

The novel displays Scott's dramatic gifts at their best. Though the language of Morton, Edith, and Evandale is sometimes stiff, the dialogue of the rest of the characters is vigorous and precisely adjusted to their various stations and backgrounds, and the language of the Covenanters, loaded with scriptural allusions, idioms, and rhythms, constitutes a particularly remarkable achievement. In addition to the characters already discussed, three others stand out. One is Sergeant Bothwell, who is descended from an illegitimate son of James VI and resents his failure to attain preferment. He is one of the novel's chief embodiments of the bullying oppression and extortion to which the Covenanters are subjected, but he is also capable of the courtesy and bravery that he regards as incumbent on one of his blood. Another is Mause Headrigg, whose compulsive declarations of her extreme Presbyterian principles are always ill-timed, to the chagrin of her pragmatic son Cuddie, who has no ambition to become a martyred Covenanter. The third is Jenny Dennison, Edith's maid. Like her mistress, Jenny has a suitor on each side of the conflict, and Scott thus creates a comic parallel to the Morton-Edith-Evandale triangle. She chooses Morton's servant Cuddie over her other suitor, a soldier in the Cavalier army, and this match foreshadows the eventual union of Edith and Morton. Jenny, however, has more vitality, resourcefulness, and charm than her mistress. She has been criticized for trying to promote Edith's marriage to the wealthy Evandale with a view to securing the future of herself, her husband, and their children. One can admit this fault and go on to point out that it is related to the success of the characterization. The most convincing characters in *Old Mortality* are those in whom Scott reveals a mixure of motivations or a blending of admirable with deplorable traits.

Rob Roy is probably the least successful of the four novels considered here. It resembles *Waverley* in that it takes a young Englishman into the Highlands during a Jacobite rising, this time that of 1715. Like Edward Waverley, Frank Osbaldistone has a romantic and poetical turn and responds eagerly to the unfamiliar world of the Highlands. Like Waverley, he has a touch of vanity and of obstinacy in his temper. Like Waverley, he is slow to understand his feelings for the heroine. That he is not as slow as Waverley was to realize that he loved Rose may be attributed to two factors: There is only one possible object for Frank's affections, not two; and that object, Diana Vernon, bears a much closer similarity to Flora, who captivated Waverley immediately, than to Rose.

Frank Osbaldistone, however, is a less interesting hero than Waverley, largely because he does not experience any serious internal conflict. In spite of his love for Diana, a committed Jacobite, he never considers supporting the Pretender. His conflicts are all external. Having angered his father by refusing to follow him into trade, Frank is sent to stay with his uncle's family in Northumberland, to be replaced in the firm by one of his cousins. Though it is understandable that his father should turn to a nephew when his son has disappointed him, it is not clear what point he has in sending Frank to Osbaldistone Hall. Frank's uncle and five of his cousins are boors with no interests beyond hunting and drinking. The sixth son, Rashleigh, is clever, villainous, ugly, and lame. He is the one chosen to take Frank's place in the firm. He had been tutor to Diana, who is his cousin on his mother's side, but had attempted to seduce her, and she has since kept him at a distance. Nevertheless, their common Jacobite sympathies remain a bond between them. Rashleigh, resenting Diana's obvious liking for Frank and smarting under an insult from him, forms a plan that will ruin the Osbaldistone firm and at the same time hasten the rising of the clans in support of the Pretender. The financial details of this scheme are not clear, and it therefore lacks credibility. This flaw in the plot is fairly serious because in *Rob Roy* commercial activity has considerable thematic importance.

Once in London, Rashleigh wins his uncle's confidence and then absconds with certain crucial documents. Frank's task is to follow him to Glasgow and then into the Highlands to recover them. It is in fact not Frank but Diana Vernon's father (whose identity is a mystery to Frank and the reader until the end of the book) who gets the documents back, and this in spite of the fact that he is also a Jacobite and might thus be expected to further rather than thwart Rashleigh's plot. Punishment comes to Rashleigh not from Frank but from the Highland chieftain Rob Roy. Rashleigh turns traitor to the Jacobites, and, after the failure of the rebellion, he arranges the arrest of Diana and her father. In the process of rescuing them, Rob Roy kills Rashleigh.

Thus, though Frank is a party to his fair share of adventures, he is too often merely a party rather than the chief actor, even though he is clearly meant to be the hero. Although Rob Roy appears at practically every crisis of the story, those appearances are intermittent, and the crises mark stages in the experience of Frank. Everything, down to the use of Frank as first-person narrator, points to him as the central character. (Everything, that is, except the title, but a writer with Scott's sense of what sells would hardly call a book *Osbaldistone*.) At too many crucial points, however, Rob Roy displaces Frank as the focus of the reader's interest. Though their relationship may appear to resemble that of Waverley and Fergus or of Morton and Burley, Morton and even Waverley are more active characters than Frank and thus are never eclipsed by Burley and Fergus to the extent that Frank is by Rob Roy. This seems to be largely a result of the bonds that unite Fergus with Waverley and Morton with Burley in a common enterprise for much of their respective stories. The cause shared by each pair of characters makes it possible for each pair to share the spotlight, so to speak, against a common background without compromising the novel's unity. Rob Roy and Frank, by contrast, do not act together in a public cause, since Frank is not a Jacobite. Furthermore, the distance between them is emphasized in the early part of the novel by the fact that, though he takes action several times in Frank's behalf, Rob Roy's identity is unknown to Frank until the novel is half over. In short, the plot keeps these characters separate as Waverley is not kept separate from Fergus nor Morton from Burley, and as a result the novel seems marred by a divided focus.

There is also a failure to unify the public and the private themes as convincingly as in the other two novels. The vagueness of the link between the ruin of the Osbaldistone firm and the rising of the clans has already been noted. A related problem is the absence of specificity about Diana Vernon's Jacobite activities. A wary reader will recognize Scott's irony in having Frank respond to an early warning about Diana with the words, "Pshaw, a Jacobite?—is that all?" There is, however, a lack of concrete detail about her role in the conspiracy. This is perhaps inevitable, given the first-person point of view and the fact that Diana keeps Frank out of the secret of the conspiracy, but it weakens the characterization of the heroine. In contrast, Flora MacIvor's political obsession is fully convincing. Diana is perhaps not meant to seem as much a fanatic as Flora, yet she too has sacrificed all personal inclination to the cause—or to her father's will. At the end of the novel, the reader learns that her father has been a central figure in the conspiracy and has often stayed at Osbaldistone Hall in the disguise of a priest, and that Rashleigh's hold over Diana resulted from his having penetrated her father's disguise. This is a fairly dramatic situation, but the reader is, so to speak, asked to do the dramatizing for himself in retrospect. The specifics about Diana's part in the conspiracy are too little too late.

Since Sir Frederick Vernon has for the reader no identity until the closing pages, he can never be more than a minor figure. Yet to him, Scott assigns the account of the actual rebellion. In the penultimate chapter, the rebellion and its collapse are perfunctorily described by Sir Frederick in less than two pages. This is a signal failure to unify the personal and historical dimensions. Instead of the climax that it should have been, the 1715 rising seems almost an afterthought.

There is, however, a good deal of effective characterization in the novel. Diana Vernon is probably the most attractive and interesting of Scott's heroines. She is well educated, strong-minded, outspoken, aggressive, and witty. She may not quite hold her own in the company to which critical opinion sometimes promotes her, the company of William Shakespeare's Beatrice and Jane Austen's Elizabeth Bennett, but the dialogue Scott gives her does indeed amply express intelligence and vitality. If there is one false note, it is Scott's allowing her finally to marry Frank, but one's reservations may be qualified by the consideration that Frank seems politically almost neutral. If he does not support the Stuarts, he is not in the debt of Hanover either. It is not quite as if Flora MacIvor had married Edward Waverley.

Diana first appears before Frank on horseback wearing "what was then somewhat unusual, a coat, vest, and hat, resembling those of a man, which fashion has since called a riding-habit." Scott several times underlines her firm and forthright behavior by comparing it to a man's. There is a much stronger masculine streak in the only other important female character in this book which has just four speaking roles for women. Rob Roy's wife Helen is a virago capable of ambushing a British troop with only a small band and of cold-bloodedly ordering the drowning of a hostage. She should have been a powerful figure, but the language she speaks is impossibly bookish and rhetorical, an objection which is not sufficiently answered by Scott's later remarking that her "wild, elevated, and poetical" style is caused by the fact that she is translating from Gaelic into English, "which she had acquired as we do learned tongues."

The characterization of Rob Roy himself is on the whole successful, despite a certain lack of impact in his first few appearances, during which a reader who has skipped Scott's unusually cumbersome prefatory material may not even realize that this is the titular character. He gains added weight by being the chief embodiment of one side of the novel's main thematic conflict. The focus of the novel is not on the Jacobite-Hanoverian struggle but on the related but distinguishable conflict between the half-barbaric feudal life of the Highland clans and the modern commercial world of trade. Rob Roy is an outlaw relying on blackmail to support himself and his followers, who acknowledge no leader but him. Their way of life breeds narrow loyalties (a point emphasized also by the judge in the trial of Fergus MacIvor). Helen MacGregor cannot "bide the sight o' a kindly Scot, if he come frae the Lowlands, far less of an Inglisher." The clansmen are a threat to peace and order because rebellion and disorder are conditions far more likely to improve their lot. As Rob Roy says of the expected uprising, "Let it come . . . and if the world is turned upside down, why, honest men have the better chance to cut bread out of it."

Rob Roy is contrasted with the Glasgow weaver and magistrate Bailie Nichol Jarvie. A business associate of the Osbaldistone firm, he accompanies Frank in his pursuit of Rashleigh. Scott makes Rob Roy and Jarvie kinsmen in order to point out the contrasts between them more sharply. These contrasts are most clearly drawn in two fine scenes, one in the Glasgow jail midway through the novel and the other near the end. In the latter scene, when Bailie Nichol Jarvie deplores the ignorance of Rob Roy's sons, the Highlander boasts, "Hamish can bring down a black-cock when he's on the wing wi' a single bullet, and Rob can drive a dirk through a twa-inch board." Jarvie retorts, "Sae muckle the waur for them baith! . . . An they ken naething better than that, they had better no ken that neither." Rob Roy scorns his kinsman's offer to take his sons as apprentices: "My sons weavers! . . . I wad see every loom in Glasgow, beam, traddles, and shuttles, burnt in hell-fire sooner!" Shortly afterward, however, he admits to Frank that he is troubled at the thought of his sons "living their father's life." That kind of life in fact remained possible for only about three more decades, for after the rising of 1745, the rule of law was extended into the Highlands and the power of the clans was permanently broken.

That defeat in effect completed the Union of England and Scotland that had been established in 1707. In Chapter 27, when Andrew Fairservice, Frank's servant, speaks disparagingly of the Union, Jarvie sternly rebukes him:

> Whisht, sir—whisht! it's ill-scraped tongues like yours, that make mischief atween neighbourhoods and nations. . . . I say, Let Glasgow flourish! . . . judiciously and elegantly putten round the town's arms, by way of by-word—Now, since St. Mungo catched herrings in the Clyde, what was ever like to gar [make] us flourish like the sugar and tobacco trade? Will ony body tell me that, and grumble at the treaty that opened us a road west-awa' yonder?

Jarvie expresses Scott's own sense of the benefits that the growing commercial activity of the eighteenth century had brought to Scotland. Emotionally, he admired the romantic and adventurous character of Rob Roy's way of life, but his reason put him finally on the Bailie's side. Jarvie states the theme in terms of honor versus credit: "I maun hear naething about honour—we ken naething here but about credit. Honour is a homicide and a bloodspiller, that gangs about making frays in the street; but Credit is a decent honest man, that sits at hame and makes the pat play [pot boil]" (chap. 26).

The Heart of Midlothian is regarded by many as Scott's best work. In additon to the familiar virtues of a fully realized specific historical milieu and a large cast of characters from a variety of social levels who create themselves through the dialogue, the novel has for its heroine one of the common people, with whom Scott's powers of characterization were at their surest, and it has a truly serious ethical theme in the heroine's refusal to lie to save the life of her younger sister. Jeanie Dean's dilemma enables Scott to examine the relation of the law to justice and to mercy.

The novel opens with an extended presentation of an actual historical event, the Porteous riots in Edinburgh in 1736. Immediately after the execution of a smuggler named Wilson, John Porteous, Captain of the City Guard, reacts to a minor disturbance among the spectators by needlessly ordering his troop to fire upon the crowd. Several people are killed and Porteous is sentenced to be hanged. On the very day set for his execution, he is reprieved by Queen Caroline. That night a mob storms the prison, the Tolbooth (to which the novel's title is a reference). Porteous is dragged out and hanged.

In Scott's version, the mob is led by George Robertson, an accomplice of Wilson, who would have died along with him had Wilson not generously made possible his escape. Robertson has another reason besides revenge on Porteous for breaking into the Tolbooth. In the prison is Effie Deans, who has been seduced by him and has borne his child. She is to stand trial under a statute which stipulates that if a woman conceals her pregnancy and then can neither produce the infant nor prove that it died a natural death, she shall be presumed to have murdered it and shall suffer the death penalty. Once inside the prison, Robertson seeks her out and urges her to make her escape in the confusion, but she refuses. (One wonders why he did not remove her forcibly, but evidently he has his hands full directing Porteous' fate.) The next night, Robertson summons Effie's sister Jeanie to a remote spot and tells her that the case can be removed from under the statute if Effie is found to have communicated her condition to anyone. Jeanie refuses to lie about her sister's having done this, and she repeats her refusal in an affecting interview with Effie just before the trial. When Effie is condemned to death, Jeanie travels on foot all the way from Edinburgh to London, wins the support of the Duke of Argyle, and persuades Queen Caroline to pardon her sister. A few days after Effie is released, she elopes with Robertson.

At this point the novel is in effect finished, or nearly so, but Scott added a fourth volume to stretch the book to the length for which he had contracted. In it, the Duke of Argyle arranges for Jeanie, her new husband Reuben Butler (a clergyman), and her father to remove to a remote part of Scotland under his protection. This pastoral coda contrasts too strongly with the tone of the rest of the novel, and there is an unfortunate emphasis on the material blessings showered on Jeanie that rather qualifies one's sense of the disinterested heroism of her achievement. The closing chapters are, to be sure, tied to the main plot by the reappearance of Effie and her husband and by the discovery of their son, now a member of a small gang of bandits. Robertson is killed in an encounter with this gang, probably by his own son. There is an interesting variation on the novel's central situation, for the son, probably actually guilty of unnatural murder as his mother Effie was not, escapes when Jeanie goes to the room where he is confined and in her compassion loosens his painfully tight bonds. If this repetition of the novel's central event, Jeanie's saving a prisoner from execution, is aesthetically interesting, it is nevertheless ethically problematic, for the youth is a lawless individual who shows no compunction at what he has done and who does not hesitate, once Jeanie has loosened his bonds, to endanger her life by setting a fire in order to effect his escape. Jeanie's mercy seems in this case ill-judged.

It is the first three volumes that contain the most effective probing of the relation of the law to justice and to mercy. Scott contrasts a number of characters, each of whom stands in a different relation to the law. Wilson is a criminal justly condemned for smuggling, but his last offense is the generous one of saving a life by enabling his young accomplice to escape, and it wins him the sympathy of the populace and sets him in sharp contrast to the enforcer of the law, the Captain of the City Guard. Porteous' excessive zeal in the performance of his office leads to the loss of life and earns him the hatred of the populace when he gives the order to fire upon the crowd. His callousness is also shown by his earlier refusal to loosen Wilson's painfully tight handcuffs on the way to the execution, pointing out that all his pain will soon be at an end.

Among the mob that punishes Porteous, Robertson is concerned to preserve order because he wishes to stress the justice of their action, yet in his own person he has much to fear from justice. He is, moreover, clearly moved more by a desire for revenge than by a true concern for justice, and also, as has already been noted, he has in Effie Deans an ulterior motive for storming the Tolbooth.

Of all the prisoners the novel describes, Effie is in the worst plight, since she is entirely innocent of the crime she is charged with and since the statute does not even require that a crime be proved to have occurred. Moreover, she is in a sense to suffer for the guilt of others, for the government wishes to make an example of her because of the increasing frequency of child murder. Also, the Queen's anger at the response to the pardon of Porteous makes a royal pardon for Effie unlikely. Her situation is rendered more hopeless by these two factors that in strict justice have no bearing on her case.

Effie is linked with Wilson in that he and she have both sacrificed themselves for Robertson. Effie staunchly refuses to reveal her seducer's identity, even when she is "offered a commutation and alleviation of her punishment, and even a free pardon, if she would confess what she knew of her lover." In her desire to protect Robertson, she goes so far as to withhold all information concerning Meg Murdockson, the woman to whom Robertson had sent her when her child was due.

Robertson clearly does not deserve her generosity (nor Wilson's, for that matter). He is completely selfish. Effie is not the first girl he has abused. Meg Murdockson had long been a servant in his family, and he had seduced her daughter Madge. When her mother put Madge's infant out of the way so it would not pose an obstacle to Madge's finding a husband, Madge lost her wits. She is one of a number of pathetic simpletons who wander through Scott's novels, a company that includes David Gellatley in *Waverley* and Goose Gibbie in *Old Mortality*. Robertson's guilt in Madge's case has far-reaching consequences, for it is anger at the prospect of Effie's taking her daughter's place that moves Meg Murdockson to spirit away Effie's infant and later to attempt to waylay Jeanie on her journey to London.

Robertson's real name is Staunton. He has been among other things an actor, and this is appropriate, for, besides being selfish, he is the rankest hypocrite. In the scene where he confronts Jeanie to explain how she can save her sister, he heaps blame on himself liberally, but it is all empty gesture and rhetoric. He expects someone else to solve the problem. Jeanie is to save Effie by telling a lie when he could do it by surrendering himself and telling the truth. When Effie has finally been sentenced, then indeed he leaps on his horse with the intention of securing her reprieve by giving himself up as the leader of the Porteous mob, but his horse loses its footing and Staunton is thrown and severly injured. Jeanie learns of this on her journey to London when, by a remarkable coincidence, she meets him in his father's house, where he is recuperating. He authorizes her to trade his life for that of her sister, but only if her own unsupported plea is refused.

When Effie is reprieved and Staunton marries her, he becomes an actor in good earnest, and so does she. Sir George and Lady Staunton live for years in fear that their past will be discovered, and his unhappiness is much aggravated by the fact that they are childless. A series of coincidences reveals that their son is not dead, but is part of a small gang of bandits in the very vicinity where Jeanie and her family now live. When Staunton arrives in search of him and is killed, Jeanie prepares the body for burial. She discovers "from the crucifix, the beads, and the shirt of hair which he wore next his person, that his sense of guilt had induced him to receive the dogmata of a religion, which pretends, by the maceration of the body, to expiate the crimes of the soul" (chap. 52). The verb *pretends* conveys Scott's view of the appropriateness of Staunton's conversion to Roman Catholicism.

Jeanie Deans, in contrast, is firmly anchored in her father's rigid Presbyterianism and has a horror of every kind of pretense or falsehood. Her principles prevent her from lying to save Effie, but her generosity enables her to accomplish what all of Staunton's empty heroics are powerless to achieve. It is interesting to consider a misunderstanding that arises between Jeanie and her father, David Deans, regarding her testifying at Effie's trial. Deans is a Cameronian, the strictest kind of Scottish Presbyterian, and his memory goes back to the battle of Bothwell Bridge and the persecutions that followed it.

He is doubtful of the propriety of even appearing in court, since doing so might seem to constitute an acknowledgement of a government that has abandoned the Solemn League and Covenant and that exercises what he regards as undue influence over the Kirk. Though Deans has never before hesitated to tell anyone what to do, in the present case he says to himself, "My daughter Jean may have a light in this subject that is hid frae my auld een—it is laid on her conscience, and not on mine—If she hath freedom to gang before this judicatory, and hold up her hand for this poor cast-away, surely I will not say she steppeth over her bounds" (chap. 18). The inconsistency is too touching and too clearly rooted in his love for Effie to be called hypocrisy. It is another instance of the conflict between principles of conduct and emotional claims, and it enriches the character and underlines his relation to the central theme.

When he attempts to convey to Jeanie his resolution of his scruples, she, who has no thought of refusing to appear in court, takes it that he is encouraging her to give false testimony. The misunderstanding increases her sense of isolation and lack of support and thus makes her behavior all the more heroic.

The heroic impact of the journey itself is marred somewhat by the melodramatic events with which Scott seeks to enliven it. The lurid coloring is overdone in the scene of Jeanie's captivity at the hands of Meg, Madge, and two underworld cronies of theirs (to whom the old woman is known as Mother Blood). Scott is more successful when he modulates into comedy in the scene in which the demented Madge, in the absence of Meg and the others, leads Jeanie to a nearby village and then into church, where Madge's fantastic behavior causes her captive considerable embarrassment. The tension between the comic elements here and the very real danger of Jeanie's situation makes a strong effect. Shortly afterward, however, the tone shifts back to melodrama with the coincidental meeting with the convalescent Staunton, and the dramatic temperature drops during one of those retrospective narratives which Scott's complex plotting often forced on him.

The climactic confrontation with the Queen is very well done. Oddly enough, although Scott often had trouble finding a convincingly natural mode of utterance for his invented characters of the upper class, for actual historical figures he often succeeded in writing dialogue that is elevated without being stilted, polished without being wooden. Such is the language of Prince Charles Edward in *Waverley*, of Claverhouse in *Old Mortality*, and of Queen Caroline here.

The psychology of the Queen as well as her language is noteworthy. Jeanie's simple plea is effective, but it is not, or not only, emotional considerations that cause the Queen to grant the pardon. Even her response to Jeanie's main speech—"This is eloquence"—suggests objective evaluation of the speech more than emotional assent, and Scott keeps the scene well clear of sentimentality by a persistent emphasis on the political factors in the Queen's decision. She is divided between resentment of the Scots for their response to her pardoning of Porteous and her inclination to remain on good terms with Jeanie's sponsor, the Duke of Argyle. Even though he is at present out of favor, her policy is based on the principle that political allies may become opponents and opponents may again become allies. Another element in the scene is her complex attitude toward Lady Suffolk, also present at the interview. The Queen has so arranged matters that Suffolk is both her chief confidante and the King's mistress. After inadvertently making a remark that the Queen construes as a reflection on herself, Jeanie rights herself with a chance reference to "the stool of repentance," the punishment in Scotland "for light life and conversation, and for breaking the seventh command." The Queen is amused at the obvious embarrassment of "her good Suffolk."

The novel as a whole indicates that although the law is an absolute necessity, it can never do more than approximate justice because it is made and administered by human beings. It is ironically the generous instincts of Effie (in protecting Staunton) and the uncompromising honesty of Jeanie that make Effie the victim of a law which, it is repeatedly suggested, is a bad law because it exacts punishment in cases where there may have been no crime. It seems unjust too that the strict enforcement in the present instance is caused by factors external to Effie's case, the rise in child murder and the royal anger over the Porteous affair. Moreover, the author tends to place the human agents who enforce the law in an unflattering light. Porteous abuses the authority vested in him. The Doomster, or executioner, is a kind of untouchable who inspires horror in everyone when he makes his ritual appearance at Effie's sentencing. Ratcliffe, a thief four times condemned to the gallows, is the only prisoner besides Effie who rejects the opportunity to escape when the mob breaks into the Tolbooth. His reason is that he wants the post of underturnkey. The authorities actually grant this audacious request after considering how valuable his knowledge of the underworld is likely to prove. Scott provides a striking emblem of the amount of practical compromise involved in the enforcing of the law when he shows Ratcliffe and Sharpitlaw, the superintendent of police, at the start of the interview in which they bargain over Ratcliffe's request: "They sate for five minutes silent, on opposite sides of a small table, and looked fixedly at each other, with a sharp, knowing, and alert cast of countenance, not unmingled with an inclination to laugh."

The scene with the Queen indicates that the prerogative of mercy that is intended to mitigate the sternness of the law or correct miscarriages of justice is likewise governed by considerations of policy and expediency. The outcome of that scene, however, shows that the gap between ideal justice on the one hand, and policy or expediency on the other, can be bridged by the selfless exertions of someone motivated simply by love.

Although the four novels discussed here are likely to appear on anyone's list of the best of Scott, they are by no means the only ones worthy of a modern reader's attention. *The Antiquary, The Bride of Lammermoor, A Legend of Montrose*, and *Woodstock* have all found advocates among modern critics. There is also a very successful third panel in what might be called the Jacobite triptych that includes *Waverley* and *Rob Roy*; *Redgauntlet*, set in the 1760's, describes the last throes of the Jacobite movement. In addition to a plot full of intrigue, it is noteworthy for its combination of letters and journals with third-person narration and for autobiographical elements in the main characters of Alan Fairford and Darsie Latimer. Obviously Scott will never again have the huge audience he enjoyed throughout the nineteenth century, but he is more than merely a chapter in literary history. In addition to establishing the genre of the historical novel and influencing nineteenth century historiography, he wrote several novels that can be judged major achievements by any but the most narrow and rigid criteria.

John Michael Walsh

Other major works

SHORT FICTION: *Chronicles of the Canongate*, 1827.

PLAYS: *Halidon Hill*, 1822; *Macduff's Cross*, 1823; *The Doom of Devorgoil*, 1839; *Auchindrane: Or, The Ayrshire Tragedy*, 1830.

POETRY: *The Eve of Saint John: A Border Ballad*, 1800; *The Lay of the Last Minstrel*, 1805; *Ballads and Lyrical Pieces*, 1806; *Marmion: A Tale of Flodden Field*, 1808; *The Lady of the Lake*, 1810; *The Vision of Don Roderick*, 1811; *Rokeby*, 1813; *The Bridal of Triermain: Or, The Vale of St. John, in Three Cantos*, 1813; *The Lord of the Isles*, 1815; *The Field of Waterloo*, 1815; *The Ettrick Garland. Being Two Excellent New Songs*, 1815 (with James Hogg); *Harold the Dauntless*, 1817.

NONFICTION: *The Life and Works of John Dryden*, 1808; *The Life of Jonathan Swift*, 1814; *Lives of the Novelists*, 1825; *The Life of Napoleon Buonaparte: Emperor of the French, with a Preliminary View of the French Revolution*, 1827.

TRANSLATIONS: *The Chase, and William and Helen: Two Ballads from the German of Gottfried Augustus Bürger*, 1796; *Goetz von Berlichingen*, 1799.

EDITED TEXTS: *Minstrelsy of the Scottish Border*, 1802-1803 (3 volumes); *A Collection of Scarce and Valuable Tracts*, 1809-1815 (13 volumes); *Chronological Notes of Scottish Affairs from the Diary of Lord Fountainhall*, 1822.

Bibliography

Crawford, Thomas. *Scott.* Rev. ed. Edinburgh: Scottish Academic Press, 1982. A revision and elaboration of Crawford's widely acclaimed study of Scott. Examines Scott's work as a poet, balladist, and novelist in a compact style.
Daiches, David. *Sir Walter Scott and His World.* London: Thames and Hud-

son, 1971. A well-written account of Scott, generously illustrated. Contains much valuable information in a readable style by an eminent scholar of Scott.

Elton, Oliver. *Sir Walter Scott*. London: Edward Arnold, 1971. Discusses Scott's poetry and the *Waverley* novels. Includes a tribute to John Gibson Lockhart, Scott's son-in-law and author of *Memoirs of the Life of Sir Walter Scott* (Edinburgh: R. Cadell, 1837-1838).

Hart, Francis R. *Scott's Novels: The Plotting of Historical Survival*. Charlottesville: University of Virginia Press, 1966. A survey of Scott's novels, generally favorable and emphasizing the author's diversity.

Johnson, Edgar. *Sir Walter Scott: The Great Unknown*. 2 vols. New York: Macmillan, 1970. Now considered the definitive biography of Scott, replacing John Gibson Lockhart's. Johnson has used the many sources and information available on Scott to present an accurate portrayal of the author. A must for the serious Scott scholar.

Lauber, John. *Sir Walter Scott*. Rev. ed. Boston: Twayne, 1989. A good introduction to Scott, ideal for the beginning student or new reader of Scott. Rather than concentrating on the *Waverley* novels, takes a "sampling" of Scott's finest works. Contains a useful bibliography.

MARY LEE SETTLE

Born: Charleston, West Virginia; July 29, 1918

Principal long fiction
The Love Eaters, 1954; *The Kiss of Kin*, 1955; *O Beulah Land*, 1956; *Know Nothing*, 1960; *Fight Night on a Sweet Saturday*, 1964; *The Clam Shell*, 1971; *Prisons*, 1973; *Blood Tie*, 1977; *The Scapegoat*, 1980; *The Killing Ground*, 1982 (revision of *Fight Night on a Sweet Saturday*); *Celebration*, 1986; *Charley Bland*, 1989.

Other literary forms
In addition to her novels, Mary Lee Settle has written several nonfiction books. Her juvenile works, *The Story of Flight* (1967) and *Water World* (1984), the latter being a parallel history of man's exploration of the sea, are not as significant as her autobiographical *All the Brave Promises: Memories of Aircraft Woman Second Class 2146391* (1966) or her historical study *The Scopes Trial: The State of Tennessee vs. John Thomas Scopes* (1972). *All the Brave Promises* describes her experiences as an American volunteer in the Women's Auxiliary Air Force of the Royal Air Force (RAF) in 1942 and 1943. *The Scopes Trial*, like *All the Brave Promises*, deals with human responses to a historical confrontation.

Achievements
As late as 1978, when she won the National Book Award in Fiction for *Blood Tie*, critics were calling Settle an "unknown" writer. With the earlier publication of four of her historical novels, some of them had praised her for research-based realism, resulting in works more respectable than the typically lurid products of that genre. Critics, however, found her complexity sometimes confusing, pointing out the changes in point of view, the flashforwards and flashbacks, and sometimes the assumption that the reader knew the history of her characters as well as the writer did. There was a lack of agreement as to whether her characters were well developed. After the completion of the Beulah Quintet in 1982 (*O Beulah Land*, *Know Nothing*, *Prisons*, *The Scapegoat*, *The Killing Ground*), however, critics recognized the depth and scope of her vision, arguing that Settle's structural complexity was justified by her aim: to present the truth about human relationships in their historical context. To her early champions, among them Malcolm Cowley and George Garrett, were added numerous other reviewers, who saw evidence of her considerable talent in her contemporary works as well as in the historical novels. To them, the award for *Blood Tie* was a belated recognition, rather than an unexpected one. When *Celebration* was published, Settle received

praise, rather than blame, for her stylistic and technical feats, and she was no longer faulted for her characterization. With such articles as that by Peggy Bach in the October, 1984, *The Southern Review*, Settle's reputation was established as a skillful, serious writer, whose approach to her material is necessitated if she is to document her own search and that of her characters for, in Bach's words, "their own personal past and the taproot that was cut."

Biography

Mary Lee Settle was born in Charleston, West Virginia, on July 29, 1918. She attended Sweet Briar College from 1936 to 1938. After serving in the RAF Women's Auxiliary Air Force during World War II, she became a free-lance writer and journalist, working briefly as an editor for *Harper's Bazaar* and later as English correspondent for *Flair*. After writing several plays, still unpublished, she turned to fiction, publishing her first novel in 1954. She was awarded Guggenheim Fellowships in 1957-1958 and in 1959-1960. She lives with her husband, writer and historian William Tazewell, in Charlottesville, Virginia, and teaches at Georgetown University.

Analysis

Whether her works are set in the present or in the past, in Europe or in West Virginia, Mary Lee Settle's preoccupations are always the same: the quest for freedom and the pursuit of love in a threatening, changing social environment. Like a Greek dramatist, she employs a background of ordinary people, who ignore the issues and the dangers of their time and place, who accept their intellectual and social prisons, blindly assuming that all is for the best, no matter what persons or what ideals they betray. In contrast to this chorus are a few exceptional people who are incapable of that blind and easy acceptance. Whatever the social cost, they insist on honesty. Whatever the political and economic cost, they seek freedom. Their ideals are ultimately democratic, for they will not judge others by narrow social standards or limit their associations by social formulas. Because they are uncompromising, they are destined to be misunderstood, ridiculed, deserted, even betrayed, but they may also be followed, admired, and loved.

Settle's novels fall into three categories: the Southern novels, such as her first two published works, *The Love Eaters* and *The Kiss of Kin*, as well as *The Clam Shell* and *Charley Bland*; the Beulah Quintet, five historical novels published between 1956 and 1982, out of chronological order; and the European novels, the award-winning *Blood Tie*, set in contemporary Turkey, and *Celebration*, set in London but tracing the past lives of its characters to Kurdistan, Hong Kong, and Africa. Before *Celebration*, Settle had finally concluded the Beulah Quintet with *The Killing Ground*, which brought her several families into the present. In *Celebration*, although her characters deal with their past, they find redemption. More than any of her other works,

Celebration moves joyfully into the future, symbolized by the central section, in which the characters of the work gather to watch the moon walk.

The Love Eaters is set in Canona, West Virginia, among the Country Club people who will appear again in the final novel of the quintet, *The Killing Ground*, Anne Randolph Potter, for example, the drawling Virginian, and her "real American" husband George Potter. The men work, talk, and drink; the women decorate their homes, plan community projects, talk, and drink. With her fine ear for dialogue, Settle captures their sterile lives by carefully recording that talk, the beauty-shop gossip blaring under the hair dryers, the brief exchanges between husbands and wives, mothers and daughters, men in the Country Club locker-room. The marriages in Canona have become the routine relationships of people who live politely in the same house, like the Potters and like their friends the Dodds, Jim and Martha. Because she was tired of the meaningless talk, Martha married Jim, and when she feels alone in their silent home, she reminds herself that she got exactly what she wanted. What Jim himself wanted was a quiet routine; knowing this, Martha has not even permitted herself to bear him a child.

The bored women of the Canona Country Club have brightened their lives by organizing an acting company, and it is through this venture that one of the two disrupting forces in *The Love Eaters* comes to Canona. As the novel opens, the itinerant director Hamilton Sacks descends from the train, accompanied by his devoted mother. Sacks is a physical and emotional cripple, who delights in "playing" the people he meets as if he were playing to an audience, as indeed he is, and who has no sense of moral responsibility for the effect that his wicked hints may have on their lives.

The second disrupting force comes, ironically, through the placid Jim Dodd. Through a letter, he has learned the whereabouts of the son whom he had by a previous marriage, about whom he had never told his childless present wife. With the arrival of charming, slender, handsome, and above all, lovable Selby Dodd in Canona, the lives of Jim and Martha are changed forever.

In Settle's modern version of *Phaedra* (c. A.D. 45-55), the passion of a menopausal woman, trapped in the aimless days and nights of a society which thinks in stereotypes and in a marriage whose value has been its placid silence, is no more surprising than the fact that George Potter keeps the local beautician as his mistress. Martha's upcountry old mother is familiar with the yearnings of middle-aged women, familiar enough to warn that infatuations with young men, while not surprising, are generally unwise. Martha is not the only one who is taken with Selby Dodd, who, as Hamilton comments, lives on love and, without exerting himself, attracts women of all ages, as well as men such as Hamilton; Martha's contemporary Anne Randolph Potter and her seventeen-year-old daughter Sally Bee Potter vie for Selby from the first time they meet him. There is, then, very little shock in speculations about Martha's feelings. It is Martha herself who inflicts the punishment upon herself, and her emphasis is not on the immorality of incestuous feelings or fear of a heroic husband—for neither moral rectitude nor heroism is common in Canona society—but on her own need for Selby's physical and emotional love. As Hippolytus, Selby is neither morally outraged nor committed to a young princess. He trifles with Sally Bee Potter under the same rules which she observes in teasing him, but no love is involved, for Selby, like Hamilton, is too narcissistic to love anyone but himself and too opportunistic to be troubled by morality. Because his long-range plans include acquiring as much of Jim's property as possible, however, Selby cannot afford to risk angering Jim, and his pose must remain that of loving son and considerate stepson.

The differences between the traditional tragic characters in this account of a stepmother's passion for her stepson and Settle's characters, who lack the tragic stature and the rigid moral sense of those in the earlier versions of the story, indicate the diminished standards of modern society, which imprisons its members within patterns which have no moral dimension, but merely the force of mindless custom. At the end of the novel, Martha at least briefly takes responsibility for Selby's death, but instead of dying, she loses her mind. Jim, too, escapes from reality; having made his dead son into a hero, he waits for Martha to become her old self.

In *The Kiss of Kin*, the imprisoning society is a Southern family, brought together for a funeral. Into this society comes Abraham Passmore, summoned to claim his inheritance and determined also to discover the wrong which his father's people once did to his mother. By the end of the novel, Abraham has forced the members of the family to admit the truth, but it is obvious that they will not therefore become honest. Only the cousin who leaves with him has been forced by the day's events to reject the family, as well as her similarly dishonest Yankee lover, in order to find her own freedom.

While entertaining, *The Kiss of Kin* is too clearly an adaptation of the light comedy which Settle had first written. Like *The Love Eaters*, it was skillfully constructed, hilariously satirical, accurate in dialogue; avoiding authorial comment, it depends upon dramatic scenes and upon the meditations of the few sensitive characters to comment upon the society which is its target. At this point, Settle made an important turn in her literary career. She produced the first of the Beulah Quintet novels, which plunged into the historical past to find the roots of that Southern society realized in her first two novels.

Settle's first two historical novels were written in chronological order. *O Beulah Land* is set in what was later to be West Virginia at the time of the French and Indian War; *Know Nothing*, in the 1840's and 1850's. It is significant that both of these novels take place just before a momentous historic event, in the first case, the American Revolution, in the second, the Civil

War. In both of them, exceptional people understand the issues of their time and respond heroically. Others either insist on living in a changeless world, clinging to a familiar pattern, or blindly refuse to admit that change is inevitable.

In *O Beulah Land*, a massacre results from the insistence of two English men, at opposite ends of the social scale, that the New World pattern is no different from the old. "Squire" Josiah Devotion Raglan steals, as he did in England; the arrogant British commander is rude, as he could afford to be in England. Unfortunately, the Indians, whose tomahawk is stolen and whose pride is offended, are not governed by Old World rules, and the massacre is the outcome. Significantly, Hannah Bridewell, a transported prostitute and thief, survives captivity by the Indians and reaches safety in the arms of a frontiersman, Jeremiah Catlett. Adapting to the New World, they create a marriage outside the church, which has not yet come to the wilderness, and later defend their home by the justifiable murder of the blackmailing Squire, who once again has miscalculated in the New World.

In the Lacey family, Settle again contrasts the selfish and the blind with those perceptive, freedom-loving individuals who refuse to enslave themselves to an old pattern. Sally Lacey, the pretentious, spoiled wife of Jonathan Lacey, refuses to adapt to frontier life. Failing in her lifelong crusade to make over her homely neighbors, Sally at last goes mad. In contrast, the printer Jarcey Pentacost has lost his shop rather than tailor his efforts to the values of a community already stagnating; for him, the frontier means freedom.

In *Know Nothing*, although the historical background is very different, the descendants of the characters in *O Beulah Land* must choose between enslavement to older patterns, which no longer suit the changing country, and emerging new patterns. Another Sally Lacey and her husband, Brandon, must move west because the plantation economic system has failed them. Unable to adapt, Brandon kills himself and Sally retreats permanently into the contemplation of her heredity. Other casualties of inherited patterns are Johnny Catlett, who cannot escape from his role as slaveowner and finally as Confederate officer; Lewis Catlett, the prisoner of his religious obsession, whose abolitionism, the result of his mother's influence, has in it no grain of compassion; Melinda Lacey and Sara Lacey, both trapped in miserable marriages from which, in a society which does not permit divorce, only death can release them. Already in *Know Nothing*, the same kind of social prisons from which American immigrants escaped have been established in the New World, and the quest for freedom has become more and more difficult.

In 1964, Viking Press published *Fight Night on a Sweet Saturday*, which was to have been the concluding work in a "Beulah Trilogy." In that book, Hannah McKarkle, who is named for the heroic Hannah of *O Beulah Land*, comes to Canona, West Virginia, originally to see her brother and then to investigate his death. During her visit, she begins to explore the past of her family and of her region, thus, in a sense, becoming Mary Lee Settle herself. Unfortunately, the publishers so cut *Fight Night on a Sweet Saturday* that Settle found the relationships obscured. Eventually, she was to add two volumes to the Beulah works, *Prisons* and *The Scapegoat*, and to rewrite *Fight Night on a Sweet Saturday*, which was published as *The Killing Ground*.

Still pursuing the democratic ideal, Settle returned to Great Britain, where she tracked down a chance reference to John Lilburne, the leader of a group of radicals, a number of whom were executed by the forces of Cromwell, who were averse to the "Leveling" principles of true egalitarians. It is the story of one of these executed radicals which Settle tells in her seventeenth century novel *Prisons*, which becomes the first novel in the Beulah Quintet, viewed chronologically. Its hero, the brave, idealistic Johnny Church, enmeshed in amoral public policy, refuses to save his own life by becoming Oliver Cromwell's agent among the men who see Johnny as a natural leader. It is the descendants of Johnny Church, both literal and spiritual, who continue to fight for freedom in Settle's historical and contemporary novels.

Meanwhile, Settle had published another novel set in the contemporary South, *The Clam Shell*, which is set among the same Country Club set as *The Love Eaters*. In Canona in 1966, Anne Randolph Potter, "Plain" George Potter, and their friends are involved in their usual rituals. This time, however, the disrupting influence is one of their own friends, the woman protagonist, who watches them watching football, drinking, and reminiscing. Unlike Martha Dodd, she learned young that she was unable to fit the mold of her friends in Canona, just as she could not fit the mold of the Virginia finishing school to which she was sent. Musing on her youth, remembering her unjust treatment at the finishing school, she realizes that she has long ago ceased wishing to be accepted by mindless, restrictive upper-class Virginia or West Virginia society. Like Abraham Passmore, she is content to be an honest exile.

In literary quality, *The Clam Shell* is one of Settle's less effective novels. Satirical and often angry, it divides its characters into two groups: those who understand life and those who, from dullness or from choice, choose not to understand but, instead, to persecute those who do.

After this simplistic novel came one of Settle's best, *Blood Tie*, a contemporary work set on a Turkish island. The protagonist, idealistic, innocent Ariadne, has come to Ceramos to recover from a mid-life divorce. There she becomes acquainted with a group of expatriates, the sensationalist Basil, a German archaeologist, a Jewish bar owner, a wealthy American girl, and the CIA agent Frank Proctor. None of the expatriates understands the language well enough to realize the disapproval, the contempt, and the ridicule with which they are viewed by the natives. Nor have the expatriates any idea of the intrigue with which they are surrounded. The archaeologist, for example, does not guess that a hunted university student is hiding in the sacred caverns which he cannot find. As the Turks manipulate the expatriates for gain, the expatriates utilize one another and the Turks for the sensations they seek. Through the corruption walks Ariadne, mothering the spoiled American girl and the mute Turkish child, struggling with her sense of rejection and with her own troublesome sexuality, unintentionally shocking the Turks, who misinterpret her actions. When she and the other expatriates at last leave the island, the Chief of Police praises her because of all the visitors only Ariadne tried to see the Turks as individuals, rather than as background figures in an exotic environment. Although Ariadne does not know it, she has made a difference to the troubled, mute child, for at last he is able to speak.

In *The Scapegoat*, published only three years after *Blood Tie*, Settle again created complex characters who have a moral sense. Foolish, innocent, and idealistic though they may be, such individuals do provide some hope for the future. Like its predecessors in the series, *The Scapegoat* takes place at a time of confrontation, on a single day, June 7, 1912, when the hostility between British mine owners and their hired thugs, on one hand, and the mines with their union leaders, on the other, results in armed conflict. In the middle of the conflict are the mine owners, Beverley and Ann Eldridge Lacey, who hope to keep their mine, their home, and their friendships apart from the approaching violence. Ironically, the idealism of their daughter Lily Ellen Lacey, home from college, leads directly to the violence. Her friendship with a young striker is exploited to inflame both the strikebreakers and the strikers. As the day develops, basically good people do evil. To save her son, Lily's friend sacrifices a new immigrant, the "scapegoat" of the title; to help the friend escape, Lily and Beverley take advantage of the death of the scapegoat, thus in a sense participating in the guilt.

In her later books, however, Settle is dealing more realistically with guilt, seemingly recognizing that in this world every act is tainted. Rather than expecting her exceptional characters to be flawless and fully cognizant of the situation in which they are placed, Settle is more compassionate toward the well meaning, even if, like Lily, they unintentionally play into the hands of clearly evil forces. Granted, ignorance cannot exempt one from guilt. Lily's service as a nurse in World War I, which results in her death, is a course deliberately chosen because she must take the responsibility for her tragic blindness. Yet in her later works, Settle castigates fewer characters for their blindness and permits more of them the possibility of redemption.

In her final volume of the Beulah Quintet, *The Killing Ground*, Settle's writer Hannah McKarkle sums up what she has learned of history. In clash after clash, people struggle for freedom. Often, as Johnny Church learned in the English Civil War, as the Laceys saw in the American mine wars, both sides in a confrontation seek power, and it is a third group which must struggle for real freedom. Whatever its pretensions, every society is made up of many who are blind, often for their own comfort, and of many who, though perceptive, are unprincipled. Because of that convenient or deliberate blindness, the rebels, the seekers for freedom, must always struggle, first to see the truth, then, and only then, to act upon it.

Because critics are now becoming aware of Settle's themes, they can justify the shifts in point of view and the movements back and forth in time which make her work difficult. In *The Scapegoat*, for example, Settle tells her story through the eyes of several different characters, whose testimony, weighed and judged by the reader, can add up to objective truth. Similarly, in *Blood Tie*, the mutual misunderstandings between the Turkish and the expatriate populations are dramatized by frequent changes in point of view, often revealing opposite interpretations of events and statements. Thus, the thematic emphasis on the pursuit of truth is exemplified by Settle's own method of revealing the truth.

Moreover, because as William Faulkner believed, the truth of any one moment involves the past of an individual, a community, a people, and because the human mind never lives purely in present consciousness, Settle's frequent shifts in time are also a technical expression of a thematic emphasis. In a comic novel such as *The Kiss of Kin*, the thrust of the work is toward the revelation of a single element in the past, and therefore the dramatic technique is effective. In a complicated novel such as *The Killing Ground* or *Blood Tie*, however, in which characters attempt to understand the present while always being conscious of the past, the shifts in time are both effective and thematically necessary.

Settle's increasing technical mastery and her developing theme of redemption are both evident in *Celebration*. The six chapters of the novel alternate between London and three distant areas where various characters once lived, Kurdistan, Hong Kong, and Africa. The process through which the main characters must go is that of the mass: an honest facing of the past, the acceptance of guilt, repentance, redemption, and joy. Each of the characters has crossed what Settle terms "the Styx," directly confronting death and despair. For Teresa Cerrutti, it was the death of her husband in Malakastan, followed by her own surgery for cancer. For Noel, Lord Atherton, it was a disastrous encounter with a Chinese lover in Hong Kong. For Ewen Stuart McLeod, it was the betrayal by his uncle, who trapped him in an unsavory African expedition and involved him in the murder of innocent people.

The movement toward a joyful future is suggested in the fourth of Settle's chapters, when her major characters and their friends together watch the moon landing, which is an affirmation of mankind's possibilities. That chapter, however, is followed by the darkest account in the novel, Ewen's African adventure, revealing man at his treacherous, murderous worst. Ewen's life was saved by the black Roman Catholic priest, Pius Deng, who is also now in London, one of the friends.

In the final chapter, there is a celebration of death and of life. The priest is killed by London muggers, but as the guilt-stricken youngest of them comments, he died in a state of grace. Furthermore, the commitment for which he had hoped, the marriage of Ewen and Teresa, concludes the novel. Under the influence of the saintly Pius and through their ever-increasing love for one another, the London friends have made the Styx not a river of death, but one of life.

Thus, in her works, Mary Lee Settle has always stressed the need for personal honesty, for emotional and political freedom, and for a democratic acceptance of others on an individual basis. In her early Southern novels, she emphasizes the stagnant, snobbish, superficial society which broke the weak and drove the strong into exile. In the Beulah Quintet and in the European novels, however, while still castigating the cruel, the selfish, and the blind, Settle has increasingly emphasized the possibility of expiation or of redemption. As her imagination has moved backward in time and outward in space, her sense of human possibilities has intensified. With *Celebration*, she seems to have expressed an honest hope for those who are willing to face life with honesty and courage; with that novel, she has also almost faultlessly synthesized her matter and her manner.

Rosemary M. Canfield-Reisman

Other major works

NONFICTION: *All the Brave Promises: Memories of Aircraft Woman Second Class 2146391*, 1966; *The Scopes Trial: The State of Tennessee vs. John Thomas Scopes*, 1972.

CHILDREN'S LITERATURE: *The Story of Flight*, 1967; *Water World*, 1984.

Bibliography

Bach, Peggy. "The Searching Voice and Vision of Mary Lee Settle." *Southern Review* 20 (October, 1984): 842-850. After outlining the various critical assessments of Settle's work, Bach supports her own insistence that it can hardly be rated too highly. In the Beulah Quintet, Settle has traced a family through three hundred years of history, showing how desperately even people beginning fresh in a new land need to have a sense of their past.

Garrett, George. "Mary Lee Settle's Beulah Land Trilogy." In *Rediscoveries*, edited by David Madden. New York: Crown, 1971. This essay, published before the completion of the Beulah Quintet, illustrates Garrett's early respect and support for Settle. In it, Garrett, himself a fine historical novelist, praises Settle's skill in handling complex structure, her vivid characters, and her grasp of history.

Joyner, Nancy Carol. "Mary Lee Settle's Connections: Class and Clothes in the Beulah Quintet." In *Women Writers of the Contemporary South*, edited by Peggy Whitman Prenshaw. Jackson: University Press of Mississippi, 1984. Stresses the theme of social rigidity and social injustice in Settle's Beulah Quintet. In these five books, which range across two continents and through three centuries, Joyner sees the repeated emphasis on class consciousness and family connections, which help to perpetuate wrongs, generation after generation, even in the supposedly classless New World. An interesting, if somewhat limited, approach.

Settle, Mary Lee. Interview by Wendy Smith. *Publishers Weekly* 230 (October 10, 1986): 73-74. This interview was prompted by the growing recognition of Settle's stature as a novelist, indicated by the paperback reissues of a number of her works. Her comments about her writing methods and her perception of the American experience, as well as her clear statement of purpose, are extremely revealing.

Speer, Jean Haskell. "Montani Semper Liberi: Mary Lee Settle and the Myths of Appalachia." In *Southern Women Writers: The New Generation*. Tuscaloosa: University of Alabama Press, 1990. Speer contends that in the Beulah Quintet one of Settle's purposes was to debunk such myths as the assumption that there is a single, easily defined Appalachian culture whose people are both ignorant and innocent. This essay argues that Settle's realistic fiction has done much to define the real Appalachia for her readers.

MARY WOLLSTONECRAFT SHELLEY

Born: London, England; August 30, 1797
Died: London, England; February 1, 1851

Principal long fiction

Frankenstein, 1818; *Valperga: Or, The Life of Castruccio, Prince of Lucca*, 1823; *The Last Man*, 1826; *The Fortunes of Perkin Warbeck*, 1830; *Lodore*, 1835; *Falkner*, 1837.

Other literary forms

Mary Shelley was a prolific writer, forced into copiousness by economic necessity. Punished by Sir Timothy Shelley, her husband Percy Bysshe Shelley's father, for her violation of his moral codes with his son, Mary Shelley was denied access to the Shelley estate for a long time after her husband's death. Her own father, William Godwin, was eternally in debt himself and spared her none of his troubles. Far from helping her, Godwin threw his own financial woes in her lap. It fell to Mary to support her son by writing, in addition to her novels, a plethora of short stories and some scholarly materials. The stories were mainly available to the public in a popular annual publication called the *Keepsake*, a book intended for gift-giving. Her stories were firmly entrenched in the popular Gothic tradition, bearing such titles as "A Tale of Passion," "Ferdinand Eboli," "The Evil Eye," and "The Bride of Modern Italy." Her scholarly work included contributions to *The Lives of the Most Eminent Literary and Scientific Men* in *Lardner's Cabinet Encyclopedia*. She attempted to write about the lives of both her father and her husband, although her efforts were never completed. She wrote magazine articles of literary criticism and reviews of operas, an art form that filled her with delight. She wrote two travel books, *History of A Six Weeks' Tour Through a Part of France, Switzerland, Germany, and Holland* (1817) and *Rambles in Germany and Italy* (1844). Shelley edited two posthumous editions of her husband's poetry (1824 and 1839) and she wrote several poetic dramas: *Manfred*, now lost, *Proserpine*, and *Midas*. She wrote a handful of poems, most of which were published in *Keepsake*. Her two novellas are *Mathilda*, unfinished and unpublished, and *The Heir of Mondolfo*, published posthumously in 1877.

Achievements

Shelley's literary reputation rests solely on her first novel, *Frankenstein*. Her six other novels, which are of uneven quality, are very difficult indeed to find, even in the largest libraries. Nevertheless, Mary Shelley lays claim to a dazzling array of accomplishments. First, she is credited with the creation of modern science fiction. All subsequent tales of the brilliant but doomed scientist, the sympathetic but horrible monster, both in high and mass culture, owe their lives to her. Even Hollywood's dream factory owes her an imaginative and economic debt it can never repay.

Second, the English tradition is indebted to her for a reconsideration of the Romantic movement by one of its central participants. In her brilliant *Frankenstein* fantasy, Mary Shelley questions many of the basic tenets of the Romantic rebellion: the Romantic faith in man's blissful relationship to nature, the belief that evil resides only in the dead hand of social tradition, and the romantic delight in death as a lover and restorer.

Finally, she has created one of the great literary fictions of the dialogue with the self. The troubled relationship between Dr. Frankenstein and his monster is one of the foundations of the literary tradition of "the double," doubtless the mother of all the doubles in Charles Dickens, Robert Louis Stevenson, and even in Arthur Conan Doyle and Joseph Conrad.

Biography

Mary Shelley, born Mary Wollstonecraft Godwin, lived the life of a great romantic heroine at the heart of the Romantic movement. She was the daughter of the brilliant feminist Mary Wollstonecraft and the equally distinguished man of letters, William Godwin. Born of two parents who vociferously opposed marriage, she was the occasion of their nuptials. Her mother died ten days after she was born, and her father had to marry for the second time in four years to provide a mother for his infant daughter. He chose a rather conventional widow, Mary Jane Clairmont, who had two children of her own, Jane and Charles.

In her childhood, Mary Shelley suffered the torments of being reared by a somewhat unsympathetic stepmother; later, she led the daughter of this extremely middle-class woman into a life of notoriety. The separation traumas in her early years indelibly marked Mary Shelley's imagination: almost all of her protagonists are either orphaned or abandoned by their parents.

Mary Shelley's stormy early years led, in 1812 and until 1814, to her removal to sympathetic "foster parents," the Baxters of Dundee. There, on May 5, 1814, when she was seventeen years old, she met Percy Bysshe Shelley, who was then married to his first wife, Harriet. By March 6, 1815, Mary had eloped with Shelley, given birth to a daughter by him, and suffered the death of the baby. By December 29, 1816, the couple had been to Switzerland and back, had another child, William, and had been married, Harriet having committed suicide. Mary Shelley was then nineteen years old.

By the next year, Mary's stepsister, Jane Clairmont, who called herself Claire Clairmont, had had a baby daughter by Lord Byron, while Mary was working on *Frankenstein*, and Mary herself had given birth to another child, Clara.

The network of intimates among the Shelley circle rapidly increased to include many literati and artists. These included, among others, Leigh and

Marrianne Hunt, Thomas Love Peacock, Thomas Jefferson Hogg, and John Polidori. The letters and diaries of the Shelleys from this period offer a view of life speeded up and intensified, life at the nerve's edge.

While the Shelleys were touring Switzerland and Italy, they sent frantic communications to their friends, asking for financial help. Mary issued frequent requests for purchases of clothing and household items such as thread. There were also legal matters to be taken care of concerning publishing, Shelley's estate, and the custody of his children from his previous marriage.

The leaves of the letters and diaries are filled with urgent fears for the safety of the Shelley children and the difficulties of what was in effect an exile necessitated by the Shelleys' unorthodox style of life. In 1818, Clara Shelley died, barely a year old, and in 1819, William Shelley died at the age of three. Five months later, a son, Percy Florence, was born, the only child of the Shelleys to grow to maturity.

In 1822, Mary Shelley's flamboyant life reached its point of desolation. Percy Shelley, while sailing with his close friend Edward Williams, in his boat, *Ariel*, drowned in the Gulf of Spezia. Mary's letters and diaries of the time clearly reveal her anguish, her exhaustion, and her despair. Her speeding merry-go-round suddenly and violently stopped.

Literary historians find themselves in debate over this point in Mary Shelley's life. Her letters and diaries record unambiguous desolation, and yet many scholars have found indications that Percy Shelley was about to leave her for Jane Williams, the wife of the friend with whom he drowned. There is also some suspicion that Mary's stepsister had recently given birth to a baby by Percy Shelley, a rumor that Mary Shelley denied. Because of Percy Shelley's mercurial nature, such speculations are at least conceivable. Against them stands Mary's diary, a purely private diary, which suggests that she would have no reason to whitewash her marriage among its confidential pages.

Mary's tragedy did not prompt warmth and help from her estranged father-in-law. He refused to support his grandson, Percy Florence, unless Mary gave the child to a guardian to be chosen by him. This she would not do, and she was rewarded for her persistence. Her son became heir to the Shelley estate when Harriet Shelley's son died in 1826. After the death, Mary's son became Lord Shelley. Just as important, however, was the warm relationship that he maintained with Mary until her death. Mary Shelley's life ended in the tranquil sunshine of family affection. Her son married happily and had healthy children. Mary seems to have befriended her daughter-in-law, and, at the last, believed herself to be a truly fortunate woman.

Analysis

Mary Shelley's six novels are written in the Gothic tradition. They deal with extreme emotions, exalted speech, the hideous plight of virgins, the awful abuses of charismatic villains, and picturesque ruins. The sins of the past weigh heavily on their plot structures, and often include previously unsuspected relationships.

Shelley does not find much use for the anti-Catholicism of much Gothic fiction. Her nuns and priests, while sometimes troublesome, are not evil, and tend to appear in the short stories rather than in the novels. She avoids references to the supernatural so common in the genre and tends instead toward a modern kind of psychological Gothic and futuristic fantasy. Like many Gothic writers, she dwells on morbid imagery, particularly in *Frankenstein* and *The Last Man*. Graphic descriptions of the plague in the latter novel revolted the reading public which had avidly digested the grotesqueries of Matthew Gregory Lewis' *The Monk* (1796) and Mr. Singer's *Wanderer of the Alps* (1796).

With the exception of *Frankenstein*, Shelley's novels were written and published after the death of her husband; with the exception of *Frankenstein*, they appear to be attempting to work out the sense of desolation and abandonment that she felt after his death. In most of her novels, Shelley creates men and particularly women who resign themselves to the pain and anguish of deep loss through the eternal hope of love in its widest and most encompassing sense. Reconciliation became Shelley's preponderant literary theme.

Frankenstein is Shelley's greatest literary achievement in every way. In it, she not only calls into the world one of the most powerful literary images in the English tradition, the idealistic scientist Victor Frankenstein and his ironically abominable creation, but also, for the one and only time, she employs a narrative structure of daring complexity and originality.

The structure of *Frankenstein* is similar to a set of Chinese boxes, of narratives within narratives. The narrative frame is composed of the letters of an arctic explorer, Robert Walton, to his sister, Mrs. Saville, in England. Within the letters is the narrative of Victor Frankenstein, and within his narrative, at first, and then at the end within Walton's narrative, is the firsthand account of the monster himself. Walton communicates to England third- and then secondhand accounts of the monster's thoroughly unbelievable existence. Here, it would seem, is the seminal point of Joseph Conrad's much later fiction, *Heart of Darkness* (1902): the communication to England of the denied undercurrents of reality and England's ambiguous reception of that intelligence. In *Frankenstein* as in *Heart of Darkness*, the suggestion is rather strong that England cannot or will not absorb this stunning new perception of reality. Just as Kurtz's fiancée almost a century later cannot imagine Kurtz's "horror," so Mrs. Saville's silence, the absence of her replies, suggests that Walton's stunning discovery has fallen on deaf ears.

The novel begins with Walton, isolated from his society at the North Pole, attempting to achieve glory. He prowls the frozen north "to accomplish some great purpose"; instead, he finds an almost dead Victor Frankenstein, who tells him a story which, in this setting, becomes a parable for Walton. Frankenstein, too, has isolated himself from society to fulfill his great expectations, and he has reaped the whirlwind.

Frankenstein tells Walton of his perfect early family life, one of complete kindness and solicitude. It is a scene across which never a shadow falls. Out of this perfection, Victor rises to find a way of conquering death and ridding himself and mankind of the ultimate shadow, the only shadow in his perfect middle-class life. Like a man possessed, Frankenstein forges ahead, fabricating a full, male, human body from the choicest corpse parts he can gather. He animates the creature and suddenly is overwhelmed by the wrongness of what he has done. In his success, he finds utter defeat. The reanimated corpse evokes only disgust in him. He abandons it in its vulnerable, newborn state and refuses to take any responsibility for it.

From that day, his life is dogged by tragedy. One by one, all his loved ones are destroyed by the monster, who at last explains that he wanted only to love his creator but that his adoration turned to murderous hate in his creator's rejection of him. Ultimately, Frankenstein feels that he must destroy the monster or, at the very least, die trying. He succeeds at both. After Frankenstein's death in the presence of Walton—the only man other than Frankenstein to witness the monster and live—the monster mourns the greatness that could have been and leaves Walton with the intention of hurling himself onto Frankenstein's funeral pyre.

The critical task regarding this fascinating work has been to identify what it is that Frankenstein has done that has merited the punishment which followed. Is the monster a kind of retribution for man's arrogant attempt to possess the secrets of life and death, as in the expulsion from Eden? Is it the wrath of the gods visited on man for stealing the celestial fire, as in the Prometheus legend, a favorite fiction of Percy Shelley? Or is this a rather modern vision of the self-destructiveness involved in the idealistic denial of the dark side of human reality? Is this a criticism of Romantic optimism, of the denial of the reality of evil except as the utterly disposable dead hand of tradition? The mystery endures because critics have suggested all these possibilities; critics have even suggested a biographical reading of the work. Some have suggested that Victor Frankenstein is Shelley's shrewd insight into her husband's self-deceived, uncritical belief in the power of his own intelligence and in his destined greatness.

Valperga, Shelley's second novel, has a fairy-tale aura of witches, princes, maidens in distress, castles, and prophecies. The author uses all these fantasy apparatuses, but actually deflates it as being part of the fantasy lives of the characters which they impose on a fully logical and pragmatic reality. The novel pits Castruccio, the Prince of Lucca, a worldly, Napoleonic conquerer, against the lost love of his youth, the beautiful and spiritual Euthanasia. Castruccio's one goal is power and military dominion, and since he is enormously capable and charismatic, not to mention lucky, he is successful. Nevertheless, that he gains the world at the price of his soul is clearly the central point of the novel.

To gain worldly sway, he must destroy Valperga, the ancestral home of his love, Euthanasia. He must also turn Italy into an armed camp which teems with death and in which the soft virtues of love and family cannot endure. His lust for power raises to predominance the most deceitful and treacherous human beings because it is they who function best in the context of raw, morally unjustified power.

In the midst of all this, Castruccio, unwilling to recognize his limits, endeavors to control all. He wants to continue his aggrandizing ways and have the love of Euthanasia. Indeed, he wants to marry her. She reveals her undying love for him, but will only yield to it if he yields his worldly goals, which he will not do. As his actions become more threatening to her concept of a moral universe, Euthanasia finds that she must join the conspirators against him. She and her cohorts are betrayed, and all are put to death, with the exception of Euthanasia. Instead, Castruccio exiles her to Sicily. En route, her ship sinks, and she perishes with all aboard. Castruccio dies some years later, fighting one of his endless wars for power. The vision of the novel is that only pain and suffering can come from a world obsessed with power.

Surely the name Euthanasia is a remarkable choice for the novel's heroine. Its meaning in Shelley's time was "an easy death"; it did not refer to the policy of purposefully terminating suffering as it does today. Euthanasia's death is the best one in the story because she dies with a pure heart, never having soiled herself with hurtful actions for the purpose of self-gain. Possibly, the import of Shelley's choice is that all that one can hope for in the flawed, Hobbesian world of *Valperga* is the best death possible, as no good life can be imagined. It is probable that this bleak vision is at least obliquely connected with the comparatively recent trauma of Percy Shelley's death and Mary Shelley's grief and desolation.

The degenerating spiral of human history is the central vision of *The Last Man*. Set in the radically distant future of the twenty-first century, this novel begins with a flourishing civilization and ends with the entire population of the world, save one man, decimated by the plague. Lionel Verney, the last man of the title, has nothing to anticipate except an endless journey from one desolate city to another. All the treasures of man are his and his alone; all the great libraries and coffers open only to him. All that is denied to him—forever, it seems—is human companionship.

The novel begins before Lionel Verney's birth. It is a flashback narrated by Lionel himself, the only first-person narrator possible in this novel. Lionel describes his father as his father had been described to him, as a man of imagination and charm but lacking in judgment. He was a favorite of the king, but was forced out of the king's life by the king's new wife, a Marie Antoinette figure. The new queen, depicted as an arrogant snob, disapproves of Verney's father and effects his estrangement from the king by working on her husband's gullible nature.

Verney's father, in ostracized shame, seeks refuge in the country, where he marries a simple, innocent cottage girl and thus begets Lionel and his sister Perdita. Verney's father can never, however, reconcile himself to his loss of status and dies a broken man. His wife soon follows, and Lionel and Perdita live like wild creatures until chance brings the king's son, Adrian, into their path. Their friendship succeeds where the aborted friendship of their fathers failed, despite the continued disapproval of the queen.

What is remarkable to the modern reader is that Shelley, having set her story two hundred years in the future, does not project a technologically changed environment. She projects instead the same rural, agrarian, hand- and animal-driven society in which she lived. What does change, however, is the political system. The political system of *The Last Man* is a republican monarchy. Kings are elected, but not at regular intervals. The bulk of the novel concerns the power plays by which various factions intend to capture the throne by election rather than by war.

Adrian and Lionel are endlessly involved with a dashing, Byronic figure named Lord Raymond, who cannot decide whether he wants life in a cottage with Perdita, or life at the top. Ultimately, Raymond, like the protagonist of *Valperga*, wants to have both. He marries Perdita and gives up all pretensions to power, but then returns with her to rule the land. Power does not make him or his wife happy.

Despite the sublimation of the power process into an electoral system, the rage for power remains destructive, degenerating finally into war. The plague which appears and irrevocably destroys mankind is merely an extension of the plague of man's will to power. Not only Raymond and Perdita, but also their innocent children, Lionel's wife, Iris, and Adrian's sister, who stayed home to eschew worldly aspirations, are destroyed. No one is immune.

Lionel's survival carries with it a suggestion of his responsibility in the tragedy of mankind. His final exile in a sea of books and pictures suggests that those who commit themselves solely to knowledge and art have failed to deal with the central issues of life. In simply abdicating the marketplace to such as Lord Raymond, the cultivators of the mind have abandoned humanity. Through Lionel, they reap a bitter reward, but perhaps the implication is that it is a just reward for their failure to connect with their fellow human beings.

A number of critics consider *The Last Man* to be Mary Shelley's best work after *Frankenstein*. Like *Frankenstein*, this novel rather grimly deals with the relationship between knowledge and evil. Its greatest drawback for modern audiences, however, is its unfortunate tendency to inflated dialogue. Every sentence uttered is a florid and theatrical speech. The bloated characterizations obscure the line of Shelley's inventive satire of man's lemminglike rush to the sea of power.

The Fortunes of Perkin Warbeck attempts to chronicle the last, futile struggles of the House of York in the Wars of the Roses. Perkin Warbeck was a historical character who claimed to be Richard, the son of Edward IV of England. Most scholars believe that Richard died in the tower with his brother Edward; Perkin Warbeck claimed to be that child. Warbeck said that he had survived the tower, assumed another identity, and intended to reclaim the usurped throne held by Henry VII.

Shelley's novel assumes that Perkin was indeed Richard and documents his cheerless history from his childhood to his execution in manhood by Henry VII. The novel attempts to explore once more man's fruitless quest for power and glory. Richard is an intelligent, virtuous young man who finds true companionship even in his outcast state, and the love of a number of women, each different, utterly committed, and true. He is unable, however, to forsake the dream of conquest and live simply. As he presses onward to claim the throne, he suffers a series of crushing losses, not one of which will he yield to as a revelation of the wrongheadedness of his quest. His rush toward the throne achieves only the death of innocent persons. When he is executed at the end of the novel, his wife Katherine is given the last words. She needs to find a way of continuing to live without him. She is urged by his adherents to forsake the world, and for his sake to live a reclusive life. Although Katherine appears only briefly in the interminable scenes of war and the grandiose verbiage through which the reader must trudge, her appearance at the end of the novel and her refusal to forsake the world in her grief are the most impressive moments in the work.

In refusing to retreat from the world, Katherine commits herself to the only true value in the novel, love, a value which all the senseless suffering of Richard's quest could not destroy. Katherine, as the widow of the gentle but misguided warrior, becomes a metaphor for the endurance of love in a world which has its heart set on everything but love. Her final, gracious words are a relaxing change from the glory-seeking bombast of the action, "Permit this to be, unblamed—permit a heart whose sufferings have been and are, so many and so bitter, to reap what joy it can from the strong necessity it feels to be sympathized with—to love." Once again, Shelley's basic idea is an enthralling one, but her execution of her plan includes a grandiose superfluity of expression and incident.

Lodore and Shelley's last novel, *Falkner*, form a kind of reconciliation couplet to end her exploration of loss and desolation. Reward for persistence in loving through the trials of death and social obliquy is her final vision. In *Lodore*, an extremely long parade of fatal misunderstandings, the central image is the recovery of a lost mother. The novel begins veiled in mystery. Lord Lodore has exiled himself and his fairylike, delicate daughter, Ethel, to the forests of Illinois in far-off America. Lord Lodore is without his wife, who has done something unnamed and perhaps unnameable to provoke this unusual separation. Reunion with her is the central action of the plot.

Lord Lodore is a perfect gentleman amid the cloddish but honest American settlers. His one goal is to produce the perfect maiden in his daughter, Ethel. Father and daughter are entirely devoted to each other. A series of flashback chapters reveal that Lady Lodore, very much the junior of Lord Lodore, had been overly influenced by her mother, who had insinuated herself between husband and wife and alienated her daughter's affections from Lord Lodore. Lord and Lady Lodore lived what life they had together always on the brink of rapproachement, but utterly confounded by the wiles of the mother-in-law, who managed to distort communicated sentiments to turn husband and wife away from each other, finally effecting a radical separation that neither Lord nor Lady Lodore wanted.

The American idyll ends for Ethel and her father when Ethel is about fifteen years old. The unwanted attentions of a suitor threaten Ethel's perfect life, and her father moves his household once more. Lodore thinks of reestablishing the bond with his estranged wife but is killed in a duel hours before departing for England. His last thoughts of reconciliation are buried with him, because the only extant will is one recorded years ago when he vindictively made Lady Lodore's inheritance dependent on her never seeing Ethel again. Ethel returns to England shaken and abandoned, but not to her mother. Instead, she lives with Lodore's maiden sister.

Ethel is wooed and won by a gentleman, Edward Villiers, coincidentally one of the few witnesses to her father's death and many years older than herself. The marriage of this truly loving couple is threatened because Edward, reared in luxury, is in reduced financial circumstances owing to the irresponsibility of his father, one of the few truly despicable characters in the novel.

Much suffering ensues, during which Edward and Ethel endeavor to straighten out priorities: Which is more important, love or money? Should they part to give Ethel a chance at a more comfortable life, or should they endure poverty for love? They choose love, but Edward is taken to debtor's prison, Ethel standing by for the conjugal visits that the prison system permits.

Through a series of chance encounters, Lady Lodore, now a seemingly shallow woman of fashion, becomes aware of Ethel's needs and of her need to be a mother to the young woman. Telling no one but her lawyer what she intends, she impoverishes herself to release Edward from prison and to set the couple up appropriately. She then removes herself to a humble country existence, anticipating the blessings of martyrdom. She is, however, discovered, the mother and daughter are reunited, and Lady Lodore is even offered an advantageous marriage to a rich former suitor who originally was kept from her by the machinations of his sisters.

Lodore includes many particulars that are close to the biographical details of the author's life: the penury and social trials of her marriage to Shelley, the financial irresponsibility of her father, and the loss of her mother. Shelley's familiarity with her material appears to have dissolved the grandiose pretensions of the previous novels, which may have sprung from her distance from their exotic settings and situations. *Lodore* has the force of life despite its melodramatic plot. If it were more widely available, it would be a rich source of interest for historians and literary scholars. It contains an interesting image of America as envisioned by the early nineteenth century European. It also contains a wealth of interest for students of women's literature.

If *Lodore* offers a happy ending with the return of a long-lost mother, then *Falkner* finds contentment in the restoration of an estranged father. Here, the father is not the biological parent, but a father figure, Rupert Falkner. The plot is a characteristic tangle of Gothic convolutions involving old secrets and sins, obdurate Catholic families, and the pure love of a young girl.

The delightful Elizabeth Raby is orphaned at the age of six under severe circumstances. Because her fragile, lovely parents were complete strangers to the little town in Cornwall to which they had come, their death left Elizabeth at the mercy of their landlady. The landlady is poor, and Elizabeth is a financial burden. The landlady keeps her only because she suspects that the now decimated, strange little family has noble connections. Thus begins a typical Shelley fiction—with abandonment, innocence, and loss of love.

The plot is set in motion by a mysterious stranger who identifies himself as "John Falkner." Falkner undertakes the guardianship of Elizabeth, not only because of her charm, but also because of an unfinished letter found in the family cottage. This letter connects Elizabeth's mother to one "Alithea." The reader comes to learn that Falkner was Alithea's lover, that he carries the guilt of her ruin and death since Alithea was a married woman, and that her husband continues to bear his wife's seducer a vindictive grudge. Happily, for the moment, Alithea's husband believes that the seducer was surnamed Rupert. Alithea's husband was and is an unsuitable mate for a sensitive woman, and the marriage was one from which any woman would have wanted to flee. Alithea's infraction was only against the letter of the marriage bond, not its spirit.

The vindictive husband has conceived a hatred for Alithea's son, Gerard, on account of Alithea's connection with "Rupert." Elizabeth, Falkner's ward, coincidentally meets and forms an attachment to Gerard. Falkner repeatedly attempts to separate them because of *his* guilty feelings. Their attachment blooms into a love which cannot be denied, and Falkner is forced to confess all to Gerard after the boy saves Falkner's life. He is the infamous Rupert, Rupert Falkner.

With the revelation comes the separation of Elizabeth and Gerard, she to stand loyally with Falkner, he to defend his father's honor. For the first time in his life, Gerard finds himself on his father's side, but familiarity breeds contempt. Gerard wants to fight a manly duel for honor, while his father wants to crush Falkner for economic gain in the legal system. Gerard finds this an inexcusable pettiness on his father's part. He then joins Elizabeth to defend Falkner in court. To do this, they will need to go to America to bring back a crucial witness, but the witness arrives and saves them the voyage: Falkner is acquitted. The legal acquittal is also metaphorical: in comparison with the ugly sins of greed, the sins of passion are pardonable.

Elizabeth, the reader knows, is also the product of an elopement in defiance of family, a sin of passion. The proud Catholic family which once spurned her decides to acknowledge Elizabeth. Gerard and Elizabeth, both wealthy and in their proper social position, marry. Falkner will have a home with them in perpetuity.

Once again, Shelley's fictional involvement in the domestic sphere tones down her customary floridity and affords the reader fascinating insights into the thinking of the daughter of an early feminist, who was indeed an independent woman herself. It can only clarify history to know that such a woman as Mary Shelley can write in her final novel that her heroine's studies included not only the "masculine" pursuits of abstract knowledge, but also needlework and "the careful inculcation of habits and order . . . without which every woman must be unhappy—and, to a certain degree, unsexed."

Martha Nochimson

Other major works

SHORT FICTION: *Mary Shelley: Collected Tales and Stories*, 1976.
PLAYS: *Proserpine*, 1922; *Midas*, 1922.
NONFICTION: *History of a Six Weeks' Tour Through a Part of France, Switzerland, Germany, and Holland*, 1817; *Lardner's Cabinet Cyclopaedia*, 1838 (Numbers 63, 71, 96); *Rambles in Germany and Italy*, 1844; *The Letters of Mary Shelley*, 1980 (Betty T. Bennett, editor, 2 volumes).

Bibliography

Baldick, Chris. *In "Frankenstein"'s Shadow: Myth, Monstrosity, and Nineteenth-Century Writing*. Oxford, England: Clarendon Press, 1987. Baldick analyzes the structure of modern myth as it has adapted and misread Shelley's novel until the film version of 1931. Focuses on Shelley's novel as itself a monster, which is assembled, speaks, and escapes like its protagonist. Also examines transformations in E. T. A. Hoffmann, Nathaniel Hawthorne, Herman Melville, and Elizabeth Gaskell, links *Frankenstein* to Thomas Carlyle, Charles Dickens, and Karl Marx, and traces the novel's influence on late Victorian stories of mad scientists, H. G. Wells, Joseph Conrad, and D. H. Lawrence. The last chapter argues that literary realism is itself a result of *Frankenstein*'s shadow. Includes footnotes, five illustrations, an appendix summarizing the novel's plot, and an index.

Forry, Steven Earl. *Hideous Progenies: Dramatizations of "Frankenstein" from Mary Shelley to the Present*. Philadelphia: University of Pennsylvania Press, 1990. Examines the influence of Shelley's novel on the history of theater and cinema from 1832 to 1930, discussing in great detail the popularization of the story until it became an enduring myth. After an introduction to the prevailing theater in London from 1823 to 1832, Forry studies the various Victorian adaptations of the novel from 1832 to 1900 and its revivals in twentieth century drama and cinema from 1900 to 1930. Provides the texts of seven dramatic adaptations of *Frankenstein*, from Richard Brinsley Peake's 1823 *Presumption* to John Lloyd Balderston's 1930 *Frankenstein*. Contains thirty-one illustrations, a list of ninety-six dramatizations from 1821 to 1986, an appendix with the music from *Vampire's Victim* (1887), a bibliography, and an index.

Kiely, Robert. *The Romantic Novel in England*. Cambridge, Mass.: Harvard University Press, 1972. An important book on Romantic prose fiction, including Shelley's Gothic romances, which analyzes in depth twelve Romantic novels to define the intellectual context of the era. Notes that concepts of reality were tested and changed by Romantic novels and Edmund Burke's ideas of the sublime modified aesthetic forms. Shelley makes a significant contribution to this general thesis, and *Frankenstein* is analyzed in detail as the focus of her chapter. Examines the story as a tragedy of suffering and superiority, in which a nightmarish experience carries moral themes. Finds a common drift toward death in most novels of this genre. Includes a set of notes and an index.

Mellor, Anne K. *Mary Shelley: Her Life, Her Fiction, Her Monsters*. London: Methuen, 1988. An important book which argues against trends of analysis which subordinate Shelley to her husband Percy Bysshe Shelley. Extends feminist and psychoanalytic criticism of *Frankenstein* to include all of Shelley's life and work, arguing that her stories are creations of the family she never enjoyed. The strength of her stories is their expression of her ambivalent desire for and criticism of the bourgeois family as an exploitation of property and women by a patriarchal ideology. Establishes Shelley's need for family, her feminist critique of science, and her analysis of the relationship between fathers and daughters. Includes eight illustrative plates, a chronology, ample notes, a bibliography, and an index.

Nitchie, Elizabeth. *Mary Shelley: Author of "Frankenstein."* New Brunswick, N.J.: Rutgers University Press, 1953. This critical biography evaluates Shelley in her own right in the milieu of people and places she knew. Assesses Shelley's temperament and talent, discussing her faults and strengths. Follows her life and career, from her earliest appearance as a self-conscious girl with a critical mind to her widowhood when she wrote largely forgotten works. Although primarily a biography, contains valuable comments on her writings, seen as art and as expressions of her life. A bibliography, an index, and six appendices, including a chronology, a list of works, a note on the unpublished novella *Mathilda*, the stage history of *Frankenstein*, and some unpublished poems, are provided.

Spark, Muriel. *Mary Shelley*. London: Constable, 1988. A revision of Spark's *Child of Light* (Essex, England: Tower Bridge, 1951) which reassesses the view that Shelley craved respectability after her husband's death. Spark skillfully narrates Shelley's life and then analyzes her writings. Argues that Shelley's pessimism was the consequence of her rationalist upbringing by William Godwin, but that she possessed an inner tranquility with which she created her novels. Concentrates on *Frankenstein* as the end of Gothic fiction for its rational exposé of Gothic mystery, on *The Last Man* as an expression of Shelley's feeling of solitude, and on *The Fortunes of Perkin Warbeck* as her challenge to learn from Sir Walter Scott's Waverley novels. Contains eight pages of illustrations, a selected bibliography, and an index.

Walling, William A. *Mary Shelley*. New York: Twayne, 1972. Contains a biographical sketch and analyzes each of Shelley's three most significant novels, *Frankenstein*, *Valperga*, and *The Last Man*. While *Frankenstein* receives the most attention, the other two novels are analyzed for their differences from it: *Valperga* is a story of political ambition and *The Last Man* examines the themes of human destruction and psychological isolation. Reviews the remaining novels (*The Fortunes of Perkin Warbeck*, *Lodore*, and *Falkner*) and briefly looks at her shorter fiction and verse. Also examines her nonfictional prose in order of importance: *Rambles in Germany and Italy*, the biographical writings, and the editions of Shelley's writings. A concluding note expresses regret that Shelley failed to fulfill her early promise. Includes a chronology, notes and references, a selected annotated bibliography, and an index.

ALAN SILLITOE

Born: Nottingham, England; March 4, 1928

Principal long fiction

Saturday Night and Sunday Morning, 1958; *The Loneliness of the Long-Distance Runner*, 1959 (novella); *The General*, 1960; *Key to the Door*, 1961; *The Death of William Posters*, 1965; *A Tree on Fire*, 1967; *A Start in Life*, 1970; *Travels in Nihilon*, 1971; *The Flame of Life*, 1974; *The Widower's Son*, 1976; *The Storyteller*, 1979; *Her Victory*, 1982; *The Lost Flying Boat*, 1983; *Down from the Hill*, 1984; *Life Goes On*, 1985; *Out of the Whirlpool*, 1987; *The Open Door*, 1989.

Other literary forms

Alan Sillitoe's short-fiction collection *The Loneliness of the Long-Distance Runner* (1959) reinforced the critical acclaim and popular recognition earned by his first novel, *Saturday Night and Sunday Morning*. The collection's title novella is now regarded as the archetypal Sillitoe narrative about a working-class protagonist fighting an indifferent, oppressive society. Sillitoe has continued to publish novellas and short stories of high quality and notable originality. While they continue his sympathetic portrayal of working-class life, his steady output of poetry reflects significant changes in mood and theme over three decades. *The Rats and Other Poems* (1960) is strident political-protest verse, brief, vivid echoes of the fiction's dark themes. Later poems develop hopeful themes: the definition of love in a postromantic age, the possibility of individual happiness amid political upheaval and oppression, and the consolation of nature. Sillitoe believes that he will ultimately be remembered for his poetry rather than his fiction. He has also written an autobiography, works of juvenile fiction, and plays.

Achievements

Sillitoe is one of the most successful of England's "Angry Young Men," who dramatically changed post-World War II literary culture. For their stark depiction of working-class life, his first novel and his first story collection received prizes: the Author's Club award in 1958 for *Saturday Night and Sunday Morning* and the Hawthornden Prize in 1960 for *The Loneliness of the Long-Distance Runner*. Critical and popular acclaim begin to wane in the 1970's, when, after a half-dozen books, Sillitoe showed little ability to go beyond the sociological themes and alienated heroes of his early work. His reputation rebounded a decade later, however, with the publication of *Her Victory*. In this and subsequent works, Sillitoe displays an enlarged gallery of characters, a facility for different narrative forms, and an awareness that young rebels remain interesting even as they age and adapt.

Biography

Alan Sillitoe was born in Nottingham, England, on March 4, 1928, one of five children born to a working-class family. In the economic depression of the 1930's, Sillitoe's father could not find steady work; the family survived by odd jobs, public assistance, and doing without. Educated in local schools until he was fourteen, Sillitoe worked at several factory jobs during the war years. These experiences convinced him that only personal rebellion and political revolution could change life for millions of Great Britain's workers. In 1946 he began a tour of duty with the Royal Air Force in Malaysia as a radio operator. Here he began to read literature and witnessed a war between Communist insurgents and the Malaysian government. A routine physical examination before discharge revealed that Sillitoe had tuberculosis. To pass the time in his hospital bed, he began writing a novel and poems.

Though he destroyed his earliest drafts, Sillitoe continued to write. After his discharge from the service, he lived, worked, and wrote in France, Spain, and Italy for a decade. This long sojourn was partly for his health and partly a rejection of England. While living in Majorca, he wrote *Saturday Night and Sunday Morning* and *The Loneliness of the Long-Distance Runner*. In 1959 he was married to Ruth Fainlight, an American poet; they have two children.

In the 1960's, Sillitoe traveled in the Soviet Union in the hope of finding that life for workers in a socialist society was better. Though his travels generated many poems and a book, he did not find the Soviet Union the political or economic solution to his complaints about Great Britain. Later, Sillitoe visited Israel and found much to admire. He continues to live, and occasionally to teach writing, in England. He has made a truce with his native land, signaled by his commentary in two books of photographs that celebrate Nottinghamshire and the southeast coast.

Analysis

Great Britain began the twentieth century a political and economic power. By 1950, two world wars and a Great Depression later, it had lost its colonial empire, its industrial leadership, and its identity as an ordered, cultured community of mutually respectful social classes. To many young writers of the postwar era, Great Britain seemed a doomed society, led by an archaic aristocracy and blighted by decaying industrial cities. That the nation seemed apathetic about its plight and lethargic about change angered them. Venting their frustration in plays, novels, poems, and short stories radically different from the social comedy and reflective character study typical of British literature, a new generation of writers such as John Braine, Kingsley Amis, John Osborne, and John Wain became known as the "Angry Young Men." Alan

Sillitoe's first works immediately identified him as one of the angriest and most artful of them. While other writers satirized the privileges of the upper class or traced the dead-end ambitions of the middle class, Sillitoe expressed the proletarian point of view. Unsparingly he threw light on the daily life of the factory worker and welfare recipient; ingeniously he reported this life— which he knew so well—through their eyes and in their words. He made Nottingham the emblem of postwar Britain.

Many critics and readers recognized immediately that *Saturday Night and Sunday Morning* and *The Loneliness of the Long-Distance Runner* were original contributions to English literature. Not only were Sillitoe's emotional intensity and subject matter distinctive, but also his narrative method fitted subject and theme perfectly. Employing as first-person narrator an articulate though not necessarily educated young worker, Sillitoe created a modified stream-of-consciousness technique. Retaining the essentials of standard written English, Sillitoe altered diction, syntax, and logic to reflect the speaker's knowledge, values, and emotions. Although reviewers have sometimes found his plots uneven and the public occasionally regards his themes as tendentious, no reader fails to appreciate the immediacy of scene and intimacy of character created by Sillitoe's method.

The main character of the novella *The Loneliness of the Long-Distance Runner*, known only by his last name, Smith, is the archetypal Sillitoe protagonist. A few weeks out of the Essex Borstal (a corrections facility for teenage offenders), he recounts the story of his arrest and incarceration. After conviction for robbing a bakery cash till, the lean, restless Smith becomes, at the Warden's urging, a long-distance runner. Every day at dawn he runs five miles, outside the prison, not to win a race in the Borstal games as the Warden wants, but for his own sense of freedom. As Smith runs, he thinks.

He thinks with anger of the "In-Laws" who run the Borstal and impose society's rules upon "Out-Laws" such as he, who work at menial jobs and get nowhere. He thinks with pride of his ability to outfox the detective investigating the bakery robbery until mere accident (a sudden rainstorm flushed the stolen money hidden in a drainpipe) linked him to the crime. He thinks with contempt of the Warden, who may be tempting him to run away and thereby get into worse trouble; Smith is confident that "I can see further into the likes of him than he can see into the likes of me." He recalls with pride the cunning way that he bettered the Warden. At the competition, Smith easily outdistances the other Borstal boys until he is in sight of the finish line. Then he runs in place, simply marking time, until the runners pass him and the Warden apoplectically sees victory snatched away.

Though this deliberate loss costs him his running privileges and earns for him extra chores, Smith has no doubt that frustrating the In-Laws is a triumph for all Out-Laws. While running provided the pleasure of being alone and free to imagine that he is sometimes "the first man" and sometimes "the last man" on earth, Smith sacrifices such pleasure because "it's war between them and me." In this war, victory is control of fate; by his cunning, Smith is sure that he controls his fate more than the In-Laws do.

Smith concludes with a boast that he has resumed stealing since his release; he is more successful and will be harder to catch. His unrelenting rebelliousness at the end leaves many readers at a disturbing impasse. Does Sillitoe mean only to cheer Smith's assertion of his own worth and indict society's inability to affect Smith's worldview? What does the future bode for the alienated individual battling an entrenched system? What happens to Smith as he matures? Does Sillitoe's vision extend beyond the terrible elation of proving dignity by spitting back?

Arthur Seaton, the twenty-four-year-old protagonist of *Saturday Night and Sunday Morning*, provides one answer. Unmarried, Arthur lives at home with his parents and siblings in a crowded neighborhood where no one has any privacy. He works in a bicycle factory, but his pleasure in craftsmanship is ruined by the bosses who worry about productivity, schedules, and the like. Arthur lives for the freedoms of the weekend: Saturday pub crawls punctuated by fights and drunken revelry; Sunday-morning lovemaking in the bed of Brenda, whose husband works nights at the factory. Through alcohol and sex Arthur asserts that he is alive and thumbs his nose at "them," those who control society and begrudge him and his class even a meager share of the wealth.

Throughout the novel Arthur teeters willingly on the brink: Brenda becomes pregnant, and he helps her through a self-induced abortion; he seduces Brenda's sister Winnie; he tries to date a single girl, Doreen, even as he woos the married sisters; he teases an annoying neighbor by shooting her with an air rifle. Not until Winnie's husband beats him badly does Arthur stop to reflect upon himself. His only visitor during convalescence is Doreen; gradually he discovers in her a woman with whom he can converse frankly and imagine the possibility of engagement and marriage.

In the final scene, as Arthur fishes and looks toward the future, he decides that life is good. Though a man, like a fish, may be hooked and dragged from the river of life by powerful outside forces, he can enjoy the passions and sensations of existence. Arthur determines not to weaken before life: he will make the world hear from him yet. The novel received high praise for its evocation of Nottingham and of industrial life's rhythms. Critics judged its protagonist as fully realized as Smith and were pleased by the resolution, even if temporary, in Arthur Seaton's life.

When Sillitoe returned to the Seaton world in *Key to the Door*, he recounted how the world hears, not from Arthur, but from his older brother Brian. Divided into four parts, the novel traces Brian's life from birth through age twenty-one. The first two parts contrast the city of Nottingham during the Depression with a farm belonging to Brian's grandfather. In Nottingham,

Brian experiences privation and turmoil as Harold and Vera Seaton struggle without hope or help to survive. At the farm, Brian experiences peace: here he learns sympathy for other people and discovers the world of books. Eventually, however, the farm is gobbled up by the city's sprawl.

The third and fourth parts contrast Brian's factory work in Nottingham during World War II with his postwar military service in Malaysia. Soldiering is ill-suited to Brian; he wears his uniform rarely and prefers chasing women. He is hostile, in fact, to his country's foreign policies and openly proclaims himself a socialist. His factory experiences justify his position: forced to perform dangerous work and seeing how bosses treat their employees, Brian becomes convinced that workers are always exploited under capitalism.

On a climb of Gunong Barat with five friends, Brian alone is strong enough to make it to the summit, but he chooses not to go alone. The view from where his friends must rest is magnificent enough. When Communist guerrillas attack the Malaysian government, British forces intervene against the insurgents. Valuing political solidarity, Brian only fires into the air and refuses to kill a guerrilla, even though his own life is threatened. Brian returns to England convinced that the world must listen to so-called radicals or face revolution. His new awareness is the key to the door of economic and political change.

The first part of the novel, expanding readers' knowledge of the Seaton family's world, received high praise, but the second part seemed devoid of literary interest. As a statement of Sillitoe's commitment to socialism and proletarian revolution, it was unequivocal. Few readers sensed that Brian's conversion was well motivated: they could follow him into anger and frustration with understanding, but not into revolution.

Though *The Death of William Posters* introduces a new protagonist, Frank Dawley, the central character seems simply an older Brian Seaton. Frank acts out the implications of Brian's political commitment. Trapped in an unhappy marriage and routine job, Frank realizes that his life requires radical restructuring. He leaves Nottingham, has a brief though serious affair with a nurse, and makes contact with an old friend, painter Arthur Handley, who shares Frank's political sympathies. Through him Frank meets Myra Bassingfield and Shelley Jones. Through Myra, Frank evolves a new understanding about love; through Shelley, an ideological mercenary, Frank develops a commitment to bring about social change through violence. Shelley helps Frank outgrow his "Bill Posters" mentality. William Posters is Frank's name for Everyworker, derived from signs on city walls threatening, "Bill Posters will be prosecuted." William Posters symbolizes society's exploitation, but Shelley shows Frank that Posters is an image of despair that only hinders revolutionary violence. Frank joins Jones in fighting on the side of Algerian rebels and, in an ambush of government mercenaries, imaginatively slays Posters as well.

Two subsequent novels, *A Tree on Fire* and *The Flame of Life*, follow Frank's revolutionary career in Algeria and upon his return to England. In his native country, Frank joins a group driven by a mystical vision of a cleansing civil war that will create a reinvigorated, socialist Great Britain. When the group splinters into factions, their plot fails. The William Posters trilogy is generally perceived as a failure, both artistically and philosophically. Frequent, repetitious arguments over political issues slow down the plot; the protagonist's failure to succeed, though clearly believing the right (that is, the author's) ideas, creates thematic confusion. The trilogy does not offer a convincing or engaging answer to the questions, What hope for Smith? How will the world hear of Arthur Seaton? What next for Brian Seaton?

The Open Door, a novel which picks up the story of Brian Seaton at age twenty-one, articulates the vision Sillitoe struggled unsuccessfully to capture in the William Posters trilogy. Like *Key to the Door*, *The Open Door* has strong autobiographical overtones. Perhaps it supplies the answers about Smith and the Seatons more convincingly because it offers what Sillitoe has lived rather than what he has abstractly concluded.

Upon his return from Malaysia, Brian is diagnosed with tuberculosis. Confined for long periods to a hospital bed, he spends his time reading great books and listening to classical music. At last he has time to educate himself. He instructs himself in French from a school primer. No longer feeling connected to his wife Pauline, whom he married before entering the service, he becomes involved first with one nurse, Rachel, and later with a second, Nora. He sees them as providing him an education of the heart even as *King Lear* educates his head. Brian begins to write; though dissatisfied enough to destroy his first efforts, he decides to become a writer. In search of kindred spirits, he joins the Nottingham literary society, only to find its members' commitment to art superficial and self-indulgent. After Lillian (another consumptive patient who had become Brian's lover) commits suicide, Brian decides to go to France alone to dedicate himself to writing.

The Open Door relies less on dramatic plot than do other Sillitoe novels, yet presents a satisfying portrait of Brian's growth as a writer. Sillitoe's tour de force in the novel is an account Brian composes of the ascent of Gunong Barat recounted in *Key to the Door*. The passage is a brilliant rendering of a budding writer's effort—powerful and trite, original and derivative by turns. Even Nottingham, so vividly realized in previous books, is blurred as Sillitoe concentrates on depicting Brian's development as a storyteller. Though still disliking England for continued exploitation of its working class, Brian remains apolitical. No longer does revolution seem a desirable or necessary path to change.

The Open Door echoes a theme of several Sillitoe novels since the Posters trilogy that inquire into the power of storytelling to blur, pleasingly and persuasively, the line between reality and fantasy, caring and alienation, solitude and community. Narrative itself is the answer to the questions about Smith, Arthur, and Brian. As long as each can speak in his authentic voice, Smith faces no impasse, Arthur knows another of life's good things, and Brian needs no gun to make the world listen.

Robert M. Otten

Other major works

SHORT FICTION: *The Loneliness of the Long-Distance Runner*, 1959; *The Ragman's Daughter*, 1963; *A Sillitoe Selection*, 1968; *Guzman Go Home and Other Stories*, 1968; *Men, Women, and Children*, 1973; *The Second Chance and Other Stories*, 1981.

PLAYS: *All Citizens Are Soldiers*, 1967 (with Ruth Fainlight; adaptation of a play by Lope de Vega); *Three Plays*, 1978.

SCREENPLAYS: *Saturday Night and Sunday Morning*, 1960; *The Loneliness of the Long-Distance Runner*, 1961; *Che Guevara*, 1968; *The Ragman's Daughter*, 1974.

POETRY: *Without Beer or Bread*, 1957; *The Rats and Other Poems*, 1960; *A Falling Out of Love and Other Poems*, 1964; *Shaman and Other Poems*, 1968; *Love in the Environs of Voronezh and Other Poems*, 1968; *Poems*, 1971 (with Ted Hughes and Ruth Fainlight); *Barbarians and Other Poems*, 1974; *Storm: New Poems*, 1974; *Snow on the North Side of Lucifer*, 1979; *More Lucifer*, 1980; *Sun Before Departure*, 1984; *Tides and Stone Walls*, 1986.

NONFICTION: *The Road to Volgograd*, 1964; *Raw Material*, 1972; *Mountains and Caverns: Selected Essays*, 1975; *The Saxon Shore Way: From Gravesend to Rye*, 1983 (with Fay Weldon); *Nottinghamshire*, 1986 (with David Sillitoe); *Every Day of the Week*, 1987.

CHILDREN'S LITERATURE: *The City Adventures of Marmalade Jim*, 1967; *Big John and the Stars*, 1977; *The Incredible Fencing Fleas*, 1978; *Marmalade Jim at the Farm*, 1980; *Marmalade Jim and the Fox*, 1984.

Bibliography

Atherton, Stanley S. *Alan Sillitoe: A Critical Assessment*. London: W. H. Allen, 1979. This study approaches Sillitoe as primarily a political novelist interesting for his diagnosis of British society's ills and his vision of revolution. Atherton studies each novel individually to understand the sociological realities of working-class life depicted in the novels. The study pays relatively little attention to the distinctive literary qualities of Sillitoe's work but offers a useful bibliography.

Nardella, Anna Ryan. "The Existential Dilemmas of Alan Sillitoe's Working Class Heroes." *Studies in the Novel* 5 (1973): 469-482. Nardella finds that Sillitoe's heroes confront not only economic or social problems but philosophical ones as well. Like all citizens of the modern world, Sillitoe's heroes face the existential challenge of finding the meaning of individual life in a hostile, ultimately absurd world.

Osgerby, J. R. "Alan Sillitoe's *Saturday Night and Sunday Morning.*" In *Renaissance and Modern Essays*, edited by G. R. Hibbard. London: Routledge & Kegan Paul, 1966. Osgerby studies the development of the protagonist Arthur Seaton, Sillitoe's archetypal hero, through the novel's structure and imagery. Sillitoe expresses Seaton's worldview through jungle imagery and depicts his growth through the motif of changing seasons.

Penner, Allen R. *Alan Sillitoe*. Boston: Twayne, 1972. Penner studies the novels in chronological order, providing thorough plot summaries and insightful analyses. Penner finds Sillitoe's work uneven in quality, with the earliest fiction his best because of its emotional intensity and narrative compression. The study concludes with an introduction to Sillitoe's poetry. Penner provides a good biographical introduction and a useful bibliography on the early fiction.

Roskies, D. M. "'I'd Rather Be Like I Am': Character, Style, and the Language of Class in Sillitoe's Narratives." *Neophilogus* 45 (1981): 308-319. Roskies analyzes Sillitoe's "character signature," his frequent use of a first-person narrator from the British working class. The narrator's speech is characterized by colloquial diction, informal delivery, recursive thought patterns, and frequent shifts of mood. Roskies concludes that the character signature is Sillitoe's distinctive contribution to contemporary fiction.

WILLIAM GILMORE SIMMS

Born: Charleston, South Carolina; April 17, 1806
Died: Charleston, South Carolina; June 11, 1870

Principal long fiction

Martin Faber: The Story of a Criminal, 1833; *Guy Rivers: A Tale of Georgia*, 1834; *The Yemassee: A Romance of Carolina*, 1835; *The Partisan: A Tale of the Revolution*, 1835; *Mellichampe: A Legend of the Santee*, 1836; *Richard Hurdis: Or, The Avenger of Blood, a Tale of Alabama*, 1838; *Pelayo: A Story of the Goth*, 1838; *The Damsel of Darien*, 1839; *Border Beagles: A Tale of Mississippi*, 1840; *The Kinsmen: Or, The Black Riders of the Congaree*, 1841 (revised as *The Scout*, 1854); *Confession: Or, The Blind Heart*, 1841; *Beauchampe: Or, The Kentucky Tragedy, a Tale of Passion*, 1842; *Helen Halsey: Or, The Swamp State of Conelachita, a Tale of the Borders*, 1845; *Count Julian: Or, The Last Days of the Goth, a Historical Romance*, 1845; *Katharine Walton: Or, The Rebel of Dorchester*, 1851; *The Sword and the Distaff: Or, "Fair, Fat and Forty,"* 1852 (revised as *Woodcraft*, 1854); *Vasconselos: A Romance of the New World*, 1853; *The Forayers: Or, The Raid of the Dog-Days*, 1855; *Eutaw: A Sequel to the Forayers*, 1856; *Charlemont: Or, The Pride of the Village*, 1856; *The Cassique of Kiawah: A Colonial Romance*, 1859.

Other literary forms

William Gilmore Simms wrote extensively in all major literary genres. He began as a poet and achieved his first widespread fame in the northern United States with his long poetic work *Atalantis: A Story of the Sea* (1832). Although he continued to write and publish his verse throughout his lifetime, and, indeed, felt himself to be a good poet, his reputation has never rested on his poetic abilities. Still, his poetry is not without interest, for Simms often reveals a sharp eye for natural detail in his descriptions, especially of the Southern landscape. His accomplishments as a writer of short fiction have only recently begun to be appreciated. His emphasis on realism can be seen in such works as "The Hireling and the Slave," and his wonderful command of folk humor can be found in such literary "tall tales" as "Bald-Head Bill Bauldy" and "How Sharp Snaffles Got His Capital and Wife." Longer stories such as *As Good as a Comedy: Or, The Tenesseean's Story* (1852) and "Paddy McGann" contain further elements of the tall tale and folklore. Simms was not a good dramatist; he wrote a number of aborted plays and, in the case of *Pelayo*, adapted a failed drama into novel form. His best play is considered to be *Michael Bonham: A Tale of Texas* (1852), which deals with the Texas war for independence.

In his nonfiction works, Simms often turned to the history of the South.

Of his four major biographies, two—*The Life of Francis Marion* (1844) and *The Life of Nathanael Greene* (1849)—grew out of his abiding interest in the Revolutionary War in the South; both men also appeared as characters in his novels. His historical writings include *The History of South Carolina* (1840), a general history of the state, beginning with its settlement; *South-Carolina in the Revolutionary War* (1853), which concentrated on that part of the state's history which he so often used in his fiction; and his contemporary account of the Civil War, *Sack and Destruction of the City of Columbia, S.C.* (1865), an inspired example of reporting. Although Simms was not always accurate or unbiased, he was a surprisingly good historian. He collected sources throughout his life, made use of private recollections and memoirs, and today his work provides a storehouse of information often overlooked by more standard historical works. Simms's combination of the factual and the imaginative in his historical romances is one of his strongest and most appealing traits.

Achievements

Although during his lifetime William Gilmore Simms's popularity as a novelist ranked second only to that of James Fenimore Cooper, his reputation steadily diminished after his death, so that by the turn of the century he was little more than a footnote in literary histories. With the University of South Carolina Press publications of *The Letters of William Gilmore Simms* (1952-1956, 5 volumes, Mary C. Simms Oliphant, editor) and the first volumes of *The Centennial Edition of the Writings of William Gilmore Simms* (1969-1975, 16 volumes, John C. Guilds and James B. Meriwether, editors), however, there has been a growing interest in his work. Still, the fact remains that Simms's contributions to the development of American literature in the first half of the nineteenth century have been much underrated. Put simply, Simms was the most important antebellum Southern man of letters. He created a body of work that is awesome in size and scope. More than eighty separate volumes were published during his life, and ongoing research is uncovering more of his writings hidden in forgotten periodicals or under various pseudonyms.

When, in 1832, Simms first traveled to New York City, he was determined to establish himself as a writer of national importance. He made the necessary publishing connections and paid homage to the leading Northern literary figures. The publication of his poetic work *Atalantis* in that year was enthusiastically received, but it and his short novel *Martin Faber*, published the following year, were still apprenticeship pieces which followed patterns set down by others. With *Guy Rivers*, *The Yemassee*, and *The Partisan*, Simms not only staked out his own literary territory but also publicly placed himself in competition on a national level. Simms was an ardent supporter of the idea that America must produce its own unique brand of writing, inspired by its own land and people and experiences. Simms's own interest lay in the South, but, as he explained in the Preface to *The Wigwam and the Cabin* (1845), by mastering sectional material, the writer could still be of national importance, since no single writer could adequately depict the country as a whole.

It was in his commitment to the South that Simms achieved his greatness. He saw the South as a land of exciting potential. He loved its rawness as well as its manners, its violence as well as its vitality. Its heritage was rich, he felt, but largely unknown to people both inside and outside the region. Thus, Simms, with his passion for history and folklore, set out to reveal this past to Southerners and Northerners alike, to correct the historical picture he found so lacking. In his romances, he helped to define the popular image of the South from precolonial times up to the American Civil War. The Northerner, Simms maintained, had no right to feel superior to his Southern brethren, but the Southerner had all too often been remiss in preserving and appreciating his own heritage.

As the political disputes between North and South intensified, Simms became a protector of a way of life he felt was being threatened. In this time of trouble, he maintained that the past held lessons for the present: the courageous spirit of the pioneer and the partisan soldier could still inspire, the inherent nobility of the manor-born ladies and gentlemen could still instruct. Thus, Simms's tales of an earlier era, marked by characters of indomitable strength, could be seen as examples for his own time.

The sheer quantity of Simms's work remains staggering and his overall achievement approaches the heroic. Although he sometimes bemoaned the lack of appreciation and support he received in the South, most of his contemporaries, despite occasional carping, freely awarded him the laurels of leadership. A less courageous and confident man would never have faced the challenges that Simms invited. Before the war, he sought, through his own example, to impart a sense of dignity to the Southern artist. For the five years he lived after the war, he struggled to rekindle the pride of a defeated people, in the midst of his own great personal tragedy. As a critic and an editor, as a poet and a writer of fiction, he worked at first with energy and enthusiasm, later out of a kind of desperation against the inevitable, but he never stinted in his devotion to art and to a world which came to lie in ruins around him.

Biography

William Gilmore Simms was born in Charleston, South Carolina, on April 17, 1806, the second son and only surviving child of William Gilmore and Harriet Ann Augusta Singleton Simms. Simms's father came from Ireland after the American Revolution and established a successful mercantile business in Charleston. His mother's family, the Singletons, had lived in the port city for generations. Her grandfather, Thomas Singleton, was one of the Charleston citizens arrested by the British authorities during their occupation and, despite his advanced age, sent in exile to St. Augustine; her father, John Singleton, had fought as a soldier on the side of the patriots. Simms's mother died in 1808, and shortly thereafter, his father, grief-stricken at the loss of his wife, left Charleston to journey westward, placing his only child in the care of his late wife's mother, Mrs. Jacob Gates (she had remarried in 1800 after the death of John Singleton in 1799). The elder Simms went on to lead what must have seemed an incredibly exciting life to his impressionable son; the boy heard tales of his father's fighting under Andrew Jackson in the Indian Wars in Florida and later at the Battle of New Orleans in the War of 1812 before settling in Mississippi, then the edge of the frontier. Thus, Simms the boy grew up surrounded by legends and dreams of almost mythical characters—the Revolutionary War heroes on the Singleton side of the family, and the pioneer-soldier he saw in his own father. Both romantic threads would run throughout Simms's writings. In addition, growing up in historic Charleston allowed him to visit sites of Revolutionary incidents in and near the city. His unflagging interest in history (especially that of South Carolina but also of foreign lands) provided a foundation for his wilder imagination, and his writings would always contain a solid understructure of fact.

Although tradition has held that Simms grew up in genteel poverty in Charleston, feeling ostracized by that aristocratic city's more prominent citizens, his father had, in fact, left him substantial property holdings, and Simms was recognized early for his achievements. Still, it is equally clear that Simms was sensitive to slight—at least partly because of boyhood loneliness after the loss of his immediate family—and his enormous artistic energy no doubt fed on this partial uncertainty.

In 1812, at the age of six, Simms began school in Charleston. He entered the College of Charleston when he was ten, and at twelve he began work in a local apothecary shop. He was already writing poetry and drama. By the age of sixteen, he had published verse in a Charleston newspaper; at seventeen he was editing a juvenile periodical, the first of many editorships he would undertake in his lifetime. The next year, 1824 to 1825, Simms spent with his father in Mississippi. Together they ranged into the wilderness, where Simms met and carefully observed the types of frontiersmen (rascals and rogues among them) and Indians which would people his romances.

When Simms returned to Charleston in 1825, he set about establishing himself as a writer. His first volume of verse, *Monody on the Death of Gen. Charles Cotesworth Pinckney* (1825), made him a prominent local talent. In 1826, he married Anna Malcolm Giles. The next year Simms was admitted to the bar and published his second and third volumes of poetry. In 1828, he bacame editor of the *Southern Literary Gazette*; in 1829, his fourth volume of verse appeared, and his fifth followed in 1830. Also in 1830, he became copartner in the Charleston *City Gazette*; in this role he figured as a leading opponent to the Nullification Movement which was dividing South Carolina into two very fractious parties. Simms's opposition brought him into serious disfavor with many important citizens, and it was an experience which he would remember with a mixture of anger and regret.

The year 1832 was a decisive one for Simms. His wife, Anna, died in February. Overtaxed by emotional and professional demands, Simms gave up his legal practice (never a foremost interest), sold the *City Gazette*, and journeyed to New York City, determined to make his way in earnest as a literary man. In New York, he formed what was to be a lifelong friendship with James Lawson. Simms would use Lawson's home as his northern base until the Civil War finally intervened; Lawson would be among the first to help Simms in the dark days after the war as well. With Lawson's encouragement and advice, Simms published his sixth volume of poetry, *Atalantis*, in 1832. When it proved extremely popular with the Northern audience, Simms followed it with his first novel, *Martin Faber*, and his first collection of short fiction, *The Book of My Lady*, both in 1833. With the publication of *Guy Rivers* in 1834 and of *The Partisan* and *The Yemassee* in 1835, Simms had announced his literary directions, as these three books were the first of his Border, Revolutionary, and Colonial romances, respectively.

The next twenty or so years were generally good ones for Simms. In 1836, he married Chevillette Eliza Roach, the daughter of a prominent land owner in South Carolina. As part of his marriage inheritance, Simms obtained "Woodlands" plantation, which became his most prized retreat, an emblem of all he saw best in the Southern way of life. The demands of his life-style made it necessary that Simms publish as much and as often as possible, but because of the laxity of copyright laws he often received far less than he was due for what he did write. Simms would travel to New York about once a year to confer with his publishers (for a time new works by Simms came out annually) and to visit old friends. He enjoyed his growing reputation as spokesman for the South. Although he was always interested in politics and acted as an informal adviser to a number of political leaders in South Carolina, he served only one term in government, as a member of the South Carolina House of Representatives from 1844 to 1846. His most notable literary position during this time was as editor of *The Southern Quarterly Review* from 1849 to 1854.

Beginning in the 1850's, Simms became a leading and increasingly strident voice in the call for Southern secession from the Union and in the defense of slavery. Unfortunately, he is too often remembered for the attitudes struck in these pronouncements, so at odds with modern understanding, at the expense of his more important creative works. As a public figure, Simms attracted the opprobrium aimed at the South as war became inevitable. His 1856 lecture tour of the North on the role of the South in the American Revolution had to be cut short when Simms enraged his audiences with his vigorous and even pugnacious arguments against the Union stand. He welcomed the final break and was confident of Southern victory, but as the war progressed, he came to see the specter of defeat.

The last years of Simms's life were tragic. In 1862, "Woodlands" was partially burned but was rebuilt through the subscriptions of appreciative South Carolinians. In 1863, his second wife died, a devastating blow to Simms, who had also lost nine of his children. In 1865, "Woodlands" was again set ablaze, this time by stragglers from General Sherman's army. Simms lost in this conflagration his private library of ten thousand volumes, considered to be the finest in the South at the time. During the five years remaining to him after the war, Simms worked as never before, as editor of two newspapers—the Columbia *Phoenix* and the *Daily South Carolinian*—and as the author of still more poems, addresses, short fiction, and serialized novels. Despite his own almost inconceivable losses, Simms did what he could to bring about the resurrection of his land and people. When he died on June 11, 1870, a world and a way of life had clearly passed with him.

Analysis

As early as 1835, in the Preface to *The Yemassee*, William Gilmore Simms attempted to define his goals as a writer. He distinguished his full-length fiction as "romances" rather than novels. Following definitions already in vogue, Simms described the novel as picturing ordinary people in everyday situations, both domestic and common. These works he traced to Samuel Richardson and Henry Fielding. The "romance," on the other hand, he saw as the modern-day equivalent to the ancient epic, drawing its inspiration and power from both drama and poetry. The romance (as practiced by writers such as Sir Walter Scott, Edward Bulwer-Lytton, and James Fenimore Cooper) was of "loftier origins" than the novel. Its characters were individuals caught up in extraordinary, uncertain, even improbable events. As Simms saw it, the writer of a romance was not as bound by strict logic as was the novelist; indeed, the romancer's ingenuity in plotting was often a strong point in the work. As critics have pointed out, a number of Simms's supposed literary sins—stock characters, absurd resolutions, inflated dialogue—resulted from the romantic tradition in which he worked rather than from a lack of art or skill.

To categorize Simms simply as a writer of romances is, however, somewhat misleading, and more recent studies have emphasized the strong sense of realism that is found in his work. During his lifetime, Simms was regularly accused of exceeding the bounds of propriety. He answered these objections on numerous occasions. In his "Advertisement" to *Mellichampe*, for example, he insisted that his purpose was to "adhere as closely as possible, to the features and the attributes of real life." Thus, although he endeavored to invest his stories with noble characters involved in stirring adventures, he wished to write neither "a fairy tale, [n]or a tale in which none but the colors of the rose and rainbow shall predominate."

This sense of realism, which must have seemed uncouth in Simms's own time, has come to be recognized as one of his strongest traits. He was clearly influenced by the "realism" of the legends and frontier tales of his youth and in the writings of the Southern and Southwestern humorists. Augustus Baldwin Longstreet's *Georgia Scenes* was published in 1835, the same year as *The Yemassee* and *The Partisan*. (Simms would himself write several brilliant "tall tales" such as "Bald-Head Bill Bauldy" and "How Sharp Snaffles Got His Capital and Wife.") Simms's sense of realism did not apply only to "low" characters and their exploits, however, as has often been implied. Simms would modify the nobility, the wisdom, even the courage of his "model characters," his aristocrats, if the story warranted it. His heroes could learn, could fail, could grow; and his villains were often surprisingly complex, capable of unexpected decency and courageous deeds.

Underlying all of Simms's romances was a strong awareness of history, of what had actually happened at the time and place about which he wrote. Simms felt free to bend fact to the demands of art, but not to misrepresent the essential truth of the situation. The *facts* of history, he said, standing by themselves, carried little weight, but the artist—the creative writer—by giving *shape* to the facts, could give them life and meaning. Thus, it is the writer who is the true historian, and it was as an "artist-historian" that Simms wrote most of his romances.

As all commentators on Simms like to point out (and as Simms himself was aware), he usually wrote too rapidly and carelessly. He simply produced too much for the good of his own reputation. His faults are often glaring, but they are usually the result of haste and little or no revision. Simms could write with clarity and precision, but he could also sacrifice both for blood and thunder. Simms was a storyteller, and his books, for all their length, keep a steady pace. When he turned his hand to psychological interpretations of characters, when he tried to "analyze the heart," he often did so with the concomitant loss of energy and drive. In his best works, however, he was able to combine complexity of character with a compelling story.

Simms wrote eight romances dealing with the Revolutionary War in the South, and as a group they represent his best work. The novels cover the period from 1775, when the first open warfare began, to 1783, when the British abandoned Charleston and the soldiers returned home to a new and difficult way of life. The internal chronology of the novels does not correspond to the sequence of their composition. "Joscelyn: A Tale of the Revolution," which was meant to be the "opening scene" in Simms's "grand drama" of the South's seven-year war of Revolution, was one of the very last works he wrote, and the only one of the eight never to appear in book form during his lifetime. It appears as volume sixteen of *The Centennial Edition of the Writings of William Gilmore Simms*. "Joscelyn" is set around the Georgia-South Carolina border and describes the early conflicts between those who joined in the growing freedom movement and those who remained loyal to the crown. It also shows that men on both sides of the issue could be motivated by cruelty as well as courage, by selfishness as well as honor.

The next three novels—*The Partisan, Mellichampe,* and *Katherine Walton*—were conceived of by Simms as a trilogy, with developing characters and overlapping plots, although each was also meant to stand as an independent work. These books cover the events of 1780, following the fall of Charleston to the British. *The Partisan* is a big, sprawling book which Simms later described as a "ground-plan," a setting of the stage for the works to come. It introduces numerous characters, both historical—Francis Marion, Lord Cornwallis, Banastre Tarleton, Horatio Gates, Baron DeKalb—and fictional—Major Robert Singleton, Colonel Richard Walton, his daughter Katharine, Lieutenant Porgy—who return in later works in the series. *The Partisan*'s story lines include the development of Marion's guerrilla forces in the swamps of South Carolina, the growth of love between Singleton and Katharine Walton, and the agony of Colonel Walton's decision to align himself with the rebel cause. The novel closes with a detailed description and analysis of the Battle of Camden (in August, 1780), wherein Gates and the Southern Continental Army were soundly defeated by Cornwallis. *Mellichampe* is set in the fall of 1780. It put less emphasis on the large historical picture and was more clearly intended as a work of fiction, although here again the "facts" of the war are not forgotten. In *Mellichampe*, Simms expands his description of Marion's role in the war, develops several minor characters found in *The Partisan*, and illustrates the "excesses of patriotism" and the necessity of honor in times of conflict. The third book of this trilogy, *Katharine Walton*, again takes up the story of Colonel Walton, his daughter, and Robert Singleton. It is set largely in Charleston during the last months of 1780 and describes the social life and attempts at rebellion in the captured city at this very trying time.

The next in the series is *The Scout*, which moves into the central region of South Carolina. It is, in some ways, the most "romantic" and melodramatic of the novels. Its plot of feuding brothers and mysterious outriders is heavy with conventions, but in its description of the marauding outlaw bands which terrorized the back country and in its discussion of Nathanael Greene's siege of the British fort at Ninety-Six (upstate South Carolina) in the summer of 1781, *The Scout* is an impressive and absorbing story. *The Forayers* and *Eutaw*, which were first conceived as one book, follow the retreat of the British from Ninety-Six to Charleston and present the events leading to the climactic battle at Eutaw Springs, South Carolina, in September, 1781, which effectively ended British rule in the state, although the battle itself was a draw.

The last of the Revolutionary War novels is *Woodcraft*, which begins in December, 1782, after the British evacuation. Its theme is the readjustment of soldiers to domestic life, and its main character is Lieutenant Porgy, the wastrel aristocrat soldier whom many feel to be Simms's most successful character. Porgy appears in five of the eight novels, but his most important role is in *Woodcraft*. Basically a comic character (Porgy is often compared to William Shakespeare's Falstaff, although such comparisons rarely go beyond surface descriptions), this fat soldier confronts the challenges of peace after the adventures of war. Born of the landed gentry, Porgy is known to have wasted his inheritance as a young man, and despite his courage and wit, he is not one of Simms's noble heroes. He is, however, among the most likable and (with reservations) the most admirable of Simms's characters, and it is his mood of reconciliation (after one final battle) and acceptance that presides over this last book. Some critics hold *Woodcraft* to be Simms's best work (although *The Forayers* and *Eutaw* might be better choices), and it certainly shows Simms at his most relaxed and amiable.

Commonly listed under the category of Simms's Border Romances are *Guy Rivers*, *Richard Hurdis*, *Border Beagles*, *Beauchampe*, *Helen Halsey*, *Charlemont*, "Voltmeier: Or, The Mountain Men," and "The Cub of the Panther." These works lack the specific historical overview of the Revolutionary War novels—they are closer to Simms's own time and are not as likely to be built around identifiable events—but they do give excellent descriptions of the frontier of the Old South—the customs, speech patterns, and life-styles of settlers, outlaws, and adventurers. The first of these, *Guy Rivers*, was Simms's first full-length novel as well. Set in the mountainous region of Georgia, where gold was being mined in the early 1800's, the story centers on the conflict between Guy Rivers, a notorious outlaw (though once a respected lawyer) and Ralph Colleton, a young South Carolinian whose own frustrations with love and family have led him to the frontier. There he meets Mark Forrester, a native of the region who helps Ralph in his "natural" education. Colleton foreshadows such later Simms's heroes as Robert Singleton, Ernest Mellichampe, and Willie Sinclair (in *The Forayers* and *Eutaw*), while Forrester anticipates Thumbscrew Witherspoon in *Mellichampe* and Supple Jack Bannister in *The Scout*, woodsmen who teach the young aristocrats the need for clear thinking and honorable actions. Rivers is the melodramatic villain of the type that would chew the scenery and threaten feminine virtue in a number of Simms's works: Barsfield in *Mellichampe*, Edward Conway in *The Scout*, Captain Inglehardt in *The Forayers* and *Eutaw*.

Richard Hurdis, the second of the Border novels, is perhaps the best of them. Set in Alabama, the story is loosely based on the outrages of John Murrell and his outlaw gang which roamed throughout Alabama and Mississippi. Simms apparently had met witnesses to or even participants in some of this gang's doings while visiting his father in Mississippi as a boy. The plot is somewhat similar to that of *The Scout*: in each novel, two brothers— one virtuous and one criminally inclined—find themselves at odds; both books are concerned with the attempts to bring outlaw bands to justice. In a sense, *Border Beagles* is a continuation of *Richard Hurdis*; a tale of bandits on the Mississippi frontier, it is generally considered a less effective story than its predecessor.

Beauchampe was Simms's retelling of the notorious Beauchampe-Sharpe "Kentucky tragedy," a murder case in which Beauchampe killed Warham Sharpe, the seducer of Margaret Cooper, whom Beauchampe had married. In 1856, Simms returned to this story in *Charlemont*, which detailed the events leading up to the "tragedy" in *Beauchampe*. Thus, *Beauchampe*, although published first, was, in Simms's words, the "sequel" to *Charlemont*. Simms's last two Border romances were both published in magazines in 1869, at the very end of his life. "Voltmeier" was published again in 1969 as volume one of *The Centennial Edition of the Writings of William Gilmore Simms*. "Voltmeier" and "The Cub of the Panther" were drawn from Simms's personal observations and experiences during trips into the mountainous regions of North Carolina, and they contain some of his best writing.

Simms dealt with the settling of South Carolina in the early eighteenth century in two important works, *The Yemassee* and *The Cassique of Kiawah*. *The Yemassee* was Simms's most popular novel, and, because of its Indian theme, was immediately compared to the works of Cooper. The novel described the 1715 Yemassee Indian War against the colonists. Simms's tale concentrates on two main characters: Governor Charles Craven (a historical figure), who takes the disguise of Gabriel Harrison for much of the book, and Sanutee, the chief of the Yemassee. Simms illustrates Sanutee's problem with sympathy and understanding—the Indian had originally welcomed the settlers and then found himself and his tribe threatened by them—but the novel finally argues in favor of the white men and the advanced civilization they bring with them. Despite *The Yemassee*'s popularity—it is still the work for which Simms is best remembered—the novel is not as impressive as *The Cassique of Kiawah*, a much later and more mature work, which deals with similar material but has received little critical attention. It has been argued that Simms's picture of the Indian was more realistic than Cooper's. He avoided the idea of the "noble savage," but often imbued his Indians with traits of courage and dignity. In addition to these two novels, Simms used colonial and Indian material in several of his shorter works found in *Carl Werner*, *The Wigwam and the Cabin*, and *The Lily and the Totem: Or, The Huguenots in Florida*.

Simms's interest in European history, especially in Spanish history, dated back to his childhood and formed the basis for four foreign romances. *Pelayo* had been conceived when Simms was seventeen as a drama on the conquest of Spain by the Moors. The play was never performed, and the material later grew into a novel. *Count Julian* was the sequel to *Pelayo*, but its publication was delayed for a number of years because its manuscript was lost for a time.

The Damsel of Darien was inspired by the adventures of Vasco Balboa, while *Vasconselos* concerned itself with Hernando DeSoto's explorations in the New World. Most critics and readers would agree that these works are among Simms's weakest.

Simms's first novel was *Martin Faber: The Story of a Criminal*. It recounts the first-person confessions of the title character, who has seduced and murdered one girl and married another, whom he then begins to suspect of adultery. Faber tells his story in prison, just before his execution. The book is a short and emotional work, and was quickly linked to William Godwin's *The Adventures of Caleb Williams: Or, Things as They Are* (1794), although its antecedents could also be found in numerous Gothic romances. Simms returned to this type of story in *Confession: Or, The Blind Heart*, which, in his introduction, Simms linked to Godwin. *Confession* was the reworking of an idea Simms had played with as a younger writer. He explained that he had forgotten the work before he found the manuscript by accident years later. As he reread it, he was "led away" by the psychological aspects of the tale. *Confession* tells of Edward Clifford, a young lawyer who is consumed by jealousy of his wife. Convinced of the worst, Clifford kills the entirely virtuous woman; when he later discovers the truth, he condemns himself to a life of wandering and self-recrimination. The similarities to Shakespeare's *Othello* (1604) are obvious, although Simms maintained that the materials were "gathered from fact."

The same interests in crime, guilt, and retribution are found throughout his other works—he was always intrigued by the psychological complexities of sinners and criminals—and it could be argued that *Beauchampe* and *Charlemont* might better be placed in this group than among the Border tales. These psychological novels, however, are not the works for which Simms is remembered. Although his constantly inquiring imagination was stirred by these situations, he was the master of scope and action rather than the kind of close analysis these topics demanded. The twists and entanglements of plot which could be overridden in his more sweeping works became all too obvious when related at a slower, more concentrated pace.

In his lasting works, Simms's long undervalued contribution to America's literary heritage is clearly evident. His was the voice of the South—the maker of its romances, the singer of its legends, the keeper of its history, and the defender of its traditions. More than any other writer, he embodied his time and place: its grandeur, its courage, and its wrongheadedness.

Edwin T. Arnold III

Other major works

SHORT FICTION: *The Book of My Lady*, 1833; *Carl Werner*, 1838; *The Wigwam and the Cabin*, 1845; *Southward Ho!*, 1854.

PLAY: *Michael Bonham: A Tale of Texas*, 1852.

POETRY: *Monody on the Death of Gen. Charles Cotesworth Pinckney*, 1825; *Early Lays*, 1827; *Lyrical and Other Poems*, 1827; *The Vision of Cortes*, 1829; *The Tri-Color*, 1830; *Atalantis: A Story of the Sea*, 1832; *Areytos: Or, Songs of the South*, 1846; *Poems Descriptive, Dramatic, Legendary and Contemplative*, 1853.

NONFICTION: *The History of South Carolina*, 1840; *The Geography of South Carolina*, 1843; *The Life of Francis Marion*, 1844; *Views and Reviews in American Literature, History and Fiction*, 1845; *The Life of Captain John Smith*, 1846; *The Life of the Chevalier Bayard*, 1847; *The Life of Nathanael Greene*, 1849; *The Lily and the Totem: Or, The Huguenots in Florida*, 1850; *South-Carolina in the Revolutionary War*, 1853; *Sack and Destruction of the City of Columbia, S. C.*, 1865; *The Letters of William Gilmore Simms*, 1952-1956 (Mary C. Simms Oliphant, editor, 5 volumes).

MISCELLANEOUS: *The Centennial Edition of the Writings of William Gilmore Simms*, 1969-1975 (John C. Guilds and James B. Meriwether, editors, 16 volumes).

Bibliography

Guilds, John Caldwell, ed. *Long Years of Neglect: The Work and Reputation of William Gilmore Simms*. Fayetteville: University of Arkansas Press, 1988. This collection brings together a dozen essays, some rather scholarly, though many suitable for the high school student. In addition to useful articles, offers a reproduction of an oil portrait of Simms.

Parks, Edd Winfield. *William Gilmore Simms as Literary Critic*. Athens: University of Georgia Press, 1961. Though the focus of this book is narrow—Simms's reviews and literary essays—it offers some insight into his creative works.

Ridgely, J. V. *William Gilmore Simms*. New York: Twayne, 1962. A good starting point for students of Simms, this short book gives a history of his career and brief comments on his major works. Contains a chronology of Simms's life and works, a useful annotated bibliography, and an index.

Wakelyn, Jon L. *The Politics of a Literary Man: William Gilmore Simms*. Westport, Conn.: Greenwood Press, 1973. Although he mostly explores the political aspects of Simms and his writings, Wakelyn now and then contributes literary insights. Contains an extensive bibliography and a photograph of Simms.

Wimsatt, Mary Ann. *The Major Fiction of William Gilmore Simms*. Baton Rouge: Louisiana State University Press, 1989. Though its discussions sometimes rise above the high school and undergraduate level, this is the most lavishly illustrated book on Simms available, with fourteen pages of pictures, maps, and photographs of Simms and the people and places associated with him.

UPTON SINCLAIR

Born: Baltimore, Maryland; September 20, 1878
Died: Bound Brook, New Jersey; November 25, 1968.

Principal long fiction

Springtime and Harvest, 1901; *Prince Hagen*, 1903; *The Journal of Arthur Stirling*, 1903; *Manassas*, 1904 (as *Theirs Be the Guilt*, 1959); *The Jungle*, 1906; *A Captain of Industry*, 1906; *The Overman*, 1907; *The Metropolis*, 1908; *The Moneychangers*, 1908; *Samuel the Seeker*, 1910; *Love's Pilgrimage*, 1911; *Sylvia*, 1913; *Sylvia's Marriage*, 1914; *King Coal*, 1917; *Jimmie Higgins*, 1919; *100%*, 1920; *They Call Me Carpenter*, 1922; *Oil! A Novel*, 1927; *Boston*, 1928; *Mountain City*, 1930; *Roman Holiday*, 1931; *The Wet Parade*, 1931; *Co-op*, 1936; *The Flivver King*, 1937; *No Pasaran!*, 1937; *Little Steel*, 1938; *Our Lady*, 1938; *World's End*, 1940; *Between Two Worlds*, 1941; *Dragon's Teeth*, 1942; *Wide Is the Gate*, 1943; *Presidential Agent*, 1944; *Dragon Harvest*, 1945; *A World to Win*, 1946; *Presidential Mission*, 1947; *One Clear Call*, 1948; *O Shepherd, Speak!*, 1949; *Another Pamela: Or, Virtue Still Rewarded*, 1950; *The Return of Lanny Budd*, 1953; *What Didymus Did*, 1954; *It Happened to Didymus*, 1958; *Affectionately Eve*, 1961.

Other literary forms

Between 1901 and 1961, Upton Sinclair wrote or rewrote more than forty novels, but in addition to his longer fiction, Sinclair also wrote and published a massive amount of nonfiction, including pamphlets, analyses of diverse subjects, memoirs, twelve plays, and letters by the thousands. The bibliography of his works is testimony to his amazing fluency, but no one who is so prolific can escape being uneven, and this is indeed the case with Sinclair. His career, which spanned more than six decades, was unified in one respect, however, for both his fiction and his nonfiction were devoted to a single aim—the achievement of social justice. Everything that he wrote was written primarily as a means to attain the end he sought, bettering the conditions of life for his fellowman. Thus, much of what Sinclair produced is not belletristic in any full sense, but propaganda to spread his ideas about politics and economics. In books such as the *The Industrial Republic* (1907), he tries to explain how socialism will be arrived at by a natural process in America; the theory is based on the premise that social revolutions are bound to be benevolent. During the period following World War I to the onset of the Depression, most of Sinclair's writing was nonfiction. In a number of books, which he called his Dead Hand series, an ironic allusion to Adam Smith's "Invisible Hand" of *laissez-faire* economics, Sinclair deals with the destructive influence of capitalism on numerous American institutions: *The Profits of Religion* (1918) treats the abuses of institutional religions, showing how the established church supports the ruling classes in exchange for economic advantages; *The Brass Check: A Study in American Journalism* (1919) details the operation of class bias in American journalism; *The Goose-Step: A Study of American Education* (1923) reveals higher education's lackeylike relationship to capitalism, fostered by grants and endowments made to the universities by wealthy families and industry. In *The Goslings: A Study of the American Schools* (1924), the same kind of servile relationship with the capitalist status quo is exposed as existing in elementary and high schools, and in *Mammonart* (1925), Sinclair shows how artists and writers down through history have been duped into serving oppressive economic and political power structures. Not even William Shakespeare, Fyodor Dostoevski, or Joseph Conrad were their own men according to Sinclair's ideological criticism. Although the Dead Hand series is flawed by an excess of socialist polemics, Sinclair did an extensive amount of research to produce each book, and though the case is overstated, there is a grain of truth in his analysis of the all-pervasive influence of the economic and political structure of America on those areas that should be most independent of such pressure—the Church, the press, the educational system, the arts.

Of more interest to the general reader are Sinclair's autobiographical works *American Outpost: A Book of Reminiscences* (1932) and *The Autobiography of Upton Sinclair* (1962), which updates his life for the thirty years intervening between the two books. In his accounts of his life, Sinclair reveals himself to be an honest but self-centered idealist. He chronicles his victories and defeats through childhood, youth, and marriage as the educational experiences of a genius; he offers in generally positive and optimistic terms his lifelong belief in progress and his hatred of social inequality and social exploitation.

Achievements

Sinclair's literary remains weighed in at eight tons when being collected for donation to Indiana University Library. Of modern American writers, he is among the most widely translated, his works having been translated into forty-seven languages in thirty-nine countries, yet his literary reputation has been on a steady decline since the 1940's, despite the fact that *The Jungle* is still widely read in high school and college classrooms. Moreover, Sinclair himself has historical importance for the role he played in the American radical movement.

Sinclair's recurring theme as a novelist was class-conflict, the exploitation of the poor by the rich, of labor by management, of the have-nots by the haves. With few exceptions, the rich are depicted as useless, extravagant, and unprincipled, while the poor are essentially noble characters who are the victims of capitalistic society. Sinclair's literary method, which came to be called "muckraking," was intended to expose the evils of such a society. Apart from *The Jungle*, which is the best-known example of this genre, there is the

Lanny Budd series—ten historical novels that trace the history of the world from 1913 to 1946. *Dragon's Teeth*, the third in the series, won the Pulitzer Prize for Fiction in 1942 by virtue of its vivid portrayal of conditions in Nazi-dominated Europe. In addition to these, the most widely read of Sinclair's novels, he produced novels on almost every topic of then-current social history, including coal strikes in Colorado in *King Coal*, exploitation by the oil industry in California in *The Wet Parade*, and the legal injustices of the Sacco-Vanzetti case in *Boston*. All of Sinclair's fiction was aimed at the middle-class liberal, whom he hoped to convert to his idealistic vision of a brotherhood of labor. Sinclair was thus a spokesman for the progressive era of American history; a chronic protestor and iconoclast, he tried to stir the conscience of his nation and to cause change. In only one case, *The Jungle*, was he successful in prompting the desired changes through legislation. As a propagandist writing in the spirit of Thomas Paine and in the idiom of Karl Marx, Sinclair made a permanent impact by what he said, if not by how he wrote, and to this day, he still serves as one of the chief interpreters of American society to other nations.

Biography

Upton Beall Sinclair was born in Baltimore, Maryland, but reared in New York. Finishing high school at the age of twelve, he was too young for college and had to wait until he was fourteen before he could enter the City College of New York. While an undergraduate, he helped support himself by writing stories and jokes for pulp magazines. In one span of a few weeks, he turned out fifty-six thousand words, an incredible feat even for a prolific prodigy such as Sinclair. In 1898, after taking his B.A. from CCNY, Sinclair enrolled as a special student in the Graduate School of Columbia University, but withdrew after a professor told him "you don't know anything about writing." In 1900, Sinclair married Meta Fuller and began work on his first novel, *Springtime and Harvest*, which was written in Canada. Shortly afterward, in 1902, he joined the Socialist party. The reception of his early fiction gave him little critical encouragement and no cash of which to speak. His first four novels brought him less than one thousand dollars, and the threat of poverty put a strain on his marriage. In 1905, Sinclair, with Jack London, formed the Intercollegiate Socialist Society, an indication of his growing political radicalism.

Sinclair's first fame came with his fifth novel, *The Jungle*; he was even invited to the White House by President Theodore Roosevelt to discuss the book. With the thirty thousand dollars that *The Jungle* earned for him, Sinclair founded a Utopian community, Helicon Colony, in New Jersey. In 1907, an arsonist burned down the Colony and Sinclair's fortune with it. This was the first actual persecution that Sinclair had experienced for professing unpopular views. In private life, he faced further difficulties; his wife divorced him in

1911; he remarried in 1913 and moved West with his new wife, Mary Kimbrough, in 1915. Continuing to write at a furious pace, Sinclair became a publisher during World War I with the *Upton Sinclair Magazine*. He also issued a series of tracts on the effects of capitalism, objecting to its effects on education, art, journalism, and literature.

Not all of Sinclair's energies went into writing. He was instrumental in creating The League for Industrial Democracy and the American Civil Liberties Union. Three times he ran for the California state legislature and three times for governor, usually on the Socialist party ticket but also as a Democrat. In *I, Governor of California and How I Ended Poverty* (1933), he set forth his platform, "End Poverty in California" or "E.P.I.C.," which explained the Depression as a result of private ownership and the economic insanity of limited production. His ideas found a large degree of public acceptance in the early days of the New Deal and he came close to being elected despite the mudslinging of his opponent. Some critics believe that the chief reason for Sinclair's decline as a novelist was his involvement in electoral politics in the 1930's. His novels of that decade are about specific political situations. *The Flivver King* attacks Ford Motor Company and makes a case for labor unions. "Little Steel" is a story about the organization of steel-mill owners against unions. "Pasaram!" is another short story from the 1930's about the brave fight in the Spanish Civil War against right-wing dictators.

During World War II, Sinclair began the historical record of his times in the Lanny Budd series. The novels in this ten-book series show the metamorphosis of the hero, Lanny, from an espouser of socialist causes to an anti-Communist, a change that reflected Sinclair's own changed sympathies.

By the decade of the 1950's, Sinclair had entered semiretirement, during which he nevertheless managed to expand his autobiography and finish six books, including a clever parody of Samuel Richardson's epistolary novel *Pamela* (1740-1741), entitled *Another Pamela*, and a biography of Jesus. In these years, Sinclair finally settled his quarrel with the status quo. In his old age, he came to approve of the American establishment's foot-dragging on civil rights and supported American intervention in Vietnam. The old radical had, like so many before him, softened his position.

Analysis

Upton Sinclair was a prodigy as a writer and wrote with great fluency and consequent unevenness. For him, the essential purpose of literature was to expose social evils and promote change; his end as a writer was the improvement of mankind's condition. Thus, his literary reputation is not really germane to what he was trying to do as a writer. His fiction has more relevance when it is regarded in a political and historical light rather than as literature per se. As the social and economic issues of his time recede into history, so does interest in those books which were simply propaganda.

Although Sinclair was regarded as a literary rebel for his iconoclastic attacks on America's economic, intellectual, and political institutions, he was not in any way an avant-garde writer in terms of style and structure. His subject was society rather than the individual human consciousness. It is necessary in any analysis of Sinclair's fiction to admit at once the defects in his writing. Most of it is journalistic in quality rather than belletristic. In fact, he deliberately wrote against the genteel tradition in American letters. Sinclair employed his rhetoric for practical results rather than to achieve poetic effects. His polemics were couched in fictional form because he believed the novel was a particularly effective medium for his idealistic radicalism.

Sinclair's first four novels were produced between 1900 and 1904. These early works were awkward but full of passionate idealism. In *Prince Hagen* and *The Overman*, which were written before Sinclair discovered socialism, there is already a conflict between the pure-minded and the corrupt oppressors, but no solutions for the problems are proposed. The ideology of socialism provided him with solutions, although Sinclair was not a traditional Socialist; to him, socialism was the purest expression of the American dream. He did not see himself as an overthrower of American values, but as a writer who was helping his countrymen return to a vision of human brotherhood.

Prior to *Manassas*, Sinclair's fiction had been based on personal experience. In this novel about the Civil War, a young Southerner, Alan Montague, the son of a Mississippi plantation owner, becomes a supporter of Abolition. The protagonist is present at many historic moments—the raid at Harper's Ferry, the bombardment of Fort Sumter—and encounters many historical figures, such as Abraham Lincoln, Jefferson Davis, Frederick Douglass, and John Brown. *Manassas* differed from Sinclair's early books in that it was more realistic and objective. As a work of art, however, *Manassas* is not remarkable. The plot is often an inert review of historical facts, the characterizations are shallow, and the story is too filled with coincidence to be plausible. Despite its flaws, *Manassas* marked a turning point in Sinclair's career. In this novel, he revealed attitudes that pointed toward his development as a writer of exposés.

In 1904, Sinclair was asked by the editor of *The Appeal*, a radical paper, to write a novel about wage-slavery and the oppressive conditions of industrial workers which would show that their plight was analogous to that of the black in the Old South. Responding to this offer, Sinclair spent two months in the meat-packing houses of Chicago talking to the workers; he visited the plants also as an official tourist, and in disguise as a worker. The impressions and information Sinclair gathered from this experience were extremely distressing to him. His personal reaction to the corruption he saw was outrage; it is his identification with the exploited workers and his naturalistic descriptions of the oppressive industrial conditions that make his next novel, *The Jungle*, so gripping.

As Sinclair explains in his autobiography, *American Outpost*, he returned to his farm in New Jersey after he had collected his data on the meat-packing industry in Chicago and started writing the novel on Christmas Day, completing it in the summer of 1905 after less than six months' work. Although it was published in serial form as it was being written, Sinclair had trouble finding a publisher for the book; it was refused by five houses before Doubleday & Company took it after their lawyers made a careful investigation to avoid any possible libel suits. When *The Jungle* was published in February, 1906, the public was horrified, not by the novel's account of the conditions of the workers as Sinclair and his socialist friends expected, but by the naturalistic descriptions of the slaughterhouses and the evidence of criminal negligence in meat inspection. *The Jungle*, like most of Sinclair's fiction, straddles genres; it is partly a novel and partly exposé journalism. Sinclair's purpose in writing the book was to protest the exploitation of the workers and to recommend socialism as a corrective ideology to capitalism; the revelations of unsanitary packing-plant procedures were only a means to those ends. Hardly a dozen pages of this long novel are explicitly concerned with the repugnant details of the slaughterhouse, yet what remains in the reader's mind long after the plot line and thematic intentions fade are the scenes of grinding up poisoned rats, children's fingers, and carcasses of steers condemned as tubercular for canning meats; and the rendering of hogs dead of cholera for a fine grade of lard. Most dramatic of all, however, was Sinclair's report that the men who served in the cooking room occasionally fell into the boiling vats and were returned to the world transubstantiated into Durham's Pure Leaf Lard. The vividness of the author's descriptions had two effects: the first was an immediate drop in meat sales across America and Europe; the second was a summons to the White House to detail the abuses in the meat industry to President Theodore Roosevelt. The outraged public brought pressure to bear on politicians, and Congress enacted the Federal Pure Food and Drug Act of 1906.

The sensational revelations of *The Jungle* have drawn attention from the book's literary qualities. *The Jungle* has been compared to the polemical late works of Leo Tolstoy and to the naturalistic fiction of Émile Zola because of its pessimistic determinism. The setting is the grim slums of Chicago and the gory stockyards. The novel tells the story of a group of recent Lithuanian immigrants who have been lured to American from their old-world villages with promises of high wages.

Jurgis Rudkus, the novel's principal character, comes to the stockyard district, along with several of his friends and relatives, expecting to realize the American dream, little aware that they have entered a jungle. Unable to speak English, the immigrants are exploited by almost everyone in power—the politicians, the police, the landlords, and the "Beef Trust" bosses. Jurgis has to pay his foreman part of his low salary to keep his job. He is cheated by a crooked real-estate agent, who sells him a house with a hidden clause which allows the mortgage company to foreclose on Jurgis. After losing his house, Jurgis and his family are afflicted with misery. His job is taken away after he is blacklisted; he serves a jail term for slugging his wife's lascivious boss, who has compromised her honor. In turn, his father dies of disease, his wife and infant son die in childbirth, and finally, he loses his last son in a drowning accident. Jurgis is left without anything; alone and in ill-health, he is a broken man. He becomes a hobo, a petty criminal, and a strike-breaking scab—the lowest form of degradation for him.

In his extremity, Jurgis for the first time reflects upon how unjustly he has been treated by society, which he begins to regard as his enemy, but his views are inchoate. One day, by chance he hears a Socialist speak. The lecture transforms his conception of the world; socialism is like a revelation, for now there is a way by which the workers of the world can win respect. With Jurgis' conversion, the novel as a narrative ends for all practical purposes. The last chapters are devoted to socialist propaganda and socioeconomic analysis. The optimistic conclusion of the novel contrasts sharply with the pessimistic naturalism of the first chapters. Ironically, and to Sinclair's disappointment, the appeal to socialism and the protest against wage-slavery did not win the hearts and minds of his audience, but his realistic portrayal of conditions in the meat-packing industry (as he once remarked) surely turned the stomach of the nation.

The Jungle will never be placed in the first rank of American fiction because of its mixture of fictional and journalistic elements, its unresolved contradictions in theme, and its melodramatic plot and bifurcated structure. Sinclair tried to do too many things at once, and was only partially successful. Most readers think that the true significance of Sinclair's achievement in *The Jungle* lies in the uncensored presentation of the conditions of working-class life. Only Stephen Crane in *Maggie: A Girl of the Streets* (1893) had dealt with slum subjects with such integrity, and Sinclair had no models to follow in depicting this strata of society. In his firsthand observations and deep compassion for the oppressed, he was breaking new ground for literary treatment, which Theodore Dreiser would follow to different purposes.

Following the success of *The Jungle* was difficult for Sinclair. He spent the next eight years trying to repeat what he had done with his first and best "muckracking" book. He produced a number of novels focused on specific problems, but at the other end of the social scale. *The Metropolis* is an exposé of conspicuous consumption among upper-class New York socialites. It is a poor book by Sinclair's own admission and is remarkable only for the absence of socialistic sermons by the author. Sinclair, like F. Scott Fitzgerald, apparently believed that money sets the very wealthy quite apart from the rest of society, but, rather than seeking rapport with his wealthy characters, as Fitzgerald did, Sinclair hoped to reform them. Another novel of this period, *The*

Money Changers, is a story of the machinations of a high financier, obviously patterned on J. P. Morgan; the story tells of the exploits of Dan Waterman, the elderly head of the Steel Trust, who creates a panic on Wall Street purely for personal revenge against a rival steel magnate. Although *The Money Changers* is not very good fiction, it does have an interesting premise, suggesting a connection between sexual desire and the drive for financial power.

Another novel of this period that deserves mention for its subject is *Love's Pilgrimage*; neofeminist in theme, this work examines the pressures on Sinclair's own marriage because of his male insensitivity to his wife's personal, sexual, and intellectual needs. The novel is also interesting for the insight it offers into Sinclair's personality, for he candidly implies that the divorce his first wife sought was deserved because he prudishly withheld from sexual relations on the theory that it would decrease his creative energy.

In 1914, Sinclair was remarried and living in California. The transition in his life resulted in a change in his writing. In the West, Sinclair was drawn back to the problems of the proletariat by labor strife in the Colorado coal mines. As a result of the attempt by the United Mine Workers to organize the miners, the govenor of Colorado had called up the state militia to break up strikes. In 1914, in the town of Ludlow, National Guard troops fired into a camp of strikers and their families, killing eleven women and two children. This shocking event outraged Sinclair as nothing had since he had witnessed the brutal conditions of the stockyards.

Following the methods he had used to collect background material for *The Jungle*, he went to Colorado, visited the miners and their families, and talked with the mining officials and labor leaders. His direct contact with the working-class people stirred his emotions and gave him a more realistic point of departure for his next novel, *King Coal*, than any he had employed since *The Jungle*. In fact, *King Coal* was an attempt to repeat the same sort of muckraking performance that had succeeded so well in the former case. Unfortunately for Sinclair, *King Coal* did not create the response aroused by *The Jungle*, a fact largely resulting from the lag time in the publication of the novel. When *King Coal* appeared in 1917, the events in Ludlow were three years old and yesterday's news. America had just entered World War I, and the nation's mind was on "doughboys" rather than on coal miners.

The poor reception of *King Coal* was a great disappointment to Sinclair, because he knew he had produced the kind of novel he wrote best. *King Coal*, while not as powerful as *The Jungle*, has the rhetorical strength and the factual validity of the earlier book. Sinclair tells the story of a rich young man named Hal Warner, who impersonates a coal miner in order to investigate working conditions in the western coal camps. He becomes a union sympathizer and labor agitator after he becomes convinced that the mine owners are denying the miners their legal rights and are cheating them out of their wages by rigged scales. After witnessing the futility of getting justice for working men inside the legal system, the miners go on a wildcat strike. Hal convinces his coworkers to join the union, and the novel ends with the lines drawn between labor and management while Hal returns to college, vowing to continue his fight for the working people of America.

Although *King Coal* is not as powerful in its naturalistic details as *The Jungle* and lacks the pessimistic determinism of that novel, it is in the opinion of most critics Sinclair's second-best effort at muckraking. If very few Americans responded to Sinclair's account of the dangers of cave-ins, coal dust, and explosions, this result may be because they were never exposed to such perils, whereas all were subject to health hazards as a result of unsanitary food processing. For this reason, the exposé of negligence in Chicago meatpacking plants had a much more profound and practical effect than the exposé of the inhuman conditions in the coal camps of Colorado.

Between World War I and the start of the Depression, Sinclair wrote two remarkable novels based on topical social or political situations. *Oil!* delves into the Tea Pot Dome and other oil scandals of the Harding Administration, and thus has considerable historical significance as well as being one of Sinclair's most readable books. *Boston*, on the other hand, represents Sinclair's best use of a contemporary event for fictional purposes. This novel enfolds the drama of the Sacco-Vanzetti case, but it also encompasses the whole of Boston's society, suggesting that the city itself was responsible for what happened in this tragic case. The central character is again from the upper classes, an elderly Back Bay aristocrat, Cornelia Thornwell, wife to a governor. Full of vitality and intelligence, she thinks that she has spent her life as an artificial adornment to a great family. She determines late in life to emancipate herself from mores and manners of the mansion, and moves out to board with the Brini family, who are honest Italian mill hands, and starts to earn her own living in a factory.

At this point, Vanzetti enters the story. During a strike in the mill, he plays an important role in keeping up the workers' spirits. He also prevents them from organizing, because as an anarchist, Vanzetti did not support unions. Afterward, Vanzetti and his friend Sacco are marked as "anarchist wops" by the police. They are picked up as suspects in a payroll robbery, and in the midst of the deportation mania of the postwar period, the city's reason and sense of justice are beclouded. The courts, judge, jury, and prosecutor seem determined to make the foreigners pay—if not for the crime, then for their politics. The climax of the novel comes when the cogs of justice bring the proletarian saints, Vanzetti and Sacco, to the electric chair with many doubts about their guilt still lingering.

Through a blending of fact and fiction, Sinclair is able to record a complex and tragic story of social injustice, although the story of the runaway grandmother does get lost in the final pages as the historical facts dominate the plot. As a novel, the two-volume *Boston* is too long except for readers with some special interest in the Sacco-Vanzetti case. As usual, Sinclair was writing for a mass audience, and the novel employs many stock characters and a melodramatic plot; furthermore, a statement of socialist doctrine forms a coda to the novel. Sinclair does, however, create a convincing portrait of Vanzetti. It is in Sinclair's account of the death of this man of dignity and intelligence that the novel gains its greatest power.

The major literary effort of Sinclair's career was launched just before the outbreak of World War II: a ten-novel series offering a fictionalized history of the Western world in the first half of the twentieth century. The series is unified by its central character, Lanny Budd, and is known collectively by his name. One of the Lanny Budd novels, *Dragon's Teeth*, won for Sinclair a Pulitzer Prize in 1943. A chronicle of Germany's slide into Nazism, *Dragon's Teeth* is a scrupulous study of the fateful years between 1930 and 1934, and reflects an extensive research effort on Sinclair's part. In fact, several critics claimed that if the book were stripped of its fictional ingredient, it might well serve as a history text.

Sinclair creates an air of impending doom as he shows how quickly Europe was led to the abyss. His protagonist, Lanny Budd, is a neutral observer traveling the Continent with his millionaire wife, Irma, who is especially obtuse about economics, politics, and national traits. She is a foil to the sensitive and intelligent Lanny, who is aware of the coming crisis. Irma and her upper-class female friends refuse to believe that their smug routine of bridge and dinner parties will be disrupted. The reader in 1942 received these opinions with a great deal of dramatic irony. Meanwhile, Lanny grows increasingly concerned about the absence of morality in the political climate of Germany. Lanny has rather improbable meetings with the big-wigs of the Nazi regime. He goes hunting with Hermann Göring, has cocktails with Joseph Goebbels, and a discussion with Adolf Hitler about the Jewish question. His interest in this topic is not merely academic, since his sister is married to one of Germany's most prominent Jews. The Jews in Germany, however, are like Irma's circle; they refuse to face the realities of Nazism. The novel ends with Lanny's contriving to help his brother-in-law escape the dragon's teeth of the Nazi menace, closing the story on an exciting climax, somewhat like that of a cliffhanger film of the 1940's.

Sinclair continued the adventures of Lanny Budd, interweaving fiction with fact as he related the sequence of world events in *World's End* which covers the years 1913 to 1919; *Between Two Worlds* deals with the events between the Versailles Treaty and the stock market crash of 1929; the author then covers the Nazi "Blood Purge" of 1934 to the Spanish Civil War in *Wide Is the Gate*; the annexation of Austria, the invasion of Czechoslovakia, and the Munich pact in *The Presidential Agent*; the fall of France in *Dragon Harvest*; and America's entry into the war in *A World to Win*. The years of Allied setbacks, 1941-1943, are covered in *Presidential Mission*; *One Clear Call* and

O Shepherd, Speak! deal with the Normandy Invasion and the defeat of the German military machine; and in the sequel to the series, *The Return of Lanny Budd*, Sinclair brings events up to 1949 and the onset of the Cold War between the United States and the Soviet Union.

As a whole, this group of novels is interesting, in part simply because the series surveys a dramatic period of history in considerable detail. Throughout the series, Sinclair's careful research is evident, but the popularity of these novels was also a result of their appeal to patriotism. America's role as the savior of civilization is increasingly emphasized in the later novels in the series. During this period, Sinclair's confidence that progress was represented by socialism and Communism was shaken by the example of the Soviet Union. Like so many early twentieth century political radicals, he became an anti-Communist in the 1950's.

Sinclair was a propagandist first and a novelist second, if propaganda is defined as an "effort directed systematically toward the gaining of support for an opinion or course of action." He wrote millions of words trying to change, improve, or expose oppressive conditions. Because Sinclair so obviously used literature for ulterior purposes and because he was so prolific, serious critics have unduly neglected him; on the other hand, he has been overrated by those foreign critics who delight in finding indictments of America by an American writer. As time puts Sinclair's contribution to American literature into perspective, it seems certain that he will never be regarded as a great novelist, but he will fairly be judged an honest, courageous, and original writer.

Hallman B. Bryant

Other major works

PLAYS: *Plays of Protest*, 1912; *Hell: A Verse Drama and Photo-Play*, 1923; *The Millennium*, 1924; *The Pot Boiler*, 1924; *Singing Jailbirds*, 1924; *Bill Porter*, 1925; *Oil!*, 1929; *Depression Island*, 1935; *Wally for Queen!*, 1936; *Marie Antoinette*, 1939; *A Giant's Strength*, 1948; *The Enemy Had It Too*, 1950.

NONFICTION: *Our Bourgeois Literature*, 1904; *The Industrial Republic*, 1907; *The Fasting Cure*, 1911; *The Profits of Religion*, 1918; *The Brass Check: A Study in American Journalism*, 1919; *The Book of Life, Mind and Body*, 1921; *The Goose-Step: A Study of American Education*, 1923; *The Goslings: A Study of the American Schools*, 1924; *Mammonart*, 1925; *Letters to Judd*, 1925; *Money Writes!*, 1927; *Mental Radio*, 1930; *American Outpost: A Book of Reminiscences*, 1932; *I, Governor of California and How I Ended Poverty*, 1933; *The Way Out—What Lies Ahead for America?*, 1933; *The EPIC Plan for California*, 1934; *What God Means to Me*, 1936; *Terror in Russia: Two Views*, 1938; *Expect No Peace!*, 1939; *A Personal Jesus*, 1952; *The Cup of*

Fury, 1956; *My Lifetime in Letters*, 1960; *The Autobiography of Upton Sinclair*, 1962.

CHILDREN'S LITERATURE: *The Gnomobile: A Gnice Gnew Gnarrative with Gnonsense, but Gnothing Gnaughty*, 1936.

Bibliography

Colburn, David R., and George E. Pozzetta, eds. *Reform and Reformers in the Progressive Era*. Westport, Conn.: Greenwood Press, 1983. An essay by Judson Grenier examines Sinclair's position as a muckraker and his role in inspiring Progressive reforms. Unlike other journalistic writers, Sinclair was personally and ideologically committed.

Dell, Floyd. *Upton Sinclair: A Study in Social Protest*. New York: AMS Press, 1970. Dell's treatment of Sinclair's career analyzes the apparent discrepancy between his literary position in the United States and throughout the rest of the world. Personal incidents and psychological insights are intertwined with evaluations and interpretations of specific works. Contains a bibliography of out-of-print books and an index.

Harris, Leon. *Upton Sinclair: American Rebel*. New York: Thomas Y. Crowell, 1975. This biography traces Sinclair's rise from obscurity to fame, with his subsequent decline in popularity. The text provides interesting information regarding source materials for some of his novels. A section of photographs, extensive notes, a list of Sinclair's books, and an index complete the book.

Mookerjee, R. N. *Art for Social Justice: The Major Novels of Upton Sinclair*. Metuchen, N.J.: Scarecrow, 1988. Mookerjee, a critic of writers of the 1930's, provides a reevaluation of *The Jungle*, *King Coal*, *Oil! A Novel*, *Boston*, and the Lanny Budd series. This slender volume is a valid reminder of the pioneer role of Sinclair in the "documentary novel." Contains a good selected bibliography.

Sinclair, Upton. *The Autobiography of Upton Sinclair*. New York: Harcourt, Brace & World, 1962. Sinclair admittedly takes a "casual and lighthearted tone" in recounting his life story and provides his own personal perceptions. He sums up the ten specific accomplishments in his life which he sees as establishing him as a champion of social justice. Indexed.

Yoder, Jon A. *Upton Sinclair*. New York: Frederick Ungar, 1975. Like some other critics, Yoder attributes Sinclair's "meager reputation" in part to his socialistic views. Five chapters in this slim volume examine various facets of the novelist's life and career. A chronology, notes, a bibliography, and an index supplement the text.

ISAAC BASHEVIS SINGER

Born: Leoncin, Poland; July 14, 1904

Principal long fiction

Sotan in Goray, 1935 (*Satan in Goray,* 1955); *Di Familie Muskat,* 1950 (*The Family Moskat,* 1950); *Der Hoyf,* 1953–1955 (*The Manor,* 1967, and *The Estate,* 1969); *Der Kunstnmakher fun Lublin,* 1959 (*The Magician of Lublin,* 1960); *Der Knekht,* 1961 (*The Slave,* 1962); *Sonim, de Geshichte fun a Liebe,* 1966 (*Enemies: A Love Story,* 1972); *Neshome Ekspeditsyes,* 1974 (*Shosha,* 1978); *Der Bal-Tshuve,* 1974 (*The Penitent,* 1983); *Der Kenig vun di Felder,* 1988 (*The King of the Fields,* 1988); *Scum,* 1991.

Other literary forms

Isaac Bashevis Singer began his literary career as a short-story writer, and his short fiction has been collected in numerous volumes, beginning with *Gimpl Tam un Anderer Dertzailungen* (1957; *Gimpel the Fool and Other Stories,* 1963). Encouraged by Elizabeth Shub, editor of children's books at Harper's, he turned to juvenile fiction in 1966; his efforts have earned for him repeated Newbery honors and a National Book Award in 1970 for *A Day of Pleasure: Stories of a Boy Growing Up in Warsaw* (1969), only the second children's book to receive this honor. His works have appeared on stage and screen, and he has published several autobiographical accounts, among them *Mayn Tatn's Bes-din Shtub* (1956; *In My Father's Court,* 1966), *A Little Boy in Search of God: Mysticism in a Personal Light* (1976), *A Young Man in Search of Love* (1978), and *Lost in America* (1980).

Achievements

In presenting Singer with the Nobel Prize for Literature in 1978, the Swedish Academy praised "his impassioned narrative art which, with roots in a Polish-Jewish cultural tradition, brings universal human conditions to life." Although he composes in a language unfamiliar to most of his readers, who depend on translations, and although he writes of a world of Polish Jewry that has vanished, he has enjoyed critical and popular acclaim among readers of all ages. Regarding himself as a storyteller rather than a preacher, he has never forgotten that the writer's first task is to entertain. Yet within his narrative he has embedded the eternal struggle of good and evil, the search for self, the desire for and fear of love. He offers no resolution, for in a universe in which God is silent certainty is impossible; yet his works challenge the reader to ponder the central questions of existence.

Biography

The son of Rabbi Pinchas Mendel and Bathsheba (Zylberman) Singer,

Isaac Bashevis Singer was born in Leoncin, Poland, in 1904. When he was four, his family moved to nearby Warsaw, where they lived at 10 Krochmalna Street. This urban shtetl, or Jewish village, of Krochmalna Street provides the setting for a number of his works, most notably *Shosha*. Here his father practiced as unofficial rabbi; the first volume of Singer's autobiography, *In My Father's Court*, describes his childhood observations and experiences, many of which also surface in his stories for both children and adults.

In 1917 the hunger and disease caused by World War I drove Singer, his younger brother (Moshe), and his mother to live with relatives in the small village of Bilgoray, near Austria. Here for the first time Singer encountered Judaism untinged with modernism. He would later comment that without the four years in Bilgoray he could have written *The Family Moskat* but never *Satan in Goray*. In Bilgoray he was also introduced to Hillel Zeitlin's *The Problem of Good and Evil* (1898), which maintains that God is silent; only human compassion can link one person with another and with the divine. This idea is central to Singer's fiction.

At his father's insistence, Singer enrolled in the Tachkemoni Rabbinical Seminary in 1921, but a year later he returned to Bilgoray, then moved to Dzikow, where his father was serving as rabbi. Here he read the stories by Rabbi Nachman of Bratzlav (1772-1810), great-grandson of the Ba'al Shem Tov, who had founded Hasidism. Though Singer would reject the happy endings of Rabbi Nachman's tales (except in his children's fiction), he adopted their pervasive supernaturalism.

Yet another shaper of Singer's fiction was his brother, Israel Joshua, eleven years his senior, who had established a literary magazine in Warsaw (*Literarische Bletter*). In 1923 Singer became proofreader for this periodical, and two years later it carried his first story, "Oyf der Elter" (in old age), a gloomy tale filled with sex and violence. In 1933 Israel Joshua went to America at the invitation of Abraham Cahan, editor of the *Jewish Daily Forward*, and Singer followed two years later, though he did not join the newspaper's staff until 1942.

Married to Alma Haimann Wassermann in 1940, Singer began to enjoy widespread recognition in 1950 with the publication in English of *The Family Moskat*, which sold thirty-five thousand copies. Saul Bellow's masterful translation of "Gimpl Tam" (1945) in the *Partisan Review* three years later brought him even more readers. Internationally recognized, he has received numerous honorary doctorates and many literary prizes, and the appearance of a new Singer book is greeted as a major literary event.

Analysis

Although he writes in Yiddish, in a number of ways Isaac Bashevis Singer differs from predecessors such as Isaac Lev Peretz, Sholem Aleichem, and Mendele Mocher Sforim. He breaks with their genteel tradition by treating sex overtly and emphasizing its role in motivating behavior. Singer's central concern also differs from that of traditional Yiddish writing, which was intended primarily for a Jewish audience and therefore dealt with questions that affected that readership. Singer's popularity derives in part from his more universal outlook. He writes about Jews because theirs is the world he knows best, but the issues he addresses are not limited to any religion or nation. Most significantly, Singer challenges the Enlightenment philosophy that has underlain Jewish literature since the eighteenth century. As Eli Katz has observed,

> The readers of classical Yiddish literature were conditioned to find in their reading indications of a rational world of progress, hope, and brotherly assistance, and the unmistakable assurance of the authors' adherence to these values. Singer describes instead an irrational, asocial universe where, as often as not, . . . the devil has the last word.

Dybbuks and demons do not appear as the stuff of superstition but rather as living beings; modernism leads to isolation rather than emancipation.

Singer does not, however, accept traditional religious solutions. His outlook derives from the Cabalistic idea that to make the world God had to withdraw Himself from part of the cosmos, to allow room for His new creation. Unlike the existentialists, Singer accepts God's existence and believes in a divine plan. The world might as well be absurd, though: the discovery of meaning is impossible, since God has withdrawn Himself and remains silent. This absence of revelation demands the exercise of free will, the perpetual search for the eternally hidden answer. Singer's heroes are those who embark on this quest for meaning. Many do not find it; indeed, most of those who think that they have, prove deluded. Discovery, however, is not crucial: the journey is everything.

Many of the concerns and ambiguities that characterize Singer's fiction are evident in his first book. Like Singer's other novels, *Satan in Goray* evokes the past, in this case seventeenth century Poland. In the aftermath of the horrors perpetrated against the Jews by Bogdan Chmielnicki and his Cossacks in 1648 and 1649, Rabbi Benish offers a traditional explanation for the recent disasters: Jews have strayed from God's way. The rabbi urges a return to observance as he leads the effort to rebuild the Jewish community. Even he, however, suffers doubt, and his inability to unify his own family reflects the larger division in the village between those accepting conventional religion and the mystics who turn to Cabala and believe the messianic claims of Sabbatai Zvi, who in 1648 had proclaimed himself the long-awaited savior of the Jews.

The appeal of such a charlatan at this time is evident. As the tormented Rechele in the novel yearns for love, even from Satan, so the beleaguered Jews will clutch at any hope for redemption. Both Goray and Rechele therefore welcome Itche Mates, an ascetic devotee of Zvi, who seizes control of the community and marries Rechele, while Rabbi Benish flees to Lublin to die. Orthodoxy has yielded to messianic heresy.

Itche Mates is soon supplanted by Reb Gedaliya, a ritual slaughterer who also believes in Zvi. In all other respects he is Mates' exact opposite, urging indulgence rather than denial and preaching the violation of all the commandments. Even news of Zvi's conversion to Islam cannot shake the faith of his adherents, who claim that the messiah will come only when the world is totally corrupt. Rechele continues to serve as the symbol of the community as Satan possesses her. Ultimately a reaction sets in; Gedaliya is rejected, and the novel concludes with a warning against any attempt to force the coming of the redeemer.

Fanaticism clearly fails. Instead of bringing salvation, it opens the way for the Devil, in whose physical presence Singer believes. Yet the attraction of a Zvi or a Gedaliya is undeniable, and orthodoxy can offer only warnings, not comfort or solutions. The Cabalist Mordecai Joseph, a bitter enemy of Rabbi Benish, repents and purges Rechele of her dybbuk, but in the process the girl dies. As Edwin Gittleman summarizes the novel, "In the Goraic universe goodness is either ineffectual, irrelevant, or non-existent, while piety is an invitation to demonic seizure, and innocence is valuable only because it is capable of being corrupted." Still, the novel is not nihilistic. God, unlike Satan, offers no answers; solutions come only at the end of time. Meanwhile the quest remains to give life whatever meaning it may have.

Singer's family chronicles—*The Family Moskat*, *The Manor*, and *The Estate*—written in part as tributes to Israel Joshua, who was a master of the form, explore more modern versions of messianism. The earlier work covers the period from about 1910 to 1939, the latter from 1863 to 1900, but the author's note to *The Estate* describes the concern of all three: "What happened in the village of Jampol, and what was discussed by a small group of self-educated youths in furnished rooms in Warsaw, became the basis of the social upheavals and the terrible disillusions of our present time."

The novels present a panoramic view of Jewish life in Poland; the works are rich in precise detail and filled with diverse characters. Each nevertheless focuses on the career of a particular figure to symbolize the fate of the Jewish community and the problem of exercising free will in the absence of certainty. In *The Family Moskat* the central figure is Asa Heshel Bannet, grandson of Reb Dan Katzenellenbogen of Tereshpol Minor. Asa's ancestors have been famous for their piety and religious learning, and he, too, has made great progress in his Hebrew studies. Even in Tereshpol Minor, though, forces of modernism intrude: Jekuthiel the watchmaker reads German philosophy and introduces Asa to skepticism. When Asa arrives in Warsaw, he is torn between tradition and change. He dresses as a Hasid but yearns for secular knowledge; he carries a letter of recommendation to Dr. Shmaryahu Jacobi of the Great Synagogue of Warsaw but also a copy of *Ethica ordine geometrico demonstrata* (1677; *Ethics*) by the great heretic Benedictus de Spinoza. Rejecting his past, Asa buys a new wardrobe that prompts Abram Shapiro to remark that he looks like a Gentile.

Yet Asa cannot escape his religion so easily. When he orders lunch in a restaurant, the owner instantly recognizes him as a Jew and insults him. The outside world will not let Asa forget his heritage, and he himself cannot escape his upbringing. Toward the end of the novel, Adele, whom Asa marries and then abandons, realizes that he has become "a living body with a dead soul." In the absence of belief, he himself is lost. All of his relationships fail, and his nihilism prompts him to conclude that death is the only savior.

The English version of the novel ends with this negative assertion, delivered as the Nazis invade Poland. The Yiddish original continues for another chapter, depicting a Passover Seder in occupied Poland. Asa, Nyumie Moskat, and Masha, who had converted to marry an anti-Semitic Gentile who later deserts her, join in an affirmation of orthodox belief. The two endings may not, however, be that different, since the Nazis, those messiahs of death, are preparing to destroy the Jewish community. Secularism and assimilation will not save the Jews, but tradition seems equally unavailing. As Asa knows, "God had drawn a veil over His secrets and would let no one pull it aside. The only question was what was to be done."

Singer's refusal to resolve this quandary is evident in the description of the Jews' expulsion from Tereshpol Minor. This exile is heralded by an essay entitled "Jews with a Mission," in which the author affirms the secularist-assimilationist creed:

> The Jewish masses love their homes. They want to live in brotherhood with their neighbors and to fight shoulder to shoulder with them for a better world, where there will be neither nations, classes, nor religions, but only one united, advancing humanity.

About a month later, when the Jews are driven from their homes, the Poles ignore the situation—it is not a gentile problem. Modern Jews may want unity, but no one will join with them. As the Jews leave Tereshpol Minor, the rabbi, Asa's grandfather, thinks, "Where are your worldly remedies? Where is your trust in the gentiles? What have you accomplished by aping Esau?" Jekuthiel, the secularist, has his own set of questions: "Where is your Lord of the Universe now? Where are His miracles? Where is your faith in Torah and prayer?" Neither traditionalists nor modernists can solve the riddle of existence.

Like Asa, Ezriel Babad in *The Manor* and *The Estate* rejects orthodoxy, choosing science as his messiah. Increasingly, though, he discovers the truth of Rabbi Jochanan's Yom Kippur sermon on the text from Isaiah, "But the wicked are like the troubled sea when it cannot rest, whose waters cast up mire and dirt." The rabbi equates Isaiah's wicked with the modernists and observes, "Man is born to serve. If he does not serve God, he serves man." Ezriel recognizes that the supposed rationalists are the most irrational people he knows. His sister, Mirale, and his friend Alexander Zipkin claim to believe in universal brotherhood but cannot find a place for Jews in their brave new world. Miriam Leibe converts to Catholicism to marry Lucian Jampoliski because she believes that in their love lies the salvation of the universe. Similarly, Ezriel begins an affair with the converted Olga Bielikov. Neither finds the happiness he or she seeks, perhaps because their love is selfish. The only successful marriage in these novels is the one arranged between the eleven-year-old Tsipele Jacoby and Rabbi Jochanan; their love grows within the confines of orthodox belief and mutual respect.

At the conclusion of *The Estate* Ezriel accepts the truth of Rabbi Jochanan's assertion that man needs to serve. For Ezriel religion is an illusion, but it is a useful one, far more benevolent than the illusions of science, socialism, or free love. The former at least offers a noble vision, while the others produce "bloody nightmares." Ezriel therefore follows his son Joziek to Israel, where he can escape Polish anti-Semitism and live as he wishes. In the absence of revelation one may choose one's reality—or one's dream. Rabbi Jochanan's son also has second thoughts about secularism as *The Estate* ends, and he may re-embrace the tradition he had abandoned in the vain hope of finding happiness in an alien culture.

Returning to tradition may provide the key to individual happiness, but Singer does not necessarily endorse that alternative. Yasha Mazur, the magician of Lublin, has developed his own religion, one that alienates him from both Jews and Gentiles. He dreams repeatedly of flying, of escaping all restrictions, and he earns his living as a tightrope walker, an occupation indicating his suspended state. He also refuses to commit himself to any one woman. Married to Esther, his wife of twenty years, he also keeps a Jewish mistress, Zeftel, and a gentile lover, Magda, as he contemplates marrying another Gentile, Emilia.

His "game of maybes and perhapses" must eventually end. Emilia insists on a decision: either he must convert and marry her, or he must end their relationship. She also requires a large amount of money so they can live abroad in comfort. Yasha therefore attempts to rob an apartment, but this master of the most intricate locks fails to open a simple safe. In his flight from the scene he slips and injures his foot, thereby ending his tightrope walking—though he had already ceased to vacillate when he chose Emilia. When he tells her what he has done, she dismisses him, and that same day he discovers that Magda, fearing rejection, has hanged herself and Zeftel has given herself to a white slaver.

Having rejected alienation and having been rejected in turn by Christianity, he turns to ascetic Judaism, walling himself up in a small brick structure that has no door. Early in the book he had joked with his wife, "What would happen if I became an ascetic and, to repent, had myself bricked into a cell without a door?" Esther replies that such action is unnecessary, to which Yasha retorts, "It all depends on what sort of passion one is trying to control."

The irony of this solution is that Yasha remains subject to doubts that drive him almost to madness, and he has chosen an isolation no less restricting than the one he endured at the beginning of the novel. Indeed, Esther suffers more from his confinement than from his earlier infidelity. Before, he always returned to her; now they are separated permanently. When he was a doubter, he would ask the religious whether they had been to heaven and seen God. Now an old friend visits and puts the same question to Yasha. Emilia, who has the last words of the novel, similarly questions Yasha's decision: "It does seem to me that you have inflicted too severe a punishment upon yourself." Yasha's last messiah, asceticism, thus appears no more satisfactory, no more true, than his earlier choices.

Singer has been accused of pessimism because his fiction often portrays characters who fail to find happiness and because he has refused to endorse a particular solution to the meaning of the universe. *The Slave* and *Enemies: A Love Story* suggest that redemption is nevertheless possible. In the former, Jacob converts Wanda despite Polish law punishing such action with death. Together they flee to the village of Pilitz, where Wanda, who takes the name of Sarah, the first convert, pretends to be a mute so that her accent and poor Yiddish will not reveal her gentile origin. Still, the Jews of Pilitz do not accept her. Singer does not confine his criticism to his twentieth century coreligionists but shows that even in the supposedly observant communities before the Enlightenment Jews failed in their responsibilities to their fellows. When Sarah, dying in childbirth, reveals her history, the community rejoices at what it regards as her disgrace. It brands her son illegitimate, refuses Wanda/Sarah burial in consecrated ground, steals Jacob's money, and surrenders him to the Christian authorities who would kill him.

Jacob escapes to Israel with his son, Benjamin, and twenty years later he returns for the bones of his wife. In Pilitz he suddenly becomes ill and dies. The gravedigger, preparing to bury him, finds the unmarked tomb of Wanda/Sarah, with her corpse preserved as a saint's would be. At last the town accepts her, and she is reunited with her husband. Through his love Jacob has redeemed Wanda from the savagery of her family and neighbors, and their mutual affection, regulated by true religious feeling, ensures the continuance of the Jewish nation through Benjamin and can even produce the miracle that ends the novel.

Enemies: A Love Story offers a similar resolution. Here the love of Yadwiga for Herman Broder provides a stay against death. A Polish peasant, Yadwiga saved Broder's life at the risk of her own during World War II; after the war the two marry and move to New York. She adopts his religion, offers to leave the United States when Broder's first wife, supposedly killed by the Nazis, appears, and continues to care for him even when he runs off with his mistress, Masha. Broder, who has rejected religion, is unworthy of her love; he deceives her and cares only for his own pleasure. Even when he learns that she is carrying his child, he remains indifferent; he has never wanted children and does nothing to help Yadwiga through her pregnancy. His nihilism prevents him from truly uniting with anyone, and at the end of the novel he vanishes. He had worked as a ghostwriter, a fitting occupation for one who has rejected life. His mistress has been as self-centered as he, and at the end of the novel she kills herself. Yet the work ends hopefully as Yadwiga delivers a girl, whom she names Masha. Yadwiga moves in with Tamara, Broder's first wife, and various people help with the newborn's needs. Concern for others thus creates a community that triumphs over the forces of destruction.

Shosha, Singer's next work, returns to pre-World War II Poland to demonstrate that sometimes even love cannot provide salvation. Modernism once more appears as a false messiah: the idealistic Communist Dora Stolnitz vanishes during the war, and the actress Betty Slonim, lacking belief, commits suicide. Yet Aaron Greidinger's love for Shosha cannot save her, either, despite her innocence and kindness. She, too, perishes in the Nazi nightmare. The novel ends with Aaron and his friend Haiml Chentshiner in a dark room waiting for the answer to the question of suffering, but no response is forthcoming.

Joseph Shapiro (*The Penitent*) would claim that the only hope for salvation lies in a return to traditional Judaism, but Singer explicitly rejects that conclusion, at least for himself. Shapiro, moreover, reveals himself as an unattractive figure. While his indictment of modernism echoes Singer's views, it goes far beyond the author's objections: Singer, for example, never has condemned history teachers, and Shapiro's analysis of great literature such as Leo Tolstoy's *Anna Karenina* (1875-1877) is highly reductive. Shapiro has fled from the United States to Israel, but he finds the Jewish state as objectionable as his previous home. Only in the isolation of Meah Shearim is he content; he imprisons himself almost as effectually as did Yasha Mazur. His conversion from secularism to religion seems questionable, too, because on the flight to Israel he tries to make love to the woman sitting next to him.

Just as *Shosha* may serve as a corrective to the two novels that preceded it, so *The King of the Fields* responds to the ultra-orthodoxy of Joseph Shapiro by showing the destructiveness of nihilism. Set in ancient Poland, the novel portrays the violence and greed of a world devoid of effectual belief. The Jewish Ben Dosa rescues a pagan, as Jacob in *The Slave* redeemed Wanda, but the focus of the novel is on Cybula, leader of the Lesniks, who tries to understand the cruelty of people and the beauty of nature. He concludes that there are many gods, but over all of them is Shmiercz, the god of death, and this nihilism drives him to suicide.

To deny God's existence is to destroy oneself, but mindless credulity is equally dangerous. The certainty of a Joseph Shapiro proves as isolating and unappealing as the view of Cybula or Asa Heshel that death is the messiah. In the absence of external authority one must, as Aaron Feitelzohn says in *Shosha*, find one's own version of grace, a version that opposes evil, rejects hate, and promotes life. Singer joked in his 1978 Nobel Prize address that he uses Yiddish because it is a dead language and so is best suited to one who writes about ghosts. More seriously, he observed that Yiddish is "the wise and humble language of us all, the idiom of frightened and hopeful humanity." That is the humanity that fills his fiction, whose search for truth he chronicles. Singer cannot accept neat solutions—hence the discomfort many readers feel with his endings. That discomfort may well be the intended response, for Singer is like the angel at the pool of Bethesda: only by troubling the waters, only by raising eternal questions, can fiction heal a frightened and hopeful humanity.

Joseph Rosenblum

Other major works

SHORT FICTION: *Gimpl Tam un Anderer Dertzailungen*, 1957 (*Gimpel the Fool and Other Stories*, 1963); *The Spinoza of Market Street*, 1961; *Short Friday and Other Stories*, 1964; *The Séance and Other Stories*, 1968; *A Friend of Kafka and Other Stories*, 1970; *A Crown of Feathers and Other Stories*, 1973; *Passions and Other Stories*, 1975; *Old Love*, 1979; *The Collected Stories*, 1982; *The Image and Other Stories*, 1985; *The Death of Methuselah and Other Stories*, 1988.

PLAYS: *The Mirror*, 1973; *Yentl, the Yeshiva Boy*, 1974 (with Leah Napolin); *Shlemiel the First*, 1974; *Teibele and Her Demon*, 1978.

NONFICTION: *Mayn Tatn's Bes-din Shtub*, 1956 (*In My Father's Court*, 1966); *A Little Boy in Search of God: Mysticism in a Personal Light*, 1976; *A Young Man in Search of Love*, 1978; *Lost in America*, 1980.

CHILDREN'S LITERATURE: *Zlateh the Goat and Other Stories*, 1966; *The Fearsome Inn*, 1967; *Mazel and Shlimazel: Or, The Milk of a Lioness*, 1967; *When Shlemiel Went to Warsaw and Other Stories*, 1968; *A Day of Pleasure: Stories of a Boy Growing Up in Warsaw*, 1969; *Elijah the Slave*, 1970; *Joseph and Koza: Or, The Sacrifice to the Vistula*, 1970; *Alone in the Wild Forest*, 1971; *The Topsy-Turvy Emperor of China*, 1971; *The Wicked City*, 1972; *The Fools of Chelm and Their History*, 1973; *Why Noah Chose the Dove*, 1974; *A Tale of Three Wishes*, 1975; *Naftali the Storyteller and His Horse, Sus, and Other Stories*, 1976; *The Power of Light: Eight Stories*, 1980; *The Golem*, 1982; *Stories for Children*, 1984.

Bibliography

Alexander, Edward. *Isaac Bashevis Singer*. Boston: Twayne, 1980. Focusing largely on the novels (in chapters 2-8), Alexander explores Singer's war with modernism and his portrayal of the vanished world of Eastern European Jewry. Includes a useful chronology and brief annotated bibliography.

Allentuck, Marcia, ed. *The Achievement of Isaac Bashevis Singer*. Carbondale: Southern Illinois University Press, 1969. A collection of twelve essays offering numerous insights into Singer's fiction. Among the best are Eli Katz's exploration of Singer's relationship to earlier Yiddish writers and Edwin Gittleman's analysis of *Satan in Goray*.

Buchen, Irving H. *Isaac Bashevis Singer and the Eternal Past*. New York: New York University Press, 1968. The first book-length study of Singer, and still useful. Focuses mainly on the novels through *The Manor*, seeing in them the repeated pattern of the prodigal son. The bibliography is especially useful for the composition and publication history of Singer's work.

Lee, Grace Farrell. *From Exile to Redemption: The Fiction of Isaac Bashevis Singer*. Carbondale: Southern Illinois University Press, 1987. Lee observes that although Singer rejects modernism and existentialism, his characters would feel at home in a play by Samuel Beckett because they seek answers that never arrive. What distinguishes Singer's fiction from that of the absurdists is a sense of hope. Hence, as Lee states, "no matter how dark the night, we ought to sit and wait, for anything is possible."

Malin, Irving, ed. *Critical Views of Isaac Bashevis Singer*. New York: New York University Press, 1969. A collection of fourteen essays followed by lengthy primary and secondary bibliographies especially helpful for the list of book reviews. The essays explore such matters as Singer's use of history, his concept of good and evil, and supernaturalism in his fiction.

_____. *Isaac Bashevis Singer*. New York: Frederick Ungar, 1972. A good introduction. Discusses the autobiographical writings, the novels, and the short stories, treating themes, characters, and symbols. Malin finds the family chronicles (which he calls "open novels") less satisfactory than the rest of Singer's fiction. Offers sound observations, but rather heavy on the italics and exclamation points.

Studies in American Jewish Literature 1 (1981). A special issue devoted to Singer, with a number of interviews as well as critical essays on all aspects of his writing.

TOBIAS SMOLLETT

Born: Dalquhurn, Scotland; baptized March 19, 1721
Died: Antignano, Italy; September 17, 1771

Principal long fiction

The Adventures of Roderick Random, 1748; *The Adventures of Peregrine Pickle: In Which Are Included Memoirs of a Lady of Quality*, 1751; *The Adventures of Ferdinand, Count Fathom*, 1753; *The Adventures of Sir Launcelot Greaves*, 1760-1761; *The Expedition of Humphry Clinker*, 1771.

Other literary forms

Tobias Smollett combined his medical practice with an active and varied career as a man of letters. His earliest, though unsuccessful, effort was as a playwright with *The Regicide: Or, James the First of Scotland, a Tragedy* (1749), published by subscription a full ten years after fruitless attempts at having it staged in London. Two other disappointments followed with his inability to secure a production for *Alceste* (1748-1749), a combination of opera, tragedy, and masque, and with the rejection of his first comedy, *The Absent Man* (1751), which was never produced or published. Both of these works have now been lost. His only success on the stage came finally with *The Reprisal: Or, The Tars of Old England* (1757), a comedy; this farce was produced by David Garrick at the Theatre Royal, Drury Lane.

Smollett's deep moral energy surfaced in two early verse satires, "Advice: A Satire" (1746) and its sequel, "Reproof: A Satire" (1747); these rather weak poems were printed together in 1748. Smollett's poetry includes a number of odes and lyrics, but his best poem remains "The Tears of Scotland." Written in 1746, it celebrates the unwavering independence of the Scots, who had been crushed by English troops at the Battle of Culloden.

As Smollett's literary career grew, his hackwork for publishers increased with translations. His most popular work among these projects was *A Complete History of England* (1757-1758) and its sequel, *Continuation of the Complete History of England* (1760-1765). He took great pride in his achievements as a historian and as a historical editor, *A Compendium of Authentic and Entertaining Voyages* (1756). A diversity of interests from medicine to politics prompted the writing of numerous pamphlets and essays. *An Essay on the External Use of Water* (1752) was a farsighted proposal for the improvement of public hygiene at Bath that caused a furor among the resort's staff and patrons.

Though his health was rapidly deteriorating from overwork, Smollett completed a thirty-five volume edition of *The Works of M. de Voltaire* (1761-1769). In the hope that a warm climate would improve his health, he traveled to France and Italy, and on returning to England published *Travels Through France and Italy* (1766). His didactic observations instructed his readers to accept England, for all its faults, as the best nation for securing happiness on earth. His last nonfiction works were *The Present State of All Nations* (1768-1769) and the political satire, *The History and Adventures of an Atom* (1749, 1769). Lewis M. Knapp offers the best modern edition of the *Letters of Tobias Smollett* (1970).

Achievements

Smollett cannot be said to have added dignity to the art of the novel in the manner of Henry Fielding's imitation of the epic, nor can it be argued that he gave form to the genre as did Samuel Richardson, yet the eighteenth century novel cannot be discussed without giving full attention to Smollett's stylistic virtuosity and satiric intent.

Smollett successfully challenged Richardson's and Fielding's substantial popular reputation by providing "familiar scenes in an uncommon and amusing point of view." In *The Adventures of Roderick Random* (commonly known as *Roderick Random*), his first novel, he displayed a thorough understanding of the distinction between the novel and the romance, of which Samuel Johnson would speak in *The Rambler* essays (1750-1752). Borrowing from Latin comedy and Elizabethan drama, Smollett created caricatures of human beings with the dexterity of William Hogarth and Thomas Rowlandson. Though his characters lack the psychological depth of Richardson's, they possess breathtaking energy and evocative power.

Only in the past twenty years has Smollett's role in the development of the English novel been fully appreciated. Recent criticism has emphasized the wrongheadedness of viewing Smollett's satiric energy as a deviation from Fielding's epic ambitions for the novel. Instead, Smollett is seen at the beginning of another tradition. Sir Walter Scott and Charles Dickens both valued Smollett's work; Dickens acknowledged his debt to Smollett's picaresque realism and comic characterization in *Pickwick Papers* (1836-1837). Among modern novelists, the savage comedy of writers as various as Evelyn Waugh and Joseph Heller is in Smollett's tradition rather than that of Fielding or Richardson.

Smollett's works continue to provoke critical inquiry. Eight books and numerous dissertations have appeared in the last two decades, as well as many articles. The Oxford English Novels series has published all five of his novels, and the University of Delaware has begun to publish its *Bicentennial Edition of the Works of Tobias Smollett*, under the editorship of O. M. Brack, with *The Expedition of Humphry Clinker* (commonly known as *Humphry Clinker*) appearing in 1979.

Biography

Tobias George Smollett was born at Dalquhurn, Dumbartonshire, in western Scotland, and baptized on March 19, 1721. He was the son of Archibald Smollett, a lawyer, who suffered from ill health, and Barbara Cunningham

Smollett, a woman of taste and elegance but no fortune. Smollett's grandfather, of whom the boy was especially proud, had been knighted by King William in 1698, and had become an influential member of the landed gentry as a local Whig statesman. When Smollett's father died only two years after his son's birth, the family suffered from lack of money.

Smollett's education, for all of his family's financial deterioration, was of superior quality though erratic. He entered Dumbarton Grammar School in 1728, remaining for five years, and received the traditional grounding in the classics. His matriculation to Glasgow University (though officially unrecorded) was interrupted when he became a Glasgow surgeon's apprentice while still attending university medical lectures. In the fall of 1739, Smollett was released from his apprenticeship to go to London; now eighteen, he had some reputation as a writer of earthy satires and doggerel. While traveling to London, Smollett carried the manuscript of a tragedy, *The Regicide*, which, he soon realized, would provide no entrée for him with the London theater managers. He is described at this time as "attractive, entertaining as a *raconteur*, and blessed with self-assurance." His future as a London man of letters uncertain, Smollett received advice from a number of Scottish physicians suggesting he continue practicing medicine. On March 10, 1740, he received a medical warrant from the Navy Board and embarked on the *H.M.S. Chichester* as a surgeon's second mate.

The author's naval experience, material used later for *Roderick Random*, began during the outbreak of war with Spain and continued through the bloody Carthagena, West Indies, expedition of 1741. Smollett returned to England in 1742, but was drawn back to Jamaica, where he resided until 1744. While living on the island, he met the daughter of an established family of planters, the Lassells; he married Anne Lassells in 1743. She is described as an affectionate and beautiful woman, in her early twenties, of considerable fortune.

Smollett, on the advice of her family, returned to London alone, where he set up a practice as a surgeon on Downing Street in May, 1744. Having never lost hope of a literary career, he worked on improving his fluency in Spanish and then began translating *Don Quixote*. The years from 1747 to 1750 were marked by considerable literary activity, numerous changes in residence, various trips abroad, a widening circle of acquaintances, and the birth of his only child, Elizabeth, in 1747.

In January, 1748, *Roderick Random* was published; this was followed by the impressive translations of Alain Le Sage and Miguel de Cervantes, and in 1749, *The Regicide* was printed. The success of *Roderick Random* was instantaneous and prolonged, with 6,500 copies sold in twenty-two months; it was to rival the popularity of Fielding's *Joseph Andrews* (1742). The success of *Roderick Random*, which was written in less than six months, became a kind of revenge on the theater managers of London. During this period,

Smollett made plans to produce *Alceste*, his opera (George Frederick Handel was contracted for the music), but this effort was to fail; only a lyric from this work survives. His comedy *The Absent Man* was submitted to David Garrick but not accepted; Smollett's failure at drama was a continuing source of frustration throughout his career.

In June, 1750, Smollett purchased his medical degree from Marischal College, Aberdeen, and in the same month moved his family to Chelsea, a fashionable London suburb. It became an ideal home for him, where both his medical practice and his writing flourished; he remained there for thirteen years until forced abroad by his health in 1763. It was in Chelsea that he wrote *The Adventures of Peregrine Pickle* (commonly known as *Peregrine Pickle*), a work of nearly 330,000 words composed at top speed in anticipation of a trip to Paris. On February 25, 1751, his second novel was published to laudatory reviews and wide popularity.

Smollett's involvement with various periodicals began during the 1750's, first as a book reviewer for the *Monthly Review* and later as editor and proprietor of the *Critical Review*. Smollett joined Oliver Goldsmith in launching the *British Magazine* (the *Monthly Repository* beginning in 1760), remaining as coeditor until 1763. With a final venture, Smollett gained public notoriety and untold enemies by agreeing to write the *Briton*, a political effort in support of Lord Bute's ministry. Of Smollett's various journalistic efforts, only the work in the *Critical Review* is exceptional; as a literary periodical, it remains one of the most significant of the last half of the eighteenth century.

In the early 1750's, Smollett was driving himself in order to escape debt. Publishing a medical paper, *An Essay on the External Use of Water*, brought him little money, and in February, 1753, his third novel, *The Adventures of Ferdinand, Count Fathom* (commonly known as *Ferdinand, Count Fathom*), was published with poor financial results. The book attracted few readers, and Smollett was forced to borrow money and to supplement his medical fees with further hackwork. The years of hack writing began in earnest with *A Complete History of England*, a translation of Voltaire's writings, a geographical reference work, and several digests of travel. The period from 1756 to 1763 destroyed Smollett's health, but his reputation as a critic and a successful writer became unquestioned. Unfortunately, this frantic production hardly kept him from debtor's prison. Returning to the novel in the *British Magazine*, Smollett published "the first considerable English novel ever to be published serially"—*The Adventures of Sir Launcelot Greaves* (commonly known as *Sir Launcelot Greaves*). In monthly installments from January, 1760, to December, 1761, the novel gave the six-penny periodical substantial popularity.

In the midst of this literary hard labor, Smollett was imprisoned for three months, having been convicted of libeling an Admiral Knowles in an article in the *Critical Review*. On his release in early 1761, Smollett continued fulfilling his contracts with certain booksellers but also traveled extensively, possibly to Dublin, even though troubled by asthma and tuberculosis. In addition to these difficulties, his spirit was nearly broken by the illness and death of his daughter in April, 1763. This final shock caused him to cut all his London ties and move his family to the Continent, hoping to calm his wife and cure his ailments in the mild climate of the south of France and Italy. He spent two years abroad, returning to England in July, 1765; the literary result of his tour was *Travels Through France and Italy.* Though ill-health plagued him he sought for the third time a consulship but was rejected; in 1768 he left England for the last time.

Arriving in Pisa, Italy, Smollett visited with friends at the University, finally settling at his country villa in Antignano, near Leghorn, in the spring of 1770, where he completed his masterpiece, *Humphry Clinker.* Immediately following its publication, he received the rave notices of friends and critics concerning the novel, but he had little time to enjoy the praise. On September 17, 1771, he died from an acute intestinal infection and was buried at the English cemetery at Leghorn.

Analysis

Tobias Smollett is not only a great comic novelist; he is also a morally exhilarating one—a serious satirist of the brutality, squalor, and hideous corruption of mankind. His definite moral purposes are firmly grounded in the archetypal topic of all novelists—man's unceasing battle for survival in the war between the forces of good and evil. Smollett insists that man defy "the selfishness, envy, malice, and base indifference of mankind"; in such a struggle, the hero will ultimately prevail and will be rewarded for his fortitude.

The principal theme of Smollett's first novel, *Roderick Random*, is the arbitrariness of success and failure in a world dominated by injustice and dishonesty. Smollett's decision to use realistic detail as a guise for his satire produces a lively and inventive work; moreover, the hero, Roderick, is not a mere picaro nor a passive fool but an intent satiric observer "who recognizes, reacts, and rebukes." The novel is organized in a three-part structure. The initial stage reveals Roderick's numerous trials as a young man; he loses his innocence during the years of poverty in Scotland, of failure in London, and of brutal experience in the Navy. The middle of the narrative embodies "the lessons of adversity" as the hero declines into near collapse. In a final brief section, Roderick recovers his physical and moral equilibrium and promotes the simple human values of friendship, love, and trust as the only viable bases for a satisfying existence.

Roderick's problem is both to gain knowledge of the world and to assimilate that knowledge. M. A. Goldberg, in *Smollett and the Scottish School* (1959), finds that "at first his responses are dictated by his indignation, by passions . . . eventually, he learns . . . to govern the emotions with reason." The struggle between these two forces is central to an understanding of eighteenth century

England and its literature. In Smollett's first novel, good sense seems a sufficient defense against the sordid viciousness of the world. Good sense, however, can only be achieved, or learned, when the hero can control his pride and passionate nature, which are inextricably linked. Equilibrium, an orderly existence, arises paradoxically from the ashes of his random adventures. This understanding develops as the hero pursues the happiness he thinks he deserves but can never fully attain; as a good empiricist, Roderick gathers knowledge from each reversal, finally achieving a "tranquility of love" with the prudent Narcissa.

In *Roderick Random*, the hero's search for happiness differs significantly from the quest of the traditional picaro. While gaining an education and suffering the rebukes of other men, Roderick remains good and effectual, unlike Don Quixote, who is powerless against cruelty. Roderick's youthful ferocity contributes to the practicality of the satire. Smollett's approach to correcting the ills of society is to allow no attack or insult to go unavenged. A thorough whipping of a bully or the verbal punishment of a pedant lifts the book beyond the picaresque and advances it past the formal verse satire. The center of the satiric discussion implicates the surroundings and not the hero, thus permitting Smollett to offer a long list of evil, self-centered figures who provide an excellent contrast to the goodness and charity of the ill-served protagonist. Only his faithful servant, Strap; his uncle, Tom Bowling; and the maid, Narcissa, join him in opposing his neglectful grandfather, the scoundrel Vicar Shuffle, the tyrannical Captain Oakum, the dandiacal Captain Whiffle, and the rapacious Lord Strutwell.

The last section of the novel provides the hero with the riches of his long quest: family, wealth, and love. The moral of the adventures follows as Roderick's recently discovered father "blesses God for the adversity I had undergone," affirming that his son's intellectual, moral, and physical abilities had been improved "for all the duties and and enjoyments of life, much better than any education which affluence could bestow." The felicity of this final chapter provides a conventional ending, but the crucial point is that Roderick, having completed a rigorous education in the distinctions between appearance and reality, is now deserving of these rewards.

The protagonist of Smollett's long second novel, *Peregrine Pickle*, reminds one of Roderick in every aspect, except that Peregrine is an Englishman, not a Scot. The supporting players are improved; among the novel's outstanding comic creations are Commodore Hawser Trunnion and the spinster, Grizzle Pickle. Often described as the best picaresque novel in English, *Peregrine Pickle* satirizes the upper classes of mid-eighteenth century England. Rufus Putney argues, in "The Plan of *Peregrine Pickle*" (1945), that Smollett "meant to write a satire on the affectations and meannesses, the follies and vices that flourished among the upper classes in order that his readers might learn with Peregrine the emptiness of titles, the sordidness of avarice, the triviality of wealth and honors, and the folly of misguided ambition."

The novel begins by sketching Peregrine's social and emotional background and introducing other principal characters. Following this introductory section, Smollett's protagonist describes his adolescence and education at Winchester and Oxford, where he becomes addicted to coarse practical jokes and to satisfying his overbearing pride. Here the hero meets Emilia, a beautiful orphan with whom he falls in love; because of his capricious nature, however, he cannot remain long with her. Having become alienated from his parents, Peregrine departs on the Grand Tour with the best wishes of his guardian, Trunnion.

Peregrine returns from France an unprincipled, arrogant rogue whose every action supports his vanity. After numerous incidents including the death of Trunnion and his replacement with the eccentric Cadwallader Crabtree as Peregrine's mentor, the hero tests the virtue of Emilia and is rebuffed. The remainder of the novel observes the long distress, the eventual imprisonment, and the final rehabilitation of the protagonist, who by now is convinced of the fraud and folly of the world. As Putney mentions, only after matriculating to the "school of adversity," which reduces his pride and vanity, can Peregrine hope to achieve wealth, marry his true love, triumph over his enemies, and retire to the country. Adversity teaches him to distinguish between the complex vices of the urban sophisticates and the simpler but more substantial pleasures of generosity and love in a rural retreat. Despite its picaresque vigor and satisfactory resolution, the novel suffers from a confusion of purposes: Peregrine's arrogance undermines the credibility of his role as a satirist of high society. Thus, Smollett's satiric intentions are blunted by his aspirations to a novel of character.

Ferdinand, Count Fathom is remembered today for its dedication, in which Smollett gives his famous definition of the novel, and for its place as the first important eighteenth century work to propose terror as a subject for a novel. In *The Novels of Tobias Smollett* (1971), Paul-Gabriel Boucé finds that the major defect of the novel is the author's "mixture of genres, without any transition brought about by unfolding of the story or the evolution of the characters." Fathom's dark cynicism informs the majority of the work, with the last ten chapters unraveling into a weak melodrama; nevertheless, Smollett's satire remains effective as a bitter denunciation of the hypocrisy and violence of elegant society. As an early contribution to the literature of terror, the novel probes the emotions of a young, virtuous girl who undergoes isolation, deprivation, and sadistic brutality at the hands of a rapacious creature. The figure of Fathom is used to undercut sentimental conventions and show their uselessness when civilized norms are forgotten.

Sir Launcelot Greaves completed serialization in December, 1761, and was published as a book in March, 1762. Because of its serial publication, the novel's structure suffers from the frequent contrivance of artificial suspense.

Recent criticism, however, has pointed to an underlying thematic unity based upon a series of variations on the theme of madness, with minute investigation into the physical, psychological, and moral aspects of the disorder. Greaves, the quixotic hero, launches a noble crusade for reform. His hopeless demand that a corrupted world listen to reason embraces Smollett's social idealism. If moral intention were the only measure of a novel's worth, then the didactic power of *Sir Launcelot Greaves* would guarantee its success; unfortunately, the delicate balance of the genre remains disordered by the force of an over-obvious moral preoccupation.

Smollett's last novel, *Humphry Clinker*, appeared in the bookstalls on June 15, 1771; Smollett had written the three volumes over a five-year period. It is his masterpiece, and it remains among the great English novels. The work was inspired by the epistles of Christopher Anstey's witty and popular *New Bath Guide* (1766). Using the epistolary method instead of the travel narrative of the early novels, Smollett characterizes his correspondents by means of their wonderfully individual letter-writing styles. Old Matthew Bramble of Brambleton Hall, Wales, travels with his household through Gloucester, Bath, London, Scarborough, Edinburgh, Cameron (Smollett country), Glasgow, Manchester, and home again. Squire Bramble suffers various physical complaints, and his ill-health makes him sensitive to the social ills surrounding him on his journey. Bramble searches for a recovery but finds himself becoming worse, not better, yet his compassionate nature remains undiminished. The journey was begun so that Bramble might distract his young niece, Lydia Melford, from a strolling actor named Wilson. The party also includes Tabitha, his aging, narrow-minded, old-maid sister; her malapropic maid, Winifred Jenkins, the classic example of the illiterate servant; and the modishly cynical nephew, Jery. En route, they adopt, much to Tabitha's delight, a Scottish veteran of Indian warfare, Obadiah Lismahago. Soon, they add Humphry Clinker to the party as a new footman; he turns out to be the natural son of Matthew.

There are three major plots to develop, and numerous minor episodes, all of which hinge upon the charcteristic picaresque device of the journey; Smollett exchanged the rogue hero for a group of picaros—Bramble and nephew Jery—who analyze and observe society. Through careful stages in letter after letter, Matthew's character is revealed to the reader, who learns to trust him as a reliable observer of society's foibles; in this respect *Humphry Clinker* is much stronger than *Peregrine Pickle*, where the satire was blunted by the protagonist's unreliability.

Smollett's satire strikes not individuals but categories of people and assorted social institutions; in particular *Humphry Clinker* is an *exposé* of the false attitudes and disordered life of the eighteenth century *nouveaux riches*. His conservative political views are displayed in Bramble's rages against an unrestricted press, politically biased juries, and the ignorance of the mob, and, as in *Peregrine Pickle*, he contrasts the folly and depravity of urban life with idealized pictures of the country.

Smollett's achievement in *Humphry Clinker* depends on his skillful use of the picaresque and epistolary traditions.His last novel is also distinguished by a warmth and tolerance not found to such a degree in his earlier works. Bramble's cynicism never becomes obnoxious to the reader; the brutality of Roderick is muted here. Smollett allows his hero to accept human society, despite "the racket and dissipation." Finally, for all his burlesque of Samuel Richardson's epistolary method, Smollett's characterization of Lydia has a depth and intensity that raises her above mere romantic convention.

In contrast to many critical reports, *Humphry Clinker* ends on a buoyant note of pure happiness, a happiness which fulfills the eighteenth century dictum of conformity to the universal order. Smollett's novels embrace moral and virtuous methods for pursuing one's goals. Passions and reason must remain in balance, and within this harmony, nature and art can moderate the demands of vice and folly.

Paul J. deGategno

Other major works

PLAYS: *The Regicide: Or, James the First of Scotland, a Tragedy*, 1749; *The Reprisal: Or, The Tars of Old England*, 1757.

NONFICTION: *The History and Adventures of an Atom*, 1749, 1769; *An Essay on the External Use of Water*, 1752; *A Compendium of Authentic and Entertaining Voyages*, 1756; *A Complete History of England*, 1757-1758; *Continuation of the Complete History of England*, 1760-1765; *Travels Through France and Italy*, 1766; *The Present State of All Nations*, 1768-1769; *Letters of Tobias Smollett*, 1970 (Lewis M. Knapp, editor).

TRANSLATIONS: *The Adventures of Gil Blas of Santillane*, 1748; *The History and Adventures of the Renowned Don Quixote*, 1755; *The Works of M. de Voltaire*, 1761-1774; *The Adventures of Telemachus, the Son of Ulysses*, 1776.

Bibliography

Bold, Alan, ed. *Smollett: Author of the First Distinction*. New York: Barnes & Noble Books, 1982. Contains four essays dealing with general issues and five concentrating on each of Smollett's major novels. Indexed.

Boucé, Paul-Gabriel. *The Novels of Tobias Smollett*. Translated by Antonia White. London: Longman, 1976. A slightly abridged version of the 1971 French study. Includes a biographical sketch, chapters on the major novels and good discussions of Smollett's realism and comic devices. Contains a chronologically arranged bibliography of secondary works from 1928 to 1975.

Grant, Damian. *Tobias Smollett: A Study in Style*. Totowa, N.J.: Rowman & Littlefield, 1977. As the title suggests, Grant ignores questions of realism and moral purpose to concentrate on what he regards as Smollett's three styles: comic, passionate, and, to a lesser extent, lyrical.

Knapp, Lewis Mansfield. *Tobias Smollett: Doctor of Men and Manners*. Princeton, N.J.: Princeton University Press, 1949. The standard life, sympathetic and detailed, but with little critical analysis of the works.

Rousseau, G. S. *Tobias Smollett: Essays of Two Decades*. Edinburgh: T. & T. Clark, 1982. Collects fifteen previously published essays and reviews on such topics as Smollett as letter writer and his role in various medical controversies of his day. Makes a good case, *inter alia*, for not regarding Smollett's novels as picaresques.

Rousseau, G. S., and Paul-Gabriel Boucé, eds. *Tobias Smollett: Bicentennial Essays Presented to Lewis M. Knapp*. New York: Oxford University Press, 1971. Includes ten essays that examine all aspects of Smollett's writings, including his voluminous, oft-neglected histories. The index allows for cross-references.

Spector, Robert Donald. *Tobias George Smollett*. 1968. Rev. ed. Boston: Twayne, 1989. The first chapter quickly surveys Smollett's minor works and the rest consider his novels. Contains a useful annotated bibliography of secondary criticism.

Wagoner, Mary. *Tobias Smollett*. New York: Garland, 1984. Provides an extensive list of editions of Smollett's works as well as an annotated bibliography of secondary material. Arranged by subject (for example, "Biographies and Biographical Material" and "The Expedition of Humphry Clinker") and therefore easy to use for locating criticism on a specific topic.

C. P. SNOW

Born: Leicester, England; October 15, 1905
Died: London, England; July 1, 1980

Principal long fiction

Death Under Sail, 1932, 1959; *New Lives for Old*, 1933; *The Search*, 1934, 1958; *Strangers and Brothers* series (includes *Strangers and Brothers*, 1940, reissued as *George Passant*, 1972; *The Light and the Dark*, 1947; *Time of Hope*, 1949; *The Masters*, 1951; *The New Men*, 1954; *Homecomings*, 1956, published in the United States as *Homecoming*; *The Conscience of the Rich*, 1958; *The Affair*, 1960; *Corridors of Power*, 1964; *The Sleep of Reason*, 1968; *Last Things*, 1970); *The Malcontents*, 1972; *In Their Wisdom*, 1974; *A Coat of Varnish*, 1979.

Other literary forms

Reflecting his various careers and interests, C. P. Snow published, in addition to his novels, a number of books, including the literary biographies, *Trollope: His Life and Art* (1975) and *The Realists* (1978), as well as many reviews and articles. He had some interest in the drama, encouraging the staging of his novels *The Affair*, *The New Men*, and *The Masters*, writing a full-length play, *The View Over the Park*, produced in London in 1950, and collaborating with his wife, Pamela Hansford Johnson, on six one-act plays published in 1951: *Spare the Rod*, *The Penguin with the Silver Foot*, *Her Best Foot Forward*, *The Supper Dance*, *To Murder Mrs. Mortimer*, and *Family Party*.

Achievements

As a man, Snow's accomplishments were many and varied; as a novelist his achievement was more limited, and yet (*ars longa*, public life frequently *breva*) probably more long-lasting. Snow the scientist and Snow the public figure cannot, however, be divorced from Snow the writer. Just as his novels drew upon his experiences in his nonliterary careers, so were his sociopolitical ideas presented in his novels. Yet, there are less of the details of "doing" science, less of the specificity of the public life than one might have expected from Snow's background had he been more of a "naturalistic" novelist, and there is less ideological content than might have been anticipated from one with Snow's strong views, had he been more of a propagandist.

Snow was rather, a realistic novelist, using his particular knowledge, background, and political ideology not primarily for their own sake, but in the service of his art. This art was conventional, relatively old-fashioned. Snow had limited patience with James Joyce and the literary avant-garde. As a *roman-fleuve*, *Strangers and Brothers* has a few interesting features, but it certainly lacks the subtlety that Snow admired in Marcel Proust. Snow did little to advance novelistic techniques; his own craftsmanship shows scant development over the course of a long writing career. His style has frequently been described as dull or pedestrian; Edmund Wilson found his novels "unreadable."

Snow implicitly defended his own style in discussing Anthony Trollope's, praising his predecessor for using language that was often intentionally made flat in order to be clear. Snow's style is certainly more serviceable than inspired. His imagery is limited and repetitious. Unity and impact are achieved through the recurrence of a limited number of images, such as those of lighted windows and rivers, but the impact is gained at the expense of a degree of monotony.

If Snow's style and imagery are little more than adequate, his plot construction is only somewhat more skillful. Unlike Trollope, whom Snow admired and to whom he has frequently been compared, Snow uses plots that are usually suspenseful; one reads his books partly to see how they will come out. This element of suspense, going back to his first published novel, a "whodunit," no doubt helps explain his having attracted a fairly wide and loyal audience, many of whom were not regular readers of novels. Snow's plots, however, are seldom particularly ingenious or original; essentially, they are a means to the revelation of character.

It is in characterization that Snow's prime virtue as a novelist lies; yet his characterizations excel only within certain limits. These limits arise from his subject matter. As has been frequently noted, Snow is particularly effective in dealing with "man in committee." This focus, related to the election, by thirteen Fellows, of a new head of their college, is central to Snow's most highly praised novel, *The Masters*. A similar focus is present in a number of his other novels, most strongly in *The Affair*. The men operate in committees because of the nature of their work—they are professionals involved in their careers, as academics, businessmen, scientists, civil servants. This *work*—not the physical labor described in a "proletarian novel" but the work of "The New Men," the professional, bureaucratic, technological, managerial, classes—is presented with knowledgeable detail to be found in hardly any other novelist. Snow's work, in effect, filled a vacuum.

Snow filled another vacuum in his treatment of love and sex. While these topics have hardly been ignored by novelists, Snow's consideration of the social dimensions of a love affair or a marriage—the effect, for example, of a particular passion upon a man's career, such as Jago's protective love, in *The Masters*, for his wife—is rare, if not unique, among modern novelists, especially as, in Snow, the passion per se, however important, is never (not even in *Time of Hope*) the central concern.

This concern is character; the conditions of work, the politicking in committee, the impact of love—all these are used to reveal character in action.

Thus, Snow is fundamentally a very traditional novelist, even though his distinctive reputation rests upon his having been a kind of contemporary social psychologist, carefully observing particular segments of modern society. While he is likely to continue to be read for some time for the picture of parts of society that his special experience allowed him to present, he may well still be read when this picture, encrusted by time, is of only historical interest. If, as seems likely, his novels do so survive, it will be because, while dealing with the time-bound particulars of their age, they were able to rise to an understanding of fundamental human motivation, and thus to enjoy the longevity of true art.

Biography

Charles Percy Snow was born on October 15, 1905, in the Midland city of Leicester, the second of four sons. His background was similar to that of his fictional persona, Lewis Eliot. Snow's family had risen to the lower levels of the middle class; his father worked as a clerk in a shoe factory. Like Eliot's father, who led a choir, Snow's father played the organ in church; when he was no longer able to do so he died soon after, at the age of eighty-four.

In school, Snow specialized in science; after graduation he worked as a laboratory assistant while he prepared for the examination which won him a scholarship, in 1925, at the University College of Leicester. He was graduated, in 1927, with First Class Honors in chemistry, and received a grant that allowed him to proceed to a Master of Science degree in physics in 1928. Subsequently, he gained a scholarship to Cambridge, where he entered Christ's College as a research student in physics, published a paper on the infrared investigation of molecular structure, and, in 1930, received a Ph.D. and was elected a Fellow of Christ's College, a post he held until 1950, serving as Tutor from 1935 until 1945.

Like the fictional Lewis Eliot, whose law career hinged upon doing well in examinations and receiving scholarships, Snow must have worked hard (as did the hero of *The Search*) and must have been driven by ambition. His lifelong friend William Cooper (H. S. Hoff) has written novels about the life of the young people in Leicester in which the young Snow appears in fictional form; this work helps confirm the autobiographical quality of Snow's *Time of Hope*. Snow himself suggests the autobiographical aspect of *The Conscience of the Rich*, writing that when he was "very poor and very young," he "was taken up by one of the rich patrician Anglo-Jewish families."

Just as Lewis Eliot changes careers, and as the narrator of *The Search* turns from science to writing, Snow also did not rest in the comfort of being a rising young scientific don. He later wrote that since eighteen or so he knew that he wanted to be a writer, and while an undergraduate he wrote a novel, never published, called *Youth Searching*. He had gone into science because it offered a practical possibility for a poor boy. Although he did good scientific work at Cambridge and published some significant papers, according to William Cooper in *C. P. Snow* (1959), when some of Snow's scientific research went wrong through oversight, he abandoned scientific experimentation and turned more to his writing.

Snow had already published his first novel, *Death Under Sail*, a detective story, in 1932; he looked on it as practice for his later, more serious fiction. The next year he published *New Lives for Old*, combining his interest in science and politics in a work of science fiction. Worried that it would hurt his scientific career, he published this novel anonymously; it has never been reprinted. The first of his "serious" novels, *The Search*, appeared in 1934; like the Lewis Eliot series, it had a significant autobiographical element.

Snow did not move away from science to a complete commitment to literature at this time; rather, he became involved in administration, starting at his college. In 1939, he was appointed to a committee of the Royal Society that was organizing scientists for the war effort. This position led to a career in civil service; during World War II, he worked with the Ministry of Labour, being responsible for scientific personnel; after the war, he recruited scientists for government service. Beginning in 1944, he was associated with the English Electric Company, becoming a member of its Board of Directors in 1947. He was a Civil Service Commissioner from 1945 until 1960.

Snow's public life led to public honors; in 1943 he was made a Commander of the British Empire; in 1957 he was knighted. In 1964, when the Labour party resumed power, Snow, making a decision different from Lewis Eliot's, was made a life peer, Baron Snow, of the City of Leicester, and served for two years as parliamentary secretary of the Ministry of Technology.

During these years of public service, Snow was, of course, also living a personal life. He married the novelist Pamela Hansford Johnson in 1950. Like Margaret Davidson in the *Strangers and Brothers* series, she had been previously married, and like Lewis Eliot, Snow became a stepfather before having a son of his own, Philip Hansford Snow, born in 1952. Lady Snow has written autobiographically; her accounts are especially interesting in suggesting the similarities and differences between her children and the fictional children presented, especially in *Last Things*, by Snow.

Both the public and the personal sides of Snow's life were reflected in the *Strangers and Brothers* series, the idea for which occurred to him, he wrote, on January 1, 1935, while he was in France. It is difficult to determine the degree to which the whole series was worked out in advance. It would seem that Snow developed early certain controlling themes, such as "possessive love" and the idea of the "resonance" of experience upon the narrator, Lewis Eliot, while remaining flexible regarding the number and nature of the volumes that would make up the series. The first volume, *Strangers and Brothers*, which was to give the title to the whole series, appeared in 1940. It was followed in 1947 by *The Light and the Dark*. The subsequent nine volumes of the series appeared at roughly two-year intervals. They continued to draw directly upon his own life, including his eye operations, his cardiac arrest, his interest in the Moors murder case, and his experience in parliament.

The course of Snow's simultaneous literary and public careers brought him increased recognition and honors, including numerous honorary degrees, and apointment as rector of the University of St. Andrews, Scotland. (Like Lewis Eliot, he postponed the first of his eye operations in order to attend this academic installation.) They also involved him in notable controversy, the most famous resulting from his Cambridge lectures in 1959, later published as *The Two Cultures and the Scientific Revolution*. Snow's position, which included a criticism of intellectuals' general lack of understanding of modern science, provoked much discussion and a strong attack, renewed in 1961 by the noted Cambridge literary critic, F. R. Leavis. In 1960, Snow, while on one of his trips to the United States, stirred up another controversy by his lectures at Harvard. In those lectures, he criticized some of the military-scientific decisions made by Winston Churchill's government during World War II.

In his later years, Snow continued to speak out on public policies. He remained a controversial figure, but he gradually acquired the image of an elderly, liberal sage, even if his sagacity was frequently questioned by both the political Left and Right. Following the completion of the *Strangers and Brothers* series, he revised it for an "Omnibus Edition" and continued his writing, publishing *The Malcontents*, *In Their Wisdom*, and ending his career, as he began it, with a detective story (of sorts), *A Coat of Varnish*. His remarkably full life ended on July 1, 1980.

Analysis

Characterization is the foundation of Snow's fiction. While theme and idea, as one might expect from a writer as political and engagé as was C. P. Snow, are important to his work, and while plot is nearly always a major source of interest, character is fundamental. It was his special approach to characterization, at once limited and complex, that allowed him to employ theme and plot, as well as style and imagery, in its service, and which made certain subject matter particularly appropriate. Consequently, his works have their own distinctive and satisfying unity.

In his study of Anthony Trollope, a writer whom he valued highly and with whom he identified in a number of ways, Snow speaks interestingly of characterization. He defines character as persona, distinguishes it from inherent, individual nature, and considers personality to be a fusion of nature and character. These distinctions are certainly relevant to Snow's own work. His starting interest is in "characters," that is, an individual's personal qualities that are conditioned by, and expressed in, social experience. Yet, recognizing that this "character" interacts with "nature," Snow, in attempting to represent a rounded picture of "personality," must demonstrate the interaction. His fiction, then, is simultaneously concerned with showing people their "character" in social situations, indicating their "nature" or personal psychology, and presenting the interplay of the two, the social character and the private nature. All men have, in differing proportions, both a private and a social side to their personalities; all are both strangers and brothers.

Given this approach, it is not difficult to understand why Snow dealt frequently with "man in committee," or why he balanced this social material with presentation of individual passions, such as Lewis Eliot's for Sheila. Work and careers, seen in relation to individual "nature" and love and sex, were the two poles to which his subject matter flowed. As the social side of personality is developed, Snow was able to suggest its changing formation. One observes, for example, Walter Luke's evolution from a brash young scientist to Lord Luke of Salcombe; his persona, but not his basic nature, changes with the years. Because an individual's "nature" is inherent (like his physiology), it is taken as a *donnée*, and its effects are dealt with. It is, for example, a given fact that Roy Calvert is a kind of "manic-depressive"; the reader discovers what the results of this nature will be, both for Calvert himself and for those with whom he interacts.

It was convenient for Snow that this approach to character was quite appropriate to the type of plotting that he apparently preferred. Most of his novels pose a question: "What will Martin decide?" "Who will be elected master?" "Will Roger Quaife succeed?" The reader, in attempting to anticipate the answer, and Snow, in providing and justifying it, must consider the personalities involved. This consideration requires some understanding of the characters' public personae, their social interactions, and their private passions. Plot, a strong element in its own right, is based on character.

Imagery also consistently reinforces Snow's binocular view of personality. The light of brotherhood wages a never-ending Manichaean conflict with the dark of private estrangement. Windows may be lit, inviting people to "come home" to social involvement, but they often walk the dark streets, locked out in their lonely individuality.

Much of Snow's style also reflects his view of personality. E. A. Levenston, in a careful study of Snow's sentence structure (*ES*, 1974), has noticed the prevalence of qualifying "interrupters." Many of these are a result of Snow's comparing the particular to the general, one man's qualities to many men's. Expressions such as "very few men, George least of all," or "Roy was not a snob, no man was less so," run throughout his work.

Thus, Snow was consistent in his craft. If this consistency imposed some limitations on his achievements, it also provided a valuable unity to his whole literary corpus.

For reasons that he later described as "obscure," Snow "signalled" that he intended to abandon his scientific career by writing "a stylised, artificial detective story very much in the manner of the day." *Death Under Sail* is a competent example of this form; it remains quite readable and in some ways foreshadows his more significant work. Told in the first person (curiously, for a book by a twenty-six-year-old, the narrator is sixty-three), it employs light and dark and also water imagery; it includes a political discussion regarding class society being justified through the ranks of the elite being open to talent; and it is concerned with friendship and the "genertion gap." More important, the plot hinges on character. While the novel's characterization is relatively superficial, it involves both social character, as seen in the interaction of a small group (the narrator, the detective, and the suspects), and the individual psychology of concealed motives. It is thus typical of Snow's novels, most of which have the element of a suspense story based on the two sides, public and private, of personality.

Snow's second published novel, *New Lives for Old*, is the weakest of his whole canon, but it is not without its virtues. The story involves the discovery of a rejuvenating process and the subsequent questions of whether the process will be suppressed, its effects on the love-lives of some of the characters, and the political implications of the discovery. These three questions are not well unified; instead of integrating the love interest and the politics, in this one instance Snow treats them as essentially separate stories, at the expense of both. The love story in the middle section becomes tedious; in the last section of the book Snow, atypically, lets a political interest stifle the story. The first part of the book, however, is fairly successful. Here, the plot is related to character, social interactions, private motivations, and moral decisions. Snow is doing what he does best. The falling-off of the work after its relatively effective beginning, however, justifies his decision not to have it reprinted; it is now a difficult book to obtain.

His third published novel, *The Search*, was slightly revised and reprinted twenty-four years after its first appearance. It is generally superior to the first two novels, and more easily related to the *Strangers and Brothers* series, especially *Time of Hope* and *Homecoming*. Although Snow warns the reader, in his Preface to the 1958 edition, that the book's narrator and protagonist, Arthur Miles, is "not much like" Snow himself, clearly there is an autobiographical element in the story of a poor boy's using his talent, determination, and scholarships to make a career in science, later to abandon it to turn to writing. The book was praised for its accurate picture of what it is like to be a scientist; in fact, very little scientific activity per se is present. Rather, professional concerns, ambitions, the relation between love and career, and the decisions made by men in committees constitute the basic material of the book. The protagonist might as easily be a barrister as a scientist. Indeed, *The Search*, while a worthwhile book in its own right, can be seen as a trying out of the material that Snow was to go on to develop in his series. The defects of *The Search* result primarily from attempting to try out too much at once; the book's construction becomes somewhat confused. The virtues arise from Snow's basing his work on personal experience; he employed, more thoroughly than in his first two published novels his skill in showing the interconnections of the personal and public aspects of personality.

The favorable reception given to *The Search* certainly encouraged Snow to continue his career as a novelist; within a year of its publication, he conceived of the series on which his reputation rests. He must have made various plans for the series as a whole; the first volume, however, did not appear until 1940, six years after *The Search*. Writing a *roman-fleuve*, as opposed to a series of individual novels, presents an author with certain problems and various opportunities. While Snow avoided some of the pitfalls, such as narrative inconsistency, he failed to take advantage of some of the potentialities of the form. The overall pattern of this series is more blurred than it need have been. This is indicated by the order in which the books were published; it is not the essentially chronological order of the "Omnibus Edition," published after the series was concluded. While this authorial rearrangement must be accepted, the fact that Snow did not originally insist on it suggests a certain random quality to the series' organization as first conceived of and executed. Furthermore, proposed systems of classification of the books within the series—as, for example, novels of "observed experience" and of "direct experience," or a novels dealing with individuals, groups, or a mixture of both—while useful, fail to make clear a compelling pattern.

Indeed, the individual volumes of the series, with the possible exception of the final *Last Things*, stand on their own and easily can be enjoyed separately. That is not to say that nothing is gained by reading them all in the order that they appear in the "Omnibus Edition." As compared, however, to a work such as Anthony Powell's *roman-fleuve*, *A Dance to the Music of Time*, *Strangers and Brothers* fails to develop the potential cumulative effect of a series.

The series form does allow the overlapping of incident and the "resonance" between events as seen and felt by the narrator, Lewis Eliot. Snow has an interesting concept here but he does too little with it. The reader does not, as in some of the novels of Joyce Cary, see the same events through different eyes; rather, one is given different accounts by a relatively consistent Eliot. The result is that events described for the second time sometimes bore the reader, at other times the reader feels cheated by the inadequacy of the first account. Only occasionally does the technique work well, as, for example, the two accounts, in *The Light and the Dark* and *The Masters*, of Roy Calvert's giving of a self-damning paper to Winslow. The first account omits material in order to focus on Calvert; subsequently, as one learns of the larger implications of the act, it takes on new meaning.

More obvious benefits of a series novel are present in *Strangers and Brothers*; the reader observes more characters, over a longer period of time, than

would normally be possible in a single volume. Snow, however, possibly in
the interest of verisimilitude, does relatively little with his opportunity. Roy
Calvert is killed off, George Passant's change is not traced; one does see
more of Martin Eliot and Francis Getliffe, but their developments, such as
they are, have little drama. There is little in Snow corresponding to the
surprises that Powell gives the reader when, for example, his villain, Wid-
merpool, makes one of his sudden appearances. Only quite rarely does Snow
make effective use of surprise, as when the elderly Hector Rose is found to
have acquired a younger, sexy wife.

The time-span of the series does, however, allow Snow to present the
succession of generations, and he does a fine job of suggesting how childhood
experiences affect parents as they react to their own children and their friend's
children. The parents' point of view is an important part of human experience,
infrequently treated in fiction; here again, in presenting parental love, Snow
effectively filled a vacuum.

A more fundamental aspect of the *roman-fleuve* is of the development of
the narrator. Lewis Eliot does change, both in his attitudes and in his style,
becoming more ironic in the later volumes. Looking back on earlier events,
such as his support of Jago in *The Masters*, he recognizes his errors. While
Eliot's development adds interest to the whole series, it would be difficult to
maintain that this interest is central.

There are two final aspects of a series novel that make *Strangers and Brothers* something other than eleven separate books—repetition and thematic
development. The former is a two-edged device. Any reader of the whole
series will be struck by the frequent repetition of certain phrases, sententious
remarks, images, and tricks of style, and can readily assemble a list. Are the
values of the repetition—interesting variations on a theme and a sense of
continuity greater than the drawback—monotony? In Snow's case, it is something of a toss-up. On balance, although many readers may be inclined to
say "Oh no! Not another lighted window," the recurring images of light and
darkness do form a pattern that unifies the series and reinforces its themes.

Finally, there is theme. Snow himself, in a note preceding *The Conscience
of the Rich*, indicated the importance of recurring themes, including "possessive love" and love of, and renunciation of, power. The list could be easily
expanded; as has been indicated, the title of the series itself points to a
fundamental thematic concern. By seeing these various themes dramatized
through different characters in differing circumstances, and learning Lewis
Eliot's reactions, the reader certainly gains a perspective that would be impossible in a single volume. Thematic perspective, then, provides the most convincing justification for Snow's series. It is a sufficient justification; the whole
is greater than the sum of the parts. That Snow's strength lay more in characterization than thematic presentation may account for the occasional failures
of the series, qua series.

A brief discussion of three of the eleven novels of the series may serve to suggest aspects of the volumes considered as individual works. *Time of Hope* is both an early novel and one that focuses upon Lewis Eliot; *The Masters*, generally the most highly regarded of the series, is from the middle period and has a "collective hero"; *Corridors of Power*, a later novel, centers on a protagonist other than Eliot.

Time of Hope was the third volume in the series; in terms of internal chronology, however, it comes first, dealing with the years 1914 to 1933, during which Lewis Eliot matures from a boy of nine to an established barrister, involved in an "impossible" marriage. Strongly unified by its plot, it is perhaps the most emotionally moving volume of the whole series, and one of the more successful.

Indicative of Snow's central concern for the interconnections of the public and private aspects of character, the title refers to both the hope for a better society that Lewis Eliot shares with George Passant's group, and the hero's private ambitions. Asked what he wants from life, Eliot, in a phrase he returns to much later in the series, replies that he wants to see a better world, spend his life not unknown, and gain love.

The suspense in the novel is based on the question of whether Eliot will succeed, whether he will at least be started on the road to realizing these hopes. The conflict and tension behind this question provide the *Angst* that contrasts to the hope. The book begins with a "homecoming," dreaded by the young Eliot. (In a clear parallel with Marcel Proust, Snow picks this up at the start of the very last volume of the series.) Just as he had reason to fear this first homecoming, Eliot later dreads subsequent returns to the woman he manages to marry. Eliot's success is mingled with failure. Through a combination of his "nature," which gives him the drive to struggle, and his social "character," which wins him the help of George Passant, Eliot's "personality" wins through on the public level: he succeeds in becoming a barrister. On the personal level, however, while he "succeeds" in marrying Sheila, his possessive love evokes no response; his marriage is personally disastrous, and a handicap to his career.

Snow in *Time of Hope* thus successfully utilizes his approach to character and his recurring themes in a self-contained story, but one which also prepares for subsequent volumes. His techniques in this volume are typical of the series: The imagery of light and darkness prevails; secondary characters, such as Herbert Getliffe, the barrister under whom Eliot trains, are well drawn; the "nature" of a major character is presented as a *donneé*. Not being shown what makes her the strange person she is, one must take Sheila's problems as given. Fortunately for the story, it is easier to do so than to accept Roy Calvert's inherent depression in *The Light and the Dark*. As a *Bildungsroman*, *Time of Hope* is more conventional than the majority of the volumes in the series. Consequently, it is both one of the more satisfactory of Snow's novels, and one of the less distinctively interesting.

While *Time of Hope* has a clear protagonist, *The Masters*, the first volume in the revised series, has no one hero. Snow is particularly good at dealing with interreactions within a group and *The Masters* has been the most highly regarded of his novels. The title refers to two "masters" or heads of a college; after the first one dies, a new one must be elected. It is on this election, involving the votes of thirteen Fellows of the college, that the plot centers. The election comes down to two candidates, Jago and Crawford. While Lewis Eliot, now one of the Fellows, supports Jago, and while the reader's sympathies are involved on this side, Snow is careful to avoid making the choice one between good and evil. There are very few outright villains in Snow's novels, and Crawford is certainly not one. Politically of the Left, but personally not so well suited for the mastership, he is contrasted to Jago, whom Eliot finds less appealing politically but much more appealing as a man. Thus, the issue is essentially between personal "nature" and public "character." The different Fellows line up on this basis, thereby reflecting their own natures and characters; their ultimate votes demonstrate the balance of these two aspects of "personality."

Interestingly, given Snow's famous dispute, following the publication of the *The Masters*, over "the two cultures," the literary and the scientific, one might see Jago, a scholar of English literature, as the humanists' candidate, and Crawford, a member of the Royal Society, as the scientists'. Snow, opposed to the split between the "cultures," does not have the Fellows vote on the basis of this split. Walter Luke, a scientist, judges by nature and sticks with Jago. Francis Getliffe, also a scientist, although recognizing Jago's virtues, is motivated by "public" principle, and supports Crawford. Eustace Pilbrow, a literary scholar, agrees with Getliffe. Nightingale, another scientist, jealous of Crawford's professional success, initially supports Jago. Paradoxically, Despard-Smith, because he identifies with Jago, supports Crawford.

Having established the initial lineup of votes, Snow skillfully shows the interactions of motives that cause some of them to shift. One particularly important consideration is the question of Jago's wife; her character, thought to be unsuitble for that of a Master's spouse, becomes an issue in the election. The personal issue here involves another form of "possessive love," and sets up a "resonance" for Eliot, who is ambivalently trapped in his marriage to Sheila. Snow handles the development of the plot and the suspense leading to the election quite effectively. In ringing so many insightful changes on the interactions of the personalities within a small group, Snow wrote what may be his own masterpiece.

In the later volumes of the series, Eliot moves from college to national and international political maneuvers; the implications are that there is not that much difference. Nevertheless, the "Tolstoyan" view of history—that individuals are secondary to the larger forces of history which is explicitly mentioned more than once in the series—is more pronounced in the later volumes. Snow suggests that with other men, probably the same policies would be carried out, the same forces would operate. Thus, the *mechanisms* of politics are of primary interest, but to understand them, one must understand the men who work and are worked by them. As Snow once said, one must understand how the world "ticks" if one is to change it for the better.

Corridors of Power, the ninth volume in the series, gives the reader a picture of how the high-level decision making that he also described in *The New Men* and questioned in *Science and Government* (1961), does operate. However deterministic its underlying historical philosophy, the novel supports the statement of one of its characters that what is important is how something is done, who it is done by, and when it is done.

The story centers on Roger Quaife, a politician committed to an "enlightened" view of the use of atomic weapons. Once again, one sees both the public and private side of a protagonist, the "nature" and "character" that interact to form Quaife's "personality"; again, however, the nature is essentially a *donneé*—Quaife is to be taken as found. Ostensibly happy in his marriage, Quaife has a mistress; she is a factor, although not a decisive one, in his political career. Snow is quite good at showing the interactions of career considerations and more personal feelings within the triangle composed of Quaife, his wife Caro, and his mistress Ellen. Sex is seen as a *relationship*, social as well as emotional and physical. In order to present this relationship, however, verisimilitude must be stretched a bit, because Lewis Eliot, the narrator, has to be in places and hear confidences from which one would expect him to be barred. Not only does Eliot learn much about private lives, but also he is rather surprisingly ubiquitous at political councils. Here, in describing some of the behind-the-scenes maneuvers, Snow is quite effective, as he is with the presentation of secondary characters, such as the member of Parliament "Sammikins," and the important civil servant, Hector Rose.

After the completion and revision of the *Strangers and Brothers* series, Snow not only worked on biographical studies (*Trollope, The Realists, The Physicists*) but also continued his novel-writing. Although the final volume in the series, *Last Things*, was diffuse in plotting, he returned, in his final novels, to the use of a strong plot line. Both *The Malcontents* and *A Coat of Varnish* are forms of the "whodunit," and *In Their Wisdom*, like *The Sleep of Reason*, maintains the reader's interest in the outcome of a law case.

The Malcontents received generally poor reviews. It does have obvious weaknesses; the dialogue, usually one of Snow's stronger points, is somewhat unconvincing. Well attuned to the talk of his cohorts, Snow's ear for the speech of contemporary youth was less acute. A more serious defect is related to the mystery-story requirement of providing a goodly number of suspects. Too many characters are introduced at the beginning; the reader has an initial problem in differentiating them, and the book gets off to a slow start. Once the story is underway, however, the narrative interest is strong. It involves the interaction of a group of seven young people, planning to take action against the Establishment. One of them is known to be an informer. Typically for a Snow novel, to appreciate fully the narrative one must consider the formative aspects of each individual's personality. Class background, family relations, ideological positions, and love interests all enter in. Diffused through seven characters, however, Snow's analysis of these factors is somewhat superficial, with the exception of Stephen Freer, whose relationship to the older generation is presented with sensitivity. An underlying sympathy for the ends, if not the means, of the young radicals informs much of the book. This sympathy, while somewhat Olympian, avoids being patronizing and becomes one of the novel's virtues.

In Their Wisdom is a more successful work. Again, to develop narrative interest, a problem is posed. In this instance, it involves an argument over a will and the results of a trial over the disputed legacy. Just as the reader's sympathy is involved, in *The Masters*, on Jago's side, here there is no question of whom to support in the contest. Julian, a selfish and opportunistic young man, is Snow's closest approach to a clear villian. By simplifying some of the characters, Snow is able to devote more attention to the others. Jenny is particularly interesting, different from characters in Snow's earlier books. In showing her life of genteel poverty and the effect upon her of the trial and its outcome, Snow once again effectively intertwines the personal and the public. Although it devotes an excessive amount of space to the House of Lords, *In Their Wisdom* is one of Snow's more successful novels.

His last novel, *A Coat of Varnish*, was a return to the detective-story genre of his first book. A less pure example of this genre than *Death Under Sail*, however, it is somewhat unsatisfactory considered simply as a mystery. The title refers to a line within the book, to the effect that civilization is a thin coat of varnish over barbarism, a notion relevant also to *The Sleep of Reason*. A fairly interesting cast of characters is introduced, but none of them is treated with the depth of analysis of which Snow was capable. Here, character is secondary to plot, and plot itself is used to comment on society. To try to work out who is guilty, one must understand motives: Money, sex, and power. In understanding these motives, one gains, Snow expects, an understanding of society. Although this is one of Snow's weaker novels, certainly not ending his career triumphantly, it does manage a degree of fulfillment of the Horatian formula, to delight and to instruct.

Perhaps one should ask for no more. Throughout his career as a novelist, Snow, although with varying degrees of success, never failed to provide a number of intelligent readers with these twin satisfactions. This may not put him in the ranks of a Leo Tolstoy or a Proust; it is, nevertheless, no small accomplishment.

William B. Stone

Other major works

PLAYS: *A View Over the Bridge*, 1950; *The Supper Dance*, 1951 (with Pamela Hansford Johnson); *Family Party*, 1951 (with Pamela Hansford Johnson); *Spare the Rod*, 1951 (with Pamela Hansford Johnson); *To Murder Mrs. Mortimer*, 1951 (with Pamela Hansford Johnson); *The Pigeon with the Silver Foot*, 1951 (with Pamela Hansford Johnson); *Her Best Foot Forward*, 1951 (with Pamela Hansford Johnson); *The Public Prosecutor*, 1969 (adaptation with Pamela Hansford Johnson).

NONFICTION: *Richard Aldington: An Appreciation*, 1938; *Writers and Readers of the Soviet Union*, 1943; *The Two Cultures and the Scientific Revolution*, 1959 (revised as *Two Cultures and a Second Look*, 1964); *The Moral Un-Neutrality of Science*, 1961; *Science and Government*, 1961; *A Postscript to Science and Government*, 1962; *Magnanimity*, 1962; *C. P. Snow: A Spectrum, Science, Criticism, Fiction*, 1963; *Variety of Men*, 1967; *The State of Siege*, 1969; *Public Affairs*, 1971; *Trollope: His Life and Art*, 1975; *The Realists*, 1978; *The Physicists*, 1981.

Bibliography

Karl, Frederick S. *C. P. Snow: The Politics of Conscience*. Carbondale: Southern Illinois University Press, 1963. A generally useful study of Snow that analyzes his novels up to and including *The Affair*. Some of the statements about him are misleading, however, and should be read with caution.

Ramanathan, Suguna. *The Novels of C. P. Snow: A Critical Introduction*. London: Macmillan, 1978. A fresh, sympathetic assessment of Snow that discusses all of his novels save his two earliest works, *Death Under Sail* and *New Lives for Old*. Notes Snow's "imaginative impulse," his understanding of the changing social scene in England over a span of fifty years, and the gradual change in his outlook from hopefulness to doom. Upholds Snow as being free from fanaticism. A recommended reading.

Shusterman, David. *C. P. Snow*. Boston: Twayne, 1975. A competent, compact study of Snow, including his early life, the controversies surrounding his nonfiction, and his literary output. Contains an in-depth analysis of the *Strangers and Brothers* series of novels, noting their interest apart from their literary value. Includes a chronology and a select bibliography.

Snow, C. P. *C. P. Snow: A Spectrum, Science, Criticism, Fiction*. Edited by Stanley Weintraub. New York: Charles Scribner's Sons, 1963. A useful introduction to Snow's life and works. The commentary covers many aspects of his fiction, criticism, and writings on science.

Thale, Jerome. *C. P. Snow*. New York: Charles Scribner's Sons, 1965. Considered an excellent secondary source on Snow that is both readable and informative. Presents Snow's work up to and including 1964. Discusses his nonfiction writings, among which are his two controversial works, *The Two Cultures and the Scientific Revolution* and *Science and Government*.

WOLE SOYINKA

Born: Abeokuta, Nigeria; July 13, 1934

Principal long fiction
The Interpreters, 1965; *Season of Anomy*, 1973.

Other literary forms
Wole Soyinka is best known as a dramatist. He has written more than twenty plays in various modes, including *The Swamp Dwellers* (1958), *The Lion and the Jewel* (1959), *A Dance of the Forests* (1960), *Madmen and Specialists* (1970, revised 1971), and *Death and the King's Horseman* (1975). He is also a director and filmmaker. He has published several collections of poetry, including *Idanre and Other Poems* (1967), *A Shuttle in the Crypt* (1972), and *Mandela's Earth and Other Poems* (1988), and the long poem *Ogun Abibiman* (1976). His nonfiction prose includes impressive books of criticism such as *Myth, Literature, and the African World* (1976) and *Art, Dialogue, and Outrage: Essays on Literature and Culture* (1988). His autobiographical works examine various aspects of his life experiences: his prison years in *The Man Died* (1972), his early life in *Aké: The Years of Childhood* (1981), and the influence of his father in *Isarà: A Voyage Around "Essay"* (1989). In addition, he has translated the Yoruba novel *Ogboju Ode Ninu Igbo Irunmale*, by D. O. Fagunwa, as *Forest of a Thousand Daemons: A Hunter's Saga* (1968).

Achievements
Soyinka is perhaps the most talented and versatile writer to have emerged during the literary flowering in Africa beginning in the 1950's. He is, without doubt, the finest dramatist; he is also an accomplished poet and has written two novels so experimental that critics are not yet sure what to make of them. While tapping numerous twentieth century fictional devices, the novels are based on his own cultural heritage, combining ritual, myth, comedy, and hard realism in a new configuration. He draws from the Yoruba mythology of his native region but makes contact with a larger public by frequent references and parallels to myths and literatures of other cultures. Not only his literary achievements but also his championing of individual freedoms have gained for him recognition both in his native Nigeria and abroad. He has received numerous awards, including first prize at the Dakar Negro Arts Festival in 1960, the John Whiting Drama Prize in 1966, the Jock Campbell Award for Fiction in 1968, and the Nobel Prize for Literature in 1986.

Biography
Akinwande Oluwole Soyinka was born July 13, 1934, at Abeokuta, in western Nigeria. A Yoruba by birth, he has studied Yoruba mythology and

theology and has made it the basis of his literary themes. His formal education, however, was British. He attended primary and secondary schools in Abeokuta and Ibadan, began his undergraduate work at University College, Ibadan, and received his bachelor of arts degree with honors in English (1957) at the University of Leeds. He has continued to be associated with various universities throughout his academic and literary career and has held lectureships, delivered papers at academic meetings, and published critical reviews and articles. His career as a dramatist began at Leeds and continued with his establishment of acting companies in Lagos and Ibadan. Aside from the theater and his own literary endeavors, he has been a political activist; the Nigerian authorities detained him in prison during the Biafran War, from August, 1967, to October, 1969. Individual freedom and social responsibility are themes in his earliest work, but his commitment to social justice became even more intense after his prison experiences and the Nigerian atrocities during the war.

Analysis

Like other novelists in Africa during the years just before and after independence, Wole Soyinka faced the question of ethnic and cultural identity. The now notorious negritude movement, begun in the 1930's, had attempted to promote a pan-African identity by distinguishing between two mentalities: the rational, methodical, categorical tendency of the industrialized Westerner and the emotional spontaneity of the African still in tune with the rhythms of nature. Many, including Soyinka, came to see this definition as a sign of cultural dependency—the African described by contrast to the dominant European culture. In his most famous remark on the subject, Soyinka declared that "the tiger does not proclaim his tigretude!" Soyinka presumably meant that the African need not be defensive about his identity; at any rate, Soyinka has proclaimed unabashedly, in all of his works, including his two novels, the indigenous source of his themes and inspiration.

As Soyinka makes clear in his book of criticism *Myth, Literature, and the African World*, his own cultural heritage is Yoruba. Drawing from its fascinating and complex mythology, Soyinka concentrates on two central events. One is the disintegration of primal oneness, which he calls Orisa-nla. In the beginning, only Orisa-nla existed, with his servant Akunda; in a moment of revolution or treachery, depending upon the point of view, Akunda rolled a boulder down the back of Orisa-nla, shattering him into the fragments that became the human race and the gods of the Yoruba pantheon; god and man were thenceforth separated from each other. Among these individuated gods, two stand out, Obatala and Ogun, as aspects of the original oneness. Soyinka uses human representations of them both in his novels. Obatala appears as the titular leader of a traditional community. While not actively pursuing the rejuvenation of society, he tries to hold things together: "He is the embodiment of the suffering spirit of man, uncomplaining, agonised, full of the redemptive qualities of endurance and martyrdom." Soyinka also includes a third human figure in the novels, a woman, who appears as the fertility principle inherent in Orisa-nla and promises continuity.

The most important god for Soyinka, however, is Ogun, whose story is central to the plots in the two novels and whose complex character makes him the most complete symbol of the original oneness. Most simply, he is the god of creation and destruction, and man is his incarnation. After the original disintegration, Ogun took upon himself the task of entering the abyss that separated men from the gods and of building a bridge across the primeval gulf to reunite them. To accomplish this task, he had to "die," to risk total disintegration of the personality (thus repeating the original fragmentation) and to reintegrate himself through an act of the will. Ogun's success was his grand triumph that man must strive to emulate. Ogun's cautionary tale does not, however, end here. At the call of human beings, he reluctantly descended to aid them, but his gift of "Promethean" fire—Ogun is the god of the forge—gave man the power of destruction as well as creation. During his sojourn among men, Ogun, as god of wine and of war, then experienced his most shameful moment, the massacre in battle, while in a drunken rage, of both friends and enemies. This destructive power of the will repeated the drunken act of Akunda and symbolizes the ever-present threat of man's own destructiveness. It is especially Ogun's personality and social roles that provide for Soyinka a rationale for contemporary events. Ogun's story proclaims the will as the crucial ethical faculty, individual heroism as the dynamic factor in social change, and the communal function of the heroic act as its sanction.

Soyinka's first novel, *The Interpreters*, is a dark comedy. The settings are the capital city of Lagos, the university city of Ibadan, and the surrounding lagoons, at a time soon after Nigeria's independence, in the early 1960's. Soyinka presents a directionless society seen mainly through the eyes of a few university-educated observers who have just returned from abroad to take up their roles, which they have yet truly to discover, in the new state. What they see is an assortment of professional people holding on to or seeking status and power; their attractive public image is but a disguised sleaziness, a combination of Old World corruption and Victorian hypocrisy. Moving through this structured society are various lost people seeking stability: an American black homosexual, an evangelical preacher, a thief, and occasional transients from outside Africa. The novel traces the lives of the five interpreters—Egbo, Sagoe, Kola, Sekoni, and Bandele—as they get in touch with themselves and their society. What sets them apart, in particular, is their refusal to accept wholesale imported Western values and mores, and a vague sense that an indigenous worldview should mold the new state. The problem is to get in touch with it and revive it. Soyinka does not offer any hope of immediate success.

Of all the interpreters, Egbo and Sekoni are most closely associated with the Ogun experience. Sagoe, Kola, and Bandele do not share the risky heroism of Ogun's nature but seem closer to the passive, suffering attitude of the god Obatala, though it is difficult and undesirable to make such identifications with any allegorical rigidity. Sagoe, the newspaper reporter whose experiences give insight into the corrupt practices of business and politics and into the religious void of modern Nigeria, suffers in the first part of the novel from inebriation and a morning hangover. He has developed an absurd philosophy of Voidancy, a solipsistic return to original oneness, a passive loss of identity. A recurring childhood memory perpetuates a Western, Manichaean split between divine and human nature. He finally agrees to abandon his philosophy and commit himself to his fiancée, Dehinwa, but Sagoe never displays any deep internal struggle. Kola is a painter who is intellectually aware of Yoruba tradition; he spends several months finishing his huge canvas, a symbolic representation of the Yoruba pantheon using contemporary models. Kola gradually recognizes his own inadequacy as an artist—Ogun is Soyinka's divine symbol of the true artist—and is almost ready to accept his role as simply a teacher of art. The painting itself would suggest, at least in the eyes of Egbo, an inadequate conception of human struggle and redemption. Kola presents Ogun (Egbo) not in his creative role as architect of order but as a drunken murderer. Bandele is the clearest image of the god Obatala. Throughout the novel, he tries to mediate among the various interpreters and to judge and encourage ethical behavior. He also tries to live a life of compromise, to prevent a complete split between the intellectuals and the rest of society. In the end, he continues his role of judge—as the traditional Oba—but strikes out at the society itself, ensuring a split, as he sarcastically accuses the hypocritical professional class of burying its own children.

Soyinka measures human character against divine behavior after the original fragmentation. Only Ogun, among all the gods, risked the loss of individuation in the abyss of transition. Egbo, the grandson and heir of a village chief, is on the edge of the abyss. The novel places two choices before him: between the power and privileges of the Osa chiefdom and a life in a modern state, and between a sensuous life with Simi, a nationally famous and beautiful courtesan, and a New World university student, a feminist rebel pregnant with his child. While he has not made either choice definitively at the end of the novel, he leans toward contemporary demands. Such a commitment would be a denial of African heritage as superficially perceived but an assertion of it in essential terms. The university student is herself a heroine, defying artificial conventions of the day and committed to her child and to her education in spite of bitter rejection by the professional elite. She is also the only person with whom Egbo has shared his religious commitment to the Yoruba gods; their night of love takes place in his sacred retreat under the bridge crossing the Ogun River. Egbo has at least three initiation experiences, all sexual, described as symbolic leaps into the abyss of death and rebirth: twice during his first night with Simi and once during his more mature "venturing" with the unnamed student girl. By the end of the novel, he knows, though he has not yet made the decision, that "he could not hold her merely as an idyllic fantasy, for the day rose large enough and he was again overwhelmed by her power of will."

While Egbo's Ogun experience is still on the level of "idyllic fantasy," Sekoni's has a degree of fulfillment and a tragic finality. Like Egbo, at the beginning of the novel he perceives the sacred through physical reality. Egbo calls the fleshy black dancer at the Club Cabana "the exaltation of the Black Immanent." For Sekoni, she is a symbol of the original oneness: It would be profane, he says in his stuttering excitement, "t-t-to bring her in c-c-conflict." In moments of inspiration, as he comes into contact with spiritual reality, his language breaks down and his stuttering increases. Sekoni's first profession is engineering. His dream is to harness the powers of nature. A flashback has him returning home aboard ship, imagining the ocean as "a deafening water-fall defying human will," and his creative fingers as shapers of bridges, hospitals, derricks, and railroads. The sea, however, proves to be too strong; the bureaucracy at home gives him a desk job and then allows him to build a rural power plant only to have it condemned by an expatriate expert. The failure drives him insane. When he is released from the mental hospital, he goes on a pilgrimage to Jerusalem (not to Mecca, as his devout Muslim father would have wished), and by putting his fingers through the broken walls of the city, he has a mystical experience. Soyinka's description of it suggests an identification between the Jewish and the African diaspora, the disintegration of traditional community, and, by implication, a repetition of the original fragmentation of Orisa-nla. Sekoni returns to Nigeria as an inspired artist. His one great work, a sculpture which he calls "The Wrestler," seems a race against time. Using Bandele as a model and a rough incident with a bouncer at the Club Cabana as the inspiration, Sekoni depicts what appears to be Ogun just beginning to relax after subduing the forces of chaos in the abyss. Kila admires and envies Sekoni's genius, his ability to create "that something which hits you foully in the stomach."

When Ogun grants such powers, however, he demands a sacrifice in return. In a symbolic scene, with obvious mythological references and a typical Soyinka setting, Sekoni dies in an automobile accident during a raging storm, near a bridge that spans a precipice. As god of the forge, Ogun is associated with automobiles and bridges and with the metal that draws down lightning from the heavens. On that chaotic night, the "dome" of heaven "cracked," and, like Ogun in the abyss, Sekoni loses his identity, literally, except as he survives in his sculpture. His death leaves the other interpreters drained of energy, searching desperately for a myth that will convince them of rebirth. That Sekoni is not reborn seems to provoke estrangement. At the end, the four remaining interpreters are no longer a close-knit group: They experience "a night of severance, every man . . . going his way." The Ogun paradigm would suggest that, since everyone is an incarnation of Ogun, the interpreters are facing the transition experience.

Like *The Interpreters, Season of Anomy* has as its major theme the reestablishment of cultural and spiritual continuity. Bandele's searing rebuke of his peers, that they are burying their own children, applies even literally to the generation in power in Soyinka's second novel. The ruling Cartel (a conglomerate of business, political, and military leaders) use their positions to exploit the country (a fictionalized Nigeria) and to intimidate, suppress, and massacre in order to maintain control. The novel's main antagonist is the innocuous-appearing community of Aiyéró, headed by the wise Pa Ahime, which perpetuates the traditional African values of community and harmony with nature. Ahime resembles the Obatala personality in his passive, suffering role as priest. Beneath his surface calm dwell "doubts upon doubts, thicker than the night" about African ideals ever overcoming the forces of exploitation. He himself, however, does not struggle actively against the forces outside the community. The conflict in the novel begins when Ofeyi, the novel's protagonist and the Ogun personality in its artistic, creative aspect, goes out into the larger world to combat the Cartel. Ofeyi is at first a propagandist jingle writer for the Cocoa Corporation, an ally of the Cartel; under the influence of Ahime and his own vision of a new Africa, however, he uses his position to undermine the corporation, until he has to resign under fire. The novel, then, presents a conflict between these two forces, creation and destruction, but the plot is a tracing of Ofeyi's growing commitment to his cause, his debate in particular over using either peaceful or military means, his eventual acceptance of violence, and his personal and communal quest for Iriyise, his mistress, whom Soyinka develops as a goddess of fertility, an aspect of Orisa-nla, who gave birth to the Yoruba pantheon. Ofeyi travels into the center of the Cartel's massacres in order to rescue Iriyise from the enemy prison and carry her, though comatose, safely back to the refuge of Aiyéró.

While the novel often operates on a realistic level—with its vivid pictures of war, for example—its language is infused with ritual and myth. Ofeyi's actions take on a ritualistic meaning and, as in ritual and myth, detailed, causal explanations are not always forthcoming. The novel does not follow a clear chronological line; it oscillates between the communal life in Aiyéró and the outside world and between the inner life of Ofeyi, his memories and reflections, and public action. The novel tries to make sense of the chaotic events through which Ofeyi moves. It judges the Cartel according to traditional values and myths. In particular, it condemns an exploitation that forgets the obligation of one generation to another. Ofeyi's subversive jingles accuse the Cocoa Corporation of milking the country dry: "They drained the nectar, peeled the gold/ The trees were bled prematurely old/ Nor green nor gold remained for the next generation." The proverb that defines the Cartel, one of its own choosing, damns it: "The child who swears his mother will not sleep, he must also pass a sleepless night." The mother (the Cartel), accusing the child of the crime, fails to acknowledge that the child is restless and screams for attention because the mother has not been nurturing him. The Cartel fails in its function of ensuring continuity from one generation to the next. Aiyéró, on the other hand, through its rituals and myths, maintains the three necessary connections, between generations, between the living and the dead, and between gods and men. Aiyéró is not a pastoral paradise; it has a reputation for its boatbuilding, uses hydroelectric power, and manufactures guns. Soyinka's notion of the idyllic community is not backward. Still, its communal ideal suggests strongly its allegorical representation of the divine world attempting to reestablish ties with the fragmented human race to achieve wholeness.

Ogun's transitional journey is the paradigm for the novel's plot and theme. Individual scenes and incidents reinforce the idea. Ofeyi's main concern is whether his actions will make any impact on history: whether the attempt to create order out of chaos is hopeless and whether his own personal contribution will soon be covered in obscurity. When he is still debating his role, sitting in a canoe on the pond that the people of Aiyéró use as a retreat for reflection, Ofeyi watches the wake quickly disappear as the waters resume their calm cover. Even "this simple rite of passage," he says, seems a meaningless challenge. Beneath the pond are centuries of history—"Slaves, gold, oil. The old wars"—and his efforts seem doomed to join them. The oil could be a promise for the future; like Ogun, Ofeyi regards resources as the raw materials of creativity. As he contemplates the Cartel's exploitation of them, he determines, through an act of the will, that victory requires "only the rightful challenger."

The novel's central symbol of the new Nigeria, as conceived by Ahime and Ofeyi, is the dam at Shage, which will, when completed, span the river into Cross-river, the region most antagonistic to Aiyéró's ideas and known for its xenophobia. Mainly Aiyéró men, living outside their native community, are engaged on the project, and Ofeyi, as ideologue, has been its inspiration. It, like Iriyise's dance performed for the workers on the construction site, celebrates the harmonious creation of power—hydroelectric power—out of natural forces. Later, however, after the Cartel has begun to react to the initiatives of the Aiyéró men and has begun to repress them, Ofeyi passes by Shage Dam on the way to Cross-river. The site is abandoned, the dam only partially finished, and dead bodies—perhaps the men of Aiyéró—lie floating in the artificial lake. The Cartel has begun its massacres. When Ofeyi first sees the crane with its rope suspended over the lake, he recalls a similar scene in Scotland and remembers his reaction to the unfinished bridge there.

It seemed to him then that all unfinished things were sublime—a Western romantic notion to which he had clung until this day at Shage Dam. Now he reevaluates that experience, according to the myth of his own culture: "It all remained unfinished, and not sublime." Ofeyi as the Ogun personality cannot accept the chaos of the abyss as the end of the creative effort. The goal must be to restore order, not aesthetically admire the incomprehensible.

When Ofeyi arrives at the bridge that will carry him into Cross-river, he, like Egbo in *The Interpreters*, bathes himself in the purifying waters. Unlike Egbo, however, he then takes the final plunge into the abyss. He enters Cross-river in search of Iriyise. As he experiences at first hand the horrors of war, he moves deeper and deeper into enemy territory and ends in Temoko Prison. He is there not because he is forced to be but because he wills to be. In the final symbolic act of the abyss, he is knocked unconscious, loses his "individuation," and then wills himself back to life. This unrealistic mythical event accompanies his simultaneous rescue of Iriyise from the prison. Their return to Aiyéró with Ahime and Demakin (the warrior aspect of Ogun) means a temporary defeat for society but a victory for Ofeyi, whose will has overcome the recurring temptation of passivity.

A common complaint against Soyinka, in spite of the high acclaim he receives for his artistry and his patriotism, is his failure to speak realistically to the issues confronting African societies. Not only does his complex, allusive style encourage elitism, but also his characters are intellectuals whose problems and solutions have little direct relationship to the larger society. Whereas Western audiences, especially critics, might be attracted to such a highly individualistic aesthetic, African readers and critics might wish for a voice that is closer to their pitch, that seems to echo their complaints. Certainly, many would wish fervently that one who is perhaps the most talented literary figure on the continent could use his gift to effect real and visible change. Nevertheless, three things must be said about Soyinka as an African spokesman. First, his novels have as their underlying theme the freedom of the individual and the use of that freedom in the interests of society. Second, he insists on African roots and traditional African concepts as rationales and sanctions for human behavior. Finally, Soyinka does not indulge in experimentation for its own sake, nor does he employ fiction merely as a medium for presenting the tensions of contemporary conflict; rather, by incorporating ritual and myth in his novels, he seeks to suggest the very communal sense that must ultimately hold the society together.

Thomas Banks

Other major works
  PLAYS: *The Swamp Dwellers*, 1958; *The Lion and the Jewel*, 1959; *The Invention*, 1959; *The Trials of Brother Jero*, 1960; *A Dance of the Forests*,

1960; *Camwood on the Leaves*, 1960 (radio play); *The Strong Breed*, 1963; *Three Plays*, 1963; *Five Plays*, 1964; *Kongi's Harvest*, 1964; *The Road*, 1965; *Madmen and Specialists*, 1970, revised 1971; *Jero's Metamorphosis*, 1973; *The Bacchae*, 1973 (adaptation of Euripides' play); *Collected Plays*, 1973, 1974 (two volumes); *Death and the King's Horseman*, 1975; *Opera Wonyosi*, 1977 (adaptation of Bertolt Brecht's play *The Threepenny Opera*).

POETRY: *Idanre and Other Poems*, 1967; *Poems from Prison*, 1969; *A Shuttle in the Crypt*, 1972; *Ogun Abibiman*, 1976; *Mandela's Earth and Other Poems*, 1988.

NONFICTION: *The Man Died*, 1972 (autobiography); *Myth, Literature, and the African World*, 1976; *Aké: The Years of Childhood*, 1981 (autobiography); "Nobel Lecture 1986: This Past Must Address Its Present," 1987; *Art, Dialogue, and Outrage: Essays on Literature and Culture*, 1988; *Isarà: A Voyage Around "Essay,"* 1989.

TRANSLATION: *Forest of a Thousand Daemons: A Hunter's Saga*, 1968 (of D. O. Fagunwa's novel *Ogboju Ode Ninu Igbo Irunmale*).

Bibliography

Adelugba, Dapo. *Before Our Very Eyes: Tribute to Wole Soyinka*. Ibadan, Nigeria: Spectrum Books, 1987. This collection of sixteen essays is divided into two parts, the first part consisting of ten personal tributes and the second of six analytical essays. Contains notes on contributors.

Graham-White, Anthony. *The Drama of Black Africa*. New York: Samuel French, 1974. Serves as a comprehensive introduction to the drama of sub-Saharan Africa, from precolonial times to the 1960's, based on European sources. Provides the context for understanding Soyinka's plays, which are discussed in one chapter. Includes notes, appendices on African drama, published plays by African authors, a chronology of African drama, and an index. Contains a preface by Dapo Adelugba.

Jones, Eldred Durosimi. *The Writing of Wole Soyinka*. 1973. Rev. ed. London: Heinemann, 1983. A comprehensive volume which examines the man and his background, one of Soyinka's autobiographies, and his plays, poetry, and fiction. Also includes a bibliography and an index.

Moore, Gerald. "Wole Soyinka: Across the Primeval Gulf." In *Twelve African Writers*. Bloomington: Indiana University Press, 1980. The introduction provides a quick overview of issues in studying African literature. The twelve authors, selected for their longevity as writers, are appraised individually and comparatively. Contains references, a bibliography of primary sources, a suggested reading list, and an index.

Okpu, B. *Wole Soyinka: A Bibliography*. Lagos, Nigeria: Libriservice, 1984. Introduction by F. Odun Balogun. Contains an extensive bibliography of Soyinka's plays, poetry, fiction, nonfiction, and translations, as well as secondary works, reviews, and a name index. A valuable research source.

Palmer, Eustace. "Negritude Rediscovered: A Reading of the Recent Novels of Armah, Ngugi, and Soyinka." *The International Fiction Review* 8 (1981): 1-11. This discussion of the concept of Negritude pays particular attention to three works: Soyinka's *Season of Anomy*, Ngugi wa Thiong'o's *Petals of Blood*, and Ayi Kwei Armah's *Two Thousand Seasons*. Includes notes.

MURIEL SPARK

Born: Edinburgh, Scotland; February 1, 1918

Principal long fiction

The Comforters, 1957; *Robinson*, 1958; *Memento Mori*, 1959; *The Ballad of Peckham Rye*, 1960; *The Bachelors*, 1960; *The Prime of Miss Jean Brodie*, 1961; *The Girls of Slender Means*, 1963; *The Mandelbaum Gate*, 1965; *The Public Image*, 1968; *The Driver's Seat*, 1970; *Not to Disturb*, 1971; *The Hothouse by the East River*, 1973; *The Abbess of Crewe: A Modern Morality Tale*, 1974; *The Takeover*, 1976; *Territorial Rights*, 1979; *Loitering with Intent*, 1981; *The Only Problem*, 1984; *A Far Cry from Kensington*, 1988; *Symposium*, 1990.

Other literary forms

In addition to her novels, Muriel Spark has produced a sizable amount of work in the areas of poetry, the short story, drama, biography, and criticism. Her volumes of poetry include *The Fanfarlo and Other Verse* (1952) and *Collected Poems I* (1967). Her first collection of short stories, entitled *The Go-Away Bird and Other Stories*, appeared in 1958, followed by *Collected Stories I* (1967) and *The Stories of Muriel Spark* (1985). *Voices at Play*, a collection of short stories and radio plays, appeared in 1961, and a play, *Doctors of Philosophy*, was first performed in London in 1962 and published in 1963. Spark's literary partnership with Derek Stanford resulted in their editing *Tribute to Wordsworth* (1950), a collection of essays on the centenary of the poet's death, and *My Best Mary: The Selected Letters of Mary Shelley* (1953). Spark and Stanford also edited *Letters of John Henry Newman* (1957) and coauthored a critical and biographical study of Emily Brontë entitled *Emily Brontë: Her Life and Work* (1953), with Spark contributing the biographical essay. She has produced a study of Mary Shelley, *Child of Light: A Reassessment of Mary Wollstonecraft Shelley* (1951, 1987), and *John Masefield* (1953). Spark also edited *Selected Poems of Emily Brontë* (1952) and *The Brontë Letters* (1954).

Achievements

Critical opinion about Spark's status as a novelist is sharply divided. In general, she has been less highly valued by American critics; Frederick Karl, for example, has dismissed her work as being "light to the point of froth" and says that it has "virtually no content." English critics such as Frank Kermode, Malcolm Bradbury, and David Lodge, on the other hand, consider Spark a major contemporary novelist. Kermode compliments her on being "obsessed" with novelistic form, calls *The Mandelbaum Gate* a work of "profound virtuosity," and considers her to be a "difficult and important artist." Bradbury, who has regarded Spark as an "interesting, and a very amusing, novelist" from the beginning of her career, now thinks that she is also a "very high stylist" whose work in the novella shows a precision and economy of form and style. In a reassessment of *The Prime of Miss Jean Brodie*, Lodge comments on the complex structure of the novel and Spark's successful experimentation with authorial omniscience.

Throughout her career, Spark has been able to combine popular success with critical acclaim. In 1951, she received her first literary award, the *Observer* Story Prize for the Christmas story "The Seraph and the Zambesi." A radio drama based on *The Ballad of Peckham Rye* won the Italia Prize in 1962, and in the same year she was named Fellow of the Royal Society of Literature. In 1965, Spark received the prestigious James Tait Black Memorial Prize for Fiction for the *The Mandelbaum Gate*.

Biography

Muriel Sarah Spark was born in Edinburgh, Scotland, on February 1, 1918, of a Jewish father, Bernard Camberg, and an English mother, Sarah Uezzell Camberg. She attended James Gillespie's School for Girls in Edinburgh, an experience that later formed the background for *The Prime of Miss Jean Brodie*. She lived in Edinburgh until 1937, when she married S. O. Spark and moved to Africa. She was divorced from Spark a year later and, in 1944, returned to England, after having lived in South Africa and Rhodesia. From 1944 to 1946, she worked in the Political Intelligence Department of the British Foreign Office, an experience she later drew upon when writing *The Hothouse by the East River*. Her interest in poetry led to her serving as General Secretary of the Poetry Society in London from 1947 to 1949 and as editor of the *Poetry Review*; in 1949, she introduced a short-lived journal entitled *Forum Stories and Poems*. In the 1950's, she began a successful career as a critic and editor which included books on William Wordsworth, Mary Shelley, Emily Brontë, John Masefield, and John Henry Newman, publishing several of these works with her literary partner and friend Derek Stanford.

The major turning point in Spark's career as a writer occurred in 1954, when she converted to Roman Catholicism. Brought up in the Presbyterian religion, she says that she had "no clear beliefs at all" until 1952, when she became "an Anglican intellectually speaking," although she did not formally join the Anglican Church until late in 1953. The Church of England was, however, a halfway house for Spark, who was an Anglo-Catholic for only nine months before her conversion to Roman Catholicism. She believes that the writings of John Henry Newman were an important factor in her move to the Catholic Church. Her conversion initially caused her a great deal of emotional suffering, and she says that her mind was, for a period of time, "far too crowded with ideas, all teeming in disorder." This feeling of mental chaos gave way later to what she has called "a complete reorganization" of her mind that enabled her to begin writing fiction. Several persons encouraged her to produce a novel, among them Graham Greene and Macmillan and Company, which was looking for new writers at the time; the result was *The Comforters*.

In 1961, Spark traveled to Jerusalem to research the background for *The Mandelbaum Gate*, and, in 1964, moved from her home in London to New York. She lived for less than a year in an apartment close to the United Nations Building, a location which later became the setting for *The Hothouse by the East River*. In 1967, she was awarded the Order of the British Empire and left England to settle in Italy. In 1982, after fifteen years in Rome, she moved to Tuscany; she continues to travel widely.

Analysis

Muriel Spark frequently uses the word "minor" to describe her achievement as a novelist, a term which, in her vocabulary, is not as derogatory as it may at first appear. She believes that the artist is by definition a "minor public servant" and claims that she chooses to write "minor novels deliberately." This characterization of the artist and of her own intentions as a writer reflects her concerns about the novel as a form and the creative process in general, issues which are present throughout her work. She has admitted that while writing her first novel, *The Comforters*, she had difficulty resigning herself to the fact that she was writing a novel, a genre which, in her opinion, was a "lazy way of writing poetry." For Spark at that time, poetry was the only true literature, while the novel was an "inferior way of writing" whose "aesthetic validity" was very much in doubt. Although she has apparently revised her earlier low estimation of the novel, she says that she still thinks of herself as a poet rather than a novelist and believes that her novels are "the novels of a poet."

Spark's distrust of the novel form also results from her suspicions about fiction's relationship to truth; she has said that she is interested in "absolute truth" and that fiction is a "kind of parable" from which a "kind of truth" emerges which should not be confused with fact. The truth which the novel can embody is similar to her definition of "legend" in *Emily Brontë: Her Life and Work*. Speaking of the literary legends which surround a writer such as Emily Brontë, she says that these stories, though not literally true, are "the repository of a vital aspect of truth" which should be accorded respect in their own right. It is imperative, however, for writers and readers to discriminate among types of truth and between life and art, a discrimination that Charmian Colston, the aged novelist in *Memento Mori*, is capable of making. She tells another character that "the art of fiction is very like the practice of deception," and, when asked if the practice of deception in life is also an art, replies, "In life . . . everything is different. Everything is in the Providence of God." Spark, who is careful to maintain this distinction in her statements about her work, has described her own novels as a "pack of lies."

Caroline Rose in *The Comforters*, who shares this distrust of fiction, struggles against being a character in a novel because she resents being manipulated by the novelist. At one point, she describes the author of the fiction as an "unknown, possibly sinister being." The writer's "sinister" nature results from his ability to create fictions which are imaginative versions and extensions of the truth rather than the truth itself; and, perhaps more important, the novelist deprives his characters of their free will and independence. As Patricia Stubbs has observed, Spark perceives a parallel between God and the novelist, and the act of creating fiction is, in a sense, "dabbling in the devil's work."

As a result, Spark's novels are filled with would-be artists and artist-figures, people who attempt to create fictions in real life and consequently bring about discord and mischief. In *The Prime of Miss Jean Brodie*, Miss Brodie begins to view the people around her as characters in a story she is creating and attempts to bring about sexual pairings and heroic deeds in her self-made "plot" with disastrous results. Both Alec Warner in *Memento Mori* and Dougal Douglas in *The Ballad of Peckham Rye* are involved in "research" into the lives of the people around them; Douglas carries his curiosity about others a step further, fictionalizing an autobiography for an actress and later becoming the author of "a lot of cock-eyed books." In two later novels, *The Public Image* and *Territorial Rights*, fictions are devised even more consciously— and are potentially more dangerous. In *The Public Image*, film actress Annabel Christopher is, for the most part, merely the product of a clever publicity campaign with its accompanying lies, distortions, and omissions. After her husband's suicide, she becomes the victim of his well-planned attempt to destroy her career, for he has left behind a group of letters which would impugn her sexual morality and destroy her carefully devised "public image." In *Territorial Rights*, Robert Leaver stages his own kidnaping and sends threatening letters filled with truth and lies to his family and friends. In addition, he leaves fragments of a "novel" he is supposedly writing which contain a sensational mixture of fact and fiction which could hurt many of the people around him. Just as these characters are guilty of trying to manipulate reality by inserting carefully constructed "fictions" into the lives of real people, Sir Quentin Oliver in *Loitering with Intent* overtly plagiarizes a fictional model to accomplish his ends. After reading Fleur Talbot's novel *Warrender Chase*, he begins to orchestrate the lives of the members of the Autobiographical Association according to its plot, an action which causes Fleur to complain that "He's trying to live out my story."

The ubiquitous "listening devices" and spying present in Spark's fiction are another aspect of her fascination with the process of creating fictions. Dougal Douglas, the artist-to-be, sells tape recorders to African witch doctors; the

Abbey in *The Abbess of Crewe* is bugged; and Curran in *Territorial Rights* has a sudden moment of paranoia in a restaurant when he wonders if his fellow diners are all spies armed with "eavesdropping devices." As the servants in *Not to Disturb* realize, recording and preserving experience allows the person doing the recording to alter, and, in a sense, to create reality. Armed with tape recorders and cameras, they are busy creating their own version of the events of an evening which culminates in the deaths of the Baron and Baroness Klopstock and their secretary; the servants are artist-figures, manipulating the plot of the story which they will soon sell to the public media. Spark sees the novelist, like the "typing ghost" who plagues Caroline Rose in *The Comforters*, as an eavesdropper who spies upon his characters and then manipulates their actions in order to create a fiction; and she peoples her novels with characters who are also engaged in this process.

Because Spark is so intent upon acknowledging her fiction as fiction, most of her novels are consciously artificial in both form and content. She has no desire to be a realistic novelist or to write the "long novel"; she said she grew bored writing her only lengthy novel, *The Mandelbaum Gate*, because of its length. Rather, she claims to speak in a "kind of shorthand" in which the narrative voice is curiously impersonal. Not surprisingly, in several novels, among them *Not to Disturb* and *The Driver's Seat*, she has experimented with her own version of the *nouveau roman*. In Spark's fiction, however, unlike that of many of the antinovelists, all details, no matter how arbitrary they at first appear, are ultimately significant. In fact, a word that appears throughout her statements about fiction and in her novels is "economy." In *The Takeover*, the narrator mentions the "intuitive artistic sense of economy" that characterizes the creative person, and Spark has emphasized her belief that the artist should carefully select only the most appropriate details in order to create meaning.

At the same time, because she believes that it is "bad manners to inflict emotional involvement on the reader," she writes novels in which the narrator's witty detachment from the subject matter signifies her goal of creating art which remains distanced from the human suffering it presents. Literature, she believes, should not continue to sympathize with the victims of violence and tyranny; art should instead abandon sentimental depictions of the human condition so that it can "ruthlessly mock" the forces which cause the individual to suffer. She believes that art needs "less emotion and more intelligence" and should aspire to become an art of satire and ridicule. The world, for Spark, is essentially absurd, and "the rhetoric of our time should persuade us to contemplate the ridiculous nature of the reality before us, and teach us to mock it."

Spark's first novel, *The Comforters*, reflects the two pivotal experiences of her life: her conversion to Roman Catholicism and her change as a writer from poet to novelist. Spark has said that in order to overcome her aesthetic skepticism about the novel form, it was necessary for her "to write a novel about somebody writing a novel." In addition, she believes that *The Comforters* is a result of the "complete reorganization" of her mind that followed her conversion and that its theme is "a convert and a kind of psychic upheaval." Caroline Rose, the novel's central character, is in the process of coming to terms with both these issues. A recent convert to Catholicism who dislikes many of her fellow Catholics, Caroline is writing a book called *Form in the Modern Novel* and trying to understand why she has begun to overhear a disembodied "novelist," complete with typewriter, who is writing a novel about her and her friends.

The Comforters is about the battle between the author and her characters, a battle in which Caroline struggles to preserve her free will in the face of the novelist's desire to control the events of the story. Caroline finds the experience of being "written into" someone else's narrative painful, just as her friend Laurence Manders protests that "I dislike being a character in your novel" when he discovers that Caroline is writing fiction which includes the story of their relationship. Caroline believes that it is her "duty" to "hold up the action" of the novel, to "spoil" it, and she asserts her right to make her own decisions, finding, however, that this is usually impossible; the predetermined "plot" of the novelist prevails.

Caroline remains unaware, however, that she in turn is capable of affecting the novel as it is being written. The narrator admits that Caroline's "remarks" continue to interfere with the book and that she does not realize her "constant influence" on the story's development. From Caroline's perspective, she has only partial knowledge of the plot, and she complains that the voices she overhears only give her "small crazy fragments" of a novel in which there may be other characters whom she does not know. In this sense, Caroline is a surrogate for Spark the novelist, a character who "discovers" the plot, as does its creator, while it is being written. As a result, *The Comforters* concludes with Caroline leaving London to write a novel which apparently will be *The Comforters*.

Spark would appear to be working out both the technique and the morality of writing fiction in her first novel. Caroline's fascination with "form in the modern novel" is also Spark's fascination, and Spark writes a story about the problems involved in writing a story: *The Comforters* is about the struggle between the novelist's will to impose form and the continued growth and development of the characters, who begin to become independent entities in the narrative, insisting upon the right to break free of the restraints of plot and situation. One of the reasons Caroline Rose gives for opposing the novelist is that Caroline "happens to be a Christian"; Spark, as a Catholic, is uneasy with the idea of the novelist "playing God" and depriving her characters of choice.

The Comforters is also about Catholicism and the recent convert's attempts to find an identity as a Catholic. Georgina Hogg, the Catholic in the novel whom Caroline particularly despises, symbolizes Caroline's (and Spark's) reservations about individual Catholics. These reservations are not, it should be emphasized, about Catholicism as a religion. Rather, Mrs. Hogg represents a Catholicism which, in the hands of a certain type of individual, becomes simply dogma. Mrs. Hogg, who lacks insight or any true feeling about her religion, uses her sense of self-righteousness to impinge upon the people around her. In the novel, she is called a "sneak," a "subtle tyrant," and a "moral blackmailer," and she is indeed guilty of all these accusations. At one point in the story, Caroline decides that Mrs. Hogg is "not a real-life character . . . merely a gargoyle"; she is so lacking in identity that she literally "disappears" when there are no other people around to perceive her existence. As several characters observe, Georgina Hogg "has no private life," a phrase which ironically underscores her lack of substance as a character and a Catholic.

Mrs. Hogg's lack of identity is a major theme of the novel, and a problem which several other characters share. Helena Manders, when she has a sudden sense of how "exhilarating" it is to be herself, actually perceives her personality as belonging to someone else. Eleanor Hogarth, as Caroline realizes, has completely lost contact with her true personality because she has for so long been satisfied with mimicking others, adopting other roles to play. Caroline's auditory hallucinations are another aspect of this problem, for she feels that her free will as an individual is being taken from her: Is she Caroline Rose, or simply a character in someone else's novel? At the same time, she is obsessed with the identity of what she calls the "typing ghost," at one point making a list entitled "*Possible identity*" which speculates about who the typist-novelist may be—Satan, a woman, a hermaphrodite, or a Holy Soul in Purgatory.

The characters' lack of identity is related to their isolation and inability to communicate with one another. "Is the world," asks Caroline, "a lunatic asylum then? Are we all courteous maniacs discreetly making allowances for everyone else's derangement?" Although she rejects this idea, *The Comforters* certainly depicts a world in which individuals search for an identity while remaining locked into a very subjective set of preconceptions about everything external to them. The way out of this trap, at least for Caroline, is to write a novel, the novel which Spark has actually written. *The Comforters* represents Spark's successful confrontation with and resolution of the issues of Catholicism, creativity, and the novel as a genre. Her interest in the novel as a form and the process of creating fictions has continued throughout her career as a novelist.

In an interview, Spark has said that the eponymous protagonist of *The Prime of Miss Jean Brodie* represents "completely unrealised potentialities," a descriptive phrase which reflects the same ambiguity with which she is treated in the novel. The story of an Edinburgh schoolmistress and her effects on the lives of six of her pupils, *The Prime of Miss Jean Brodie* concentrates on the relationship between Jean Brodie and Sandy Stranger, the student who eventually "betrays" her. Like many other characters in Spark's fiction, Miss Brodie begins to confuse fact and fiction, and it is when Sandy perceives that her teacher has decided that Rose Stanley must begin an affair with art teacher Teddy Lloyd that Sandy realizes that Jean Brodie is no longer playing a game or advancing a theory: "Miss Brodie meant it." As David Lodge notes in his article on the novel in *The Novelist at the Crossroads* (1971), Sandy and Jenny intuitively understand when their fiction, a made-up correspondence between Miss Brodie and music teacher Gordon Lowther, should be buried and forgotten; unlike her students, Jean Brodie does not know when fantasies should be discarded.

In addition to seeing herself as an artist-figure who can manipulate the lives of her students and lovers, Jean Brodie is also guilty, in Sandy's eyes, of serious religious and political errors. Although she has not turned to religion at the time, a very young Sandy is frightened by her vision of all the "Brodie set" in a line headed by their teacher "in unified compliance to the destiny of Miss Brodie, as if God had willed them to birth for that purpose." Later, Sandy is horrified to discover that her former teacher "thinks she is Providence" and that she can see the beginning and the end of all "stories." Jean Brodie's lack of guilt over any of her actions results from her assurance that "God was on her side"; she elects herself to grace with an "exotic suicidal enchantment" which drives her to the excesses that eventually result in her forced retirement. Jean Brodie's view of herself as "above the common moral code," a phrase she applies to Rose, her chosen surrogate for an affair with Teddy Lloyd, is related to her political views as well. An early admirer of Benito Mussolini and Adolf Hitler whom Sandy later characterizes as a "born fascist," she sees herself as duty-bound to shape the personalities and the destinies of the young girls around her. "You are mine," she says to her "set," whom she has chosen to receive what she calls the "fruits of her prime," which will remain with the girls "always," a prophecy which is partially true.

The complexity of *The Prime of Miss Jean Brodie* lies in the fact that Jean Brodie is not simply a villainous character who oversteps her bounds as a teacher and begins to exert a potentially corruptive force on the young people entrusted to her. Although she flirts with Fascism (after the war she calls Hitler "rather naughty"), she at the same time encourages a fierce individualism in her chosen students, who, as the headmistress of the Marcia Blaine School for Girls sadly learns, are totally lacking in "team spirit." She makes good her promise to "put old heads on young shoulders" and creates the "capacity for enthusiasm" for knowledge that remains with several of her students for life. The lecture to her girls on her theory of education—"It means a leading out. To me education is a leading out of what is already there in the pupil's soul. . . . Never let it be said that I put ideas into your heads"—is, like the portrait of Jean Brodie that Spark presents in the novel, open to several interpretations. Although in the later years of her prime, Miss Brodie *does* attempt to put "ideas" into the girls' heads, at the same time she bequeaths to her students a knowledge of and sensitivity to art, culture, and ideas that would have been impossible in a more conventional educational situation.

Just as *The Prime of Miss Jean Brodie* is about "unrealised potentialities," Miss Brodie also communicates to her students a knowledge of the unlimited potential inherent in all experience. In her late thirties, Jenny Gray has an experience that reawakens a memory of her "sense of the hidden possibility in all things" that she felt as an eleven-year-old student under the tutelage of Jean Brodie. More important, however, is the teacher's influence on Sandy Stranger. In his book on Spark, Derek Stanford says that "Truth, for Muriel Spark, implies rejection," and Sandy laments in the novel that she has had nothing, particularly in the religious realm, to react against or reject. Jean Brodie finally provides this catalyst, and Sandy's decision to "put a stop" to her results from a variety of reasons: her moral indignation over Miss Brodie's "plans" for Rose and Joyce Emily, sexual jealousy of Teddy Lloyd's continued infatuation with her teacher, and her awakening sense of Christian morals.

As an adult, however, Sandy acknowledges that Jean Brodie was her most important formative influence and in a sense responsible for the course her life has taken. Her conversion to Catholicism and taking of the veil are the result of her affair with Teddy Lloyd, an affair she instigates in order to subvert Jean Brodie's plans. Although Spark does not indicate the exact subject of the psychological treatise that has made Sandy famous, other than the fact that it concerns the nature of "moral perception," its title, "The Transfiguration of the Commonplace," reveals that it in some way deals with the mind's ability to alter everyday reality. Clearly, this topic owes a debt to Jean Brodie's communication to her students of the endless "possibilities" which surrounded them and is a reflection of Jean Brodie's constantly changing nature in the novel. The narrator observes that, unlike her colleagues, Miss Brodie is in a "state of fluctuating development"; like her students, her "nature was growing under their eyes, as the girls themselves were under formation." One element of Jean Brodie's "prime" is her nonstatic personality, and the problem, of course, is the direction in which the changes take place. As the narrator notes, "the principles governing the end of her prime would have astonished herself at the beginning of it."

In *The Prime of Miss Jean Brodie*, Spark is at the height of her powers as a novelist, and nowhere else in her fiction is she more in control of her subject. The "flash-forwards" which occur throughout the novel cause the reader to concentrate on the characters' motivations and interrelationships rather than on any intricacies of the plot, and Spark makes use of the principle of "economy" which she so values on almost every page, providing only the most telling details of the story while refraining, for the most part, from any authorial interpretation. In fact, the idea of economy is an important thematic element in the book. Sandy is first fascinated by the economy of Jean Brodie's fusing her tales of her dead lover, Hugh, with her current associations with Gordon Lowther and Teddy Lloyd, and later she is angered and intrigued by the economy of the art teacher's paintings, which make Jean Brodie's students resemble their teacher. When Sandy betrays Miss Brodie to the headmistress, she uses this principle after concluding that "where there was a choice of various courses the most economical was the best." Both in form and style, *The Prime of Miss Jean Brodie* shows Spark utilizing her own "intuitive artistic sense of economy."

In *The Driver's Seat*, Spark writes her revisionist version of the *nouveau roman*. She has said that she disagrees with the philosophical tenets of the antinovel, and she adopts many of its techniques to prove the invalidity of its philosophy. Although *The Driver's Seat* initially appears to be filled with randomly chosen, objectively described phenomena, ultimately the novel denies the entire concept of contingency. As Frank Kermode states in *The Sense of an Ending* (1966), Spark's fiction is not about any kind of "brutal chaos" but rather presents a "radically non-contingent reality to be dealt with in purely novelistic terms." Every event, every description becomes, in the light of the ending of *The Driver's Seat*, significant.

The novel concerns a young woman named Lise who leaves her home in northern Europe to travel south. Spark carefully fails to specify which cities are involved in order to create the same impersonal, anonymous air in the novel that characterizes Lise's world in general. The purpose of her journey is to find a man to murder her, and in this story Spark inverts the typical thriller: the "victim" relentlessly stalks her murderer and finally "forces" him to act. Lise, who has abandoned the sterile loneliness of her former existence symbolized by her apartment, which "looks as if it were uninhabited," takes control of her life for the first time and decides to take the most dramatic final step possible. In the opening scene, she shouts at a salesgirl who attempts to sell her a dress made of nonstaining fabric because, having already decided that she is to be stabbed to death, she wishes for clothing which will provide the more lurid touch of bloodstains. At the conclusion of the scene, Lise again shouts at the salesgirl "with a look of satisfaction at her own dominance over the situation," and the remainder of the novel is about Lise's carefully planned murder and the trail of information and clues she leaves for Interpol all across Europe.

Unlike Caroline Rose in *The Comforters*, whose response to being a character in a novel is to write a novel about characters in a novel, Lise actually wrests control of the plot from the narrator, who is forced to admit ignorance of her thoughts and intentions. "Who knows her thoughts? Who can tell?"

asks the narrator, who is even unsure as to whether or not Lise tints her hair or the reason she attracts so much attention. As a result, the narrator is forced to give only external information, but this information is, as the reader begins to realize, all pertinent to the outcome of the novel. Only at the conclusion, after Lise's death, does the narrator seem privy to the interior knowledge accessible to the omniscient author.

One of the most important themes in *The Driver's Seat* is, as in many other Spark novels, the inability of people to communicate with one another. In the majority of the conversations, no logical connections are made between the participants, who remain isolated in their own worlds of obsessional concerns. It would even appear that the more sane the individual, the less likely it is that any communication can take place. Instead, it is the more psychotic characters who are capable of nonverbal, intuitive understanding. Lise realizes immediately, as does Richard, that he is the man who is capable of murdering her, and he initially avoids any conversation with her. The three men who do converse with her, Bill, Carlos, and the sickly looking man on the plane, are not, as she phrases it, "her type"; this is because they attempt to communicate verbally with her. As Lise says of the salesman in the department store, "Not my man at all. He tried to get familiar with me. . . . The one I'm looking for will recognize me right away for the woman I am, have no fear of that." The verb "sense," which is used several times in the novel, signifies the subterranean, psychotic apprehension of other people which is the only perception taking place in *The Driver's Seat*.

Although most of Mrs. Friedke's conversations with Lise have the same illogical, uncommunicative structure that characterizes the other dialogues, she does momentarily enter Lise's realm of supernatural perception. She buys a paper knife for her nephew Richard similar to the one Lise decides against purchasing at the beginning of her journey, and this gift becomes the weapon Richard uses to murder Lise. She also prophetically insists that "you and my nephew are meant for each other . . . my dear, you are the person for my nephew." It is at this point that Lise reveals how she will recognize the man for whom she is searching.

In a phrase that tells a great deal about her past life, she says that she will know him not as a feeling of "presence" but as a "lack of absence." Malcolm Bradbury, in his essay on Spark in *Possibilities: Essays on the State of the Novel* (1973), says that Spark's fiction "conveys significant absences, a feeling of omission, and so has considerable resemblances to a good deal of contemporary art, including the *nouveau roman*." Lise's search for a "lack of absence" is a statement about the emptiness and lack of meaning in her own existence and the type of novel Spark has chosen to write about her: the form of the antinovel is used to comment both on the psychosis of the main character and the failure of the *nouveau roman* to deal with the ultimate significance of phenomena. In the *nouveau roman*, the present tense frequently signifies the meaninglessness and ephemerality of events; in *The Driver's Seat*, the present tense is used to create a world of terrifying inevitability in which the smallest details become integral elements in Lise's carefully plotted death.

Spark calls *The Driver's Seat* "a study, in a way, of self-destruction," but also admits that the novel is impossible for her to describe. She says that she became so frightened while writing the story that she was forced to enter a hospital in order to complete it. The fear the novel inspired in her—and many readers—cannot be explained simply by Lise's self-destructiveness; Lise's decision to assert herself, to play god with her life independent of any control by the novelist or a higher power, also contributes to the frightening dimension of the novel. Spark, who has said that she believes that "events are providentially ordered," creates a character who decides to *become* providence and the author of her own story; unlike Jean Brodie, who mistakenly thinks she can see the "beginning and the end" of all stories, Lise successfully orchestrates the novel's conclusion.

In *Loitering with Intent*, Spark's heroine, novelist Fleur Talbot, frequently quotes from Benvenuto Cellini's *The Autobiography of Benvenuto Cellini* (c. 1558-1560): "All men . . . who have done anything of merit, or which verily has a semblance of merit . . . should write the tale of their life with their own hand." *Loitering with Intent* is the fictional autobiography of its "author," Fleur Talbot, and a meditation by Spark on her own career as a novelist; it is, in addition, a meditation on the creative process and the relationship between fiction and autobiography. Spark shows that she has come a long way from her early distrust of the novel: *Loitering with Intent* is a paean to the artistic, fiction-making sensibility. Although the habitual tension between life and art and the danger of confusing the two are still present in this novel, Spark firmly comes down on the side of art, defending it against individuals who would seek to "steal" its myth and pervert its truth.

Fleur Talbot frequently comments on "how wonderful it is to be an artist and a woman in the twentieth century." At the conclusion, she admits that she has been "loitering with intent"; that is, she has used her observations about the people and events around her as fictional material, taking joy both in the comic and tragic occurrences in the lives of the individuals who become characters in her own "autobiography." "I rejoiced in seeing people as they were," she says, and the word "rejoice" occurs many times in the novel as Fleur repeatedly uses Cellini's phrase, saying that she "went on her way rejoicing." In her later life she is accused by her friend Dottie of "wriggling out of real life," but Fleur makes no apologies for the way in which she handles the relationship between her life and her creativity; instead, *Loitering with Intent* calls into question the use "real" people make of the fictions of others.

Fleur becomes the secretary of Sir Quentin Oliver, head of the spurious Autobiographical Association he has formed in order to bring people together to compose their memoirs. Like the character of Warrender Chase in the novel Fleur is in the process of completing, Sir Quentin begins to exert a devastating influence on the Association's members, psychologically manipulating them not for blackmailing purposes but for the enjoyment of pure power. Instead of encouraging them to fictionalize their autobiographies, as Fleur attempts to do, Sir Quentin begins to fictionalize their lives with tragic results. Fleur says that

> I was sure . . . that Sir Quentin was pumping something artificial into their real lives instead of on paper. Presented fictionally, one could have done something authentic with that poor material. But the inducing them to express themselves in life resulted in falsity.

Fiction, when acknowledged as fiction, can help the individual to comprehend reality more clearly, as Fleur notes when she tells a friend that she will have to write several more chapters of *Warrender Chase* before she will be able to understand the events of the Autobiographical Association. In the same way, she says that one can better know one's friends if they are imaginatively pictured in various situations. Sir Quentin, however, inserts "fictions," frequently stories and events taken from Fleur's novel, into the lives of the Association's members.

The relationship between Sir Quentin and Fleur symbolizes the battle between life and art that is waged in *Loitering with Intent*, for Fleur accuses him of "using, stealing" her myth, "appropriating the spirit" of her legend, and trying to "live out the story" she creates in *Warrender Chase*. Although she believes that it is wrong for Sir Quentin to take her "creation" from her, she in turn believes that he may well be a creation of hers, particularly when he begins to resemble her character Warrender Chase as the story progresses. She takes pride in saying that she could almost "have invented" Sir Quentin and that at times she feels as if she *has* invented him; in fact, this feeling so persists that she begins to wonder if it is Warrender Chase who is the "real man" on whom she has partly based the fictional character of Sir Quentin. From Fleur's point of view, this kind of inversion of life and art is necessary and productive for the artistic process and is not dangerous because it results in a bona fide fiction that acknowledges itself as fiction; Sir Quentin's appropriation of her "myth," however, is dangerous because he refuses to acknowledge the fictiveness of his creation. One irony of this situation is editor Revisson Doe's refusal to publish *Warrender Chase* because it too closely resembles the activities of the Autobiographical Association: Sir Quentin's literal and figurative theft of Fleur's novel almost results in its never becoming a work of art available to the public.

The relationship between life and art has another dimension in *Loitering with Intent*. In this novel, Spark is also concerned with the psychic potential of the artist, the ability of the creative imagination to foresee the future in the process of creating fictions. Just as Fleur remarks that writing a novel or imagining her friends in ficitional situations helps her to understand them better, so does the artist often predict the future while constructing a work of art. At the end of the novel, Dottie admits that Fleur had "foreseen it all" in *Warrender Chase*, and the events of *Loitering with Intent* do bear an eerie resemblance to the plot of Fleur's first novel. In her book on Emily Brontë, Spark said that "Poetic experience is . . . such that it may be prophetic." In *Loitering with Intent*, Fleur uses reality as raw material for her novel, while Sir Quentin attempts to use art to tamper with the lives of real people; at another level, however, Fleur's poetic imagination perceives and creates future events.

Loitering with Intent also permits Spark to look back on her life as a novelist and defend many of her fictional techniques. Fleur's philosophy of art is, to a great degree, Spark's philosophy, and Fleur's descriptions and explanations of her craft could easily be addressed by Spark directly to her readers. Like Spark, Fleur is a believer in economy in art, observing "how little one needs . . . to convey the lot, and how a lot of words . . . can convey so little." Fleur does not believe in authorial statements about the motives of her characters, or in being "completely frank" with the reader; in fact, "complete frankness is not a quality that favours art." She defends herself against the charge of writing novels that are called "exaggerated" by critics and states that her fiction presents "aspects of realism." The novel, she believes, is not a documentary transcription of reality but should always seek to transform its subject. "I'm an artist, not a reporter," she informs her readers.

Fleur also answers the critics who in the past have accused Spark of treating her material in a flippantly detached manner. She says that she treats the story of Warrender Chase with a "light and heartless hand" which is her method when giving a "perfectly serious account of things" because to act differently would be hypocritical: "It seems to me a sort of hypocrisy for a writer to pretend to be undergoing tragic experiences when obviously one is sitting in relative comfort with a pen and paper or before a typewriter." At one point in the novel, Spark even challenges the "quality" of her readers, having her narrator remark that she hopes the readers of her novels are of "good quality" because "I wouldn't like to think of anyone cheap reading my books."

The most significant theme of *Loitering with Intent*, however, is joy: the joy the artist takes in the everyday reality that contributes to the imaginative act, and the euphoria the artist feels in the act of creation. Spark has indeed traveled a great distance from her early suspicions of the fiction-making process and of the novel as form.

In her three novels since *Loitering with Intent—The Only Problem*, *A Far Cry from Kensington*, and *Symposium*—Spark has continued to play variations of her characteristic themes. *The Only Problem* centers on the problem of evil: how can a just God "condone the unspeakable sufferings of the world"? Spark's protagonist, Harvey Gotham, an eccentric Canadian millionaire, wrestles with this question in a treatise on the Book of Job. Harvey's study is repeatedly interrupted as a consequence of the escapades of his young wife, Effie, who joins a terrorist group, kills a French policeman, and is herself eventually shot and killed by the police during a raid on a terrorist hideout. The intrusion of these events helps Harvey to appreciate the ultimate inscrutability of the human condition. Here again Spark celebrates the fiction-making process: in contrast to scholars who attempt to rationalize Job's story or abstract the philosophical issues from it, Harvey recognizes the unique power to the story itself. Spark's novel is thus a "commentary" on Job that remains true to the spirit of the original.

A Far Cry from Kensington, like *Loitering with Intent*, draws on Spark's experiences in postwar London. *A Far Cry from Kensington* is a retrospective first-person narrative; from the vantage point of the 1980's, the narrator recalls events which took place in 1954 and 1955. She was then in her late twenties, a war widow who had married at age eighteen a man whom she had met only a month before. Throughout the narrative other characters address her as Mrs. Hawkins (her married name), rather than by her given name, and she is regarded as a reliable confidante—in part, she suggests, because she was then rather fat. (As she loses weight, she begins to lose the roles which others have assigned to her.)

The backdrop of the story is the London publishing scene, especially its dubious fringe. The narrator's encounters with a variety of publishers and literary hangers-on are deftly sketched; also figuring in the plot are devotees of "radionics," a pseudoscience employing a device similar to Wilhelm Reich's orgone box. In particular, Mrs. Hawkins jousts with a hack writer and an adept of radionics, Hector Bartlett, whom she dubs a *pisseur de copie*. Initially, this conflict might seem to be merely a matter of aesthetics, and Bartlett—with his absurd pretensions and truly awful writing—merely a figure of comedy, yet he is shown to be an agent of evil, responsible for the death of a troubled woman. Unsettled by this mixture of nostalgia and satire, light comedy and metaphysical probing, the reader is never allowed to become comfortable. Evidently, this is Spark's intention.

Symposium, focusing on a dinner party in Islington, offers a similarly unsettling mixture, for which the reader is duly prepared by an epigraph from Plato's *Symposium* that suggests the interdependence of comedy and tragedy. There is talk of the "evil eye" (reminiscent of the occult machinations of Hector Bartlett in *A Far Cry from Kensington*). The concept is absurd, and yet as the narrative progresses there is evidence that one of the women present at the party genuinely possesses this maleficent power. In this novel, more than ever, Spark manipulates her characters with detachment: the reader is always aware that this is a performance. Yet if Spark's novels are coolly ironic entertainments, they are also oblique parables which explore with obsessive persistence the nature of evil.

Angela Hague

Other major works

SHORT FICTION: *The Go-Away Bird and Other Stories*, 1958; *Voices at Play*, 1961 (with radio plays); *Collected Stories I*, 1967; *The Stories of Muriel Spark*, 1985.

PLAY: *Doctors of Philosophy*, 1963.

POETRY: *The Fanfarlo and Other Verse*, 1952; *Selected Poems of Emily Brontë*, 1952 (edited); *Collected Poems I*, 1967.

NONFICTION: *Tribute to Wordsworth*, 1950 (edited with Derek Stanford); *Child of Light: A Reassessment of Mary Wollstonecraft Shelley*, 1951, 1987; *Emily Brontë: Her Life and Work*, 1953 (with Derek Stanford); *John Masefield*, 1953; *My Best Mary: The Selected Letters of Mary Shelley*, 1953 (edited with Derek Stanford); *The Brontë Letters*, 1954 (edited); *Letters of John Henry Newman*, 1957 (edited with Derek Stanford).

CHILDREN'S LITERATURE: *The Very Fine Clock*, 1958.

Bibliography

Bold, Alan, ed. *Muriel Spark: An Odd Capacity for Vision*. Totowa, N.J.: Barnes & Noble Books, 1984. A compilation of essays by various authors, each with a different slant, which offers a comprehensive introduction to Spark. Contains well-selected and lively criticism.

Kemp, Peter. *Muriel Spark*. New York: Barnes & Noble Books, 1975. A lucid and sensitive study of Spark's work up to 1974. Contains an excellent analysis of her novels from *The Comforters* to *The Hothouse by the East River*.

Richmond, Velma Bourgeois. *Muriel Spark*. New York: Frederick Ungar, 1984. A valuable resource on Spark which includes commentary on her plays. Chapter 8, "The Darkening Vision," gives sound interpretations of *The Driver's Seat*, *The Public Image*, and *Not to Disturb*.

Walker, Dorothea. *Muriel Spark*. Boston: Twayne, 1988. An informative and relatively current study on the main themes of Spark's work, with emphasis given to the wit and humor of her characters. The extensive bibliography is particularly helpful.

Whittaker, Ruth. *The Faith and Fiction of Muriel Spark*. New York: St. Martin's Press, 1982. A definitive look at Spark and the relationship between the secular and the divine in her work. This scholarly study, with its extensive bibliography, is a fine source for reference and critical material on Spark.

CHRISTINA STEAD

Born: Rockdale, Australia; July 17, 1902
Died: Sydney Australia; March 31, 1983

Principal long fiction

Seven Poor Men of Sydney, 1934; *The Beauties and Furies*, 1936; *House of All Nations*, 1938; *The Man Who Loved Children*, 1940, 1965; *For Love Alone*, 1944; *Letty Fox: Her Luck*, 1946; *A Little Tea, A Little Chat*, 1948; *The People with the Dogs*, 1952; *Dark Places of the Heart*, 1966; *The Little Hotel*, 1974; *Miss Herbert: The Suburban Wife*, 1976; *I'm Dying Laughing: The Humourist*, 1986.

Other literary forms

Christina Stead began her career with a volume of short stories, *The Salzburg Tales* (1934), and she has contributed short stories to both literary and popular magazines. A posthumous collection, *Ocean of Story: The Uncollected Short Stories of Christina Stead*, was published in 1985. Her volume *The Puzzleheaded Girl* (1967) is a collection of four novellas. Her other literary output includes reviews and translations of several novels from the French. She also edited two anthologies of short stories, one with her husband William Blake. The *Christina Stead Anthology*, edited by Jean B. Read, was published in 1979.

Achievements

Stead is considered to be in the first rank of Australian novelists; in 1974, she received Australia's Patrick White Award. One of Stead's novels, *The Man Who Loved Children*, received special critical acclaim. Stead resisted critics' attempts to represent her as a feminist writer, but she has received attention from feminist critics for her depiction of women constricted by their social roles.

Biography

Christina Ellen Stead's parents were David George Stead, a naturalist and fisheries economist, and Ellen Butters Stead, who died of a perforated appendix when Christina was two years old. David Stead then married Ada Gibbons, a society woman, and they had six children to whom Stead became big sister. Stead trained at the Sydney Teachers College, where she became a demonstrator in experimental psychology. As a public school teacher, she taught abnormal children and administered psychological tests in the schools. Stead suffered voice strain, however, and she later saw it as a symptom of her being unfit for the work. Like Teresa Hawkins in *For Love Alone*, Stead studied typing and shorthand to embark on a business career. In 1928, she left Sydney, sailing on the *Oronsay* for England. In London and Paris, she worked as a grain clerk and a bank clerk, experiences that became background for her novel about finance, *House of All Nations*. By that time, Stead had met the economist and writer, William Blake (born William Blech), whom she married in 1952. Stead settled in the United States from 1937 to 1946, publishing several novels and working for a time as a writer with Metro-Goldwyn-Mayer in Hollywood. At the end of World War II, Stead returned to Europe with Blake, living in various places on the Continent and returning to England when she feared that she was losing her feel for the English language. In 1968, Stead's husband died, and a few years later, in 1974, she returned to live with one of her brothers in Australia. She died in Sydney on March 31, 1983, at the age of eighty.

Analysis

Christina Stead was preeminently a novelist of character. She identified herself as a psychological writer, involved with the drama of the person. Her stories develop out of the dynamics of characters asserting their human energy and vigor and developing their wills. Stead established personality and communicated its energy and vitality through her creation of a distinctive language for each character. This individuating language is explored in the characters' dialogues with one another (Sam Pollit talking his fantastic baby talk to his children), in their interior monologues (Teresa Hawkins, walking miles to and from work, meditating on her need to find a life beyond the surface social conventions), and in letters (the letter to Letty Fox from her former lover, who wants his money back after she has had an abortion). The language establishes the sense of an individual person with obsessions and characteristic blindnesses. One gets to know the quality of the mind through the texture of the language. Christopher Ricks expressed Stead's accomplishment by saying that she re-creates the way people talk to themselves "in the privacy of [their] skulls." His phrase gives the sense of how intimately and deeply the language belongs to the person: it is in the skull and the bone.

In her novel *Letty Fox*, Stead has Letty sum up her adventures to date by saying, "On s'engage et puis on voit." The statement (roughly translated as "one gets involved and then one sees") is an existentialist one that reconciles what critics see as two forces in Stead's fiction: a preoccupation with character that links her to nineteenth century novelists, and an analysis of social, psychological, and economic structures behind individual lives that links Stead to her contemporaries.

The phrase "On s'engage et puis on voit" sums up Stead's method. First, she immerses the reader in the particular atmosphere of the character's mind and world; only then does she lead the reader to see a significance behind the individual passion. The phrase implies that one cannot see clearly by being disengaged, looking down on the human spectacle with the detachment of an objective physical scientist. Instead, one must become part of that experience, seeing it as a participant, in order to understand its reality. Some of the constant preoccupations of Stead's characters include family, love, marriage, money, and individual power.

Stead's masterpiece, as critics agree, is the larger-than-life depiction of a family, *The Man Who Loved Children*. Out of print for twenty-five years, the book has enjoyed a second life because of a partly laudatory review by the poet Randall Jarrell that was included as an introduction when the novel was reissued. *The Man Who Loved Children* immerses its readers in the life of the Pollit family, in its swarming, buzzing intimacy. The father, Sam Pollit, is a garrulous idealist who advocates eugenics for the unfit but who fantasizes for himself babies of every race and a harem of wives who would serve his domestic comfort. On the surface, Sam's passions are his humanitarian ideals and his love for his children, but his underlying passion is what Geoffrey Chaucer said women's was—his own way or his own will. Sam is an egotistical child himself; he sees only what he wants to see. His characteristic talk is his overblown, high-sounding rhetoric expressing schemes to right the world and the fanciful, punning baby talk, whining and wheedling, that he uses with the children.

Henny, wife to Sam and stepmother to Louisa, is Sam's compulsive antagonist, worn down with childbearing and the struggle to manage the overextended household. Henny's passion is to survive, to fight dirt and debt and the intermittent sexuality that involves her in continual childbearing. Henny's characteristic talk is insult and denunciation, castigating with graphic details and metaphors the revolting sights, sounds, smells, tastes, and touches that assault her. Stead emphasizes Henny's eyes in descriptions of the fierce eyeballs in her sockets and her mouth in descriptions of her incessantly drinking tea and mouthing insults.

Stead's way of explaining the unbridgeable gap between the minds and sensibilities of the marriage partners is to say that they have no words in common. Sam's abstraction can never communicate with Henny's particularity. They have no words that they understand mutually, and so for most of the book the two characters communicate with each other only through messages relayed by the children or by terse notes concerning household necessities. In spite of that essential gap, a sixth child is conceived and born to the couple during the novel, and the resources of the household are further strained, finally to the breaking point.

What brings the family to destruction is a complex of causes, many of which are fundamentally economic. The death of David Collyer, Henny's once rich father, is a blow to the family's fortunes. The family loses its home, and Henny's creditors no longer expect that her father will pay her debts. Collyer's death also leaves Sam without a political base in his government job, and Sam's enemies move to oust him. The money crisis is intensified by Sam's refusal to fight for his job. Instead, he retires to their new ramshackle home to do repairs and to play with the children. Sam grandly waits to be exonerated, while Henny struggles to keep the family fed and clothed.

Another cause of the breakup of the family is the birth of Sam and Henny's newest baby. Part of the trouble is economic: the new child means more expenses when Henny had promised her money-conscious eldest son Ernie that there would be no more children. The birth also brings an anonymous letter charging falsely that the child is not Sam's because Sam has been away in Malaya for several months. The letter, filled with spite, probably has been sent by one of Henny's disappointed creditors, but it exacerbates the mutual resentment of the couple and drives them closer and closer to serious violence against each other. (The pregnancy has not only invaded Henny's body and multiplied her worries, but it has also cost her her lover, who deserts her when he hears of the pregnancy. Henny is more than ever in Sam's power.)

A pivotal character in the fierce struggle between the parents is Louisa, oldest daughter of Sam and stepdaughter of Henny. Louisa's emergence from childhood upsets the hierarchy of the household. The man who "loved children" does not love them when they question his authority and threaten his position as "Sam the Bold," leader of the band of merry children. In retaliation, Sam calls Louisa names from "Loogoobrious" to "Bluebeak." In disputing Sam's ability to make it rain (his cosmic power), Louisa and Ernie— who is quick to jump in with what he has learned in school about evaporation—introduce norms from the world outside the family.

By the end of the novel, the family tears itself apart. Sam is unconsciously comparing himself to Christ and seeing Nature as his bride, while he says that women are "cussed" and need to be "run" and that he will send Henny away and keep the children. When Louisa asks for freedom to be sent to her dead mother's relatives in Harper's Ferry, Sam says that he will never let her leave, that she must not get married but must stay and help him with the children and his work. The quarreling between the parents increases until Louisa thinks that they will kill each other. The quarrels become physical battles, and Henny screams to the children to save her from their father. In despair, Ernie makes a dummy out of his clothes and hangs himself in effigy. Sam teases and humiliates the children, insisting that they stay up all night and help him boil down a marlin, an image that is reminiscent of Henny with its staring eye, deep in its socket, and its wound in its vitals.

Louisa sees the two parents as passionate and selfish, inexorably destroying each other and the children, completely absorbed in their "eternal married hate." To save the children, Louisa considers poisoning both parents. Sam provides both the rationale, that the unfit should make room for the fit, and the means, cyanide that he ghoulishly describes as the bringer of death. Louisa succeeds in getting the grains of cyanide into only one large cup of tea when Henny notices what she has done and drinks it, exonerating Louisa and saying "damn you all." Even with Henny dead and Louisa's confession of her plan and its outcome, Sam refuses to believe her and refuses to let her go. Louisa's only escape is to run away, thus seizing her freedom.

The power of the novel derives partly from the archetypal nature of the conflicts—between parents and children for independence; between man and woman, each for his own truth and identity; between parents for their children, their objects of greatest value. The power also results from the particularity of the characterization, the metaphors that Stead employs to communicate the nature of each family member, and the astounding sense of individual language mirroring opposed sensibilities.

The epigraph to another Stead novel, *Letty Fox: Her Luck*, says that one can get experience only through foolishness and blunders. The method which Letty follows in her adventures puts her in the stream of picaresque heroes; the novel's subtitle, "her luck," makes more sense with reference to the notion of a submission to experience, to one's fate, than it does with reference to the common meaning of "luck" as "good fortune." Letty's "luck" is that she survives and learns something about the ways of the world.

Stead once said that in *For Love Alone*, the novel which preceded *Letty Fox*, she wrote about a young girl of no social background, who tries to learn about love, and that readers did not understand the story. Thus, in *Letty Fox*, she gave American readers a story which they could understand: the story of a modern American girl searching for love and trying to obtain status through marriage.

In both novels, the social structure tells young women that they have no valid identity except through the men they marry. In *For Love Alone*, Teresa Hawkins, like her friends, fears becoming an old maid. Even though Letty Fox has had a series of lovers and a series of responsible, interesting jobs, she does not feel validated without the security of marriage.

This firmly held conventional belief is belied by Letty's own family situation. Her beloved father Solander has a mistress, Persia, with whom he has lived faithfully for many years. The family women wonder how Persia can hold Solander without a paper and without a child. On the other hand, Mathilde, Letty's mother, has the marriage title but little else. She has three daughters—Letty, Jacky, and the much younger Andrea, conceived in a late reconciliation attempt—but Persia has Solander.

Like the picaresque hero, on her own, Letty learns the ways of the world. She truly loves Luke Adams, who tantalizes her with pretended concern for her youth and innocence and fans her fascination with him. She lives for a summer with a married man and has an abortion for which she must repay him. Originally confused by Lucy Headlong's interest in her, Letty refuses a lesbian affair with her. Letty sees a range of choices in the lives of the women around her: from her sister Jacky, in love with an elderly scientist, to her younger sister Andrea, sharing the early maternal experience of her friend.

Letty wants the security of marriage, but the men she knows do not want to make serious commitments. In *For Love Alone*, Teresa remarks on the short season for the husband hunt, with no time for work or extended study. In the marriage market for the comparatively long season of seven years, Letty does not catch a husband, even when her vicious cousin Edwige does.

Except in the matter of marriage, Letty trusts her own responses and takes credit for her own integrity. When her lover Cornelius is about to leave her for his mistress in Europe and his wife, Letty faces him with the truth of relationships from a woman's point of view. She tells Cornelius that she has got ambition and looks. She works for men, and she is their friend. She suffers without crying for help and takes responsibility for her life. Yet she sees men run after worthless, shiftless women and honor the formality of marriage when there is no substance to their relationships with them. All of these facts might be just part of the injustice of the world, but Cornelius and many other men Letty knows also expect that she should be their lover and yet admit that there is no love involved but only a relationship of mutual convenience. Like the British poet William Blake, Letty sees prostitution as an invention of men who have tried to depersonalize the most intimate relationship between people. Letty affirms the reality of the sexual experience in its intimacy and its bonding.

With all her clear sight and all her independence, however, Letty does not feel safe and validated until she is married to her longtime friend Bill Van Week. Ironically, Letty marries Bill when he has been disinherited by his millionaire father, so the security Letty attains is not financial. In summing up her life to date, Letty does not claim total honesty, but—like a typical picaresque hero—she does claim grit. She says that with her marriage, her journey has begun. Here Stead limits the awareness of her character. At the end of the novel, Letty says that marriage gives her not social position but self-respect. In this retreat, Letty joins the social mainstream but denies her individual past experience. Self-respect is not an award; it is not issued like a diploma or a license. Letty, who may stand up very well to the practical problems of real life with Bill, is by no means liberated, and her awareness is finally limited.

Published in Britain as *Cotter's England*, *Dark Places of the Heart* is an exploration of the influence of Nellie Cotter Cook on the people around her—her family, friends, and acquaintances. A central concern is the relationship between Nellie and her brother Tom, a jealous relationship with which Nellie seems obsessed. Like Michael and Catherine Baguenault, the brother-sister pair in *Seven Poor Men of Sydney*, Nellie and Tom seem too close to each other, too intimately attuned to each other's sensibilities. In their battles, Nellie calls Tom a man out of a mirror, who weaves women into his life and then eats their hearts away. Tom calls Nellie a spider, who tries to suspend a whole human being on a spindly thread of sympathy. Tom also criticizes

Nellie's bent for soul-saving, saying that it gets people into trouble.

The motif of hunger and starvation runs through the novel. When Tom brings a chicken to the family home in Bridgehead, no one in the family knows how to cook it. When George goes away to Italy, he writes that Nellie should buy cookery books, a suggestion that she scorns. Seemingly exhibiting a strange kind of hunger, Nellie craves followers who will make her destiny. Nellie and Tom's battles often center on Tom's relationships with women, which precipitate a tug-of-war between Nellie and Tom for the love of the woman in question. Many allusions and incidents in the novel suggest that Nellie's interest is lesbian. Nellie begins her luring of these women by demanding their friendship and, ultimately, by forcing them to prove their loyalty through death. Such demands literalize the existentialist definition of love, that the lover puts the beloved beyond the value of the world and his life, making that beloved his standard of value, his absolute. The demand is messianic, and in this novel the cost is the suicide of Caroline Wooler, after her witnessing what seems to be a lesbian orgy. Caroline climbs a building under construction and jumps to her death.

Nellie views Caroline's death as a personal triumph. At the end of the novel, with her husband dead, Nellie goes with the window-washer Walter to a temple, a "Nabob villa," where she explores "problems of the unknowable." Like Sam Pollit, who at his worst compared himself to Christ, Nellie Cook is drawn finally to outright mysticism, an interest that combines, in Nellie's case at least, a fascination with death, a craving for a high destiny, and an uncontrollable urge to manipulate other people. It seems that for Stead, the "dark places of the heart" make people dissatisfied with their humanity.

Kate Begnal

Other major works

SHORT FICTION: *The Salzburg Tales*, 1934; *The Puzzleheaded Girl*, 1967; *Ocean of Story: The Uncollected Short Stories of Christina Stead*, 1985.

ANTHOLOGIES: *Modern Women in Love*, 1945 (with William Blake); *Great Stories of the South Sea Islands*, 1956.

MISCELLANEOUS: *Colour of Asia*, 1955 (translated); *The Candid Killer*, 1956 (translated); *In Balloon and Bathyscaphe*, 1956 (translated).

Bibliography

Bader, Rudolf. "Christina Stead and the *Bildungsroman*." *World Literature Written in English* 23 (1984): 31-39. Argues that feminist or Australian nationalistic treatments of Stead's work limit its richness, and that the real strength of her fiction emerges when it is considered within the international literary tradition on which Stead depended. To develop this point, Bader shows how three of Stead's novels—*For Love Alone, Letty Fox*, and

The Man Who Loved Children—draw from a Germanic form, the *Bildungs-roman* (a novel that records the education of a young person).

Brydon, Diana. *Christina Stead*. London: Macmillan, 1987. While admitting that she has presented Stead's work from an essentially feminist perspective, Brydon qualifies this stance by examining Stead's fiction as about both sexes in varied social relationships. Provides a thorough examination of all the novels and includes a chapter entitled "Stead and Her Critics," which throws interesting light on Stead's critical reception. Also contains an extensive secondary bibliography.

Jarrell, Randall. "An Unread Book." Introduction to *The Man Who Loved Children*, by Christina Stead. New York: Holt, Rinehart and Winston, 1965. This first serious and thorough critical examination of Stead's work incorporates many of the themes on which subsequent critics enlarge. Jarrell, a distinguished American poet, praises the novel for its record of a family, its inventive style, and its account of the artist's development: He predicts that the novel, which first appeared in 1940, will be widely read and appreciated by future audiences in this new edition.

Lidoff, Joan. *Christina Stead*. New York: Frederick Ungar, 1982. The earliest full reading of Stead's fiction from a feminist perspective, this book concentrates on *The Man Who Loved Children* and *For Love Alone*. Examines what Lidoff calls Stead's "domestic gothic" and how this technique reveals the long suppressed rage of women. Also examines Stead's characters as wanderers, more fearful of a patriarchal home than of homelessness. Includes an interview, a chronology, and an extensive secondary bibliography.

Ross, Robert L. "Christina Stead's Encounter with 'The True Reader': The Origin and Outgrowth of Randall Jarrell's Introduction to *The Man Who Loved Children*." In *Perspectives on Australia*, edited by Dave Oliphant. Austin: University of Texas Press, 1989. Relies entirely on fifty years of correspondence between Stead and Stanley Burnshaw, her New York editor and friend. Outlines Stead's literary career, focusing on the re-publication of *The Man Who Loved Children* in 1965, with an introduction by the American poet Randall Jarrell. Shows, through her letters, the great delight Stead took in Jarrell's introduction, which she considered the impetus for her novel's rediscovery. Also tells of her reaction to sudden fame after years of literary oblivion and recounts the unhappy period following her husband's death.

Sheridan, Susan. *Christina Stead*. Bloomington: Indiana University Press, 1988. While conceding that Stead disclaimed feminism and always insisted that she was not a feminist writer, Sheridan creates a dialogue between Stead's major novels and contemporary feminist literary theory. Intends not to argue that Stead's work is feminist, but to uncover feminist themes in it. The study rejects other critical approaches that place the novels in the naturalistic or international tradition.

Williams, Chris. *Christina Stead: A Life of Letters.* Melbourne: McPhee Gribble, 1989. This admirable and first full-length biography of Stead depends in large part on unpublished materials, including Stead's letters and early drafts of stories, and on interviews with friends and family members. Provides a detailed account of her childhood in Australia and stresses the importance of men in Stead's life, including her father, who was the model for the main character in *The Man Who Loved Children,* and her husband, William Blake, on whom she depended for stability. Concludes with a record of her final years, after Blake's death, during which she battled against loneliness and alcoholism and was unable to write.

WALLACE STEGNER

Born: Lake Mills, Iowa; February 18, 1909

Principal long fiction

Remembering Laughter, 1937; *The Potter's House*, 1938; *On a Darkling Plain*, 1940; *Fire and Ice*, 1941; *The Big Rock Candy Mountain*, 1943; *Second Growth*, 1947; *The Preacher and the Slave*, 1950; *A Shooting Star*, 1961; *All the Little Live Things*, 1967; *Angle of Repose*, 1971; *The Spectator Bird*, 1976; *Recapitulation*, 1979; *Joe Hill*, 1980; *Crossing to Safety*, 1987.

Other literary forms

Wallace Stegner has also published two collections of short fiction, *The Women on the Wall* (1950) and *The City of the Living* (1956); two biographies, *Beyond the Hundredth Meridian: John Wesley Powell and the Second Opening of the West* (1954) and *The Uneasy Chair: A Biography of Bernard DeVoto* (1974); a collection of critical essays, *The Writer in America* (1951); a historical monograph, *The Gathering of Zion: The Story of the Mormon Trail* (1964); and two volumes of personal essays on the Western experience. *Wolf Willow: A History, a Story, and a Memory of the Last Plains Frontier* (1962) and *The Sound of Mountain Water* (1969). Stegner has also published a number of edited works, both nonfiction and fiction.

Achievements

Stegner has had three distinct audiences since the start of his career: the popular magazine audience; readers interested in modern American literature; and a regional audience interested in the culture and history of the American West. Since the 1930's, he has published seventy-two short stories, with fifty of them appearing in such magazines as *Harper's*, *Mademoiselle*, *Collier's*, *Cosmopolitan*, *Esquire*, *Redbook*, *The Atlantic*, *The Inter-Mountain Review*, and the *Virginia Quarterly*. Bernard DeVoto, Van Wyck Brooks, and Sinclair Lewis recognized his talent early, and DeVoto was instrumental in encouraging Stegner to continue writing. Stegner has enjoyed a solid critical reputation as a regional American writer concerned largely with the problems and themes of the Western American experience.

He has also won numerous honors throughout his career. He was elected to the American Academy of Arts and Sciences and the National Academy of Arts and Letters, and he was awarded fellowships by Phi Beta Kappa, the Huntington Library, The Center for Advanced Studies in the Behavioral Sciences, and by the Guggenheim, Rockefeller, and Wintergreen Foundations. In 1937, he won the Little, Brown Novelette Prize for *Remembering Laughter*. He also won the O. Henry Memorial Award for short stories in

1942, 1948, and 1950, and in 1971 he won the Pulitzer Prize for Fiction for his *Angle of Repose*. Other awards for his work include the Houghton Mifflin Life-in-America Award in 1945 and the Commonwealth Club Gold Medal in 1968. In 1981, he became the first recipient of the Robert Kirsch Award for Life Achievement in the *Los Angeles Times* Book Awards.

As a master of narrative technique and a respected literary craftsman, Stegner has had the opportunity to influence many young writers associated with the Stanford University Creative Writing Program, where he taught from 1945 to 1971, including Eugene Burdick, one of the authors of *The Ugly American* (1958), Ken Kesey, and Thomas McGuane. His own theory of literature is rather traditional and appears in his only extended piece of criticism, *The Writer in America*. The creative process, he believes, is basically the imposition of form upon personal experience. The committed writer must discipline himself to the difficult work of creation, choosing significant images from the insignificant and selecting significant actions for his characters. The writer must change the disorderliness of memory into symmetry without violating his readers' sense of what is true to life.

Biography

Wallace Earle Stegner was born on February 18, 1909, in Lake Mills, Iowa, the second son of George and Hilda Paulson Stegner. He was descended from Norwegian farmers on his mother's side and unknown ancestors on his father's side. His father was a drifter and a resourceful gambler—a searcher for the main chance, the big bonanza. In Stegner's early years, the family moved often, following his father's dream of striking it rich, from Grand Forks, North Dakota, to Bellingham, Washington, to Redmond, Oregon, to East End Saskatchewan, where they lived from 1914 to 1921. East End left him with memories of people and landscapes that played an important role in *The Big Rock Candy Mountain*. The family moved in 1921 to Salt Lake City, Utah, where Stegner attended high school and began college. Here, Stegner went through the pains of adolescence and, although not himself a Mormon, he developed a strong attachment to the land and a sympathy for Mormon culture and values which are reflected in his later books such as *Mormon Country* (1942), *The Gathering of Zion*, and *Recapitulation*.

From 1925 to 1930, Stegner attended the University of Utah, where he balanced his interest in girls and his studies with a job selling rugs and linoleum in the family business of a close friend. By a fortunate chance, he studied freshman English with Vardis Fisher, then a budding novelist, and Fisher helped stimulate Stegner's growing interest in creative writing. In 1930, he entered the graduate program at the University of Iowa, completing his M.A. in 1932 and completing his Ph.D. in 1935 with a dissertation on the Utah naturalist Clarence Dutton, entitled "Clarence Edward Dutton: Geologist and Man of Letters," later revised and published as *Clarence Edward Dutton:*

An Appraisal by the University of Utah in 1936. This work fed his interest in the history of the American West and the life of the explorer John Wesley Powell, the subject of his *Beyond the Hundredth Meridian*. Teaching English and creative writing occupied him for several years, beginning with a one-year stint at tiny Augustana College in Illinois in 1934. Next, he went to the University of Utah until 1937, moving from there to teach freshman English at the University of Wisconsin for two years. He also taught at the Bread Loaf School of English in Vermont for several summers and enjoyed the friendship of Robert Frost, Bernard DeVoto, and Theodore Morrison. In 1940, he accepted a part-time position at Harvard University in the English writing program. There, during the Depression, he was involved in literary debates between the literary left led by F. O. Matthiessen, and the conservative DeVoto.

In 1945, Stegner accepted a professorship in creative writing at Stanford University, where he remained for twenty-six years until his retirement in 1971. The Stanford years were his most productive; he produced a total of thirteen books in this period. In 1950, he made an around-the-world lecture tour, researched his family's past in Saskatchewan and Norway, and spent much of the year as writer-in-residence at the American Academy in Rome. He was also an active environmentalist long before ecology became fashionable. During the Kennedy Administration, he served as Assistant to the Secretary of the Interior (1961) and as a member of the National Parks Advisory Board (1962).

Analysis

Wallace Stegner is a regional writer in the best sense. His settings, his characters, and his plots derive from the Western experience, but his primary concern is with the meaning of that experience. Geographically, Stegner's region runs from Minnesota and Grand Forks, North Dakota, through Utah and Northern Colorado. It is the country where Stegner lived and experienced his youth. Scenes from this region appear frequently in his novels. East End, Saskatchewan, the place of his early boyhood, appears as Whitemud, Saskatchewan, in *The Big Rock Candy Mountain*, along with Grand Forks and Lake Mills, Iowa, his birthplace. Salt Lake City figures prominently in *Recapitulation* and *The Preacher and the Slave*, the story of Joe Hill, a union martyr. *Wolf Willow*, furthermore, is historical fiction, a kind of history of East End, Saskatchewan, where he spent his early boyhood, and *On a Darkling Plain* is the story of a much decorated and seriously wounded veteran of World War I who withdraws from society in an isolated shack on the plains outside of East End.

In a much larger sense, Stegner is concerned with the spiritual West—the West as an idea or a consciousness—and with the significance of the Western values and traditions. He is also concerned with the basic American cultural conflict between East and West and with the importance of frontier values in American history. Bo Mason, modeled after Stegner's father, the abusive head of the Mason family in *The Big Rock Candy Mountain*, is an atavism, a character who may have been at home in the early frontier, who searches for the elusive pot of gold—the main chance of the Western myth. Never content with domestic life or with stability, Bo Mason, like George Stegner, moves his family from town to town always looking for an easy fortune. As a man of mixed qualities—fierce pride, resourcefulness, self-reliance, and a short, violent temper—he is ill at ease in the post-frontier West, always chafing at the stability of community and family ties. He continually pursues the old Western myth of isolated individualism that preceded twentieth century domestication of the region. He might have made a good mountain man. Stegner stresses his impact on his family and community and shows the reader the basic tragedy of this frontier type trapped in a patterned world without easy bonanzas.

In *Angle of Repose*, Stegner explores the conflict between the values of self-reliance, impermanence, and Western optimism and the Eastern sense of culture, stability, and tradition. In a way, this is the basic conflict between Ralph Waldo Emerson's party of hope (the West) and the party of the past (the East). He also explores the idea of community as a concept alien to the Western myth. Indeed, community as the close-knit cooperation between individuals is shown in Stegner's work as the thing that ended the frontier. In *The Big Rock Candy Mountain* and in *Recapitulation*, there is a longing for community and a pervasive feeling that the Mason family is always outside the culture in which it exists, particularly in Utah, where Mormon culture is portrayed as innocent, solid, stable, and as a result attractive. Mormon life is characterized by the absence of frontier individualism and by a belief in permanence and group experience, an anomaly in the Western experience.

A third major concern throughout Stegner's work is his own identity and the meaning of Western identity. Bruce Mason in *The Big Rock Candy Mountain* is much concerned with his relationship as an adolescent to the Utah culture and its sense of community.

Stegner's fifth novel, *The Big Rock Candy Mountain*, is an obviously autobiographical account of his childhood and adolescence. A family saga, the novel follows the history of the rootless Mason family as it follows the dreams of Bo Mason, a thinly disguised version of Stegner's father, as he leads them to Grand Forks, North Dakota, to the lumber camps of Washington, then back to Iowa and up to Whitemud, Saskatchewan, and finally to Salt Lake City and Reno. Family identity problems are played out against the backdrop of an increasingly civilized and domesticated West against which the self-reliant and short-tempered character of Bo Mason stands out in stark relief. His qualities, which might have had virtues in the early settlement of the West, create family tensions and trauma that cause Bruce Mason (Stegner) to develop a hatred for his father only partially tempered by a grudging respect. Bo Mason relentlessly pursues the American dream and the Western myth of easy success rooted in the early frontier: he endlessly pursues the Big Rock Candy Mountain.

Throughout this odyssey, the family longs for stability and community, for a place to develop roots. Even in Salt Lake City, where Bruce spends his adolescence, Bo keeps the family changing houses to hide his bootlegging business during the Prohibition period. His activities in the midst of puritanical Mormon culture only highlight the contrast between the Masons and the dominant community. Even in his later years, Bo pursues his dream in Reno by operating a gambling house.

Stegner vividly illustrates how this rootless wandering affects family members. Else, Bo's wife, representing the feminine, domesticating impulse, is a saintly character—long-suffering, gentle, and protective of her two sons. She longs for a home with permanence but never finds it. Her initial good nature and mild optimism eventually give way to pessimism as resettlements continue. Three of the family members die: Else is destroyed by cancer; Chet, the other son, who is defeated by both marriage and career, dies young of pneumonia; and Bo, with all his dreams shattered and involved with a cheap whore after Else's death, shoots himself. Only Bruce is left to make sense of his family's experiences, and he attempts to understand his place in the family saga as he strives to generalize his family's history. In the final philosophical and meditative chapters, Stegner tries to link Bruce (and therefore himself) to history, to some sense of continuity and tradition. His family history, with its crudeness and tensions, is made to represent the history of the frontier West with its similar tensions and rough edges. Bruce, who long sought solace and identity in books, excels in school and finally follows the civilized but ironic path of going to law school at the University of Minnesota. He has, finally, reached a higher level of culture than his family ever attained. *The Big Rock Candy Mountain* has achieved a reputation as a classic of American regionalism, while it also deals with broader national themes and myths.

Angle of Repose, published in 1971 and awarded the Pulitzer Prize for Fiction, is regarded by many critics as Stegner's most finely crafted novel. The metaphoric title is a mining and geological term designating the slope at which rocks cease to fall, the angle of rest. Stegner uses it to apply to the last thirty years of the marriage of Susan Burling and Oliver Ward, two opposite personalities, after their often chaotic early married years. This ambitious work, covering four generations, is a fictionalized biography of the turn-of-the-century writer and illustrator Mary Hallock Foote (1847-1930) and her marriage to Arthur De Wint Foote, an idealistic pioneer and self-educated mining engineer.

Lyman Ward, the narrator, was reared by his grandparents Susan Burling Ward and Oliver Ward, fictionalized versions of the Footes, and is a retired

history professor from Berkeley who was crippled in middle age by a pro-
gressively arthritic condition. He has been transformed by the disease into a
grotesque creature who loses first his leg and then his wife Ellen, who runs
off with the surgeon who amputated Lyman's leg. Bitter and disillusioned by
his wife's behavior and his son Rodman's radical idealism and contempt for
the past, he retires to Grass Valley, California, to write his grandparents'
biography. Here, he is assisted by Shelly Hawkes, a Berkeley dropout who
shares Rodman's attitude toward history.

As he reads through his grandparents' correspondence, he simultaneously
recounts the development of their marriage and discovers the dynamics of
their personalities. Susan Ward, cultured, educated in the East, and artistically
talented, marries Oliver Ward, an idealistic mining engineer, her second
choice for a husband. Without having resolved her disappointment at his lack
of culture and appreciation for the arts, she marries him and begins two
decades of following him through the West as he looks for professional and
financial success in the unstable mining industry. The years in New Almeden,
California, Leadville, Colorado, Michoacán, Mexico, and southern Idaho
increasingly wear Susan down, despite brief interludes of stability and the
frequent company of other Eastern scientists and engineers during her Western exile.

In Boise Canyon, Idaho, as Oliver's grand irrigation project falls apart,
Susan falls into infidelity with Frank Sargent, Oliver's colorful assistant, and
steals away to the countryside under the pretext of taking five-year-old Agnes
Ward for a walk. Soon, Agnes' body is found floating in a nearby canal, and
the day after her funeral, Frank Sargent commits suicide. Suspecting the
worst, Oliver leaves his wife for two years until persuaded to return. For the
remaining fifty years of their marriage, Oliver treats her with a kind silence
and lack of physical affection, never truly forgiving her infidelity. Lyman
learns that his grandparents' angle of repose was not the real thing, not a
time of harmony, but a cold truce full of human weakness. His naïve image
of his grandparents based on childhood memories is undercut as he comes to
understand them in a more sophisticated way. He learns to respect their
strength and complexity.

Lyman's discoveries are all the more poignant because of the similarities
between his grandparents' experience and his own relationship with an
unfaithful wife who has broken trust, and who, it is implied, will seek a
reconciliation. As in *The Big Rock Candy Mountain*, the two main characters
symbolize two conflicting impulses in the settlement of the West—Oliver, the
dreamer and idealist, pursuing his vision of success in a world with few amen-
ities, and Susan, the finely cultured Easterner, yearning for stability and
society. Lyman discovers links between his family's past and present and
encounters universals of history such as suffering and infidelity which are
more poignant to him because he discovers them in his own family history.

Finally, the novel suggests that frontier values and the civilizing impulses need their own angle of repose. In essence, American experience has not yet reached its angle of rest; frontier and domestic values lie instead in a kind of uneasy truce.

A continuation of the family saga played out in *The Big Rock Candy Mountain*, *Recapitulation*, published in 1979, is the moving drama of Bruce Mason's return to Salt Lake City to face his past. Toward the end of a successful career as a diplomat in the United States Foreign Service, Mason returns to the scene of his turbulent adolescence and the death of his family to attend his maiden aunt's funeral. Upon his arrival at the funeral home, the attendant presents him with a message to call Joe Mulder, his best friend in high school and in college at the University of Utah. Bruce was virtually a member of Joe's family for three years during the time when his father's bootlegging business threatened to jeopardize his social life.

Bruce remembers the 1920's and his adolescence before the stock market crash. Trying to find himself, he slowly remembers the time when he was an outsider in Mormon country, a time when he found many of the values that sustained him after the death of his family. Well-liked in high school by his teachers, Bruce was also picked on by the bigger boys and the less able students and acutely embarrassed by the family's house, which doubled as a speakeasy. His first major romance with Nola, a Mormon country girl who was half Indian, led to his first sexual encounter. Bruce was infatuated with her but knew her intellectual limits—that ideas put her to sleep and art bored her. Throughout the narrative, he recounts the disintegration of his family during his adolescence.

Stegner stresses Bruce's close relationship with Joe Mulder, but Bruce is emotionally incapable of meeting Joe because he hates being treated as "The Ambassador," a visiting dignitary—a title that would only exaggerate the changes and losses of the past forty-five years. In a sense, he finds that he cannot go home again. He would have nothing in common with Joe except memories of adolescent love affairs, and youthful myths. Their past could never be altered or renewed.

A second major theme in *Recapitulation* is the need to belong to some larger community. The Mormon sense of community, whatever its intellectual failings, is viewed nostalgically. Bruce envies the close-knit families of his friends. Nola's family, for example, seems like a tribe, a culture unto itself full of unspoken values and understandings. His decision to attend law school in Minnesota irrevocably removes him from Nola, Utah, his adolescence, and ultimately from his chance to belong. When he returns to Utah, he is in the later stages of a successful but lonely adult life. His first job out of law school was in Saudi Arabia—a place without available women. He finally becomes a Middle Eastern specialist and a permanent bachelor.

Stegner ends the novel with Bruce, lonely, nostalgic, and emotionally incomplete, unable to make contact with Joe Mulder and with his past in a satisfying way. Even though the act of thinking through his past has served him therapeutically, he will continue as a diplomat, making formal contacts with people, living in the surface world of protocol, unable to connect emotionally with people. As the last of his family, he is a solitary figure, a man of deep feelings which he is unable to express. He is, finally, a man who has partially tamed the frontier restlessness and anger of his father and risen above his family's self-destructive tendencies. Still, Bruce carries on the family's feeling of rootlessness, in a more formal, acceptable way. In the Foreign Service, he never develops roots and is shifted from one diplomatic post to another. In a more formal sense than his father, Bruce is still a drifter. Stegner ends the novel fittingly with Bruce Mason being called back to the diplomatic service as United States Representative to an important OPEC meeting in Caracas, Venezuela, reluctantly pulled away from his efforts to understand his past.

Crossing to Safety introduces a new set of characters but also is about coming to terms with the past. Larry and Sally Morgan are a young couple who have moved to Madison, Wisconsin, because Larry has been given a teaching post for a year at the university there. Almost magically, they meet a personable young couple like themselves, Sid and Charity Lang, who also turn out to be very generous. In these Depression days, security is the most sought-after item, and all the young academics vie furiously for tenure. Yet, the Langs (though engaged as furiously in the contest as any) bestow on the Morgans a friendship rare in this backbiting atmosphere—wholehearted, sincere, and giving. Envy and jealousy are not part of their emotional makeup, though they do have their problems. Charity comes from an academic household (her father is a professor), and she wants the same for her family, including a professorship for her husband, who, however, really wants only to write poetry.

Stegner's portrayal of this lifelong friendship is neither idealistic nor blind. He reveals the human sides to his characters, keeping this paragon of *amicitia* from being falsely perfect. The ups and downs of their lives are relayed through flashback: Larry and Sally have come to visit the Langs because Charity is dying from cancer. Larry and Sally's life has not been without tragedy either. The summer after bearing their first child, Sally contracts polio and is crippled by it.

Ultimately, Larry becomes a successful writer, while Sid never becomes successful either as an academic or as a poet. Belying her name—for she is a strong personality at best, harsh and unyielding at worst—Charity never really forgives Sid for his failure. Yet, Stegner concentrates on the love these people have for one another through thick and thin, creating a compelling story without resorting to tricks of subterfuge or violence to sustain the reader's interest. For Stegner's great strength lies in knowing people; he knows their quirks and foibles so well that they come alive on the page without being demeaned or caricatured. In addition, his feeling for mood and setting are twin talents that infuse his writing with life, placing Stegner firmly on the shortlist of great American novelists.

Richard H. Dillman

Other major works

SHORT FICTION: *The Writer's Art: A Collection of Short Stories*, 1950 (edited with Richard Scowcroft and Boris Ilyin); *The Women on the Wall*, 1950; *The City of the Living and Other Stories*, 1956; *Collected Stories of Wallace Stegner*, 1990.

NONFICTION: *An Exposition Workshop*, 1939 (edited); *Readings for Citizens at War*, 1941 (edited); *Mormon Country*, 1942; *One Nation*, 1945 (with the editors of *Look*); *Look at America: The Central Northwest*, 1947; *The Writer in America*, 1951; *Beyond the Hundredth Meridian: John Wesley Powell and the Second Opening of the West*, 1954; *This Is Dinosaur: The Echo Park and Its Magic Rivers*, 1955 (edited); *The Exploration of the Colorado River of the West*, 1957 (edited); *Report on the Lands of the Arid Region of the United States*, 1962 (edited); *Wolf Willow: A History, a Story, and a Memory of the Last Plains Frontier*, 1962; *The Gathering of Zion: The Story of the Mormon Trail*, 1964; *Modern Composition*, 1964 (edited, 4 volumes); *The American Novel: From Cooper to Faulkner*, 1965 (edited); *The Sound of Mountain Water*, 1969; *The Uneasy Chair: A Biography of Bernard DeVoto*, 1974; *Ansel Adams: Images 1923-1974*, 1974; *The Letters of Bernard DeVoto*, 1975 (edited); *One Way to Spell Man*, 1982; *The American West as Living Space*, 1987; *On the Teaching of Creative Writing: Responses to a Series of Questions*, 1988 (edited by Edward Connery Lathem).

ANTHOLOGIES: *Stanford Short Stories, 1946*, 1947 (with Richard Scowcroft); *Great American Short Stories*, 1957 (with Mary Stegner); *Selected American Prose: The Realistic Movement*, 1958; *Twenty Years of Stanford Short Stories*, 1966.

Bibliography

Baker, John F. "Wallace Stegner." *Publishers Weekly* 232 (September 25, 1987): 85-86. This interview with Stegner was done after the publication of *Crossing to Safety*. Stegner talks about his work on that novel and about his writing in general.

Burrows, Russell. "Wallace Stegner's Version of Pastoral." *Western American Literature* 25 (May, 1990): 15-25. In this article, Burrows discusses the importance of the topic of ecology in Stegner's fiction. The article includes some discussion of *Crossing to Safety*, but a more in-depth review (by Jackson J. Benson) of that book follows Burrows' article. Includes reference notes and a bibliography.

Lipson, Eden Ross. "Back to Work After Bora-Bora." *The New York Times Book Review* 92 (September 20, 1987): 14. This interview with Stegner includes his reflections on writing *Crossing to Safety* as well as a discussion of that novel.

Mosher, Howard Frank. "The Mastery of Wallace Stegner." *The Washington Post*, October 4, 1987. This review of *Crossing to Safety* includes some biographical information on Stegner as well as an in-depth discussion of the novel.

Robinson, Forrest Glen, and Margaret G. Robinson. *Wallace Stegner*. Boston: Twayne, 1977. Part of Twayne's United States Authors series, this volume provides a brief chronology of personal and professional events in Stegner's life and some general biographical information. After a discussion of his work, there are primary and secondary bibliographies and an index.

GERTRUDE STEIN

Born: Allegheny, Pennsylvania; February 3, 1874
Died: Neuilly-sur-Seine, France; July 27, 1946

Principal long fiction

Three Lives, 1909; *The Making of Americans*, 1925; *Lucy Church Amiably*, 1930; *A Long Gay Book*, 1932; *Ida, a Novel*, 1941; *Brewsie and Willie*, 1946; *Blood on the Dining-Room Floor*, 1948; *Things As They Are*, 1950 (later as *Quod Erat Demonstrandum*); *Mrs. Reynolds and Five Earlier Novelettes, 1931-1942*, 1952; *A Novel of Thank You*, 1958.

Other literary forms

Any attempt to separate Gertrude Stein's novels from her other kinds of writing must be highly arbitrary. Stein thought the novel to be a failed literary form in the twentieth century, claiming that no real novels had been written after Marcel Proust and even including her own novelistic efforts in this assessment. For this and other reasons, it might be claimed that few, if any, of Stein's works are novels in any traditional sense. In fact, very few of Stein's more than six hundred titles in more than forty books can be adequately classified into any traditional literary forms. Her philosophy of composition was so idiosyncratic, her prose style so seemingly nonrational, that her writing bears little resemblance to whatever genre it purports to represent. Depending on one's definition of the novel, Stein wrote anywhere between six and twelve novels, ranging in length from less than one hundred to 925 pages. The problem is that none of Stein's "novels" has a plot in any conventional sense, that few have conventionally developed and sustained characters, and that several seem almost exclusively autobiographical, more diaries and daybooks than anything else. It is not any easier to categorize her other pieces of writing, most of which are radically *sui generis*. If references to literary forms are made very loosely, Stein's work can be divided into novels, autobiographies, portraits, poems, lectures, operas, plays, and explanations. Other than her novels, her best-known works are *The Autobiography of Alice B. Toklas* (1933); *Tender Buttons* (1914); *Four Saints in Three Acts* (1934); *Lectures in America* (1935); *Everybody's Autobiography* (1937); and *Portraits and Prayers*, 1934.

Achievements

Whether towering or crouching, Stein is ubiquitous in contemporary literature. A child of the nineteenth century who staunchly adhered to many of its values halfway through the twentieth, she nevertheless dedicated her creative life to the destruction of nineteenth century concepts of artistic order and purpose. In her own words, she set out to do nothing less than to kill a century, to lay the old ways of literary convention to rest. She later boasted that "the most serious thinking about the nature of literature in the twentieth century has been done by a woman," and her claim has great merit. During the course of her career, Stein finally managed to convince almost everyone that there was indeed some point, if not profundity, in her aggressively enigmatic style. The ridicule and parody that frustrated so much of her early work had turned to grudging tolerance or outright lionizing by 1934, when Stein made her triumphant American lecture tour; for the last fifteen or so years of her life, she was published even if her editor had not the vaguest idea of what she was doing (as Bennett Cerf later admitted he had not). On the most concrete level, Stein's distinctive prose style is remarkably significant even when its philosophical dimensions are ignored. William Gass has observed, Stein "did more with sentences, and understood them better, than any writer ever has."

More important was Stein's influence on other leaders in the development of modernism. As a student of William James, a friend of Alfred North Whitehead and Pablo Picasso, Stein lived at the center of the philosophical and artistic revolutions of the twentieth century. She was the natural emblem for modernism, and in her person, career, and legend, many of its salient issues converged. In the light of more recent developments in the novel and in literary theory, it has also been argued that Stein was the first postmodernist, the first writer to claim openly that the instance of language is itself as important as the reality to which it refers. Among major writers, Ernest Hemingway was most obviously influenced by his association with her, but her genius was freely acknowledged by F. Scott Fitzgerald, Sherwood Anderson, and Thornton Wilder. William Saroyan explained her influence most directly when he asserted that no American writer could keep from coming under it, a sentiment reluctantly echoed by Edmund Wilson in *Axel's Castle* (1931), even before Stein's great popular success in the mid-1930's.

Biography

Gertrude Stein was born on February 3, 1874, in Allegheny, Pennsylvania, but she was seven before her family settled into permanent residence in Oakland, California, the city she was later to describe as having "no there there." Her birth itself was contingent on the deaths of two of her five brothers and sisters: her parents had decided to have only five children, and only after two children had died in infancy were Gertrude and her older brother, Leo, conceived. Identity was to become one of the central preoccupations of her writing career, and the tenuous nature of her own birth greatly influenced that concern.

Stein's early years were comfortably bourgeois and uneventful. Her father, a vice-president of the Union Street Municipal Railway System in San Francisco, was authoritarian, moody, aggressive, but vacillating, and he may have helped foster her sense of independence, but he undoubtedly left her annoyed by him in particular and by fatherhood in general. Her mother barely figured in her life at all: a pale, withdrawn, ineffectual woman, she left most of the rearing of her children to governesses. By the time Stein was seventeen, both parents had died and she had grown even closer to her immediate older brother, Leo. In 1893, she entered Harvard Annex (renamed Radcliffe College the following year), thus rejoining Leo, who was a student at Harvard. There, Stein studied with William James and Hugo Munsterberg and became involved in research in psychology. Together with the great influence exerted on her thinking by William James, this early work in psychology was to provide her with both a subject and a style that would continue in many forms throughout her career. She was awarded her A.B. by Harvard in 1898, almost a year after she had entered medical school at The Johns Hopkins University. Her interest in medicine rapidly waned, and she left Johns Hopkins in 1901, failing four courses in her final semester.

After leaving medical school, Stein spent two years moving back and forth between Europe and America. During that time, she was involved in an agonizing love affair with another young woman student at Johns Hopkins, May Bookstaver. The affair was painfully complicated, first by Stein's naïveté, then by the presence of a more sophisticated rival for May's love, Mabel Haynes. The resulting lover's triangle led Stein, in an effort to understand May, to begin formulating the theories of personality that dominated her early writing. The frustration and eventual despair of this lesbian relationship profoundly influenced Stein's view of the psychology of personality and of love. Most directly, Stein's troubled affair with May Bookstaver provided her with many, if not most, of the concerns of three of her books, *Q.E.D.*, *The Making of Americans*, and *Three Lives*, the first two of which she began while living in New York in the winter of 1903.

After a brief stay in New York, she lived with Leo, first in Bloomsbury in London, and then, beginning in 1903, in Paris at 27 rue de Fleurus, the address she was to make so well-known to the world. In Paris, Gertrude and Leo became more and more interested in painting, buying works by new artists such as Henri Matisse and Picasso. Leo's preference was for works by Matisse, while Gertrude favored the more experimental works of Picasso, marking the beginning of a distancing process that would lead to Leo's complete separation from his sister in 1913. Leo was bright, opinionated, and fancied himself by far the greater creative talent of the two, but his brilliance and energy never produced any creative or significant critical work, and he grew to resent both his sister's independent thinking and her emerging ability to write. Later in his life, he would dismiss Gertrude as "dumb," her writing as "nonsense."

In 1907, Stein met another young American woman in Paris, Alice Toklas, and Alice began to displace Leo as the most important personal influence in

Gertrude's life. Alice learned to type so she could transcribe Stein's hand-written manuscripts, beginning with portions of *The Making of Americans* in 1908. In 1909, Alice moved in with Gertrude and Leo at 27 rue de Fleurus, and by 1913, Alice had replaced Leo as Gertrude's companion and as the manager of her household. Stein later referred to her relationship with Alice as a "marriage," and few, if any, personal relationships have ever influenced a literary career so profoundly. Apart from providing Stein with the persona for her best-known work, *The Autobiography of Alice B. Toklas*, Alice typed, criticized, and valiantly worked to publish all of Stein's work for the rest of her career and for the twenty years that Alice lived after Stein's death. While it is doubtful that Alice was directly responsible for any of Stein's writing, her influence on its composition and on Stein's life was tremendous.

Gertrude and Alice spent the first months of World War I in England as houseguests of Alfred North Whitehead, returning to Paris briefly in 1914, then spending more than a year in Spain. They joined the war effort in 1917 when Stein ordered a Ford motor van from America for use as a supply truck for the American Fund for French Wounded, an acquisition which began Stein's lifelong fascination with automobiles, particularly with Fords. She and Alice drove this van, named "Auntie," until the war ended, work for which she was later awarded the Medaille de la Reconnaissance Française.

Modernism had burst on the American consciousness when the Armory Show opened in New York in 1913, and this show, which had confronted Americans with the first cubist paintings, also led to the association in the public mind of Stein's writing with this shockingly new art, particularly since Stein's first periodical publications had been "Matisse" and "Picasso" in *Camera Work*, the year before. Stein's mammoth, 925-page novel, *The Making of Americans*, was published in 1925, and in 1926, she lectured at Oxford and Cambridge, attempting to explain her idiosyncratic writing style. Her "landscape" novel, *Lucy Church Amiably*, appeared in 1930, but it was in 1933, with the publication of the best-selling *The Autobiography of Alice B. Toklas*, that Stein first captured the public's interest. She became front page news the following year when her opera *Four Saints in Three Acts* was first performed and when she embarked on a nationwide lecture tour, later described in *Everybody's Autobiography* and *Lectures in America*.

Stein and Toklas spent World War II in Bilignin and then in Culoz, France. While Stein and Toklas were both Jewish, they were never persecuted by occupying forces, owing in part to the influence of Bernard Fay, an early admirer of Stein's work who directed the Bibliothèque Nationale for the Vichy regime. When, after the war, Fay was sentenced to life imprisonment for his Vichy activities, Stein was one of his few defenders. That her art collection survived Nazi occupation virtually intact can only have been through Fay's intercession. During the war, Stein finished another novel, *Mrs. Reynolds* (unpublished), and *Wars I Have Seen* (1945), an autobiographical work. Her

novel *Brewsie and Willie*, a series of conversations among American GIs, was
published in 1945.

Stein died following an operation for cancer in the American Hospital in
Neuilly-sur-Seine, France, on July 27, 1946. While Alice Toklas' account of
Stein's last words may be apocryphal, it certainly is in keeping with the spirit
of her life. As Alice later reconstructed their last conversation, Stein had
asked her "What is the answer?" Then, when Alice remained silent, Stein
added, "In that case, what is the question?"

Analysis

While Gertrude Stein's persistence finally earned her access to readers, it
could never guarantee her readers who would or could take her strange writing
seriously. As a result, more confusing and contradictory information surrounds her career than that of any other twentieth century writer of comparable reputation. Usually responding in any of four basic ways, readers and
critics alike seemed to view her as (1) a literary charlatan of the P. T. Barnum
ilk, interested in publicity or money rather than in art; (2) something of a
naïve child-woman incapable of comprehending the world around her; (3) a
fiery-eyed literary revolutionary, den mother of the avant-garde; or (4) an
ageless repository of wisdom and genius. Ultimately, the reader's acceptance
or rejection of these various categories will greatly determine his or her
response to Stein's writing, which forces the reader to make as many cognitive
choices as does that of any major writer.

Stein's many explanations of her writing further complicate its interpretation: even her "explanations" frustrate as much as they reveal, explicitly
setting her up in cognitive competition with her reader, a competition suggested by her favorite cryptogram, which works out to read: "I understand
you undertake to overthrow my undertaking." Stein proposes a rhetoric not
of misunderstanding, but of antiunderstanding; that is, her "explanations"
usually argue precisely against the desirability of explaining.

As Stein bluntly put the matter, "understanding is a very dull occupation."
"Understanding" has a special denotation for Stein, sometimes meaning as
little as paying attention to or reading. "To understand a thing means to be
in contact with that thing," she proclaimed. Central to her mistrust of explanations and interpretations was Stein's often anguished belief that her
thoughts could never really be matched to anyone else's. She was deeply
troubled by this doubt as she wrote *The Making of Americans*, referring in
that work to "the complete realization that no one can believe as you do
about anything" as "complete disillusionment in living." Starting from this
assumption that no one can ever really understand what someone else says
or writes because of the inherent ambiguity of language, Stein not only decided
to force her readers to confront that ambiguity, but also claimed it as a primary
virtue of her writing. She announced triumphantly that "if you have vitality

enough of knowing enough of what you mean, somebody and sometimes a great many will have to realize that you know what you mean and so they will agree that you mean what you know, which is as near as anybody can come to understanding any one." Stein's focus here is on relationships or process rather than on product—on the act of trying to become one with, rather than focusing on the ultimate result of that act.

Stein's thinking about understanding manifests itself in a number of distinctive ways in her writing, as do her theories of perception and of human psychology. Moreover, during the nearly fifty years of her writing career, her style developed in many related but perceptibly different stages, such as her "cubist" or her "cinema" phases. As a result, no single analysis can do more than describe the primary concerns and features of one of her stylistic periods. There are, however, three central concerns that underlie and at least partially account for all of the stages in the development of her style. These concerns are with the value of individual words, with repetition as the basic rhythm of existence, and with the related concept of "movement" in writing. Her articulations of these central concerns all run counter to her reader's expectations about the purpose and function of language and of literature. Her writing surprised her readers in much the same way that her penchant for playing only the black keys on a piano surprised and frustrated all but the most patient of her listeners.

One of Stein's goals was to return full meaning, value, and particularity to the words she used. "I took individual words and thought about them until I got their weight and volume complete and put them next to another word," she explained of seemingly nonsense phrases such as "toasted Susie is my ice cream," or "mouse and mountain and a quiver, a quaint statue and pain in an exterior and silence more silence louder shows salmon a mischief intender." This sort of paratactic juxtaposition of seemingly unrelated words rarely occurs in Stein's novels, but represents a problem for her reader in many other ways in her writing. She frequently chose to stress or focus on a part or aspect of the object of her description that the reader normally does not consider. The "things" Stein saw and wrote of were not the "things" with which readers are familiar: where another observer might see a coin balanced on its edge, Stein might choose either of the descriptive extremes of seeing it literally as a thin rectangle, or figuratively as the essence of money. Characteristically, her most opaque parataxis refers to essences or processes rather than to objects or static concepts.

A related quirk in Stein's style results from her intellectual or emotional attachment to particular words and phrases at certain stages of her career. As she admitted in *The Making of Americans,*

> To be using a new word in my writing is to me a very difficult thing. . . . Using a word
> I have not yet been using in my writing is to me a very difficult and a peculiar feeling.

Sometimes I am using a new one, sometimes I feel a new meaning in an old one, sometimes I like one I am very fond of that one that has many meanings many ways of being used to make different meanings to everyone.

Stein said she had learned from Paul Cézanne that everything in a painting was related to everything else and that each part of the painting was of equal importance—a blade of grass as important to the composition of the painting as a tree. She attempted to apply these two principles to the composition of her sentences, taking special delight in using normally "overlooked" words, arguing that articles, prepositions, and conjunctions—the transitive elements in grammar—are just as important and more interesting than substantives such as nouns and verbs. Her reassessment both of the value of words and of the conventions of description resulted in what Michael J. Hoffman in *The Development of Abstractionism in the Writings of Gertrude Stein* (1965) has described as Stein's "abstractionism." It also resulted in her including in her writing totally unexpected information in perplexingly paratactic word-strings.

A second constant in Stein's style is the pronounced repetition of words, phrases, and sentences, with no change or with only incremental progressions of sounds or associations. Works such as *The Making of Americans* and *Three Lives* contain long passages in which each sentence is a light variation on some core phrase, with great repetition of words even within a single sentence. Stein termed this phenomenon "insistence" rather than repetition, citing her former teacher, William James, as her philosophical authority. James's argument in his *The Principles of Psychology* (1890) that one must think of the identical recurrence of a fact in a fresh manner remarkably resembles Stein's contention that "in expressing anything there can be no repetition because the essence of that expression is insistence, and if you insist you must each time use emphasis and if you use emphasis it is not possible while anybody is alive that they should use exactly the same emphasis." Repetition or insistence is perhaps the central aspect of what has been called Stein's "cinema style," based on her claim that in writing *The Making of Americans* she was "doing what the cinema was doing." She added that her writing in that book was "like a cinema picture made up of succession and each moment having its own emphasis that is its own difference and so there was the moving and the existence of each moment as it was in me."

Stein's discussion of "what the cinema was doing" appears in her *Lectures in America* and also suggests the third basic concern of her writing: movement. By "movement," she referred not to the movement of a message to its conclusion or the movement of a plot or narrative, but to "the essence of its going" of her prose, a timeless continuous present in the never-ending motion of consciousness. Stein also credits Cézanne with discovering this concern, "a feeling of movement inside the painting not a painting of a thing moving but the thing painted having inside it the existence of moving." She seemed to understand Cézanne's achievement in terms of William James's model of consciousness as an ever-flowing stream of thought. Accordingly, she used her writing not to record a scene or object or idea (products of thought), but to try to capture the sense of the process of perceiving such things. Stein's subject is almost always really two things at once: whatever attracted her attention—caught her eye, entered her ear, or crossed her mind—and the mobile nature of reality, particularly as it is perceived by human consciousness. In fact, Stein was usually more concerned with the nature of her own perception and with that of her reader than she was with its objects. She wanted to escape the conventions of linguistic representation, arbitrary arrangements similar to the "rules" for perspective in painting, and to present "something moving as moving is not as moving should be." As confusing as her resulting efforts sometimes are, her concern with motion makes sense as an attempt to mimic or evoke the nature of consciousness as she understood it.

From James at Harvard and possibly from Henri Bergson in Paris, Stein had learned that the best model for human consciousness was one that stressed the processual, ever-flowing nature of experience. She added to this belief her assumption that the essence of any subject could only be perceived and should only be represented through its motion, echoing Bergson's claim that "reality is mobility." Unfortunately, this belief led her writing into one of its many paradoxes: she could only attempt to represent the continuous stream of experience through the segmented, inherently sequential nature of language. Streams flow; words do not. Instead, they proceed one by one, like the cars pulled by a train engine. While James would certainly have objected to Stein's sequential cinema model as an approximation of the stream of consciousness, her motion-obsessed writing probably suggests the flow of consciousness as well as does any literary style.

Written in 1903, but put out of her mind until 1932, and not published until 1950, Stein's *Quod Erat Demonstrandum* (first published as *Things as They Are*) is her most conventional novel. Its sentences employ no unexpected syntax or diction, its central concerns are clear, its time scheme is linear, and its characters are conventionally drawn. If anything, Stein's style in this first novel is markedly old-fashioned, including highly formal sentences that frequently sport balanced serial constructions. "Adele vehemently and with much picturesque vividness explained her views and theories of manners, people and things, in all of which she was steadily opposed by Helen who differed fundamentally in all her convictions, aspirations and illusions." While its conventional style (crudely reminiscent of that of Henry James) is completely unlike that of any other Stein novel, *Q.E.D.* is a very significant work for the consideration of Stein's career. Apart from convincingly refuting the suspicion of some of her detractors that Stein was incapable of rational writing, this book establishes her preoccupation with psychological typecasting and vaguely hints at the importance of repetition in her thinking and writing.

Q.E.D. charts the growth, turbulence, and eventual dissolution of the relationships among three young women: Adele, the book's central consciousness, an obviously autobiographical figure; Helen Thomas, the object of Adele's love; and Mable Neathe, Adele's calculating rival for Helen's affection. These three characters closely parallel Stein, May Bookstaver, and Mabel Haynes, and the story of their relationship is the story of Stein's first, agonizing love affair. While the novel follows these three young women for three years, not much happens. Most of the book relates conversations and correspondence between Adele and Helen, showing Adele's torment first from her not yet understood desire for Helen, then from her growing realization that she is losing Helen to Mabel. Of principal interest to the reader is Stein's self-characterization in her portrayal of Adele.

Three Lives is easily Stein's best-known and most respected piece of fiction. Technically three novellas, this work is unified by its three subjects, by its central concern with the nature of consciousness, and by its attempt to blend colloquial idioms with Stein's emerging style, here based largely on her understanding of Cézanne's principles of composition, particularly that "one thing was as important as another thing." "The Good Anna," "Melanctha," and "The Gentle Lena" are the three sections of this work. Anna and Lena are poor German immigrants who patiently work as servants in Bridgepoint, Baltimore; Melanctha is a young black woman who discovers sexuality and love, then turns from a frustrating relationship with a sincere young black doctor to a dissipative affair with a gambler. Since all three women are essentially victimized by their surroundings and die at the end of their stories, this work is deterministic in the naturalist tradition, but *Three Lives* marks the transition from naturalism to modernism as Stein departs from nineteenth century literary conventions. She abandons conventional syntax to try to follow the movement of a consciousness rather than of events, and she develops a new narrative style only partially tied to linear chronology. The result is an interior narrative of consciousness in which Stein's prose style serves as the primary carrier of knowledge. Through the rhythms of her characters' speech and the rhythms of her narration, Stein gives her reader a sense of the basic rhythms of consciousness for these three women—what Stein would elsewhere refer to as their "bottom natures."

Possibly Stein's most widely celebrated piece of writing, "Melanctha" recasts the anguishing love triangle of *Q.E.D.* into the conflict between Melanctha and Jeff Campbell, whose inherently conflicting "bottom natures" or personality types parallel the conflict between Helen and Adele in the earlier work. "Melanctha" has been praised by Richard Wright, among others, as one of the first realistic and sympathetic renderings of black life by a white American author, but Melanctha's race is actually incidental to Stein's central concerns with finding a style to express the rhythms of personality and the frustrating cycles of love.

While it was not published until 1925, Stein's *The Making of Americans* occupied her as early as 1903 and was in fact begun before *Q.E.D.* and *Three Lives*. This mammoth novel began as a description of the creation of Americans from a representative immigrant family: "The old people in a new world, the new people made out of the old, that is the story that I mean to tell, for that is what really is and what I really know." Stein's projected family chronicle soon lost its original focus, becoming first a history of everyone, then a study of character types rather than of characters. Leon Katz, who has worked with this book more than has anyone else, calls it "a massive description of the psychological landscape of human being in its totality." Although the book ostensibly continues to follow events in the lives of two central families, the Herslands and the Dehnings, its real concern is almost always both larger and smaller, ranging from Stein's questions about her own life and identity to questions about the various personality types of all of humanity. As Richard Bridgman suggests, this is "an improvised work of no identifiable genre in which the creator learned by doing," one "full of momentary wonders and botched long-range schemes, lyrical outbursts and anguished confessions." Accordingly, Bridgman concludes that *The Making of Americans* is best thought of "not as a fictional narrative nor a philosophic tract, but as a drama of self-education." In a way, the book chronicles the "making" of Gertrude Stein, presenting a phenomenology of her mind as it works its way through personal problems toward the distinctive "cinema style."

Underlying a great part of the writing in this book is Stein's belief that human personality consists of variations on a few basic "bottom natures" or kinds of identity which can be perceived through a character's repeated actions. "There are then many things every one has in them that come out of them in the repeating everything living have always in them, repeating with a little changing just enough to make of each one an individual being, to make of each repeating an individual thing that gives to such a one a feeling of themselves inside them." There are two basic personality types, "dependent independent" and "independent dependent," polarities identified in part by the way the person fights: the first kind by resisting, the second by attacking. Concerns with character-typing dominate the book's first two sections, "The Dehnings and the Herslands" and "Martha Hersland," (the character most closely modeled on Stein's own life), while the third section, "Alfred and Julia Hersland," contains mostly digressions about contemporary matters in Stein's life. The fourth section, "David Hersland," becomes a meditation on the nature of aging and death ("He was dead when he was at the beginning of being in middle living."), and the final section, "History of a Family's Progress," is—even for Stein—an incredibly abstract and repetitive series of reflections on the concerns that had given rise to the novel. This final section contains no names, referring only to "some," "any," "every," or "very many."

Stein later described her efforts in this book as an attempt "to do what the cinema was doing"; that is, to give a sense of motion and life through a series of highly repetitive statements, each statement only an incremental change from the preceding one, like frames in a strip of film. One of the main effects of this technique is to freeze all action into a "continuous present." Not only do Stein's sentences exist in overlapping clusters, depending more for their meaning on their relationships to one another than on individual semantic content, but also her verbs in *The Making of Americans* are almost exclusively present participles, suspending all action in the present progressive tense. "The business of Art," Stein later explained, "is to live in the actual present, that is the complete actual present, and to express that complete actual present." As a result, while *The Making of Americans* does ostensibly present a history of four generations of the Hersland family, there exists in it little or no sense of the passage of time. Instead, the book presents a sense of "existence suspended in time," a self-contained world existing quite independently of the "real world," a basic modernist goal that has also become one of the hallmarks of postmodernism.

A 416-page version, abridged by Stein, was published in 1934, but has not been accepted by Stein scholars as adequately representative of the longer work. For all its difficulty, *The Making of Americans* is one of modernism's seminal works and an invaluable key to Stein's literary career.

Described by its author as "a novel of Romantic beauty and nature and which Looks Like an Engraving," *Lucy Church Amiably* shares many characteristics with Stein's best-known opera, *Four Saints in Three Acts*, and with the several works she called "geographies." The book was Stein's response to the area around Belley, France, where she and Alice spent many summers. Stein's title plays on the existence of the church in a nearby village, Lucey. As Richard Bridgman has observed, Lucy Church refers throughout the book to both that church and to a woman who resembles a relaxed Gertrude Stein. As Bridgman also notes, "the book is essentially a long, lyric diary," with Stein including in it information about the geography, residents, and flora of the surrounding area. This information appears, however, in Stein's distinctive paratactic style:

> In this story there is to be not only white black tea colour and vestiges of their bankruptcy but also well wishing and outlined and melodious and with a will and much of it to be sure with their only arrangement certainly for this for the time of which when by the way what is the difference between fixed.

This novel can perhaps best be thought of as a pastoral and elegiac meditation on the nature of place.

In 1939, Stein's novel for children, *The World Is Round*, was published, with illustrations by Clement Hurd. The book focuses on a series of events in the lives of a nine-year-old girl, Rose, and her cousin, Willie. These events are more enigmatic than dramatic, but seem to move both children through several kinds of initiations. Identity worries both Rose and Willie ("Would she have been Rose if her name had not been Rose and would she have been Rose if she had been a twin"), as does the contrast between the uncertainties of their lives and the advertised verities of existence, emblemized by the "roundness" of the world. Comprising both the children's meditations and their songs, the book is, for Stein, relatively conventional. Although its sentences are highly repetitive and rhythmic, they present a compelling view of a child's consciousness, and Stein scholars agree on the importance and success of this little-known work.

Originally intended as "a novel about publicity," *Ida, a Novel* expands many of the concerns of *The World Is Round*, extending them from Ida's birth well into her adult life. As is true of all of Stein's novels, there is not anything resembling a plot, and many of the things that happen in Ida's life are surrealistically dreamlike. "Funny things" keep happening to the young Ida, and while the nature of these things is never explained, most of them seem to involve men. Frequently, these men have nothing at all to do with her, or they only glance at her, but Ida sees them as vaguely threatening, and insofar as her novel can be said to have a central concern, it is with certain problems of sexuality. Although Stein later described Ida as having been based on the Duchess of Windsor, this connection is only superficial, and Ida is better seen as another in the long line of Stein's autobiographical characters.

Stein's novel, *Brewsie and Willie*, redirected her revolutionary spirit from literary to social and economic problems. In this series of conversations among American GIs and nurses awaiting redeployment from France to the United States after World War II, Stein pessimistically considered the future of her native land. Stein had long held that the United States was "the oldest country in the world" because it had been the first to enter the twentieth century. By 1945, she felt that America had grown "old like a man of fifty," and that its tired, middle-aged economic system had become stale and repressive. In *Brewsie and Willie*, she describes that economic system as "industrialism," portraying a stultifying cycle of depleting raw materials for overproduction and installment buying. This cycle also locked the worker into "job thinking," making of him a kind of automaton, tied to his job, locked into debt, and, worst of all, robbed of freedom of thought. Through conversations involving Brewsie (Stein's spokesman), Willie, and several other GIs and nurses, Stein portrays an apprehensive generation of young Americans who see the potential dangers of postwar America but who fear they do not "have the guts to make a noise" about them. These conversations cover a wide range of subjects, from a comparison of French and American baby carriages to the tentative suggestion that the American system must be torn down before "pioneering" will again be possible.

Stein makes little or no effort in this book to differentiate the voices of her speakers, but she does rather amazingly blend her own voice with those of the GI's. The result is a style that is characteristically Stein's but that also has the rhythm and the randomness of overheard conversation. Often overlooked, *Brewsie and Willie* is one of the most remarkable documents in Stein's writing career.

However idiosyncratic Stein's writing may seem, it must be remembered that a very strong case can be made for its substantial philosophical underpinnings. To her way of thinking, language could refuse few things to Stein, and the limitations of language were exactly what she refused to accept. She bent the language to the very uses that process philosophers such as James and Bergson and Whitehead feared it could not be put. Her stubborn emphasis on the individual word—particularly on transitive elements—her insistent use of repetition, and her ever-present preoccupation with the essential motion of words were all part of Stein's monumental struggle with a language she felt was not accurately used to reflect the way people perceive reality or the motion of reality itself. In a narrow but profound sense, she is the most serious realist in literary history. Stein was not a philosopher—her magpie eclecticism, associational flights, and thundering *ex cathedra* pronouncements ill-suited her for systematic explanation—but in her writing a wealth of philosophy appears.

Brooks Landon

Other major works

PLAYS: *Geography and Plays*, 1922; *Operas and Plays*, 1932; *Four Saints in Three Acts*, 1934; *Lucretia Borgia*, 1939; *In Savoy: Or, Yes Is for a Very Young Man (A Play of the Resistance in France)*, 1946; *The Mother of Us All*, 1947; *Last Operas and Plays*, 1949; *In a Garden: An Opera in One Act*, 1951; *Selected Operas and Plays*, 1970.

POETRY: *Tender Buttons: Objects, Food, Rooms*, 1914; *Two (Hitherto Unpublished) Poems*, 1948; *Bee Time Vine and Other Pieces: 1913-1927*, 1953; *Stanzas in Meditation and Other Poems: 1929-1933*, 1956.

NONFICTION: *The Autobiography of Alice B. Toklas*, 1933; *Matisse, Picasso, and Gertrude Stein, with Two Shorter Stories*, 1933; *Portraits and Prayers*, 1934; *Lectures in America*, 1935; *Narration: Four Lectures*, 1935; *The Geographical History of America*, 1936; *Everybody's Autobiography*, 1937; *Picasso*, 1938; *What Are Masterpieces*, 1940; *Wars I Have Seen*, 1945; *Reflections on the Atomic Bomb*, 1973; *How Writing Is Written*, 1974.

CHILDREN'S LITERATURE: *The World Is Round*, 1939.

Bibliography

Bridgman, Richard. *Gertrude Stein in Pieces*. New York: Oxford University Press, 1970. Still an indispensable source, this was the first book to look critically at the whole Stein canon and to analyze its genesis. Bridgman remains immune from the many statements Stein made to explain her own work and arrives at honest and independent—if not always completely acceptable—judgments.

Chessman, Harriet Scott. *The Public Is Invited to Dance: Representation, the Body, and Dialogue in Gertrude Stein.* Stanford, Calif.: Stanford University Press, 1989. Perhaps the best overall assessment to date of the conscious artistry of Stein, with special attention to her keen ear for the language of common people.

Doane, Janice L. *Silence and Narrative: The Early Novels of Gertrude Stein.* Westport, Conn.: Greenwood Press, 1986. Strong on the development of Stein's unique narrative voice with its focus on the speech of working-class women. Demonstrates Stein's sensitivity to nuance.

Dubnick, Randa. *The Structure of Obscurity: Gertrude Stein, Language, and Cubism.* Urbana: University of Illinois Press, 1984. Applies structuralist critical theories to an analysis of Stein's writing, connecting her selection (word choice) and combination (syntactic ordering) to the two major movements in Cubist painting, the analytical and the synthetic.

Hoffman, Michael J., ed. *Critical Essays on Gertrude Stein.* Boston: G. K. Hall, 1986. The most current collection of writing on Stein, representing varied points of view. A good starting point for beginners.

_____. *Gertrude Stein.* Boston: Twayne, 1976. A useful book with strong analyses of Stein's writing and interesting sidelights on its production and its relationship to the avante garde movements of the period. Especially strong on cubist influences.

Mellow, James R. *Charmed Circle: Gertrude Stein and Company.* New York: Praeger, 1974. A deeply felt and pleasing illustrated book by one of Stein's scholarly admirers. Contains interesting, detailed discussions of her writing, her family background and relationships, her association with artists and writers in Paris over fifty years, and her enduring relationship with Alice B. Toklas.

Neuman, Shirley, and Ira B. Nadel, eds. *Gertrude Stein and the Making of Literature.* Boston: Northeastern University Press, 1988. Offers some of the most current feminist readings of Stein, clarifying the innovations that originated with Stein and had a sweeping influence on later writers including Ernest Hemingway, Ford Madox Ford, and Sherwood Anderson.

Steiner, Wendy. *Exact Resemblance to Exact Resemblance.* New Haven, Conn.: Yale University Press, 1978. Perhaps the best book available for linking Stein's modernism to her interest in and study of psychology and philosophy.

Walker, Jayne L. *The Making of a Modernist: Gertrude Stein from "Three Lives" to "Tender Buttons."* Amherst: University of Massachusetts, 1984. Walker emphasizes the influences that the art movements had on Gertrude Stein as a writer during the early years of her literary endeavors, giving special attention to impressionism and cubism.

JOHN STEINBECK

Born: Salinas, California; February 27, 1902
Died: New York, New York; December 20, 1968

Principal long fiction

Cup of Gold, 1929; *The Pastures of Heaven*, 1932; *To a God Unknown*, 1933; *Tortilla Flat*, 1935; *In Dubious Battle*, 1936; *The Red Pony*, 1937, 1945; *Of Mice and Men*, 1937; *The Grapes of Wrath*, 1939; *The Moon Is Down*, 1942; *Cannery Row*, 1945; *The Wayward Bus*, 1947; *The Pearl*, 1947; *Burning Bright*, 1950; *East of Eden*, 1952; *Sweet Thursday*, 1954; *The Short Reign of Pippen IV*, 1957; *The Winter of Our Discontent*, 1961; *Acts of King Arthur and His Noble Knights*, 1976.

Other literary forms

In addition to his seventeen novels, John Steinbeck published a story collection, *The Long Valley* (1938), and a few other uncollected or separately printed stories. His modern English translations of Sir Thomas Malory's Arthurian tales were published posthumously in 1976. Three plays he adapted from his novels were published as well as performed on Broadway: *Of Mice and Men* (1938), *The Moon Is Down* (1943), and *Burning Bright* (1951). Three of the six film treatments or screenplays he wrote—*The Forgotten Village* (1941), *A Medal for Benny* (1945), and *Viva Zapata!* (1952, 1975)—have been published; the other three also were produced as films—*Lifeboat* (1944), *The Pearl* (1945), and *The Red Pony* (1949), the latter two adapted from his own novels. His nonfiction was voluminous, and much of it remains uncollected. The more important nonfiction books include: *Sea of Cortez* (1941, 1951), *Bombs Away* (1942), *A Russian Journal* (1948), *Once There Was a War* (1958), *Travels With Charley* (1962), *America and Americans* (1966), *Journal of a Novel* (1969), and *Steinbeck: A Life in Letters* (1975).

Achievements

From the publication of his first bestseller, *Tortilla Flat*, in 1935, Steinbeck was a popular and widely respected American writer. His three earlier novels were virtually ignored, but the five books of fiction published between 1935 and 1939 made him the most important literary spokesman for the Depression decade. *In Dubious Battle*, *The Red Pony*, and *Of Mice and Men* established him as a serious writer, and his master work, *The Grapes of Wrath*, confirmed him as a major talent. During these years, his popular and critical success rivaled that of any of his contemporaries.

Although his immense popularity, public recognition, and the impressive sales of his works persisted throughout his career, Steinbeck's critical success waned after *The Grapes of Wrath*, reaching a nadir at his death in 1968, despite his Nobel Prize for Literature in 1962. During World War II, his development as a novelist faltered for many reasons, and Steinbeck never recovered his artistic momentum. Even *East of Eden*, the work he thought his masterpiece, proved an artistic and critical failure though a popular success. Since his death, Steinbeck remains widely read, both in America and abroad, while his critical reputation has enjoyed a modest revival. Undoubtedly the appreciation of his considerable talents will continue to develop, as few writers have better celebrated the American dream or traced the dark lineaments of the American nightmare.

Biography

John Ernst Steinbeck was born on February 27, 1902, in Salinas, California. The time and place of his birth are important because Steinbeck matured as an artist in his early thirties during the darkest days of the Depression, and his most important fictions are set in his beloved Salinas Valley. In one sense, Steinbeck's location in time and place may have made him a particularly American artist. Born just after the closing of the frontier, Steinbeck grew up with a frustrated modern America and witnessed the most notable failure of the American dream in the Depression. He was a writer who inherited the great tradition of the American Renaissance of the nineteenth century and who was forced to reshape it in terms of the historical and literary imperatives of twentieth century modernism. Steinbeck's family background evidenced this strongly American identity. His paternal grandfather, John Adolph Steinbeck, emigrated from Germany, settling in California after serving in the Civil War. His mother's father, Samuel Hamilton, sailed around Cape Horn from northern Ireland, finally immigrating to the Salinas Valley. John Ernst Steinbeck and Olive Hamilton were the first-generation descendants of sturdy, successful, and Americanized immigrant farm families. They met and married in 1890, settling in Salinas, where the father was prominent in local business and government, and the mother stayed home to rear their four children— three daughters and a son, the third child named for his father. The Steinbecks were refined, intelligent, and ambitious people who lived a quiet middle-class life in the small agricultural service town of Salinas.

Steinbeck seems to have enjoyed a happy childhood, and in fact he often asserted that he did. His father made enough money to indulge him in a small way, even to buy him a red pony. His mother encouraged him to read and to write, providing him with the classics of English and American literature. At school, he proved a popular and successful student and was elected president of his senior class.

After graduation from Salinas High School in 1919, Steinbeck enrolled at Stanford University. His subsequent history belies the picture of the happy, normal young man. He was soon in academic difficulties and dropped out of college several times to work on ranches in the Salinas Valley and observe "real life." His interests were varied, but he settled on novel-writing as his ambition, despite his family's insistence that he prepare for a more prosaic career. This traumatic rejection of middle-class values would prove a major force in shaping Steinbeck's fiction, both his social protest novels and his lighter entertainments such as *Cannery Row*.

Leaving Stanford without a degree in 1925, Steinbeck sojourned in New York for several months, where he worked as a laborer, a newspaper reporter, and a free-lance writer. Disillusioned in all his abortive pursuits, Steinbeck returned to California, where a job as winter caretaker of a lodge at Lake Tahoe provided the time to finish his first novel, *Cup of Gold*. The novel, a romance concerned with the Caribbean pirate Henry Morgan, was published by a small press directly before the crash of 1929, and it earned the young writer little recognition and even less money. In 1930, he married Carol Henning and moved with her to Los Angeles and later to Pacific Grove, a seaside resort near Monterey, where he lived in his parents' summer house. Still supported by his family and his wife, the ambitious young writer churned out the manuscripts of several novels.

A friend, Edward F. (Ed) Ricketts, a marine biologist trained at the University of Chicago, encouraged Steinbeck to treat his material more objectively. Under Rickett's influence, Steinbeck modified his earlier commitment to satire, allegory, and romanticism and turned to modern accounts of the Salinas Valley. Steinbeck's next two novels, *Pastures of Heaven* and *To a God Unknown*, are both set in the Valley, but both still were marked by excessive sentimentality and symbolism. Both were virtually ignored by the public and the critics. Steinbeck's short fiction, however, began to receive recognition; for example, his story "The Murder" was selected as an O. Henry Prize story in 1934.

Tortilla Flat, a droll tale of Monterey's Mexican quarter, established Steinbeck as a popular and critical success in 1935. (Unfortunately, his parents died just before he achieved his first real success.) The novel's sales provided money to pay his debts, to travel to Mexico, and to continue writing seriously. His next novel, *In Dubious Battle*, established him as a serious literary artist and began the period of his greatest success, both critical and popular. This harshly realistic strike novel followed directions established in stories such as "The Raid," influenced by the realistic impulse of American literature in the 1930's. Succeeding publications quickly confirmed this development in his fiction. His short novels *The Red Pony* and *Of Mice and Men* followed in 1937, his story collection, *The Long Valley*, in 1938, and his epic of the Okie migration to California, *The Grapes of Wrath*, in 1939. His own play version of *Of Mice and Men* won the Drama Critics Circle Award in 1938, and *The Grapes of Wrath* received the Pulitzer Prize in 1940. Steinbeck had become one of the most popular and respected writers in the country, a spokesman for an entire culture.

In 1941, Pearl Harbor changed the direction of American culture and of

John Steinbeck's literary development. During the war years, he seemed in a holding pattern, trying to adjust to his phenomenal success while absorbing the cataclysmic events around him. Steinbeck's career stalled for many reasons. He left the California subjects and realistic style of his finest novels, and he was unable to come to terms with a world at war, though he served for a few months as a front-line correspondent. Personal developments paralleled these literary ones. Steinbeck divorced his first wife and married Gwen Conger, a young Hollywood starlet; no doubt she influenced his decision to move from California to New York. Steinbeck began to write with an eye on Broadway and Hollywood.

Steinbeck was forty-three when World War II ended in 1945; he died in 1968 at the age of sixty-six. Over those twenty-three years, Steinbeck was extremely productive, winning considerable acclaim—most notably, the Nobel Prize in Literature in 1962. Yet the most important part of his career was finished. The war had changed the direction of his artistic development, and Steinbeck seemed powerless to reverse his decline.

Again, his personal life mirrored his literary difficulties. Although Gwen Conger presented him with his only children—Tom, born in 1944, and John, born in 1946—they were divorced in 1948. Like his first divorce, this one was bitter and expensive. In the same year, his mentor Ricketts was killed in a car accident. Steinbeck traveled extensively, devoting himself to film and nonfiction projects. In 1950, he married Elaine Scott, establishing a supportive relationship which allowed him to finish his epic Salinas Valley novel *East of Eden*.

Steinbeck tried again and again to write his way back to the artistic success of his earlier years, notably in *The Wayward Bus*, but his commercial success kept getting in the way. *East of Eden*, Steinbeck's major postwar novel, attempted another California epic to match the grandeur of *The Grapes of Wrath*. Although the book was a blockbuster best-seller, it was an artistic and critical failure. Steinbeck himself seemed to recognize his own decline, and in his last years he virtually abandoned fiction for journalism.

Of his last novels, only *The Winter of Our Discontent* transcends mere entertainment, and it does not have the literary structures to match its serious themes. Despite the popularity of nonfiction such as *Travels with Charley*, despite awards such as the Nobel Prize and the United States Medal of Freedom, despite his personal friendship with President Lyndon Johnson as a supporter of Vietnam, Steinbeck was only the shell of the great writer of the 1930's. He died in New York City on December 20, 1968.

Analysis

John Steinbeck remains a writer of the 1930's, perhaps *the* American writer of the 1930's. Although his first novel, *Cup of Gold*, was published in 1929, its derivative "Lost Generation" posturing gives little indication of the masterpiece he would publish at the end of the next decade, *The Grapes of Wrath*. Steinbeck developed from a romantic, imitative, often sentimental apprentice to a realistic, objective, and accomplished novelist in only a decade. The reasons for this change can be found in the interplay between a sensitive writer and his cultural background.

A writer of great talent, sensitivity, and imagination, John Steinbeck entered into the mood of the country in the late 1930's with an extraordinary responsiveness. The Depression had elicited a reevaluation of American culture, a reassessment of the American dream: a harsh realism of observation balanced by a warm emphasis on human dignity. Literature and the other arts joined social, economic, and political thought in contrasting traditional American ideals with the bleak reality of breadlines and shantytowns. Perhaps the major symbol of dislocation was the Dust Bowl; the American garden became a wasteland from which its dispossessed farmers fled. The arts in the 1930's focused on these harsh images and tried to find in them the human dimensions which promised a new beginning.

The proletarian novel, documentary photography, and the documentary film stemmed from similar impulses; the radical novel put more emphasis on the inhuman conditions of the dislocated, while the films made more of the promising possibilities for a new day. Painting, music, and theater all responded to a new humanistic and realistic thrust. The best balance was struck by documentary photographers and filmmakers: Dorothea Lange, Walker Evans (James Agee's associate), and Arthur Rothstein in photography; Pare Lorentz, Willard Van Dyke, and Herbert Kline in film. As a novelist, Steinbeck shared this documentary impulse, and it refined his art.

In Dubious Battle tells the harsh story of a violent agricultural strike in the "Torgas Valley" from the viewpoint of two Communist agitators. Careful and objective in his handling of the material, the mature Steinbeck provided almost a factual case study of a strike. In a letter, he indicated that this was his conscious intention:

> I had an idea that I was going to write the autobiography of a Communist. Then Miss McIntosh [his agent] suggested I reduce it to fiction. There lay the trouble. I had planned to write a journalistic account of a strike. But as I thought of it as fiction the thing got bigger and bigger . . . I have used a small strike in an orchard valley as the symbol of man's eternal, bitter warfare with himself.

For the first time, Steinbeck was able to combine his ambition to write great moral literature with his desire to chronicle his time and place.

Significantly, the novel takes its title from John Milton's *Paradise Lost* (1667) in which the phrase is used to describe the struggle between God and Satan, but it takes its subject from the newspapers and newsreels of the 1930's. The underlying structure demonstrates the universal struggle of good and evil, of human greed and selfishness versus human generosity and idealism.

Jim, the protagonist killed at the conclusion, is obviously a Christ figure, an individual who has sacrificed himself for the group. Here, Steinbeck needs no overblown symbolic actions to support his theme. He lets his contemporary story tell itself realistically and in documentary fashion. In a letter, he describes his method in the novel: "I wanted to be merely a recording consciousness, judging nothing, simply putting down the thing." This objective, dispassionate, almost documentary realism separates *In Dubious Battle* from his earlier fiction and announces the beginning of Steinbeck's major period.

Of Mice and Men was written in 1935 and 1936 and first published as a novel in 1937 at the height of the Depression. Steinbeck constructed the book around dramatic scenes so that he could easily rewrite it for the stage, which he did with the help of George S. Kaufmann. The play opened late in 1937, with Wallace Ford as George and Broderick Crawford as Lennie. A movie version, directed by Lewis Milestone (*All Quiet on the Western Front*, 1931; *Rain*, 1932; and so on), with Burgess Meredith and Lon Chaney, Jr. in the central roles, appeared in 1939. The success of the play and film spurred sales of the novel and created a wide audience for Steinbeck's next book, *The Grapes of Wrath*.

Like his classic story of the "Okie" migration from the Dust Bowl to the promised land of California, *Of Mice and Men* is a dramatic presentation of the persistence of the American dream and the tragedy of its failure. His characters are the little people, the uncommon "common people," disoriented and dispossessed by modern life yet still yearning for a little piece of land, that little particle of the Jeffersonian ideal. Lennie is the symbol of this visceral, inarticulate land-hunger, while George becomes the poet of this romantic vision. How their dream blossoms and then dies is Steinbeck's dramatic subject; how their fate represents that of America in the 1930's and after becomes his theme. His title, an allusion to the Scottish poet Robert Burns, suggests that the best laid plans "of mice and men often gang a-gley"; so the American vision had gone astray in the Depression decade Steinbeck documented so movingly and realistically.

The Red Pony involves the maturation of Jody Tiflin, a boy of about ten when the action opens. The time is about 1910 and the setting is the Tiflin ranch in the Salinas Valley, where Jody lives with his father, Carl, his mother, Ruth, and the hired hand, a middle-aged cowboy named Billy Buck. From time to time, they are visited by Jody's grandfather, a venerable old man who led one of the first wagon trains to California. "The Gift," the first section of the novel, concerns Jody's red pony, which he names Gabilan, after the nearby mountain range. The pony soon becomes a symbol of the boy's growing maturity and his developing knowledge of the natural world. Later, he carelessly leaves the pony out in the rain, and it takes cold and dies, despite Billy Buck's efforts to save it. Thus Jody learns of nature's cruel indifference to human wishes.

In the second part, "The Great Mountains," the Tiflin ranch is visited by a former resident, Gitano, an aged Chicano laborer reared in the now vanished hacienda. Old Gitano has come home to die. In a debate which recalls Robert Frost's poem "The Death of the Hired Man," Carl persuades Ruth that they cannot take Old Gitano in, but—as in Frost's poem—their dialogue proves pointless. Stealing a broken-down nag significantly named Easter, the old man rides off into the mountains to die in dignity. Again, Jody is faced with the complex, harsh reality of adult life.

In "The Promise," the third section, Jody learns more of nature's ambiguous promises when his father has one of the mares put to stud to give the boy another colt. The birth is complicated, however, and Billy Buck must kill the mare to save the colt, demonstrating that life and death are inextricably intertwined. The final section, "The Leader of the People," ends the sequence with another vision of death and change. Jody's grandfather comes to visit, retelling his time-worn stories of the great wagon crossing. Carl Tiflin cruelly hurts the old man by revealing that none of them except Jody is really interested in these repetitive tales. The grandfather realizes that Carl is right, but later he tells Jody that the adventurous stories were not the point, but that his message was "Westering" itself. For the grandfather, "Westering" was the source of American identity. With the close of the frontier, "Westering" has ended, and the rugged Westerners have been replaced by petty landholders such as Carl Tiflin and aging cowboys such as Billy Buck. In his grandfather's ramblings, Jody discovers a sense of mature purpose, and by the conclusion of the sequence, he too can hope to be a leader of the people.

The Red Pony traces Jody's initiation into adult life with both realism and sensitivity, a balance which Steinbeck did not always achieve. The vision of the characters caught up in the harsh world of nature is balanced by their deep human concerns and commitments. The evocation of the ranch setting in its vital beauty is matched only in the author's finest works, such as *Of Mice and Men*. Steinbeck's symbols grow naturally out of this setting, and nothing in the story-sequence seems forced into a symbolic pattern, as in his later works. In its depiction of an American variation on a universal experience, *The Red Pony* deserves comparison with the finest of modern American fiction, especially with initiation tales such as William Faulkner's *The Bear* (1942) and Ernest Hemingway's Nick Adams stories.

Responding to a variety of social and artistic influences, Steinbeck's writing had evolved toward documentary realism throughout the 1930's. In fiction, this development is especially clear in *In Dubious Battle*, *Of Mice and Men*, and *The Long Valley*. Even more obvious was the movement of his nonfiction toward a committed documentation of the social ills plaguing America during the Depression decade. Steinbeck's newspaper and magazine writing offered detailed accounts of social problems, particularly the plight of migrant agricultural workers in California's fertile valleys. The culmination of this development was *Their Blood Is Strong* (1938), a compilation of reports originally written for the *San Francisco News* and published with additional text by Steinbeck and photographs by Dorothea Lange originally made for the Farm Security Administration.

It is significant that Steinbeck first conceived of *The Grapes of Wrath* as just such a documentary book. In March, 1938, Steinbeck went into the California valleys with a *Life* magazine photographer to make a record of the harsh conditions in the migrant camps. The reality he encountered seemed too significant for nonfiction, however, and Steinbeck began to reshape this material as a novel, an epic novel.

Although his first tentative attempts at fictionalizing the situation in the agricultural valleys were heavily satiric, as indicated by the early title *L'Affaire Lettuceberg*, Steinbeck soon realized that the Okie migration was the stuff of an American epic. Reworking his material, adding to it by research in government agency files and by more journeys into the camps and along the migrant routes, Steinbeck evolved his vision. A grand design emerged; he would follow one family from the Oklahoma Dust Bowl to California. Perhaps this methodology was suggested by the sociological case histories of the day, perhaps by the haunted faces of individual families which stared back at him as he researched in Farm Security Administration files.

In discussing his plans for his later documentary film, *The Forgotten Village* (1941), Steinbeck remarked that most documentaries concerned large groups of people but that audiences could identify better with individuals. In *The Grapes of Wrath*, he made one family representative of general conditions. The larger groups and problems he treated in short interchapters which generalized the issues particularized in the Joad family. Perhaps the grand themes of change and movement were suggested by the documentary films of Pare Lorentz (later a personal friend), *The Plow That Broke the Plains* (1936) and *The River* (1938), with their panoramic geographical and historical visions. Drawing an archetypal theme from Sir Thomas Malory, John Bunyan, John Milton, and the Bible—the ultimate source of his pervasive religious symbolism—Steinbeck made the journey of the Joads into an allegorical pilgrimage as well as a desperate race along Route 66. During this journey, the Joad family disintegrates, but the larger human family emerges. Tom Joad makes a pilgrim's progress from a narrow, pessimistic view to a transcendental vision of American possibilities. The novel ends on a note of hope for a new American dream.

The Grapes of Wrath was a sensational best-seller from the beginning. Published to generally favorable reviews in March, 1939, it was selling at the rate of more than twenty-five hundred copies a day two months later. Controversy helped spur sales. As a semidocumentary, its factual basis was subject to close scrutiny, and many critics challenged Steinbeck's material. Oklahomans resented the presentation of the Joads as typical of the state (many still do), while Californians disapproved of the depiction of their state's leading industry. The book was attacked, banned, burned—but everywhere it was read. Even in the migrant camps, it was considered an accurate picture of the conditions experienced there. Some 430,000 copies were sold in a year, and in 1940, the novel received the Pulitzer Prize and the Award of the American Booksellers Association (later the National Book Award). Naturally, all the excitement attracted the attention of Hollywood, in spite of the fact that the controversy over the novel seemed to preclude a film version, or at least a faithful film version. Nevertheless, Darryl F. Zanuck produced and John Ford directed a faithful adaptation starring Henry Fonda in 1940; the film, like the novel, has become a classic, and it gave Steinbeck's vision of America in the 1930's even wider currency.

Indeed, Steinbeck's best work was filmic in the best sense of that word—visual, realistic, objective. These qualities nicely balanced the allegorical and romantic strains inherent in his earlier fiction. During World War II, however, his work, much to its detriment, began to cater to the film industry. In fact, much of his postwar writing seems to have found its inspiration in Hollywood versions of his work. His own screen adaptation of an earlier story, *The Red Pony* (1949), proves a sentimentalized reproduction of the original. Still, he was occasionally capable of recapturing his earlier vision, particularly in his works about Mexico—*The Pearl* and *Viva Zapata!*

Mexico always had been an important symbolic place for Steinbeck. As a native Californian, he had been aware of his state's Mexican heritage. Even as a boy, he sought out Chicano companions, fascinated by their unconcern for the pieties of WASP culture; he also befriended Mexican fieldhands at the ranches where he worked during his college summers. Later, his first literary success, *Tortilla Flat*, grew from his involvement with the *paisanos* of Monterey, people who would today be called Chicanos.

For Steinbeck, Mexico was everything modern America was not; it possessed a primitive vitality, a harsh simplicity, and a romantic beauty—all of which are found in *The Pearl*. Mexico exhibits the same qualities in the works of other modern writers such as Malcolm Lowry, Aldous Huxley, Graham Greene, Hart Crane, and Katherine Anne Porter. All of them lived and worked there for some time, contrasting the traditional culture they discovered in Mexico with the emptiness of the modern world. Steinbeck also was fascinated by a Mexico still alive with social concern. The continued extension of the Revolution into the countryside had been his subject in *The Forgotten Village*, and it would be developed further in *Viva Zapata!* For Steinbeck, Mexico represented the purity of artistic and social purposes that he had lost after World War II.

This sense of the writer's personal involvement energizes *The Pearl*, making it Steinbeck's best work of fiction in the years following the success of *The Grapes of Wrath*. At the beginning of the novella, the storyteller states: "If this story is a parable, perhaps everyone takes his own meaning from it and reads his own life into it." The critics have read Steinbeck's short novel in a number of ways, but strangely enough, they have not considered it as a parable of the author's own career in the postwar period. Much like Ernest Hemingway's *The Old Man and The Sea* (1952), *The Pearl* uses the life of a simple fisherman to investigate symbolically an aging artist's difficult maturation.

Steinbeck was presented with the tale during his Sea of Cortez expedition in 1940. In his log, he recounts "an event which happened at La Paz in recent years." The story matches the basic outline of *The Pearl*, though Steinbeck made several major changes, changes significant in an autobiographical sense. In the original, the Mexican fisherman was a devil-may-care bachelor; in *The Pearl*, he becomes the sober young husband and father, Kino. Steinbeck himself had just become a father for the first time when he wrote the novella, and this change provides a clue to the autobiographical nature of the parable. The original bachelor thought the pearl a key to easy living; Kino sees it creating a better way of life for the people through an education for his baby son, Coyotito. If the child could read and write, then he could set his family and his people free from the social and economic bondage in which they toil. Kino is ignorant of the dangers of wealth, and *The Pearl* is the tale of how he matures by coming to understand them. Steinbeck, too, matured from his youthful innocence as he felt the pressures of success.

As in his best fiction of the 1930's Steinbeck fuses his universal allegory with documentary realism. Perhaps planning ahead for a screenplay, Steinbeck's prose in the novel often takes a cinematic point of view. Scenes are presented in terms of establishing shots, medium views, and close-ups. In particular, Steinbeck carefully examines the natural setting, often visually contrasting human behavior with natural phenomena. As in his best fiction, his naturalistic vision is inherent in the movement of his story; there is no extraneous philosophizing.

Steinbeck's characters in *The Pearl* are real people in a real world, but they are also universal types. Kino, the fisherman named for an early Jesuit explorer, Juana, his wife, and Coyotito, their baby, are almost an archetypal family, like the Holy Family in a medieval morality play. Kino's aspirations are the same universal drives to better himself and his family that took the Okies to the California valleys. Like the Joads, this symbolic family must struggle at once against an indifferent natural order and a corrupt social order. Unfortunately, aside from the screenplay of *Viva Zapata!*, Steinbeck would never again achieve the fusion of parable and realism which energizes *The Pearl*.

In his Nobel Prize speech of 1962, Steinbeck indicated what he tried to accomplish in his work:

The ancient commission of the writer has not changed. He is charged with exposing our many grievous faults and failures, with dredging up to the light our dark and dangerous dreams, for the purpose of improvement.

No writer has better exposed the dark underside of the American dream, but few writers have so successfully celebrated the great hope symbolized in that dream—the hope of human development. Steinbeck's best fictions picture a paradise lost but also posit a future paradise to be regained. In spite of his faults and failures, John Steinbeck's best literary works demonstrate a greatness of heart and mind found only rarely in modern American literature.

Joseph R. Millichap

Other major works

SHORT FICTION: *Saint Katy the Virgin*, 1936; *The Long Valley*, 1938.
PLAY: *Burning Bright*, 1951.
SCREENPLAYS: *The Forgotten Village*, 1941; *Lifeboat*, 1944; *A Medal for Benny*, 1945; *The Pearl*, 1945; *The Red Pony*, 1949; *Viva Zapata!*, 1952.
NONFICTION: *Their Blood Is Strong*, 1938; *The Forgotten Village*, 1941; *Sea of Cortez*, 1941 (with Edward F. Ricketts); *Bombs Away*, 1942; *A Russian Journal*, 1948 (with Robert Capa); *Once There Was a War*, 1958; *Travels with Charley*, 1962; *Letters to Alicia*, 1965; *America and Americans*, 1966; *Journal of a Novel*, 1969; *Steinbeck: A Life in Letters*, 1975 (Elaine Steinbeck and Robert Wallsten, editors).

Bibliography

Fontenrose, Joseph. *John Steinbeck: An Introduction and Interpretation*. New York: Holt, Rinehart and Winston, 1963. A biographical introduction to Steinbeck, followed by an examination of the biological and mythical elements in his work and the thematic movements of his fiction. Contains a useful chronology, a selected bibliography, and an index.
Hughes, R. S. *John Steinbeck: A Study of the Short Fiction*. Boston: Twayne, 1989. Divided into three sections: Steinbeck's short stories, the author's letters exploring his craft, and four critical commentaries. A good study of some of his lesser known works which includes a chronology, a lengthy bibliography, and an index.
Kiernan, Thomas. *The Intricate Music: A Biography of John Steinbeck*. Boston: Little, Brown, 1979. The first full-length biographical study of Steinbeck. Kiernan pieces together the writer's remarkable life through solid research, interviews, and personal conversations.
Lisca, Peter. *The Wide World of John Steinbeck*. New York: Gordian Press, 1958. An indispensable guide to Steinbeck's work, published in 1958 and then updated with an "Afterword" examining the writer's last novel *The Winter of Our Discontent* (1961). Admired and imitated, Lisca's work set

the standard for future Steinbeck studies.

McCarthy, Paul. *John Steinbeck*. New York: Frederick Ungar, 1980. A short
biographical approach to Steinbeck's work that examines each novel against
the forces that shaped his life. Includes a useful chronology, notes, a bibliography, and an index.

RICHARD G. STERN

Born: New York, New York; February 25, 1928

Principal long fiction

Golk, 1960; *Europe: Or, Up and Down with Schreiber and Baggish*, 1961; *In Any Case*, 1962 (reissued as *The Chaleur Network*, 1981); *Stitch*, 1965; *Other Men's Daughters*, 1973; *Natural Shocks*, 1978; *A Father's Words*, 1986.

Other literary forms

In addition to his novels, Richard Stern has published several well-received collections of short fiction: *Teeth, Dying, and Other Matters* (1964), *1968: A Short Novel, an Urban Idyll, Five Stories, and Two Trade Notes* (1970), *Packages* (1980), and *Noble Rot: Stories, 1949-1988* (1989). He has published three miscellanies, comprising essays, reviews, reflections, journal excerpts, interviews, and even a bit of poetry: *The Books in Fred Hampton's Apartment* (1973), *The Invention of the Real* (1982), and *The Position of the Body* (1986). His three plays—*The Gamesman's Island* (1964), *Dossier: Earth. Twenty-four Blackouts from the Middle Electric Age* (1966), and *Reparations* (1958)—have not found a large audience. Stern has also edited two anthologies, *American Poetry of the Fifties* (1967) and *Honey and Wax: The Powers and Pleasures of Narrative* (1966), further testimony to his wide range of abilities and interests.

Achievements

Stern's fiction has been compared to that of Saul Bellow by a number of critics. There are a number of similarities between the two writers, but the differences are, perhaps, more important. Stern does use literary and historical allusions and analogies in the manner of Bellow, but he is not a novelist of ideas as Bellow decidedly is. Stern, in contrast to Bellow, continues to exploit the resources of the traditional novel. His interest is more in character and theme than in the dialectic of ideas. This traditional stance may have limited Stern's audience and his recognition as a writer. He has, however, received some prestigious awards. He received the Longwood Foundation Award in 1960, the Fiction Award of the National Institute of Arts and Letters in 1968, the Carl Sandburg award for Fiction in 1979, and the Award of Merit for the Novel in 1985, and he has been both a Rockefeller and a Guggenheim Fellow. The major complaint about Stern's novels is that they are too consciously allusive or mythical; they lack the confessional note and the excess of feeling so characteristic of contemporary fiction. Marcus Klein is helpful, however, in revealing what Stern's fiction does contain:

> In a time when serious American fiction has tended toward extreme personal assertion and extravagance of manner, Richard G. Stern has been composing a body of work which is notable for its detailed craftsmanship, its intricacy, and its reticencies.

Biography

Richard Gustave Stern was born in New York City on February 25, 1928. He was graduated Phi Beta Kappa from the University of North Carolina, Chapel Hill, in 1947, receiving an M.A. from Harvard University in 1949 and a Ph.D. from the University of Iowa in 1954. He has been a member of the faculty at the University of Chicago since 1955 and has been a visiting lecturer at such institutions as the University of Venice, Harvard University, and the University of Nice. He lives in Chicago, Illinois.

Analysis

In an interview, Robert L. Raeder noted that Richard Stern's "books and stories seemed to lack a center, a common denominator." Stern replied that he adheres to a theory of art in which the artist "detaches" himself from his creations and rejects the Romantic approach, wherein the author includes his own life, opinions, and feelings. Stern immerses himself not only in the personalities of the characters he invents but also in their occupations and milieus. Accordingly, Stern's novels explore the mind and world of a professor of biology, a famous sculptor, a journalist, and a television producer. There is no trace of the author in these diverse creations; nor is there any trace of autobiography in characters who display a very limited range of perception, such as Hondorp in *Golk* or Edward Gunther in *Stitch*.

Despite this diversity, however, there are a few constants in Stern's fiction. One of these is the city. His characters are constantly observing, describing, and identifying their fates with the great cities they inhabit, whether it be the New York of *Golk*, the Venice of *Stitch*, or the Cambridge of *Other Men's Daughters*. Another recurring feature of Stern's novels is their lack of conclusive resolution: What happens to the main characters is a sort of ironic modulation, a subtle change of perception rather than a marked change in character or fortune. Marcus Klein has described the movement of a typical Stern novel as one in which a private man becomes involved in the public world and in the process becomes involved in "contingencies" with which he must deal. "His modest success is that he has become potentially moral."

Stern's first novel, *Golk*, is the tale of a private and reclusive man. Hondorp, who is thrust into the public world by a chance encounter with Golk and his film crew in a bookstore. Up to this point, Hondorp has spent his time wandering around New York City and watching television at home with his father. Suddenly, he is on television and a public figure; he accepts a job with Golk's television crew and joins them in their "Golks," which are the tricks played on unsuspecting people who are filmed in absurd situations. The television program based on these secret glimpses of ordinary people becomes very successful, and the show receives a network contract. Yet Golk, the producer and planner of the show, has larger ambitions: He starts to expose senators, union officials, and bureaucrats. At this point, Golk's empire begins to crumble under the attacks by the politicians and network officials. The climactic moment comes when Hondorp and his girlfriend, Elaine, betray Golk and take over the program. They justify the betrayal with the highest of motives: It is a continuation "of Golk's work." Yet their victory—and their marriage—is short-lived; without the eccentric vision of Golk, the show flounders and is canceled. At the end of the book, everyone returns to his earlier state; Golk is now merely one of the crowd, as he "fits" everywhere; Elaine has gone back to her brutal husband; and Hondorp becomes once more the empty person he was at the beginning, with "all trace of his ambition, all desire for change gone absolutely and forever."

Most critics of the novel have emphasized Stern's satire on the invasion of privacy and the baleful influence of television. Stern, however, suggests that this reading ignores the primary thrust of the novel. According to Stern, *Golk* "deals in large part with genius and its epigones and the nature of contemporary exploitation in its great theater, post-war New York." Golk, then, is, for all of his eccentricities, an authentic original; he pushes his created form to its limits, and, in doing so, encounters the wrath of the establishment. Golk scares them, but his second-rate imitator, Hondorp, takes no risks and eventually fails to excite the audience. Even though Golk has lost his position, he remains a presence; he "fits," while Hondorp does not belong anywhere.

Stern's next important novel, *In Any Case*, also deals with betrayal. The protagonist, Samuel Curry, discovers in a book by a French priest an accusation that his son, Bobbie, has betrayed the Chaleur Network, a group of French, English, and Americans working against the Nazis in the early 1940's. Curry is an unlikely hero; he is comfortable and established in France, and the thought of involving himself in the murk of the recent war is repugnant to him. He first seeks out Bobbie's accuser, Father Trentemille, and confronts him, but he receives no satisfaction: Trentemille simply repeats the charges. He then tries two survivors of the "Network," one of whom defends Bobbie, while the other repeats the accusation. He has better luck with Bobbie's girlfriend in the Network, Jacqueline, who asserts her belief in Bobbie's innocence, although she can offer no proof. He has even better luck with German sources and discovers that the real traitor is an agent whose code name is Robert. Robert is described as a professional agent, one who "doesn't even have sides. He's a sphere." When Samuel Curry confronts Robert, he finds that the matter is more complicated than he had thought. He believes that Robert is a "decent" man and goes into business with him. The climax of the novel comes when Curry decides that he must expose Robert and ask Father Trentemille for a retraction. His motives for this action, however, are complex. He believes that he is punishing Robert for his own "delinquency" in rehabilitating Bobbie's name and because Robert has become a rival for Jacqueline's affections. The result of this series of betrayals is surprisingly tranquil. Robert is exposed, but he is not punished. Samuel Curry and Jacqueline marry and are living on the Riviera and expecting the birth of a child in a few months. Not only is Bobbie's name cleared but also his father and the girl he loved have united to repair the loss of his death—a very satisfying ending.

Stern has spoken of how he drew upon and altered the factual background for *In Any Case*. His source was a factual account of the work of the underground in France. Stern makes it into a moral tale in which "the discoverer finds in himself a treasonous impulse which is related to the official traitor's." This impulse begins when Curry sees the divergence between motive and result, of intention and action. "Action would be too easy a way into the current, too much a short cut to judgment." Curry's own intentions and actions during the war and in his relationship with his son hinder any judgment he might make or any action he might take. Stern's comment on his original title for the novel makes his intention clear. "The idea was that the hero always eschewed an active role because 'in any case' there was so much to be said for either side that to take sides was to simplify the issue. To seek relief in action." Curry seeks this sort of "relief" at the end of the novel when he can no longer control the complexities he discovers.

In *Stitch*, Stern returns to the theme of "genius and its epigones." The protagonist, Edward Gunther, is an American who has left his advertising job to find himself and culture in Europe. He has, however, no sensitivity to or perception of art; he spends his time, instead, in eating, chasing women, and brooding. His wife and children are left behind in a hotel in Venice while he searches for the European experience. His opposite, the genius, is Thaddeus Stitch, an American sculptor who has lived in Italy for many years and is recovering from a prison sentence for supporting Fascism; he is obviously modeled on Ezra Pound. Stitch is now quite old and unable to create great art, but his monuments surround him on his island. Edward and Stitch are brought together by their common interest in Nina, a young American poet. Nina is the opposite of Edward; Nina is a poet, not a cultural hanger-on like Edward, and her epic poem has some of the connections with the past that Stitch's work does. Edward is measured and found wanting by these comparisons. As Stitch remembers creating or re-creating monuments of unaging intellect, and as Nina creates, Edward is literally swelling up with the weight he has gained and the assertions of his ego. His only encounter with Stitch ends with a curt dismissal from the master, and his only encounter with Stitch's art produces only pseudoinsights; he describes the island as "beautiful wreckage." Edward's personal life is also a disaster: His wife finds out about his adulteries and throws him out of the house. He finds cultural salvation in the pompous essays he writes and in the possibility of a place with a foundation. The novel comes to an end with Edward's return to the United States. He is teaching at a secondary school in Santa Barbara while waiting for a foundation position. He does hear news of those he left behind in Europe—news which unsettles him. Nina has married and had her epic poem published; Stitch remains in Venice and was the one who introduced Nina to her husband; Edward's wife has divorced him and has found a new partner. Edward is watching the funeral services for President John F. Kennedy as his dreams of finding himself and Europe fade into nothingness.

In *Stitch*, Stern takes the theme of genius and its epigones much further than he did in *Golk*. The genius of this novel is much more credible; some of the best parts of the book are the descriptions of Stitch's art. The epigone is also more credible: Edward is not merely a nullity who is suddenly placed in a position of power but also a chilling example of the cultural middleman who would not recognize an authentic work of art if he tripped over one. The debate between Edward and Nina over Stitch's art, and art in general, defines the differences between the genius and the epigone. Nina sees the problem in life and in art. "Attempts to be what we aren't. Overprizing our singularity. Egoism. Imperceptivity in situations solved long ago. Failure to adapt. The bloodline runs from the world to art's expression of it." Yet Edward never can escape his egoism, and he remains a bundle of unfulfilled and inexpressible longings.

Other Men's Daughters traces the changes in a relationship and a family, a theme in nearly all of Stern's fiction, especially the later works. The protagonist is a very attractive and settled man, Dr. Merriwether. He is a professor at Harvard Medical School, and he lives in Cambridge in a house passed down to him from his ancestors. He is jolted out of this settled life when a young girl, Cynthia Ryder, comes to him one day for a prescription for the Pill. They meet a few times and eventually become lovers. Dr. Merriwether— Stern emphasizes his title and position rather than his personal identity— resists for a while, but they become deeply involved. When Cynthia returns to Swarthmore, they correspond and keep the relationship alive. They manage to meet when Merriwether delivers a paper in New York and when Cynthia can come to Cambridge, but Merriwether manages simultaneously to keep his domestic life intact. This balance is upset, however, when Cynthia accompanies Merriwether to Italy, where he is reading a paper. Merriwether adds a few "speculations" to his formal paper and is then attacked by an American scientist who tells him to "go back to your child whore and let the rest of us do serious work." The public exposure continues when *Newsweek* prints an item linking Merriwether and Cynthia; this brings Cynthia's father on the scene to confront the couple. The confrontation between Mr. Ryder and Merriwether is reminiscent of *In Any Case*; Mr. Ryder does not despise Merriwether but is, instead, drawn to the seriousness and character he sees in him. He does, however, require Cynthia to undergo psychiatric therapy and for the lovers not to meet for a period. The reaction of Merriwether's wife, Sarah, from whom he has long been emotionally estranged, is angry and bitter. Egged on by her lawyer, she starts acrimonious divorce proceedings, and Merriwether loses all of his comfort and the routines he has established over the years. There are some touching moments, such as the Merriwethers' last Christmas together and the parents' breaking the news of their divorce to the younger children; the mood moves away from bitterness once the painful process has been completed. The last chapter of the novel reunites Merriwether and Cynthia in Colorado. The new environment helps Merriwether to overcome the earlier dislocations, and he has some tender moments with his two youngest children. The last note is a very positive one. "The depth of love after loss. The way of human beings. . . . Linkage. Transmission. Evolving."

Other Men's Daughters emphasizes character and setting more than theme. Stern's portrayal of Robert Merriwether—he acquires a first name when he immerses himself in the private world of relationships—and his world is very full. Even Merriwether's scientific specialty, thirst, is exactly appropriate. Furthermore, Stern also renders Sarah's point of view with an impressive sympathy and fidelity. She reveals that the apparently perfect home and family is a façade that hides long-held feelings of resentment and hatred. In the late twentieth century, divorce may be what marriage was to Jane Austen in the nineteenth century, the essential social transaction to be represented in the novel.

Natural Shocks begins where *Other Men's Daughters* ends; the protagonist, Frederick Wursup, is a new journalist who has been divorced for three years. He now lives across from his children and former wife, and he spends much time peeping into his wife's apartment to see what is happening. This intrusion on privacy is directly related to Wursup's occupation as a journalist, and there are many examples in the book of Wursup's destructive private revelations. He recalls an interview with a famous Hollywood director for *Life* magazine and feels "disgusted" at his unwarranted invasion of the man's privacy. His attempt to help a friend who is having political problems with a forthcoming magazine article revealing that the friend's father is on welfare only makes matters worse. A mutual friend, Knoblauch, sees a central problem in such writing: "The intimacies would be converted into publicity, benevolently but beyond recall. All but the hardest or deepest people would find that unbearable." After establishing the theme of the public revelation of private events and feelings, the novel shifts to deal with the most essential "natural shock," death. Wursup is looking for a topic on which to write, and his editor suggests that he look into the newly popular subject of death. When Wursup visits the hospital to talk to some dying patients, however, he becomes involved in the life of one of them, Cicia Buell. Because of his involvement, or the irreducible nature of death, Wursup finds it difficult to translate the interview with Cicia into his usual brand of journalism. Other shocks follow: His father and a friend commit suicide because of age or anxiety; the reason is never made clear. Wursup's wife remarries, which dislocates his sense of order. He tries to retreat to a Maine island to find some rest and peace; his idyll is interrupted, however, by the news that Cicia is dying. By the time he arrives at the hospital, she is dead, and the novel ends on a note of darkness unrelieved by any saving insight.

The themes are clear in *Natural Shocks*; death and privacy are interwoven throughout the novel. What is more difficult is coming to terms with the main character, Fred Wursup. He is an engaging and witty character, but his prying into people's lives for material for his journalism is disturbing. It is no accident that the book begins and ends with Wursup spying on his former wife's apartment. Wursup does have an epiphany: "Wursup himself had surrendered Cicia upstairs. She was almost as far away as Poppa and Mona. He'd toss off that article for Mike Schilp now. It was just another verbal turn." The people whose lives he has touched have become a product to be marketed. His recognition is, perhaps, what distinguishes him from other revealers of the private life.

A Father's Words is another investigation of domestic life, although the conflict is now not between husband and wife but between parent and children. The father, Cy Riemer, is amicably divorced from his first wife; his four children are in their twenties and, with one exception, settled. Jack is the oldest child and the recipient of most of his father's words; he is a habitual liar and self-deceiver whose unstructured life is a constant source of dismay and disruption to his father. Cy is always encouraging his son to become respectable. When Jack is working in a "bucket shop" selling books by phone, his father suggests that he get a job in a publishing company. Yet Jack resists the advice and continues on his disorderly way. He only impinges on his father's life when he suggests that Cy accept personal advertisements for his scientific newsletter. Cy is in financial difficulty and lets Jack handle it, although he feels soiled by the ads. Jack marries Maria Robusto, the daughter of a pornographic film king, and starts working for a commodities broker, so his father is temporarily relieved. Cy has trouble, however, with his other children. The next oldest, Jenny, has written a Ph.D. thesis on the "Wobbling" family in literature. The youngest son, Ben, has published a book called *The Need to Hurt*, which claims that human personality is formed at the fetal stage. Both works are attacks on Cy's fatherhood and his concept of family. The conflict with Jack comes to a head when Cy confronts Jack in a run-down tenement in New York. Again, Cy's words do not help, and Jack seems to give up on their relationship and on himself. "Face it, Dad. I'm finished. I'm never going to be what you want me to be." There are, however, two important reversals at the end of the novel. First, only a few years later, Jack becomes successful; he is the creator of a television situation comedy which features an addled father who creates problems which the wise son has to solve. It is another attack upon Cy's fatherhood and a curious metamorphosis of their relationship. The second reversal is that Cy has, once more and against all odds and sense, become a father. He resists at first and asks his then girlfriend, Emma, to get an abortion, but at the end he leaves Jack and looks forward to "coming home to a new family."

Cy seems, at first glance, to be an ideal parent. He encourages, instructs, and supports all of his children. Yet the words he directs toward his children to accomplish these tasks are resented by his children. Jenny accuses him of "the destructiveness that's there with the generosity and love." She believes that her father does not want anyone to "rival" him and so he cuts down each of the children. Furthermore, the children's success is based on the defeat of the father, in Jack's television show, Jenny's thesis, or Ben's book. The theme, then, is the oppressive burden of a father's love, inevitably felt no matter how the father treats the child; each child in the novel must win his independence by supplanting the father in some way. It must be said that this conflict and its resolutions are given a witty rather than oppressive treatment by Stern. In addition, Cy does not, finally, bend under the weight of this conflict but accepts and looks forward to it.

Richard Stern has created a body of work that is equal to that of any of his contemporaries. He was stereotyped early in his career as a follower of Saul Bellow and as a Jewish novelist. Those labels never did fit Stern, and they have become even less accurate as his work has developed. He has moved from such strongly thematic novels as *Golk* and *In Any Case* to novels that emphasize character and plot. Stern's ability to create not only credible characters but also their environment is most impressive. His novels are, as one critic has said, "in the great tradition of moral realism."

James Sullivan

Other major works

SHORT FICTION: *Teeth, Dying, and Other Matters*, 1964; *1968: A Short Novel, an Urban Idyll, Five Stories, and Two Trade Notes*, 1970; *Packages*, 1980; *Noble Rot: Stories, 1949-1988*, 1989.

PLAYS: *Reparations*, 1958; *The Gamesman's Island*, 1964; *Dossier: Earth. Twenty-four Blackouts from the Middle Electric Age*, 1966.

ANTHOLOGIES: *Honey and Wax: The Powers and Pleasures of Narrative*, 1966; *American Poetry of the Fifties*, 1967.

MISCELLANEOUS: *The Books in Fred Hampton's Apartment*, 1973; *The Invention of the Real*, 1982; *The Position of the Body*, 1986.

Bibliography

Bergonzi, Bernard. "Herzog in Venice, I." *New York Review of Books* 5 (December 9, 1965): 26. Bergonzi claims that the hero of *Stitch* is modeled on Ezra Pound. He likes the novel but is uneasy about Stern's evocation of literary myths.

Flower, Dean. "The Way We Live Now." Review of *Natural Shocks*, by Richard G. Stern. *The Hudson Review* 31 (Summer, 1978): 343-355. This review is generally negative. Flower argues that the suffering of the protagonist, Wursup, is sometimes too great, and that it is hard to discover the real Wursup in contrast to his public image.

Kenner, Hugh. "*Stitch*: The Master's Voice." Review of *Stitch*, by Richard G. Stern. *Chicago Review* 18 (Summer, 1966): 177-180. A very favorable review, in which Kenner praises Stern's originality and his ability to construct a novel out of discrete parts. Kenner also calls the book an act of homage to Ezra Pound.

Raban, Jonathan. "Lullabies for a Sleeping Giant: New Fiction." Review of *Other Men's Daughters*, by Richard G. Stern. *Encounter* 43 (July, 1974): 73-77. A very negative review, in which Raban accuses Stern of wasting his style and skill on a trite story.

Stern, Richard G. "A Conversation with Richard Stern." Interview by Eliot Anderson and Milton Rosenberg. *Chicago Review* 31 (Winter, 1980): 98-108. The interview focuses on Stern's *Natural Shocks*. Stern speaks of his interest in death as a fictional subject and the problems of writing about a hero who does not have a dramatic fate.

LAURENCE STERNE

Born: Clonmel, Ireland; November 24, 1713
Died: London, England; March 18, 1768

Principal long fiction

The Life and Opinions of Tristram Shandy, Gent., 1759-1767; *A Sentimental Journey Through France and Italy*, 1768.

Other literary forms

Laurence Sterne began his literary career with political pieces in the *York-Courant* in 1741. Two years later, he published a poem, "The Unknown World," in *The Gentleman's Magazine* (July, 1743). His song, "How Imperfect the Joys of the Soul," written for Kitty Fourmantel, appeared in Joseph Baildon's *Collection of New Songs Sung at Ranelagh* (1765), and a four-line epigram, "On a Lady's Sporting a Somerset," was attributed to Sterne in *Muse's Mirror* (1778). His sermons were published in three installments: two volumes in 1760, another two in 1766, and a final three volumes in 1769. A political satire entitled *A Political Romance* was published in 1759 but quickly suppressed. After Sterne's death, *Letters from Yorick to Eliza* appeared in 1773, and his daughter arranged for the publication of *Letters of the Late Rev. Mr. L. Sterne to His Most Intimate Friends* (1775, 3 volumes). These volumes include an autobiographical *Memoir* and the *Fragment in the Manner of Rabelais*. In 1935, Oxford University Press published the definitive edition of Sterne's letters, edited by Lewis Perry Curtis. The *Journal to Eliza*, composed in 1767, was not published until 1904.

Achievements

When Sterne went to London in March, 1760, he was an obscure provincial parson. He rode as a guest in Stephen Croft's cart, and he brought with him little more than his "best breeches." Two months later, he returned to York in his own carriage. Robert Dodsley, who the year before had refused the copyright of *The Life and Opinions of Tristram Shandy, Gent.* (commonly called *Tristram Shandy*) for 50 pounds, now gladly offered Sterne 250 pounds for the first two volumes, 380 pounds for the next two, as yet unwritten, and another 200 pounds for two volumes of sermons. The famous artist William Hogarth agreed to provide a frontispiece to the second edition of Volume I and another for Volume III; Joshua Reynolds painted Sterne's portrait. Like Lord Byron, Sterne could have said that he awoke to find himself famous. As Sterne did say, in a letter to Catherine Fourmantel, "I assure you my Kitty, that Tristram is the Fashion." Despite the carpings of a few—Horace Walpole thought *Tristram Shandy* "a very insipid and tedious performance," and Samuel Richardson thought it immoral—the novel was the rage of London, inspiring so many continuations and imitations that Sterne had to sign the later volumes to guarantee their authenticity.

After the novel's initial popularity, sales did drop off. In Book VIII, Tristram complains that he has "ten cart-loads" of Volumes V and VI "still unsold." Dodsley abandoned publication of the work after Volume IV, and Sterne's new publisher, Thomas Becket, complained in April, 1763, that he had 991 copies of Volumes V and VI unsold (from a printing of four thousand). Samuel Johnson's famous comment, though ultimately incorrect, probably reflected the opinion of the day: "Nothing odd will do long. *Tristram Shandy* did not last." Even Sterne may have tired of the work; the volumes grew slimmer, and Volume IX appeared without its mate, Volume X having, in Sterne's apt words for an obstetrical novel, "miscarried."

Yet *Tristram Shandy* has lasted. It retains its readership, even if it has continued to justify Sterne's complaint of being "more read than understood." Twentieth century readers have made great, perhaps exaggerated, claims for the novel, seeing it as the harbinger of the works of Marcel Proust, James Joyce, and Albert Camus, who, it is said, derived from Sterne the concept of relative time, the stream of consciousness, and a sense of the absurd. Even if one discounts such assertions, there can be no question of the work's importance in the development of the novel or of *Tristram Shandy*'s place in the first rank of eighteenth century fiction.

Less has been claimed for *A Sentimental Journey Through France and Italy* (commonly called *A Sentimental Journey*), yet this work, apparently so different and so much simpler than *Tristram Shandy*, greatly influenced Continental, especially German, literature of the Romantic period. Though critics debate the sincerity of the emotions in the work, eighteenth century readers generally did not question Yorick's sentimentality, which contributed to the rise of the cult of sensibility exemplified by such works as Henry Mackenzie's *The Man of Feeling* (1771) and Sarah Morton's *The Power of Sympathy* (1789). Because of its brevity, its benevolence, and its accessibility, *A Sentimental Journey* has enjoyed continued popularity since its first appearance. Though lacking the stature of *Tristram Shandy*, it remains a classic.

Biography

Laurence Sterne was born in Clonmel, Tipperary, Ireland, on November 24, 1713. On his father's side, he could claim some distinction. His great-grandfather, Richard Sterne, had been Archbishop of York, and his grandfather, Simon Sterne, was a rich Yorkshire country squire. Roger Sterne, Laurence's father, was less distinguished. Sterne describes his father as "a little smart man—active to the last degree, in all exercises—most patient of fatigue and disappointments, of which it pleased God to give him full measure." Sterne added that his father was "of a kindly, sweet disposition, void of all design." Many have seen Roger Sterne as the model for Uncle Toby

Shandy. At the age of sixteen, Roger joined the Cumberland Regiment of Foot, and on September 25, 1711, he married Agnes Nuttall. Agnes, according to her son, was the daughter of "a noted sutler in Flanders, in Queen Ann's wars," whom Roger married because he was in debt to her father. Actually, she may have been the daughter of a poor but respectable family in Lancashire.

From his birth to the age of ten, Sterne led a nomadic life, wandering from barracks to barracks across Great Britain. During these years, he may have acquired some of the military knowledge that appears throughout *Tristram Shandy*, or at least that fondness for the military which marks the work.

When Sterne was ten, his uncle Richard sent him to school near Halifax, in Yorkshire, and in 1733, Sterne's cousin sent him to Jesus College, Cambridge, where his great-grandfather had been a master and where both his uncle Jaques and his cousin had gone. At Cambridge, Sterne met John Hall, who later renamed himself John Hall-Stevenson. Hall-Stevenson was to be one of Sterne's closest friends throughout his life; his library at "Crazy Castle" would furnish much of the abstruse learning in *Tristram Shandy*, and he would himself appear in both that novel and *A Sentimental Journey* as "Eugenius," the sober adviser. While at Cambridge, Sterne suffered his first tubercular hemorrhage.

After receiving his bachelor's degree in January, 1737, Sterne had to choose a profession. Since his great-grandfather and uncle had both gone into the Church, Sterne followed their path. After Sterne served briefly in St. Ives and Catton, his uncle Jaques, by then Archdeacon of Cleveland and Canon and Precentor of the York Cathedral, secured for him the living of Sutton on the Forest, a few miles north of York. A second post soon followed; Sterne received the prebend of Givendale, making him part of the York Cathedral chapter and so allowing him to preach his turn there.

At York, Sterne met Elizabeth Lumley, a woman with a comfortable fortune. Their courtship had a strong sentimental tinge to it. Indeed, if Sterne actually wrote to Elizabeth the letters that his daughter published after his death, his is the first recorded use of the word *sentimental*, and the emotions expressed in these letters foreshadow both *A Sentimental Journey* and the *Journal to Eliza*. Even if these letters are spurious, Sterne's description of his courtship in the *Memoirs* is sufficiently lachrymose to rival the death of Le Fever in *Tristram Shandy*. Unfortunately for Sterne, he, unlike Tristram, did go on; on March 30, 1741, he married Elizabeth. The unfavorable portrait of Mrs. Shandy owes much to Sterne's less than sentimental feelings toward his wife, whom he called in March, 1760, the "one Obstacle to my Happiness."

The year 1741 was also important for Sterne because it marked his first appearance in print. His uncle Jaques was a strong Whig, and he recruited his nephew to write in support of the Whig candidate for York in that year's election. Sterne wrote, the Whig won, and Sterne received the prebend of

North Newbold as a reward. The Whig success was, however, short-lived. When the Walpole government fell in 1742, Sterne wrote a recantation and apology for his part in "the late contested Election," and thereby earned the enmity of his uncle, an enmity which ended only with Jaques's death in 1759.

For the next eighteen years, Sterne lived as a typical provincial clergyman, attending to the needs of his parishioners and publishing two sermons. One of these, "For We Trust We Have a Good Conscience," Sterne reprints in its entirety in the second volume of *Tristram Shandy*. In 1751, he received the commissaryship of Pickering and Pocklington, despite his uncle's efforts to secure this position for Dr. Francis Topham. Sterne and Topham collided again in 1758, when Topham attended to include his son in a patent and thus secure for him a post after his own death. When the dean of York Cathedral blocked the inclusion, a pamphlet war ensued. Sterne fired the final shot; his *A Political Romance* so squashed Topham that he agreed to abandon the fray if Sterne would withdraw his pamphlet. Sterne did withdraw *A Political Romance*, but he was not finished with Topham, who was to appear in *Tristram Shandy* as Phutatorius and Didius.

A Political Romance is little more than a satirical squib, but it shows that Sterne was familiar with the works of Jonathan Swift. In its use of clothes symbolism as well as in its severity it recalls *A Tale of a Tub* (1704), and it shows that Swift's work was running in Sterne's head between 1758 and 1759. He was making other use of Swift, too. On May 23, 1759, Sterne wrote to Robert Dodsley, "With this You will receive the Life & Opinions of *Tristram Shandy*, which I choose to offer to You first." By this time, the first volume of the novel was finished. Although Dodsley refused the copyright for the 50 pounds Sterne requested, Sterne continued to write, completing a second volume and revising the first to remove "all locality" and make "the whole . . . more saleable," as he wrote to Dodsley several months later.

Salable it was. The York edition sold two hundred copies in two days when it appeared in December, 1759, and when Sterne went up to London, he was told that the book was not "to be had in London either for Love or money." Dodsley, who had been unwilling to risk 50 pounds on the copyright, now purchased it for 250 pounds, gave another 380 pounds to publish the still unwritten Volumes III and IV, and yet another 200 pounds for two volumes of Sterne's sermons. Sterne was honored by the great. Thomas Gray wrote to Thomas Wharton, "Tristram Shandy is still a greater object of admiration, the Man as well as the Book. One is invited to dinner, where he dines, a fortnight beforehand."

In March, 1760, Sterne also succeeded to the curacy of Coxwold, a better position than his earlier one at Sutton. In May, 1760, he therefore settled at Coxwold, renting Shandy Hall from Earl Fauconberg. Here he worked on the next two volumes of *Tristram Shandy*, which he brought to London at the end of the year. In 1761, he repeated this pattern, but he did not return to Yorkshire after delivering the manuscript of Volumes V and VI. Having suffered a tubercular hemorrhage, he set off for the warmer, milder air of France.

There he repeated his earlier triumph in London, and he incidentally acquired materials for Book VII of *Tristram Shandy* and *A Sentimental Journey*. Sterne remained in France for almost two years; when he returned to England, he hastily wrote the next two volumes of *Tristram Shandy*, which appeared in January, 1765. In October of that year, he brought twelve sermons to London rather than more of his novel. After leaving the manuscript with his publisher, he again set off for the Continent; he would combine the adventures of this trip with those of his earlier one in writing *A Sentimental Journey*.

In June, 1766, Sterne was back in Coxwold, where he wrote what proved to be the last installment of *Tristram Shandy*. This he brought with him to London in late December; shortly after his arrival, he met Eliza Draper, the wife of an East India Company clerk twenty years her senior. Though initially unimpressed witn her, Sterne was soon madly in love. When Sterne met her, she had already been in England some two years, and she was to return to India less than three months later, yet she was to color Sterne's last year of life. Before she sailed on the *Earl of Chatham* on April 3, 1767, Sterne visited her daily, wrote letters to her, drove with her, exchanged pictures with her. After their separation, Sterne continued his letters; those he wrote between April 13 and the beginning of August, 1767, comprise the *Journal to Eliza*. When he broke off this journal with the words "I am thine—& thine only, & for ever" to begin *A Sentimental Journey*, her spirit haunted that work, too, as the Eliza upon whom Yorick calls.

By December, Sterne had finished the first half of *A Sentimental Journey* and again set off for London and his publisher. On February 27, 1768, *A Sentimental Journey*, Volumes I and II, appeared. Less than a month later, on March 18, Sterne died. He was buried in London on March 22; on June 8, 1769, he was reinterred in the Coxwold churchyard in Yorkshire.

Analysis

Readers may be tempted to see Laurence Sterne's works either as *sui generis* or as eighteenth century sports that had no mate until Marcel Proust and James Joyce. In fact, Sterne was very much a product of his age. His humor owes much to such earlier writers as François Rabelais, Miguel de Cervantes, Michel de Montaigne, Sir Thomas Browne, and Jonathan Swift, all of whom influenced his experimentation with the form of the newly emerged novel. Even this experimentation is typical of the age. Thomas Amory's *The Life and Opinions of John Buncle Esquire* (1756-1766) may have suggested to Sterne his complete title *The Life and Opinions of Tristram Shandy, Gent.* Like *Tristram Shandy*, Amory's book is full of digressions, and its narrator is conceited.

Sterne's experimentation did go beyond the traditional; one need look no farther than the typography, the varying length of the chapters in *Tristram Shandy*—from four lines to sixty pages—or the unusual location of certain conventional elements—for example, the placing of *Tristram Shandy's* Preface after the twentieth chapter of Book III or Yorick's writing the Preface to *A Sentimental Journey* after Chapter Six. At the same time, Sterne relied on the conventions of the novel. He is meticulous in his descriptions of clothing, furniture, and gesture. His characters are fully developed: they walk, sometimes with a limp, they cough, they bleed, they dance. From Swift, Daniel Defoe, and Samuel Richardson, Sterne took the first-person narrator. From Richardson, he adopted the technique of writing to the moment; from Henry Fielding, he got the idea of the novel as a comic epic in prose. From numerous sources—Rabelais, Cervantes, and Swift, to name but three—he learned of the satiric potential of the genre.

A Political Romance reveals Sterne's powerful satiric abilities, but this work has little in common with the novels. True, the personal satire of the pamphlet does persist. Sterne lampoons Dr. Burton (Dr. Slop), Dr. Richard Meade (Dr. Kunastrokius), and Francis Topham (Phutatorius, Didius) in *Tristram Shandy*; Tobias Smollett (Smeldungus) and Samuel Sharp (Mundungus) in *A Sentimental Journey*. For the most part, though, Sterne is after bigger game. As he wrote to Robert Dodsley, the satire is general; and, as he wrote to Robert Foley some years later, it is "a laughing good tempered Satyr," another distinction between the novels and the pamphlet.

The objects of this general satire are several: system-makers of all types, pedants, lawyers, doctors, conceited authors, prudes, self-deceivers. A common thread uniting all these satiric butts is folly, the folly of believing that life should conform to some preconceived notion, of trying to force facts to fit theories rather than the other way around.

Sterne's insistence on common sense and reason is consistent with the Augustan tradition, which itself is rooted in Anglican beliefs that Sterne emphasized in his sermons as well as in his fiction. Although Sterne's satire is good-tempered, it attacks man's tendency to evil, a tendency noted in Article IX of the Thirty-nine Articles of the Anglican Church. Like his fellow Augustans, Sterne saw this tendency to evil in many spheres. Like them, therefore, he attacked these deviations from the norm as established by religion and reason (which for Sterne are the same), by nature, by tradition, and by authority. The characters in *Tristram Shandy* and Yorick in *A Sentimental Journey* (who is the only sustained character in that work) are laughable because they deviate from the norm and because they refuse to accept their limitations.

Sterne repeatedly reminds the reader of man's finiteness. Thus, death haunts the novels: in *Tristram Shandy*, Toby, Walter, Mrs. Shandy, Yorick,

Trim, and Bobby are all dead, and Tristram is dying. In *A Sentimental Journey*, a resurrected Yorick sees death all around him—a dead monk, dead children, a dead ass, dead lovers. Another, less dramatic symbol of the characters' limitation is their inability to complete what they begin. *Tristram Shandy* and *A Sentimental Journey* remain fragments. Trim never finishes his tale of the King of Bohemia and his seven castles. Walter never finishes the *Tristrapaedia*. Obadiah never goes for yeast. Yorick never finishes the story of the notary. Nor can characters communicate effectively with one another: Walter's wife never appreciates his theories; Toby's hobbyhorse causes him to understand all words in a military sense; Dr. Slop falls asleep in the middle of Trim's reading; Yorick in *A Sentimental Journey* never pauses long enough to develop a lasting friendship.

Death, the prison of the self, the petty and great disappointments of life— these are the stuff of tragedy. Yet, in Sterne's novels they form the basis of comedy, for the emphasis in these novels is not on the tragic event itself but rather on the cause or the reaction. Bobby's death, for example, is nothing to the reader, not only because one never meets Bobby alive but also because one quickly becomes involved in Walter's oration and Trim's hat. In *A Sentimental Journey*, Sterne focuses on Yorick's reaction to Maria rather than on her poignant tale: consequently, one laughs at Yorick instead of crying with Maria. The prison of words that traps the characters is not the result of man's inherent isolation but rather of a comic perversity in refusing to accept the plain meaning of a statement. The tragic is further mitigated by its remoteness. Though Tristram writes to the moment, that moment is long past; Tristram's account is being composed some fifty years after the events he describes, and Yorick, too, is recollecting emotions in tranquility. The curious order of *Tristram Shandy* and the rapid pace of *A Sentimental Journey* further dilute the tragic. Yorick dies in Book I but cracks the last joke in Book IX. Yorick has barely begun a sentimental attachment with a *fille de chambre* in Paris when he must set off for Versailles to seek a passport. Though the disappointments, interruptions, failures, and deaths recur, individually they quickly vanish from view. What remains are the characters, who are comic because they refuse to learn from their failures.

Sterne's world is therefore not tragic; neither is it absurd. In the world of the absurd, helpless characters confront a meaningless and chaotic world. For Sterne, the world is reasonable; he shares the Augustan world view expressed so well by Alexander Pope: "All Nature is but Art, unknown to thee,/ All Chance Direction which thou canst not see." The reasonableness of the world is not, however, to be found in the systematizing of Walter Shandy or the sentimentalism of Yorick. People can live in harmony with the world, Sterne says, only if they use common sense. The comedy of these novels derives in large part from people's failure or laziness to be sensible.

In *Aspects of the Novel* (1927), E. M. Forster writes: "Obviously a god is hidden in *Tristram Shandy* and his name is Muddle." There is no question that the muddle is present in the novel. Chapters Eighteen and Nineteen of Book IX appear as part of Chapter Twenty-five. The Preface does not appear until the third volume. There are black, marbled, and white pages. In Book IV, a chapter is torn out and ten pages dropped. Uncle Toby begins knocking the ashes out of his pipe in Book I, Chapter Twenty-one, and finishes this simple action in Book II, Chapter Six. The novel begins in 1718 and ends, if it may be said to end, in 1713. Although called *The Life and Opinions of Tristram Shandy, Gent.*, the novel recounts the life of Uncle Toby and the opinions of Walter Shandy.

One must distinguish, though, between the muddle that the narrator, Tristram, creates, and the ordered universe which Sterne offers. Theodore Baird has demonstrated that one can construct an orderly sequence of events from the information in *Tristram Shandy*, beginning with the reign of Henry VIII (III,xxxiii) through the wounding of Trim in 1693 (VIII,xix; II,v), the siege of Namur at which Toby is wounded in 1695 (I,xxv), the conception and birth of Tristram Shandy in 1718 (I-III), the death of Bobby (1719; IV,xxxii and v,ii), the episode of Toby and the fly (1728; II,xii), the death of Yorick (1748; I,xii), and the composition of the novel (1759-1766). Tristram does attempt to impose some order upon these events; the first five and a half books trace his life from his conception to his accident with the window sash and his being put into breeches. He then breaks off to recount the amours of Uncle Toby, which again appear essentially in sequence, with the major exception of Book VII, Tristram's flight into France.

Although Tristram attempts to order these events, he fails. He fails not because life is inherently random or absurd, but because he is a bad artist. He pointedly rejects the advice of Horace, whose *Ars Poetica* (13-8 B.C., *The Art of Poetry*) was highly respected among eighteenth century writers. He will not pause to check facts and even refuses to look back in his own book to see whether he has already mentioned something; this is writing to the moment with a vengeance. He refuses to impose any order at all upon his material, allowing his pen to govern him instead of acting the part of the good writer who governs his pen.

In governing his pen, the good writer carefully selects his material. Many a man has told a plain, unvarnished tale in less space than Tristram, but Tristram cannot decide what is important. Must one know what Mrs. Shandy said to Walter on the night of Tristram's begetting, which, incidentally, may not be the night of Tristram's begetting at all, since the night described is only eight months before Tristram's birth rather than nine—does Tristram realize this fact? Does one need so vivid an account of how Walter falls across the bed upon learning of Tristram's crushed nose? Is it true that one cannot understand Toby's statement, "I think it would not be amiss brother, if we rung the bell," without being dragged halfway across Europe and twenty-three years back in time? Such details serve the purpose of Tristram's creator by highlighting the follies of a bad writer, but they hardly help Tristram proceed with his story.

Tristram's failure to select his material derives in part from laziness. "I have a strong propensity in me to begin this chapter very nonsensically, and I will not balk my fancy," he writes (I,xxiii), for it requires intellectual effort to balk a fancy. In part, too, this failure to select reflects Tristram's belief that everything concerning himself is important. His is a solipsistic rendering of the humanist's credo, "*Homo sum, humani nihil a me alienum puto*"—I am a man, and nothing that relates to man can be foreign to me. He is confident that the more the reader associates with him, the fonder he (the reader) will become. Hence, the reader will want to know about his failure with Jenny, about his aunt Dinah's affair with the coachman, about his attire as he writes, about his casting a fair instead of a foul copy of his manuscript into the fire. Tristram sets out to write a traditional biography, beginning with a genealogy and proceeding to birth, education, youthful deeds that foreshadow later achievements, marriage, children, accomplishments, death, and burial. He becomes so bogged down in details, however, that he cannot get beyond his fifth year. The episode of Toby and the fly must substitute for a volume on education, and the setting up of his top replaces an account of his youthful deeds.

Although Tristram refuses to impose any system on his writing, he is a true son of Walter Shandy in his willingness to impose systems on other aspects of his world. He devises a scale for measuring pleasure and pain, so that if the death of Bobby rates a five and Walter's pleasure at delivering an oration on the occasion rates a ten, Walter proves the gainer by this catastrophe. Tristram has another scale for measuring his own writing; he awards himself a nineteen out of twenty for the design of the novel. Tristram attaches much significance to the way he is conceived, believing that one's conception determines his entire life. His declared method of describing character is similarly reductive, focusing strictly on the individual's hobbyhorse. He has a theory on knots, on window-sashes, and on the effect of diet on writing. Tristram thus serves as a satire on systematizers as well as on bad writers.

The more obvious butt of Sterne's satire on system-makers is Walter Shandy. The Augustan Age has also been called the Age of Reason, and Sterne recognizes the importance of reason. At the same time, the Augustans recognized that a person's reason alone is often an insufficient guide because it can be corrupted by a ruling passion, as Yorick's sermon in *Tristram Shandy* reveals. Tristram fails as an author because he trusts exclusively to his own logic instead of following conventional guidelines. Walter Shandy is another example of one who becomes foolish because of his reliance on his own reason. Like Pope's dunces, Walter is well read, and like Pope's dunces, he fails to benefit from his learning because he does not use common sense. He will look in the Institutes of Justinian instead of the more obvious, and more reliable, catechism—part of Sterne's joke here is that the source Walter cites does not contain what he wants. Walter will consult Rubenius rather than a tailor to determine of what cloth Tristram's breeches should be made. From his reading and reasoning he develops a host of theories: that Caesarian birth is the best way of bringing a child into the world, that Christian names determine one's life, that auxiliary verbs provide a key to knowledge. Each of these theories rests on a certain logic. Walter is correct that no one would name his child Judas. From this true observation, though, he erects a most absurd theory, proving Tristram's statement that "when a man gives himself up to the government of a ruling passion,—or, in other words, when his Hobby-Horse grows headstrong,—farewell cool reason and fair discretion" (II,v). Neither Walter nor his son will rein in his hobbyhorse, and, as a result, they become ridiculous.

They may also become dangerous. While Walter is busily engaged in composing his *Tristrapaedia* that will codify his theories of child rearing, Tristram grows up without any guidance at all. Walter is willing, indeed eager, to have his wife undergo a Caesarian operation because he believes that such an operation will be less harmful to the infant than natural childbirth. That such an operation will cause the death of Mrs. Shandy is a fact that apparently escapes him.

Even the benign and lovable Uncle Toby makes himself ridiculous by yielding to his hobbyhorse. Not only does this hobbyhorse lead him into excessive expense and so deprive him of money he might put to better use, but also it keeps his mind from more worthwhile occupations. Repeatedly, Sterne, through Tristram, likens Toby's garden battlefield to a mistress with whom Toby dallies; the Elizabethan sense of hobbyhorse is precisely this—a woman of easy virtue. As Tristram notes early in the novel, when "one . . . whose principles and conduct are as generous and noble as his blood" is carried off by his hobbyhorse, it is better that "the Hobby-Horse, with all his fraternity, (were) at the Devil" (I,viii). Deluding himself that he is somehow contributing to the defense of England, Toby blinds himself to the real horrors of war. Wrapped up in his military jargon, he isolates himself verbally from those around him; a bridge or a train has only one meaning for him. No less than Tristram, he is betrayed by words, but in his case as in Tristram's the fault lies not with the words but with the individual betrayed.

Nor is Toby's hobbyhorse dangerous to himself alone. It keeps him away from the Widow Wadman and so prevents his fulfilling his legitimate social responsibilities of marrying and begetting children; his hobbyhorse renders him sterile even if his wound has not. This hobbyhorse also comes close to rendering Tristram sterile, for Trim removes the weights from the window sash to make cannon for Toby's campaigns.

Each of the major characters is trapped in a cell of his own making. Tristram can never finish his book because his theory of composition raises insurmountable obstacles. The more he writes, the more he has to write. Walter's and Toby's hobbyhorses blind them to reality and prevent their communicating with each other or anyone else. The Shandy family is well named; "shandy" in Yorkshire means crackbrained. Significantly, the novel begins with an interrupted act of procreation and ends with sterility. As in Pope's *The Dunciad* (1728-1743), the uncreating word triumphs because of human folly.

Sterne's vision is not quite as dark as Pope's, though; the novel ends not with universal darkness but with a joke. Yorick, the voice of reason and moderation, remains to pull the reader back to reality. Yorick is a jester, and the role of the jester is to remind his audience of the just proportion of things as well as to make them laugh. Yorick does not put a fancy saddle on a horse that does not deserve one. He will destroy a sermon because it is too bad (unlike Tristram, who destroys a chapter because it is too good). He makes only modest claims for his sermons and is embarrassed even by these (unlike Tristram, who repeatedly proclaims himself a genius). Yorick thus offers in word and deed an example of living reasonably and happily.

Sterne offers a second consolation as well. Even though characters isolate themselves with their hobbyhorses, even though they cannot or will not understand one another's words, they can and do appreciate one another's feelings. These emotional unions are short-lived, but they are intense and sincere. Walter will continue to make fun of Toby even after promising not to, but at the moment the promise is made, the two are united spiritually and physically. Tristram and Jenny quarrel, but they also have their tender moments. Trim looks for a carriage in a book by shaking the leaves, and he mistakes fiction for reality in a sermon, but he allows his parents three halfpence a day out of his pay when they grow old. The benevolence that Sterne urged in his sermons is capable of bridging self-imposed isolation. Though one laughs at the characters in *Tristram Shandy*, one therefore sympathizes with them as well; one sees their weaknesses but also their underlying virtue. Though they have corrupted that virtue by yielding to a natural tendency to evil, they redeem themselves through their equally natural tendency to kindness.

Tristram Shandy offended many contemporary readers because of its bawdy tales; reviewers much preferred such seemingly sentimental episodes as the death of Le Fever and urged Sterne to refine his humor. *A Sentimental Journey* superficially appears to have been written to satisfy these demands. It is full of touching scenes, of tears, of charity, of little acts of kindness. Moreover, in a letter to Mrs. William James in November, 1767, Sterne describes the novel as dealing with "the gentle passions and affections" and says his intention is "to teach us to love the world and our fellow creatures better than we do." Sterne's letters, and especially his *Journal to Eliza*, reveal him as a man of feeling, and *Tristram Shandy* satirizes all aspects of human life except for benevolence. Sterne's sermons reinforce his image as a believer in the importance of charity. As a Latitudinarian, he believed that the Golden Rule constitutes the essence of religion, that ritual and church doctrine, while important, are less significant than kindness. Since Yorick in *Tristram Shandy* is Sterne's spokesman, it is tempting to see Yorick in *A Sentimental Journey* as having the same normative function. Though the narrator of *Tristram Shandy* is a dunce and a satiric butt, can one not still trust the narrator of *A Sentimental Journey*?

No. In a famous letter to Dr. John Eustace, Sterne thanks Eustace for the gift of a curious walking stick: "Your walking stick is in no sense more shandaic than in that of its having *more handles than one.*" Readers could regard *Tristram Shandy* as total nonsense, as a collection of bawdy stories, as a realistic novel, as a satire on the realistic novel, or as a satire on the follies of mankind. Sterne's second novel, too, is "shandaic." The reader can see it as a tribute to the popular spirit of sentimentality, or he can view it as a satire of that spirit. Yet a careful reading of the book will demonstrate why Sterne wrote to the mysterious "Hannah" that this novel "shall make you cry as much as ever it made me laugh." In other words, Sterne is sporting with rather than adopting the sentimental mode.

The object of Sterne's laughter is Yorick. The Yorick who recounts his travels is not the same normative parson as appears in *Tristram Shandy*. He is by now twice dead—dead in William Shakespeare's *Hamlet* (1600-1601) and dead again in *Tristram Shandy* some fifteen years prior to the events of *A Sentimental Journey*. This second resurrection may itself be a joke on the reader, who should recall Yorick's death in Book I of the earlier novel.

This revived Yorick bears a great similarity to Tristram. He is, for one thing, a systematizer. He establishes three degrees of curses; he discovers "three epochas in the empire of a French woman" ("Paris"); he is able to create dialogues out of silence; he derives national character not from "important matters of state" but rather from "nonsensical minutiae" ("The Wig—Paris"). Like Tristram, too, Yorick is vain. He gives a sou to a beggar who calls him "My Lord *Anglois*" and another sou for "*Mon cher et très charitable Monsieur.*" He does not worry about being unkind to a monk but is concerned that as a result a pretty woman will think ill of him.

Even his style, though less difficult to follow than Tristram's, bears some similarities to that of Sterne's earlier narrator. In the midst of the account of his adventures in Versailles, Yorick introduces the irrelevant anecdote of Bevoriskius and the mating sparrows, thus combining Tristram's habit of digressing with Walter's love of abstruse learning. Yorick later interpolates an account of the Marquis d'E****, and while telling about Paris he presents a "Fragment" that does nothing to advance the story. Like Tristram, too, Yorick cannot finish his account, breaking off in mid-sentence. Apparently, he is more governed by his pen than governing.

Yorick also reminds the reader of the narrator in Swift's *A Tale of a Tub*, who believes that happiness is the state of being well deceived. Yorick is disappointed to learn that his small present to Le Fleur has been sufficient only to allow his servant to buy used clothes: "I would rather have imposed upon my fancy with thinking I had bought them new for the fellow, than that they had come out of the *Rue de friperie*" (Le Dimanche—Paris"). Instead of inquiring about the history of the lady at Calais, he invents a pleasant account of her until he gets "ground enough for the situation which pleased me" ("In the Street—Calais"). He deceives himself into believing that he is accompanying a pretty *fille de chambre* as far as possible to protect her when actually he wants her company. Even his benevolence is self-deception. He conjures up images to weep over—a swain with a dying lamb, a man in the Bastille, an imaginary recipient of charity. When in this last instance he confronts the reality, his behavior is hardly benevolent, though.

Sterne is not satirizing benevolence as such. In his sermons "The Vindication of Human Nature" and "Philanthropy Recommended" he rejects the notion that man is inherently selfish and stresses his belief in man's natural benevolence. Yet he had to look no farther than his own nose to discover that benevolence can become a hobbyhorse that can carry a person away from the path of reason. Yorick's hobbyhorse of benevolence is no less dangerous than Uncle Toby's or Walter Shandy's. Yorick will weep over a carriage, over a dead ass, over a caged starling. He admits that he does not even need an object for his sympathy: "Was I in a desert, I would find out wherewith in it to call forth my affection" ("In the Street—Calais"). Real human misery, however, he cannot understand. He can weep over his imagined prisoner in the Bastille, but he cannot imagine the real suffering there. He can be callous to the poor, but never to a pretty young woman.

Yorick's benevolence is thus a compound of self-deception and lust. He will give no money to the poor monk until he wants to impress a pretty woman. He gives a sou to a beggar with a dislocated hip, but he gives an unsolicited crown to a pretty *fille de chambre*, and he gives three *louis d'or* to a pretty grisette. He imagines that in offering to share his chaise with another pretty young lady, he is fighting off "every dirty passion" such as avarice, pride, meanness, and hypocrisy. Actually, he is yielding to desire.

True benevolence is guided by reason, and it is not a thing of the moment only, as Sterne points out in his sermon on the Good Samaritan. Yorick's benevolence is impulsive and short-lived. The cry of a caged starling moves him greatly: "I never had my affections more tenderly awakened," he says ("The Passport—The Hotel at Paris"). The hyperbole of the language is itself a warning of Yorick's inability to temper emotion with reason. After such a reaction, his attitude changes abruptly; Yorick buys the starling but never frees it. After tiring of it, he gives it away to another as callous as himself. At Namport, he mourns for a dead ass and praises its owner for his kindness, adding, "Shame on the world! . . . Did we love each other, as this poor soul but loved his ass—'twould be something" ("Namport—The Dead Ass"). By the next page, Yorick is sending his postillion to the devil. Yorick goes out of his way to find the mad Maria, whom Sterne had introduced in Book VII of *Tristram Shandy*. He weeps with Maria at Moulines; she makes such an impression on him that her image follows him almost to Lyon—an entire chapter!

Yorick is humorous because, like Tristram, Walter, and Toby, he is the victim of his hobbyhorse. He gallops away from reason, failing to examine his motivation or to temper his sudden fanciful flights. In "Temporal Advantages of Religion," Sterne provides a picture of the ideal Christian traveler. "We may surely be allowed to amuse ourselves with the natural or artificial beauties of the country we are passing through," Sterne notes, but he warns against being drawn aside, as Yorick is, "by the variety of prospects, edifices, and ruins which solicit us." More important, Yorick forgets the chief end of man's earthly sojourn: "Various as our excursions are—that we have still set our faces towards Jerusalem . . . and that the way to get there is not so much to please our hearts, as to improve them in virtue." Yorick has come to France for knowledge, but he learns nothing. His benevolence is much closer to wantonness than to virtue; it is fitting that he ends his account in the dark, grasping the *fille de chambre*'s end of Volume II.

In *A Sentimental Journey*, as in *Tristram Shandy*, Sterne mocks excess. He shows the folly that results from the abdication of reason. Though he introduces norms such as Yorick in *Tristram Shandy* or the old soldier in *A Sentimental Journey*, the ideal emerges most clearly from a depiction of its opposite—perverted learning, bad writing, unexamined motives. When Sterne came to London in 1760, Lord Bathurst embraced him as the heir to the Augustan satirists; Lord Bathurst was right.

Joseph Rosenblum

Other major works

NONFICTION: *A Political Romance*, 1759; *Letters from Yorick to Eliza*, 1773; *Sterne's Letters to His Friends on Various Occasions, to Which Is Added His History of a Watch Coat*, 1775; *Letters of the Late Rev. Mr. L. Sterne to His Most Intimate Friends*, 1775 (3 volumes); *In Elegant Epistles*, 1790; *Journal to Eliza*, 1904.

RELIGIOUS WRITINGS: *The Sermons of Mr. Yorick*, 1760, 1766 (Vols. I-IV); *Sermons by the Late Rev. Mr. Sterne*, 1769 (Vols. V-VII).

Bibliography

Cash, Arthur Hill. *Laurence Sterne*. 2 vols. London: Methuen, 1975-1986. The definitive biography. The first volume follows Sterne's life to early

1760 and offers many details about his role in the religious and political affairs of York. The second volume treats Sterne the author. Presents a realistic picture freed from Victorian strictures and romantic glosses. The appendices provide a series of portraits and of letters never before published.

_____. *Sterne's Comedy of Moral Sentiments: The Ethical Dimension of the Journey.* Pittsburgh: Duquesne University Press, 1966. Comparing Sterne's sermons with *A Sentimental Journey Through France and Italy,* Cash finds a moral stance in the novel, one that condemns Yorick for excessive sentimentality. Sterne laughs at Yorick, at himself, and at mankind for abandoning reason.

Cash, Arthur Hill, and John M. Stedmond, eds. *The Winged Skull: Papers from the Laurence Sterne Bicentenary Conference.* Kent, Ohio: Kent State University Press, 1971. A collection of essays on a range of subjects, including Sterne's style, his reputation outside England, and his fictional devices. Includes some helpful illustrations.

Farrell, William J. "Nature Versus Art as a Comic Pattern in *Tristram Shandy.*" *English Literary History* 30 (1963): 16-35. Points out numerous instances of Tristram's authorial failures, which are caused by his failure to distinguish between art and reality. Sees Tristram as object of Sterne's satire, not as his alter ego.

Hartley, Lodwick. *This Is Lorence: A Narrative of the Reverend Laurence Sterne.* Chapel Hill: University of North Carolina Press, 1943. Still the best general introduction to the man and his work. In a sprightly biography for the general reader, Hartley quotes generously from Sterne and sets him clearly in his age.

Myer, Valerie Grosvenor, ed. *Laurence Sterne: Riddles and Mysteries.* New York: Barnes & Noble Books, 1984. Contains eleven essays on *The Life and Opinions of Tristram Shandy, Gent.*, covering such matters as the nature of Sterne's comedy, the intellectual background of the novel, and Sterne's influence on the work of Jane Austen. Includes a brief annotated bibliography.

New, Melvin. *Laurence Sterne as Satirist: A Reading of "Tristram Shandy."* Gainesville: University of Florida Press, 1969. Sees Sterne as a satirist in the tradition of Alexander Pope and Jonathan Swift; the novel "is ultimately directed against human pride." Sterne is not Tristram; he uses the narrator to satirize pride and folly.

Putney, Rufus D. "The Evolution of *A Sentimental Journey.*" *Philological Quarterly* 19 (1940): 349-369. Treats the novel as a hoax in which readers could find the sentimentality they were seeking, while Sterne could create the humorous fiction he wanted to write.

Stedmond, John M. *The Comic Art of Laurence Sterne: Convention and Innovation in "Tristram Shandy" and "A Sentimental Journey."* Toronto:

University of Toronto Press, 1967. Sterne's novels highlight the comic distance between aspiration and attainment that is endemic in human existence. Provides helpful readings of the novels and an appendix recording Sterne's direct borrowings.

ROBERT LOUIS STEVENSON

Born: Edinburgh, Scotland; November 13, 1850
Died: Apia, Samoa; December 3, 1894

Principal long fiction

Treasure Island, 1883; *Prince Otto*, 1885; *The Strange Case of Dr. Jekyll and Mr. Hyde*, 1886; *Kidnapped*, 1886; *The Black Arrow*, 1888; *The Master of Ballantrae*, 1888; *The Wrong Box*, 1889; *The Wrecker*, 1892 (with Lloyd Osbourne); *Catriona*, 1893; *The Ebb-Tide*, 1894 (with Lloyd Osbourne); *Weir of Hermiston*, 1896 (unfinished); *St. Ives*, 1897 (completed by Arthur Quiller-Couch).

Other literary forms

In addition to his novels, Robert Louis Stevenson published a large number of essays, poems, and short stories, most of which have been collected under various titles. The best edition of Stevenson's works is the South Seas Edition (32 volumes) published by Scribner's in 1925.

Achievements

A man thoroughly devoted to his art, Stevenson was highly regarded during his lifetime as a writer of romantic fiction. Indeed, few, if any, have surpassed him in that genre. Combining a strong intellect and a wide-ranging imagination with his ability to tell a story, he produced novels that transport the reader to the realms of adventure and intrigue. After his death, his literary reputation diminished considerably, until he was regarded primarily as a writer of juvenile fiction, unworthy of serious critical attention. With the growth of scholarly interest in popular literature, however, Stevenson is sure to enjoy a revaluation. Certainly his narrative skill speaks for itself, and it is on that base that his literary reputation should ultimately rest. Anyone who has vicariously sailed with Jim Hawkins in quest of buried treasure or sipped a potion that reduces intellect to instinct with Henry Jekyll can vouch for the success of Stevenson as a writer and agree with what he wrote in "A Gossip of Romance" (1882): "In anything fit to be called reading, the process itself should be absorbing and voluptuous; we should gloat over a book, be rapt clean out of ourselves, and rise from the perusal, our mind filled with the busiest kaleidoscopic dance of images, incapable of sleep or of continuous thought."

Biography

The only child of Thomas and Margaret (Balfour) Stevenson, Robert Louis Stevenson was born on November 13, 1850, in Edinburgh, Scotland. He was in poor health even as a child, and he suffered throughout his life from a tubercular condition. Thomas, a civil engineer and lighthouse keeper, had hopes that Stevenson would eventually follow in his footsteps, and the youngster was sent to Anstruther and then to Edinburgh University. His fragile health, however, precluded a career in engineering, and he shifted his efforts to the study of law, passing the bar in Edinburgh in 1875.

Even during his preparation for law, Stevenson was more interested in literature, and, reading widely in the essays of Michel de Montaigne, Charles Lamb, and William Hazlitt, he began imitating their styles. Their influence can be seen in the style that Stevenson ultimately developed—a personal, conversational style, marked by an easy familiarity.

Between 1875 and 1879, Stevenson wandered through France, Germany, and Scotland in search of a healthier climate. In 1876, at Fontainebleau, France, he met Fanny Osbourne, an American with whom he fell in love. She returned to California in 1878, and in that same year became seriously ill. Stevenson set out immediately to follow her. Traveling by steerage, he underwent considerable hardships on his journey, hardships that proved detrimental to his already poor health. In 1880, he married Fanny and settled for a few months in a desolate mining camp in California. After a return to Scotland, the couple journeyed to Davos, Switzerland, for the winter.

Again returning to Scotland in the spring, Stevenson worked on his novel, *Treasure Island*. Moving back and forth between Scotland and Switzerland was not conducive to improved health, and Stevenson decided to stay permanently in the south of France. Another attack of illness, however, sent him to Bournemouth, England, a health resort, until 1887, during which time he worked assiduously on his writing. In August of that year he sailed for America, settling at Saranac Lake in New York's Adirondacks. There he wrote *The Master of Ballantrae* in 1889. He finally settled in the islands of Samoa in the South Seas, a setting that he used for *The Wrecker* and *The Ebb-Tide*. He died there on December 3, 1894, ending a short but productive life.

Analysis

By the time that Robert Louis Stevenson published his first novel, *Treasure Island*, the golden age of Victorianism in England was over. The empire was far-flung and great, but the masses of England had more immediate concerns. The glory of the Union Jack gave small comfort to a working class barely able to keep its head above water. If earlier novelists wrote for the middle-class reader, those of the last twenty years of the century revolted against the cultural domination of that class. Turning to realism, they dealt with the repression caused by a crushing environment. Stevenson, however, disdained moral and intellectual topics, preferring the thin, brisk, sunny atmosphere of romance. Consequently, he stands apart from such figures as Thomas Hardy, Arnold Bennett and George Gissing.

In "A Humble Remonstrance," Stevenson spoke of the function of a writer of romance as being "bound to be occupied, not so much in making stories true as in making them typical; not so much in capturing the lineament of each fact, as in marshalling all of them to a common end." Perhaps, then, Stevenson should be seen not simply as an antirealistic writer of romance, but as a writer whose conception of realism was different from that of his contemporaries.

In his study of Stevenson, Edwin Eigner points out that the novelist's heroes are drawn from real life and are usually failures. Moreover, says Eigner, "very few of the characters, whether good *or* evil, manage even to fail greatly." Stevenson himself wrote in his essay "Reflection and Remarks on Human Life" that "our business in this world is not to succeed, but to continue to fail, in good spirits." His own ill-health may have caused him to see life in terms of conflict, and in his case a conflict that he could not win. This element of failure adds a somber dimension to Stevenson's romances—a note of reality, as it were, to what otherwise might have been simply adventure fiction. It is the element of adventure superimposed on reality that gives Stevenson's writing its peculiar character. A writer's stories, he remarked, "may be nourished with the realities of life, but their true mark is to satisfy the nameless longings of the reader, and to obey the ideal laws of the daydream." In doing this, the writer's greatest challenge, according to Stevenson, is to give "body and blood" to his stories. Setting, circumstance, and character must all fall into place to give a story the power to make an impression on the mind of the reader—"to put the last mark of truth upon a story and fill up at one blow our capacity for sympathetic pleasure." In this way a story becomes more than merely literature; it becomes art.

Stevenson regarded the tales of the *Arabian Nights* as perfect examples of the storyteller's art: tales that could captivate the reader in his childhood and delight him in his old age. Such was the goal that he sought in his own works: to bring the reader to the story as an involved spectator, who does not shy away from the unpleasantries or the villainy, but finds in witnessing them the same pleasure he does in witnessing the more optimistic and uplifting aspects of the piece. Perhaps this is Stevenson's greatest achievement: he illustrates with his stories a sometimes forgotten truth—"Fiction is to the grown man what play is to the child."

"If this don't fetch the kids, why, they have gone rotten since my day," Stevenson wrote in a letter to Sidney Colvin on August 25, 1881. He was speaking of *Treasure Island*, the novel on which he was then at work. He need not have worried, for since its publication it has been a favorite of children everywhere—and, indeed, of many adults. Stevenson wrote the book, according to his own account, in two bursts of creative activity of about fifteen days each. "My quickest piece of work," he said. The novel was begun as an amusement for his stepson Lloyd Osbourne, then twelve years old. Upon its completion in November of 1881, the novel was serialized in the magazine *Young Folks*; since it did not raise circulation to any degree, it was not considered particularly successful. The book was an altogether different story.

As a tale of adventure, *Treasure Island* stands as one of the best. Buried treasure has always had an aura of mystery and intrigue about it, and this case is no exception. Young Jim Hawkins is the hero of the novel; the adventure starts when Bill Bones, an old seaman, comes to Jim's father's inn, the Admiral Benbow, to wait for a one-legged seaman, who does not arrive. Bones does have two other visitors: a seaman named Black Dog, whom he chases away after a fight, and a deformed blind man named Pew, who gives him the black spot, the pirates' death notice. Bones is so frightened that he dies of a stroke. In the meantime, Jim's father has also died, leaving Jim and his mother alone. Opening Bones's locker, they find an oilskin packet that Jim gives to Squire Trelawney and Dr. Livesey.

Finding in the packet a treasure map, Trelawney and Livesey decide to outfit a ship and seek the treasure. Jim is invited to come along as cabin boy. Just before they sight the island where the treasure is supposed to be, Jim overhears the ship's cook, the one-legged Long John Silver, and some of the crew plotting a mutiny. When Silver and a party are sent ashore, Jim smuggles himself along to spy on them.

When Trelawny and Livesey learn of Silver's duplicity, they decide to take the loyal crew members and occupy a stockade they have discovered on the island, leaving the ship to the pirates. Unable to take the stockade, Silver offers a safe passage home to its defenders in return for the treasure map. The offer is refused, and, after another attack, the party in the stockade is reduced to Trelawney, Livesey, Captain Smollett, and Jim. Jim rows to the ship, shoots the only pirate on board and then beaches the ship. Returning to the stockade, he finds his friends gone and Silver and the pirates in control. Silver saves Jim's life from the other pirates and reveals the treasure map, which Dr. Livesey had given him secretly when the former had come to treat some of the wounded pirates. What Silver does not know is that Ben Gunn, the lone resident of the island, has already found the treasure and moved it to his own quarters. When the pirates find no treasure, they turn on Jim and Silver, but Gunn and Jim's friends arrive in time to rescue them. The ship is floated by the tide, and Jim, his friends, and Silver leave the island. Silver jumps ship with only a bag of coins for his efforts, but the rest of the group divide the treasure. "Drink and the devil had done for the rest."

Though Jim may be the hero of the novel, it is Long John Silver who dominates the book. He is an ambiguous character, capable of murder, greed, and double-dealing on the one hand and magnanimity on the other. He was Stevenson's favorite character—and the one who ultimately raises the book from a pedestrian adventure story to a timeless, mythically resonant tale which has absorbed generations of readers. The unifying theme of *Treasure Island* is man's desire for wealth. Trelawney and Livesey may be more moral in society's eyes than Silver, but their motivation is certainly no higher. As for Jim, he cannot, like Silver, give a belly laugh in the face of such a world and go off seeking another adventure. One such adventure is enough for Jim, and that one he would rather forget.

Serialized in *Young Folks* in 1883, *The Black Arrow* was labeled by Stevenson as "tushery," a term he and William Henley used for romantic adventures written for the market. In a letter to Henley in May, 1883, he said, "Ay, friend, a whole tale of tushery. And every tusher tushes me so free, that may I be tushed if the whole thing is worth a tush." Stevenson had hopes, however, that *The Black Arrow* would strike a more receptive note in *Young Folks* than did *Treasure Island*, and in this respect, his hopes were realized.

Though it lacks the depth of *Treasure Island*, *The Black Arrow* was enormously popular in its time and does not deserve its critical neglect. Set in the fifteenth century against the background of a minor battle of the Wars of the Roses and the appearance of the infamous Richard, Duke of Gloucester, the story recounts the adventures of Dick Shelton as he attempts to outwit his scheming guardian, Sir Daniel Brackley. An unscrupulous man, Sir Daniel has fought first on one side of the war and then on the other, adding to his own lands by securing the wardships of children orphaned by the war.

Planning to marry Dick to Joanna Sedley, an orphaned heiress, Sir Daniel has ridden away to take charge of the girl. In his absence, Moat House, his estate, is attacked by a group of outlaws led by a man with the mysterious name of John Amend-All, who pins a message to the church door of Moat House swearing vengeance on Sir Daniel and others for killing Dick's father, Henry Shelton.

Dick, deciding to remain quiet until he can learn more of the matter, sets out to inform Sir Daniel of the attack. In the meantime, Joanna, dressed as a boy, has eluded Sir Daniel. On his way back to Moat House, Dick meets Joanna in the guise of "John Matcham." Unaware that Sir Daniel has planned the marriage and unaware that John is Joanna, Dick offers to help his companion reach the abbey at Holywood. They eventually arrive at Moat House, where Dick learns that John is really Joanna and that his own life is in danger. He escapes and, after a lengthy series of intrigues and adventures, saves the life of Richard of York, Duke of Gloucester, and rescues Joanna from Sir Daniel, who is killed by Ellis Duckworth (John Amend-All). Dick then marries Joanna and settles at Moat House.

As an adventure story, *The Black Arrow* is thoroughly sucessful. The movement from episode to episode is swift, and the reader has little opportunity to lose interest. The love story between Dick and Joanna is deftly handled, with Joanna herself a delightfully drawn character. Still, the novel does not venture beyond the realm of pure adventure. Like many adventure stories, it is often contrived and trivial, but this fact does not detract from its readability.

Stories and theories abound regarding the writing of *The Strange Case of Dr. Jekyll and Mr. Hyde*. In "A Chapter of Dreams" (1888), Stevenson himself gave an account of the composition of the novel, explaining that "for two days I went about racking my brain for a plot of any sort; and on the second night I dreamed the scene at the window; and a scene afterwards split in two, in which Hyde, pursued for some crime, took the powder and underwent the change in the presence of his pursuers. All the rest was made awake, and consciously." The whole, according to Stevenson, was written and revised within a ten-week period.

The novel is based on the idea of the double personality in every man, an idea with which Stevenson had long been concerned. Referring to Jekyll, he said to Will H. Low, a painter, that "I believe you will find he is quite willing to answer to the name of Low or Stevenson." Not the first to use the idea in literature, Stevenson does give it a different twist. Hyde is not the double of the sinner, a conscience as it were, but, as one reviewer put it, Hyde is a personality of "hideous caprices, and appalling vitality, a terrible power of growth and increase."

As the story opens, Richard Enfield and Mr. Utterson, a lawyer, are discussing the activities of a Mr. Hyde, who has recently trampled down a small child. Both friends of Dr. Henry Jekyll, they are perturbed that the latter has named Hyde as heir in his will. A year later, Hyde is wanted for a murder, but he escapes. Soon after, Dr. Jekyll's servant Poole tells Utterson of strange goings on in his employer's laboratory. He is concerned that possibly Jekyll has been slain. Poole and Utterson break into the laboratory and find a man dead from poison. The man is Edward Hyde. A note in the laboratory contains Jekyll's confession of his double identity.

Early in life, he had begun leading a double existence: a public life of convention and gentility and a private life of unrestrained vice. Finally, he discovered a potion that transformed him physically into Edward Hyde, his evil self. Though Jekyll wanted desperately to be rid of Hyde, he was not strong enough to overcome his evil side. He finally closed himself in his laboratory, seeking a drug that would eliminate Hyde. Failing in his search, he committed suicide.

As an exploration into the darkest recesses of the human mind, *The Strange Case of Dr. Jekyll and Mr. Hyde* is skillfully constructed. Not only are Jekyll and Hyde presented in a haunting fashion, but Utterson also is a character brought clearly to life. The plot, sensational though it is, does not rely on the standard Gothic claptrap to hold the reader. On the contrary, the story is subtly undertold, and the reader is drawn into the horror of it by Stevenson's penetrating imagination and his easy mastery of language and style. The reader, said one reviewer, "feels that the same material might have been spun out to cover double the space and still have struck him as condensed and close knit workmanship. It is one of those rare fictions which make one understand the value of temperance in art."

Stevenson completed *Kidnapped* in the spring of 1886, intending it originally as a potboiler, and it surely has all the ingredients of high adventure: a stolen inheritance, a kidnaping, a battle at sea, and several murders. Having gained an interest in Scottish history from his travels through the Highlands, Stevenson used as his principal source of historical information *Trial of James Stewart* (1753), a factual account of the 1752 Appin murder trial.

Kidnapped is the story of David Balfour, whose only inheritance from his father is a letter to Ebenezer Balfour of Shaws, David's uncle. On the way to see Mr. Rankeillor, the family lawyer, to get the true story of the inheritance, David is tricked and sent off on a ship for slavery in the American colonies. He meets Alan Breck, an enemy of the monarch because of his part in a rebellion against King George, and, though David is loyal to the king, the two become fast and true friends. Escaping from the ship, they have numerous adventures, finally returning to Scotland, where David learns the truth of the inheritance. His father and uncle had both loved the same woman; when David's father married the woman (David's mother), he generously gave up his inheritance to his brother Ebenezer. Ebenezer knew that such an arrangement would not hold up legally, and thus he tried to kill David. David accepts Ebenezer's offer of two-thirds of the income from the inheritance, and, with the money, he helps Alan reach safety from the king's soldiers who are pursuing him.

Kidnapped is rich in its depiction of the Scottish Highlands, and the novel's dialogue is particularly effective. The contrast between David, a Lowlander and a Whig, and Alan, a Highlander and a Jacobite, for example, is well drawn. Ignoring their differences, the two, like Huck and Jim in Mark Twain's *The Adventures of Huckleberry Finn* (1884), prove that their friendship is more important than geographical and political differences.

Whatever Stevenson thought of *Kidnapped*, his friend Edmund Gosse thought it the "best piece of fiction that you have done." Many would argue with Gosse's statement. While it perhaps has more human interest than does *Treasure Island*, it lacks the sharpness and force of Stevenson's masterpiece.

Although not as well known as *Treasure Island* and *Kidnapped*, *The Master of Ballantrae* is considered by many to be Stevenson's best novel. Stevenson himself saw it as a "most seizing tale," a "human tragedy." Despite his preoccupation with character delineation in the story, he still regales the reader with a plethora of adventurous incidents. Set in eighteenth century Scotland, *The Master of Ballantrae* recounts the story of two brothers as they compete for title and love. When Stuart the Pretender returns to Scotland in 1745 to claim the English throne, Lord Durrisdeer decides to send one son to fight with Stuart and to keep one at home, hoping that way to make his estate secure regardless of the outcome of the struggle. James, Master of Ballantrae and his father's heir, joins Stuart, and Henry remains behind. When news of

Stuart's defeat and James's death comes, Henry becomes Master of Ballantrae. He marries Alison Graeme, who had been betrothed to James.

James, however, is not dead, and, after adventures in America and France, returns to Scotland. Goading Henry and pressing his attentions on Alison, James soon angers his brother to the point of a midnight duel. Henry thinks that he has killed James, but again the latter escapes death—this time going to India. He surprises Henry once more by showing up alive at Durrisdeer. Taking his family, Henry secretly leaves for America, but James, with his Indian servant Secundra Dass, follows. Searching for treasure that he buried on his previous trip to America, James falls sick and dies, but Henry, thinking his brother able to return at will from death, goes to the grave one night and sees Secundra Dass performing strange ministrations over James' exhumed body. Although the servant is unable to revive James, Henry believes that he sees his brother's eyes flutter and dies from heart failure. Thus, both Masters of Ballantrae are united in death.

The Master of Ballantrae, perhaps more than any other of Stevenson's novels, goes beyond the bounds of a mere adventure story. Adventure is a key element in the book, but the characters of James and Henry Durie are drawn with such subtlety and insight that the novel takes on dimensions not usually found in Stevenson's works. Like Long John Silver in *Treasure Island*, James Durie is not an ordinary villain. Henry, who moves from a kind of pathetic passivity in the first part of the novel to a villainy of his own, is unable to assume the true role of Master of Ballantrae. Overmatched and possessed by James, he lacks the dash and charm and strength of personality that makes the latter the real Master of Ballantrae. "In James Durie," wrote one reviewer, "Mr. Stevenson has invented a new villain, and has drawn him with a distinction of touch and tone worthy of Vandyke." With all the attributes of a hateful fiend, James nevertheless has a wit and a courage that are captivating.

Perhaps the novel does, as Stevenson himself feared, leave the reader with an impression of unreality. Still, whatever its shortcomings, *The Master of Ballantrae* has all the trademarks of Stevenson's fiction: an intricately and imaginatively designed plot, power of style, clear evocation of scene, and lifelike characters. G. K. Chesterton felt that Stevenson was the "first writer to treat seriously and poetically the aesthetic instincts of the boy." In his own way, Stevenson contributed a fair number of readable and memorable works to the English literary heritage, and that heritage is the richer for it.

Wilton Eckley

Other major works

SHORT FICTION: *The New Arabian Nights*, 1882; *More New Arabian Nights*, 1885; *The Merry Men and Other Tales and Fables*, 1887; *Island Nights' Enter-*

tainments, 1893.

PLAYS: *Deacon Brodie*, 1880; *Macaire*, 1885 (with William Ernest Henley); *The Hanging Judge*, 1914 (with Fanny Van de Grift Stevenson).

POETRY: *Moral Emblems*, 1882; *A Child's Garden of Verses*, 1885; *Underwoods*, 1887; *Ballads*, 1890; *Songs of Travel and Other Verses*, 1896.

NONFICTION: *An Inland Voyage*, 1878; *Edinburgh: Picturesque Notes*, 1878; *Travels with a Donkey in the Cévennes*, 1879; *Virginibus Puerisque*, 1881; *Familiar Studies of Men and Books*, 1882; *The Silverado Squatters: Sketches from a Californian Mountain*, 1883; *Memories and Portraits*, 1887; *The South Seas: A Record of Three Cruises*, 1890; *Across the Plains*, 1892; *A Footnote to History*, 1892; *Amateur Emigrant*, 1895; *In the South Seas*, 1896; *The Lantern-Bearers and Other Essays*, 1988.

Bibliography

Calder, Jenni. *Robert Louis Stevenson: A Life Study.* New York: Oxford University Press, 1980. Calder's intention is to explain Stevenson as an author and individual, rather than merely to present biographical facts. A well-documented study containing thirty-four illustrations. Also includes a chronological list of Stevenson's works.

──────────, ed. *The Robert Louis Stevenson Companion.* Edinburgh: Paul Harris, 1980. Forty-one illustrations accompany eight articles by different authors on the life and work of Stevenson. Some of the authors knew Stevenson personally. These topical articles were written between 1901 and 1979.

Daiches, David. *Robert Louis Stevenson and His World.* London: Thames and Hudson, 1973. A standard popular biography written in chronological and narrative style. Complete with 116 illustrations and a chronological page of events pertinent to Stevenson.

Hammond, J. R. *A Robert Louis Stevenson Companion: A Guide to the Novels, Essays, and Short Stories.* London: Macmillan, 1984. The first three sections cover the life and literary achievements of Stevenson and contain a brief dictionary which lists and describes his short stories, essays, and smaller works. The fourth section critiques his novels and romances, and the fifth is a key to the people and places of Stevenson's novels and stories.

Hennessy, James Pope. *Robert Louis Stevenson.* London: Jonathan Cape, 1974. Provides anecdotal episodes within a biographical narrative. Light reading with thirty illustrations.

Knight, Alanna. *The Robert Louis Stevenson Treasury.* London: Shepherd-Walwyn, 1985. An extremely useful compendium, arranged in eight parts with twenty-eight illustrations. Contains four maps: of Scotland, France, the South Seas, and the United States, as they pertained to Stevenson's life. Includes an alphabetized index of his works, letters, and characters, as well as works published about him in text, film, and radio. Also covers people and places which factored in his life.

Swearingen, Roger G. *The Prose Writings of Robert Louis Stevenson*. Hamden, Conn.: Archon Books, 1980. A complete (350-entry) chronological list of Stevenson's prose writings—from his earliest childhood until his death in 1894—which is concerned with his literary activity as his career progressed. The data includes the first appearance of each work, with its particular history of development, and actual locations of the works today.

ROBERT STONE

Born: Brooklyn, New York; August 21, 1937

Principal long fiction
A Hall of Mirrors, 1967; *Dog Soldiers*, 1974; *A Flag for Sunrise*, 1981; *Children of Light*, 1986.

Other literary forms
Reflecting his particular interest in film, Robert Stone wrote *WUSA* (1970), a screenplay based on his novel *A Hall of Mirrors*; with Judith Roscoe, he also wrote *Who'll Stop the Rain* (1978), a screen adaptation of *Dog Soldiers*. Stone has contributed short stories, articles, and reviews to such periodicals as *The Atlantic*, *Harper's Magazine*, *The New York Times Book Review*, and the *Manchester Guardian*. Notable among these pieces is "The Reason for Stories: Toward a Moral Fiction," which appeared in *Harper's Magazine* in June, 1988.

Achievements
Stone received a Wallace Stegner fellowship to Stanford University in 1962 and a Houghton Mifflin literary fellowship in 1967 for a promising first novel. In 1968 he won the William Faulkner Foundation Award for *A Hall of Mirrors*, a "notable first novel"; reviewers praised his narrative skill, facility for language and dialogue, and strength of characterization. *Dog Soldiers*, in turn, won the National Book Award for 1975 and established Stone's importance as a significant American novelist. In 1979 the Writers Guild of America nominated *Who'll Stop the Rain* for best script adapted from another medium. In 1982 *A Flag for Sunrise* received the John Dos Passos prize for literature and the American Academy and Institute award in literature, was nominated for the American Book Award, the National Book Critics Circle Award, and the PEN/Faulkner Award, and was runner-up for the Pulitzer Prize in Fiction. In 1983 Stone received a National Endowment for the Arts fellowship and a grant from the National Institute of Arts and Letters. Stone is an established artist of high caliber, a political and social critic whose skill has merited comparisons with Graham Greene, Joseph Conrad, John Dos Passos, and Nathanael West.

Biography
Robert Stone was born in south Brooklyn, New York, on August 21, 1937, the son of Gladys Catherine Grant, an elementary school teacher, and C. Homer Stone, who abandoned his family during Stone's infancy. A product of orphanages and Catholic schools, the young Stone, having offended the Mar-

ist Brothers by his drinking and his militant atheism, joined the United States Navy's amphibious force before high school graduation. His childhood experiences taught him about the rootless, the psychotic, the irresponsible, and the hypocritical, while his military service prepared him to write credibly of military life, language, and style. While attending New York University from 1958 to 1960, he worked as a copyboy, caption writer, and then editorial assistant for the *New York Daily News,* and on December 11, 1959, he was married to social worker Janice G. Burr. The Stones dropped their conventional life and ended up in New Orleans, where Stone worked at menial jobs for a while, read his own poetry to jazz accompaniment in a French Quarter bar, and moved with the beatnik crowd. His daughter was born at Charity Hospital (a son, Ian, was born later). His experiences in that city provided material for his first novel, *A Hall of Mirrors.*

The Stones became friends with Jack Kerouac and others of the emerging bohemian scene in New York City, and with Ken Kesey while Stone was studying and then teaching creative writing at Stanford University in California. His involvement in the drug culture led to his joining the Merry Pranksters' bus in its 1964 cross-country trip.

Stone wrote for the *National Mirror* in New York City from 1965 to 1967 and then free-lanced between 1967 and 1971. A Guggenheim fellowship paid his way to London, England. Later, after two months spent gathering material in Saigon, South Vietnam, for his second novel, he moved on to Hollywood, California, to help write the script for *Dog Soldiers.* Next he began a teaching career as a writer-in-residence, mainly at Princeton University but also at Amherst College, Stanford University, the University of Hawaii at Manoa, Harvard University in Cambridge, Massachusetts, the University of California at Irvine, New York University, and the University of California at San Diego. During the 1970's he interrupted this itinerant teaching to travel to Central America three times and to write his third novel. His fourth novel grew out of his experiences with the Hollywood film scene.

Stone retained his friendship with Kesey, and continued to write short stories and articles for popular journals, as well as novels: his fifth is set in New England, where he resides.

Analysis

Intrigued by the exotic and by disappointed promises of wealth or adventure, Robert Stone writes as a disillusioned American romantic, whose characters unsuccessfully pursue the American Dream in New Orleans, Vietnam, Southern California, Mexico, or Central America. Their failure to choose wisely and to accept responsibility, however, turns their dreams of wealth to ashes, destroys their personal lives, and creates nightmares. Their plight has paralleled that of the national culture as it coped with shattered ideals and governmental corruption in the 1960's and after. In many ways, Stone's works have paralleled the concerns and obsessions of the baby-boom generation.

A Hall of Mirrors, for example, takes a sharp, satirical look at romantic pessimism in the face of racial prejudice and right-wing extremism in the 1960's. M. T. Bingamon, a "superpatriot" demagogue, exploits the racist fears of poor whites aided by Brother Jensen, alias Farley the Sailor, a con man, philosopher, and supposed missionary, head of the Living Grace Mission. A cynical misfit and drifting disc jockey, Rheinhardt, and a naïve and idealistic social worker of wealthy Southern parentage, Morgan Rainey, become pawns in Bingamon's power plot. Rheinhardt espouses Bingamon's cause to preserve his position as the rock disc jockey of WUSA, while Rainey conducts a "welfare" census that brings only pain and loss to those whom he seeks to help. The final third of the novel is an apocalyptic Armageddon, a surreal and nightmarish description of the violent, racist "patriotic" rally the station sponsors and of the ensuing riot. Rheinhardt's parody of reactionary speeches sums up the illusions negated by Stone's novel: "The American way is innocence. In all situations we must and shall display an innocence so vast and awesome that the entire world will be reduced by it. American innocence shall rise in mighty clouds of vapor to the scent of heaven and confound the nations!" Stone's characters have lost their innocence, and all is emptiness, ashes, and betrayal, as the coldhearted and cold-blooded dominate. Ultimately, Rainey is seriously wounded in the madness of the political rally, but Rheinhardt drifts on. His girlfriend, a basically decent woman brought low by circumstances and misplaced affections, is stunned by Rheinhardt's indifference and, picked up for vagrancy, commits suicide in her jail cell. Rheinhardt, Geraldine, and Rainey's private hall of mirrors reflects the American nightmare wherein civilization proves a farcical hell, dreams are distorted, and action fails.

Dog Soldiers and *A Flag for Sunrise*, in turn, capture the naïve cynicism of failed upper-middle-class idealists of the 1970's and their involvement in romanticized drug-dealing or revolutionary plots. *Dog Soldiers* depicts the tragic costs of the Vietnam War in its ongoing effects back home: the difficulty of telling friend from foe, the disintegration of moral certainties, loyalties, and conscience. It argues that the war poisoned American values and produced a loss of faith that infects the survivors. In the novel, former marine Ray Hicks, a drug smuggler from Vietnam, finds in the United States love, betrayal, craziness, and ambiguity. His trusted friend John Converse, a journalist on assignment to Vietnam, enlists his aid to smuggle three kilograms of pure heroin home from Vietnam for a share of the anticipated forty-thousand-dollar profit. Converse classifies Hicks as a usable "psychopath" but does not understand that he himself has been set up from the beginning. Consequently, when Hicks contacts Converse's wife, Marge, a ticket girl for a pornographic cinema and a Dilaudid addict, he finds himself waylaid by hoods and fleeing for his life. Converse too is threatened, tortured, and then forced to deal with a less than honest federal "regulatory" agent, Antheil, who, in on the deal since its Vietnam origins, runs the hoods with "a certain Bohemian flair." As Hicks and Marge flee across Southern California, they meet an array of fringe characters from Hicks's past, characters who make him conclude, "It's gone funny in the states." Hicks envisions himself a serious man, a modern samurai with a worthy illusion, riding the wave until it crashes, but his romantic obsession with Marge and his strong sense of loyalty doom him. After a confused battle scene, heightened by the sounds of Vietnam battles blasted out over loudspeakers, Hicks discovers an escape route but is badly wounded when he returns to rescue Marge and help reunite her with her husband.

The final line of Dieter, Hicks's mentor, sums up the message in all Stone's novels: "We're in the dark ages." The self-centered, amoral Converse, dreaming of personal profit at the expense of friendship and loyalty, confirms this view when he attempts to renege on his agreement to meet Hicks in the desert on the far side of the mountains and then dumps the heroin to save himself. Converse is another of Stone's survivors: an egocentric creature who has sacrificed human feelings and human values to maintain his life. Federal agent Antheil, in turn, epitomizes moral ambiguity as he confiscates for personal profit the smuggled heroin. Ultimately, Stone demonstrates that the end result of the war's by-product, heroin, is nightmare and death—"a chain of victims."

A Flag for Sunrise, set in the fictional Central American country of Tecan, attacks American interference in such countries. As it does so, it continually draws parallels with Vietman through the memories of the central observer, Frank Holliwell, onetime Central Intelligence Agency operative, now a wandering professor. By exploring the fate of Americans whose lives become entangled in Tecanecan politics, Stone sums up the diverse motives that draw Americans into conflicts that they only vaguely understand. The end result of such involvement is inevitably negative: the importation of the worst from North American culture, support of cruel and murderous regimes, destruction and death. The novel ends with the statement that "a man has nothing to fear . . . who understands history," yet Stone's characters continually fail to understand history in any of its contexts. A bored and frustrated Roman Catholic nun, the beautiful Sister Justin Feeney, is ordered to close her failed mission and to return to the United States, yet she self-righteously volunteers to aid the revolutionary wounded; the result is that she is senselessly battered to death by a crazed Tecanecan lieutenant. Pablo Tabor, a paranoid psychotic on a rampage of killing, finds his destiny: death underwater. A curious, burned-out drifter, anthropologist Frank Holliwell feels alive only when caught up in the mystery and the horror of conflicts in the threatening and oppressive tropics, but cannot explain why. Holliwell finds survival of the fittest the only value, but concludes that outsiders have "no business down there." Everyone is searching for what only the revolutionaries seem to have—a "flag" or purpose—but all are betrayed, tortured, and killed.

Children of Light depicts the selling-out in the 1980's of the dreams of the 1960's: potential artists, novelists, and actors lose their vision and give in to crass commercialism. Stone's characters have buried themselves in drugs, fantasies, sex, and a wealthy life-style that leaves them unfulfilled, alienated from their marital partners, their children, and their art. Gordon Walker, once a Shakespearean actor and now a Hollywood writer, writes the screenplay of Kate Chopin's *The Awakening* (1899) and, after his wife's desertion, comes to Bahia Honda, Mexico, to recapture his past bittersweet romance with actress Lee Verger in order to rediscover who he was and what he can still be. Verger, in turn, acts out as her own reality the marital and personal conflicts of her screen character Edna Pontellier. Verger refers to herself and Walker as "Children of Light," the film generation, sitting in darkness and staring at the lighted screen. As "Children of Light," Verger and Gordon cannot distinguish between true relationships and those projected in their art. The "real" Walker and Verger are but empty shadows on the screen.

Verger has given up her medical treatment because it interfered with her acting; she has driven away her psychiatrist husband with her psychic projects and struggled to please director, producer, and press and to deal with sexual advances, blackmail, and threats. At the same time, she has puzzled over the suicide of her screen character, and eventually she accepts suicide as her own destiny. Walker, in contrast, ever the survivor—no matter the cost—returns to family and home and shoddy career. Stone provides no answers to his characters' plight; it is too late.

Most of Stone's characters are blind to their inner motives and to the destructive results of their acts. Converse, in *Dog Soldiers*, says, "I don't know what that guy did or why he did it. I don't know what I'm doing or why I do it or what it's like. . . . Nobody knows. . . . That's the principle we were defending over there [Vietnam]. That's why we fought the war." Stone's characters ask one another what they are worth and find the answer depressing: "A little cinder in the wind, Pablo—that's what you are." A number of them contemplate or commit suicide.

Overall, Stone's characters are self-destructive men and women of their times, hooked on alcohol, drugs, greed, or egocentricity, paying the price of national and personal ignorance and irresponsibility. They are rootless wanderers of mind and world—sometimes violent, often at the end of their tether, engaging in various forms of sophistry, rationalization, equivocation, or indifference. There is a sense of a cultural breakdown, of misplaced dreams, of despair and loss of hope. Caught up in movements beyond their understanding, they continually betray one another without guilt and without self-knowledge.

In *A Flag for Sunrise* Stone's final image of the world is the cold, hostile one of the sea: at times delicate and beautiful, but always predatory. In fact,

Stone relies on this image throughout his canon, with his metaphors and images repeatedly connecting humans to fish and the bleak bottom-of-the-ocean competition. Thereby he captures a sense of cosmic menace, nihilism, and conflict: race wars in *A Hall of Mirrors*, Vietnam and drug wars in *Dog Soldiers*, crazed killers and guerrilla warfare in *A Flag for Sunrise*, war against inner demons in *Children of Light*. His true villains are casual, feckless individuals who act without thinking or feeling and survive at the cost of others' pain and death.

Stone is one of the most impressive novelists of his generation because of his journalist's sharp eye for detail and for short, intense dramatic scenes, his poet's ear for dialogue, his English teacher's sense of the subtle nuances of language, images, and interlocking patterns, his imaginative drive, and, most important, his commitment to understanding and facing up to the moral ambiguities of America and Americans.

Andrew Macdonald
Gina Macdonald

Other major works

SCREENPLAYS: *WUSA*, 1970; *Who'll Stop the Rain*, 1978 (with Judith Roscoe).

Bibliography

Epstein, Jason. "Robert Stone: American Nightmares." In *Plausible Prejudices: Essays on American Writing*. New York: W. W. Norton, 1985. Epstein delineates the violence and destruction in Stone's works and attacks Stone's pessimism.

Jones, Robert. "The Other Side of Soullessness." *Commonweal* 113 (May 23, 1986): 305-306, 308. Jones shows how Stone chronicles, with cinematic vividness, the country's decay through the voices of its burnt-out cases, always in distant locales, and shows how dangerous and careless people are with one another. In *Children of Light* Stone tries to mirror the American cultural breakdown but provides only meaningless choices.

Moore, L. Hugh. "The Undersea World of Robert Stone." *Critique: Studies in Modern Fiction* 11, no. 3 (1969): 43-56. Moore's thesis is that Stone's recurring images and metaphors of fish-seafloor-evolution are vital to theme and character. They capture a movement toward a new man who can cope with a nightmare environment: cold, immoral. In this hostile world, to survive is immoral, but there is no other choice but despair and death.

O'Brien, Tim, and Robert Stone. "Two Interviews: Talks with Tim O'Brien and Robert Stone." Interview by Eric James Schroeder. *Modern Fiction Studies* 30 (Spring, 1984): 135-164. In this interview Stone talks about the background and research for his books, his sense of American values, his personal interpretation of some of his characters, and the changes in his own perceptions.

Stone, Robert. Interview by Maureen Kaguezian. *TriQuarterly* 53 (1982): 248-258. Stone discusses his characters as representative of different aspects of the American condition, the background out of which his novels grew, his dissatisfaction with the limitations of film and short story, his interest in "the convolutions and ironies of events," and, most particularly, the problem of living in a "meaningful moral way in a world which is apparently godless."

_____. "Robert Stone." Interview by Charles Ruas. In *Conversations with American Writers*. New York: Alfred A. Knopf, 1984. An intriguing interview in which Stone discusses his early influences, the drug culture, the counterculture movement, his writing process, his goals and values, and his characters and plots.

HARRIET BEECHER STOWE

Born: Litchfield, Connecticut; June 14, 1811
Died: Hartford, Connecticut; July 1, 1896

Principal long fiction

Uncle Tom's Cabin: Or, Life Among the Lowly, 1852; *Dred: A Tale of the Great Dismal Swamp*, 1856; *The Minister's Wooing*, 1859; *Agnes of Sorrento*, 1862; *The Pearl of Orr's Island*, 1862; *Oldtown Folks*, 1869; *Pink and White Tyranny*, 1871; *My Wife and I*, 1871; *We and Our Neighbors*, 1875; *Poganuc People*, 1878.

Other literary forms

In 1843, Harriet Beecher Stowe gathered a number of her sketches and stories into a volume called *The Mayflower: Or, Sketches of Scenes and Characters of the Descendants of the Pilgrims* (1843). For forty years thereafter, she published short fiction and miscellaneous essays in magazines. In *A Key to Uncle Tom's Cabin* (1853), she assembled a mass of sources and analogues for the characters and incidents of her most famous novel. Her 1869 *The Atlantic* article "The True Story of Lady Byron's Life," and a subsequent elaboration, *Lady Byron Vindicated* (1870), caused a sensation at the time. She also published a geography for children (1833, her earliest publication, issued under her sister Catharine's name), poems, travel books, collections of biographical sketches, and a number of other children's books.

Stowe's stories and sketches remain readable. Her best collection, *Sam Lawson's Oldtown Fireside Stories* (1872), differs from the novel *Oldtown Folks* mainly in degree of plotlessness. Selections from Stowe's frequently long and chatty letters can be found in the *Life of Harriet Beecher Stowe* (1889), written by her son Charles Edward Stowe, and in more recent biographies, but hundreds of her letters remain unpublished and scattered in various archives.

Achievements

Known primarily today for her antislavery novel *Uncle Tom's Cabin*, Stowe also interpreted the life of her native New England in a series of novels, stories, and sketches. Along with Ralph Waldo Emerson and Oliver Wendell Holmes, she contributed to the first issue of the *The Atlantic* (November, 1857) and for many years thereafter contributed frequently to that Boston-based magazine. As an alert and intelligent member of a famous family of Protestant ministers, she understood the Puritan conscience and outlook as well as anyone in her time, and as a shrewd observer of the commonplace, she deftly registered Yankee habits of mind and speech. All of her novels feature authentic New England characters; after *Uncle Tom's Cabin* and *Dred*, she turned to settings which included all six New England states. Despite a contradictory idealizing tendency, she pioneered in realism.

One of the first American writers to apply a talent for dialect and local color to the purposes of serious narrative, she exerted a strong influence on Sarah Orne Jewett, Mary Wilkins Freeman, and other regionalists of the later nineteenth century. Without a doubt, however, her greatest achievement was the novel which, beginning as an intended short serial in a Washington anti-slavery weekly, the *National Era*, forced the American reading public to realize for the first time that slaves were not only a national problem but also people with hopes and aspirations as legitimate as their own. Critics as diverse as Henry Wadsworth Longfellow, Heinrich Heine, William Dean Howells, and Leo Tolstoy in the nineteenth century, and Edmund Wilson and Anthony Burgess in the twentieth, have used superlatives to praise *Uncle Tom's Cabin*.

Biography

When Harriet Elizabeth Beecher was born on June 14, 1811, the seventh child of Lyman and Roxana Beecher, her father's fame as a preacher had spread well beyond the Congregational Church of Litchfield, Connecticut. All seven Beecher sons who lived to maturity became ministers, one becoming more famous than his father. Harriet, after attending Litchfield Academy, a well-regarded school, was sent to the Hartford Female Seminary, which was founded by her sister Catharine—in some respects the substitute mother whom Harriet needed after Roxana died in 1816 but did not discover in the second Mrs. Beecher. In later years, Harriet would consistently idealize motherhood. When Catherine's fiancé, a brilliant young man but one who had not experienced any perceptible religious conversion, died in 1822, the eleven-year-old Harriet felt the tragedy. In 1827, the shy, melancholy girl became a teacher in her sister's school.

In 1832, Lyman Beecher accepted the presidency of Lane Seminary in Cincinnati, Ohio, and soon Catharine and Harriet had established another school there. Four years later, Harriet married a widower named Calvin Stowe, a Lane professor. In the years that followed, she bore seven children. She also became familiar with slavery, as practiced just across the Ohio River in Kentucky; with the abolitionist movement, which boasted several notable champions in Cincinnati, including the future Chief Justice of the United States Supreme Court, Salmon P. Chase; and with the Underground Railroad. As a way of supplementing her husband's small income, she also contributed to local and religious periodicals.

Not until the Stowes moved to Brunswick, Maine, in 1850, however, did she think of writing about slavery. Then, urged by her brother Henry, by then a prominent minister in Brooklyn, New York, and by other family members in the wake of Congress's enactment of the Fugitive Slave Act, and spurred by a vision she experienced at a church service, she began to construct

Uncle Tom's Cabin. Even as a weekly serial in the *National Era*, it attracted much attention, and its publication in 1852 as a book made Stowe an instant celebrity. After that year, from her new base in Andover, Massachusetts, where her husband taught, she twice visited Europe, met Harriet Martineau, John Ruskin, the Brownings, and Lady Byron, among others, and the scope of her fame increased even further.

Stowe wrote another slavery novel, *Dred*, and then turned her literary attention to New England. The drowning of her son Henry, a Dartmouth student, in the summer of 1857, marred for her the successes of these years. In the fall of 1862, infuriated by the lack of British support for the North in the Civil War and skeptical that President Lincoln would fulfill his promise to issue a proclamation of emancipation, Stowe visited Lincoln, who is reported to have greeted her with the words, "So this is the little lady who made this big war." She left Washington satisfied that the president would keep his word.

Following Calvin Stowe's retirement from Andover, the family moved to Hartford, the winters usually being spent in northern Florida. Two of the most sensational scandals of the post-Civil War era involved Stowe, the first arising when she published an imprudent and detailed account of Lord Byron's sins as revealed to her some years earlier by the now deceased widow of the poet, the second being an adultery suit brought against her brother Henry in which Stowe characteristically defended him to the hilt. The Byron affair in particular turned many people against her, although her books continued to be commercial successes throughout the 1870's. The most severe personal abuse ever directed at a respectable nineteenth century woman bothered Stowe far less than another personal tragedy: the alcoholism and eventual disappearance of her son Fred in San Francisco, California, in 1870.

In the last twenty-three years of her life, Stowe became the central attraction of the Hartford neighborhood known as Nook Farm, also the home of Charles Dudley Warner and Mark Twain, the latter moving there in part because of its Beecher connections. Her circle of friends included Annie Fields, wife of *The Atlantic* publisher; George Eliot, with whom she corresponded; and Holmes, always a staunch supporter. In her final years, her mind wandered at times, but she was still writing lucid letters two years before her death on July 1, 1896, at the age of eighty-five.

Analysis

In 1869, after finishing her sixth novel, *Oldtown Folks*, Harriet Beecher Stowe began a correspondence with George Eliot by sending her a copy. Although an international celebrity, Stowe wanted the approval of this younger and less famous woman who had contributed notably to a movement just beginning to be critically recognized: literary realism. Like Stowe, Eliot came from a deeply religious background and had formed a union with an unromantic, bookish, but supportive man. Unlike the American novelist, Eliot had rejected religion for rationalism and romanticism for realism. Had Calvin Stowe's first wife not died, it would have been unthinkable for Harriet Beecher to live with him as Eliot did with George Henry Lewes. In life, the former Miss Beecher cheerfully married the unexciting scholar; in *The Minister's Wooing*, she would not permit her heroine Mary Scudder to marry her scholarly suitor (as Eliot's Dorothea Brooke in *Middlemarch* was permitted to marry hers, Dr. Casaubon).

Stowe's hope, in a measure fulfilled, that Eliot would like *Oldtown Folks* may be taken as signifying her desire to be recognized as a realist, even though her own realism was strongly tinged with the romanticism Eliot had come to despise. The young Harriet Beecher had probably learned something from John Bunyan's *The Pilgrim's Progress* (1678, 1684), but most of her other reading—*The Arabian Nights*, Cotton Mather's *Magnalia Christi Americana* (1702), and the works of Sir Walter Scott and Lord Byron—had little to teach an incipient realist. Nor did American literature in the 1830's, when she began to write, furnish any likely models. As a result, the reader finds in her works a mingling of realistic and romantic elements.

Stowe's settings, particularly the New England ones, ring true. She understood her cultural roots, and she proved able to recollect childhood impressions almost photographically. She possessed a keen ear for dialect and a sharp eye for the idiosyncrasies of people she scarcely seemed to have noticed until they turned up in her writing. She used the novel to probe urgent social issues such as slavery and women's rights. Although she liked nature and worked hard at describing it accurately, she disdained her native region's characteristic transcendental interpretations of it. She displayed the realist's aversion to mystery, mysticism, and the legendizing of history.

On the other hand, the romantic tendencies of Stowe's fiction stand out against its realistic background. Her heroines are invariably saintly, as are certain of her black males such as Uncle Tom and, in *Dred*, Uncle Tiff. Her recalcitrant heroes often undergo rather unconvincing conversions. Occasionally, she introduces a mythic, larger-than-life character such as Dred. In common with most of the generation of American realists who followed her, she never renounced the heroic but sought to demonstrate its presence among humble and common people. Her heroes differ from those of Twain, William Dean Howells, and Henry James, however, in drawing their strength from a firm Christian commitment: Stowe's piety has been something of an impediment to her modern readers.

The looseness of plotting about which Stowe's critics have complained so much derives in large measure from her inability to develop convincing central characters in most of her novels. Four of her last five novels have plural nouns—words such as *neighbors* and *folks* and *people*—in their titles, but even *Uncle Tom's Cabin* is not about Uncle Tom in the sense that Charles

Dickens' *David Copperfield* (1849-1850) or Gustave Flaubert's *Madame Bovary* (1857) is about its title character. In fact, Stowe changed the title of *Dred* for a time to *Nina Gordon*, a more central character but one who dies many chapters from the end. *My Wife and I* and *Oldtown Folks* are narrated by relatively colorless central characters.

One of Stowe's most persistent and indeed remarkable narrative traits also works against her realism on occasions. As she confides at the beginning of Chapter forty-four of *Dred*, "There's no study in human nature more interesting than the aspects of the same subject in the points of view of different characters." That she periodically allowed this interest to distract her from the task at hand is clear. Although she experimented with different points of view—omniscient, first-person, dramatic, and circulating (the last primarily through the use of the epistolary method)—she worked before the time when novelists such as Joseph Conrad, James Joyce, and William Faulkner developed techniques capable of sustaining this kind of interest. It should be pointed out that Stowe uses the expression "points of view" in the sense of "opinions," and she is more likely to present the conflict of opinions through conversations than through living, breathing embodiments of motivating ideas.

It is as a realist before her time that Stowe is most profitably considered. Even where her realism does not serve a socially critical purpose, as it does in *Uncle Tom's Cabin* and *My Wife and I*, she makes her readers aware of the texture, the complexity, of social life—particularly the conflicts, tensions, and joys of New England community life. Understanding how people grow from their geographic, social, religious, and intellectual roots, she is able to convey the reality of isolated Maine coastal villages and the jaunty postwar Manhattan of aspiring journalists. In her best work, she depicts evil not as the product of Mephistophelean schemers or motiveless brutes but of high-minded people incapacitated by a crucial weakness, such as the irresolute Augustine St. Clare of *Uncle Tom's Cabin*, the temporizing Judge Clayton of *Dred*, and the imperceptive Dr. Hopkins of *The Minister's Wooing*.

Uncle Tom's Cabin: Or, Life Among the Lowly, remains one of the most controversial of novels. Extravagantly admired and bitterly detested in the 1850s, it still arouses extreme reactions more than a century later. An early barrage of challenges to its authenticity led Stowe to work furiously at the assembling of *A Key to Uncle Tom's Cabin* the next year. In 262 closely printed, double-columned pages, she impressively documented horrors that verified "the truth of the work." This book unfortunately encouraged the development of an essentially nonliterary mass of criticism, with the result that the novel early gained the reputation of a brilliant piece of propaganda—even President Lincoln supposedly accepting the Civil War as its legacy—but unworthy of serious consideration on artistic grounds.

It did not help the novel's cause that the inevitable later reaction against this enormously popular story coincided with the effort, spearheaded by Henry James, to establish the novel as a form of art rather than as a mere popular entertainment. A writer who strove too singlemindedly for mere verifiability did not merit consideration as an artist. In the same year that *Uncle Tom's Cabin* began appearing serially, Nathaniel Hawthorne—James's chief example of the American artist—prefaced his *The House of the Seven Gables* (1851) with a firm declaration of its imaginary basis which contrasted sharply with his attempt to provide a "historical" one for *The Scarlet Letter* one year earlier. Hawthorne's star as a writer of fiction gradually rose; Stowe's sank. Like "Old Ironsides," the vigorous youthful poem of Stowe's staunch friend of later years, *Uncle Tom's Cabin* was relegated to the status of a work that made things happen—important historically but damned by that very fact to the region of the second-rate.

In *A Key to Uncle Tom's Cabin*, Stowe herself called *Uncle Tom's Cabin* "a very inadequate representation of slavery," but her excuse is significant: "Slavery, in some of its workings, is too dreadful for the purposes of art." She was acknowledging a problem that would continue to bedevil realists for most of the rest of the century. The most prominent spokesman for realism, Howells, agreed with her, and until the 1890's, realists would generally exclude things considered "too dreadful." As late as 1891, Thomas Hardy induced mass revulsion by allowing his heroine to be raped in *Tess of the D'Urbervilles* (1891) while referring to her in his subtitle as "a pure woman."

Stowe sandwiched the story of Uncle Tom, the meek Christian capable of turning the other cheek even to the sadistic Simon Legree, between the resolute George and Eliza Harris' escape from slavery and the Harris family's fortuitous reunion at the end of the novel. If the plot is untidy and contrived, a number of the individual characters and episodes have remained among the most memorable in fiction. The famous scene in which Eliza crosses the Ohio River ice in early spring is "true" not because the feat had been accomplished (although Stowe knew it had) but because she makes the reader feel Eliza's desperation, the absolute necessity of the attempt, and the likelihood that a person who grew up in her hard school would develop the resources to succeed.

The meeting between Miss Ophelia and Topsy illustrates Stowe's talent for dramatizing the confrontation of stubborn viewpoints. Sold down the river by his first owner, Tom has rescued the angelic daughter of Augustine St. Clare and has been installed to the St. Clare household. Miss Ophelia, a Vermont cousin of St. Clare, has been brought south to take care of Eva, whose mother is languidly incompetent. St. Clare despises slavery but feels powerless to resist it; Ophelia's intransigent New England conscience will not permit her to acquiese in it. After listening to a considerable amount of her antislavery rhetoric, St. Clare gives his cousin a little black girl rescued from alcoholic parents. Ophelia is revolted by Topsy, so utterly different from the golden, cherubic Eva. Topsy, shrewd and skeptical beyond her years, embodies the insidiousness of slavery itself. Neither was premeditated but simply "grow'd" and now must somehow be dealt with as found. Ophelia must find room in her heart for the little "black spider" or lose face with her cousin. Her struggle with Topsy—and with her own physical aversion—is fierce and richly comical, and its successful outcome believable.

For the modern reader, the death scenes in the novel are more of a problem. Little Eva's protracted illness and beatific death exactly pleased the taste of Stowe's time. Today, her father's senseless and sudden death as a result of his attempt to mediate a tavern brawl seems more like real life—or would if Stowe had not permitted St. Clare to linger long enough to undergo a deathbed religious conversion. Modern reaction to Stowe's climactic scene is complicated by the hostility of writers such as James Baldwin to the character of Uncle Tom, who, in dying at the hands of Legree's henchmen, wins their souls in the process. Whether or not the conversion of Sambo and Quimbo convinces today's reader, Tom's character has been firmly established, and he dies in precisely the spirit the reader expects.

Far less satisfactory is the subsequent escape of two of Legree's slaves from his clutches. Stowe did nothing beforehand to induce belief in a brutal master who could melt into helpless impassivity at the sight of a lock of his dead mother's hair. Finding it expedient to make Legree superstitious, she established this side of his character belatedly and ineptly, and she failed to understand that her conception of the power of motherhood was not universally shared.

In short, the reader's admiration is interrupted by idealistic and sentimental material that does not support Stowe's goal of depicting life as it was. Nor is this inconsistency surprising. No American had ever written such a novel: realistic in impulse and directed at a current social problem of the greatest magnitude. She had no models and could not, like Twain after her, draw upon experiences as Missourian, journalist, western traveler, and—before he wrote his greatest books—neighbor of Stowe and reader of her work.

Like Twain and Howells after her, Stowe did not banish Romanticism from her novels, but her commitment to realism is clear. Thirty years before Twain boasted of his accomplishments with dialect in *The Adventures of Huckleberry Finn* (1884), and nearly two decades before Bret Harte popularized the concept of local color, Stowe used dialects—not with perfect consistency but not for the conventional purpose of humor either. For the first time in major American fiction, dialect served the purpose of generating a credible environment for a serious narrative. In the process, she changed the perceptions of hundreds of thousands of readers forever.

Within a year, the book had made Stowe internationally known. When, after several years of minor literary activity, she returned to the subject of slavery, events were unfolding that led inexorably to war. Her brother Henry was outraging North and South alike by holding his own mock slave auction in his Brooklyn church. John Brown was launching his personal Civil War in Kansas. In the chamber of the United States Senate, abolitionist Charles Sumner was nearly beaten to death by a Southern colleague. Stowe herself had been busy with antislavery petitions and appeals.

From this context emerged *Dred*, a more somber novel. As it opens, Nina Gordon has returned to her North Carolina plantation from New York upon the death of her father. She has dallied with several suitors but has sense enough to prefer Edward Clayton, an idealistic young lawyer from another part of her native state. After successfully prosecuting a white man who had hired and then physically abused Nina's domestic slave Milly, Clayton's ambition to counteract such abuses legally is checked when an appeals judge—a man of undoubted probity and, ironically, Claytons' own father—reverses the earlier decision on the grounds that no slave has any rights under state law. Meanwhile, Nina's attempt at benign management of her plantation is set back by the appearance of her wastrel brother Tom, who especially enjoys tormenting her able quadroon steward Harry. Although bearing a strong resemblance to George Harris of *Uncle Tom's Cabin*, Harry is different in two important ways. First, Stowe develops the frustration of this educated and sensitive man much more thoroughly. Second, Harry is, unknown to Nina, the Gordon children's half-brother.

When Nina dies in a cholera epidemic, Tom asserts control over the plantation, and Clayton returns home with the resolve to press for changes in a legal code that permits a man to own and mistreat his own brother. Harry is driven to rebel and flee into the nearby swamp, where he falls under the influence of Dred, whom the author styles after the son of the famous black rebel Denmark Vesey, but who resembles even more closely that other noted rebel, Nat Turner.

What happens next exemplifies Stowe's familiarity with the clergy and her talent for controversy. Invited by his uncle to a Presbyterian ministers' conference, Clayton seeks there the moral support for legal reform. Even though he finds one minister passionately committed to rights for slaves, the majority of the brethren turn out to be complacent trimmers, and Clayton learns that he can expect no help in that quarter. Stowe strategically places the conference between two scenes of desperation, both of which illustrate the social system's assault on the family. In the former, Uncle Tiff, the black guardian of two white children whose father is a shiftless squatter on the Gordon plantation, vows to preserve them from the corrupting influence of their slatternly stepmother and takes them to Dred's hidden fastness in the swamp. In the latter, another quadroon Gordon offshoot, Cora, confesses in court to the murder of her own two children to "save" them, as she puts it, from being sold away.

In the swamp, Tiff and the children are succored by Dred, who is one of Stowe's most bizarre creations: half Robin Hood, half self-appointed executioner for the Lord. Too mythic a hero for a realistic novel, Dred unfortunately develops quickly into a very tedious one too, ranting interminably in his guise of Old Testament prophet. Even he is no match, however, for the committed Christian Milly, although she can accomplish no more than the postponement of his planned revenge against the hated whites. When Tom Gordon organizes a party to ransack the swamp for Dred and Harry, the former is killed, and Harry and his wife, along with Tiff and his young charges, escape to the North. In an obviously Pyrrhic victory, Clayton, baffled by his neighbors in his attempt to educate the slaves on his own estate, takes them off to Canada, where they continue to work for him in their freedom.

Tiff is another saintly domestic slave, but he has no power to reclaim any Sambo or Quimbo from degradation. There are no spectacular personal conversions in *Dred* and no hope of any social one. Milly, who has had to endure the loss by death or sale of all her numerous children, seems to win a legal victory over a cruel master and a moral one over the vindictive fugitive Dred, but both turn out to be illusory. Not only the fugitive blacks but also Clayton the hero must leave the country. If *Uncle Tom's Cabin* stands as a warning to a divided society, *Dred* is a prophecy of disintegration.

Stowe's next two novels have much in common. Both *The Minister's Wooing* and *The Pearl of Orr's Island* are anchored in New England coastal communities, and both put Yankee manners and speech on display. Each novel boasts a saintly heroine who effects the conversion of a dashing young man with a strong affinity for the sea. Although the former novel paints Newport, Rhode Island, less colorfully than the latter does coastal Maine, *The Minister's Wooing* is a more carefully constructed novel which analyzes New England character more profoundly.

More than any other Stowe novel, *The Minister's Wooing* focuses on its principals: Samuel Hopkins, Congregationalist minister of Newport, and Mary Scudder, daughter of Hopkins' widowed landlady. In several respects, the minister is the historical Dr. Hopkins, learned protégé of the great Jonathan Edwards, eminent theologian in his own right, and vigorous opponent of slavery in a town consecrated to the slave trade. In the 1780's, when the novel is set, however, the real Hopkins was in his sixties and possessed a wife and eight children; Stowe makes him middle-aged and a bachelor. Another celebrity of the time plays a significant role: Aaron Burr in the years before he became senator, vice-president, and killer of Alexander Hamilton in a duel. Burr is depicted as a charming, unscrupulous seducer of women—a distortion of the historical Burr, no doubt, but one based on the man's reputation.

Stowe's motive for involving these men in her story of pious young Mary Scudder is utterly serious. As friend and student of Edwards, Hopkins represents the stern, uncompromising Puritan past. As Edwards' worldly and skeptical grandson, Burr stands for the repudiation of the past. Mary's choice is not—what would be easy for her—between Hopkins and Burr but between Hopkins and her young lover James Marvyn, who resembles Burr only in his impatience with the hard and incomprehensible doctrines of his forebears. James has grown up with Mary but has gravitated to the sea, and is not quite engaged to her when he is reported lost in a shipwreck. Mrs. Scudder thereafter nudges Mary toward a union with the unexciting minister, himself an admirer of the young lady's ardent—if for his taste too sunny—Christianity.

Stowe neatly balances the claims of Hopkins's exacting Old Testament theology and Mary's simpler faith in the loving kindness of Jesus. In comforting the lost James's mother, long appalled by the minister's remorseless logic and now driven to near-psychosis by her son's supposed death, Mary's cheerful faith receives its first test. She also befriends an aristocratic young Frenchwoman—Burr's intended victim—and learns of the world of adulterous intrigue. As in her previous novels, Stowe introduces a black servant who has looked on life long and maintained a practical Christianity that is proof against all temptation to despair. Having been freed by her master, Mr. Marvyn, under the minister's influence, Candace works freely for the Marvyns and venerates Dr. Hopkins, not failing, however, to draw Mrs. Marvyn gently from "the fathomless mystery of sin and sorrow" to the "deeper mystery of God's love." Meanwhile, Mary's faith deepens, Stowe probably raising more than a few Protestant eyebrows by likening her explicitly to the Virgin Mary, who "kept all things and pondered them in her heart."

In real life, Catharine Beecher's beloved did not survive his shipwreck, and Stowe's elder sister agonized long over the possibility of his having died unregenerate. In life, Henry Stowe did not miraculously escape drowning. James Marvyn, on the other hand, after a considerable interval in which he inexplicably fails to notify either Mary or his family of his survival, returns a week before Mary's scheduled wedding with the minister. After having promised herself to Hopkins, Mary will not of course renege, so it falls to Miss Prissy, her dressmaker and friend, to approach the formidable theologian with the fact—which he is incapable of divining—that James is Mary's true love. Miss Prissy is one of Stowe's well-conceived realistic characters; an incurable gossip and a hypocrite in her professed admiration for the minister's sermons, she is nevertheless willing to assume the unpleasant initiative on behalf of her friend. Apprised of the true situation, the minister releases Mary and promptly marries her to Marvyn.

As she had in her first *The Atlantic* short story, Stowe depicts in this novel the psychology of bereavement; what she refuses to present is not death itself but the possibility of a good-hearted lad's dying unregenerate. She demonstrates how the rigorous faith of a Hopkins can be a barrier, even a poison, to the unstable, but of the efficacy of Christianity to restore lost lambs, she can conceive no doubt. Even the heterodox Burr nearly succumbs to Mary's entreaties to reform. Stowe's less saintly believers, such as Miss Prissy, and her magnanimous skeptics, like Augustine St. Clare of *Uncle Tom's Cabin*, are more credible. As for Hopkins, willing to jeopardize his church financially and socially by his insistence that the most influential of his parishoners renounce his connections with the slave trade, his final renunciation of Mary is quite consistent with his previous rock-ribbed selflessness.

Oldtown Folks, at which Stowe worked in the postwar years and published whole in 1869—for she refused to serialize it in the usual way—repeats many of the concerns of *The Minister's Wooing* and even reintroduces Jonathan Edwards' grandson, here known as Ellery Davenport. Longer, more varied, and much more rambling, this novel contains a considerable amount of Stowe's best writing. In the Preface, her narrator, Horace Holyoke, vows to "interpret to the world the New England life and character of the early republic." Today, no one would choose a loose, leisurely narrative to achieve such an ambition, and perhaps no one but Stowe would have attempted it in the 1860's. It is no coincidence that *Oldtown Folks* attracted the attention of Perry Miller, the distinguished twentieth century interpreter of the New England tradition.

The Minister's Wooing had been a theological novel in which no one had very much fun. As if to redress the deficiency, Stowe widens her focus, invests this work with more of the engaging minor characters of *The Pearl of Orr's Island*, and shows her villagers enjoying themselves. Her twenty-seventh chapter, "How We Kept Thanksgiving at Oldtown," which has become an anthology piece in recent years, argues that Oldtown (based on her husband's hometown of Natick, Massachusetts) has fun precisely because the inhabitants take human life seriously enough "to believe they can do much with it." Sam Lawson—Stowe's most famous character outside *Uncle Tom's Cabin*—far from exemplifying the protestant work ethic, is the town idler, universally valued for his skill at "lubricating" with his humorous andecdotes and relaxed manner the "incessant streampower in Yankee life." By contrast, the character most devoted to work, Miss Asphyxia Smith, is easily the most hateful character in the book.

Sam also serves the tenuous plot interest by coming upon two of its three principals (Narrator Horace Holyoke is the other) in an abandoned house to which they had fled from Miss Asphyxia's clutches, for, like Uncle Tiff's young charges in *Dred*, Harry and Tina Percival have been successively deserted by their scalawag father and subjected to the slow death of their mother. Tina, who is adopted by Mehitabel Rossiter, a woman of no physical beauty but much strength of character and intellect, grows into a beautiful, kindhearted, but willful woman—exactly the type favored by the unprincipled Davenport. Harry grows up as Horace's companion in the nearby Holyoke household.

Tina, not knowing that Davenport numbers among his previous victims Ellen Rossiter, Mehitabel's younger sister, marries him, and it appears that Stowe will not permit her protagonist the usual eleventh-hour rescue. Tina endures ten years with the erratic Davenport, generously adopting his daughter by Ellen Rossiter, but then, in a switch on the Aaron Burr story, Davenport is killed in a duel. Two years (but only three paragraphs) later, Tina and Horace marry and settle in Boston. At the end of the novel, the Horace Holyokes are discoverd back in Oldtown visiting its most durable inhabitant, Sam Lawson.

Any synopsis leaves untouched the merits of *Oldtown Folks*: the interplay of its varied and vital minor characters and the development of its seduction theme. Of the former, Miss Asphyxia, "a great threshing-machine of a woman"; Horace's peppery grandmother, "a valiant old soul, who fearlessly took any bull in life by the horns, and was ready to shake him into decorum"; and Lawson, half nuisance, half good neighbor, are only three of the most memorable. As seducer, Davenport takes advantage of several factors: the intransigence of Calvinism in its death throes, embodied in brilliant but outdated theorizers such as this novel's version of Hopkins, Dr. Stern; the Calvinist legacy of neurosis, skepticism, and rebellion (Miss Rossiter, Tina, and Davenport himself); and the ineffectuality of well-intentioned observers such as Horace and Harry. Thwarted by orthodoxy, which has become a cruel instrument in the hands of its conservative defenders, and averse to the rationalism that played such a large part in the creation of the new republic, the Oldtowners are easily taken in by Davenport, who has turned the passion and intellectual energy inherited from Edwards and the rest of his Puritan forebears to the service of selfish and worldly ends.

In *My Wife and I* and its sequel, *We and Our Neighbors*, Stowe turns to contemporary Manhattan life, a frivolous and even more worldly existence dotted nevertheless by young men and women of impulses Stowe characterizes as Christian but which may strike today's reader as more generally humanitarian. The full spectrum of views on women's rights is on display, including a conviction, expressed by a young woman struggling for the opportunity to study medicine, that "marriage ought never to be entered on as a means of support." The main business of the two novels, however, is to educate Harry Henderson for marriage and thus to provide a base of operations for his wife, who dedicates herself to neighborliness and charitable offices. Stowe retains her observant eye and spicy descriptive powers, but her narrator cannot "interpret" the Gilded Age as Horace Holyoke in *Oldtown Folks* could interpret post-Revolutionary New England.

Pink and White Tyranny, the story of a man who married and must endure a selfish and demanding woman, must rank, along with the earlier *Agnes of Sorrento*, among Stowe's weakest books. Finally, in *Poganuc People*, she returns to the milieu of *The Minister's Wooing*, *The Pearl of Orr's Island*, and her Oldtown books. Poganuc is the Litchfield of her childhood and Dolly Cushing her closet approximation to an autobiographical heroine. The principal conflict is not between the old religion and the new worldliness but between entrenched Congregationalism and upstart Episcopalianism. The novel begins and ends at Christmas when the liturgical and social differences between the two denominations stand out most sharply. Like Maggie Tulliver in Eliot's *The Mill on the Floss* (1860) Dolly is precocious, sensitive, and consequently often uncomfortable, but instead of developing the crises of her heroine's maturation, as does Eliot, Stowe whisks her off to a fashionable Boston marriage with a successful merchant, after which the author makes a final survey of the Poganuc people going about their business under the immemorial elms of the village.

Stowe seldom brought her psychological insights to bear on the development of her main characters, with the result that the less important ones invariably seem more convincing. Whether because her most productive years antedated the time of the realistic novel and particularly the psychological novel, or because she felt too strongly the nineteenth century prohibition against a woman exploring the conflicts and repressions of her own life, Stowe left unwritten what might have constituted her richest vein of realism. She never wrote a novel expressing what it felt like to be a vocationless Harriet Beecher approaching womanhood or the second Mrs. Calvin Stowe struggling with sickness, poverty, and the multitudinous demands of husband and children. The woman who wrote of domesticity in her time avoided calling attention to its tensions, exactions, and restrictions. Whatever else family life meant to Stowe, it helped prepare her to do what no American novelist had done before: write powerfully and feelingly about slavery.

Robert P. Ellis

Other major works
SHORT FICTION: *The Mayflower: Or, Sketches of Scenes and Characters of the Descendants of the Pilgrims*, 1843; *Sam Lawson's Oldtown Fireside Stories*, 1872.

POETRY: *Religious Poems*, 1867.

NONFICTION: *Sunny Memories of Foreign Lands*, 1854; *Lady Byron Vindicated*, 1870; *Palmetto Leaves*, 1873.

CHILDREN'S LITERATURE: *First Geography for Children*, 1833 (published under sister Catharine's name).

MISCELLANEOUS: *A Key to Uncle Tom's Cabin*, 1853.

Bibliography
Boydston, Jeanne, Mary Kelley, and Anne Margolis. *The Limits of Sisterhood: The Beecher Sisters on Women's Rights and Woman's Sphere*. Chapel Hill: University of North Carolina Press, 1988. A superb study of Stowe and her sisters, Catharine and Isabella. Brief but insightful essays address each woman as an individual and as a sister. Primary documents are ap-

pended to each chapter, providing excellent resources. Illustrations, careful documentation, and a detailed index make this an invaluable text.

Lang, Amy Schrager. *Prophetic Woman: Anne Hutchinson and the Problem of Dissent in the Literature of New England.* Berkeley: University of California Press, 1987. An excellent feminist study, focusing on *Uncle Tom's Cabin* and Stowe's role in the history of Puritan suppression of women who achieve public notice. Stowe's novel constitutes a culmination in this process and presents a model of women as moral superiors who represent the possibility of a future without slavery.

Showalter, Elaine. "Piecing and Writing." In *The Poetics of Gender*, edited by Nancy K. Miller. New York: Columbia University Press, 1986. Showalter analyzes patchwork as a feminist lexicon in women's culture. In Stowe's novels, the relationship between material culture (piecing) and literary production (writing) is found in the novels' narrative designs of sketches or short "pieces" that resemble the popular Log Cabin quilts of alternating light and dark fabrics.

Stowe, Charles Edward. *Life of Harriet Beecher Stowe.* Boston: Houghton Mifflin, 1889. Written by her seventh child, this is the first full-length biography of Stowe, drawn from her letters and her journal. Though not critical, it offers extensive excerpts of her personal writings and of correspondence from other renowned writers. An annotated primary bibliography and a detailed index are included.

Sundquist, Eric J., ed. *New Essays on "Uncle Tom's Cabin."* Cambridge, England: Cambridge University Press, 1986. An excellent collection of essays on Stowe's most famous novel. The insightful introduction discusses changing literary theories as they relate to *Uncle Tom's Cabin*. The six diverse contributions by notable scholars include analyses of genre and gender issues. A selected bibliography also notes additional criticism.

Tompkins, Jane. *Sensational Designs: The Cultural Work of American Fiction, 1790-1860.* New York: Oxford University Press, 1985. Tompkins addresses *Uncle Tom's Cabin* from the perspective of "the politics of literary history." Nineteenth century popular domestic novels represent attempts to reorganize culture from a woman's perspective, and Stowe's novel is representative of "America's religion of domesticity" as empowerment of women. An excellent and influential study.

Wagenknecht, Edward. *Harriet Beecher Stowe: The Known and the Unknown.* New York: Oxford University Press, 1965. Analyzes Stowe's various personal roles (daughter, wife, mother, woman) and professional roles (writer, reformer), and includes a brief biography and an evaluative bibliographic essay.

JESSE STUART

Born: W-Hollow, Riverton, Kentucky; August 8, 1907
Died: W-Hollow, Riverton, Kentucky; February 17, 1984

Principal long fiction

Trees of Heaven, 1940, *Taps for Private Tussie*, 1943; *Foretaste of Glory*, 1946; *Hie to the Hunters*, 1950; *The Good Spirit of Laurel Ridge*, 1953; *Daughter of the Legend*, 1965; *Mr. Gallion's School*, 1967; *The Land Beyond the River*, 1973; *Cradle of the Copperheads*, 1988.

Other literary forms

Jesse Stuart initially gained prominence as a poet. His first collection, *Harvest of Youth* (1930), contained eighty-one poems, which are considered largely juvenilia. His second collection, *Man with a Bull-Tongue Plow* (1934), was composed of 703 poems written in sonnetlike forms (Stuart did not always hold strictly to the sonnet structure). The book was a popular and critical success and brought Stuart his first recognition. His next volume of poetry, *Album of Destiny* (1944), was less well-received, although Stuart considered it his best. Subsequently, he published three other books of verse: *Kentucky Is My Land* (1952), *Hold April* (1962), and *The World of Jesse Stuart: Selected Poems* (1975).

Stuart was also a prolific short-story writer. From his more than three hundred published short stories, Stuart gathered several collections, including *Head o' W-Hollow* (1936), *Men of the Mountains* (1941), *Tales from the Plum Grove Hills* (1946), *Clearing in the Sky and Other Stories* (1950), *Plowshare in Heaven: Tales True and Tall from the Kentucky Hills* (1958), *Save Every Lamb* (1964), *My Land Has a Voice* (1966), and *The Best-Loved Short Stories of Jesse Stuart* (1982). "Huey the Engineer," a story first published in *Esquire* (August, 1937), was later printed in an anthology, *The Best Short Stories of 1938*. It is generally agreed that Stuart's best work has been in the short story.

Stuart's biographical and autobiographical writings, which are among his most important, include *Beyond Dark Hills* (1938), *The Thread That Runs So True* (1949), *The Year of My Rebirth* (1956), and *God's Oddling* (1960). In addition, he has written several books for children, including *The Beatinest Boy* (1953), *A Penny's Worth of Character* (1954), *Red Mule* (1955), *The Rightful Owner* (1960), and *Andy Finds a Way* (1961).

Achievements

As a writer, Stuart was both a spokesman for and a popularizer of Appalachia, a region and people that have long bewildered and fascinated the rest of the nation. In some ways, Stuart was responsible for, if not creating, then strengthening and prolonging a number of the myths and stereotypes which have beleaguered this area, although Stuart insisted that he rarely exaggerated the truth. Stuart himself seems larger than life, and since so much of his fiction is heavily dependent on his own life, it is difficult to determine where the actual leaves off and the imaginative begins. There was Stuart as the mountain boy from a large, poor family, who worked his way through school fired by a need for knowledge; then, as an educator who returned to his region and almost single-handedly (and sometimes two-fistedly) brought learning into a backward land; and finally as an extremely successful writer who scribbled poems by the bushel while plowing fields, who produced novels in a few weeks' time, and who gained a reputation as a true primitive, a writer who created as a force of nature. Still, there is no denying the impressive scope of Stuart's achievements. A man of boundless energy and enthusiasm, he established himself as perhaps the foremost American regionalist writer of the twentieth century.

Stuart was labeled as an original from the time of his first important work, *Man with a Bull-Tongue Plow*, in 1934. He claimed to have written these poems primarily for his own pleasure, as reflections and observations on the world of nature in which he lived; but when they were published, their vitality, apparent artlessness, and obvious sincerity captivated a large section of the literary establishment and the reading public. Stuart, the writing mountain man, was called "a modern Robert Burns," the kind of easy pigeonholing which reveals a misunderstanding of both men. When Stuart followed the poems with a collection of stories (*Head o' W-Hollow*), a book of autobiography (*Beyond Dark Hills*), and an impressive novel (*Trees of Heaven*), he had declared himself a writer to be reckoned with. The recognition and awards came quickly. In 1934, he received the Jeannette Sewal Davis poetry prize of one hundred dollars for *Man with a Bull-Tongue Plow* (beating out such other contenders as Ezra Pound and William Carlos Williams). In 1937, he was awarded the John Simon Guggenheim Literary Award for his poetry and short stories. In 1941, he was given the Academy of Arts and Sciences Award for *Men of the Mountains*, his second short-story collection. In 1943, his second novel, *Taps for Private Tussie*, was chosen for the Thomas Jefferson Southern Award of $2500 as the best Southern novel of the year. *The Thread That Runs So True*, which detailed Stuart's experiences as a young teacher in a one-room schoolhouse, was selected by the National Educational Association as the "most important book of 1949" written on the subject of education (the president of the NEA, Jay Elmer Morgan, called it "the best book on education written in the last fifty years"). In 1954, Stuart was named poet laureate of Kentucky; in 1955, he was given the Centennial Award for Literature by Berea College. The recognition which meant the most to Stuart came in 1961, when the 1960 Fellowship of the Academy of American Poets was bestowed on him for "distinguished service to American poetry."

Biography

Hilton Jesse Stuart was born on August 8, 1907, in W-Hollow in Greenup County, a very mountainous and, at the time, relatively isolated section of Kentucky which Stuart would use as the locale for most of his writings. He was the first child of Mitchell and Martha Hilton Stuart; six other children followed, but two died in infancy from pneumonia. Stuart's father's family had lived in Kentucky for generations. They were a clannish people—"Tall Figures of the Earth," in Stuart's own words. His grandfather, Mitchell Stuart, had fought in the Civil War, and Stuart honored this individualistic and often cantankerous old man in one of his first poems, "Elegy for Mitch Stuart," published by H. L. Mencken in *The American Mercury* in 1934. Stuart's father was a quieter man than "Mitch" Stuart; he worked as a coal miner, railroad man, and farmer, and his influence on his son was immense. Stuart used him as the prototype for some of his most impressive characters, and described his relationship with his father in his autobiographical *Beyond Dark Hills* and in *God's Oddling*, a biography of his father. His mother's family came to Kentucky from North Carolina and were apparently more "cultured"; it was she who encouraged her son to read and first supported him in his continuing quest for education.

The Stuarts moved from farm to farm throughout W-Hollow when Jesse was a boy, a way of life which gave him a sympathy for the plight of the landless. When he was seventeen, Stuart's enthusiasm for learning earned him the position of teacher in a one-room school, two years before he was graduated from Greenup High School. Following graduation in 1926, Stuart left the mountains, working for a short time in a carnival; then undergoing military training at Camp Knox, Kentucky; and finally spending an unhappy period in the Ashland, Kentucky, steel mills. Later in 1926, he was accepted at Lincoln Memorial University (Harrogate, Tennessee), where he studied under Professor Harry Harrison Kroll, a published writer and one of Stuart's greatest influences. While at Lincoln Memorial, with Kroll's encouragement, Stuart began writing poems, some of which were published in the school newspaper. After being graduated in 1929, Stuart returned to the mountains and served a year as principal and teacher of Warnock High School. In 1930, his first book, *Harvest of Youth*, was privately published; Stuart dedicated it to Harry Harrison Kroll.

In September of 1931, Stuart entered Vanderbilt University to undertake a master's degree in English. There he met such beginning writers as Robert Penn Warren and John Crowe Ransom, and he studied under his most important mentor, Donald Davidson. Stuart's year at Vanderbilt was a time of trial. He was working part-time to support his studies, he was homesick for the mountains, and he was uncertain of his future. When he was assigned by Professor Edwin Mims to write an autobiographical paper, Stuart complied with a work of more than three hundred pages, which, when revised several years later, became *Beyond Dark Hills*. Mims was impressed by Stuart's talents, rough though they were, and further encouraged him to continue his writing. Still, the year was largely one of frustration, capped by a dormitory fire which destroyed most of Stuart's possessions and his nearly finished thesis on the writings of John Fox, Jr. Thus, Stuart left Vanderbilt without a degree, but with experience, inspiration, connections, and material which he would use in his later work.

In September of 1932, Stuart became superintendent of Greenup County schools, but after a year spent embroiled in political turmoil, resigned to become principal of McKell High School, where he incorporated many of his then-radical educational theories. While serving as principal of McKell, from 1933 to 1937, he published *Man with a Bull-Tongue Plow* and *Head o' W-Hollow*. He also began to lecture throughout the country on matters of education and literature. In 1937, Stuart received a Guggenheim Fellowship and traveled to Scotland after obtaining a year's leave of absence from McKell, but when he returned in April of 1938, he found that a new administration had reneged on the agreement. Following another year's teaching in Ohio (just across the state line), while continuing his fight with the Kentucky school authorities (during which time his life was threatened and he was once actually beaten by an assailant), Stuart quit teaching in disgust and returned to farming. On October 14, 1939, he married Naomi Deane Norris; their only child, Jessica Jane, was born in 1942.

Stuart wrote about many of these experiences in two of his major books, *Beyond Dark Hills* and *The Thread That Runs So True*. After his retirement from teaching, he devoted a greater part of his time to his career as a writer and lecturer. His first novel, *Trees of Heaven*, appeared in 1940; his second, *Taps for Private Tussie*, in 1943, proved his greatest success, financially and critically, and was a main selection of the Book-of-the-Month Club. From 1944 to 1945, Stuart served in the United States Naval Reserves, but continued to write. In 1954, he suffered a near-fatal heart attack after one of his many lectures and was left practically helpless for a year. Stuart described the experience in his "journal," *The Year of My Rebirth*. In 1956, he again returned to the field of education, serving as principal once more at McKell High School for the year, a time he discussed in a late novel, *Mr. Gallion's School*. In 1960-1961, he taught at the American University in Cairo, Egypt, in part because of his desire to challenge the spread of communism in this region. In 1962-1963, he undertook a seven-month lecture tour overseas for the State Department for the same reasons. In 1966, Stuart became writer-in-residence at Eastern Kentucky University. Stuart spent his last years in W-Hollow, the world he made his own. He died there in February, 1984.

Analysis

Jesse Stuart's works are a part of the rich literary heritage drawn from the people and traditions of the Appalachian Mountains. He is grouped with such writers as George Washington Harris, Mary Noailles Murfree, John Fox, Jr., Elizabeth Madox Roberts, James Still, Wilma Dykeman, and Harriette Arnow as creators (and sometimes debunkers) of one of America's most lasting stereotypes, the Southern mountaineer or "hillbilly." Of these writers, Stuart surely stands at the head, for he has captured the imagination and sympathy of the reading public as has none of the rest.

There are several reasons for Stuart's abiding popularity. His writings are, for the most part, easily accessible. His main interest is in telling a story or relating an emotion, and he does so with simplicity of style and directness of approach. Indeed, Stuart's works are rarely overtly analytical; his characters are not introspective, which has led to charges of an anti-intellectual strain in his writings. Certainly, Stuart does tend to answer complex problems with easy solutions: if a man is determined, brave, and honest, Stuart suggests, the greatest challenge will be overcome. His autobiographical works especially emphasize this idea, and, in truth, such solutions seem to have been borne out in Stuart's own life.

Stuart also has proven popular because of the uniqueness and inherent romance of his material. As Stuart presents them, his characters are a primitive people, in some ways unspoiled by the corruptions of the outside society, but often in need of the civilizing influences that such a society can offer through education. Thus, some of these people, such as Theopolis Akers in *The Good Spirit of Laurel Ridge*, glory in their separation from the rest of the world, while others, like so many of the Tussie clan, are desperately in need of some edifying influence. Because these characters are drawn in broad strokes and are easily labeled as "good" or "bad" (perhaps "worthy" or "worthless" would be more appropriate terms), they exist more as character types, clothed in the charm of dialect and locale, than as real, breathing people. Still, Stuart is capable of surprising subtlety in his work, a quality often overlooked by some of his critics. He can force his readers to question their initial judgments of such characters as Anse Bushman in *Trees of Heaven*, Grandpa Tussie in *Taps for Private Tussie*, and even Theopolis Akers in *The Good Spirit of Laurel Ridge*.

The land plays an all-important role in Stuart's works. He attended Vanderbilt University at the time of the Agrarian-Fugitive Movement (*I'll Take My Stand* was published by Twelve Southerners in 1930, the year before Stuart arrived), and he came into contact with a number of its leaders, but Stuart never became a disciple himself. Although he agreed with many of the ideas of the movement, Stuart felt that "their farming was on paper," whereas he had farmed in order to eat. His writings, however, always reflect the importance of place in a man's life, and *Man with a Bull-Tongue Plow* is essentially a celebration of the land and man's relationship with it. He clearly admired characters such as Theopolis Akers, Deutsia Huntoon in *Daughter of the Legend*, and Tarvin Bushman in *Trees of Heaven*, who live in harmony with nature and draw their strength and their morality from the world-spirit. In Stuart's work, nature can be dangerous to the unwary, but it offers peace and wisdom to those who approach it with respect.

Perhaps Stuart's greatest strength as a writer is his fine sense of the comic. He has been linked to such humorists as A. B. Longstreet, G. W. Harris, Mark Twain, Erskine Caldwell, and William Faulkner, and rightfully so. His most serious books, such as *Mr. Gallion's School*, are among his weakest, while *Taps for Private Tussie*, his comic masterpiece, continues to delight. Stuart's humor is basically good-natured. He laughs at the foibles of man, enjoys his foolishness, and shakes his head at absurdities. He rarely condemns. Even in a satirical work such as *Foretaste of Glory*, in which he recounts the many hypocrisies to which men are given, Stuart deals gently with his characters. His comedy derives from the tall-tale tradition and is at its best when it ventures into that region wherein the absurd and the tragic coexist.

Although Stuart achieved honor and success in almost every form of literature, he was most effective in the short story. Despite his early fame as a poet, his verse has never received the attention it warrants. His novels generally are loosely structured; they tend to be episodic and uneven as he moves from one event to the next. His plots also rely heavily on convention or cliché. Still, in his large body of writing, Stuart created a unique fictional world, peopled with characters recognizably his own. It is a world that is likely to last.

Stuart wrote *Trees of Heaven* in 1939 after returning from Europe. He married Naomi Deane Norris while writing the book, and their romance is reflected in the love story of Tarvin Bushman and Subrinea Tussie. *Trees of Heaven* is a big, rambling book, less a well-constructed novel than a conglomeration of facts, observations, tales, and characterizations built around a very simple plot. Anse Bushman is a prominent landowner and farmer, one who takes great pride in the quality of his work and the number of his possessions. Boliver Tussie is a squatter who lives on the land that Anse owns. The two men are antithetical to each other. Anse works—and drives others to work—to such a degree that labor and ownership have become obsessions to him. Boliver opts for a more relaxed, indeed, indolent approach to life, unburdened by responsibility. The conflict arises when Tarvin Bushman, the only child still living with Anse, falls in love with Subrinea Tussie, Boliver's beautiful daughter. Through Tarvin's intervention, Anse agrees to take on the Tussies as sharecroppers, although he first compels Boliver to sign a contract specifying what he can and cannot do while living on Anse's land. The contract is an attempt to control not only the Tussies' work habits but their moral and social behavior as well. Although Boliver is offended by some of these demands, he is in no position to argue with Anse; thus, he agrees to stop drinking, to avoid dancing, and to abstain from fathering any more children until the harvest is over. Two such differing life-styles cannot coexist peacefully, and when Anse becomes suspicious of his son's relationship with Subrinea and becomes convinced that the Tussies are taking advantage of his generosity, he evicts the family and takes their crops. After an accident, however—Anse is almost killed by a falling tree limb—he becomes a wiser, more tolerant man. Tarvin and Subrinea (who is already pregnant) marry, and, as the book ends, they are going to bring back the Tussies to work the land once again.

Although Anse Bushman is the central character of this novel and the one for whom the reader has the most sympathy and respect, he is by no means an entirely admirable character. His emphasis on work has driven away his other children, and his wife, Fronnie, has succumbed to premature aging. Indeed, toward the end of the book, she is clearly teetering on the edge of madness, haunted by nightmares of Anse's spiritual damnation and fearful that Tarvin will be caught up by his father's obsessions. Anse is a dictatorial old man who cannot balance his love of family with his greed for land. Still, Stuart does not present him as a villain; the reader can understand Anse and generally sides with him in his struggle against the Tussies. At the same time, the Tussies are more likable than one might expect. Their shiftlessness is a relief from Anse's discipline, but they are quite capable of hard work when the occasion demands and show a true love of the land on which they have lived for generations. In fact, Boliver Tussie is a farmer equal to Anse Bushman, although he is usually careless and negligent. The Tussies are a convincing thorn in Anse's side, but he is wrong in his attempt to impose his life-style on them.

It is difficult to label *Trees of Heaven* as either a romantic or realistic novel, for it contains elements of each. The love story between Tarvin and Subrinea is idyllic and is the weakest part of the novel, while Stuart's detailed and factual discussions of farming and sheep raising interfere with the progress of the plot. The description of the Tussies and their kind—families that have become inbred over the years and that are capable of viciousness and violence—is sometimes at odds with their basically comic role in the book. The threat of bloodshed runs throughout the story, but it is generally averted through the author's manipulations.

Trees of Heaven is narrated in the present tense and is structured around the change of the seasons. Both devices give it a sense of timelessness, as if the characters, the place, and the actions were occurring in the present in their own world. The use of present tense sometimes leads to repetition and oversimplification, however, and its effectiveness is not sustained throughout the book. Still, *Trees of Heaven* is an impressive first novel, a work of considerable art and scope.

Stuart's second novel, *Taps for Private Tussie*, is generally considered to be his best. Certainly it is his most successful comic work, although the tale it tells is marked by numerous tragic events. Indeed, Stuart claimed that he wrote the story as a "sad thing" and was surprised that others laughed at the antics it described. The book is more carefully constructed than *Trees of Heaven* and is effectively held together through the use of a first-person narrator, a young boy who tells the story with an appealing mixture of naïveté and native wisdom.

Private Kim Tussie is reported killed in action during World War II, and his family sets about burying the returned body. Like the Tussies in *Trees of Heaven*, this branch of the family is also made up of squatters. At the beginning of the book, they are living in a schoolhouse abandoned for the summer. The immediate family is composed of Kim's parents, Grandpa and Grandma Tussie, his wife, Vittie, his unmarried brother, Mott, and the boy-narrator, Sid. When Vittie collects Kim's ten-thousand-dollar insurance policy, the Tussies are able to fulfill their long-held dreams. First, they move from the schoolhouse (from which they are being evicted) to a "mansion," a fourteen-room house on the outskirts of town. Then they buy furniture for each of the rooms to replace that which has been destroyed on leaving the schoolhouse. Soon, as Grandma has predicted, other Tussies begin to arrive, hoping to benefit from Grandpa's "good fortune." The first of these is Uncle George, Grandpa's brother, who has been married five times. Others follow until finally there are forty-six Tussies living in the house. George and Mott have, by this time, begun vying for the attentions of Aunt Vittie, and as George grows more successful, Mott turns increasingly to drink.

After a period of communal living, the Tussies are again turned out of their home, which they have destroyed through their careless behavior, because Grandpa has lost his relief benefits, upon which they had depended. With the last of the insurance money, Grandpa buys a small piece of land, and the family moves into a run-down shack for the winter. Uncle George marries Vittie; Sid is forced to begin school; and Mott sinks into dissipation. Grandpa learns the pride of ownership and plans to farm the following spring, while Sid discovers the joy of education and begins to consider his future, but these plans are upset when Mott kills two of his cousins while drunk and is himself killed by Uncle George. Grandpa then prepares for his own approaching death and confines himself to bed, awaiting the end. At this point, hope returns with the appearance of Kim himself, who was not killed after all, and who stands ready to take Grandpa's place as the head of the remaining group. Uncle George is tracked down by a posse, Sid learns that Vittie is his mother, and the novel ends with a mixture of death and regeneration.

Taps for Private Tussie is an extremely enjoyable book. Grandpa Tussie is one of Stuart's most successful and memorable characters, a good and loving man despite his weaknesses. Sid Tussie comes from a long line of boy-narrators in American literature, including, most obviously, Huckleberry Finn, but also those boys in the works of Sherwood Anderson, William Faulkner, and

Erskine Caldwell. Once again Stuart displays his sympathies for a basically unsympathetic group of people. Stuart distinguishes Sid from the Tussies through the revelation that he does not have Tussie blood and is therefore "superior" (he is smarter and more ambitious than the average Tussie). The book acts as a satire on the welfare system: Grandpa Tussie has so long depended on his relief check that he has forgotten the satisfaction of self-sufficiency; when he rediscovers it in the land, it is too late. Stuart often shows man at his worst—fawning, lying, killing—but *Taps for Private Tussie* finally offers hope of renewal. The Kim who left for war was, as Sid remembers, a vicious and hateful man; the one who returns has been reborn and shows the boy kindness and understanding. Grandpa must die, but Sid will begin to live with a new sense of self.

Foretaste of Glory was begun while Stuart served in the Navy during World War II and was developed from stories he remembered and told about his home. It was not published until 1946, and it was poorly received by the people in Greenup County, Kentucky, who took the book as an affront. It recounts the events of one night—September 18, 1941—in Blakesburg, Kentucky, when the night sky is set ablaze by the uncommon appearance of the aurora borealis. Most of the townspeople are convinced that the display prefigures the end of the world, the Second Coming. Stuart examines the reactions of selected characters when faced with their apparent Day of Judgment. The book is constructed in an episodic manner, although some characters do appear in more than one episode, and certain ideas are repeated as Stuart mocks social distinctions, political alliances (as in *Taps for Private Tussie*), and basic hypocrisies. Stuart was attempting in this work to capture an overall sense of the community, in much the same manner as Sherwood Anderson did in *Winesburg, Ohio* (1919). The book is a satire, for most of the characters reveal their deceits and admit their sins as they await the arrival of the Lord, but the tone is not malicious. The author is more understanding and amused than cruel or vindictive. Although the book has been highly praised by some readers, its very concept finally limits its effectiveness. The narratives become redundant, the episodes are uneven, and the excitement is simply not sustained.

Although Stuart considered *The Good Spirit of Laurel Ridge* the best novel he had written, it is a flawed work. Its plot and too many of its characters are unconvincing, although many readers have been charmed by its view of natural man in the natural world. The story is insubstantial. Theopolis Akers has lived all of his life on Laurel Ridge. His wife is dead; his daughter, Lucretia, was taken away from him when she was a child because of his drinking; and his simpleminded son, Jack, roams the land and appears only in the spring to see the butterflies. As the book begins, Op has undergone a cataract operation, and Lucretia has come to live with him as he regains his sight. Although the operation is successful, she decides to stay in the mountains with her father. A pretty girl, she is soon being courted by a local mountain swain, Hootbird Hammertight, but she is more interested in a mysterious stranger who is hiding out in the hills, a figure Op declares to be the ghost of Ted Newsome, a young man murdered for love many years ago. Op is convinced that spirits—both good and bad—inhabit this area of the mountains, and in his tales and memories he insists on the otherworldliness of Laurel Ridge.

Op's way of life has been disturbed by Lucretia's arrival, although her father comes to accept her. When, however, in a completely unrealistic plot contrivance, two other relatives—Alfred and Julia Pruitt, Lucretia's city cousins—arrive, Op finds himself pushed to the limits. Alf Pruitt is set up as a foil to Op, his city ways and suburban dread placed in stark contrast to Op's natural acceptance of life. Alf most fears the atom bomb, but modern civilization in general has driven him to distraction. Through Op's influence and in a series of mildly comic adventures, Alf learns the importance of nature, but he remains a nervous, essentially unhappy man. Finally, it is revealed that the ghost "Ted Newsome" is really a soldier Lucretia had known in the city. He is AWOL because he mistakenly believes that he has killed a man in a fight, and both he and Lucretia have come to Laurel Ridge to escape. When the military police track him down, just as he is about to be hanged by a group of angry mountaineers, the officer explains that the soldier has killed no one and that he can make amends with a brief prison sentence. Thus, he and Lucretia return to the city. Alfred and Julia also return, having benefited from their stay in the hills, although ultimately unable to adapt to such a rough way of life. Op is again left alone, a man at peace with himself.

The Good Spirit of Laurel Ridge is filled with the folklore of the hills, and Op Akers is a good storyteller and describer of these tales and customs. The plot, however, is so conventional and the ending such a cliché that the book's potential charm is never fully realized. Stuart's satire on the modern world, exemplified in Alf Pruitt, is much too heavy-handed and obvious to work for long. Despite its popularity, *The Good Spirit of Laurel Ridge* is not one of Stuart's better works.

Generally considered Stuart's weakest novel, *Daughter of the Legend* in fact contains some of his best writing. Again, the plot of the novel is slight. The narrator, Dave Stoneking, a lumberjack, tells of his tragic love for Deutsia Huntoon, a Melungeon living in the mountains of eastern Tennessee. After a courtship in which Deutsia introduces Dave to a finer appreciation of nature than he has so far held, they are married and enjoy an idyllic winter together. In the spring, however, Deutsia dies in childbirth, and Dave leaves the land of the Melungeons a rather bitter man. The book is notable for two reasons. First, in his discussion of the Melungeon people, Stuart calls for racial compassion and understanding. The Melungeons are people of mixed heritage, and when Dave marries into their race, he suffers the discriminations they have long felt. His attempts to rectify these injustices give the book a contemporary social awareness missing from many other works by Stuart. In addition, *Daughter of the Legend* includes one of Stuart's finest comic episodes in the chapter dealing with the death and burial of Sylvania, a six-hundred-pound seller of moonshine. Although Stuart had written this tale as a short story years before, it fits smoothly into the novel and presents an ironic counterpoint to the more sentimental death of Deutsia.

Mr. Gallion's School is a semifictional account of Stuart's experiences as principal of McKell High School, to which he returned in 1956 following his heart attack. George Gallion is a thinly disguised version of Stuart himself. Against great odds, Mr. Gallion attempts to restore order and a sense of worth to the school. He must fight not only the defeatist attitudes of the students and teachers but also a corrupt and ineffectual political system which uses the schools as pawns in its power game. That Mr. Gallion succeeds so completely in his fight illustrates the weaknesses of the book. On a strictly realistic level, Stuart oversimplifies both the problems and the solutions. Indeed, the book often becomes a treatise on the author's theories of education. While *Mr. Gallion's School* holds the reader's attention, it is by no means one of Stuart's best novels.

Although Jesse Stuart has been the subject of numerous studies, he has never been accorded the kind of intensive scholarly study one might expect. This is caused, no doubt, by his reputation as a "popular" writer. His often romantic and sentimental picture of the Appalachian Mountains has come under attack in the past few decades, especially by many of the younger writers and critics from the area, who see Stuart as having helped to create the misleading and often condescending image of the mountaineer. Stuart's skills as a writer were considerable, however, and among his many publications are works which will continue to be read and admired.

Edwin T. Arnold III

Other major works

SHORT FICTION: *Head o' W-Hollow*, 1936; *Men of the Mountains*, 1941; *Tales from the Plum Grove Hills*, 1946; *Clearing in the Sky and Other Stories*, 1950; *Plowshare in Heaven: Tales True and Tall from the Kentucky Hills*, 1958; *Save Every Lamb*, 1964; *My Land Has a Voice*, 1966; *Come Gentle Spring*, 1969; *Come Back to the Farm*, 1971; *Votes Before Breakfast*, 1974; *The Best-Loved Short Stories of Jesse Stuart*, 1982.

POETRY: *Harvest of Youth*, 1930; *Man with a Bull-Tongue Plow*, 1934; *Album of Destiny*, 1944; *Kentucky Is My Land*, 1952; *Hold April*, 1962; *The World of Jesse Stuart: Selected Poems*, 1975.

NONFICTION: *Beyond Dark Hills*, 1938; *The Thread That Runs So True*, 1949; *The Year of My Rebirth*, 1956; *God's Oddling*, 1960; *To Teach, To Love*,

1970; *My World*, 1975; *The Kingdom Within: A Spiritual Autobiography*, 1979; *Lost Sandstones and Lonely Skies and Other Essays*, 1979; *If I Were Seventeen Again and Other Essays*, 1980.

CHILDREN'S LITERATURE: *Mongrel Mettle: The Autobiography of a Dog*, 1944; *The Beatinest Boy*, 1953; *A Penny's Worth of Character*, 1954; *Red Mule*, 1955; *The Rightful Owner*, 1960; *Andy Finds a Way*, 1961.

Bibliography

Blair, Everetta Love. *Jesse Stuart: His Life and Works*. Columbia: University of South Carolina Press, 1967. An early, full-length study of Stuart's work, somewhat limited in discussing his poetry but more satisfying in dealing with his fiction and autobiography, both of which have had larger audiences in the years since World War II. Contains a helpful index and a selected bibliography, both of value to high school and college students.

Bogart, Max. *A Jesse Stuart Reader*. New York: McGraw-Hill, 1963. Offers a good sample of Stuart's major work: stories, biography, and poetry. Aimed at the young person who might want help in reading Stuart, containing a foreword as well as commentary and study questions at the end, designed to stimulate thought and suggest writing topics. Although an older text, it is still readable and relevant.

Foster, Ruel E. *Jesse Stuart*. New York: Twayne, 1968. This excellent volume concentrates on Stuart as an imaginative writer who has created a "fictional place," as William Faulkner did. Puts into perspective both Stuart's primitivism and his anti-intellectualism and attempts to assess his place in American letters. Calls him a poet of a "vanished way of life" and genuinely folkloric, but not "synthetically folksy." Stuart emerges as a figure in the tradition of Walt Whitman and Edgar Lee Masters: energetic, democratic, and committed to his art.

LeMaster, J. R. *Jesse Stuart: Kentucky's Chronicler-Poet*. Memphis, Tenn.: Memphis State University Press, 1980. This full-length book concentrates on Stuart as a poet, although he has more often been admired as a popular writer for his prose. LeMaster's definition of poet is an inclusive one, however, meaning more nearly a *Dichter* (a writer of fiction) than a versifier. Stuart has an ear for sounds and an eye for images, and ballads and stories are an essential ingredient of his art. Helpful index is provided.

Richardson, H. Edward. *Jesse: The Biography of an American Writer*. New York: McGraw-Hill, 1984. While this study is chiefly a full-length portrait of an American regionalist and educator, it is objective, as well as appreciative and tolerant. More than five hundred pages long, containing sixteen pages of photographs, a bibliography of Stuart's sixty-one published works, and a select bibliography of secondary sources.

THEODORE STURGEON
Edward Hamilton Waldo

Born: Staten Island, New York; February 26, 1918
Died: Eugene, Oregon; May 8, 1985

Principal long fiction

The Dreaming Jewels, 1950 (also known as *The Synthetic Man*, 1957); *More Than Human*, 1953; *I, Libertine*, 1956 (as Frederick R. Ewing); *The Cosmic Rape*, 1958; *Venus Plus X*, 1960; *Some of Your Blood*, 1961; *Voyage to the Bottom of the Sea*, 1961; *Alien Cargo*, 1984; *Godbody*, 1986.

Other literary forms

While Theodore Sturgeon was not as prolific as some of the science-fiction fraternity, he wrote more than 190 short stories, 130 articles, and a number of radio and television scripts. His short fiction was assembled in many collections, ranging from *Without Sorcery* (1948) to *The Golden Helix* (1980).

Achievements

Theodore Sturgeon's work was once called "the single most important body of science fiction by an American to date." A founder of modern American science fiction, he contributed to the genre's transition from underground to mainstream literature. He was the recipient of Argosy (1947), International Fantasy (1954), Nebula (1970), and Hugo (1971) awards.

Biography

Theodore Sturgeon was born Edward Hamilton Waldo, on February 16, 1918, on Staten Island, New York. His parents were divorced, and, after his mother remarried in 1929, his name was legally changed when he was adopted by his stepfather. After he was graduated from high school, where his career as a gymnast was ended by rheumatic fever, he finished a term at Penn State Nautical School and then spent three years at sea. During that time he began to write, producing some forty conventional short stories for McClure's Syndicate before turning to science fiction, which he began to publish in John W. Campbell, Jr.'s *Astounding Science Fiction* in 1939.

Sturgeon recalled that science fiction was "the pornography of its day" and recounted how his stepfather discovered and destroyed his 1935 issues of *Amazing*. When he took up science fiction, Sturgeon was making a commitment to a literary form which promised little prestige and very modest financial returns. He married in the same year he launched his science-fiction career and contributed regularly to *Unknown* and *Astounding Science Fiction* in order to support his family. Although he produced highly regarded stories, such as "It" (1940) and "Microcosmic God" (1941), he had to seek employment outside of writing to earn a living.

After operating a hotel in the British West Indies in 1940, Sturgeon worked as a door-to-door salesman, as assistant chief steward at Fort Simonds, and as a bulldozer operator. In 1942, he pursued the latter occupation in Puerto Rico. Except for *Killdozer*, a novelette about a machine possessed by a malignant force, his literary output declined sharply between 1942 and 1944, when he returned to the United States and became a copy editor. These were difficult years for Sturgeon, financially and emotionally. Not until 1946, after his marriage ended in divorce, did he fully resume his career under the encouragement of John Campbell.

While continuing to write, Sturgeon tried his hand at running a literary agency and producing advertising copy. The first substantial public recognition for his work came in 1947 when he won a thousand-dollar prize for "Bianca's Hands." (The runner-up in the contest, sponsored by the British magazine *Argosy*, was Graham Greene.) "Bianca's Hands" had been written on Sturgeon's honeymoon years earlier but had found no market because of its bizarre treatment of a "passionate human attachment." Its acceptance marked a turning point for Sturgeon, which was closely followed by the publication of the first of his many anthologies, *Without Sorcery* (1948), with an introduction by Ray Bradbury.

As he entered the period of his greatest creativity, Sturgeon's personal life again underwent change, with a second marriage in 1949 and a third in 1951. His output of fiction was unabated, however, with *The Dreaming Jewels*, his first novel, appearing in 1950, and *More Than Human*, published in 1953, winning the 1954 International Fantasy Award, a confirmation of his rank as one of America's foremost writers of science fiction. His stories continued to be anthologized in his own collections and those of others, and he engaged in a broad range of literary activity, from a hoax with Jean Shepard, *I, Libertine* (1956), published under the name Frederick R. Ewing, to a fictional case history of vampirism, *Some of Your Blood* (1961), and a novel depicting an androgynous utopia, *Venus Plus X* (1960).

As a major author of speculative fiction, he helped to create a climate of acceptance for the genre among the general public. In his book reviews for the *National Review* (1961-1973), for example, he explained and defended his art while introducing some of contemporary science fiction's finest authors to an audience who might otherwise not have learned of them. He was involved in science fiction's growth in other media also, in 1966 moving to Los Angeles to write for *Star Trek*. Late in his life, he published little new fiction, but he continued to compile anthologies of his previous work for new audiences. He married for the fourth time in 1969. Sturgeon was living in Eugene, Oregon, at the time of his death in 1985.

Though Sturgeon deplored the "inexcusable invasions into . . . authors' most intimate motivations" by academic critics, there are nevertheless certain definite biographical influences on his work. Beverly Friend called him "a highly personal writer drawing from his own suffering for his craft." She cites his parents' divorce, his estrangement from his stepfather, his illness in adolescence, and his marital and professional problems as sources for his art.

Analysis

Theodore Sturgeon once said, "All great literature is great because it is fable—because it creates typical and archetypical characters and situations which can be applied outside the work to illuminate the human condition." He repeatedly insisted that he did not undervalue the science of science fiction, but he clearly inclined toward minimizing technology as a focus for his work; rather, he concentrated upon fable, often premising his work on occult matters upon which science has had little to say. He said that "in teaching, reviewing, and enjoying science fiction, my emphasis is always on the fiction." This is, he explained, "because I like writers to be read and remembered and (when they can) to move people and shake them; to ignite, to increase their ability to share their visions and their joy and their terror, as well as their knowledge." Sturgeon's criteria for art were more affective than cognitive, and he generally concentrated upon rites of passage rather than technological extrapolation.

Whatever Sturgeon's premise for a story, scientific, psychological, or occult, he wished the work to reflect essential human experiences: "love, and pain, and greed, and laughter, and hope, and above all loneliness." Loneliness is most significant, since he asserted that "what I have been trying to do all these years is to investigate this matter of love, sexual and asexual," and his major fictions are fables of growth toward community and maturity.

The four science-fiction novels which are the heart of Sturgeon's work (*The Dreaming Jewels*, *More Than Human*, *The Cosmic Rape*, and *Venus Plus X*) develop the idea that "our strange species has two prime motivating forces: sex, of course, and worship." Throughout his writing, the latter is the more important, and Sturgeon was unwilling to see the highest self-sacrificial and altruistic acts as having any foundation in sexuality. Sturgeon's center of worship, however, is not to be found outside man but in humanity.

Sturgeon's first novel, *The Dreaming Jewels*, is an exploration of what it means to be human. Its premise is the creation of a "synthetic man" by the action of alien crystals which have a deep collective life of their own, apparently unrelated to the affairs of men. These crystals, seemingly without purpose, "dream" objects into existence, sometimes imperfectly, creating freaks and monsters, and sometimes—when they are mating—perfectly, creating creatures with the power of self-transformation. Such materials are better suited to psychological symbolism than scientific discussion. This is precisely the direction of Sturgeon's art; since he found "more room in inner space than in outer space," his fables are essentially paradigms of psychological growth which begin with the frustrations and alienation of youth and end in maturation and integration. On a number of occasions, he defined science fiction in terms of the derivation of the word "science" from the Latin "to know." "Science fiction is knowledge fiction," he wrote, adding that "by far most of the knowledge is psychological."

In *More Than Human*, Sturgeon makes significant use of syzygy, a concept of nonreproductive union signified by a strange word. A collective identity is formed by a group of persons who retain their individuality while contributing to a gestalt which has the ultimate promise of a god. The collective person remains distinctly human, however, and the worship due it is finally worship of humanity. Here the components of the human being, conscience being the highest, are integrated and raised to the highest power. So, too, in a novel which deals directly with sexuality, *Venus Plus X*, the integration of the human personality and worship become paramount, with Sturgeon using androgyny as a symbol of wholeness and providing his utopia's inhabitants with a religion which worships the promise of man.

The form of Sturgeon's novels can present the critical reader with problems. Sturgeon is perhaps most at home as a writer of short stories, and his techniques of composition reflect at times an incomplete transition to the novel's demands. He seemingly pieces together sections which finally form the whole. This is not to say that the structuring of his books is unskillful, for he does finally bring to focus elements which run through them in parallel directions. Also, such a method can be seen as organic to Sturgeon's themes of integration, with loosely related parts finally encompassed in a total vision. Whatever a reader's verdict on form, however, his principal response will probably be to Sturgeon's handling of theme.

Sturgeon's work takes seriously his claim that "the best of science fiction is as good as the best of any modern literature—articulate, poetic, philosophical, provocative, searching, courageous, insightful." He once complained that though the finest science-fiction writers "open their veins into their typewriters, taking their craft and their readers seriously, they seem to be categorically disqualified from the serious attention of mainstream critics and readers." Fortunately, this is no longer the case, in part because of Sturgeon's fables of human nature.

The reprinted title of *The Dreaming Jewels* is *The Synthetic Man*, a title which more clearly reflects the subject matter of Sturgeon's first novel but which loses some of the symbolic suggestiveness of the original. Paul Williams has commented that the work is in part based on Sturgeon's resentment of his stepfather and has pointed out the significance of the dream to the creative act of writing science fiction. To this might be added the importance of jewel symbolism in the light of Sturgeon's view of science fiction as "knowledge fiction."

Jewels often symbolize arcane knowledge and spiritual transformation; here they are connected with an unconscious dream-power that can be brought to light for good or ill, and in which reside keys to transformation and regeneration. Contesting for this power are Horty, the "synthetic man," and Pierre Monetre, a most thoroughgoing misanthrope who would delight in the destruction of mankind. Horty's victory over Monetre (called "maneater" by his subordinates) comes about through his capacity to tap the power of the unconscious, and through the willing sacrifice of Zena, whose education of Horty to human values keeps him from becoming like the alienated Monetre.

Horty's potential alienation comes from abuse by a cruel stepfather, Armand Bluett, a figure Sturgeon has himself identified with "a lot of bitterness and hostility that I wanted to get out." Bluett's viciousness results in the accidental loss of three of Horty's fingers, and the young boy flees after bidding farewell to Kay Hallowell, a girl whose love balances Bluett's hatred. In his flight, Horty is befriended by carnival people, especially Zena, a midget, who notices the boy's sympathetic connection with his only possession, a jack-in-the-box with strange jewels for eyes. These gems prove to have had their effect on the child, gradually transforming him into a creature capable both of communicating with the inner life of the jewels and of transforming himself at will.

Horty's identity is hidden from Monetre, who owns the carnival. Zena disguises him as a girl and warns him never to reveal that he has regenerated his three lost fingers, which Monetre had treated upon his arrival. During his years with the carnival, Horty fails to grow and is only forced to leave when the owner discloses some curiosity about his hand. After leaving, he discovers his gift of transformation, which is useful when he encounters Armand Bluett, now a judge, victimizing Kay Hallowell. Horty cools off the sexually aggressive Bluett by taking Kay's place and slicing off his regenerated fingers, at which sight Bluett passes out. Horty thus becomes the woman who represents love for him so that he might perform a sacrificial mutilation which is both saving and vengeful.

In a series of improbable events, Kay comes under the power of Bluett and Monetre, who is clearly contrasted with Horty. While both are brilliantly gifted, Horty's mind, under Zena's guidance, has been shaped by "humanity and the extensions of humanity," as against Monetre's, which has been twisted by hatred and desire for power. In the confrontation between Horty and Monetre in a psychic duel, Zena sacrifices herself, instructing Horty to use his power to destroy jewel-created creatures. Since Monetre's character is so inhuman, he is assumed to be one. Ironically, Monetre is biologically human, without possessing any spirit of humanity, while Zena, a synthetic creature, sacrifices herself. In the end, however, Horty kills his adversary, resurrects Zena, who becomes his wife, and assumes Monetre's identity while traveling about trying to undo some of the harm he has done.

Sturgeon has assessed *The Dreaming Jewels* as "a rotten novel." Its chief faults are a terribly contrived plot and a style which lacks the energy of the best of his stories of the 1940's. The use of psychological materials is compelling, however, making it one of Sturgeon's most popular works. Horty's series of transformations are representative of his possession of the secret of the unconscious, the capacity to convert revenge into sacrificial love, whose highest exemplar is Zena. The novel moves from mutilation to regeneration, from revenge to love, with Horty progressing toward wholeness by overcoming alienation and linking the transforming power of the unconscious to positive human values.

More Than Human, Sturgeon's second and best novel, has at the center of its three-part structure a section entitled "Baby Is Three," which was published separately a year before the novel appeared. According to Sam Moskowitz, Sturgeon wrote a proloque and epilogue to this section to compose the novel. Like *The Dreaming Jewels*, "Baby Is Three" is about an alienated superman, fifteen-year-old Gerry Thompson, who in a strong first-person narration relates his visit to a psychiatrist, to whom he reveals his murder of his guardian, Miss Alicia Kew. Gerry also explains that he is part of a composite being, *homo gestalt*, a uniting of persons with extraordinary telepathic and telekinetic powers. Gerry has the capacity to probe the minds of others— he does this with the psychiatrist to make sure that he will not remember his visit—but he lacks human sympathy and moral awareness.

Sturgeon once said that "you cannot write stories about ideas—which is why so much hard-core, nuts-and-bolts science fiction fails as literature." In *More Than Human*, however, he is fortunate in combining a powerful idea with a sure grasp of style and an effective structure. The first section of the novel, "The Fabulous Idiot," focuses on Lone (a shortened form of *alone*), who is an idiot in the root sense of the word. He is aware of himself alone. He gradually becomes aware of others, first through Miss Kew's sister, Evelyn, who along with Alicia had been the victim of a demonically sexually repressive father, and then through the Prodds, a pathetic couple who take him in, and whose retarded child, "Baby," becomes the center of the gestalt being.

Lone becomes aware of a human community to which he has at least rudimentary obligations and of a more specialized group, composed of abandoned or runaway children, to which Gerry belongs, and which is destined to become a new being. By the end of the novel, this group has become a potential god, "not an exterior force, not an awesome Watcher in the sky, but a laughing thing with a human heart and reverence for its origins." In the book's last section, "Morality," Hip Barrows, the being's final component, its conscience, confronts and converts the ruthless Gerry; Hip sees himself as "an atom and his gestalt as a molecule. He saw these others as cells among cells, and he saw the whole design of what, with joy, humanity would become." His response is a "sense of worship." He participates in a vision not unlike that shared by many Romantic writers of the nineteenth century, what Walt

Whitman's follower R. M. Bucke called "Cosmic Consciousness." Sturgeon said that the willingness of science-fiction writers to treat religious themes, "to invent and extrapolate and regroup ideas and concepts in this as in all other areas of human growth and change delights me and is a source of my true love for the mad breed." *More Than Human* is Sturgeon's best illustration that such themes can be explored profitably.

More Than Human, like *The Dreaming Jewels*, traces the progress of the growth and integration of the person. In each novel, characters move from alienation to wholeness, but in *More Than Human*, the key conflict between misanthropy and humanity is handled with greater dramatic skill. In general a more sophisticated work in conception and structure, *More Than Human* manages to present the idea of a collective entity without losing sight of individual characters or the dynamics of personality. As a speculative fiction, it deserves the praise and popularity it has enjoyed.

The Cosmic Rape also employs the gestalt theme of *More Than Human*, extending the union to all of mankind, which in turn is joined to Medusa, an intergalactic composite creature. While the underlying theme of the book is essentially the same as that of *More Than Human*, it is by no means as successful. Its premises are extrapolated in far less believable fashion, and its structure is not dramatically engaging. Intercut scenes, which range from the United States to Rome to Africa, are skillfully coordinated, but character development suffers in the effort to show individuals becoming a part of the whole.

In *The Cosmic Rape*, Sturgeon attempts to put love into the largest terms, but, ironically, he employs a character most unlikely to initiate cosmic harmony. One Dan Gurlick, a loathsome bum, has become an atom in Medusa by ingesting a sort of seed concealed in a fragment of hamburger. Through him, Medusa seeks to take over the Earth telepathically. Medusa is at first thwarted, having dealt only with collective minds elsewhere in the universe. This lack in humanity is repaired, however, as psychic unity among men appears as they cooperate in the destruction of invading machines created by Medusa. In the course of attaining collective consciousness, a variety of characters emerge from sexual repression and exploitation or social alienation to sacrifice themselves. Notable is the metamorphosis of Guido, a misfit who has turned to anarchism because his musical genius has been suppressed by a wicked stepfather.

Ultimately, Medusa is joined to the human collective mind. This connection occurs when Gurlick, himself excluded from the universal intelligence, is permitted to act out the sexual fantasies which Medusa has used to control him. What Gurlick intends as rape is welcomed by a woman now sexually liberated as a part of a larger design; likewise, the joining of humanity to Medusa is transformed from rape to consent. Medusa is in fact possessed by humanity rather than possessing it.

The Cosmic Rape extends the ideas of *More Than Human* as far as they can go. Unfortunately, the extrapolation is ultimately too fanciful and the dramatic power of Sturgeon's myth of human integration is diffused. There is a sense of his recognition of this in his next book, which he calls "a tract"; the social criticism of *Venus Plus X* gives ballast to an imagination which had overextended itself.

Sturgeon responded to the charge that "science fiction is characteristically asexual and unaware of love in its larger and largest senses." He believed that this impression had sometimes arisen because writers of science fiction often "work in geological or astronomical time rather than in biographical or historical perspective." Sturgeon had dealt with themes of love in both cosmic and personal perspectives in his earlier novels, but in *Venus Plus X* he turned to utopian fiction to keep the action on a more human scale.

Though Sturgeon had written stories on sex before—"The World Well Lost" (1953) deals with homosexuality, for example—*Venus Plus X* is his most extended statement on sexism and sexual taboos. While the book has been praised for its pioneering study of sex roles, preceding Ursula K. Le Guin's much discussed *The Left Hand of Darkness* (1969) by nine years, *Venus Plus X* is also notable for its skillfuly ironic employment of science-fiction conventions and for its handling of the symbolism of androgyny.

The novel is structured in alternating chapters of action which are connected only by theme. The first set of chapters deals with suburban life and the questions of sexual identity posed to America in the 1950's. Along with standard problems of sex-role definition for children and general sexism, there are hints of change; Herb Raile comes to realize how Western culture has degraded women and catches glimpses of the significance of androgyny in the style of a rock singer. Contrasted with suburban America is Ledom (*model* inverted), a utopia founded upon the fact that its inhabitants are biologically hermaphrodites. Here, sex-role definition is no problem, and the wholeness of the human being in assuming all social duties is stressed. Against the predatory capitalism and commercialized worship of the suburbs are posed charitable religion and universal sharing.

Androgyny is used by Sturgeon as a symbol of wholeness. Like the universal man of *More Than Human*, androgyny can be found in mystical thought as signifying the primordial unity of mankind. In order to stress this aspect of his work, Sturgeon provides the Ledomites with a religion that is an ecstatic celebration of the child. "We keep before us," says the guide to this utopia, "the image of that which is malleable and growing—of that which we have the power to improve. We worship that very power in ourselves, and the sense of responsiblity which lives with it." Here again is Sturgeon's drive toward totality, a worship of human potential, yet in order to present this theme, he undercuts a number of science-fiction conventions to make his readers more aware of the symbolic nature of his statement.

The reader discovers that the book's nominal hero, Charlie Johns, is not a time-traveler as he first believes. Ledom does not exist in the distant future as it first appears; rather, it is a society hidden from the eyes of men. The Ledomites wish to test the reaction of the outside world to their culture, and use Charlie Johns's responses as a gauge. After overcoming his initial bewilderment, Charlie embarks on a course of education, learning that Ledom's technical superiority consists in a machine that can inscribe thought patterns and has revolutionized learning, and a power supply that makes the community self-sufficient. Charlie's approval of technology comes to a screeching halt, however, when he discovers that the hermaphroditism of Ledomites is biologically engineered. His reaction convinces utopian planners that the world is not ready for the revelation of Ledom.

Charlie now regards Ledom as a den of perversion and indicates that it ought to be destroyed. His education, however, has been limited: he has not detected the hints throughout that the whole culture is symbolic, that its essence is "transition." It has been designed to preserve human values while the outside world destroys itself. The novel's disquisition on religion, in fact, suggests that if one human generation could adopt the religion of Ledom, it would be saved. No hermaphroditism would be necessary for a sense of human wholeness.

The final emphasis given Ledom's symbolic nature is the revelation that Charlie Johns is not actually Charlie Johns at all, but merely a collection of his memories, obtained when he was dying after a plane crash and inscribed on the previously blank mind of a biological control. The plot, however, first permits Johns to attempt the standard escape from a dystopia. He finds the one girl who has not been biologically altered, and he tries to leave in what he thinks is a time machine. When he does so, the Ledomites are forced to tell him the truth. He and his girl therefore take up life somewhere between the two worlds, trying to sort out their identities, presumably overcoming the sexism of the man Charlie was, and learning from the wisdom of Ledom. At the same time, on the other side, Herb Raile is working his way slowly and painfully to gain some of Ledom's values.

In spite of some dated writing in the sections on suburbia in the 1950's, this is a book which powerfully anticipates many of the themes taken up by feminists in the 1960's and 1970's. Sturgeon also made fine use of the conventions of utopian fiction only to undercut them, which is most appropriate to his major points about the nature of dynamic evolutionary change throughout his fiction. Utopia, he wrote, "must be life-oriented and recognize that life is change, which is why utopias, be they by Plato or Sir Thomas More, or Joanna Russ, have hidden in them the characteristics of the necropolis." He avoided this by permitting his own utopia to self-destruct, leaving behind the impact of its symbols, and providing in *Venus Plus X* what Sturgeon saw in William Golding's *Lord of the Flies* (1954), "a fable of cultural structures, with a meaning—a 'moral' if you like—far greater than the narrative itself."

Henry J. Lindborg

Other major works

SHORT FICTION: *Without Sorcery*, 1948; *E Pluribus Unicorn*, 1953; *A Way Home*, 1955; *Caviar*, 1955; *A Touch of Strange*, 1958; *Aliens 4*, 1959; *Beyond*, 1960; *Sturgeon in Orbit*, 1964; . . . *And My Fear Is Great/Baby Is Three*, 1965; *The Joyous Invasions*, 1965; *Starshine*, 1966; *Sturgeon Is Alive and Well*, 1971; *The Worlds of Theodore Sturgeon*, 1972; *To Here and the Easel*, 1973; *Sturgeon's West*, 1973; *Case and the Dreamer*, 1974; *Visions and Venturers*, 1978; *The Stars Are the Styx*, 1979; *The Golden Helix*, 1980.

Bibliography

Friend, Beverly. "The Sturgeon Connection." In *Voices for the Future: Essays on Major Science Fiction Writers*, edited by Thomas D. Clareson. Vol. 1. Bowling Green, Ohio: Bowling Green University Popular Press, 1977. A stimulating discussion of the themes and formal structures of Sturgeon's fiction.

Hassler, Donald M. "Images for an Ethos, Images for Change and Style." *Extrapolation* 20 (Summer, 1979): 176-188. An analysis of Sturgeon's themes of love, loneliness, newness, and the nature of change in relation to his ethics and versatile technique. The works discussed include "Microcosmic God," "Slow Sculpture," *More Than Human*, and *The Cosmic Rape*.

Lawler, Donald L. "Theodore Sturgeon." In *Twentieth-Century American Science Fiction Writers*, edited by David Cowart and Thomas L. Wymer. Vol. 8 in *Dictionary of Literary Biography*. Detroit: Gale Research, 1981. An interesting and informative biography and critical analysis of Sturgeon's fiction. Includes photographs and selected primary and secondary bibliographies.

Moskowitz, Sam. "Theodore Sturgeon." In *Seekers of Tomorrow: Masters of Modern Science Fiction*. New York: Harper & Row, 1966. A discussion of Sturgeon's early fiction through *More Than Human*, with emphasis on his virtuoso style and inventiveness. Includes brief summaries of many Sturgeon plots.

Sackmary, Regina. "An Ideal of Three: The Art of Theodore Sturgeon." In *Critical Encounters: Writers and Themes in Science Fiction*, edited by Dick Riley. New York: Frederick Ungar, 1978. A discussion of Sturgeon's frequent use in his fiction of groupings of threes to develop his themes of isolation, loneliness, love, wholeness, and unity. Includes notes for the essay.

WILLIAM STYRON

Born: Newport News, Virginia; June 11, 1925

Principal long fiction

Lie Down in Darkness, 1951; *The Long March*, 1952 (serial), 1956; *Set This House on Fire*, 1960; *The Confessions of Nat Turner*, 1967; *Sophie's Choice*, 1979.

Other literary forms

Until 1990, William Styron had the curious distinction of being among the few major modern literary figures who bear discussion in only a single genre—in his case, the novel. Except for a slight and rather odd play, *In the Clap Shack* (1972), and a collection of essays, *This Quiet Dust* (1982), Styron's four major novels and his short one, *The Long March*, constituted his entire significant production.

In 1990, however, the publication of *Darkness Visible: A Memoir of Madness* was widely hailed. A candid and insightful recounting of Styron's personal battle with severe clinical depression, *Darkness Visible* was an immediate popular success.

Achievements

Until the publication of *The Confessions of Nat Turner* in 1967, Styron was well known in literary circles as a young novelist of great talent but largely unrealized potential. *The Confessions of Nat Turner*, riding the crest of a wave of social activism in the late 1960's and capitalizing on a national interest in black literature and history, gave Styron a major popular reputation as well as making him the center of a vitriolic controversy between academic and literary critics on one side, who tended to see the novel as an honest attempt to come to terms with history, and a small group of strident black critics on the other hand who questioned, often abusively, the ability of any white writer to deal with the black experience, and who called Styron's portrait of Nat Turner unflattering and inaccurate. The book and the debate it engendered made Styron a major voice in twentieth century fiction, as well as a rich man.

Despite the twelve-year hiatus between the publication of *The Confessions of Nat Turner* and that of *Sophie's Choice*, Styron's reputation grew, particularly in terms of his role as an interpreter of the South. *Lie Down in Darkness* was recognized as one of the finest presentations in fiction of the modern Southern family, haunted by memory, guilt, and time, and *The Confessions of Nat Turner* came to be seen as representative of the concern of Southern writers with the burden of history. *The Confessions of Nat Turner* was accepted as a rhetorically beautiful evocation of the past, whatever its historical inaccuracies.

The publication of *Sophie's Choice* in 1979 cemented Styron's position as one of the major figures of contemporary literature. Although several major critics had reservations about the novel, its ambitious confrontation of a moral theme of enormous implication—the Holocaust—and Styron's compelling, lyrical prose made the novel the literary event of the year. With *Sophie's Choice*, some of Styron's lifelong concerns as a novelist become clearer: the unanswerable problem of pain and suffering, the elusive nature of memory, the ambiguous legacy of history.

Biography

William Styron was born June 11, 1925, in Newport News, Virginia, which he later called "a very Southern part of the world." His mother, Pauline Margaret Abraham Styron, was from the North, but his father, William Clark Styron, a shipyard engineer, came from an old, if not aristocratic, land-poor Virginia family, and Styron remembers his grandmother telling him as a little boy of the days when the family owned slaves, a memory he was to incorporate years later into *Sophie's Choice*. Styron's father was a "Jeffersonian gentleman," liberal in his views for a Southerner, who implanted in his son much of the philosophical curiosity which characterized the young Styron's novels. His mother, a gentling influence, died when Styron was twelve after a long, painful siege with cancer, an experience which was also to leave a mark on his fiction in the form of an almost obsessive concern with physical pain and suffering and the vulnerability of the flesh. After his mother's death, Styron began "going wild," and his father sent him to an Episcopal boys' school in Middlesex County, where he was an indifferent student but a voracious reader. Graduating, he enrolled in Davidson College during World War II but soon dropped out to enlist in the marines.

Styron's stint in Officers Candidate School marked the beginning of his writing career, for while there, he enrolled in a creative writing course at Duke University under William Blackburn, whom Styron acknowledges as the most powerful formative influence on his work. One of his stories, about a Southern lynching, similar in tone and execution to William Faulkner's "Dry September," appeared in a student anthology, Styron's first published fiction. At the tail end of the war, Styron was commissioned and sent to the Pacific, arriving on the island of Okinawa after the fighting was over. Styron was to speak later of his sense of guilt at not having seen action, as well as his feeling of horror at the waste and destruction of the war and the terrible, almost casual way in which life could be lost. Back in America, Styron resumed his program at Duke and was graduated in 1947. He took a job in New York as an associate editor in the book division at McGraw-Hill. His senior editor and immediate superior was Edward C. Aswell, the august second editor of

Thomas Wolfe and an éminence grise to rival Maxwell Perkins; Aswell was to appear grotesquely as "The Weasel" in an autobiographical passage in *Sophie's Choice* nearly thirty years later. The callow young Styron found McGraw-Hill humorless and confining, and after six months he was fired.

Living in a Brooklyn boarding house on a tiny legacy from his grandmother, Styron took another creative writing course, this time from Hiram Haydn at the New School for Social Research. He began work on his first novel, *Lie Down in Darkness*, the story of a star-crossed upper-middle-class Southern family whose failure to find love and meaning in life drives the sensitive daughter, Peyton Loftis, to insanity and suicide. The complex treatment of time in the novel and its high Southern rhetoric showed the influence of William Faulkner, whom Styron had been reading intensely, but *Lie Down in Darkness* was manifestly the work of a powerful and original talent. Styron found that the writing of the book, although exhausting, went surprisingly fast, and he finished it and saw it accepted for publication by Bobbs-Merrill before he was recalled by the marines for service in the Korean War. The novel was published in 1951. Styron was then on active reserve duty, from which he was eventually discharged for an eye problem, but which became the basis for his second novel, *The Long March*.

Lie Down in Darkness was an immediate critical success and a moderate popular one, winning the prestigious Prix de Rome in 1952. At that time, Styron had decamped to Paris and fallen in with a young crowd of American expatriate intellectuals, many of whom would later make names for themselves in literature. George Plimpton and Peter Matthiessen were at the center of a moiling, motley, talented crowd that included Harold Humes, John P. C. Train, Donald Hall, and, on the fringe, writers such as James Baldwin, James Jones, and Irwin Shaw. In 1952 and 1953, the group began compiling a literary magazine, *The Paris Review*, which was to become one of the most influential literary periodicals of the postwar period. Plimpton became the first editor and Matthiessen the fiction editor, and Styron wrote the statement of purpose for the first issue. He also gave the periodical one of the first of its famous "Writers at Work" interviews. It was recorded by Matthiessen and Plimpton at Patrick's, the *Paris Review* crowd's favorite bar, and in it Styron claimed that "this generation . . . will produce literature equal to that of any other generation . . ." and that "a great writer . . . will give substance to and perhaps even explain all the problems of the world. . . ." From the start, his ambitions were large.

Although he later said he drank enough brandy in bistros to develop a *crise de foie*, and spent months in the summer of 1952 on a sybaritic "Ovidian idyll" on the Riviera with Humes, Styron was also writing at top speed during this period. In just six weeks, he wrote a novella based on his marine corps training-camp experience, *The Long March*, and it was accepted for publication in the fall by *discovery*, a literary magazine (Knopf would publish it as a book *The Long March* four years later). In 1953, he used the money from his Prix de Rome to travel in Italy, an experience that laid the groundwork for his 1960 novel of expatriates, *Set This House on Fire*, and during this time he met Rose Burgunder, a Jewish poet with some family money from Baltimore, whom he soon married. They returned to America, to Roxbury, Connecticut, which has been Styron's home ever since, and where he began work on the "big novel" that he planned to follow up the success of *Lie Down in Darkness*.

This was *Set This House on Fire*, a sprawling account of American intellectuals living a life of self-indulgence and self-destruction in postwar Italy. The book contained fine lyrical passages of description, particularly of the physical beauty of Italy and the horrifying squalor and suffering of its people, but as Styron later admitted, the novel was seriously flawed—undisciplined and melodramatic. The reviews were very mixed, and some of them savage. Styron's former friend, Norman Mailer, called *Set This House on Fire* "a bad, maggoty novel," suggesting that Styron could "write like an angel about landscape, but like an adolescent about people." The novel was better received by Styron's European critics—it is still highly regarded in France— but Styron was wounded by his first really bad press, and he retreated to Roxbury to work on his next book, a novel he resolved to make so thoroughly a work of craftsmanship as to defy criticism.

The Confessions of Nat Turner took years to research and write, and true to Styron's expectations, it was immediately acclaimed as a masterpiece. For years, Styron had had his mind on Nat Turner's 1831 slave rebellion as a subject for fiction. It had taken place close to his own Tidewater Virginia home, and Styron saw the suffering, the violence, and the misunderstanding of the revolt as emblematic both of the South's guilt and pain and of his personal concerns as a writer. Styron claimed that reading Albert Camus' *The Stranger* (1942) furnished him with the technique he was to use in presenting Nat Turner's story—the narrative persona reflecting from jail—and there is no doubt that much of the novel's perspective on black people and black problems was derived from Styron's friend, the black writer James Baldwin, who was a guest of Styron for months while he was writing *Another Country* (1962), Baldwin's first major novel about black/white relations. Styron called *The Confessions of Nat Turner* "less an 'historical novel' than a meditation on history," but despite almost unanimous critical accolades, including the praise of Baldwin, who suggested that the novel might be considered the beginning of a black/white "mutual history," Styron became the target of a group of black critics who protested vehemently the right of a white man to consider himself qualified to interpret the black experience. These critics assaulted Styron in print, accused him of racism and of attempting to demean the reputation of a great hero of black history, and hounded him at meetings, readings, and lectures, rising up and screaming "filthy honky liar," among less kindly epithets. Ironically, Nat Turner, as Styron presented him, was a strong and sensitive character, unquestionably the hero of the novel, but so volatile was the political climate of America in the late 1960's that for some critics, any black character who was not a warrior saint was unacceptable as a fictional creation, particularly the creation of a white writer.

The critical assaults provoked by the *The Confessions of Nat Turner* left Styron bruised, but he was encouraged by the praise for the novel's powerful rhetoric and masterly structure, not to mention its enormous financial success. Of the controversy, he said, "It really had very little effect on me . . . largely because of the fact that I knew that it was politically motivated and hysterical, and that I had not violated any truth that a novelist is capable of doing." He turned to new work, first to a lengthy projected novel exploring the psyche of a career army officer, which he finally shelved, then to *Sophie's Choice*. The book began as an autobiographical reminiscence of his aimless days as a junior editor at McGraw-Hill, when he found himself frustrated artistically, philosophically, and sexually. As he worked through his memories in the character of his narrator, Stingo, whose fictional background is almost identical to Styron's own, he found his real theme: the life and eventual death by suicide of a woman who survived the Nazi concentration camps, but emerged terribly scarred emotionally. This woman, the Sophie of the title, becomes the vehicle through which Stingo confronts the potential horror of life, and through whom he matures.

Sophie's Choice was five years in the writing, but Styron was richly rewarded when it was finally published in 1979. A few critics, notably John Gardner, raised questions about its structure, and about the sometimes jejune intrusions of the shallow Stingo, but for the most part the novel was accepted as a fine and satisfying offering by a major writer. "It has the feel of permanence," Peter Prescott wrote. The gratifyingly large sales were capped by a spectacular sale of the film rights. In 1983, Meryl Streep won an Academy Award for Best Actress for her portrayal of Sophie in that film.

In 1985, Styron was hospitalized with acute clinical depression. His struggle to overcome his suicidal feelings and to return to health are recounted in his memoir *Darkness Visible*, published five years later. Styron credited the peaceful seclusion of his hospital stay and the loving patience of his wife and grown children (three daughters and a son) as the principal factors in his recovery. After the publication of *Darkness Visible*, he returned to his work on a novel set in World War II.

Analysis

The informing patterns of William Styron's fiction are by no means self-evident, and they may not yield themselves readily to the casual critic. Unlike William Faulkner, whom he often resembles in style and technique, his subjects are radically diverse—a doomed Southern family, the intellectual jet set of American expatriates, a historical slave revolt, the horror of the Holocaust. He can shift stylistically from the direct "plain' style" of *The Long March* to the purple rhetoric of sections in *Set This House on Fire*, and he moves easily from romantic abstraction to concrete objectivity.

Styron is preeminently, almost self-consciously, a writer of "big" novels of weighty moral significance—a fictional *homme sérieux*, as the French say (which may account for some of Styron's great popularity with French critics). The eternal verities embody themselves relentlessly in Styron's writing. Death, suffering, the silence of God—grave truths lumber ponderously and insistently at the reader in each novel, mercifully relieved by flashes of humor and lyrical passages of poetic beauty, which spare Styron the gray fate of being a sort of American Thomas Mann. Still, the metaphysical predominates in Styron's books.

Strongly underlying all of his novels is a concern with the past, not so much in the form of the passage of time, but rather an awareness that it is either lost or potentially reclaimable. Each of the four major novels moves from the present to the past in an attempt to explain or understand how things came to be as they are. *Lie Down in Darkness*, with its relentless burrowing in the Loftis family past, looks backward to explain Peyton's death. In *Set This House on Fire*, Peter Leverett moves very deliberately into the past in pursuit of a piece of himself that is missing, and his whole purpose in dredging up the Italian incidents that form the body of the novel is to reveal the past so that he may deal with the present. Both *The Confessions of Nat Turner* and *Sophie's Choice* are historical novels concerned with the actual past and with what Robert Penn Warren has called "the awful burden of history."

Styron's fiction is historical, but in an intensely personal and psychological way. Each exploration of the past is filtered through the consciousness of a protagonist—Milton Loftis, Cass Kinsolving, Nat Turner, Sophie—and strongly colored by the neuroses of those characters. The alcoholism of Milton and Cass, Nat's brooding rage, and Sophie's aching guilt over her murdered child—at the core of each novel is psychological exploration rather than historical exposition. Historical process is only the context within which individual psychologies grope for resolution. Each of Styron's characters lives on the verge of apocalyptic catastrophe, always on the edge of mental breakdown. Each of his protagonists is close to outright insanity. Two actually commit suicide (Peyton and Sophie); Nat Turner essentially does; and Cass Kinsolving of *Set This House on Fire* is only saved from it by the thinnest of margins. His people may be constantly close to madness, yet Styron makes the reader feel that the madness is legitimate, for his characters search for meaning in a mad world, and only when they fail to find it do they become deranged. Peyton Loftis' loveless family, Nat Turner's unjust world, and the horrors of the concentration camp for Sophie are atmospheres in which genuine sanity is difficult, if not impossible. Perhaps the most representative Styron "hero," though, is Cass Kinsolving of *Set This House on Fire*, the only protagonist who is a philosopher as well as a sufferer. Cass's madness derives from his contemplation of the horror of human life and misery, and he staggers drunkenly around postwar Italy demanding a teleological answer for the chaos of existence in which God is silent; "you can shake the whole universe and just get a snicker up there."

Perhaps it is this tendency to project the struggles of his characters beyond the ordinary world and to magnify them to the borders of melodrama that gives all of Styron's novels powerful religious overtones. Some of this tendency derives from Styron's own Episcopalian background, which is strongly echoed in the style of *Lie Down in Darkness* and *Set This House on Fire* and is particularly evident in the rhetoric of Nat Turner, who is stylistically more Anglican than Baptist. The central problem in these novels is the conspicuous absence of God from human life. Styron's world is one in which, as Cass says in *Set This House on Fire*, "God has locked the door and gone away to leave us to write letters to Him." They are unanswered. By the time Styron comes to reflecting on the horror of the Holocaust in his last book, it seems no answer is possible.

This is Styron's theme—the absence of God and the meaninglessness of life. Consistently, he approaches it through a single technique, the presentation and contemplation of pain and suffering. Styron's novels are a catalog of the slings and arrows of outrageous fortune, some physical, some mental, and some simply the result of an empathic identification with the suffering state of mankind.

On its most elemental level, Styron's depiction of suffering is as pure physical pain. Peyton Loftis is tortured by the ache in her womb, the soldiers of *The Long March* by the agony of their exhausted bodies, Nat Turner by the cold of his cell and the torments of his imprisonment, and Sophie by the tortures of the concentration camp. In *Set This House on Fire*, physical suffering is Styron's primary metaphor for the pain of man's empty relationship with the universe, and the novel is shot through with characters in various stages of suffering from "abuse of the carnal envelope."

Vivid as the physical suffering of Styron's characters is, it is nothing compared to their mental and emotional anguish. Often, this mental anguish derives from their acute sense of alienation—from one another and from God. Milton Loftis, Peyton, Cass Kinsolving, Nat Turner, and Sophie writhe painfully and actively, aware of a pervasive emptiness in their lives.

The structural complexities of *Lie Down in Darkness*, combined with the florid rhetoric of the novel, obscure for many readers the essentially simple causality which underlies the book. It is the story of how and why Peyton Loftis becomes insane and kills herself, tracing the roots of her tortured madness to her father's weakness and her mother's inability to love. Peyton's father, Milton, showers her with an excessive adoration that is one facet of his alcoholic self-indulgence; he smothers his daughter with a sloppy, undemanding adulation that counterpoints his wife Helen's psychotic frigidity. Helen is only able to show love in terms of compulsive formal discharge of parental obligations, bitterly resentful of the martyr role she has chosen to play. Eventually, Peyton instinctively rejects both her father's almost unnatural affection and her mother's unnatural lack of it. By the time Peyton cuts herself loose, however, she has been emotionally crippled, unable to accept any genuine love from a series of lovers, including the Jewish artist she marries and who might have brought her peace. She retreats deeper and deeper inside herself, watching first other people and finally the real world recede before her disintegrating mind. The last major section of the novel is her tormented, insane monologue, a brilliant tour de force reminiscent of the Benjy sections of Faulkner's *The Sound and the Fury* (1929).

When *Lie Down in Darkness* was published in 1952, it was widely hailed as a significant addition to the "Southern" school of writing led by Faulkner, Ellen Glasgow, Flannery O'Connor, and Thomas Wolfe. Thematically, *Lie Down in Darkness* is not a markedly "Southern" novel. Although the Loftis family is from Tidewater, Virginia, and there are mannerisms described in the book that are definitively Southern, Milton Loftis' weakness, his wife's cold rage, and their daughter's breakdown are in no way regional. The story could as easily be that of a New England family, such as Eugene O'Neill's Manions. What is actually distinctive about the tragedy of the Loftises is how much it is exclusively their own, rather than a product of the dictates of fate or society. In this respect, the novel differs from Styron's later works, in which he increasingly attributes man's sufferings to forces beyond the individual.

If Styron traces a source of the Loftis family's deterioration, it is perhaps in their life-style. On one level, *Lie Down in Darkness* is almost a novel of manners, for in keeping with the Loftises' "country club" lives, much of the novel delineates social activity—parties, dances, dinners. Emblematic of this are three scenes in which Milton, Helen, and Peyton go through the motions of conventional social rituals while they are torn by violent emotions lying beneath the facade of meaningless behavior. The first of these is a dance at the country club at which Peyton tries to play the role of belle-of-the-ball while her father makes drunken love to his mistress in a cloakroom and Helen seethes at both father and daughter in a jealous rage. Later, a Christmas dinner turns into a grotesque, painful fiasco, as Helen screams insults at her daughter while Milton slobbers drunkenly. Finally, Peyton's wedding becomes a nightmare when Milton again gets drunk and sloppy, and Helen, as always thinly concealing a bitter resentment of Peyton, finally cracks, screaming "Whore!" at her daughter. In a rage, Peyton claws her mother's face with her nails and flees the family forever.

The loss of love, or rather the failure to find it, informs the entire book. The three Loftises grope at one another in despair, reaching out to one another in their separate, psychologically crippled ways for an understanding and affection that will bring them some sort of emotional peace. That peace, though, is impossible because their psychic natures are flawed beyond redemption. Sigmund Freud spins the plot: Milton loves Peyton not wisely, but too well, as she uncomfortably senses, so his love of her must always seem unrequited, and he is destined to be deserted by her at the last; Helen suffers a patent jealous hatred for Peyton, who has a capacity for love that Helen lacks, and who is stranded between the two poles of her parents' emotional inadequacy. The result is endless pain and ultimately annihilation. As Milton wails, "It was awful not to be able to love. It was hell."

It is not hell, though, but obliteration—nothingness—that truly underlies this novel. In the opening scene, Milton meets the train that brings Peyton's body home for burial. The final scene is her throwing herself to her death from a New York City rooftop. Everything between, the whole body of the novel, is an explanation of that death, and the knowledge of Peyton's unavoidable extinction hangs heavily during the entire book. The title is taken from Sir Thomas Browne's gloomy *Hydriotaphia: Or Urn Burial* (1658), a seventeenth century meditation on the inevitability of death, and the "darkness" of the title is that of the grave. Images of death haunt the dreams of the tortured characters, and the reader is never allowed to forget the ultimate negation implicit in the agony of life.

The agony of life, more than the nullity of death, became the focus of Styron's fiction following *Lie Down in Darkness*. His short novel *The Long March* serves almost as a précis for the motif of pain that came to dominate Styron's writing. Not much longer than a substantial short story, *The Long March* stands between the turgid psychological weight of *Lie Down in Darkness* and the ponderous solemnity of *Set This House on Fire* like a breath of fresh air. Short, clean, concise, and plotted without a wasted word, this unpretentious novella contains some of Styron's most disciplined and readable prose. He trimmed away all the heavy rhetorical and philosophical baggage of his "big" novels, leaving before the reader only his lean and awful central subject—pain and suffering. Appropriately, the pain here is of the most basic and primitive sort—pure physical agony. Stylistically, Styron's writing of the book in 1952 was anomalous in the development of his career, for it was at this period that he was gearing up to write *Set This House on Fire*, and the stylistic and structural complexities of *Lie Down in Darkness* were being inflated to match the ambitious range of the novel to come.

Like the best of Ernest Hemingway, *The Long March* is deceptively simple—a step-by-step account of a thirty-six-mile forced march inflicted on some marine reserves by their mindless officers and endured by the men with varying degrees of courage or cowardice, acceptance or rejection, but mainly endured with pain. The march itself is relentlessly real for the reader on page after page, the physical pain of the characters becoming a kind of rhythmic pattern in the book. If the novel has a "message," it is embodied in the final lines, in which Captain Mannix, who has undergone the march protesting its sadistic insanity, swollen and aching, confronts a sympathetic barracks maid who asks if it hurts: "His words [were] uttered . . . not with self-pity, but only with the tone of a man who, having endured and lasted, was too weary to tell her anything but what was true. 'Deed it does,' he said."

After the critical success of *Lie Down in Darkness* and the artistic success of *The Long March*, there followed the better part of a decade before the 1960 publication of *Set This House on Fire*. Comfortably ensconced in Roxbury, Connecticut, prosperous, rearing a family, and moving into the center of the New York literary world, Styron's reputation grew steadily, although his literary output did not. His house, along with George Plimpton's New York City apartment, became one of the new camping grounds for the old *Paris Review* crowd, and Peter Matthiessen, James Jones, and James Baldwin were frequent visitors. Throughout the late 1950's, word of his forthcoming "big" novel spread as Styron gave private readings from it, and the publication of *Set This House on Fire* was eagerly awaited.

The novel was indeed big; actually, it sprawled embarrassingly. In place of the personal, family tragedy of *Lie Down in Darkness*, Styron broadened his scope by giving the suffering in this novel a universal dimension and by exploring the metaphysical bases of it. It is not a family that suffers, but the world. The reader sees this world through the eyes of Peter Leverett, a Styron surrogate, but the real protagonist is Cass Kinsolving, a sensitive, drunken American artist in Italy in the 1950's who is aghast by the suffering of humanity. Much of the story is told to Leverett (and the reader) by Cass, who looks for the ultimate implications of every grain of sand. Looking back, he tells Leverett that he remembers Italy as "an infinity of remembered pain," and he finds divine aspects even in his drunkenness: "God surely had clever ways of tormenting a man, putting in his way a substance whereby He might briefly be reached, but which in the end . . . sent Him packing over the horizon trailing clouds of terror." To achieve this broadened projection, Styron enlarges his cast of characters, heightens his rhetoric, and throws the whole show on an enormous stage. A vast parade of people moves through *Set This House on Fire*, many of them poor, sick, or abused, the rest venal and contemptible. The action is lifted from the commonplace to the melodramatic; rape, murder, and mystery dominate. The characters, except for Leverett and Cass's bovine, Faulknerian wife, Poppy, are exotic. Mason Flagg is a monstrous idiot typifying Victor Hugo's Quasimodo of *The Hunchback of Notre Dame* (1831). He is the "super bastard" aesthete rich boy, whose cultivated corruption is nauseating but still rich and strange. Cass deteriorates theatrically, staggering about and raving lines from Greek tragedy, a far cry from the humdrum drunkard Milton Loftis.

Heightened rhetoric is Styron's principal method of extending the scope of

Set This House on Fire. Much of the novel reads like Gothic Thomas Wolfe, from Mason's mother's description of "the horror" of her son's expulsion from prep school to Leverett's account of one of the book's several nightmares: "an abomination made of the interlocking black wings of ravens crawling and loathsome with parasites . . . a country in cataclysm and upheaval." Cass spends much of the book in deliberate blasphemy, "raving at that black, baleful, and depraved Deity who seemed coolly-minded to annihilate His creatures," when he is not suffering from delirium tremens and seeing visions of a boiling sea, or giant spiders on Mt. Vesuvius.

This rhetoric not only complements, but makes possible, the projection of much of the novel on a dream level. Styron had done this before, in a Freudian fantasy of Helen Loftis', in one of Peyton's lover's dreams of babies burning in hell, and in Peyton's entire closing soliloquy. In *Set This House on Fire*, though, the use of dream, vision, and hallucination is so pervasive that much of the novel approaches phantasmagoria. Leverett dreams of a malevolent fiend for several pages, and has recurrent, elaborately described nightmares; Cass is repeatedly haunted, and his drunken ordeal ends with an extended vision of disaster, a passage drawing heavily on Dante and the Book of Revelation. So extensive is Styron's use of dramatic and fantastic imagery that it is often difficult to tell whether he is presenting the reader with a metaphor or a dream, and at one point, when Cass describes himself first making love to a beautiful girl, then suddenly "groping for an answer on some foul black shore," it is impossible to tell whether he is just thinking or hallucinating again. Cass himself probably does not know.

Although they differ in scope and ambition, *Lie Down in Darkness* and *Set This House on Fire* are essentially the same kind of novel. Both are studies in personal alienation and deterioration. Both work through an elevated rhetoric and through psychological revelation. Although *Set This House on Fire* reaches self-consciously for transcendence and philosophical universality, the novel centers upon the psychological aberrations of two characters, Cass Kinsolving and Mason Flagg: similar to the tragedy of the Loftis family in *Lie Down in Darkness*, it is still their individual tragedies rather than a universal one. It may have been the critical failure of *Set This House on Fire* that led Styron to shift from his probing of purely personal disaster, or perhaps it was an increasingly sensitive social conscience that was responsible.

Styron called *The Confessions of Nat Turner* "a meditation on history." Its subject is not only the character of Nat, but also the meaning of slavery itself—what it does to people, and to society. Like Styron's previous novels, the book is a contemplation of horror, with a protagonist who becomes a victim of that horror, but in this case, the horror is not a purely personal one. Significantly, unlike the Loftises and Cass Kinsolving, Nat does not deteriorate, but grows through the course of the book as his comprehension of society and life grows. Nat Turner is the richest and most psychologically complex of Styron's characters, and the historical subject matter of the work is filtered through his sensitive consciousness to produce a visionary "meditation" on the world of slavery, dreamlike in quality and poetic in execution. Southern Virginia of the 1830's, the novel's world, is very much a projection of Nat's mind—a mind produced by that world, and savaged by it.

To develop the subtlety of Nat's mind, Styron drew on all his technical and rhetorical resources. His mastery of time-shifts and dream sequences, already amply demonstrated, was enhanced in this novel, and he explored a variety of rhetorical styles, varying from rural black dialect to a high Anglican style echoing Joan Didion's *A Book of Common Prayer* (1977) for Nat's more poetic utterances. Nat's mind ranges with astonishing virtuosity over his universe—the natural world, the complexities of human relations, the elusive mysteries of God, and the bitterness of mortality. An enormously sophisticated narrative persona, Nat moves fluidly across time, contemplating the painful mystery of the past, represented by his long-dead African grandmother, and of the future, represented by his own forthcoming death. Nat tells the entire novel in flashback, remembering his abortive slave rebellion and the personal and historical events leading up to it, constantly trying to cipher out the meaning of those events. The novel is a study of the growth of knowledge and of the growth of Nat's mind. In the introspective isolation of his anguished imprisonment, he reconstructs his lifelong struggle to understand the meaning of existence. He recalls his progression from childhood, when he had no comprehension of what slavery meant, to an early adult period when he accepted his condition either bitterly or philosophically, to a final understanding of slavery in personal, societal, and moral terms. Ironically, as Nat becomes more morally and aesthetically sensitive, he becomes more insensitive in human terms, gravitating toward an acceptance of the violence that finally characterizes his revolt. Only a sudden, visionary conversion to a God of love at the end of the novel saves him from closing the book as an unrepentant apostle of retributory cruelty.

In the process of expanding his knowledge and developing his terrible vision of deliverance from slavery by violence, Nat becomes the spokesman for two familiar Styron themes—the complexity of human psychology and the mystery of human suffering. The most self-searching of Styron's characters, Nat exhaustively explores the ambivalence and ambiguity of his feelings about race, sex, religion, and violence. Although he casts himself convincingly as a Christian prophet, Nat is no simplistic fundamentalist, for he recognizes in his own emotional turmoil personal depths that he can plumb with only partial understanding. His psychology is the battleground of conflicting feelings, symbolized by his powerful attraction to his master's gentle daughter and his vitriolic hatred for all she represents. When he eventually kills her, neither he nor the reader can discriminate his motives. She dies imploring, "Oh, Nat, it hurts so!", and his realization of her pain is the climax of his apprehension of the myriad pains of all mankind, particularly those of his own people. In this concern, he is representative of all Styron's protagonists.

It is almost impossible to deal with *The Confessions of Nat Turner* without mentioning the storm of controversy that followed its publication and success. A number of critics, primarily black, maintained that the novel was historically inaccurate (for example, it portrayed Nat as having homosexual tendencies, but never mentioned that there are records indicating that the real Nat Turner had a wife). Styron was also accused of demeaning a black hero, in that his Nat has reservations about his mission and is squeamish about wholesale slaughter. The real complaint against Styron, though, most thoroughly summarized in a casebook edited by John Henrik Clarke, *William Styron's Nat Turner: Ten Black Writers Respond* (1968), was that he was a white man attempting a theme that should be the sole province of black writers. In answer to the historical criticism, Styron and his defenders point out that *The Confessions of Nat Turner* is a work of fiction which does not pretend to be straight history, and that it violates no factual information known to Styron at the time of writing. The second complaint, that it degrades a black hero, is more difficult to understand. Unquestionably, Styron, like any true artist, presents his hero with his neuroses, self-doubts, and weaknesses. In the main, however, Nat is without doubt a positive and even heroic character, arguably the most admirable in all Styron's fiction. Only a critic in search of a black plaster saint *sans peur et sans reproche* could consider the creation of as rich and sensitive a character as Nat a slur. Regrettably, though, some readers are still looking for a black Natty Bumppo, however anachronistic he may seem in modern literature. As to the argument that Styron is not black, Homer did not serve at Troy nor was Molly Bloom's soliloquy written by a woman.

Styron's novel *Sophie's Choice* was some twelve years in the works, if somewhat less in the writing, and is in every way as ambitious a novel as *The Confessions of Nat Turner*, although its rank in the Styron canon is still in question. Having dealt in earlier novels with suicide, physical agony, existential despair, and slavery, Styron chose the Holocaust as the logical next state of human misery suitable for artistic contemplation. For a long time, Styron had been moving his narrative personae closer toward the subjects of his novels, introducing clearly autobiographical narrators in *The Long March* and *Set This House on Fire*, and making *The Confessions of Nat Turner* an intensely personal first-person narrative. For *Sophie's Choice*, Styron turned to the confessional form plied by novelists as various as Saul Bellow and Norman Mailer and poets such as Robert Lowell. The narrator of *Sophie's Choice*, a young Southerner named Stingo, is, for all intents and purposes, indistinguishable from the young Styron. A young artist *manqué* in New York, Stingo meets and is fascinated by a beautiful survivor of a Nazi concentration camp, Sophie, who is permanently psychologically scarred by the horror she has undergone, the most ghastly aspect of which was being forced to decide which of her two children would live and which would die. Stingo is the ultimate naïf: sexually, emotionally, morally, and artistically immature. As he comes to know Sophie, he comes to know himself. Stingo is an artist in search of a subject, as Styron evidently felt that he himself had been. Styron's problems with finding subject matter commensurate with his talents as a technician have been pointed out by William Van O'Conner in "John Updike and William Styron: The Burden of Talent" (1964) and by other critics. Styron himself acknowledged his concern with finding a fit subject for his early fiction, but he also felt that a concern with pain had been central to his earlier work. In 1970, he said, "Consciousness of pain and suffering has informed my work. . . . I hope my present work will not be so preoccupied." At that time, he was working on his military novel "The Way of the Warrior," which he eventually abandoned to write a book that returned to the pain motif with a vengeance, along with the other *leitmotiv* of *Sophie's Choice*, that of the artist's finding of himself.

The emotional pain of Peyton Loftis is alienation from family and love. Cass Kinsolving suffers from guilt brought on by self-hatred and contemplation of human suffering. Nat Turner's ultimate pain derives from his isolation from all mankind and God. Sophie and Stingo suffer the pain of guilt. Stingo, the apotheosis of Styron's autobiographical WASP characters, feels he has not "paid his dues," suffered as others have suffered, and he learns of Sophie's anguished life with a guilty voyeurism. Sophie's guilt has a specific origin in her hideous choice to doom one of her children. She also feels ashamed that in Auschwitz she somehow "suffered less" since she was the commandant's mistress and finally survived when others died. Constantly and compulsively her mind plays over the fates of those dead—her little girl, her tortured friends, and the gassed millions whom she never knew. Even memories of her murdered husband and of her father, both of whom she despised, bring her reproach and grief. The knowledge that she did what she had to gives no relief. She says, "I see that it was—beyond my control, but it is still so terrible to wake up these many mornings with the memory of that, having to live with it . . . it makes everything unbearable. Just unbearable." Soon, she will kill herself to stop the pain.

After Sophie's death, the shattered Stingo, who had just become her lover, walks on the beach trying to find some sort of personal resolution and acceptance of a world in which horror and anguish such as Sophie's exist. Her message, though, has been clear: there is no resolution. Madness and suffering of the magnitude represented by the Holocaust can be neither accepted nor understood. Sophie, like Herman Melville's Ishmael, realizes that "there is a wisdom that is woe, and there is a woe that is madness." Stingo has come to know it, too.

With the death of Sophie, Styron seems to have come full circle in his exploration of human suffering and his search for meaning in a flawed and painful world. Both Sophie and Peyton Loftis find death to be the only release from lives so agonizing and painful as to be unbearable. In both his first novel and this one, Styron leads the reader to the edge of the grave and points to it as the goal of life—"therefore it cannot be long before we lie down in darkness, and have our light in ashes." The crucial difference between *Sophie's Choice* and *Lie Down in Darkness*, however, is the character of Stingo, who like Ishmael escapes to tell the tale. The earlier novel leaves the reader in desolation, but the latter, through Stingo, holds forth the possibility of an alternative existence, one not horribly haunted by the knowledge of pain. Stingo's life is hardly one of euphoria, but it is a tenable existence compared to Sophie's untenable one. To some degree, Stingo has paid his dues through her; he has come to know pain and evil through her sacrifice, and therefore he is sadder and wiser, but not destroyed as she is. His survival counterpoints her destruction; the novel that Stingo will write grows out of her ashes and becomes her immortality.

Sophie's Choice is not a cheerful novel, or even an affirmative one, but it is not nihilistic. Perhaps Stingo's optimism at the close is unjustified. A number of critics feel that when Stingo walks on the beach after Sophie's death and finds the morning "excellent and fair," anticipating his own promising career, Styron is simply tacking on an upbeat ending hardly defensible in view of the horror explored by the novel. Similarly, Cass Kinsolving in *Set This House on Fire* never satisfies his thirst for metaphysical answers to terrible questions, but simply decides to stop thirsting and take up fishing. Whether convincing or not, though, Stingo's survival leaves William Styron's literary career pointed in a new direction, away from the contemplation of pain and the abyss.

John L. Cobbs

Other major works
PLAY: *In the Clap Shack*, 1972.
NONFICTION: *This Quiet Dust*, 1982; *Darkness Visible: A Memoir of Madness*, 1990.

Bibliography
Clarke, John Henrik, ed. *William Styron's Nat Turner: Ten Black Writers Respond*. Boston: Beacon Press, 1968. Each of the essays attacks Styron's version of the slave rebellion as ahistorical, inaccurate, or racist.
Fossom, Robert, H. *William Styron: A Critical Essay*. Grand Rapids, Mich.: Wm. B. Eerdmans, 1968. Contains critical discussions of Styron's fiction up to *The Confessions of Nat Turner*.
Friedman, Melvin J. *William Styron*. Bowling Green, Ohio: Bowling Green University Popular Press, 1974. Friedman defends Styron against the charge of racism in his treatment of Nat Turner and compares Styron's fiction to

the *nouveau roman* of Alain Robbe-Grillet.

Friedman, Melvin J., and Irving Malin, eds. *William Styron's "The Con-fessions of Nat Turner": A Critical Casebook*. Belmont, Calif.: Wadsworth, 1970. Contains essays and historical material relating to the rebellion of Nat Turner. Most of the essays support Styron's portrayal of the historical figure.

Morris, Robert K., and Irving Malin, eds. *The Achievement of William Sty-ron*. Athens: University of Georgia Press, 1975. Provides essays by various critics on Styron's fiction up to *Sophie's Choice*. The essay by Morris and Malin on Styron's career as a visionary novelist is an excellent introduction to his work. Includes an extensive and very useful bibliography.

Pearce, Richard. *William Styron*. Minneapolis: University of Minnesota Press, 1971. In this pamphlet, Pearce gives a very brief life of Styron and dis-cusses his major fictional works, praising the neglected novella *The Long March*. Includes a brief bibliography.

Ratner, Marc L. *William Styron*. New York: Twayne, 1972. A brief biography and an analysis of Styron's novels up to *The Confessions of Nat Turner*. Ratner discusses Styron's relationship with the South and the social im-plications of his work. Contains a good bibliography.

JONATHAN SWIFT

Born: Dublin, Ireland; November 30, 1667
Died: Dublin, Ireland; October 19, 1745

Principal long fiction

A Tale of a Tub, 1704; *Gulliver's Travels*, 1726 (originally entitled *Travels into Several Remote Nations of the World, in Four Parts, by Lemuel Gulliver, First a Surgeon, and Then a Captain of Several Ships*).

Other literary forms

Jonathan Swift's oeuvre includes a large and important body of verse, best assembled in *The Poems of Jonathan Swift* (1958), edited by Harold Williams. His letters may be found in *The Correspondence of Jonathan Swift*, also edited by Williams. Outstanding among a variety of political writings are Swift's contributions to *The Examiner* (1710-1711), the treatise called *The Conduct of the Allies* (1711), and the important *The Drapier's Letters to the People of Ireland* (1724-1735). His prose, collected in *The Prose Works of Jonathan Swift* (1939-1968), is a fourteen-volume collection edited by Herbert Davis.

Achievements

It is generally conceded that Swift is the greatest English satirist, possibly the most brilliant ironist and acerb wit in any language. Yet the force of his satiric barbs has rendered him controversial, and many critics have retaliated against his potent quill by claiming that Swift is wreckless, uncontrolled, spiteful, insensate, heathenish, and insane. Such rash responses merely demonstrate the powerful effect his writing instigates.

Swift is not an overt lampooner, diatribe-monger, or name-caller. Curiously, he never utilizes the direct approach: he almost always speaks through a defective mouthpiece, a flawed, self-incriminating persona who forges a case against himself. Indeed, Swift is to be remembered as a grand satiric mimic, finely shaping and generating the voices of knaves and fools alike (the "modern" hack writer in *A Tale of a Tub*, the ignorant serving-woman Frances Harris, the idiot astrologer Isaac Bickerstaff, the callous and mathematical Modest Proposer, the proud but demented simpleton Lemuel Gulliver).

Swift's ear for clichés and inflections of dullness is almost perfect, and an author such as Herbert Read (in *English Prose Style*, 1928) hails Swift as the inevitable and clear master of "pure prose" style. Swift is, without doubt, the major satirist in prose, yet he is also a first-rate light poet (in the manner of Horace and the coarser Samuel "Hudibras" Butler), and, if anything, his reputation as a poet is rising. Furthermore, Swift wrote political pamphlets with ruthless force, and his prose in sermons, letters, and treatises is virile and direct. Finally, Swift should not be forgotten as wit and jester. He invented a child-language when corresponding with Stella, wrote mock-Latin sayings, devised wicked epigrams, created paraphrases of Vergil and Ovid, and could even toy with versifying when devising invitations to dinner. In a word, Swift is the all-around English expert in straightforward exposition—especially when it is bent to provoke savage mockery and the *jeu d'esprit*.

Biography

Jonathan Swift was born in Dublin on November 30, 1667, after the death of his father, a lower-middle class Anglo-Irishman. His grandfather, the Reverend Thomas Swift, had been a vicar in Herefordshire. His father, Jonathan, had settled in Ireland to work as a steward of the King's Inns in Dublin. His mother was Abigail Erick, the daughter of a Leicestershire clergyman. Swift's mother had entrusted her young son to a nurse; the nurse had spirited the infant Swift away from Ireland for several years, and though he was eventually returned, Jonathan was peculiarly linked with Ireland throughout his life. In any case, it was his fancy to picture himself a lonely outcast amid barbarians. He attended Kilkenny School in his youth and Trinity College, Dublin, obtaining a Bachelor's degree in 1686. He spent most of the following decade at Moor Park, Surrey, in the household of Sir William Temple, the distinguished Whig statesman. It was at Moor Park that Swift met, in 1689, the child of Esther Johnson (whom Swift later immortalized as "Stella"), the daughter of Temple's widowed housekeeper. Swift helped in supervising her education and inaugurated a lifelong (and little understood) relationship, for Stella later immigrated to Dublin and spent her life near the Anglican Dean Swift. Naturally, under Temple's aegis, Swift hoped for introductions and advancement, but little came of promises and possibilities; and in 1694, he returned to Dublin long enough to be ordained an Anglican priest (in 1695). He subsequently was reunited with Temple until the latter's death in 1699. Thereafter, he returned to Ireland as chaplain to the Earl of Berkeley. His reputation for talent and wit was rapidly growing.

Swift's great political period took place in London from 1708 to 1714. He became the chief spokesman, apologist, and pamphleteer for the powerful Tory leaders then in power, Robert Harley and Henry St. John Bolingbroke. Their fall and disgrace ushered in a lengthy era of Whig dominance that permanently drove Swift back to what he must have considered exile in Ireland. Swift had been finally rewarded (although he would have perceived it as a paltry recognition) with the Deanery of St. Patrick's Cathedral in Dublin, where he served for the remainder of his life. His powerful satires had earned him powerful enemies, and significant advancement in the Church or in England was never permitted to him.

In any event, Swift served with precision, justness, and rectitude as a clergyman, and continued throughout his career to be an admirable satirist and wit. He even elected to champion the rights of the maltreated Irish, and he came to be admired as their avatar and protector, a "Hibernian Patriot."

In his last years, Swift suffered increasingly from deafness and vertigo (the results of a lifelong affliction by Ménière's Syndrome, a disease of the inner ear), which resulted in senility, and most likely a stroke. Guardians were appointed in his last years, and he died in 1745, shortly before his seventy-eighth birthday.

Swift's last ironic jest was played upon mankind in his will, which committed the bulk of his estate to the founding of a "hospital" for fools and madmen, just as he had pronounced the plan in his *Verses on the Death of Dr. Swift*, 1731:

> He gave the little Wealth he had,
> To build a House for Fools and Mad;
> And shew'd by one satyric Touch,
> No Nation wanted it so much

Analysis

Initially, it must be noted that Jonathan Swift's "fictions" are nothing like conventional novels. They seldom detail the "adventures" of a hero or even a protagonist and never conclude with his romantic achievement of goals or fulfillment of desires. Indeed, Swift is the great master of fictionalizing non-fiction. His satires always purport to be something factual, humdrum, diurnal, unimaginative: a treatise, a travel diary, an annotated edition, a laborious oration, a tendentious allegory, a puffed-out "letter-to-a-friend." Extremist Protestant sects condemned fiction, and "projectors" and would-be investi-gators in the dawning Age of Science extolled the prosaic, the plodding, the scholarly, the methodical, and the factual. At the same time, urban population growth and the rise of the middle class created a growing new audience, and printing presses multiplied in accordance with demand. Many "popular" and best-seller art forms flourished: sermons, true confessions, retellings (and Second Parts) of hot-selling tales and political harangues, news items, hearsay gossip, and science all became jumbled together for public consumption, much of which led to spates of yellow journalism. Throughout his life Swift rebelled against such indelicacies and depravities, and his satiric procedure included the extremist parody of tasteless forms—*reductio ad absurdum*. It was by such means that Swift secured his fame as an author.

Doubtless his most dazzling prose performance of this kind was his earliest, *A Tale of a Tub*, which appeared anonymously in 1704. (Swift, in fact, pub-lished most of his satires anonymously, although his work was usually instantly recognized and acclaimed.) *A Tale of a Tub* is actually a "medley" of pieces imitating the penchant for an author's combining fiction, essays, letters, verse, fragments, or anything to enable him to amass a booklength manuscript. It contained "The Battle of the Books," a wooden allegorical piece in the manner of Aesop's Fables, detailing the "quarrel of ancients versus moderns" and a fragmentary treatise upon "The Mechanical Operation of the Spirit," trussed up in the inept form of a casual letter to a friend.

The treatise mocked the new "scientific" trend of reducing all things to some species of Cartesian (or Newtonian) materialism. Rather comically, it deploys in a blasé manner the language of ancient Greek and Roman atomists—Democritus and Epicurus—as if they were contemporary modernists. Indeed, one pervasive theme throughout this volume is the ridiculousness of the modernist position of "independence"—although they might be ignorant of the past, the ideas and genres of classical antiquity keep recurring in their works, a fact which belies the Moderns' supposed originality (even while demonstrating that, as a result of solipsism, their form and control disintegrate into chaos).

Clearly, the titular piece, "A Tale of a Tub," is Swift's early masterpiece, and one of the great (and most difficult) satires in any language. In its pages, an avowed fanatic "modern" aspires to "get off" an edition, to tout and sell himself, to make money, to demonstrate his uniqueness and, however evanescently, tyrannically to be "the latest modern." He seeks to reedit an old tale of three brothers and their adventures. Naturally, he decorates and updates such a version to give it the latest cut and fashion, the style and wit and jargon of the moment. (It is perhaps an accident that this tale of the dissensions of Peter, Martin, and Jack parallels the vicissitudes of the history of Christianity, as it splinters into differing and quarreling religious sects. The Modern appears ignorant of historical sense.)

The new version of the old story, however, is fragmented: every time the Modern's imagination or his fancy supplies him with a spark, he promptly follows his rather meandering Muse and travels into an elaboration, an annotation, or a digression. In fact, the opening fifty pages of the work is cluttered with the paraphernalia of "modern" publishing: Dedications, Publisher's Comments, Introductions, Apologies, and Gratulations, Notes to the Second Edition, Acknowledgements, Prefaces, and Forewords. Thereafter, when such a cloud of ephemeral formalities would seem to have been dispensed with, the author still manages to interject a plethora of digressions—afterthoughts, asides, cute remarks *à propos* of nothing, commentary, snipings at critics, obsequious snivelings for the reader, canting pseudophilosophy for the learned, and pity and adoration for himself. In no time at all, the entire tale is awash in detours, perambulations, and divagations.

This modern storyteller is nothing if not effervescent, boorish, and chronically self-indulgent. He claims that his pipe dreams and diversions are in essence planned excursions and in fact deliberately philosophic meditations, rich with allegorical meanings. The opposite is also true, and the Modern's Tub is like an empty cart—rattling around most furiously in its vacuity, making the most noise. Furthermore, the digressions become unwieldy. The tale is disrupted more and more frequently and the digressions become longer and longer. The Modern is his most penetrating in the trenchant Section IX—a digression in praise of madness—as he coyly confesses that his reason has been overturned, his intellectuals rattled, and that he has been but recently confined. The continued multiplication of digressions (until they subvert sections of the tale) and the finale when the Modern loses his notes and his ramblings give out entirely are easily understood as the wanderings of a madman—a Modern who suppresses the past, memory, reason, and self-control.

If Swift's warning about the growing taste for nowness, modernity, and things-of-the-moment appears madcap and farcical, it is nevertheless a painfully close nightmare preview of future fashions, fantasms, and fallacies that subsequently came to be real.

A Tale of a Tub clearly demonstrates several of Swift's most common fictional ploys and motifs. Some representative of the depraved "moderns' is usually present, always crass, irreligious, ignorant, arrogant, proud, self-adulatory, concerned with the events of the moment. Indeed, Swift was fond of scrupulously celebrating every April 1 as All Fool's Day, but he also recognized April 2: All Knave's Day. He doubtless felt that both halves of mankind deserved some token of official recognition. Yet Swift also favored mixing the two: he frequently shows readers that a man who is manipulator, conman, and knave in one set of circumstances is himself conned, befooled, and gulled in another. As such, the Modern reveals an unexpected complexity in his makeup; he also illustrates the era (as Swift imagines it) that he inhabits; a period overfull of bad taste and poor writing which are the broad marks of cultural decadence.

In the work of a satirist, the world is regularly depicted as cyclic in historic periods, and usually in decline. Swift and Sir William Temple both stressed some trend toward decay in the modern era, and spoke often of barbarians and invasions; it was a type of satiric myth suitable to the disruptive fictions that the satirist envisions. In Section IX of *A Tale of a Tub*, the Modern vacillates between viewing all mankind as being "curious" or "credulous," as busy probers, analysts, and excavators, and the superficial and the inert: knaves versus fools. As is typical of Swift, the fool and knave personas are infused with enough familiar traits to suggest that all men partake of either. Further, Swift entraps his reader by implying that there are no other categories: one is either fool or knave or both. His irony is corrosive and inclusive, capturing the reader in its toils. In that sense, Swift is deliberately disruptive; he seeks to startle and to embroil the reader in his fictions about stupidity and depravity. To such an end, he tampers with logic to make his case appear substantial and manipulates paradox to keep his readers off balance. Such techniques lend Swift his volatile force.

These strategies are to be found in Swift's best verse; the same may be said for his two great, ironic short-prose pieces: *An Argument Against Abolishing Christianity* (1708) and *A Modest Proposal for Preventing the Children of Poor*

People in Ireland from Being a Burden to Their Parents (1729). Both of these works seek to shock the reader and to propose the discomforting, the alarming, the untenable.

Swift's undisputed masterpiece is the *Travels into Several Remote Nations of the World, in Four Parts, by Lemuel Gulliver, First a Surgeon, and Then a Captain of Several Ships*, better known as *Gulliver's Travels*. This fictional work accommodates all of Swift's perennial themes and does so effectually. First, the work is perhaps the definitive study of new middle-class values, specifically the preoccupation with slang, cash, smug self-righteousness, self-assertion, and self-gratulation. Second, it might not be considered a "novel" in the conventional sense of the term, but it is a delightfully fact-filled simulation of adventure fiction, and it stems assuredly from the satiric picaresque tradition (in Spain and France) that greatly contributed to the formulation of modern novelistic techniques and themes.

Swift's Lemuel Gulliver (a mulish gull) is a model representative of the fool and the knave: he aspires to befool others but nevertheless befuddles himself. His medium is the very popular literary genre of the travelogue or record of a "voyage of discovery." The genre grew popular through its Cartesian emphasis upon an inductive observer-self and the romantic subject of adventures in far-off lands. Such a travelogue format allows the narrator to take his readers on a vicarious journey of adventure and concludes by suggesting that the traveler has fulfilled the pattern of the *Bildungsroman* and has attained education, growth, experience, and Aristotelian *cognitio* (insight, maturation, the acquisition of new knowledge). As might be expected in an exemplary case manipulated by Swift, Gulliver is anything but the apt learner. He is a crass materialist for whom experiences consist of precise measurements of objects observed, a tedious cataloging of dress, diet, and customs, and an infinite variety of pains in note-taking, recording, transcribing, and translating. He is superficiality and rank objectivity incarnate. Naturally, therefore, his everyday mean density prevents his acquisition of any true understanding.

Gulliver is a minor physician, the mediocre little man, anxious, like Daniel Defoe's Robinson Crusoe, to make sight-seeing tours and to acquire cash. His first of four voyages carries him to the land of six-inch mites, the Lilliputians, and his Second Voyage to the land of gargantuan giants, the Brobdingnagians. Gulliver remains myopic in either location, for he can hardly consider that little midgets can (and do) perpetuate monstrous deeds; and, once he perceives that the giants are rather tame, he leaps to the conclusion that they are infinitely superior to other human types (even though their political and social institutions are no better than they should be, given the quirks and flaws of human nature).

In sum, the tour from very small to very large merely stimulates in Gulliver a sense of wondrous contrast: he expects in these different worlds wondrous differences. Amusingly, what the reader finds is much the same, that is the uneven and imperfect human nature. Equally amusing, Gulliver behaves much the same himself in his attempts to ingratiate himself with his "superiors": he aspires to become a successful competitor in all worlds as a "titled" nobleman, a Nardac, a "courtier" with "connections" at court. Like many middle-class people, he is a man in the middle, aspiring above all for upward mobility, mouthing the commonplaces of the day, utterly incapable of judging men and events. He is also the worst sort of traveler; he is a man who sees no farther than his own predilections and preconceptions and who imitates all the manners that he sees around him. Actually, the realms of big and little are merely distortions of the real world. Here, one of the work's central ironies is found in the fact that Gulliver could have learned as much, or as little, if he had stayed at home.

The world of sizes is replaced in the Third Voyage by the world of concepts: the muddled peoples he visits are victims of mathomania and abstraction-worship. At the same time, it is revealed that the world of the past, like the world of the present, has been tainted and corrupt. Even the potentially ideal Struldbruggs—immortals who live forever—are exposed as being far from lucky. They are, rather, especially accursed by the afflictions of impotence, depression, and senility. Swift has, with cartoon facility, carted Gulliver all around the world, showing him the corrosive face of fallen humanity, even among the various robbers, cowards, pirates, and mutineers that had beset him as he traveled in European ships; but Gulliver does not see.

The stage is properly set for the Fourth Voyage. Utilizing his favorite ploys of reversal and entrapment, Swift puts Gulliver into a land of learned and rational horses (the Houyhnhnms) and debauched hairy monkey-like beasts (the Yahoos). Once again, there is no middle ground: all in this world is rational horse or wolfish (and oafish) bestiality. Obviously, Gulliver chooses the equestrian gentlemen as his leaders and masters. (Indeed, throughout all the voyages, Gulliver the conformist has been in quest of a staid position and "masters" who will tell him what to do and grant him praise and sustenance for his slavish adulation.)

Slowly it is revealed, however, the Yahoos are men: Gulliver *is* a debased, gross, and deformed member of the Yahoo tribe; as Swift sweetly and confoundingly phrases it, Gulliver is a "perfect yahoo." The horses themselves rebuff this upstart, and Gulliver, who has undergone every other sort of ignominy in the course of his travels, is finally evicted as an undesirable alien from the horsey paradise. At last, Gulliver thinks he has learned a lesson; he aspires to be a horse, and, back in Europe, he shuns the human species and favors the environs of straw and stables. He has hardly acquired the rationality of his leaders and appears quite mad. Swift's ultimate paradox seems to imply that men can "know" about reason and ideals but can never master or practice them. Yet, even here, Swift cruelly twists the knife at the last moment, for the fond Gulliver, several years later, is revealed as slowly forgetting his intense (and irrational) devotion to the Houyhnhnms and is slowly beginning to be able to tolerate and accept the loathly human race that he had earlier so intransigently spurned. Gulliver cannot even stick to a lesson painfully and rudely learned during many years; he has neither the brains, drive, ambition, nor consistency to keep him on any course. Gulliver's travels eventually get him nowhere.

In sum, *Gulliver's Travels* makes a huge tragicomical case for the absurdity of pretentious man. Gulliver is fool enough to believe that he is progressing and knave enough to boast about it, and to hope to gain some position and affluence from the event. Yet, at his proudest moments, he is little more than a driveller, a gibbering idiot who is raveningly insane. Gulliver's painful experiences and the brute instruction his readers acquire are a caustic finale to much of the heady and bold idealism of the Renaissance, and a cautionary plea for restraint in an era launched on celebrating reason, science, optimism, and enlightenment. Time has shown that Swift was largely right; blithe super-confidence in man, his sciences, and his so-called "progress" is very likely to come enormously to grief. *Gulliver's Travels* speaks to everyman because it addresses crucial issues about the human condition itself.

John R. Clark

Other major works

POETRY: *Cadenus and Vanessa*, 1726; *Verses on the Death of Dr. Swift*, 1731; *On Poetry: A Rapsody*, 1733; *The Poems of Jonathan Swift*, 1937, 1958 (Harold Williams, editor, 3 volumes).

NONFICTION: *A Discourse of the Contests and Dissensions Between the Nobles and the Commons in Athens and Rome*, 1701; *The Battle of the Books*, 1704; *An Argument to Prove That the Abolishing of Christianity in England May, as Things Now Stand, Be Attended with Some Inconveniences, and Perhaps Not Produce Those Many Good Effects Proposed Thereby*, 1708; *A Project for the Advancement of Religion, and the Reformation of Manners By a Person of Quality*, 1709; *The Conduct of the Allies and of the Late Ministry, in Beginning and Carrying on the Present War*, 1711; *A Proposal for Correcting, Improving and Ascertaining the English Tongue, in a Letter to the Most Honourable Robert Earl of Oxford and Mortimer, Lord High Treasurer of Great Britain*, 1712; *The Public Spirit of the Whigs, Set Forth in Their Generous Encouragement of the Author of the Crisis*, 1714; *A Letter from a Lay-Patron to a Gentleman, Designing for Holy Orders*, 1720; *The Drapier's Letters to the People of Ireland*, 1735; *A Modest Proposal for Preventing the Children of Poor People of Ireland from Being a Burden to Their Parents or the Country, and for Making Them Beneficial to the Public*, 1729; *The History of the Four Last Years of the Queen, by the Late Jonathan Swift DD, DSPD*, 1758; *Journal to Stella*, 1766, 1768; *Letter to a Very Young Lady on*

Her Marriage, 1797; *The Correspondence of Jonathan Swift*, 1963-1965 (Harold Williams, editor, 5 volumes).

MISCELLANEOUS: *Miscellanies in Prose and Verse*, 1711; *Miscellanies*, 1727-1733 (by Swift, Alexander Pope, and other members of the Scriblerus Club, 4 volumes); *A Complete Collection of Genteel and Ingenious Conversation, According to the Most Polite Mode and Method Now Used at Court, and in the Best Companies of England, in Three Dialogues, by Simon Wagstaff Esq.*, 1738; *Directions to Servants in General . . .* , 1745; *The Prose Works of Jonathan Swift*, 1939-1968 (Herbert Davis, editor, 14 volumes).

Bibliography

Ehrenpreis, Irvin. *Swift: The Man, His Works, and the Age*. 3 vols. Cambridge, Mass.: Harvard University Press, 1962-1983. A monumental biography that rejects long-held myths, provides much new information about Swift and his works, and relates him to the intellectual and political currents of his age.

Hunting, Robert. *Jonathan Swift*. Rev. ed. Boston: Twayne, 1989. In this revision of his earlier book on Swift, Hunting incorporates recent scholarship to provide an overview of Swift's life and his major works. Includes a chronology and a selective, annotated secondary bibliography.

Nokes, David. *Jonathan Swift, A Hypocrite Reversed: A Critical Biography*. Oxford, England: Oxford University Press, 1985. Draws heavily on Swift's own writings, offering a good introduction for the general reader seeking information about his life and works. Nokes views Swift as a conservative humanist.

Quintana, Ricardo. *The Mind and Art of Jonathan Swift*. 1936. Reprint. London: Oxford University Press, 1953. One of the standards of Swift criticism, concentrating on the public Swift. Examines his political activities and writings, tracing the intellectual sources of his thought. Includes synopses of his major works and provides a useful historical background. The 1953 edition contains additional notes and an updated bibliography.

Rawson, Claude. *The Character of Swift's Satire: A Revised Focus*. Newark: University of Delaware Press, 1983. Presents eleven essays by Swift scholars, including John Traugatt's excellent reading of *A Tale of a Tub*, Irvin Ehrenpreis on Swift as a letter writer, and F. P. Lock on Swift's role in the political affairs of Queen Anne's reign.

Real, Hermann J., and Heinz J. Vienken, eds. *Proceedings of the First Münster Symposium on Jonathan Swift*. Munich: Wilhelm Fink, 1985. Includes twenty-four essays on all aspects of Swift's work, each preceded by an abstract. Indexed for cross-referencing.

WILLIAM MAKEPEACE THACKERAY

Born: Calcutta, India; July 18, 1811
Died: London, England; December 24, 1863

Principal long fiction

Catherine: A Story, 1839-1840 (as Ikey Solomons, Jr.); *The History of Samuel Titmarsh and the Great Hoggarty Diamond*, 1841 (later as *The Great Hoggarty Diamond*, 1848); *The Luck of Barry Lyndon: A Romance of the Last Century*, 1844; *Vanity Fair: A Novel Without a Hero*, 1847-1848; *The History of Pendennis: His Fortunes and Misfortunes, His Friends and His Greatest Enemy*, 1848-1850; *Rebecca and Rowena: A Romance upon Romance*, 1850 (as M. A. Titmarsh); *The History of Henry Esmond, Esquire, a Colonel in the Service of Her Majesty Q. Anne*, 1852 (3 volumes); *The Newcomes: Memoirs of a Most Respectable Family*, 1853-1855; *The Virginians: A Tale of the Last Century*, 1857-1859; *Lovel the Widower*, 1860; *The Adventures of Philip on His Way Through the World, Shewing Who Robbed Him, Who Helped Him, and Who Passed Him By*, 1861-1862; *Denis Duval*, 1864.

Other literary forms

William Makepeace Thackeray's career as a satirist and journalist contributed to his novelistic style. His works appeared in a number of periodicals, including *The National Standard*, which he owned, *The Constitutional*, for which he was Paris correspondent, and *The New Monthly Magazine*. More important, however, the bulk of his writing appeared in *Fraser's Magazine* and in *Punch*, until, in 1860, he became editor of the *Cornhill Magazine*. In many of his reviews, short stories, burlesques, and travel writings, he adopts facetious pen names that reveal the snobbish preconceptions of his personae. "The Yellowplush Correspondence" appeared in *Fraser's Magazine* in 1837-1838 as the supposed diary of Charles James Yellowplush, an illiterate footman who betrays all of the social prejudices of his employers. The story was later published as *Memoirs of Mr. Charles J. Yellowplush* in 1856. Thackeray assumed two pseudonyms for some of his comic pieces. As Michael Angelo Titmarsh, Thackeray published *A Legend of the Rhine* (1845), *Mrs. Perkin's Ball* (1847), and *The Rose and the Ring: Or, The History of Prince Giglio and Prince Bulbo* (1855) among others, in addition to some nonfiction works such as *The Paris Sketch-Book* (1840), *The Irish Sketch-Book* (1843), and *Notes of a Journey from Cornhill to Grand Cairo . . .* (1846); as George Savage Fitz-Boodle, an aging and susceptible bachelor, Thackeray wrote *The Fitz-Boodle Papers* (1852), *The Confessions of George Fitz-Boodle* (1843), and *Men's Wives* (1852). "Punch's Prize Novelists," which appeared in *Punch* magazine, was a series of parodies of popular novelists of the day, such as Benjamin Disraeli and James Fenimore Cooper, and was perhaps even more effective than the burlesque *Catherine* (which he wrote as Ikey Solomons, Jr.). Thackeray's other achievements include *The English Humorists of the Eighteenth Century* (1853) and *The Four Georges: Sketches of Manners, Morals, Court and Town Life* (1860); a number of tales and short stories, including *A Shabby Genteel Story* (1857), and a series of ballads and verses, such as the nostalgic "The Ballad of Bouillabaisse" (1849).

Achievements

Long remembered as a social satirist *par excellence*, Thackeray wrote more in the manner of Henry Fielding than of Samuel Richardson and more in the realistic vein than in the style of the "novel of sensibility," that production of the early nineteenth century that sought to achieve heightened emotional effects at the expense of believable plot and characterization. Both in his miscellaneous writings and in his first great novel, *Vanity Fair*, Thackeray sought to counter the kind of melodramatic and pretentious entertainment provided by such authors as Edward Bulwer-Lytton, William Harrison Ainsworth, and even the early Charles Dickens. He attempted, instead, to make his readers see through the social and literary hypocrisy that, as he believed, characterized the age. To this end, he adopted a number of pseudonyms in his early essay writing, pseudonyms that can be said to foreshadow the personae he used in his fiction.

In reviewing both art and literature for such magazines as *Fraser's Magazine* and *The New Monthly Magazine*, Thackeray adopted the Yellowplush and Titmarsh signatures; he was thus able to ridicule in a lively way what he found false. His reviews were no less devastating to the current trend of idolizing criminals and rogues, as seen in the series of popular "Newgate Novels." As Ikey Solomons, Jr., he produced *Catherine*, the tale of a murderess, but even here, his attempt to deglamorize the account was mitigated by his growing sympathy for his created characters. Again, *A Shabby Genteel Story* attempted to deal with the middle class in unvarnished terms. His first sustained narrative, *The Luck of Barry Lyndon*, features an Irish adventurer recounting his own life; the novel follows the rise and fall of its picaresque hero to illustrate the specious nature of worldly success. Perhaps most telling in his ten-year preparation for fiction writing were two series that appeared in *Punch*. "The Snobs of England" was a series of verbal portraits of social types, most drawn for their pretension; "Punch's Prize Novelists" was a collection of parodic rewritings of popular novelists' works.

In his sustained works, however, Thackeray leaves his readers not with a collection of isolated vignettes but with a panoramic study of mankind under the guidance of a witty persona whose satirical bent is tempered by the realization that he himself partakes of the foibles of his own characters. Thackeray's characteristic persona derives not only from Fielding and his prefaces to the various books of *The History of Tom Jones, a Foundling*

(1749), but also from Samuel Johnson, who ends *The History of Rasselas, Prince of Abyssinia* (1759) by suggesting that since an ideal world is impossible, a wise individual will stoically accept the one that exists. Certainly, Thackeray's experimentations with the persona in *The History of Henry Esmond, Esquire*, for example, a novel written in the memoir form, laid the groundwork for such masters of psychological realism and irony as Henry James and James Joyce. In addition, Thackeray's experimentations with the generational form, in which several novels are melded together through the familial relationships of their characters, look forward to such productions as John Galsworthy's *The Forsyte Saga* (1922). In presenting the affairs of Henry Esmond's grandsons and the development of the beautiful Beatrix Esmond into a worldly old woman in *The Virginians*, he was also implicitly exploring the kind of genetic and environmental influence that the naturalists defined as determinism.

While many modern readers are perhaps not as comfortable as their nineteenth century forebears with the conception of the authorial voice as a constant, even necessary factor in the plot, Thackeray nevertheless remains noteworthy, especially in his early novels, both for the realistic renderings of individuals in all social walks and for his moral standpoint, best expressed in the Preface to *Vanity Fair* as a charitable outlook on human foibles.

Biography

William Makepeace Thackeray was born on July 18, 1811, in Calcutta, India. His father, Richmond Thackeray, pursued a family career in the East India Company; his mother, Anne Becher, traced her ancestry back to a sixteenth century sheriff of London. The senior William Makepeace Thackeray and John Harman Becher had extensive interests in India. After his father's death in 1815, Thackeray's mother married Major Henry Carmichael-Smith, a former suitor. As was the custom, Thackeray was sent to England at the age of five for reasons of health and education. His unhappy, early experiences at the Arthurs' school and at Chiswick were later rendered in "Dr. Birch and his Young Friends" (1849). At Cambridge, as a member of a privileged class, he was trained in the standards and preconceptions that he later pilloried in his *The Book of Snobs* (1848, 1852) and in many other works. He was left with a distaste for bullying and with a distrust of his own intellectual abilities. After two years at Cambridge, Thackeray abandoned the pursuit of academic honors. Although he believed that his education had, on the whole, served him ill, it nevertheless had given him a background in history and culture, a double appreciation that is well evidenced in *The History of Henry Esmond, Esquire*; it also convinced him of his social status, although his expensive aristocratic habits were to prove difficult to control.

The gentle satire evident in *Vanity Fair*'s Pumpernickel chapters reflect Thackeray's happy six-month tour of Germany before he undertook to study law in London. While the discipline soon proved not to his taste, his life as a gentleman of fashion (a life that included large gambling debts) was congenial, at least until the collapse of many of the Indian commercial houses reversed his inheritance prospects. Almost relieved to be forced to make his own way, Thackeray decided to develop his talent for drawing, making friends with Daniel Maclise and being tutored by George Cruikshank. While in Paris studying art, he met and married Isabella Shawe, the daughter of a Colonel in the Indian army. He endeavored to support his family through journalistic activities, even offering to illustrate Charles Dickens' *Pickwick Papers* (1836-1837). His friendship with Daniel Maginn made his "Yellowplush Papers" welcome in the columns of *Fraser's Magazine*, whose readers were regaled with the malapropisms of a rascally footman. In addition, he wrote for the London *Times* and for a number of obscure journals. His first long attempt at fiction was *Catherine*, a parody of the "Newgate Novel"; in quick succession he produced *A Shabby Genteel Story* and *The Paris Sketch-Book*.

In 1840, Thackeray was visited by domestic calamity; upon the birth of their third daughter, his wife, Isabella, went insane and required institutionalization. The child-rearing was assumed by Thackeray's parents, leaving him to recoup his writing career, initially with *The Great Hoggarty Diamond* and shortly with contributions to *Punch* and the *Morning Chronicle*. During these middle years, Thackeray solaced himself for the want of domestic connections with a series of friendships with old Cambridge acquaintances such as Alfred Tennyson and W. H. Brookfield, as well as with journalistic brethren such as Francis Sylvester Mahoney (the "Father Prout" of *Fraser's Magazine* fame) and with Dickens himself, whom Thackeray could, however, never accept as a "gentleman." His travel literature was published at this time. His connection with *Punch*, begun in 1842, was an important one. From contributing fillers, he went on to write a number of series; moreover, Thackeray's rivalry with the other principal writer, Douglass Jerrold, was to affect the course of *Punch's* publishing history, turning the tide from radicalism and democracy to a Whiggish conservatism of which Dickens himself much disapproved.

The year 1847 was crucial for Thackeray. He began to parody novels for *Punch* in the "Punch's Prize Novelists" series, he began a long platonic affair with Jane Brookfield, and he published *Vanity Fair*, the novel that has achieved abiding interest for its panoramic social view and its narrator's satircal viewpoint. His four-year relationship with Jane Brookfield certainly affected his writing; much of the nostalgia and agonizing provoked by the affair are reproduced in *The History of Henry Esmond, Esquire*. Just as important was his entreé into aristocratic circles, for he, along with his daughters Anny and Minnie, with whom he had set up an establishment in Kensington, were welcome not only at Holland House but also in the demirep world of Lady Blessington. Leaving his daughters was the only blight on his first American tour in 1852, when he lectured about "English Humorists of the Eighteenth Century" and marveled at the way in which the *nouveau riche* mingled with the best society.

Upon his return, Thackeray entered the height of the London social season and visited his daughters in Paris. He began *The Newcomes*, a novel much interrupted by illness but, even as its title suggests, much influenced by his social experiences. His work on the "Four Georges," an indictment of the House of Hanover as well as of the monarchy and the upper classes, indicated his changed attitudes. After his second American tour (undertaken, like the first, to provide stipends for his daughters), Thackeray not only published *The Virginians*, but also became editor of *Cornhill Magazine*, a project that allowed him to move "out of novel-spinning back into the world" of the essay. The periodical was an immediate success, publishing such authors as Anthony Trollope and George Henry Lewes. Although Thackeray retired as editor in 1862, he continued to publish his "Roundabout Papers" there until the year after. Indeed, his last unfinished novel, *Denis Duval*, appeared in *Cornhill Magazine* posthumously in 1864, after Thackeray had died on December 24, 1863, in London.

Analysis

While William Makepeace Thackeray may indeed be best known as the author of *Vanity Fair*, to examine all of his novels is to understand why his contribution to the history of the novel is singular. His use of the intrusive narrator, although presaged by Henry Fielding, was developed so carefully that it became a new form of fiction, a "genuine creation of narrative experiment," as critic Alexander Welsh calls it. In addition, his panoramic realism—although creating that anathema of Henry James, the novel that is "a loose and baggy monster"—explored, both seriously and satirically, a number of topics from which other Victorian writers shied away, such as married life and the development of the middle-class gentleman.

Quite aside from the interest generated by the story line, many of Thackeray's novels offer explanations of the art of creating fiction as well as criticism of some of his contemporaries' inadequacies. When Amelia in *Vanity Fair*, for example, tries to visualize George's barracks, the doors are closed to her, for the romantic imagination is in all respects inadequate to the exigencies of real life. In *The Newcomes*, Thackeray compares his method of character-building to the work of the paleontologist who discovers a series of bones and who must construct the habits, behavior, and appearance of his subject from a mere skeleton. He thereby suggests that any such "reality" is merely an illusion, for like the paleontologist, the author must work with probabilities. Insofar as his characters follow a probable course of events, they are true to life and, in a sense, interact without the help of the author. That Thackeray meant his novels to be something more than believable illusionary worlds is clear when his conclusions are examined. In *The Newcomes*, for example, Thackeray retreats at the end from Pendennis' narrative to suggest that the sentimental world he has created has no basis in fact, although the reader may believe so if he wishes to delude himself, and in the well-known ending to *Vanity Fair*, Thackeray puts his "puppets"—his characters—back into their box.

Rather than following Samuel Taylor Coleridge's idea of "willing suspension of disbelief," Thackeray is philosophical, inviting the reader into a reconsideration of his own or of conventional beliefs and preconceptions. Certainly, Thackeray's satire is operative here, particularly in his *Punch* series, in *Catherine*, and in *The Luck of Barry Lyndon*, in which he deliberately spoofed popular historical, crime, and romantic novels, respectively. The reader is asked to look at more than literary conventions, however; he is asked to examine his own degree of hypocrisy and snobbery. In so doing, the reader is reminded again and again that if he laughs at his neighbors, he condemns himself. Thackeray's work is thus truly homiletic, both in a literary and in an extraliterary sense. Unlike many of his predecessors, he examined in detail the difficulties occasioned not only by marriage but also by other personal relationships; rather than assuming that a novel should end with marriage, he makes it his subject. Certainly, his personally tragic domestic situation and his affair with Jane Brookfield are reflected in Rachel Esmond's trials with her reckless husband in Henry Esmond's growing love for her. In the family chronicle *The Newcomes*, Thackeray looks at the misery occasioned by parental marriage choices; Mrs. Mackenzie (known as the "Campaigner"), a strong-minded virago who runs her daughter's life, is modeled on Mrs. Shawe, Isabella's termagant mother. Finally, in *The Virginians*, he traces the development of family characteristics and family ties.

Another one of the many senses in which Thackeray's novels are educative is the way in which he redefines the word "gentleman" to apply not to a member of a particular social class, but rather to one who possesses a set of personal characteristics, such as clear-sightedness, delicacy, generosity, and humanitarianism. His upper-class upbringing in India as well as his Cambridge education coupled with his love of the high life would seem to mitigate against such a redefinition, but, in fact, it is the greengrocer's son, Dobbin, in *Vanity Fair* who is the gentleman, rather than the pompous, vain George Osborne, and it is Colonel Newcome who, despite his misguided attempts to settle his son Clive's happiness, emerges as the paradigmatical enemy to snobbery and to greed.

Vanity Fair, whose title is taken from John Bunyan's *The Pilgrim's Progress*, (1678, 1684), proved to be Thackeray's most successful novel. Indeed, its attention to realistic detail and its panoramic sweep, to say nothing of the constant presence of the author-cum-narrator, caused many reviewers to label Thackeray "the Fielding of the nineteenth century." While neither the initial reviews nor the sales were immediately promising, interest in the serial grew steadily until the publication of the hard-backed volume guaranteed the author a financial as well as a critical success. Rivaling Thackeray at the time was Charles Dickens, whose *Dombey and Son* (1848) appealed to a wide audience; even Thackeray himself, upon reading the number containing little Paul's death, despaired about writing "against such power." Thackeray, however, had his own power, that of the saritist who created "A Novel Without a Hero" and thus ran counter to his readership's expectations, and that of the moralist who included his reader and himself in his reflective view of society.

The hero that *Vanity Fair* must do without is the typically romantic hero. George Osborne (whose first name conjures up the dandified Regency court) is handsome, dashing, and well-loved, but he is also vain, shallow, and pompous. After Joseph Sedley has gone bankrupt, George marries the pining Amelia Sedley only at the urging of his friend William Dobbin; during their honeymoon, he engages in a flirtation with Becky Sharp, herself newly married to Rawdon Crawley. Killed at the battle of Waterloo, George is cherished as a hero only by Amelia. Dobbin is at the other extreme: gangly, awkward, and low in social standing, he is nevertheless possessed of compassion and understanding, yet he is so blinded by his selfless love for Amelia that he does not see until the end of the novel on how slight a character he has set his affection. Even Rawdon, who develops from a typical "heavy dragoon" who lives by his gambling into an affectionate father for his neglected son, lacks intellectual acumen, and, after his separation from Becky, accepts the post that her prostitution to Lord Steyne earned him.

As A. E. Dyson suggests, Thackeray is indeed writing "an irony against heroes"—and against heroines as well. Amelia and Becky are as different as George and Dobbin. Initally, Amelia seems to be a conventional heroine, but the reader who views her in that light will be shocked to discover that he is idealizing the passivity, self-sacrifice, and hero-worship that are the earmarks of neuroticism, the three characteristics well seen in her treatment of her son Georgy, who is absurdly spoiled despite Amelia's and her parents' penury. No wonder, then, that readers preferred "the famous little Becky puppet" for her wit and ambition. From the moment she rides away from Miss Pinkerton's finishing school, leaving Dr. Johnson's dictionary lying in the mud, her energy in making a place for herself in society is impressive. Failing to entangle Amelia's brother Jos, she eventually marries Rawdon, the favorite of his wealthy aunt, and only repines when Lord Crawley himself proposes—too late. She turns her very bohemianism into an asset as she gains entry into the best society, and while she claims that she too could be a "good woman on £5000 a year," her energy in luring dupes to Rawdon's card table, wheedling jewels from Lord Steyne, being presented to the king, and playing charades at a social affair, belies her claim. As John Loofbourow shows, as Becky comes into social ascendency, Amelia declines into obscurity. Amelia lacks Becky's energy, while Becky lacks Amelia's morality. In the end, when

Dobbin has won his prize, Becky has devolved into a female picaresque rogue, traveling across the Continent from disreputable gaming table to questionable boarding house. Neither she nor Amelia qualifies as a heroine.

It is Thackeray's Preface that reveals the moral purpose behind his satire. Posing as the "Manager of the Performance," Thackeray reminds his readers that they are embarked on a fictional journey through an emblematic Vanity Fair, an evocation related only partly to the original in Bunyan's work. Vanity Fair, for Thackeray, is a representation of the human condition; it is not for the reader, like Bunyan's Christian, to pass through and eschew its lures, but rather to experience it "in a sober, contemplative, not uncharitable frame of mind," for the reader and author alike are part of the fair. Thackeray's comments throughout serve the purpose of distancing the reader from the characters and forcing him to judge not only the created "puppets" but also his own preconceptions. If everyone is indeed part of the fair, to condemn the booth-owners' hypocrisy, or social climbing, or snobbery, or mendacity, is to condemn one's own failings. To be possessed of "charity"—to be able to pity others with the same care one has for oneself—this, Thackeray suggests, is the best that can be expected when the puppets are put back in the box.

The subtitle of *The History of Pendennis*—"His Fortunes and Misfortunes, His Friends and His Greatest Enemy"—gives ample indication that the novel is a *Bildungsroman*. As Juliet McMaster points out, however, it is also a *Künstlerroman*; that is, a tale about the development of an artist. It is perforce autobiographical, detailing as it does the way in which a young man learns enough about the world and himself to become a writer of "good books." The novel is important in a study of Thackeray's technique, presenting, as it does, the background for the persona who was to narrate *The Newcomes* and showing Thackeray's struggles with Victorian prudery. Indeed, in his Preface he complains that his readers, unlike those of Fielding, are unwilling to accept a truthful portrayal of human beings unless they are given "a conventional simper." Thackeray's reviewers, however, welcomed the novel, their only complaint being the cynicism with which he endowed Pen. Such cynicism refutes Henry James, Sr.'s remark that Thackeray "had no ideas," for Thackeray's wryness results from a consideration of political and religious turmoil, from the "skepticism" brought about by the 1848 French Revolution, and from the controversy occasioned by the Oxford movement and Cardinal John Henry Newman's conversion from Anglicanism to Catholicism. Clearly, one reason for Thackeray's contemporary appeal was that he reflected the very doubts of his own readers, for whom belief was an exercise in paradox.

The tension between the heart and the world that animates *The History of Pendennis* is well represented by the frontispiece to the first volume, in which a youthful figure is clasped on one side by a woman representing marital duty and on the other by a mermaid representing the siren lure of worldly temptations. Within the dictates of the plot, the same tension is demonstrated by the demands of Pen's sentimental mother, Helen Pendennis, who urges her son to marry the domestic Laura, her ward, and those of his uncle, Major Pendennis, who is willing to blackmail his acquaintance, Sir Francis Clavering, so that Pen can have a seat in Parliament and the hand of Clavering's wealthy but artificial daughter Blanche. Between the two, Pen must, as McMaster points out, find his own reality; he must acquire "his uncle's keen perception without the withering selfishness" and participate in his mother's world of emotions without engaging in "romantic illusion." Pen's education progresses primarily through his amours, but also through his choice of career, for to be a writer, he must determine the relationship between fact and fiction.

Pen's abiding interest in the nature of experience makes his involvement with an actress allegorical in nature. His first affair is with Emily Costigan (known as "the Fotheringay"), an Irish actress older than he and one who plays her parts serenely unconscious of their philosophical implications; her ignorance Pen passes off as "adorable simplicity." Extricated by his uncle, who "lends" Emily's father a small sum in return for Pen's love letters, Pen next enters Oxbridge, and then, influenced by his roommate, George Warrington, determines to study law and to become a writer. His affair with Fanny Bolton, the daughter of his landlady, is again one of an attraction to "adorable simplicity," and his consequent illness a kind of purgation. His attachment to Blanche Clavering is more serious and more dangerous, for Blanche is a social "actress" with whom Pen plays the role of world-weary lover. With her he believes he has matured because he is willing to compromise with disillusionment. His real moment of maturity comes, however, when he finds that he cannot put up with his uncle's worldliness, for in discovering that Clavering's second marriage is bigamous and that the Baronet is paying blackmail money to his wife's first husband, the Major in turn blackmails Clavering to give up his seat in Parliament to Pen and to cede his estate to Blanche.

Pen's responsible decision to honor his proposal to Blanche despite the resultant scandal is, in fact, unnecessary, for she jilts him for a more suitable match, freeing him to marry Laura, whose steadfast, honest devotion represents the alternative to Blanche's sham affection. Laura, in fact, is Pen's muse, his living "laurel wreath"; she has insight and a critical faculty that force Pen to come face to face with himself. With her, Pen finally frees himself from both romantic illusion and worldly disillusionment.

Like Dickens, who turned from the largely unplotted "loose and baggy monsters" of his novelistic apprenticeship to produce the tightly controlled *Dombey and Son*, Thackeray moved from the looseness occasioned by serial publication to the careful construction of *The History of Henry Esmond, Esquire*, more commonly known as *Henry Esmond*. While the novelist Anthony Trollope agreed with Thackeray that the book was his "*very* best," initial critical reaction was mixed, ranging from high praise for Thackeray's realism to a scandalized outcry against what Gordon Ray calls the "emotional pattern" of the work—Esmond's marriage to Lady Castlewood, his cousin and senior by eight years. All agreed, however, that the novel was profoundly moving. Much of its power is owing to its genesis: written when Thackeray was recovering from his alienation from Jane Brookfield, the novel reflects his own emotional current, his nostalgia, his suffering, and his wish-fulfillment. In addition, *Henry Esmond* may be read on many levels—as historical fiction, as novel of manners, and as romance.

Superficially, Thackeray might seem an unlikely figure to write a historical novel, inasmuch as he composed a series of parodies of "costume dramas" (as he called them) for *Punch* and inasmuch as the historical novel was going out of fashion by 1852. Nevertheless, because Thackeray was steeped in seventeenth century history, the work has a verisimilitude that, in the view of some critics, allowed him to outstrip even Sir Walter Scott. The point of view he adopts, that of the first-person narrator, adds to the illusion. This tour de force is accomplished with a success that even Henry James, the master of psychological realism, might envy. The entire story is presented from the limited point of view of Esmond, the cheated heir of the Castlewood estate, who is adopted by his cousins, falls in love with the beautiful but irresponsible Beatrix Esmond, and for her sake joins the Jacobite cause; then, when Beatrix becomes the Pretender's mistress, he realigns himself on the side of the Stuarts, marries Beatrix's mother, and emigrates to America.

That Thackeray could, through a limited narrator, represent the complexity of Lady Castlewood's growing love for the innocent and unconscious Henry is remarkable in its own right. Thackeray's own memories of his boyhood helped him to re-create Henry's loneliness; his relationship with Jane Brookfield shaped his characterization of Lady Castlewood. As John Tilford points out, Thackeray prepares carefully for the marriage, doubtless aware that it challenged many readers' expectations and moral assumptions. Through nuances of dialogue, Rachel Castlewood's awareness of her feelings and of Henry's is revealed. A number of crucial scenes prepare for the denouement: Rachel's hysterical reaction to Henry's early affair with the blacksmith's daughter, an affair that brings smallpox to the family; her vituperation of Henry as he lies in prison for his involvement in a duel that killed Lord Castlewood, whose drinking, gambling, and hunting had contributed to a loveless marriage; and, finally, her overwhelming joy when she sees Henry after his long period of military service.

One early criticism of the novel was recorded by William Harrison Ainsworth, with whom Thomas Carlyle joined in objecting to the exultation of "sentiment above duty" in the novel; other critics found the comparison between the excitement of romantic love and marital unhappiness to be dangerous. The more sophisticated analysis of McMaster registers an "ironic tension" between "Rachel's moral rectitude and . . . the psychological damage" it can cause.

Like Henry James's Mme. de Mauves, Rachel is possessed of a cool virtue based on a conviction of moral and intellectual superiority; as McMaster suggests, she may indeed welcome evidence of her husband's coarseness as a way of rationalizing her affection for Henry and may therefore be responsible for exacerbating her husband's untoward behavior. Thackeray does give both sides: while Castlewood, like Fielding's Squire Western, is rough and careless, pursuing a prodigal, adulterous life once his wife has lost her beauty to smallpox, he accuses her of pride and of a blighting coldness, and pleads for "the virtue that can forgive." Even Beatrix complains that her mother's saintliness provided so impossible a model that she was driven to ambitious selfishness. Such complaints themselves sound like rationalizations, however, for at the end of the novel, Rachel has undergone a long period of repentance. Having sent her temptation—Henry—away, she lives with the renunciation of happiness while he matures. Upon his return, then, she is no longer an angel, but, as he says, "more fondly cherished as woman perhaps than ever she had been adored as divinity."

Subtitled *The Memoirs of a Most Respectable Family*, *The Newcomes* is a novel of manners that explores the way in which four generations of a nouveau riche family acquire social respectability. The novel, the first third of which is densely packed with background material and consequently slow-moving, is a deliberate return to the serial format that Thackeray had abandoned in *Henry Esmond*. While some modern critics object to the pace of this "monster," nineteenth century reviewers believed that with this novel, Thackeray had outstripped even Dickens, whose antiutilitarian manifesto, *Hard Times* (1854), was running concurrently. To be sure, a number of reviewers noted some repetition in theme and characters, a charge against which Thackeray defended himself in the "Overture" but admitted to in private, acknowledging a failure of invention because of sheer exhaustion. One such "repetition," which is, in fact, a way of extending the scope of the novel, is that Pendennis is the "editor" of the Newcome memoirs. This device allows Thackeray not only to assume an objective stance from which his satire is more telling, but also to criticize the very social punctiliousness that Pendennis reveals, thereby achieving an advanced form of psychological analysis.

What provides the novel's "unifying structural principle," as McMaster notes, is "the repetition of the mercenary marriage and its outcome between various couples." This theme, however, is a manifestation of the larger examination of the nature of "respectability," as the subtitle implies. For Barnes Newcome, the banker, for the aristocratic Lady Kew, and even for her granddaughter, Ethel Newcome, affection and generosity are weighed against wealth and social position and found wanting. The touchstone figure is Colonel Thomas Newcome, Barnes's half brother; unworldly, honest, and loving, he is seen by Gordon Ray as a model of Christian humility. The underlying cynicism of the novel is underscored by the inability of the characters to gain happiness, whether they satisfy their acquisitiveness or rebel against such a value, for Thackeray reminds his readers that real fulfillment only exists in "Fable-land."

To pursue the marriage theme is to understand that in Thackeray's world even the best intentions go awry. Certainly, the unhappiness that accrues in some relationships seems self-created: while the joining of money and class in Barnes's marriage to Lady Clara Pulleyn satisfies the dictates of the marriage market, Barnes's brutality drives his wife to elope with a former suitor. In contrast, Clive Newcome, the Colonel's son, is forbidden by Lady Kew to marry Ethel because his profession as an artist is unacceptable. Even Clive himself is infected by the view, for he neglects his modest muse to devote himself to society. For his part, the Colonel, seeing Clive's unhappiness, schemes to marry him to the sweet but shallow Rosey Mackenzie, the niece of his old friend James Binnie. The loveless though well-intentioned match is unhappy, for Clive longs for Ethel's companionship and the couple is tormented by the dictatorial Mrs. Mackenzie after the Colonel's bankruptcy.

Ethel, like Becky Sharp and Beatrix Esmond, is a complex heroine, one who, through much trial and error, weans herself from the respectable avarice she was reared to accept. In love with Clive despite her relations' objections, she nevertheless admits that she delights in admiration, fine clothes, and jewelry, and, although she despises herself for it, that she enjoys being a coquette. Her fine sense of irony about the marriage market, however, prompts her to wear a "sold" ticket pinned to her dress, much to the annoyance of her respectable relatives. At first affianced to Lord Frank Kew, she breaks the engagement; then, capitulating to social pressure, pursues the feeble-minded Lord Farintosh, only to repent at the last moment when the devastation of Barnes's marriage, on which her own is to be patterned, is borne in upon her. In revulsion from her family's values, she devotes herself to Barnes's children and manages to divert some of the Newcome fortune to the impoverished Colonel and his son.

Ethel's "conversion" and Rosey's death do not, however, lead necessarily to a happy ending, for in the years of following Ethel hopelessly, of neglecting his painting, and, finally, of engaging in a loveless marriage, Clive has become less resilient, more demoralized. Indeed, a conventional ending to *The Newcomes* would be as unwieldy as the happy denouement that Dickens was persuaded to tack on to *Great Expectations* (1860-1861). All Thackeray does promise is that in "Fable-land . . . Ethel and Clive are living most comfortably together." As McMaster points out, "poetic justice does not operate in life, however it operates in romance and fairytale." In the end, Thackeray refuses to cater to weak sentimentality.

Written while Thackeray was fighting a lingering illness, *The Virginians* is a long, formless novel, many of whose characters appear in earlier works. The weight of critical opinion, both contemporary and twentieth century, implies that Thackeray, as he well suspected, was at the end of his fictional powers. To Walter Bagehot, the novelist merely presented an "annotated picture," and, indeed, many complained about the plethora of details that substituted for imaginative creation. Thackeray's habit of digressing grew more pronounced, aided by his failure to preserve a distance between himself and his persona for the second half of the novel, the sardonic George Warrington. Connected with such digressions was Thackeray's increasing propensity to justify himself in the eyes of his critics; such justification introduced in a work of fiction was as gratuitous, many felt, as the air of mordant rumination that colored the novel.

On the other hand, Thackeray's supporters cited his adept portraiture of character and his classical style. Geoffrey Tillotson's suggestion that all of Thackeray's works are like one long novel well represents this point of view. In reviving earlier characters and in introducing their descendants, Thackeray studies the development of character traits as well as repetitive familial situations. Beatrix Esmond, for example, having been mistress to the Pretender and the King and having buried two husbands, one a bishop, reappears as a fleshy old woman with a caustic tongue and piercing black eyes. The enigmatic George Washington in *The History of Pendennis* reappears in the person of his namesake; George and Henry Warrington are twin sons of Rachel, Henry Esmond's daughter.

Unfortunately, Thackeray was unable to pursue his original plan, which was to place the brothers on opposite sides in the Revolutionary War and to insert real-life sketches of such figures as Oliver Goldsmith and Dr. Samuel Johnson. The American section was foreshortened, although Thackeray's prodigious reading in American history lends it a remarkably realistic air— so realistic that some American readers were initially incensed that George Washington should be portrayed in so commonplace a light. The book falls into halves, the first reserved for the English adventures of the innocent, gullible Henry. As Gordon Ray points out, the theme, although difficult to discern, is "the contrast between American innocence and Old World corruption."

Henry becomes involved with his cousins at Castlewood, who welcome him as the heir of the Virginia estates, on the supposition that George has died in the battle of Fort Duquesne. Enticed into a proposal by the elderly Maria and encouraged to dissipate his fortune by his infamous cousins, Henry is rescued from debt by his twin, who had not died but was taken prisoner by the French. Deceived by his fortune-seeking relatives, Henry returns to Virginia to marry the housekeeper's daughter. The second half, narrated by George, details his adventures in London. Kept on short funds by his mother, he marries Theo Lambert, the daughter of the gentlemanly General Lambert, a figure much like Colonel Newcome.

Even a brief plot outline of *The Virginians* reveals a number of Thackeray's recurring themes. The attraction of young men to older women is one: just as Henry Esmond married Rachel, many years his senior, so his grandson becomes attached to Maria, and, conversely, so his mother, Mrs. Esmond Warrington, becomes attached to a much younger suitor. The dogmatic and clinging nature of the parent-child relationship is another, much-explored theme: Hetty Lambert gives up her love for Harry to nurture the General, who is loathe to let either of his daughters leave; Mrs. Esmond Warrington throws impediments in the way of George's marriage to Theo; even George himself meditates on his fear that his own daughters will eventually marry. In the final analysis, while *The Virginians* is justly faulted for its digressiveness, Thackeray's treatment of character and his mellow, pure style grant to this work what Gordon Ray calls "a modest vitality."

Overshadowed in modern assessments by his great contemporaries, Dickens and George Eliot, Thackeray is an essential figure in the history of the English novel, and his masterpiece, *Vanity Fair*, is among the great novels in the language. It is with this work that Thackeray is assured a place among the great authors in British literature.

Patricia Marks

Other major works

SHORT FICTION: *The Yellowplush Papers*, 1937-1938; *Some Passages in the Life of Major Gahagan*, 1838-1839; *Stubb's Calendar: Or, The Fatal Boots*, 1839; *Barber Cox and the Cutting of His Comb*, 1840; *The Bedford-Row Conspiracy*, 1840; *Comic Tales and Sketches*, 1841 (2 volumes); *The Confessions of George Fitz-Boodle, and Some Passages in the Life of Major Gahagan*, 1841-1842; *Men's Wives*, 1843 (as George Savage Fitz-Boodle); *A Legend of the Rhine*, 1845 (as M. A. Titmarsh); *Jeame's Diary: Or, Sudden Wealth*, 1846; *The Snobs of England, by One of Themselves*, 1846-1847 (later as *The Book of Snobs*, 1848, 1852); *Mrs. Perkin's Ball*, 1847 (as M. A. Titmarsh); *'Our Street,'* 1848 (as M. A. Titmarsh); *A Little Dinner at Timmins's*, 1848; *Doctor Birch and His Young Friends*, 1849 (as M. A. Titmarsh); *The Kickleburys on the Rhine*, 1850 (as M. A. Titmarsh); *A Shabby Genteel Story and Other Tales*, 1852; *The Rose and the Ring: Or, The History of Prince Giglio and Prince Bulbo*, 1855 (as M. A. Titmarsh); *Memoirs of Mr. Charles J. Yellowplush [with] The Diary of C. Jeames De La Pluche, Esqr.*, 1856.

PLAY: *The Wolves and the Lamb*, 1854.

POETRY: *The Chronicle of the Drum*, 1841.

NONFICTION: *The Paris Sketch Book*, 1840 (as M. A. Titmarsh, 2 volumes); *The Irish Sketch Book*, 1843 (as *M. A. Titmarsh*, 2 volumes); *Notes of a*

Journey from Cornhill to Grand Cairo, by Way of Lisbon, Athens, Constantinople and Jerusalem, Performed in the Steamers of the Penninsular and Oriental Company, 1846 (as M. A. Titmarsh); *The English Humourists of the Eighteenth Century*, 1853; *Sketches and Travels in London*, 1856; *The Four Georges: Sketches of Manners, Morals, Court and Town Life*, 1860.

Bibliography

Bloom, Harold, ed. *William Makepeace Thackeray*. New York: Chelsea House, 1987. This critical anthology brings together major essays on Thackeray's main novels. Includes a chronology and a bibliography.

Carey, John. *Thackeray: Prodigal Genius*. London: Faber & Faber, 1977. Takes a thematic approach, concentrating on his earlier writings and the shaping of Thackeray's imagination, especially its obsessive quality. The last two chapters relate this theme to the later fiction, *Vanity Fair* in particular. Indexed.

Colby, Robert A. *Thackeray's Canvass of Humanity: An Author and His Public*. Columbus: Ohio State University Press, 1979. Colby seeks to capture Thackeray's "Protean" personality as expressed in his fiction. A very full text which contains a chronology.

Hardy, Barbara. *The Exposure of Luxury: Radical Themes in Thackeray*. London: Peter Owen, 1972. Takes a thematic approach to Thackeray's fiction, seeking to demonstrate the satiric and revolutionary feeling behind it. The themes covered include love, feasting, art and nature, and the exploitation of art.

Peters, Catherine. *Thackeray's Universe: Shifting Worlds of Imagination and Reality*. Boston: Faber & Faber, 1987. Relates Thackeray's fiction to his life, stressing particularly Thackeray's challenge to his society. A selected bibliography is provided.

PAUL THEROUX

Born: Medford, Massachusetts; April 10, 1941

Principal long fiction

Waldo, 1967; *Fong and the Indians*, 1968; *Murder in Mount Holly*, 1969; *Girls at Play*, 1969; *Jungle Lovers*, 1971; *Saint Jack*, 1973; *The Black House*, 1974; *The Family Arsenal*, 1976; *Picture Palace: A Novel*, 1978; *The Mosquito Coast*, 1982; *Half Moon Street: Two Short Novels*, 1984; *O-Zone*, 1986; *My Secret History*, 1989; *Chicago Loop*, 1991.

Other literary forms

In addition to a steady stream of novels, Paul Theroux has also published three collections of short stories, *Sinning with Annie* (1972), *The Consul's File* (1977), and *World's End* (1980); a volume of criticism, *V. S. Naipaul: An Introduction to His Work* (1972); two travel books, *The Great Railway Bazaar: By Train Through Asia* (1975) and *The Old Patagonian Express: By Train Through the Americas* (1979); and two collections of children's stories, *A Christmas Card* (1978) and *London Snow: A Christmas Story* (1980). In addition to his books, Theroux has also written numerous reviews and articles, many of them based on his perceptions of events in the non-Western world; these are to be found in newspapers and periodicals such as *The New York Times Magazine*, the *Sunday Times* (of London), *Harper's*, and *Encounter*.

Achievements

It is in the quirky nature of fame that Theroux, a prolific writer of novels, should be better known for his travel writing than for his fiction. *The Great Railway Bazaar* became a best-seller in 1975, gaining for Theroux both popular and commercial success. A second travel book, *The Old Patagonian Express*, published four years later, firmly established his popular reputation. Both offer the reader elegant and humane examples of a genre widely practiced between the world wars but not much seen today.

In the long run, however, Theroux's achievement will rest upon his fiction. At forty, Theroux has earned a reputation as a serious novelist. He has won a small share of awards for his work, including four Playboy Editorial Awards for fiction (1972, 1976, 1977, and 1979), the Literature Award from the American Academy of Arts and Letters (1977), and the Whitbread Prize for Fiction (for *Picture Palace*, 1978). In 1982, he won the James Tait Black Award and the *Yorkshire Post* Best Novel of the Year Award for *The Mosquito Coast*. In 1984, Theroux was inducted into the American Academy and Institute of Arts and Letters. *The Mosquito Coast* was filmed, starring Harrison Ford, in 1986; *Half Moon Street* was also turned into a film in 1986, starring Sigourney Weaver and Michael Caine.

Theroux writes in the best tradition of English literature, demonstrating a mastery of fictional conventions as well as a willingness to grapple with some of the thornier issues of modern life. Critics have compared him to, among others, Charles Dickens, Joseph Conrad, Somerset Maugham, Graham Greene, and Evelyn Waugh. Interested in neither the splashy innovations of a Donald Barthelme nor the lurid headline material of a Norman Mailer, Theroux will nevertheless be a novelist to follow as he continues to engage the essential dilemmas of the late twentieth century.

Biography

Paul Edward Theroux was born of French-Canadian and Italian parentage in Medford, Massachusetts, in 1941, the third of the seven children of Albert and Anne Theroux. Literature and writing were important aspects of his early life. Albert Theroux, a leather salesman, read daily to the family from the classics and encouraged the publication of family newspapers. For his efforts, he was rewarded with two novelists: Paul, and his brother Alexander.

After conventional public schooling and a B.A. in English from the University of Massachusetts, Theroux volunteered for the Peace Corps in 1963 to escape the draft. He taught English in Malawi for two years until he was expelled for his unwitting involvement in the convolutions of African politics. From Malawi, Theroux went to Makerere University in Kampala, Uganda, where he lectured on seventeenth century English literature and maintained a careful political stance during the beginnings of Idi Amin's rise to power. At Makerere, Theroux met V. S. Naipaul, who became for a time his literary mentor. Theroux left Uganda in 1968 after being trapped in a street riot and went to Singapore, where he spent the next three years lecturing at the university.

Throughout this period, Theroux was writing prodigiously, both fiction and reportage, which he published in a variety of journals, both African and European. In 1967, he married Anne Castle, then also a teacher, and fathered two sons, Louis and Marcel. In 1972, judging himself able to earn his living by his pen alone, Theroux gave up teaching and moved his family to London, where he still lives most of the time, summering on Cape Cod.

The Catholic background, the leftish political interests, the ten years in Africa and Asia, the friendship with V. S. Naipaul—these heterogeneous influences have all left their mark on Theroux's fiction. At the same time, one notes how Theroux secularizes, liberalizes, and makes contemporary the Catholic ethic; turns the African experience into a metaphor for all social experience; and absorbs and makes his own the lessons of Naipaul.

Analysis

Paul Theroux approaches his major theme—the ethical behavior of man in society—by way of postcolonial Africa and Southeast Asia, in stories that explore cultural interaction and the meaning of civilization. The three early African novels, *Fong and the Indians*, *Girls at Play*, and *Jungle Lovers*, set the scene, as it were, and suggest the terms for nearly all of his later fiction. These African novels offer not only a fictional portrait of the Third World struggling toward independence, but also a metaphor for all modern society and social ethics. In the apparently simpler world of East Africa, where white ex-patriot confronts black African, where Chinese meets Indian meets German meets American meets Australian, Theroux explores the ways individuals interact to form a social unit and the results, often absurd, of attempts to impose foreign values and ideas of civilization upon the primitive life of the jungle.

Although the later novels leave behind the specifically African setting, they continue to explore the theme of civilization versus jungle, expanding in particular upon the moral and ethical implications of certain kinds of social behavior. *The Family Arsenal* and *Saint Jack* provide instructive examples. In the former, Valentine Hood, an American ex-diplomat from Vietnam living in London, is struck by the domesticity displayed by the members of the terrorist band with which he lives: it is like a family. From this insight develop both the central theme of that novel and its plot structure. In *Saint Jack*, Jack Flowers creates a secular religion out of "giving people what they want." In *The Black House* and *The Mosquito Coast*, Theroux separates his protagonists from society to explore the meaning of exile, foreignness, and individualism. Yet, underlying all of these fictions will be found the basic assumption that every human experience, from death to redemption, from fear to loneliness, from love to murder, must be understood in a social context.

Fong and the Indians, the first of Theroux's African novels, is the witty tale of the business partnership between Sam Fong, a Chinese grocer, and Hassanali Fakhru, the Indian entrepreneur who rents him the store, supplies his goods, and, when business is poor, even becomes his customer. Fakhru dominates Fong's economic life, manipulating it for his own benefit by taking advantage of Fong's innocent incompetence as a businessman. Yet as the plot unfolds, it becomes clear the the relationship between Fong and Fakhru is far from one-sided. Moreover, it also becomes clear that this relationship is representative of all social and economic relationships. Each individual in a society suffers limitations of understanding that arise both from his own prejudices and from his cultural heritage. When two people meet to do business, they may well be speaking different languages, either literally or metaphorically. Misunderstandings are unavoidable, and the outcome of any action is unpredictable: good intentions may or may not result in good consequences; the same is true of bad intentions. Chaos and absurdity reign when no one quite understands what anyone else is doing.

The plot of *Fong and the Indians* is an intricate comedy of errors involving Fong, the unwilling grocer; Fakhru, the capitalist swindler; and two CIA agents on a mission to convert suspected Communists. The fiction works as both a satirical portrait of African society today and an allegory in which the grocery business, the swindles, and the "good will" mission—artifices of civilization—are, in the context of African reality, revealed to be absurd. In *Fong and the Indians*, Theroux explores "civilization"; in later books, *Jungle Lovers*, *Girls at Play*, *The Black House*, and *The Mosquito Coast*, he explores the meaning of "Africa"—the reality of the jungle. At no time does Theroux become an apologist for the Third World, elevating primitive civilization over modern. Rather, he turns "jungle" into a metaphor for man's natural environment: the jungle is both dangerous and nurturing; it demands that its inhabitants concentrate upon basic human needs. Although the metaphor is most easily understood when Theroux sets his story in the literal jungle of Africa or Central America, there is "jungle" too in South London, in an English village, even in Florida.

In *Fong and the Indians*, Fakhru swindles Sam Fong by convincing him that canned milk represents a victory of civilization. In Africa, however, canned milk makes no sense. Africans do not need it; Europeans prefer the fresh milk from Nairobi. Fong's only hope of becoming rich rests upon the wild improbability that the milk train will one day be wrecked. Aware of the absurdity, Fong accepts both the hope and the improbability of its fulfillment. Fong triumphs because he learns to love what he does not understand. He has the patience to submit, to accommodate his life to the requirements of survival. His change of diet, from the traditional Chinese cuisine he has maintained for all his thirty-seven years in Africa to a free, native one based on bananas and fried locusts, is at once a measure of his economic decline and an assurance of his ultimate triumph.

Theroux's ethic, then, appears to be based upon the virtue of inaction. Because human understanding is limited, all events appear ambiguous. Even innocently motivated attempts to improve the lot of humanity may prove unexpectedly destructive, such as Marais' attempt to bring revolutionary ideals to Malawi in *Jungle Lovers*, Valentine Hood's murder to rid the world of Ron Weech in *The Family Arsenal*, or even Maud Coffin Pratt's photographs of the pig feast and of her brother and sister in the mill in *Picture Palace*. Because all events are ambiguous, it is impossible to predict which actions will prove evil and which actions will prove good. Therefore, the only possible moral strategy is to take no action at all, to be patient and accommodate oneself to the unknowable mystery of the jungle.

Inaction, however, should not be confused with selfish laziness; rather it is an active, morally motivated inaction akin to the traditional Christian virtue of patience. Patience redeems the absurdity of the modern world, protecting man from despair and leading ultimately to a triumph of innocence and virtue that will in turn redeem society. This is the lesson of *Saint Jack*.

A middle-aged, balding, American ex-patriot, full of muddle, fear, and loneliness, Jack Flowers jumps ship in Singapore. A stranger and a misfit, Jack sees no hope of rescue; he does not believe in miracles. He is modern man making a realistic appraisal of his chances in an unfriendly and dangerous world. Yet Jack wrests from this vision of despair an ad-lib ethic based upon fulfilling the desires of others. He becomes what others would have him be. Condemning no one, pardoning all, Jack participates in each man's unique fantasy. In the public world, he is called a pimp—he may even be a spy— but in his own private world, Jack is a saint: thoroughly reliable and incapable of cultural misunderstanding. He gives to each what every man needs— pleasure, security, and forgiveness—and stands ready with whatever is needed to meet even an unexpected desire—be it pornographic pictures, the kind attentions of a good girl, or a game of squash. Jack shapes his own needs to match his companion's: he is the perfect friend and protector.

Jack's tattooed arms, emblazoned with Chinese obscenities and curses disguised as flowers, symbolize the way he eases the pain of human loneliness and fear by providing an illusion of hope and friendship and the reality of a temporary pleasure taken in safety. Pity, compassion, and a stubbornly innocent vision of human needs save Jack himself from doing evil and redeem the actions of all those he takes care of, even General Maddox himself.

The terms of this novel are coyly religious—Saint Jack, the manager of Paradise Gardens—but God is not really present in Singapore. What might in a Christian fiction be termed grace, is here good luck, and even Jack's redeeming power itself results, in the end, from his own fantasy. The effect is, on the one hand, tongue in cheek, and on the other, quite serious. Theroux appears to be walking the delicate line between a modern recognition that, in this absurd world, good and evil are meaningless categories and a common-sense realization that people need moral categories and at least an illusion of meaning in order to survive relatively sane.

The search for meaning and moral categories provides both the theme and the structure of *The Family Arsenal*. When the story opens, Valentine Hood has come to live with a group of unrelated people in South London. Their domesticity makes them a parody of the typical middle-class family: Mayo, the mother, a thief; Valentine, the father, a murderer; and Murf and Brodie, the teenage children, terrorist bombers. Early in the novel, many odd characters are introduced: Ralph Gawber, an accountant with a fondness for puzzles and a doomsday foreboding; Araba Nightwing, a radical actress who plays Peter Pan; Ron Weech, the hoodlum whom Hood chases and murders; Lorna Weech, his wife; Rutter, a gunrunner; and Lady Arrow. Initially, the relationships among these characters appear obscure if not irrelevant; yet as the plot develops, groupings take shape until the reader discovers, with Valentine Hood, that all are inextricably bound together by all sorts of dirty secrets, making them, in the words of one character, like one big family no one can quit.

The puzzlelike structure of this novel parodies the conventional thriller plot. Its purpose is, however, not action-packed adventure, but rather the slow revelation that, as Hood has suspected all along, inaction is best because all events (be they murder, theft, or bombing) are morally ambiguous. Thus, Hood changes from social avenger to listener. He develops an innocent vision of pity and love akin to Jack Flowers' that not only reveals the human bonds among all members and classes of society but also redeems his own guilt and saves at least some from the dangers and death that threaten them. By the end of the story, all is discovered and characters are regrouped into more pleasing families based on love rather than convenience.

Paralleling the revelation of relationships in the plot of *The Family Arsenal* is Hood's changing perception of the artistic organization of the stolen Van der Weyden that hangs in Mayo's closet. Mayo stole the painting believing that its theft would signal the beginning of social revolution. It does not: the world cares little about stolen artworks except as an interesting excuse for a headline. Yet, in an unexpected and very personal way, the painting does, in the end, play a revolutionary role in the story: it becomes the symbolic focus for the way art can organize seemingly disparate shapes and colors into a single beautiful whole. The Van der Weyden, like the tattoos on Jack's arms, suggests the resemblance between the personal vision of innocence that can redeem through pity and love and the vision of the artist that can change brutal reality into beauty.

The most extensive development of this theme occurs in *Picture Palace*, which becomes less a song of triumph for the artist's vision than a warning of the danger that arises when that vision becomes separated (as it necessarily must) from its real social context. Civilization versus the jungle, art versus reality—in Theroux's fiction these themes become almost versions of each other. The ethical effects of efforts by either art or civilization to improve human society are always unclear, dependent as much upon luck as fantasy. Instinctively, Maud Coffin Pratt seems to realize this tenet and locks away her photograph of Phoebe and Orlando in an incestuous embrace: to her, the picture represented love and innocent fulfillment, but when her brother and sister find it, they see only their own guilt and death. Unlike Jack Flowers (who can grab back his photographs of General Maddox) or Valentine Hood (whose revelations of family secrets save them in the end), Maud's personal vision of innocence redeems no one; indeed, it backfires completely, and she is left alone at the end of her life, famous but anonymous.

In *The Mosquito Coast*, Theroux returns to the jungle milieu to explore further the consequences of extreme individualism, the separation of self from society and environment. With his perpetual motion ice machine, Allie Fox expends a mad energy trying to produce icebergs in order to impress the Indians with the superiority of his civilized genius. Needless to say, whether he floats the ice downstream to a native village or carries it by sledge across the mountains, the ice melts: the impressiveness of civilization disappears in the heat of the sun. Relying completely upon his own creativity, Fox, the Yankee inventor, may be seen as a type of the artist. His attempt to impose his personal vision of utopia upon the brutal reality of the jungle fails utterly; his story reads as a warning of the danger of art without social context.

Like Sam Fong's canned milk in *Fong and the Indians*, Fox's ice machine in *The Mosquito Coast* represents an absurd attempt to civilize the jungle; yet Fong is rewarded with riches (the milk train does wreck), while Fox dies mad and beaten on the beach of Central America. Both may be seen as emblems of modern man, alone in a strange land, possessing nothing, trying to shape a life out of events that are mysterious, ambiguous, possibly dangerous, and probably absurd. Their differing responses to the jungle environment determine their different ends and provide the reader with the key to Theroux's view of social ethics.

Allie Fox rejects patience and accommodation; he rejects the mystery and the ambiguity of the jungle. He will build a bugless outpost of civilization; he would rather starve than eat a banana. In Theroux's world, it is poetic justice that Fox should misinterpret events and bring about the ruin of all that he has built. With true tragic irony, Fox learns from his failure not the value of accommodation, but only the need for an increased purity, an increased separation from the jungle, a separation doomed to failure. If Fong is the comic face of humanity, then Fox must be the tragic face.

With *O-Zone*, Theroux fashions a future in which major American cities are sealed off from one another and aliens stalk the now-deserted outside. Despite Theroux's descriptive skills, however, critics disliked *O-Zone*—mainly because it had very little plot, which they believed had been sacrificed for Theroux's love of narrative (turned to better use in his travel writing).

About *My Secret History*, on the other hand, critics complained because the narrative takes the first third of the book to really begin. A long novel that is really six novellas grouped together, it follows a young man from Massachusetts who moves to Africa and, from there, to England. Andrew Parent (who changes his first name to "Andre" while in college) starts out as an altar boy in Boston, becoming first a Peace Corps volunteer in one African country, then a teacher in another African country, before finally deciding to become a writer, ultimately moving to London.

Ultimately, Andre becomes an international womanizer, as well as a successful writer, and the last chapter/novella concentrates on his facing the consequences of what he has done to his life. Theroux's cosmopolitan experiences are what fuel his characters, and that he draws from his own life is only natural for a writer; yet, some critics have believed that his work is too self-referential—that is, thinly disguised autobiography. Pointing to his mentor V. S. Naipaul's 1987 autobiographical novel *The Enigma of Arrival*, they have wondered whether *My Secret History* is a midlife crisis *roman à clef*.

Theroux's work, however, cannot be so easily categorized or dismissed. The progression of Theroux's novels since 1967 demonstrates a marked coherence of interest and an increasing complexity of thematic and structural development. Although Theroux draws freely from the modern storehouse of pornography, violence, and antiheroism, he displays at the same time a real if not profound interest in some of the classic themes of Western literature—the source of good and evil, the use of pity and love in society, art, and reality. Technically, his work shows a similar melding of popular fiction (the Gothic horror story, the thriller) with the structure and conventions of the classic novelists.

Linda Howe

Other major works

SHORT FICTION: *Sinning with Annie and Other Stories*, 1972; *The Consul's File*, 1977; *World's End*, 1980; *The London Embassy*, 1982.

PLAY: *The Autumn Dog*, 1981.

SCREENPLAY: *Saint Jack*, 1979 (with Peter Bogdanovich and Howard Sackler).

NONFICTION: *V. S. Naipaul: An Introduction to His Work*, 1972; *The Great Railway Bazaar: By Train Through Asia*, 1975; *The Old Patagonian Express: By Train Through the Americas*, 1979; *The Kingdom by the Sea: A Journey Around Great Britain*, 1983; *Sailing Through China*, 1983; *The Imperial Way*, 1985 (with Steve McCurry); *Sunrise with Seamonsters: Travels and Discoveries, 1964-1984*, 1985; *Patagonia Revisited*, 1985 (with Bruce Chatwin); *Riding the Iron Rooster: By Train Through China*, 1988.

CHILDREN'S LITERATURE: *London Snow: A Christmas Story*, 1949; *A Christmas Card*, 1978.

Bibliography

Barth, Ilene. "A Rake's Progress on Four Continents." *Newsday* June 1, 1989. This review of *My Secret History* gives a detailed plot summary of this lengthy novel. Barth compares it to Theroux's "prickly travelogues," noting the similarities between his fiction and his life.

Burns, Jim. "The Travels of Theroux: 17 Books Pay for a Lot of Train Tickets." *Herald Examiner* (Los Angeles) May, 1988. This interview with Theroux provides a good sketch of what motivates him to write, to travel, and to write about traveling. Some biographical information is also included.

Coale, Samuel. *Paul Theroux*. Boston: Twayne, 1987. Part of Twayne's United States Authors series, this book provides a comprehensive look at Theroux's work as well as providing a chronology of events in the author's life. Includes references for each chapter and a bibliography of both primary and secondary sources and an index.

Glaser, E. "The Self-Reflexive Traveler: Paul Theroux on the Art of Travel and Travel Writing." *Centennial Review* 33 (Summer, 1989): 193-206. This article provides more insight into what motivates Theroux's writing and traveling. This in-depth profile and interview of Theroux is invaluable in the light of the scarcity of book-length works about him; includes some references.

J. R. R. TOLKIEN

Born: Bloemfontein, South Africa; January 3, 1892
Died: Bournemouth, England; September 2, 1973

Principal long fiction

The Hobbit, 1937; *The Lord of the Rings*, 1955 (includes *The Fellowship of the Ring*, 1954; *The Two Towers*, 1954; *The Return of the King*, 1955); *The Silmarillion*, 1977; *The Shaping of Middle-Earth*, 1986; *The Lost Road and Other Writings*, 1987; *The Return of the Shadow: The History of "The Lord of the Rings," Part One*, 1988.

Other literary forms

J. R. R. Tolkien's novels represent only a small part of the complicated matrix from which they evolved. During his lifetime, he published three volumes of novellas and short stories, *Farmer Giles of Ham* (1949), *Tree and Leaf* (1964), and *Smith of Wootton Major* (1967). Some of these tales had originally been bedtime stories for his own children, such as the posthumous *The Father Christmas Letters* (1976). *The Silmarillion* (1977) and *Unfinished Tales of Numenor and Middle-Earth* (1980) both contain stories Tolkien composed early in his life, material that sets the stage for the events in his novels. His poetry collections, *Songs for the Philologists* (1936), *The Adventures of Tom Bombadil* (1962), and *The Road Goes Ever On: A Song Cycle* (1967), link Tolkien's poetic formulations of Middle-earth's themes with the historical and linguistic themes of which both his professional work and much of his dreams were made, "the nameless North of Sigurd of the Völsungs, and the prince of all dragons." Tolkien's academic publications dealt with the history of the English language and Middle English literature: *A Middle English Vocabulary* (1922) and editions of *Sir Gawain and the Green Knight* (1925) with E. V. Gordon and the *Ancrene Wisse* (1962). His seminal essay "Beowulf: The Monsters and the Critics" (1936) and his only play, *The Homecoming of Beorhtnoth Beorhthelm's Son* (1953), offer fresh interpretations of ancient English epic poems.

Tolkien's novels have been adapted for cinema and television, and many, though not all, of his fragmentary stories, articles, and letters have been published since his death. His histories of Middle-earth, a remarkable invented mythology comprising chronicles, tales, maps, and poems, were edited as a series by his son, Christopher Tolkien. Volumes include *The Book of Lost Tales* (parts 1 and 2, 1983-1984), *The Lays of Beleriand* (1985), *The Shaping of Middle-Earth*, and *The Lost Road and Other Writings*.

Achievements

Tolkien's fiction dismayed most of his fellow scholars at the University of Oxford as much as it delighted most of his general readers. Such reactions sprang from their recognition of his vast linguistic talent, which underlay both his professional achievements and his mythical universe. Tolkien led two lives at once, quietly working as an Oxford tutor, examiner, editor, and lecturer, while concurrently Middle-earth and its mythology were taking shape within his imagination.

For twenty years after he took First Class Honours in English Language and Literature at Oxford, Tolkien's teaching and linguistic studies buttressed his scholarly reputation. Editing the fourteenth century text of *Sir Gawain and the Green Knight* with E. V. Gordon helped bring Tolkien the Rawlinson and Bosworth Professorship of Anglo-Saxon at Oxford in 1925. His lecture "Beowulf: The Monsters and the Critics" approached the Anglo-Saxon epic poem from an entirely new perspective and is considered a landmark in criticism of Western Germanic literature. As he was shaping his linguistic career, however, Tolkien was also formulating an imaginary language, which as early as 1917 had led him to explore its antecedents, its mythology, and its history, all of which he molded into the tales of *The Silmarillion*. Over the years, he shared them with friends, but he never finished putting them into a unified structure.

His preoccupation with Middle-earth and the practical demands of his teaching distracted Tolkien from scholarship, and between his celebrated essay *On Fairy Stories* in 1939 and his edition of the Middle English *Ancrene Wisse* in 1962, Tolkien published only fiction, a circumstance acknowledged with polite forbearance by most of Oxford's scholarly community, although his novels eventually met with astonishing popular success. *The Hobbit*, originally a children's story, was published in 1937 after a six-year gestation, and by 1949, *The Lord of the Rings* was complete. Its sales, though steadily increasing after its publication in 1954-1955, did not soar until 1965, when an unauthorized American printing proved a disguised blessing, resulting in a campus cult responsible for the sale of three million copies by 1968.

Most critics of *The Lord of the Rings* have not achieved moderation. As W. H. Auden observed, "People find it a masterpiece of its genre, or they cannot abide it." Auden himself and C. S. Lewis, Tolkien's Oxford friend, headed the "masterpiece" faction, while Edwin Muir in England and Edmund Wilson in America deplored Tolkien's style and aims.

Honorary fellowships, an honorary Doctorate of Letters from Oxford and a C.B.E. from Queen Elizabeth all descended upon Tolkien with the unexpected wealth of his last years, which were nevertheless darkened by his reluctance to complete *The Silmarillion*. His reputation rests not on his academic talent or scholarly production, nor even on his brilliant linguistically oriented "mythology for England," but upon the novels that began as tales for his children and blossomed into a splendid imaginative tree of fiction whose roots feed upon the archetypes of northern European civilization and whose leaves shelter its finest aspirations.

Biography

John Ronald Reuel Tolkein was born in Bloemfontein, South Africa, on January 3, 1892. The piano-manufacturing firm of his father's family, originally from Germany, had gone bankrupt, and the elder Tolkien had taken a South African bank position in hopes of improving his shaky finances. Tolkien's mother, Mabel Suffield, joined her husband at Bloemfontein, but when the climate strained Ronald's health, she took their two sons home to England in 1895. Less than a year later, Arthur Tolkien died in South Africa, leaving his widow and children nearly penniless.

In the summer of 1896, Mabel Tolkien rented a rural cottage at Sarehole Mill, close to Birmingham, and for the next four years she taught her boys French, Latin, drawing, and botany, to save school expenses. Much later, Tolkien called these "the longest-seeming and most formative part" of his life. Mabel Tolkien's attraction to Roman Catholicism led to her conversion in 1900, and she moved to a Birmingham suburb from which Ronald began to attend one of England's then leading grammar schools, King Edward's, on a scholarship. His mother's unpopular religion meant that she and her sons received even less help from her own family and the Tolkiens than previously, and her health began to decline rapidly. In 1904, she died at thirty-four, leaving her children in the care of Father Francis Morgan, her friend and pastor. Tolkien's devotion to his mother was inextricably intertwined with his own Catholic faith, and both played vital roles in the development of his fiction.

At sixteen, Ronald Tolkien looked back upon a series of grievous losses: his father, whom he considered as "belonging to an almost legendary past"; the Sarehole countryside he loved; his mother, whom he considered a martyr to her faith. Not surprisingly for a lonely boy, Tolkien fell in love early when he met Edith Bratt, another orphan, in his Birmingham boarding house. She was three years older than he, and she had just enough inheritance to support herself modestly while she dreamed of becoming a musician. Recognizing the boy's scholarly talent and fearing for his future, Father Morgan finally stopped all communication between Ronald and Edith until Ronald was twenty-one. Tolkien himself commented thirty years later, "Probably nothing else would have hardened the will enough to give such an affair (however genuine a case of true love) permanence."

The early fascination with language Tolkien's mother had fostered led him to the ancient languages of the North, Finnish, Welsh, and Old Icelandic, as well as the Anglo-Saxon and Middle English in which he specialized. At Oxford, he was steeped in an all-male academic atmosphere, and when he and Edith were reunited in 1913, they seemed to have little in common. On the eve of his military departure to France in 1916, however, they were married. After some months on the Western Front, Tolkien convalesced from trench fever in England until the Armistice.

In a military hospital in 1917, Tolkien began "The Book of Lost Tales" which would become *The Silmarillion*, as he envisioned it, "a body of more or less connected legend." By 1923, it was essentially complete, but he could not seem to bear finishing it—and losing it. From then on, he looked outward to the male academic company of his fellows at Oxford and inward to Middle-earth, which rapidly became his refuge and his strength. All at once, in the late 1920's, from "the Suffield side of his personality" came a startling thought: "In a hole in the ground there lived a hobbit," and for the rest of Tolkien's creative life, the "hobbit" and his adventures against the backdrop of Middle-earth and its myths dominated his attention.

Toward the end, he said, "The Silmarils are in my heart," and of *The Lord of the Rings*, "It is written in my life-blood." Perhaps little room seemed to remain in Tolkien's life for Edith, his companion for more than fifty years, but at his death in 1973, the names of Beren and Lúthien, taken from the chief story of *The Silmarillion* and carved upon the Tolkiens' headstones, testified to great sacrifices and greater love for all time to come.

Analysis

Looking back around 1951 upon his Middle-earth, J. R. R. Tolkien commented, "I do not remember a time when I was not building it . . . always I had the sense of recording what was already 'there,' somewhere: not of inventing." He conceived of fantasy as a profound and powerful form of literature with intense philosophical and spiritual meaning, serious purposes, and eternal appeal. He believed the imagination, the mental power of making images, could be linked by art to "sub-creation," the successful result of image-making, and so he regarded the genuine artist as partaking in the Creator's divine nature.

Three major factors of Tolkien's personality and environment combined to shape the theory of fantasy underlying his novels, as first enunciated in the essay "On Fairy-Stories" (1938). His love of language for its singular rewards, his brief delight in the English countryside at Sarehole, and his shattering experience of trench warfare during World War I all provided the seeds for his three longest pieces of fiction. They also contributed to the points of view, astonishingly nonhuman and yet startingly convincing, of *The Silmarillion*, *The Hobbit*, and *The Lord of the Rings*, where Elves and Hobbits illuminate the world of Men.

Even as a boy, Tolkien had been enchanted by Welsh names on railway coal cars, a sign of his unusual linguistic sensitivity, and as a mature scholar, he devoted himself to the mystery of the word in its northern manifestations. In "On Fairy-Stories," he wrote that "*spell* means both a story told, and a formula of power over living men." Tolkien cast his spells in the building blocks of words drawn from the imaginary languages he had been constructing as long as he could remember. The two languages he formulated for his Elves, the Elder Race, both derived from a common linguistic ancestor as human languages do, and this "nexus of languages" supplied the proper names for his novels, so that despite their considerable length and complication they possess "cohesion, consistency of linguistic style, and the illusion of historicity." The last was possibly the greatest achievement of Tolkien's mastery of language in his novels, fostering vital credence in his imaginary world. He felt that the finest fairy stories "open a door on Other Time, and if we pass through . . . we stand outside our own time, outside Time itself, maybe." In his own childhood, a "troublous" one Tolkien said, he had "had no special 'wish to believe'"; he instead "wanted to know," as, perhaps, do his readers, aided by the resonance of his masterful use of words.

The memory of his years at Sarehole, the happiest of his boyhood, gave Tolkien an abiding love of nature, "above all trees," which formed the basis for one of his principal concepts, "the inter-relations between the 'noble' and the 'simple.'" He found "specially moving" the "ennoblement of the ignoble," a theme which recurs throughout his fiction. Tolkien's Elves practice love and respect toward nature, as do his Hobbits, "small people" connected closely to "the soil and other living things" who display both human pettiness and unexpected heroism "in a pinch." The Elves, Hobbits, and good Men are countered in Tolkien's Middle-earth by the threat of the machine, by which he meant "all use of external plans or devices," as opposed to "the development of inner powers or talents." The evil of the machine in Tolkien's eyes (he did not own a car after World War II) derived from the misguided human desire for power, itself a rebellion against the Creator's laws, a Fall from Paradise, another recurring theme in his fiction.

The horrors of World War I must have struck Tolkien as evil incarnate, with new military technology that devastated the countryside, struck down the innocent, and left no place for chivalry, heroism, or even common decency. Unlike Andrew Lang, an early Scottish collector of fairy tales, who felt children most often ask, "Is it true?", Tolkien declared that children far more often asked him of a character, "Was he good? Was he wicked?" Tolkien shared G. K. Chesterton's conviction that children "are innocent and love justice; while most of us are wicked and naturally prefer mercy." The child's stern perception of right and wrong, as opposed to the "mercy untempered by justice" which leads to "falsification of values," confirmed Tolkien's long-held inclination toward the steely world of the northern sagas, where human heroism faces inevitable defeat by the forces of evil, and the hero, according to Edith Hamilton, "can prove what he is only by dying." From his basic distrust of the machine and his firsthand memories of Verdun, Tolkien drew one of the major lessons of his fiction: "that on callow, lumpish and selfish youth peril, sorrow, and the shadow of death can bestow dignity, and even sometimes wisdom."

Reconciling this harsh northern *Weltbild* with his Roman Catholic faith did not seem to be difficult for Tolkien. An indispensable element of his theory of fantasy is the "sudden joyous 'turn'" of a "eucatastrophic" story, a moment in fiction accompanied by "a catch of the breath, a beat and lifting of the heart, near to (or indeed accompanied by) tears." By inserting the "turn" convincingly into his tale, the sub-creator "denies universal final defeat" and give "a fleeting glimpse of Joy, Joy beyond the walls of the world, poignant as grief." Hence, Tolkien believed that such a joy was the "mark of the true fairy story," the revelation of truth in the fictional world the sub-creator built. It might even be greater,"a far-off gleam or echo of *evangelium* in the real world." Tolkien was able to see the Christian Gospels as "the greatest and most complete conceivable eucatastrophe," believing that in fantasy the human sub-creator might "actually assist in the effoliation and multiple enrichment of creation."

Tolkien's *The Silmarillion*, *The Hobbit*, and *The Lord of the Rings*, form, as he always hoped, one coherent and archetypal whole. His "creative fantasy" effectively shows the three dissimilar faces his theory demanded: "the Mystical towards the Supernatural; the Magical towards Nature; and the Mirror of scorn and pity toward Man." Man's "oldest and deepest desire," the "Great Escape" from death, is satisfied in Tolkien's major fiction, not by denying Mortality but by accepting it gracefully as a gift from man's Creator, a benefit to man that Tolkien's immortal Elves envied. The Elves' own magic is actually art, whose true object is "sub-creation" under God, not domination of lesser beings whose world they respectfully share. Scorn for fallen men (and fallen Elves and Hobbits as well) abounds in Middle-earth, but pity, too, for guiltless creatures trapped in the most frightful evil Tolkien could envision, evil that he believed arises "from an apparently good root, the desire to benefit the world and others—speedily—and according to the benefactor's own plans." Middle-earth lives forever in Tolkien's novels, and with it an affirmation of what is best, most true, and most beautiful in human nature.

Both in Tolkien's life and in the chronology of Middle-earth, the tales of *The Silmarillion* came first, but the book was not published until four years after his death. The volume called *The Silmarillion* contains four shorter narratives as well as the "Quenta Silmarillion," arranged as ordered chronicles of the Three Ages of Tolkien's middle-earth by his son Christopher, following his father's explicit intention.

Tolkien began parts of *The Silmarillion* in 1917 after he had been invalided home from France. The work steadily evolved after more than forty years, and, according to Christopher Tolkien, "incompatibilities of tone" inevitably arose from his father's increasing preoccupation with theology and philosophy over the mythology and poetry he had originally favored. Tolkien himself never abandoned his work on *The Silmarillion*, even though he found himself unable to complete it. As Christopher Wiseman had suggested to Tolkien, "Why these creatures live to you is because you are still creating them," and so Tolkien painstakingly revised, recast, and polished these stories, unwilling to banish their characters from his imagination.

The Silmarillion opens with "Ainulindalë," a cosmogonical myth revealing the creation of Middle-earth by God ("Iluvatar") in the presence of the Valar, whom Tolkien described as angelic powers. He wanted "to provide beings of the same order . . . as the 'gods' of higher mythology" acceptable to "a mind that believes in the Blessed Trinity." The universe to which Middle-earth belonged was set in living motion by music, "beheld as a light in the darkness."

The short "Valaquenta" enumerates the individual Valar, whose personal responsibilities covered all created things of Middle-earth, stopping short of the act of creation itself. One of the Valar, Melkor, rebelled in the First Age; Tolkien believed that "there cannot be any 'story' without a fall." Melkor "began with the desire of Light, but when he could not possess it for himself alone, he descended . . . into a great burning." One of Melkor's servants was Sauron, who later embodied evil in the Third Age of Middle-earth.

The twenty-four chapters of the "Quenta Silmarillion" recount the legendary history of the immortal Elves, the First-Born of Iluvatar, whom Tolkien elsewhere called "rational incarnate creatures of more or less comparable stature with our own." After writing *The Lord of the Rings*, Tolkien clearly indicated that the Elves were "only a representation of an apprehension of a part of human nature" from which art and poetry spring, but, he said, "that is not the legendary mode of talking." The Elves originally share the Paradise of the Valar, Valinor, but the Elves suffer a fall from that grace in the "Quenta Silmarillion," the rebellion and exile to Middle-earth of one of the great families of Elves, led by their chief, the artificer Fëanor, who has captured the primal light of Iluvatar in the three Silmarils. Tolkien described these great jewels as aglow with the "light of art undivorced from reason, that sees things both scientifically (or philosophically) and imaginatively (or subcreatively) and 'says that they are good'—as beautiful." Fëanor's lust to possess the Silmarils for himself leads to their capture by Melkor, and in the struggle to redeem them, splendid deeds are performed by Beren, a Man of Middle-earth beloved of the Elvish princess Lúthien. Tolkien called this "the first example of the motive (to become dominant in Hobbits) that the great policies of world history . . . are often turned . . . by the seemingly unknown and weak." The union of Beren and Lúthien is the first between mortal Man and immortal Elf; they win Paradise together, and eventually Earendil the Elven Mariner closes the "Quenta Silmarillion" by bringing the gem Beren painfully rescued from Melkor to the land of the Valar. His Silmaril was set into the sky as its brightest star, while the others were lost in the depths of the earth and sea, and the First Age of Middle-earth came to its end.

Tolkien saw the Second Age of Middle-earth as dark, and he believed "not very much of its history is (or need be) told." The Valar continued to dwell at Valinor with the faithful Elves, but the exiled Elves with Fëanor were commanded to leave Middle-earth and live in the lonely Isle of Eressëa in the West. Some of them, however, ignored the order and remained in Middle-earth. Those Men of Middle-earth who had aided the Elves to redeem the Silmarils were given the Atlantis-like realm of Númenor as their reward, as well as lifespans three times the normal age of Men. Though Melkor was chained, his servant Sauron remained free to roam Middle-earth, and through his evil influence, both Men of Númenor and the Delaying Elves came to grief.

The decay of Númenor is told in the "Akallabeth," an illustration of Tolkien's belief that the inevitable theme of human stories is "a Ban, or Prohibition." The long-lived Númenoreans were prohibited by the Valar from setting foot on "immortal" lands in the West. Their wrongful desire to escape death, their gift from Iluvatar, causes them to rebel and bring about their own watery destruction through the worship of Sauron, Melkor's servant. At the same time, the Elves who delayed in Middle-earth suffered the painful consequences of their flawed choice. Tolkien said they "wanted to have their cake without eating it," enjoying the perfection of the West while remaining on ordinary earth, revered as superior beings by the other, lesser races. Some of them cast their lot with Sauron, who enticed them to create three Rings of Power, in the misguided hopes of making Middle-earth another Valinor. Sauron secretly made another ring himself, one with the power to enslave all the others. The ensuing war between Sauron and the Elves devastated Middle-earth, but in the Last Alliance of Elves and Men against Sauron, the One Ring was lost. Tolkien calls this the "catastrophic end, not only of the Second Age, but of the Old World, the primeval age of Legend."

The posthumous collection called *The Silmarillion* ends with Tolkien's résumé "Of the Rings of Power and the Third Age," which introduces the motives, themes, and chief actors in the next inevitable war between Sauron and the Free Peoples of Middle-earth. Although *The Hobbit* and *The Lord of the Rings* have proved vastly more popular, and both can be enjoyed without the complicated and generally loftily pitched history of *The Silmarillion*, its information is essential to a thorough understanding of the forces Tolkien set at work in the later novels. Even more important, *The Silmarillion* was for Tolkien, as his son Christopher has said, "the vehicle and depository of his profoundest reflections," and as such, it holds the bejewelled key to the autobiography Tolkien felt was embedded in his fiction.

Around 1930, Tolkien jotted a few enigmatic words about "a hobbit" on the back of an examination paper he was grading. "Names always generate a story in my mind," he observed, and eventually he found out "what hobbits were like." The Hobbits, whom he subsequently described as "a branch of the specifically *human* race (not Elves or Dwarves)," became the vital link between Tolkien's mythology as constructed in *The Silmarillion* and the heroic legend that dominates *The Lord of the Rings*. Humphrey Carpenter, Tolkien's official biographer, believes that Bilbo Baggins, hero of *The Hobbit*, "embodied everything he [Tolkien] loved about the West Midlands." Tolkien himself once wrote, "I am in fact a hobbit, in all but size," and beyond personal affinities, he saw the Hobbits as "rustic English people," small in size to reflect "the generally small reach of their imagination—not the small reach of their courage or latent power."

Tolkien's Hobbits appear in the Third Age of Middle-earth, in an ominously quiet lull before a fearful storm. Sauron had been overthrown by the Elf-lord Gil-galad and the Númenorean King Elendil, but since evil is never completely vanquished, Sauron's creatures lurk quietly in the north of Middle-earth, Mordor, while a few Elves keep watch on its borders. Descendants of a few Númenoreans were saved from their land's disaster (Atlantean destruction was a recurrent nightmare for both Tolkien and his son Christopher), and they rule in the Kingdoms of Arnor in the North of Middle-earth and Gondor of the South. The former Númenoreans are allies of the Homeric Riders of Rohan, whose human forefathers had remained in Middle-earth when Númenor came to be. The three Elven Rings of Power secretly guard Rivendell and Lothlórien, which Tolkien called "enchanted enclaves of peace where Time seems to stand still and decay is restrained, a semblance of the bliss of the True West."

The Hobbits live in The Shire, in "an ordered, civilised, if simple rural life." One day, the Hobbit Bilbo Baggins receives an odd visitor, Gandalf the Wizard, who sends Bilbo off with traveling dwarves in search of Dragon's Gold, the major theme of the novel. In the process, Tolkien uses the humble Hobbit to illustrate one of his chief preoccupations, the process by which "small imagination" combines with "great courage." As he recalled from his months in the trenches, "I've always been impressed that we are here, surviving, because of the indomitable courage of quite small people against impossible odds."

Starting from the idyllic rural world of The Shire, *The Hobbit*, ostensibly a children's book, traces the typical quest of the northern hero about whom Tolkien himself had loved to read in his youth. Gandalf shares certain characteristics with the Scandinavian god Odin, said to wander among men as an "old man of great height," with a long grey cloak, a white beard, and supernatural powers. Gandalf, like Odin, understands the speech of birds, being especially fond of eagles and ravens, and his strange savage friend Beorn, who rescues the Hobbits at one critical point, recalls the berserkers, bearskin-clad warriors consecrated to Odin who fought with superhuman strength in the intoxication of battle. The Dwarves of Middle-earth distinctly resemble their Old Norse forebears, skilled craftsmen who made treasures for the gods. Smaug the Dragon, eventually slain by the human hero Bard, is surely related to "the prince of all dragons" who had captured Tolkien's boyish imagination. The Germanic code of the *comitatus*, the warrior's fidelity unto death, celebrated in the tenth century Anglo-Saxon poem "The Battle of Maldon," inspired Tolkien's only play and applies to *The Hobbit*, too, since Bilbo's outward perils are overshadowed by the worst threat of all to the northern hero, the inward danger of proving a coward. After Bilbo overcomes his fear and slays a giant spider, "he felt a different person, and much fiercer and bolder in spite of an empty stomach."

Bilbo's hard-won self-knowledge allows him to demonstrate the "indomitable courage of small people against great odds" when he saves Dwarves, Men, and Elves from suicidal war against one another. *The Hobbit* far exceeded its beginnings as a bedtime story for Tolkien's small sons, since it is also a fable about the child at the heart of every man, perceiving right and wrong as sternly as did the heroes of the North.

In late 1937, at the suggestion of his British publisher, Tolkien began a sequel to *The Hobbit*. To the East, a malignant force was gathering strength in the Europe that even the mammoth sacrifices of World War I had not redeemed from oppression, and while Tolkien often cautions against interpreting his works allegorically, the apprehensive atmosphere of prewar England must have affected his own peace of mind. He described his intention in *The Lord of the Rings* as "an attempt to . . . wind up all the elements and motives of what has preceded." He wanted "to include the colloquialism and vulgarity of Hobbits, poetry and the highest style of prose." The moral of this novel, not a "trilogy" but, he stressed, "conceived and written as a whole," was "obvious": "that without the high and noble the simple and vulgar is utterly mean; and without the simple and ordinary the noble and heroic is meaningless."

The Lord of the Rings is a vast panoramic contest between good and evil, played out against the backdrop of Tolkien's mythology as presented in *The Silmarillion*. The One Ring of Sauron, long lost, was found by little Bilbo Baggins, and from him it passed to his kinsman Frodo, who becomes the central figure of the quest-in-reverse: having found the Ring, the allied Men, Elves, Dwarves, and Hobbits must destroy it where it was forged, so that its power can never again dominate Middle-earth. Another quest takes place simultaneously in the novel, as the mysterious Strider who greets the Hobbits at Bree on the first stage of their perilous journey is gradually revealed as Aragorn, son of Arathorn and heir to Arnor in the North, descendant of Elendil who kept faith with the Valar; he is the human King of Middle-earth who must reclaim his realm. Sauron's minions rise to threaten the Ringbearer and his companions, and after many adventures, a great hopeless battle is fought before the Gates of Mordor. As Tolkien stated in "Of the Rings of Power and the Third Age," "There at the last they looked upon death and defeat, and all their valour was in vain; for Sauron was too strong." This is the paradoxical defeat-and-victory of the northern hero, whose glory is won in the manner of his death. As a practicing Christian, though, Tolkien had to see hope clearly in the ultimate struggle between right and wrong, "and help came from the hands of the weak when the Wise faltered." Frodo the Hobbit at last managed to carry the Ring to Mount Doom in spite of Sauron, and there it was destroyed, and "a new Spring opened up on Earth."

In retrospect, Tolkien acknowledged that another central issue of *The Lord of the Rings* was "love in different modes," which had been "wholly absent from *The Hobbit*." Tolkien considered the "simple 'rustic' love" between Sam, Frodo's faithful batman, and his Rosie was *"absolutely essential"* both to the study of the main hero of the novel and "to the theme of the relation of ordinary life . . . to quests, to sacrifice, causes, and the 'longing for Elves,' and sheer beauty." The evidence of Tolkien's own life indicates the depth of his ability to love, like Beren, always faithful to his Lúthien. Such love that made all sacrifice possible forms the indestructible core of *The Lord of the Rings*, which moved C. S. Lewis to speak of "beauties which pierce like swords or burn like cold iron . . . a book that will break your heart."

Love exemplified in two important romances softens the necromancy and the battles of *The Lord of the Rings*: the poignant "mistaken love" of Eowyn for Aragorn, as Tolkien described it, and the novel's "highest love-story," the tale of Aragorn and Arwen, daughter of Elrond, leader of the Elves of Middle-earth. Eowyn is niece to Theoden, King of Rohan, the land of the horsemen Tolkien patterned after ancient Anglo-Saxon tribes he had first encountered through William Morris' *House of the Wolfings* (1889). In Theoden's decline, the shield-maiden Eowyn gives her first love to the royalty-in-exile she senses in Aragorn, and though he in no sense encourages her, Eowyn's tragedy is one only he can heal once he is restored as King. In contrast, Tolkien merely alludes to the love of Aragorn and Arwen in *The Lord of the Rings*, since it seems almost too deep for tears. Arwen must forsake her Elven immortality and join Aragorn in human death. Like Tolkien's own love for Edith, Aragorn's for Arwen is temporarily prevented from fruition until he can return to her in full possession of his birthright. The shadow of her possible loss lends stature to the characterization of Aragorn, the hero of *The Lord of the Rings*.

In 1955, Tolkien observed that "certain features . . . and especially certain places" of *The Lord of the Rings* "still move me very powerfully." The passages he cited sum up the major means by which the novel so strongly conveys love, redemption, and heroism achieved in the face of overwhelming odds. "The heart remains in the description of Cerin Amroth," he wrote, the spot where Aragorn and Arwen first pledged their love and where, many years later at the beginning of his fearful quest, "the grim years were removed from the face of Aragorn, and he seemed clothed in white, a young lord tall and fair." Tolkien magnifies this small epiphany of love through the eyes of the Hobbit Frodo. Another key episode, the wretched Gollum's failure to repent because Sam interrupts him, grieved Tolkien deeply, he said, for it resembled "the *real* world in which the instruments of just retribution are seldom themselves just or holy." In his favorite passage, however, Tolkien was "most stirred by the sound of the horses of the Rohirrim at cockcrow," the great "turn" of *The Lord of the Rings*, a flash of salvation in the face of all odds that comes beyond hope, beyond prayer, like a stroke of unexpected bliss from the hand of the Creator.

The "turn" that makes *The Lord of the Rings* a "true fairy-story" in Tolkien's definition links fidelity to a vow, a Germanic value, to the Christian loyalty that animated many of the great Anglo-Saxon works Tolkien had spent his scholarly life studying. By weaving the immensely complex threads of Elves, Hobbits, Men, and Dwarves into his heroic legend of the last great age of Middle-earth, he achieved a valid sub-creation, sharing in the nature of what for him was most divine.

For almost fifty years, mostly in the quiet academic atmosphere of Oxford, Tolkien built his resounding tales of "a body of more or less connected legend, ranging from the large and cosmogonic, to the level of romantic fairy-story." He consciously dedicated it simply "to England; to my country." The intellectual absorption with language he had always enjoyed gave him the starting-place for his mythology, which he implemented in *The Silmarillion*, whose unifying theme is the Fall of Elves and Men. His brief happiness in the English countryside at Sarehole and his West Midlands family background seem to have provided him the landscape from which *The Hobbit* grew, perhaps his most approachable "fairy-story" for both children and adults, illustrating the happiness to be gained from simplicity and the acceptance of the gift of mortality. The chivalric dreams of noble sacrifice shattered for Tolkien's generation by World War I were redeemed for him by his realization that the humble may effectively struggle against domination by the misguided technological values of modern civilization. The heroic legend of *The Lord of the Rings* best illustrates Tolkien's resolution of the conflict between the northern values he had admired from youth and the Roman Catholic religion of hope and consolation to which he was devoted. Tolkien wanted to illuminate the simplest and the highest values of human existence, found in a human love that accepts and transcends mortality. Tolkien's "mythology for England," a unique gift of literature and language, has earned its immense popular success by appealing to man's eternal desire to understand his mortal lot. As Hilda Ellis Davidson commented of the great northern myths, so like Tolkien's own, "In reaching out to explore the distant hills where the gods dwell and the deeps where the monsters are lurking, we are perhaps discovering the way home."

Mitzi M. Brunsdale

Other major works

SHORT FICTION: *Farmer Giles of Ham*, 1949; *Tree and Leaf,* 1964, revised

1988; *The Tolkien Reader*, 1966; *Smith of Wootton Major*, 1967; *The Father Christmas Letters*, 1976; *Unfinished Tales of Numenor and Middle-Earth*, 1980 (Christopher Tolkien, editor); *The Book of Lost Tales*, 1983-1984.

PLAY: *The Homecoming of Beorhtnoth Beorhthelm's Son*, 1953.

POETRY: *Songs for the Philologists*, 1936 (with E. V. Gordon et al.); *The Adventures of Tom Bombadil*, 1962; *The Road Goes Ever On: A Song Cycle*, 1967; *The Lays of Beleriand*, 1985.

NONFICTION: *A Middle English Vocabulary*, 1922; *Sir Gawain and the Green Knight*, 1925 (edited with E. V. Gordon); *Ancrene Wisse: The English Text of the Ancrene Riwle*, 1962 (edited); *The Letters from J. R. R. Tolkien*, 1981; *The Monsters and the Critics, and Other Essays*, 1983.

MISCELLANEOUS: *Finn and Hengest: The Fragment and the Episode*, 1983.

Bibliography

Carpenter, Humphrey. *Tolkien: A Biography*. London: Allen & Unwin, 1977. Written with access to Tolkien's unpublished letters and diaries, this mostly chronological narrative traces the development of the world of Middle-earth from Tolkien's philological work. Balances the details of his rather pedestrian life with the publishing history of Tolkien's writings. An extensive section of black-and-white photographs, a detailed bibliography, a family genealogy, and an index add to the value of this standard biography.

Crabbe, Katharyn W. *J. R. R. Tolkien*. Rev. ed. New York: Continuum, 1988. A study of Tolkien's writings (including a chapter on *The Silmarillion* and another on the posthumous History of Middle-earth series) unified by a vision of "the quest." After a brief biographical chapter, Crabbe considers Tolkien's use of languages to delineate character in his major works. Argues that his quest was for a suitable preChristian mythology which could ground the imaginative works of the future in a great mythic past for his beloved Britain.

Foster, Robert. *The Complete Guide to Middle-earth: From "The Hobbit" to "The Silmarillion."* Rev. ed. New York: Ballantine, 1978. An alphabetical annotated compendium of each of the proper names in Tolkien's major works, including persons, places, and things, with page references to standard editions of each work. An invaluable reference, written from a perspective within the world created by Tolkien. The guide provides translations of Middle-earth tongues, chronologies as appropriate, and masterful summaries of complex events.

Isaacs, Neil D., and Rose A. Zimbardo, eds. *Tolkien and the Critics: Essays on J. R. R. Tolkien's "The Lord of the Rings."* Notre Dame, Ind.: University of Notre Dame Press, 1968. A collection of fifteen original and reprinted critical articles dealing with *The Lord of the Rings* as literature. Among the contributors, C. S. Lewis offers a paean to the author, critic Edmund Fuller allows that Tolkien's work lifts one's spirits, and translator Burton Raffel calls most of Tolkien's poetry "embarrassingly bad." An index of Middle-earth references completes a lively and accessible volume.

Rogers, Deborah Webster, and Ivor A. Rogers. *J. R. R. Tolkien*. Boston: Twayne, 1980. A short, popular study of Tolkien's literary sources, his short stories, and his novels: *The Hobbit, The Silmarillion,* and *The Lord of the Rings* trilogy. The authors find in Tolkien's high fantasy a kind of high realism, expressing the deepest human yearnings for hope, courage, and love. Contains extensive notes, a chronology, an index, and an annotated bibliography (including recordings).

Shippey, T. A. *The Road to Middle-Earth*. Boston: Allen & Unwin, 1982. An exploration of Tolkien's works from a philological perspective. Shippey, a friend of Tolkien and himself a philologist, sees the creation of Middle-earth as an outworking of Tolkien's study of word origins and sounds, and not as the result of some master design for a new myth. An appendix on Tolkien's sources, detailed notes, an index, and the reprinting (with translations) of three Old English and one Gothic poem by Tolkien enhance this scholarly study.

ANTHONY TROLLOPE

Born: London, England; April 24, 1815
Died: London, England; December 6, 1882

Principal long fiction

The Macdermots of Ballycloran, 1847; *The Kellys and the O'Kellys*, 1848; *The Warden*, 1855; *Barchester Towers*, 1857; *The Three Clerks*, 1858; *Doctor Thorne*, 1858; *The Bertrams*, 1859; *Castle Richmond*, 1860; *Framley Parsonage*, 1860-1861; *Orley Farm*, 1861-1862; *The Small House at Allington*, 1862-1864; *Rachel Ray*, 1863; *Can You Forgive Her?*, 1864; *Miss Mackenzie*, 1865; *The Belton Estate*, 1865-1866; *The Claverings*, 1866-1867; *The Last Chronicle of Barset*, 1867; *Phineas Finn, the Irish Member*, 1867-1869; *He Knew He Was Right*, 1868-1869; *The Vicar of Bullhampton*, 1869-1870; *The Eustace Diamonds*, 1871-1873; *Phineas Redux*, 1873-1874; *The Way We Live Now*, 1874-1875; *The Prime Minister*, 1875-1876; *The American Senator*, 1876-1877; *Is He Popenjoy?*, 1877-1878; *John Caldigate*, 1878-1879; *The Duke's Children*, 1879-1880; *Dr. Wortle's School*, 1880; *Ayala's Angel*, 1881; *The Landleaguers*, 1882-1883; *Mr. Scarborough's Family*, 1882-1883.

Other literary forms

Anthony Trollope's novels were frequently serialized in various periodicals such as *Cornhill Magazine* and *The Fortnightly Review*. They appeared subsequently in a two- or three-volume format. Trollope wrote several books of cultural reportage which were more than mere travelogues: *The West Indies* (1859), *North America* (1862), *Australia and New Zealand* (1873), and *South Africa* (1878), along with the more impressionistic *Travelling Sketches* (1865-1866). Three volumes of short stories appeared: *Lotta Schmidt and Other Stories* (1867), *An Editor's Tales* (1870), and *Why Frau Frohmann Raised Her Prices and Other Stories* (1882). He wrote sketches of clerical men in *Clergymen of the Church of England* (1865-1866) and detailed biographies of William Makepeace Thackeray, a longtime friend (1879), and Lord Palmerston, the prominent politician (1882). His own *Autobiography* appeared posthumously in 1883. He tried his hand at classical translation in an edition of *The Commentaries of Caesar* (1870). Trollope's letters were edited by Bradford A. Booth (1951) but 205 complete and three fragmentary letters remain unpublished at Princeton University. *The Oxford Trollope* (1948), in multiple volumes, edited by Michael Sadleir and Frederick Page, is the most complete edition of his novels.

Achievements

Trollope was acknowledged during his lifetime as a prominent though not necessarily a weighty or enduring writer. He wished to entertain and he did so, at least until the late 1860's when *He Knew He Was Right* turned out to be a failure. His posthumous reputation was harmed by his *Autobiography*, which claimed that he wrote automatically, that his characters were imitations of commonly observed types, that he transcribed reality without much aesthetic control, and that he forced his production by his methodical habits of composition whatever the circumstances. These admissions brought upon him the wrath of the next generation of writers in the 1880's and 1890's who were imbued with more aesthetic doctrines of carefully contrived and consistent viewpoints, detailed representation of interior states, a conscious interplay of ideas, and a complex style to suit a more complex method of storytelling.

Later, Trollope suffered from those who deemed him a pedestrian realist padding his work with creaking plots, flat characters, prosaic situations, and dull prose. He was, and still is for much of the public, the novelist of a single work, *Barchester Towers*, but other writers and critics have not forgiven him for writing more than thirty novels and setting himself a goal to exceed in quantity if not in quality. Despite what seems to be a simple theory of fiction—the writer tries as closely as possible to make the reader's experience approximate his own, to make his characters and events appear to parallel actual life—Trollope was more sophisticated than he allows.

Walter Kendrick finds that before Trollope's *He Knew He Was Right*, his inner thought is not distinguished from outer events, consciousness is presented chronologically; and characters, at least by implication, appear without authorial intervention. Afterward, character becomes "a zone of space on a canvas" with changes of age, feeling, and appearance even while outside the narrative. Various linear plots create a spatial unity for the reader, and they become a mosaic on which the character exists. Fiction writing becomes a subject in the novel, and the characters are a warning against efforts to define their existence with the narrative. This view sees the characters as a complex interplay between narrative and reader. Nathaniel Hawthorne had a very different view of Trollope, equating him to a giant hewing a great lump out of the earth as the earth's inhabitants go about the business of putting it under a glass case. This comment leads, unfortunately, in the direction of Henry James's evaluation after Trollope's death that he had "a great deliberate apprehension of the real" but that his "great fecundity is gross and importunate."

Trollope is a mixture of several kinds of writer, sometimes realistic in the sociological way of Honoré de Balzac, analyzing class and caste, sometimes a comedian of manners and mores like Henry Fielding, at times a sentimental melodramatist like Charles Dickens, fairly often an ironist deliberately breaking fictional illusions like Thackeray, often introspective if not as equally learned as George Eliot, and periodically a brilliant chronicler of dementia like Joseph Conrad. This mixture is what creates havoc with critical response. Trollope is a master of convincing and accurate dialogue, good at retrospective interior analysis, and gifted with varieties of ironic voices. The building of his reputation, aided by Michael Sadleir's biography in the 1920's, was materially assisted by *The Trollopian* (now *Nineteenth Century Studies*), a journal devoted to studies of his novels, further work by scholars, such as Ruth apRoberts, Robert M. Polhemus, and James R. Kincaid, and new critical techniques, which have given Trollope his present reputation as a leading English novelist.

Biography

Anthony Trollope, born on April 24, 1815, in London, seems to have owed his boisterous energy, booming voice, quarrelsome touchiness, and reticent sensitivity, to a childhood of off-handed upbringing. C. P. Snow refers to him as "weighed down by 20 years of neglect and humiliation." His father was a tactless and impractical barrister who had pretensions about being a landowner in Harrow. There, he established his family in an elegant though quickly declining farm, Julians, later the model for the experimental Orley Farm in the novel of that name. Trollope's mother, Frances, was the driving force of the family; she was closer to Trollope's oldest brother, Tom, than to Anthony: Anthony received neither much encouragement nor much regular affection from her. After starting his education at Sunbury School, with a brief stint at Harrow, Anthony was sent to Winchester, his father's old school, for three years. In 1827, the family was forced to move into a smaller house in Harrow for financial reasons.

Meanwhile, his mother made the acquaintance of a zealous Utopian reformer, Fanny Wright, and went with her and three of her children—Henry, Cecilia, and Emily—to America. Their experiences there border on black comedy. Among other misfortunes, Frances, without past experience or common sense, started a fancy emporium or bazaar in Cincinnati, the building evolved into a grand structure modeled upon an Egyptian temple. The enterprise only succeeded in making the family penniless. Through the efforts of a painter friend, her husband, and son Tom, they managed to piecemeal their way home to England.

Anthony was removed from Winchester in 1830, which deprived him of the chance to enter Oxford University from which he might have entered into the clergy, the usual course at that time. He returned as a day student to Harrow School where the intense and entrenched snobbery made the shabby boy the butt of ridicule and persecution, and perhaps began his lifelong pattern of irritability. Also at that time, Trollope's father sank into petty miserliness and self-pitying moroseness, becoming more obsessively preoccupied with his scholarly work, an ecclesiastical encyclopedia.

The success of Frances' *The Domestic Manners of the Americans* (1832), a book adversely critical of American society, temporarily kept the family from bankruptcy, but her husband's financial mismanagement created more debts.

To prevent his arrest for bankruptcy in 1834, the family, without Anthony, went to Bruges, Belgium. Any possible happiness they might have found was destroyed by tuberculosis, which killed Anthony's father, brother Henry, and sister Emily between 1834 and 1836. Frances Trollope was obviously too occupied with nursing to pay much attention to Anthony, but she did get him a tutoring position in Belgium for a short time. He returned to England where he survived in squalid lodgings in Marylebone, London, at a clerk's job in the main post office for seven years. At age twenty-six, he got the chance which changed his life, obtaining the post of deputy surveyor, the overseer of mail service, in western Ireland.

At Banaghar, he found a comfortable social milieu for the first time, though his manner with carriers and postmasters was brusque and his temper was at times violent. Trollope became a man jovial with companions, truculent with superiors, bullying with inferiors, and tender with close friends and family. In 1842, he married Rose Heseltine, an Anglo-Irish woman. Her bank-manager father, like one of Trollope's own shady characters, was an embezzler. A trusted partner, Rose handled Trollope's financial affairs, edited his manuscripts, and accompanied him on his journeys around the world. The portraits of solid, sensible, and compassionate wives and mothers found throughout his work, such as Lady Staveley in *Orley Farm*, suggest the type of woman Trollope had found in Rose.

Irish scenery and politics, and the models of his mother and his brother, Tom, led Trollope to his own fiction writing. Thus, not coincidentally, his first two novels have an Irish theme. In these years, Trollope also began rearing a family, two sons. Henceforth, Trollope's career ran on a dual path, pursuing his duties for the postal service and his writing.

Posted to southwest England in 1851 to correct faults in rural delivery, Trollope and his family led a roving existence for three years until he became his own boss as full surveyor in Belfast, at age thirty-nine. The experience of sleepy country towns and a current topic—the Anglican Church's misuse of endowed charity funds to create sizable incomes for administrators—resulted in the writing of *The Warden*, finished in Belfast and published in 1855; it was his first major success. When Trollope moved his family to Dublin, he established a daily routine of writing. The successor to *The Warden*, *Barchester Towers*, his best-known novel, is a social comedy in the eighteenth century mock-heroic vein of Henry Fielding or Oliver Goldsmith.

During a visit to see his mother and brother in Italy, Trollope met a young American woman, Kate Field, and began a long and close friendship, mostly carried out by correspondence. C. P. Snow thinks that Trollope was impressed by the independent and self-assertive woman, who was rather unlike English women. Intrigued by Kate's advocacy of feminine freedom, in *Orley Farm* (1862), Trollope presents a woman who affronts social and moral conventions by an act of forgery to save the inheritance of her infant son. The motivation

is a bit slick, but the fact that the resolute heroine succeeds against a determined male antagonist suggests that Kate's independence was sympathetically
perceived.

Trollope went to North America during the early Civil War (1861-1862);
a trip which resulted in a travel book. Like his mother's work, the book took
a negative stance toward American institutions. He then published, among
others, *Rachel Ray*, *The Last Chronicle of Barset*, and *The Claverings*, which
gained Trollope his biggest sales price ever. His works were also being serialized in various periodicals, such as *The Fortnightly Review*. It became
obvious, however, that Trollope's continued output led him to repeat themes
and recycle characters.

Immersed as he was in writing and somewhat resentful of his position at
the post office, Trollope resigned in October, 1867, after the offer of the
editorship of a new journal, *St. Paul's Magazine*. He continued to do some
work on behalf of the post office, however, since he went to Washington to
negotiate a postal treaty in 1868. Trollope ran *St. Paul's Magazine* for three
years before it went under financially. He was not temperamentally suited to
deal with authors.

In his own writing, Trollope tended, as Walter Kendrick sees it, to turn
toward more sensational materials, which other authors had discarded, but
he was also experimenting in the psychological novel. In *He Knew He Was
Right*, Trollope treats the subject of insanity and he presents a fascinating
study of psychosis. Ruth apRoberts praises the novel for its economy and the
supporting relationships of closely knit characters. Yet, Trollope's work began
to command less popular attention, and he increasingly turned to the political
world. He created Phineas Finn, an Anglo-Irish politician, who appears in
the novel of that name in 1869 and reappears in *Phineas Redux*, part of the
loose series sometimes referred to as the Palliser novels. Trollope, however,
did not give up what is really his chief subject: conflict between the sexes.

In 1871, having sold Waltham House and given up his editorship, Trollope
and his wife embarked on an eighteen-month visit to New Zealand and a stay
with their son, Fred, a relatively unprosperous sheep-farmer in Australia.
Trollope continued to write during their stay in the primitive sheep-station.
A travel commentary and materials for *John Caldigate* were the result of the
voyage, as well as further work on the novel *The Eustace Diamonds*. The
Trollopes then settled in London where he wrote on the current topic of "the
condition of England" in *The Way We Live Now* and *The Prime Minister*.
Trollope presented his skeptical views about the ability of a democratic society
to govern itself effectively.

The final stage of Trollope's life was a restless one in his sixties. He took
another trip to Australia for eight months in 1875, returning through the
United States and meeting with Kate Field. Then, he immediately went to
South Africa to inspect the Boer territory with the encroaching British set-

tlement based on gold and diamond exploitation. The Trollopes again
returned to the land by moving into a refined farmhouse at Hartung, near
Hastings, where Trollope worked on his autobiography. Along with other
fiction, he wrote a mystery novel, *Mr. Scarborough's Family*, which was serialized before his death but published posthumously in 1883. Farm living
sparked Trollope's asthma which drained his energy, thus causing him to
return to London. He was enjoying club life, dinners, and letters to his son,
Henry, who was also a writer, when Trollope suffered a sudden stroke in the
fall of 1882 that left him paralyzed, and a month later, on December 6, 1882,
he died, at the age of sixty-seven.

Analysis

Recent criticism of Anthony Trollope has acknowledged his affinity with
comic satirists of the eighteenth century, and this affinity is reflected in his
best-known work, *Barchester Towers*. There are two distinct worlds in the
novel: that of London vanity, represented by Mr. Slope, the London preacher
who comes to Barchester as the protégé of Mrs. Proudie; and that of the
smaller, conservative rural world, represented by Archdeacon Grantly of
Barchester Cathedral who opposes Mr. Slope with "high and dry" Anglicanism. At the end, Slope is rejected but so is the siren of the comic interlude,
Signora Madeleine Vesey Neroni, daughter of the gentlemanly but parasitic,
self-indulgent Dr. Vesey Stanhope, canon of the Cathedral.

The novel is concerned with the pursuit of Eleanor Bold, a young prosperous widow and daughter of Mr. Harding, by Obadiah Slope, a brash and
unctuous social climber. The newly vacant position of warden provokes a
struggle between the Grantly forces and the Proudie forces (including Mr.
Slope), with Mrs. Proudie, at the head. In this strand of the plot, the mock-
heroic or mock-epic combat parodies the Miltonic epic tradition, with Grantly
and his supporters as the rebel angels struggling against the tyrant Mrs.
Proudie, with Slope as a kind of fallen angel. Slope is first supported by Mrs.
Proudie in his efforts to prevent the return of the vacant post to Harding,
but Slope, in his effort to attain favor with Eleanor Bold, eventually gets the
position for Harding.

Slope is emasculated by Signora Neroni, who transfixes him with her bright
eyes and silvery laughter during rural games and festivities at Ullathorne, the
ancient seat of the Thornes and center of a static pastoral world. Seduced by
her witchery, he is humiliated by this demoniac Eve and defeated by Eleanor's
godlike rebuff, who slaps his face as he presses his suit upon her. Further,
he incurs the wrath of his patroness, Mrs. Proudie, with his attentiveness to
Signora Neroni, who, although crippled, rules from a couch where she resides
in state like Cleopatra. In this world of sham battles, Grantly celebrates his
triumph, including a dean's position for Mr. Harding in a solemn conclave of
the clergy.

The disputants in these mock-exercises practice their feints around innocent third parties: Bishop Proudie between Slope and Mrs. Proudie; Quiverful, the other candidate for the wardenship, a pathetically comic father of numerous children, between his determined wife and Slope; and Harding between Slope and Grantly. In this formally ordered structure, it is appropriate that Eleanor and Frances Arabin, the naïve Oxford academician, be matched by Miss Thorne, reaffirming the power of the old order, yet still contending with Proudies. The marriage of Eleanor and Arabin asserts the two worlds, old and new, country and city, innocent and corrupt.

The novel has a rich galaxy of minor characters. For example, there is Bertie Stanhope, the dilettante sculptor, who is pressed into proposing to Eleanor, but he undermines his own courtship by the candid admission of his motives; Mr. Harding, the unwilling tool of both Slope and Grantly, who takes such delight in the cathedral music that he mechanically saws an imaginary cello during moments of partisan plots and counterplots; and Mrs. Quiverful, who functions like a wailing chorus in a Greek tragedy, piteously reminding the world and Mrs. Proudie of the cruel difficulties of pinched means and a large family. Although Trollope did write important novels on more serious themes, *Barchester Towers* remains his best known, with its effective comic scenes, the balletlike entrances and exits, the lively irony, and the mock-heroic bathos. The orchestration of speaking styles ranging from the pomposity of the Archdeacon to the vacuity of Bertie Stanhope is another example of the buoyancy and playful wit that Trollope achieved only intermittently thereafter.

Orley Farm was written during Trollope's middle period. Its central situation revolves around the plight of Lady Mason, the second wife of a rich man, who, twenty years earlier, forged a codicil to her dying husband's will so that it leaves Orley Farm, her sole economic support, to her and her young child, Lucius. The possession of the farm has become a matter of regret, as the suspicions of the legitimate heir, Joseph Mason, otherwise the inheritor of considerable wealth, eventuate in a trial to break the will. The effort fails only because Lady Mason commits perjury. Using the omniscient viewpoint, Trollope shows both her guilt and her anguish in trying to provide security for her infant son. Lucius, as the novel opens, is a proud, priggish young man given to notions of scientifically reforming agricultural practice; he is well-educated, theoretical, and self-righteous.

The novel's unusual perspective poses two main themes: first, how justice can be accomplished, and second, whether justice can actually be achieved. In setting human rights against legal rights, Trollope portrays Lady Mason's crime in the light of vested interests and the selfish motives of various people. Like C. P. Snow in a novel such as *The Masters* (1951), Trollope displays in *Orley Farm* an abstract ideal distorted and transformed by human emotions, calculations, and egotism. Joseph Mason is more concerned with defeating

Lady Mason than enjoying the actual property; Sir Peregrine Orme, a highly respected landowner, proposes marriage to Lady Mason in order to extend the protection of his name, but even he is forced to realize the stain upon his honor if the truth should come out, and after Lady Mason refuses his offer, he, having been told the damning truth, keeps his promise to support her in her new trial. Another perspective is provided through Mr. Dockwrath, the country lawyer who discovers the evidence which necessitates the new trial, hopes it will prove lucrative and will enhance his legal reputation. Lady Mason's solicitor, Mr. Furnival, carefully avoids definite knowledge of her guilt, though he suspects it, while also wishing she were proven guilty so that he might forgive her with pleasure. A less selfish attitude is seen in Edith Orme, Sir Peregrine's widowed daughter-in-law, who recognizes with compassion the necessity for Lady Mason's crime and the suffering it has entailed for her.

Trollope reveals some of his other typical thematic concerns in the subplots of *Orley Farm*. He explores various attitudes toward marriage and money in the romances of Peregrine Jr., Lucius Mason, and Felix Graham, a poor barrister, with a variety of modern young women. The women's responses to the gentlemen's advances run from prudent calculation of worldly advantages to prudent reticence in acknowledging love until family wisdom approves it. Also, Trollope's impulses toward indulgence of children are exemplified in Lord and Lady Staveley, who, having made their way without worldly advantages, are willing to offer the same chance to their children by permitting the engagement of a daughter to Felix Graham, whose success has been impeded by his honesty. Trollope's conservatism is revealed through the reluctance of these young people to avow their love until they have consent from the Staveleys.

With regard to the central theme of moral and legal justice, purely through the oratorical skills of the trial lawyer, Lady Mason is found innocent of perjury, a finding wholly incorrect. The trial frees the guilty, turns the truthful into villains, makes the innocent bear the burden of deceit, challenges the loyalty of lawyers, and implicates the idealists posturings. The system has turned Lady Mason's desperate chicanery into heroism. It is somewhat anticlimactic that Trollope has the pure Edith Orme take Lady Mason to her heart and, from a sense of Christian charity, refuse to render judgment against her.

Meanwhile, Lady Mason's greatest trial has been alienation from Lucius who, unaware of her guilt, has attempted vigorous countermeasures to defend her honor rather than respecting her dignified silence. His discovery of the truth cuts deeply into his priggish pride, destroys his dreams of becoming a gentleman-farmer, and makes him restore the farm to Joseph Mason before departing abroad with his mother. Again, Trollope makes an ambivalent statement through this conclusion. Although forgiveness implies repentance and restitution, Lady Mason has not been, at least in public, repentant, and the restitution is as much a matter of pride as of justice. The effect is a tacit denial of Lady Mason's innocence and thus the aborting of the whole effort to save her reputation.

If the power of money, or the distortions of human choice and desire which money brings, is Trollope's major concern, the warfare of the sexes and the frustrations which that warfare brings are secondary themes in his novels. *Can You Forgive Her?*, the first of the Palliser series—which includes *Phineas Finn*, *Phineas Redux*, and *The Prime Minister*, each grounded in politics—raises the issue of what sort of love a woman wishes in marriage or indeed whether marriage is a suitable institution. The novel presents the case of Alice Vavasour, a "new woman" who does not know what she wants in life but resents the demands of social propriety. She especially resents the expectation that she accept the marriage proposal of John Grey, whom she really does love, merely because everyone knows him to be a suitable partner. Her cousin, the heiress Lady Glencora McCluskie, has married Plantagenet Palliser, the dull younger son of a ducal family, to support his Liberal political career with her money; but she has fallen in love with the handsome Burgo Fitzgerald, an unconventional, ruinous, yet passionate charmer. Alice reinstitutes her former affection for her cousin George Vavasour, another charmingly irresponsible man who needs her money to campaign to keep his seat in Parliament. For Alice, the masculine excitement of politics makes George attractive, although she honestly admits his desire for her money.

The novel has low-comedy relief in Alice's aunt, Arabella Greenow, and her two suitors, a grocer with money and a retired military officer without it. Arabella means to have her own way, giving her lovers only as much liberty as she desires, choosing the officer because of "a sniff of the rocks and the valleys" about him. The comedy underscores the desire of Alice and Glencora, who, if they had a choice, would put themselves at the mercy of weak men.

In a melodramatic turn of the main plot, George knocks down his sister, Kate, for refusing to assist him in overturning their grandfather's will, which had left all the family property to her. This turn of the plot demonstrates, through George's furious masculine rage, the falsity of the normal economic subjugation of women, which has been reversed in Kate's case. Arabella Greenow, for her part, is also financially independent and can bargain her way into a satisfactorily romantic liaison balancing "rocks and valleys" against "bread and cheese."

Glencora, aware of being sold into matrimony, almost runs off with Burgo but is dissuaded at the last minute by the vigilance of Alice, who makes clear to Plantagenet the temptation he has given to his wife by his conduct. In an improbable reversal that displays Trollope's own romanticism, Plantagenet sacrifices his political hopes for a cabinet appointment in order to take her away from the scenes of her misery after she has confessed her infatuation.

Indeed, he is even willing to provide Burgo, who becomes a frequenter of gambling tables, with an allowance at her behest when they encounter him abroad.

Plantagenet can make a sacrifice for Glencora because he has money and social position; George Vavasour, by contrast, is defeated in politics and exiled for lack of money. John Grey, meanwhile, has interposed himself in Alice's arrangement with George so that her fortune is not at stake. This conduct, chivalrous in one sense, paternalistic in another, results in George's challenging him to a duel. The Victorian world is not that of Regency rakes, however, and George's blustering challenge is physically rebuffed, and he is sent away degraded. Alice finally accepts John Grey in a contrite mood. although Grey has kindly intentions, Alice's undefined longings for autonomy anticipate those Henrik Ibsen made memorable through Nora Helmer in *A Doll's House* (1879), where Nora sacrifices love in the effort to mould her own destiny.

If the future of his heroines seems to lie within conventional marital arrangements or respectable spinsterhood secured by inherited money, Trollope's questioning title for the novel seems to turn the issue of feminine aspiration somewhat ambivalently to the reader. He has shown women challenging the decorum of prudent emotions and affections based on money, but only the ungenteel Mrs. Greenow succeeds in mastering her destiny through financial manipulation.

In *The Eustace Diamonds*, Trollope shows the psychologically damaging effects of survival in an upper-class and aristocratic hierarchy. A society that channels affections and loyalties in terms of property and money, where people struggle for ascendancy, domination, and power, while subscribing to romantic illusions of unfettered expression and creative self-development. The narrator ironically undercuts the Romantic pretensions as the novel delineates the unrealistic strategies of men and women coping with the moral corruption of social ambition. They seek security, status, prestige, and elegance while evincing pretentiousness, snobbery, envy, and parasitism. Trollope takes an anarchic pleasure in those egotistical characters who subvert institutions by undermining the rules of conduct, stretching them to the point of fatuity.

In the novel, Lizzie Eustace appropriates the diamonds without specific authority from her late husband, Sir Florian, and uses them as weapons against the respectable family lawyer, Mr. Camperdown, and the man she intends as her second husband, the morally honorable Lord Fawn. The diamonds become a symbol of Lizzie's inner rage against the world, a rage arising from self-doubt prompted by the excessive demands of her own idealized views of herself. While denying that ownership of the necklace gives her any pleasure, Lizzie simultaneously insists that she will throw the diamonds away while guarding them zealously. When the box in which she ostentatiously houses them is stolen, Lizzie claims that the necklace has been stolen as well. The lie is psychologically predictable. The diamonds exemplify her attitudes toward herself, toward Lord Fawn whom she despises for his complete disdain of the diamonds, and toward Frank Greystock, her champion before the world, whom she has lured away from his serious attentions to Lucy Morris. The supposed theft is Lizzie's symbolic punishment for a guilt which will be lessened if the diamonds are believed stolen, but it is also an aggrandisement of her own self-esteem since secretly she knows they are still in her possession. The diamonds, however, are stolen in a second robbery, which ends Lizzie's control of the situation.

Lizzie's desire for social domination gains dimension through the narrator's ironic moral judgment and through the close-ups of the omniscient viewpoint that reveal her own rationalizations and fears. Seeking support, Lizzie confesses to Lord George, hoping that he will be cynically brutal, but instead she receives his weak acknowledgment of her supposed cunning. When the police discover the truth, Lizzie prefers the illusion of submitting to the police administrator to the reality of confronting her own self-destructive behavior. Lizzie then tries desperately to reestablish control by triumphing over someone: she reproaches Mrs. Carbuncle, her friend; breaks her engagement with Lord Fawn, ignoring his earlier efforts to end the relationship and pretending to be heartlessly jilted, offers herself to Lord George, who also refuses her; and finally bids for the attentions of Frank Greystock through his need for money, yet Frank is simply provoked into promising he will abandon her utterly if she persists.

Yielding to a fantasy logic, Lizzie entertains a marriage proposal from Mr. Emilius, an impudent and sanctimonious popular preacher whom she had once refused. She deliberately accepts him knowing that he is a fraud and admitting that his bogus qualities attract her. Lizzie's limited knowledge of how the world operates is supported by Emilius's brazen effrontery, which will offer her a new chance for social domination.

The secondary characters are drawn with an equal sense of psychological aberration. For example, there is the cynical honesty of Lord George, which conceals a fearful vacillation that abhors responsibility yet is resolute in pushing his companion, Sir Griffin Tewett, into marriage with Lucinda Roanoke. Alternately submissive and aggressive, he turns vindictive in denouncing Lizzie for the damage she has caused his reputation by creating suspicions of his complicity in her concealment of the necklace. He is also forgiving, on the other hand, of Mrs. Barnacle, his former mistress, for her good intentions in encouraging her niece, Lucinda, to marry for money. Lord George appears cognizant of obligations assumed by others though irresolute in taking them upon himself. Further, he shows the unreality of Lizzie's dreams; but his own conduct is the model of a romantic neurosis. Other examples of psychologically crippled characters are Lucinda, who suffers from strong sexual repression and emotional sterility, and Sir Griffin, cool, vindictive, and arrogant, who is repelled by anyone who would love him.

These characters are set up in contrast to the more conventional ones, such as Mrs. Hittaway, who reflect the pathological tendencies that a materialistic society encourages. The baffled efforts of Lizzie, Lord George, Sir Griffin, and Lucinda to deal with destructive self-deception reflect the results of social forces inhibiting real creative growth in understanding. V. S. Pritchett has criticized Trollope for being "a detailed, rather cynical observor of a satisfied world," and that "we recognize that he [Trollope] has drawn life as people say it is when they are not speaking about themselves." C. P. Snow commented that an exploratory psychological writer such as Trollope "has to live on close terms with the blacker—including the worse—side of his own nature." *The Eustace Diamonds* is the record of Trollope's endurance of a mental nature that was divided. Pritchett has accused Trollope of not capturing or presenting the depth of moral experience. This may reflect a demand for a more complex style, a more intensive depiction of the intricacies of moral struggle, and a more insistent emphasis on values. Snow, however, perceived the simple, direct style as cutting out everything except the truth. Trollope was not temperamental or self-advertising, but as a novelist, he covers a wide range of social, institutional, and religious issues and controversies constituting the fabric of Victorian society. He dramatizes the moral and intellectual dilemmas often arising from them and has considerable insight as well as the ability to present the sheer flux of mental life, which anticipates later developments in the work of James Joyce, Virginia Woolf, and Dorothy Richardson.

Roger E. Wiehe

Other major works

SHORT FICTION: *Tales of All Countries*, 1861, 1863; *Lotta Schmidt and Other Stories*, 1867; *An Editor's Tales*, 1870; *Why Frau Frohmann Raised Her Prices and Other Stories*, 1882.

NONFICTION: *The West Indies*, 1859; *North America*, 1862; *Clergymen of the Church of England*, 1865-1866; *Travelling Sketches*, 1865-1866; *The Commentaries of Caesar*, 1870 (translation); *Australia and New Zealand*, 1873; *South Africa*, 1878; *Thackeray*, 1879; *Lord Palmerston*, 1882; *Autobiography*, 1883; *The Letters of Anthony Trollope*, 1851 (Bradford A. Booth, editor).

Bibliography

Edwards, P. D. *Anthony Trollope: His Art and Scope*. New York: Pantheon Books, 1978. Each one of Trollope's forty-seven novels is mentioned in an attempt to locate his most and his least successful novels and their typical characteristics. Includes a select bibliography and an index.

Hall, N. John, ed. *The Trollope Critics*. Basingstoke, England: Macmillan, 1981. Of a number of critical anthologies, this is probably the best for introductory purposes. Includes twenty leading Trollope critics and covers a wide range of topics. An excellent bibliography is provided.

Halperin, John. *Trollope and Politics*. New York: Macmillan, 1977. This study focuses on each of the six Palliser novels and includes several more general chapters. Contains a select bibliography and indexes.

Pollard, Arthur. *Anthony Trollope*. Boston: Routledge & Kegan Paul, 1978. Pollard seeks to put all of Trollope's novels and a variety of miscellaneous works within the context of his life and time. Stresses Trollope's evocation of his age and his guiding moral purpose. Includes an index.

Wright, Andrew. *Anthony Trollope: Dream and Art*. Basingstoke, England: Macmillan, 1983. This brief study of fifteen of Trollope's novels sees them as contemporary fictions, transfiguring life in a certain way. Contains a bibliography and an index.

MARK TWAIN
Samuel Langhorne Clemens

Born: Florida, Missouri; November 30, 1835
Died: Redding, Connecticut; April 21, 1910

Principal long fiction

The Gilded Age, 1873 (with Charles Dudley Warner); *The Adventures of Tom Sawyer*, 1876; *The Prince and the Pauper*, 1881; *The Adventures of Huckleberry Finn*, 1884; *A Connecticut Yankee in King Arthur's Court*, 1889; *The American Claimant*, 1892; *Tom Sawyer Abroad*, 1894; *The Tragedy of Pudd'nhead Wilson*, 1894; *Personal Recollections of Joan of Arc*, 1896; *Tom Sawyer, Detective*, 1896; *The Mysterious Stranger*, 1916 (revised as *The Chronicle of Young Satan*, 1969, by Albert Bigelow Paine and Frederick A. Duneka); *Simon Wheeler, Detective*, 1963.

Other literary forms

In addition to his novels, Mark Twain wrote a great deal of short fiction, which can be divided, although often only very arbitrarily, into short stories, tales, and humorous sketches. One of the best examples of his short stories is "The Man That Corrupted Hadleyburg," and one of the best examples of his humorous sketches is "The Celebrated Jumping Frog of Calaveras County." Somewhere between the story and the sketch are tales such as "Captain Stormfield's Visit to Heaven." Twain also wrote speeches and essays, both humorous and critical. Representative of his best satiric essays, which range from the very funny to the very sober, are "Fenimore Cooper's Literary Offenses" and "To the Person Sitting in Darkness." The first of these is a hilarious broadside against Cooper's style and invention in which Twain is obviously enjoying himself while at the same time continuing his ongoing war against the romanticizing of the past. "To the Person Sitting in Darkness," considered by some to be his finest piece of invective, is his attack upon what he saw as the exploitation of the Philippines following the Spanish-American War by, in his words, "The Blessings-of-Civilization Trust." Early in his career, he wrote the travel sketches and impressions, *The Innocents Abroad* (1869) and *A Tramp Abroad* (1880), and later, *Following the Equator* (1897). Two of his most important books are autobiographical, *Life on the Mississippi* (1883) and *Mark Twain's Autobiography*, published after his death in various editions in 1924.

Achievements

The coincidental appearance of Halley's comet in the years of Twain's birth and death, 1835 and 1910, has been much remarked. A historical event, however, in contrast to the cosmic one, occurring very near the midpoint of his life, provides a better symbol for his career and his achievement than does the mysterious, fiery comet. In 1869, at Promontory Point, Utah, a golden spike was driven to complete the first North American transcontinental railroad. The subsequent settling of the great midwestern center of the continent and the resulting transformation of a frontier society into a civilized one, a process people thought would take hundreds of years, was to be effected in several decades. Twain's life spanned the two Americas, the frontier America that produced so much of the national mythology and the emerging urban, industrial giant of the twentieth century. At the heart of Twain's achievement is his creation of Tom Sawyer and Huck Finn, who embody that mythic America, midway between the wilderness and the modern super-state.

Tom and Huck, two of the nation's most enduring characters, give particular focus to Twain's turbulent, sprawling, complex career as journalist, humorist, entrepreneur, and novelist. The focus is dramatic because the two characters have made their way into the popular imagination with the abiding vitality of legend or folklore. They have been kept before generations of Americans in motion pictures, television, cartoons, and other popular art forms as well as in their original form in the novels. The focus is also symbolic because of the fundamental dualism which the two characters can be seen to represent on the personal, the literary, and the cultural planes.

On the personal plane, Tom and Huck represent aspirations so fundamental to Twain's life as to make them seem rather the two halves of his psyche. Like good and bad angels, they have been taken to represent the contending desires in his life: a strong desire for the security and status of material success on the one hand, set against the deeply ingrained desire for freedom from conventional social and moral restraints on the other. It has been conjectured that riverboat piloting was perhaps the most satisfying of Twain's occupations because it offered him high degrees of both respectability and freedom. Although the character of Tom, the symbol of perennial boyhood, can be easily overburdened by this perspective, there is in him the clear outline of the successful, settled, influential man-of-affairs-to-be. If Tom had grown up, he might well have made and lost a fortune in the publishing business and through investments in the Paige typesetter. He almost certainly would have been a successful professional or businessman. He would likely have traveled abroad and would have been eager to associate with nobility at every opportunity. It is relatively easy to imagine Tom growing up. It is instructive to realize that it is almost impossible to imagine Huck's doing so.

On the literary plane, the two may also be seen as representing contending forces, those of the two principal literary schools of the period, the Romantic and the realistic. Surely, Twain's pervasive attacks upon romantic literature are somewhat compulsive, reminiscent of Nathaniel Hawthorne's preoccupation with the Puritans. Both protest too much. Twain is one of America's foremost Romantics, even if he did see himself as a realist, and even if he did engage much of his time in puncturing the sentimental balloons of the disciples of Sir Walter Scott, Cooper, and the graveyard poets. He was both Romantic and realist, and Tom and Huck emerge almost allegorically as symbols of the two major literary schools of the late nineteenth century.

Tom as the embodiment of socially conforming respectability and as a disciple of Romantic literature contrasts illustratively with Huck as the embodiment of the naturally free spirit, who is "realistic" in part because of his adolescent honesty about such things as art, royalty, and the efficacy of prayer. It is the symbolic dualism on the historical plane, however, that brings into sharpest focus the nature of Twain's central and most enduring achievement. On the historical plane, his two central characters reflect most clearly Twain's principal legacy to posterity: the embodiment in fiction of that moment in time, a moment both real and imaginary, given some historical particularity by the driving of the golden spike at Promontory Point in 1869, when America was poised between the wilderness and the modern, technological state. In this context, Tom represents the settlements that were to become the towns and cities of the new century, and Huck represents the human spirit, freer, at least in the imagination, in the wilderness out of which the settlements were springing. At the end of *The Adventures of Huckleberry Finn*, Twain sends Huck on that impossible mission that has been central to the American experience for centuries, when he has him decide to "light out for the territory" before Aunt Sally can "adopt" and "civilize" him.

Twain the humorist and satirist, Twain the silvermining, Paige-typesetting entrepreneur, Twain the journalist, the family man, the anguished, skeptical seeker after religious faith—all must be taken into consideration in accounts of the nature of his achievements. Without Tom Sawyer and Huck Finn, he would have made his mark as a man of his time, a man of various and rich talents. Most likely, his reputation would rest today largely upon his talents as a humorist and satirist, and that reputation still figures largely in assessment of his overall achievement. With Tom and Huck, however, his achievement is given the depth and dramatic focus of a central contribution to the national mythology. Huck's "voice" is frequently compared to the voice of Walt Whitman's "Song of Myself." Such comparisons rest in part upon rhetorical similarities between the two voices, similarities in what has been called the "vernacular mode." More significantly, they derive from the similarities of the achievements of the poet and the novelist in the establishing of historically and culturally distinctive American "voices" in poetry and fiction. Tom Sawyer and Huck Finn loom large on the nineteenth century literary horizon. They stand, along with Cooper's Natty Bumppo and Chingachgook, Hawthorne's Hester Prynne and Arthur Dimmesdale, and Whitman's persona in "Song of Myself," as the principal characters of the emerging national literature. Twain's contribution to that body of literature is at the deepest center of his achievement as a major American writer.

Biography

Mark Twain was born Samuel Langhorne Clemens in Florida, Missouri, in 1835. He first used the pen name "Mark Twain," taken from the river boatmen's cry for two fathoms of safe water, in 1862.

Twain's father was a Virginia lawyer, and the family was of poor but respectable Southern stock. In 1839, the family moved to Hannibal, Missouri, the Mississippi River town that provided the source material and background of some of Twain's best-known fiction. After his father died in 1847, Twain left school to become an apprentice in the printing shop of his brother, Orion. From 1855 to 1856, Twain worked as a journeyman printer in St. Louis, New York, Philadelphia, Keokuk, and Cincinnati. Between 1857 and 1860, he acquired much of his knowledge of the Mississippi River as a pilot, beginning that short though richly productive career under the tutelage of a senior pilot, Horace Bixby. He was a Confederate volunteer for several months after the Civil War began. In 1861, he left for the Nevada territory with his brother Orion, where he drifted into prospecting and journalism, beginning his career as a reporter with the *Virginia City Territorial Enterprise*, and continuing it with the San Francisco *Morning Call*.

Twain's literary career and the beginning of his fame might be said to have begun in 1865 with the publication in the New York Saturday Press of "The Celebrated Jumping Frog of Calaveras County." As a journalist, he went to the Sandwich Islands in 1866 and to Europe and the Holy Land in 1867. The latter of the two provided him with the experiences which he shaped into his first book, *The Innocents Abroad. Roughing It*, his narrative of pioneers striving to establish civilization on the frontier, appeared in 1872, and his first novel-length fiction, written with Charles Dudley Warner, *The Gilded Age*, came in 1873.

In 1870, Twain married Olivia Langdon. They finished their Hartford mansion and moved into it in 1871. Their infant son Langdon died in 1872, the year Susy, their first daughter, was born. Her sisters, Clara and Jean, followed in 1874 and 1880. Twain's most productive years as a novelist came in this middle period when his daughters were young and he was prospering. *The Adventures of Tom Sawyer*, *The Prince and the Pauper*, *The Adventures of Huckleberry Finn*, and *A Connecticut Yankee in King Arthur's Court*, were all written during this highly productive period.

By 1890, Twain's financial fortunes were crumbling, mostly owing to bad investment in a publishing firm and in the Paige typesetter. In 1891, Twain closed the Hartford mansion, sold the furniture, and went to Europe to economize. While he was lecturing in Europe, his daughter Susy died, and his wife, Livy, shortly afterward suffered a nervous collapse from which she never recovered. Twain blamed himself for bringing on his beloved family the circumstances that led to both tragedies. His abiding skepticism about human nature deepened to cynicism and found expression in those dark stories of his last years, "The Man That Corrupted Hadleyburg," "The Mysterious Stranger," and in the essay "What Is Man?" He died in 1910 at the age of seventy-four in Redding, Connecticut.

Analysis

It is instructive to note that the most pervasive structural characteristic of Mark Twain's work, of his nonfiction as well as his fiction, is dualistic. That observation is not worth much without detailed application to specific aspects of particular works, but even before turning to particulars, it is useful to consider how many "pairs" of contending, conflicting, complementary, or contrasting characters, situations, states of being, ideas and values run through Twain's work. One thinks immediately of Tom and Huck, of Huck and Jim, of Huck and Pap, of Aunt Sally and Miss Watson, of the prince and the pauper, of the two sets of twins in *The Tragedy of Pudd' nhead Wilson*. One thinks of boys testing themselves against adults, of youth and adulthood, of the free life on the river contrasted with the settled life of the river towns, of the wilderness and civilization, of the promises of industrial progress against the backdrop of the humbler, traditional rural setting, of Eden and everything east of Eden, and, finally, of good and evil.

The tonal quality of Twain's works is also dualistic. "The Celebrated Jumping Frog of Calaveras County" is almost pure fun. "The Mysterious Stranger," published after Twain's death, is almost pure gloom. Most of Twain's fiction comes between the two, both chronologically and thematically. Except for *The Gilded Age*, which he wrote with Charles Dudley Warner, the novels, from *The Adventures of Tom Sawyer* to the final two, *The Tragedy of Pudd' nhead Wilson* and *Personal Recollections of Joan of Arc*, fall within the thematic and tonal extremes established by the short fiction. That is, Tom's adventures take place in the hallowed light of innocence and virtue beyond the reach of any truly effective evil forces, while Roxy's adventures in *The Tragedy of Pudd' nhead Wilson*, are of almost unrelieved gloom. *The Adventures of Huckleberry Finn* is midway between the extremes, with its blending of the light and affirmation that shine so brightly in Twain's childhood idyll with the darkened vision of the later years.

Nearly everyone agrees that *The Adventures of Tom Sawyer*, Twain's second novel, is an American classic, and nearly everyone agrees that there is no accounting for its success. It is at the same time a novel of the utmost simplicity and of deep complexity. The novel is a marvelous boy's adventure story, a fact given perspective by Twain's observation that "it will be read only by adults." That is, the essence of childhood can be savored only after the fact, only after one has passed through it and can look back upon it. Popularizations of Tom's adventures are produced for children, but the continuing vitality of the novel depends upon the adult sensibility and its capacity and need for nostalgic recollection. Twain plays on all the strings of that sensibility as he guides the reader through Tom's encounters with the adult world, represented by Aunt Polly and Judge Thatcher, through Tom's romance with Becky, and finally to the adventurous triumph over evil in the person of Injun Joe.

Aunt Polly is the perfect adult foil for a perfect boyhood. Not only does she provide the emotional security that comes from being loved in one's place, but she also serves as an adult Tom can challenge through his wits, thereby deepening his self-confidence about his place in the adult world. The fence whitewashing episode is surely one of the best-known in American literature. In it, Tom not only outwits his friends, whom he dupes into whitewashing the fence for him, but also successfully challenges the adult world which, through Aunt Polly, assigned the "boy's chore" to him in the first place. The episode also provides Twain an opportunity to exercise his irony, which, in contrast to much that was to come in the later fiction, is serenely gentle here. Judge Thatcher represents the secure, if somewhat pompous, authority of the adult world beyond the domestic circle. The much desired recognition of that authority is achieved with decisive pomp when the Judge makes the treasure found in the cave legally Tom's and Huck's.

The romance with Becky is almost pure idyll, although the young lovers' descent into the cave inevitably raises speculations about deeper implications. While Injun Joe as evil incarnate is believable enough to raise the hair along the back of the necks of adults as well as children, especially when the torch goes out in the cave, there is never any doubt that Tom and Becky will be saved, that good will triumph—never any doubt, that is, for the adult sensibility, secure beyond the trials and tribulations of adolescent infatuation and terror.

The book as childhood idyll is really a simple matter, but that does not diminish the significance of that dimension of the work. Rather, it affirms an understanding of the book's success on that level. There is more to be considered, however, especially in terms of the companion piece to come, *The Adventures of Huckleberry Finn*. The poignance of *The Adventures of Tom Sawyer* is attributable in part to the fact that it is an imaginative reconstruction of youthful experience from the perspective of early middle age. The actual historical frame of the re-creation adds its own deeply poignant dimension to the book. The American national experience was clearly in the transitional state between frontier and modern society when the novel was published in 1876. Twain's idyll of boyhood is set in a time and place in history calculated to deepen the significance of the adult's backward recollection of a time of innocence and joy. The American wilderness was never Eden, but that image has haunted the American imagination from at least the time of James Fenimore Cooper's creation of his frontiersman, Natty Bumppo, down to at least the time of Robert Frost's creation of his travelers through the dark, lonely woods.

Finally, in part because it is one of those many pairings of characters so pervasive in Twain's work, Tom's relationship with his half-brother Sid should be noted. The relationship is instructive in that it foreshadows that of the later Tom-Huck relationship. Sid is the "good" boy who serves as Twain's foil for Tom's adventuresome independence. While Tom is never good in the subservient, lap-dog sense that Sid is, there is a kind of lateral movement of his character from the early to the later novel; in *The Adventures of Tom Sawyer*, Tom plays off the foil of Sid's pious "respectability," while in *The Adventures of Huckleberry Finn*, Tom, himself, has moved over to provide a similar foil for Huck's freedom.

Unlike its predecessor, *The Prince and the Pauper* is a "children's book" which has remained simply that, a book for children. Twain professed to have taken great joy in the writing of it, probably in part because of the relief he felt upon completing the troublesome *A Tramp Abroad*. His wife and children admired the book, as did William Dean Howells and the reviewers for the New York *Herald*, the Boston *Transcript*, *The Atlantic*, and the *Century*. Nevertheless, the novel holds little interest for the mature reader except in terms of its relationship to the two superior novels which preceded and followed it.

Its plot hinges upon one of Twain's most explicit pairings, that of Prince Edward with the pauper Tom Cantry. The switching of these look-alike adolescents in the England of Henry VIII allows the Prince to learn what poverty and hardship are like in the alleyways of his kingdom and the pauper to satirize, through his innocence, the foibles of royalty and court life. Neither the satire nor the compassion, however, ring true. It is almost as if Twain were finding his way from his first classic to his second through this experiment, set in a time and place far removed from his native Mississippi River valley.

With that contrast in mind, it is perhaps reasonable to see the prince and the pauper as another Sid and Tom, another Tom and Huck, all of the sets representing at various removes those two basic drives of Twain's nature for respectability and freedom. Huck and Tom Cantry, the pauper, are "freer" than are Tom and Prince Edward, although the relationships are not that simple, since the members of each pair are attracted like magnetic opposites to their mates. This attraction is made most explicit in *The Prince and the Pauper*, where the two actually exchange places. Later in his career, in *The Tragedy of Pudd'nhead Wilson*, Twain made a comparably explicit exchange with wholly tragic consequences. In *The Prince and the Pauper*, it is all play with little consequence at all except for the exigencies of a contrived, melodramatic plot. Twain's truest pairing, that of Huck and Jim, was yet ahead of him.

The Adventures of Huckleberry Finn is almost universally hailed as Twain's best book, as well as one of the half dozen or so American classics of the nineteenth century. This is not to say that the novel is without defects. The ending, in particular, presents some very real problems, structurally, thematically, and rhetorically. The very high place of the novel, however, is generally conceded. This success depends upon several considerations. In the first place, the novel continues the mythic idyll of American boyhood begun with *The Adventures of Tom Sawyer*. That connection and that continuation by itself would have insured the book a place in the national archives if not the national heart. Most agree, however, that its success derives from even deeper currents. *The Adventures of Huckleberry Finn* is Twain's best book because, for whatever reasons, he brought together in it, with the highest degree of artistic balance, those most fundamental dualities running through his work and life from start to finish. The potentially destructive dualities of youth and age, of the need for both security and freedom, of the wilderness and civilization, of innocence and corruption, all are reconciled by means of an aesthetic transformation. Historical, realistic dualities as well as psychological and moral dualities are brought into an artistic synthesis, into a novel, the most distinctive feature of which, finally, is its own modal duality, played out in the terms of a delicate balance between lyricism and satire.

Huck's relationship with Jim, the runaway slave, is central to the novel's narrative, to its structure, and to its theme. Escaping "down" the river, a cruel irony in itself, provides the episodic structure, which is the narrative thread that holds together the developing relationship between the two runaways on the raft. The escape, the quest for freedom, is literal for both Huck and Jim as they flee from Pap and Miss Watson. It may also be seen as symbolic on several planes: historical, philosophical, and moral. The historical setting of the novel is that pivotal era in American history when the new nation was being carved out of the wilderness. The flight down the river is a flight from the complexities of the ever-expanding, westward-moving settlements of the new civilization. The continuing vitality of the novel depends in part upon the survival in the twentieth century of the need for that imaginative escape. Like Henry David Thoreau's Waldon Pond, Huck's Mississippi River, originally an escape from what may now seem some of the simpler strictures of society, continues to serve the American psyche as an imaginative alternative to modern civilization.

The philosophical dimensions of the rapidly disappearing frontier are those of nineteenth century Romanticism. Celebrating their freedom on the raft from the legal and social strictures of the town along the river, Huck and Jim are at the same time affirming the central Romantic thesis concerning man's need to return to nature and to the natural self. There are two kinds of Romanticism in the novel: that which Tom espouses in his adolescent preoccupation with adventure, and that which Huck practices on the river under the stars and, most significantly, in the final resolution of the problem of Jim as a runaway slave. Twain holds up Tom's bookish Romanticism as childish at best and, for the most part, as silly. This attack on Romanticism—a secondary theme in *The Adventures of Huckleberry Finn*, where Twain sends the derelict steamer, the *Walter Scott*, to its destruction on a sandbar—was one of Twain's lifelong preoccupations. It was continued with a vehemence later in *A Connecticut Yankee in King Arthur's Court*, but its deep-running, destructive potential for Twain is harnessed in *The Adventures of Huckleberry Finn*. The satire is there, but it is in the largely playful terms of the antics of the King and the Duke, their mangling of Shakespeare, and the graveyard art of Emmaline Grangerford. This playful treatment of one of his serious themes results in part from the fact that Twain is here working a deeper vein of Romanticism in the person of his supreme fictional creation, Huck.

The moral climax of the novel comes in chapter 31, when Huck decides that he will "go to hell" rather than turn in Jim. The difficulties with the ending of the book derive largely from that relatively early resolution of its central theme. Shortly thereafter, Huck is reunited with Tom, who is responsible for all the preposterous plans to save Jim, who, ironically, no longer needs to be saved. There are real problems here with the plot, with motivation, and with the prose itself, which is no longer sustained by the lyricism of Huck's accounts of life on the raft. The artistic achievement of the climax, however, makes such problems pale into relative insignificance. Twain embodies in Huck and dramatizes in his decision a principle line of American political and moral thought which has its roots in Thomas Jefferson and Thomas Paine, its "philosophical" development in Ralph Waldo Emerson and Thoreau, and its aesthetic transformation at the hands of Twain and Whitman. Huck is the embodiment of both the political and the Romantic ideals of the common man, with no past or roots, whose principal guide is experience rather than tradition. He is one of the principal literary symbols of that fundamental American mythical dream of moral rejuvenation in the Edenic wilderness of the "new" continent. He stands at the center of nineteenth century American literature and at the center of Twain's achievements.

In *The Adventures of Huckleberry Finn*, Twain's attack upon the romantic glorification of the past is a peripheral theme. In *A Connecticut Yankee in King Arthur's Court*, it is central and devastating, both in the novel itself and in its signaling of the direction in which Twain's thought and creative energies were heading. Although this too is a boy's book of a kind, there is about it none of the idyllic radiance of *The Adventures of Tom Sawyer* nor the harmonious balancing of opposites of *The Adventures of Huckleberry Finn*. Rather, there is finally outright war between the forces of the feudal past and those of the progressive present, with considerable ambiguity about which is to be considered the good and which the evil.

There is no doubt that the reader's sympathies at the outset are with the Yankee mechanic, Hank Morgan, who, after a blow on the head, wakes up in King Arthur's England of A. D. 528. After saving himself from execution as a witch by "prophesying" a total eclipse of the sun, he vies successfully with Merlin for power and prestige at court. He is like Huck in his commonsense responses to life in general, and in particular to the romantic claims of the feudal society in which he finds himself. He is unlike Huck in his vigorous progressivism, in his determination to bring the fruits of nineteenth century democracy and technology to feudal England. He introduces explosives, sets up schools to train workmen in the mechanical arts, gives instruction in journalism to his page with an eye to a national press, and stretches telephone lines haphazardly across the countryside. His talents, taken for magic for the most part, earn for him the title "Boss," and the abiding enmity of Merlin, whom he replaces at court. He plans to declare a republic after Arthur's death, and the sixth century kingdom enjoys all the fruits of progress: schools, trains, factories, newspapers, the telephone and telegraph. The end of the story, however, just before Hank returns to his own century, pictures anything but the envisioned utopia. Arthur dies in a battle with Lancelot, Camelot is reduced to shambles, and Hank fortifies himself in a castle against the surviving chivalry of England. One of his final concerns is with the pollution caused by the dead bodies piled in the trenches around his fortress. The repressive, superstitious nightmare of feudal society has been compounded by the fearful efficiency of nineteenth century technology.

The ambiguity of the ending of the novel is symptomatic. The artistic balance of *The Adventures of Huckleberry Finn* is no longer in evidence. Twain, always something of an allegorist, was by 1889 becoming more and more a polemicist, increasingly more interested in conflicts between abstract ideas and values than in the development and portrayal of human characters in all their complexities. Hank can be identified with Huck in terms of their common sense and their human values, but the big difference between them is that Huck's chief concern is with another human being while Hank's is with an abstraction called feudalism.

Twain was to do some of his most important writing in the last two decades of his life, including short fiction and social and moral criticism. His best novels, however, were completed in 1876 and in the 1880's. Of those coming after 1889, *The Tragedy of Pudd'nhead Wilson* is the most readable and the most consistent with the principal direction of his deepening cynicism about the "damned human race." The novel's only really interesting character is Roxy, a slave woman who switches her son with that of her owner Percy Driscoll to save her child from eventually being sold "down river." The whole of the dark tale that follows indicates, in Maxwell Geismar's words, how much "irony and tragedy have taken over the center stage in [Twain's] comic proscenium of life."

Lloyd N. Dendinger

Other major works

SHORT FICTION: *The Celebrated Jumping Frog of Calaveras County, and Other Sketches*, 1867; *Mark Twain's Sketches: New and Old*, 1875; *The Stolen*

White Elephant and Other Stories, 1882; *The £1,000,000 Bank-Note and Other New Stories*, 1893; *The Man That Corrupted Hadleyburg and Other Stories and Essays*, 1900; *A Double Barrelled Detective Story*, 1902; *King Leopold's Soliloquy: A Defense of His Congo Rule*, 1905; *The $30,000 Bequest and Other Stories*, 1906; *A Horse's Tale*, 1907; *The Curious Republic of Gondour and Other Whimsical Sketches*, 1919; *The Adventures of Thomas Jefferson Snodgrass*, 1926; *The Complete Short Stories of Mark Twain*, 1957 (Charles Neider, editor).

PLAYS: *Colonel Sellers*, 1874; *Ah Sin, the Heathen Chinee*, 1877 (with Bret Harte).

NONFICTION: *The Innocents Abroad*, 1869; *Roughing It*, 1872; *A Tramp Abroad*, 1880; *Life on the Mississippi*, 1883; *Following the Equator*, 1897 (also known as *More Tramp Abroad*); *How to Tell a Story and Other Essays*, 1897; *My Debut as a Literary Person*, 1903; *Extracts from Adam's Diary*, 1904; *Eve's Diary, Translated from the Original Ms*, 1906; *What Is Man?*, 1906; *Christian Science*, 1907; *Extract from Captain Stormfield's Visit to Heaven*, 1909; *Is Shakespeare Dead?*, 1909, *Mark Twain's Speeches*, 1910; *Mark Twain's Letters*, 1917 (2 volumes); *Europe and Elsewhere*, 1923 (Albert Bigelow Paine, editor); *Mark Twain's Autobiography*, 1924, 1959 (2 volumes); *Sketches of the Sixties*, 1926 (with Bret Harte); *Mark Twain's Notebook*, 1935 (Albert Bigelow Paine, editor); *Letters from the Sandwich Islands, Written for the Sacramento Union*, 1937; *Letters from Honolulu, Written for the Sacramento Union*, 1939; *Mark Twain in Eruption*, 1940; *Mark Twain's Travels with Mr. Brown*, 1940; *Washington in 1868*, 1943; *The Love Letters of Mark Twain*, 1949; *Mark Twain to Mrs. Fairbanks*, 1949; *Mark Twain of the Enterprise, 1862-1864*, 1957; *Mark Twain-Howells Letters*, 1960; *Mark Twain's Letters to Mary*, 1961; *Letters from the Earth*, 1962; *The Complete Essays of Mark Twain*, 1963; *The Forgotten Writings of Mark Twain*, 1963; *Mark Twain's Letters from Hawaii*, 1966; *Mark Twain's Letters to His Publishers, 1867-1894*, 1967; *Clemens of the Call: Mark Twain in San Francisco*, 1969; *Mark Twain's Correspondence with Henry Huttleston Rogers, 1893-1909*, 1969; *A Pen Warmed-Up in Hell: Mark Twain in Protest*, 1972; *Mark Twain's Notebooks and Journals*, 1975-1979; *Mark Twain Speaking*, 1976 (Paul Fatout, editor).

MISCELLANEOUS: *The Writings of Mark Twain*, 1968 (25 volumes).

Bibliography

Clemens, Susy. *Papa: An Intimate Biography of Mark Twain*. Edited with an introduction by Charles Neider. Garden City, N.Y.: Doubleday, 1985. An extremely comic family portrait written by Twain's precocious thirteen-year-old daughter, with comments and correspondence by Twain himself.

Giddings, Robert, ed. *Mark Twain: A Sumptuous Variety*. Totowa, N.J.: Barnes & Noble Books, 1985. A useful collection of critical essays about

Twain and his works.

Lauber, John. *The Inventions of Mark Twain*. New York: Hill & Wang, 1990. Very well-written and often humorous, this biography reveals Twain as an extremely complex, self-contradictory individual. Includes an annotated bibliography.

Long, E. Hudson, and J. R. LeMaster. *The New Mark Twain Handbook*. New York: Garland, 1985. A very useful work which discusses Twain's career, his development as a mythic figure, and the literature on his life and writings. Each section contains an extensive bibliography.

Miller, Robert Keith. *Mark Twain*. New York: Frederick Ungar, 1983. Links events in Twain's life to critical analyses of his major works and summarizes viewpoints of Twain scholars. Miller also offers his own conclusions about Twain's attitudes. Includes a helpful chronological table.

Paine, Albert Bigelow. *Mark Twain: A Biography*. 3 vols. New York: Harper and Brothers, 1912. Though long out-of-print, this remains the standard, and best, biography of Twain.

ANNE TYLER

Born: Minneapolis, Minnesota; October 25, 1941

Principal long fiction

If Morning Ever Comes, 1964; *The Tin Can Tree*, 1965; *A Slipping-Down Life*, 1970; *The Clock Winder*, 1972; *Celestial Navigation*, 1974; *Searching for Caleb*, 1976; *Earthly Possessions*, 1977; *Morgan's Passing*, 1980; *Dinner at the Homesick Restaurant*, 1982; *The Accidental Tourist*, 1985; *Breathing Lessons*, 1988.

Other literary forms

In addition to her novels, Anne Tyler has published more than forty short stories, including several in *Harper's*, *Mademoiselle*, *The New Yorker*, *Seventeen*, and the *Southern Review*. There is no collection to date, although two stories appeared in the O. Henry Prize volumes for 1969 and 1972 and others in the first edition of the Pushcart Prize anthology (1976), *Best American Short Stories* (1977), *Stories of the Modern South* (1978, 1981), *The Editor's Choice: New American Stories* (1985), *New Women and New Fiction* (1986), *Louder than Words* (1989), and several anthologies of American literature published by major publishing houses for use in college and university courses. Tyler has also written several autobiographical and personal essays, one for *The Washington Post* in 1976 and another for *The Writer on Her Work* (1980), edited by Janet Sternburg. Since 1975, her reviews of current fiction, criticism, and biography have appeared in major newspapers and magazines, including the *Boston Globe*, the *Chicago Sun-Times* and the *Chicago Tribune*, the *Detroit News*, *The New Republic*, *The New York Times Book Review*, *USA Today*, and *The Washington Post*.

Achievements

Despite praise for the truth of her characterizations and her eye for details, Tyler did not receive much national recognition for her fiction until the publication of her sixth novel, *Searching for Caleb*. Prior to 1976, the largest segment of her audience was in the South, although her short stories appeared in prestigious national magazines throughout the 1960's and 1970's. All of her novels, except *A Slipping-Down Life*, have been published abroad. Besides English editions, translations into Danish, French, German, Italian, and Swedish have appeared. Still, the American academic and critical communities were slow to appreciate Tyler's work. Her strong supporters include John Updike, who has favorably reviewed her novels for *The New Yorker*, beginning with *Searching for Caleb*, and Reynolds Price, Tyler's professor at Duke University, who has also reviewed her work.

Since 1976, Tyler has gained increasing recognition. In 1977, the American Academy and Institute of Arts and Letters cited her as a novelist of excellence and promise. *Earthly Possessions* and *Morgan's Passing* also received largely favorable national reviews. While a few critics, including Updike, expressed some disappointment in *Morgan's Passing*, the Writers Workshop of the University of Rochester awarded it the sixth annual Janet Heidinger Kafka prize for fiction by an American woman.

With the publication of *Dinner at the Homesick Restaurant*, her first novel to make the best-seller list, Tyler at last acquired full national stature. Benjamin DeMott's front-page notice in *The New York Times Book Review* pointed to the novel's wit and the depth of Tyler's psychological insight and characterizations. DeMott saw the book as clear evidence of Tyler's having joined the ranks of major novelists. Updike reiterated this praise, citing *Dinner at the Homesick Restaurant* as a work of considerable power. As a result of this increasing recognition and praise, scholarly studies of Tyler's work, including her early novels, began to appear. Tyler's reputation as a major contemporary American novelist was fixed with the publication of *The Accidental Tourist*, which won the 1985/1986 National Book Critics Circle Award for fiction. The successful film version of the novel increased Tyler's popularity with the reading public. *Breathing Lessons* was nominated for the National Book Award and won the 1989 Pulitzer Prize for fiction.

Biography

Anne Tyler was born in Minneapolis, Minnesota, on October 25, 1941, to Phyllis Mahon, a social worker, and Lloyd Parry Tyler, an industrial chemist. She was the oldest of four children, the only girl. Both parents were Quakers dedicated to finding an ideal community, a quest that produced the theme of frustrated idealism in Tyler's fiction. As a consequence of her parents' idealism, Tyler spent most of her early years from infancy until age eleven in various rural Quaker communes scattered throughout the Midwestern and Southern United States. When she was six, the family was settled in Celo, North Carolina—a large, isolated valley commune virtually independent of the outside world and unquestionably the setting for Tyler's short story "Outside," which appeared in the *Southern Review* in 1971.

Tyler has written of the impact of her early years on her fiction. Unable to sleep at night and needing to amuse herself, she began telling herself stories at age three. Her isolation in the rural communes in which she lived as a child contributed to the themes of isolation and community dominant in her novels. Additionally, growing up in North Carolina, where she spent summers tying tobacco, she listened carefully to the stories of the tobacco handlers and tenant farmers. Later, she was able to capture the cadences of everyday speech in her fiction, realizing that the stories these workers told could form the basis for literature. She was also to rely heavily on the North Carolina tobacco country as the setting for her early novels, especially *The Tin Can Tree* and *A Slipping-Down Life*.

When Tyler was eleven, she and her family moved to Raleigh, where they finally settled into an "ordinary" middle-class existence. There, Tyler attended Broughton High School and received encouragement in her writing. She also discovered the work of Eudora Welty, which was to have great influence on Tyler's own fiction.

In September, 1958, Tyler entered Duke University as an Angier Duke Scholar majoring in Russian. She was encouraged by Reynolds Price, who taught her freshman composition and later introduced her to his agent. At Duke, Tyler helped edit the *Archive* (the student literary magazine), published three early stories there, acted in several productions of the Wesley Players, and learned a great deal about the craft of fiction from reading Leo Tolstoy and the other major Russian novelists. She twice received the Anne Flexner award for creative writing at Duke and was graduated Phi Beta Kappa, just three years after entering, in 1961.

In September, 1961, Tyler began work on a master's degree in Russian at Columbia University, an experience that provides some of the background for *If Morning Ever Comes*. She completed the coursework for the degree but quit before writing her thesis. The following summer she spent in Maine, supporting herself by working on a schooner and proofreading for a local newspaper.

In 1962, Tyler returned to Duke University as the library's Russian bibliographer. That fall, she met her future husband, Taghi Modarressi, an Iranian child psychiatry student at the Duke Medical Center. The couple married in May, 1963, three months after the publication of Tyler's first short story in a national magazine. They moved to Montreal, Canada, that spring; during their four years there, Tyler wrote her first novel, taught herself Persian in anticipation of living in Iran, and worked as a librarian at the McGill University law library. In September, 1965, she gave birth to her first child, Tezh, a girl. The publication of *The Tin Can Tree* followed the next month.

In June, 1967, the Modarressis moved to Baltimore, Maryland, where they have settled. While Tyler's short stories continued to appear frequently in national publications between 1965 and 1970, her third novel was not published until January, 1970, first in condensed form in *Redbook* and later that same year in its entirety by Alfred A. Knopf. Between *The Tin Can Tree* and *A Slipping-Down Life* came one other book—*Winter Birds, Winter Apples*—which remains unpublished. A second daughter, Mitra, was born in November, 1967, in Baltimore. A dedicated mother and a productive, organized writer, Tyler managed her dual careers for years by writing in the mornings while her children were at school. Although her two daughters moved to other cities while attending college, Tyler and her husband continue to live in Baltimore.

Analysis

In *The Writer on Her Work*, Anne Tyler discusses the importance of her having lived as a child in "an experimental Quaker community in the wilderness." For her, this early experience of isolation and her later effort "to fit into the outside world" provided the "kind of setting-apart situation" the writer requires for aesthetic distancing. Tyler's early isolation and struggle to belong also provided both the style and material for her fiction: the ironic distance characteristic of her prose as well as the subject of the individual's relationship to the community, particularly to other members of one's own household and family. Most of Tyler's short fiction and all of her novels published to date, from *If Morning Ever Comes* to *Breathing Lessons*, concern the intricacies of family relationships and the isolation of the individual within the family. For Tyler, families clearly provided not only her major source for learning about the world as a child, but also fertile ground for studying how people endure the pain of loss and disappointment of life, adjust to living with others, and yet continue to love. All of the major conflicts and central themes of her novels evolve from this concern with the family and the individual's relationship to the community.

In this regard, Tyler falls clearly within the Southern literary tradition with its emphasis on family life and history. As Paul Binding points out in *Separate Country: A Literary Journey Through the American South* (1979), Tyler, like her mentor Reynolds Price, relies on interaction and "badinage between members of a family or between people who know one another well in order to illuminate personality." Tyler does not, however, evoke or write of a regional past. She focuses on the present, narrating the past to provide a personal or familial, not a regional history. Nor are her characters and families symbolic figures. They are, instead, idiosyncratic personalities, truthfully depicted, memorable yet atypical. In all but her first three novels, moreover, Tyler's setting is not the small towns and rural landscapes so often considered synonymous with Southern life. Rather, her terrain is the border city of Baltimore and the decay and transience of modern urban life. Price, in fact, has said that she is the closest thing the South has to an urban novelist, indicating Tyler's somewhat unusual position among late twentieth century American writers: a Southerner with a traditional interest in family, community, and the past; a modern woman fascinated with change and drawn to urban life; a writer with faith in man's ability to love and endure yet keenly aware of the difficulties of contemporary life, particularly the failure of communication within the family.

In her concern for familial relationships, Tyler's novels raise the existential issues of freedom and commitment. Significantly, hers is a compassionate art without explicit moral judgment—an absence of judgment for which some critics have faulted her. The effect of this gentle portrayal of serious themes is ironic: the disturbing failure of Tyler's characters to understand fully and to be understood by those they love is counterbalanced by a witty, carefully detailed style. Violence is usually absent from her work as well, and so are the grotesques found in the fiction of Flannery O'Connor and Carson McCullers. The most disfigured character in Tyler's work—Evie Decker, the fat teenager in *A Slipping-Down Life* who carves a local rock singer's name in her forehead—is compassionately portrayed. Like Eudora Welty, Tyler populates her novels with ordinary people, all of whom, she comments in *The Writer on Her Work*, are mildly eccentric in some way and "have something unusual" at their centers, something "funny and strange" and "touching in unexpected ways." From Ben Joe Hawkes in *If Morning Ever Comes*, who reads upside down to relieve boredom, to the elusive and difficult black sheep of her fictional families—Caleb and Duncan Peck, Morgan Gower, and Cody Tull—Tyler warmly and humorously portrays a wide spectrum of fascinating yet ordinary human beings.

Tyler's view of human nature, her talent for realistically capturing generations of squabbling families, her keen ear for dialogue, and her interest in character and the isolation of the individual within the family derive from various sources. Her own "setting apart" experience in the North Carolina wilderness, her early childhood habit of telling herself bedtime stories for rest and amusement, and her long periods listening to tenant farmers' stories contributed substantially to her art. Shy, quiet, and keenly observant, she listened carefully to the stories the workers told. Later, she could call up the words of her own characters. "Having those voices in my ears all day," she has written, "helped me to summon up my own characters' voices." Additionally, with Reynolds Price as her teacher and Eudora Welty as a model, Tyler saw early in her career the rich source of literary materials offered by commonplace experience. Paul Binding also cites the influence of Tyler's study of the Russian masters, particularly Ivan Turgenev and Anton Chekhov, as a basis for her tolerant and warm portrayal of multiple generations of entangled and eccentric families. Finally, perhaps most prominent is Tyler's own witness to her parents' idealism, their quest for a perfect community throughout her youth, and later their apparently easy adjustment to an ordinary existence in a middle-sized Southern city. Like her own father, whom she describes in *The Writer on Her Work*, the heroes of Tyler's novels are those who are "infinitely adapting" and always "looking around . . . with a smile to say, 'Oh! So this is where I am!'" They are complex people, enriched and deepened by experience—Elizabeth Abbott in *The Clock Winder*, Justine Peck in *Searching for Caleb*, Charlotte Emory in *Earthly Possessions*, Jenny Tull in *Dinner at the Homesick Restaurant*, and Maggie Moran in *Breathing Lessons*, best represent the type—able to enjoy life because they view themselves and others with tolerance and wit.

In an interview with Clifford Ridley for the *National Observer*, Tyler commented that she did not particularly "like either" of her "first two books" because "they seem so bland." Ben Joe Hawkes, the hero of *If Morning Ever Comes*, is "a likable guy; that's all you can say about him." While it is true that Ben Joe lacks the zaniness and interest which some of Tyler's later characters exhibit, his struggle to deal with his family, to recognize both his own independence and theirs, and to come to terms with the past and the psychological distance that isolates people even within an intimate group, provides a basis for understanding Tyler's later work and her place within the Southern literary tradition. *If Morning Ever Comes* had its origins in two short stories: "I Never Saw Morning," which appeared in the April, 1961, *Archive* and was later collected in *Under Twenty-Five: Duke Narrative and Verse, 1945-1962* (1963), edited by William Blackburn; and "Nobody Answers the Door," which appeared in the fall, 1964, issue of the *Antioch Review*. Both involve incidents suggested by the novel but occurring prior to the time of its opening. With the novel, they indicate Tyler's strong sense of the continuity of her characters' lives.

As in later novels, the plot and subject of *If Morning Ever Comes*, Ben Joe's five-day journey home to Sandhill, North Carolina, from Columbia University where he is a law student, evolve from family conflict. The family of women Ben Joe has left behind—six strikingly independent sisters, a proud mother, and a spry, 78-year-old grandmother, the first of Tyler's zanies—fail to tell him what is happening at home. Jenny, the family letter-writer, is all business. No one mentions the illegitimate son that Ben Joe's father left behind with a mistress when he died, nor the support payments Ben Joe personally delivered for years before he left for New York. The family treats lightly even the fact that Ben Joe's oldest sister, Joanne, has taken her child, left her husband, and returned home after seven years. Their behavior and their failure to understand Ben Joe's concern and worry point clearly to the theme of the individual's isolation within the family, here a male in an entire family of women.

On the surface, *If Morning Ever Comes* is a simply structured novel covering less than a week in the life of its hero. As one critic has observed, however, going home is "only partly a spatial relocation." Ben Joe, like other Southern literary heroes, "from Quentin Compson to Jack Burden," must return home "to embrace the spiritual crisis" created by an unsettled past and attempt to forge a future shaped by that very past. In this regard, *If Morning Ever Comes* is clearly a Southern novel. That it draws on a sharp contrast between the peaceful North Carolina setting and the briskness of New York, as well as the hero's discomfort and sense of dislocation in the North, is also suggestive of Tyler's Southern literary roots.

Although not widely reviewed nor acclaimed, *The Tin Can Tree* is a moving novel which expands and deepens Tyler's treatment of family relationships and the individual's struggle to remain committed in the face of significant loss and change. Just as Ben Joe Hawkes in *If Morning Ever Comes* remained committed to his family despite their pride and reticence, and to his father's memory despite the elder Hawkes's unfaithfulness, so also the characters in *The Tin Can Tree*, the members of three separate families sharing one house— the Pikes, the Greens, and the Potters—must deal with the commonly experienced grief at the death of the Pikes's six-year-old daughter, Janie Rose, adjust, and resume the task of living. Tyler's achievement here is that she captures eight different characters' varying responses to grief while avoiding the sentimental and maudlin. She opens the novel with the close of the funeral service, thus deliberately focusing on life, rather than death, and the resumption of the tasks of everyday living.

In addition to this theme of grief, *The Tin Can Tree* explores the background and interactions of James and Ansel Green and Joan Pike, Janie Rose's cousin. The study of James's commitment to his ailing brother Ansel, the two brothers' alienation from their family, and Joan's distance from her own elderly parents as well as her unresolved romantic involvement with James, give the novel a depth lacking in *If Morning Ever Comes*, with its heavy focus on one central character. As one reviewer noted, *The Tin Can Tree* illustrates Tyler's talent for bringing "into focus a remarkable range of human traits and emotions." Lou Pike's depressive withdrawal and immobility after her daughter's death, her husband's worried yet practical concern, their son Simon's sense of rejection and neglect, Joan's uncertainty and anger at James and his brother Ansel—all acquire full portraiture. A love of detail permeates the book, from the Potter sisters' eccentric way of wearing hats and gloves even when visiting only at the other end of the porch to the details of Janie Rose's behavior, her "tin can tree" made in honor of God during a religious period and her wearing layer upon layer of underwear on "her bad days." Such details make the characters real and Janie Rose's death more immediate and painful.

The Tin Can Tree is also the first Tyler novel to draw explicitly on the author's tobacco-field experience. Joan Pike, a school secretary, spends part of her summers handing tobacco in the warehouses, as Tyler herself did as a teenager. Besides providing elements of plot and characterization, the Tobacco Road landscape mirrors the sterility of the characters' lives following Janie Rose's death and provides a spokesman for the novel's theme. "Bravest thing about people, Miss Joan," one of the tobacco tiers says, "is how they go on loving mortal beings after finding out there's such a thing as dying." Unlike Erskine Caldwell, whose stereotypical white trash characters are often farcical grotesques, Tyler deepens the Tobacco Road landscape by a compassionate, detailed account of the grief of several families at the death of a child. Hers is a fiction of psychological insight, not a document for social change. *The Tin Can Tree*, as one critic observed, is "a novel rich in incident that details the closing of a family wound and the resumption of life among people stunned by the proof of mortality."

In her third novel, *A Slipping-Down Life*, Tyler returned to the existential themes of the individual's isolation, his struggle for identity, and the lack of understanding and meaningful communication among people living closely together. Set in the fictional towns of Pulqua and Farinia, North Carolina—suspiciously similar to the actual town of Fuquay-Varina near Raleigh—it was the last of the Tyler's books set entirely in North Carolina but also the first to portray the barrenness of familial relationships in a clearly modern setting. While most of *If Morning Ever Comes* and all of *The Tin Can Tree* are set in peaceful, remote areas where family life, though troubled, seems unaffected by distinctly modern problems, *A Slipping-Down Life* draws heavily on the impact of modern American culture and media on family life. Also, where Tyler's first two novels covered only a few days in the lives of the principal characters, *A Slipping-Down Life* chronicles one full year in the life of its heroine—a fat, dowdy, teenage girl named Evie Decker—indicating a development in Tyler's ability to handle character over an extended period of time.

Originating in a "newspaper story about a 15-year-old girl in Texas who'd slashed 'Elvis' in her forehead," the novel traces Evie's barren interaction with her father, her only living relative, as well as the development and dissolution of a relationship with a local rock singer named Bertram "Drum-strings" Casey, the first of Tyler's unadmirable yet likable antiheroes—exploitative and selfish yet touchingly shy and dependent on his parents and Evie. Evie's entanglement with Drum, leading eventually to their marriage, is tragically initiated by her carving the name "Casey" in her forehead with a pair of nail scissors, and ends, equally as tragically, with the couple's separation, the death of Evie's family, and her discovery of Casey in bed with another woman. Throughout, Evie thinks of herself as though she were acting on a stage set, taking her cues from the soap operas she watches daily with Clotelia, the Deckers' sullen maid and Evie's sometime chiding surrogate mother. Like Joan Pike in *The Tin Can Tree* and later Tyler heroines—Justine Peck in *Searching for Caleb* and Charlotte Emory in *Earthly Possessions*—Evie is an only child faced with growing up alone in a dark, stifling household and creating an identity without the companionship and aid of siblings or understanding parents.

Besides its characterizations, *A Slipping-Down Life* is also noteworthy for capturing at least part of the American experience in the 1960's: the lonely world of teenagers, the generation gap, the high-school student's unending quest for popularity and romance, as well as a small town's tawdry local rock scene, featuring the chilled air in a roadside house, painfully loud music, necking couples, and the smell of stale beer. As one reviewer observed, *A Slipping-Down Life* captures "a *way* of life, a way that is tacked upon teenage bulletin boards, sewn to dresses 'decorated with poodles on loops of real chain,' enclosed in high-school notebooks containing *Silver Screen* magazine."

Tyler's first three novels all involve some type of journey home during which a central character confronts both the distance between himself and his family as well as the difficulties of unresolved past conflicts. Ben Joe's journey from New York to Sandhill in *If Morning Ever Comes* fits this pattern, as do James Green's trip to Caraway, North Carolina, in *The Tin Can Tree*, and, in *A Slipping-Down Life*, Evie Decker's return to her father's house following his death. A similar trip occurs in *The Clock Winder*. A novel characterized by Sarah Blackburn as having all the "virtues" of Southern writing—"an easy, almost confidential directness, fine skill at quick characterization, a sure eye for atmosphere, and a special nostalgic humor"—*The Clock Winder* was at the time of its publication Tyler's most ambitious work, tracing the intricate relationships of a large cast of characters over an entire decade. It was also her first novel set in Baltimore.

The diverse, eccentric, eight-member Emerson family of Baltimore and their one adopted member, Elizabeth Abbott, clearly form one of those "huge," "loving-bickering" Southern families Tyler told Clifford Ridley she hoped to create in writing *If Morning Ever Comes*. Mrs. Emerson—a skinny, fragile widow—is unrelenting in nagging her children about their neglected duties to her. She is, consequently, estranged from all but one: Timothy, a pressured medical student who, with his twin Andrew, is one of the most neurotic disturbed characters in Tyler's novels. Into this entangled, crisis-prone family, Elizabeth Abbott brings the very skills she is unable to practice with her own family in Ellington, North Carolina. Tolerant, practical, dextrous, and witty—the first of Tyler's "infinitely adapting" heroines based on her own father—Elizabeth is a handyman and a godsend for the nervous Mrs. Emerson. In Ellington, she is a bumbler, a rebellious college dropout, and a painful reminder of failure to her minister father. Her life at home is bleak, ordinary, and restricted. Commitment to the Emersons, despite their family feuds, offers interest and freedom from the Abbott family's dicta, an opportunity to form a new identity and life free of reminders of past mistakes.

Besides expanding character, setting, and timeframe, *The Clock Winder* is unusual among Tyler's first four works for its use of violence and its experimentation with point of view. Timothy Emerson commits suicide by shooting himself in Elizabeth's presence, sending her home to her family for several years. Later, after her return to Baltimore, his twin shoots her, though he causes only a flesh wound. Also, where earlier Tyler novels used omniscient point of view focusing largely on one major character—the exception is *The Tin Can Tree*, in which Joan Pike and James Green serve alternately as centers of consciousness—*The Clock Winder* shifts perspective among many characters, some of them minor. In one chapter, the reader witnesses the succession of disconnected thoughts, the confusion of physical sensations, and the temporal disorientation accompanying Mrs. Emerson's stroke. Another presents the views of the youngest Emerson, Peter, who appears only in the final chapter of the novel. These shifts in point of view result in an intimate portrait not only of the novel's central character, Elizabeth, but also of the Emersons— a varied, contrasting family of idiosyncratic individuals.

With *Celestial Navigation*, Tyler moved her novels to a totally urban landscape. Eight months after the novel's publication, she told a Duke University audience that she "could no longer write a Southern novel" since she had lived away from the South too long to capture realistically the "voices" and behavior of the people who live there. Set almost exclusively in a seedy Baltimore boardinghouse "smack in the middle" of a deteriorating inner-city neighborhood, *Celestial Navigation* is Tyler's portrait of the artist. It covers thirteen years in the central character's life, expanding the study of character development found in earlier novels and illustrating her increasing skill in handling point of view. The various boarders narrate firsthand their experiences and relationships to other residents. Additionally, since it focuses largely on boarders rather than kin, somewhat like *The Tin Can Tree* with its three families unrelated by blood, and since it includes the common-law marriage of its hero, *Celestial Navigation* redefines the meaning of family ties as characterized in Tyler's novels. It also intensifies the isolation of the protagonist. Jeremy Pauling, the artist-hero of the novel and the owner of the rooming house, is so reclusive that for years he has not left the city block where he lives. His principal ties are not with his two sisters in Richmond, neither very understanding of his peculiar artistic temperament, but with the boarders with whom he lives.

The caring family of boarders the novel studies, however, are essentially isolated strangers living in private rooms. They are mostly older people with severed family connections or no remaining kin. Ironically, they exhibit more tolerance and unquestioning respect for the peculiarities and privacy of one another than do many blood-related members. Mrs. Vinton, an aged spinster who works in a bookstore, stays on to care for Jeremy years after the others move or die, yet she never interrupts his trancelike states or work. With the other boarders—the elegant widow Mrs. Jarrett, the nubile Mary Tell, the young Olivia, and the fractious old Mrs. Somerset shuffling about in slippers— Mrs. Vinton is a testament to Tyler's talent for realistically capturing a gallery of idiosyncratic yet identifiably ordinary people.

The real achievement of *Celestial Navigation*, though, is Jeremy Pauling. He is one of Tyler's minor grotesques. A pale, pudgy sculptor, he rarely speaks and withdraws for days at a time to his secluded bedroom-studio. The novel works as Jeremy's story, however, partly because Tyler gives him a full range of emotions—including sexual attraction to several female boarders and a love for the children he has by his common-law marriage. She also views him with both compassion and humor and lets the reader see him from several points of view. Tyler shifts to third-person point of view to narrate Jeremy's chapters, since Jeremy himself is incapable of communicating his impressions in the coherent manner of the other characters. Tyler has said that the character of Jeremy is based in part on a shy, easily flustered little man she helped one day in the library where she worked, but she added several of her own traits to the character: a dread of telephones and doorbells (something retained from her isolated childhood) and, most important, her own artistic vision, an eye for the "smallest and most unnoticed scenes on earth," very much like those details Tyler captures in *Celestial Navigation*.

Searching for Caleb marked a turning point in Tyler's career. It was her first novel to receive national recognition, at a time when Tyler's own reviews began to appear in national publications. As Walter Sullivan commented in 1977 when reviewing *Searching for Caleb* for the *Sewanee Review*, Tyler "retained" in her work "a kind of innocence . . . a sense of wonder at all the crazy things in the world and an abiding affection for her own flaky characters." *Searching for Caleb* was also evidence that Tyler had retained her Southern literary roots and her delight in huge families and the range of human characters those families produce. Something of a combined family history and detective story, the novel is Tyler's most ambitious work to date, tracing five generations of one large, dichotomous, and extremely long-lived clan, the Pecks of Baltimore, from the 1880's through 1973. As in *The Clock Winder* and *Celestial Navigation*, Tyler shows her strong fascination with urban life, a result perhaps of her own early life in remote areas. She also returns to Roland Park, one of Baltimore's oldest residential neighborhoods and the main setting of *The Clock Winder*.

As the title suggests, *Searching for Caleb* involves a quest for the vanished Caleb, the great uncle of the novel's protagonists, Duncan and Justine Peck, and the half-brother of their grandfather, Daniel Peck. Representing one side of the family, Caleb, Justine, and Duncan are outcasts of a sort: spirited, talented, imaginative, and free individuals unable or unwilling to live as family rules dictate. Caleb becomes a musician, Justine a fortune-teller. Duncan, her husband and first cousin, leads an unsettled life as a mechanic and jack-of-all-trades, foreshadowing Morgan Gower, the hero of *Morgan's Passing*. Like Morgan, Duncan dismays his family.

The other side of the family, the Pecks of Roland Park, headed by Daniel, are uniformly humorless and restricted. The women, though educated, are unthreatening; the men, all attorneys educated at Johns Hopkins, drive black Fords and dress in Brooks Brothers suits. They are, above all, clannish, living side by side in similar Roland Park houses. For them, family tradition and training—in effect, the past—are inescapable. Even Daniel's late-life quest for his half-brother evolves from his ties to family and an unsettled conflict. It represents a delayed response to the question frequently asked in his childhood: "Daniel, have you seen Caleb?"

Searching for Caleb, like Tyler's earlier novels, also illustrates the author's belief in the need for human adaptability, tolerance, and love. Justine epit-

omizes the philosophy. She weathers a dark and uncertain childhood with a
depressive mother, frequent moves with her restless husband, the death of
both parents and her grandfather, and the loss of her one daughter in marriage
to a Milquetoast minister. Yet, she remains spirited and continues to love her
family. She insists on visiting Roland Park, a longing Duncan cannot understand, and she is committed to finding Caleb, not only out of a love of travel
and adventure but also to share the experiences with her grandfather and to
find her own roots. With its focus on community and family and its delineation
of the unsettled conflicts of the past impacting on the present, *Searching for
Caleb* indicates Tyler's own roots in the family of Southern literature.

When it appeared in 1977, *Earthly Possessions* was Tyler's most unfavorably
received novel. Among disapproving reviewers, Roger Sale in *The New York
Times Review of Books* saw the book as "a cartoon" of sorts, with the life of
Charlotte Emory, the protagonist, "reduced . . . by her own hand" until all
"possible anguish is . . . lost." The reason for this response is no doubt the
sardonic nature of Charlotte herself, an entrapped housewife who sets out to
leave her husband but gets kidnapped instead in a bungled bank robbery.
Such reversals characterize Charlotte's life and have led her to "loosen" her
hold so that she sees everything from an ironic distance. Charlotte, moreover,
is the novel's only narrator, and she tells her life-story in chapters alternating
perfectly with those narrating her experiences with Jake Simms, her kidnapper, on their trip south from Clarion, Maryland, Charlotte's hometown. Along
the way, Tyler captures the fragmentation and transience of modern life,
reflected in a string of drive-in restaurants, banks, and movies. The triumph
of the novel is not, as in earlier Tyler works, characterization, but the pan-
orama of contemporary American life that the book captures during this
journey of hostage and kidnapper.

With its contrapuntal chapters, *Earthly Possessions* is Tyler's most highly
structured novel, the first to be told entirely in the first person by one narrator.
The result is an artificial temporal arrangement and a restricted focus, one
lifetime as compared with those of eight or nine Emersons, five generations
of Pecks. Also, the reader is always in the presence of two somewhat unsavory
characters: a nail-biting, minor league criminal and a stoical, cynical woman.
All might have come from the pen of Flannery O'Connor but for the touchingly human flaws Tyler draws. Neither Jake nor Charlotte, despite their
failings, is morally culpable. What they share is a common, impractical desire
for freedom from the entanglements of life: for Charlotte, marriage complete
with a house full of relatives and in-laws, rooms of furniture (earthly possessions), even sinners from the mourner's bench at her husband's church;
for Jake, jail for a petty crime and a pregnant girl friend. Heading south to
rescue Mindy Callendar, Jake's Kewpie-doll girl friend, from a home for
unwed mothers, Jake, Charlotte realizes, is like herself "criss-crossed by
strings of love and need and worry." Even Charlotte and Jake's relationship

grows into a type of commitment. Eventually the two share the driving as well as their troubles. Any "relationship," Tyler told Marguerite Michaels in an interview for *The New York Times Book Review*, even one "as bizarre as" that of "a bank robber and hostage could become . . . bickering [and] familiar. . . . Anything done gradually enough becomes ordinary."

Earthly Possessions, despite its problems, shares with *The Tin Can Tree* and *Celestial Navigation* a redefinition of family ties. With Tyler's other novels, it also illuminates the problems and conflicts of the individual within a close relationship, whether familial or not, and focuses on the eccentric nature of ordinary lives, the ordinariness of the bizarre.

In her eighth novel, Tyler returned to the heart of Baltimore for her setting and to a central character, Morgan Gower, who is strikingly eccentric. Reviewers compared him with Saul Bellow's Henderson and Joseph Heller's Major Major. He also resembles Duncan Peck as well as other Tyler protagonists. Like those heroes, Morgan is in conflict with his family: seven daughters who find him embarrassing, a slovenly though good-natured wife, a senile mother, and a depressed, inert sister. Like Ben Joe Hawkes, Morgan feels trapped and misunderstood in a house cluttered with "the particles of related people's unrelated worlds" and full of women with whom he is unable to communicate satisfactorily. While his family insists on going about life unconsciously, Morgan, spirited and highly inventive, faces a mid-life crisis that calls for a change. He must also come to terms with his past, the consequences of marrying Bonny for her money as well as his father's inexplicable suicide when Morgan was a teenager. Like Duncan Peck, Morgan is a kind of mechanical genius who takes up various projects, then drops them—"a tinkering, puttering, hardware sort of man." Like the renegade Pecks, he eventually abandons his Baltimore family to take up a new life and identity with a traveling amusement company.

Despite these resemblances to other Tyler heroes, Morgan is a unique creation, the product of Tyler's maturing vision of life. Her understanding of his sexual attraction to a young puppeteer and her portrayal of his frustration with his wife suggest a depth of insight into the problems of marriage, a depth lacking in the early *If Morning Ever Comes*. Morgan is also a complex character, a genuine impostor who tries on identities complete with appropriately matching costumes. At times he is "Father Morgan, the street priest of Baltimore"; at other times, he is an immigrant with family still abroad, a doctor who delivers a baby in the backseat of a car—any role in which people will accept him. Though most of this role-playing is harmless, Morgan is an anti-hero lacking a firm identity, a modern eccentric who revels in the anonymity and emptiness of decaying city neighborhoods and a man who assumes a false identity to take up life with another man's wife without benefit of divorce. Not surprisingly, reviewers found it difficult to like Morgan, but few found him unbelievable.

Tyler's increasing skill in capturing and making believable such a character testifies to her maturation as a writer. As John Leonard commented in *The New York Times* when reviewing the novel, readers "are obliged to care" about Tyler's "odd people" "because their oddities are what we see at an angle in the mirror in the middle of a bad night." Drawing from selected everyday scenes covering twelve years in Morgan's life, Tyler roots her novel firmly in the here and now. Morgan becomes believable because he is not always posing. He reads the morning paper over coffee, affectionately slaps his wife on her rear end, smokes too much, attends a daughter's wedding, despairs over a quarrel-filled family vacation, works in a hardware store, and comes down with a terrible cold. Tyler's is a realistic art illuminating family conflict and solidly based in the ordinary details of life.

Of all Tyler's novels, *Dinner at the Homesick Restaurant* most inspires comparison with the work of Flannery O'Connor. The title is reminiscent of O'Connor's wit and irony, and the mood of the novel, as one reviewer noted, is that of "O'Connor's Gothic South" with its "sullen, psychic menace." At her best, as in *Celestial Navigation*, Tyler captures the pain, anxiety, and isolation beneath the surface of ordinary lives. At times, however, particularly in *Earthly Possessions* but also *Morgan's Passing*, she treats this pain lightly, thus denying a sense of genuine struggle. In *Earthly Possessions*, Charlotte is flippant and ironic; in *Morgan's Passing*, Morgan is a zany, the mood quick and light. *Dinner at the Homesick Restaurant*, representing what John Updike called a "darkening" of Tyler's art, presents the other side of the coin from *Morgan's Passing*, not only in mood but also in story line. Its focus is not the husband who abandons his family to find a new life, but the family he left behind. It is a stunning psychological portrait of the Tulls, Pearl and her three children, and the anger, guilt, hurt, and anxiety they feel growing up in an uncertain world without a father. All carry their pain through life, illustrating more profoundly than any of Tyler's earlier books the past's haunting influence on the present.

Covering thirty-five years, three generations of Tulls, the novel opens with Pearl on her deathbed. This first chapter, reminiscent of Katherine Anne Porter's short story, "The Jilting of Granny Weatherall," depicts Pearl as a stoical, frightened woman who has weathered a youth filled with dread of being an old maid, a quick marriage, and a lonely struggle to rear three "flawed" children: Cody, the oldest boy, a troublemaker from childhood, "prone to unreasonable rages"; Jenny, the only girl, "flippant" and "opaque"; Ezra, his mother's favorite, a gentle man who has not "lived up to his potential," but instead has become the ambitionless owner of the Homesick Restaurant. Not one of Pearl's children has turned out as she wished. Consequently, she, like other Tyler characters, feels "closed off" from her family, the very children to whom she has devoted her life. Later chapters reveal why, focusing on each of the children in turn and tracing the evolution of their lives as well as their fear of their mother's rages. All, like their mother, end up in some way "destroyed by love."

Tyler's compassionate portrayal of her characters and her characteristic humor do mitigate the darkness of this novel. Although Pearl, her forehead permanently creased from worry, verbally and physically abuses her children, Tyler lets the reader understand the reasons for Pearl's behavior, even though he may not forgive her, and shows a far mellower Pearl in old age. Jenny, after struggling through medical school, two marriages, and a nervous break-down, is nursed back to health by her mother. Cody spares no expense in caring for his family, even though he is unable to forgive Pearl for mistreating him as a child. The teenager Cody plays cruel but funny tricks on his brother Ezra—partly out of resentment of Ezra's being the favorite, but also from Cody's own pain and sense of rejection. Taking slats from Ezra's bed, Cody strews the floor with pornographic magazines so Pearl will think Ezra the kind of disappointment she finds Cody to be. Later, after stealing Ezra's sweetheart, he recognizes not only his guilt but also his love for his brother. These tales fill out the dark psychological portrait Tyler draws, making *Dinner at the Homesick Restaurant*, like many of Tyler's earlier books, a confirmation of life's difficulty as well as of the value of love.

A mood of dark comedy pervades *The Accidental Tourist*. It is the only Tyler work in which a murder occurs, and a sense of the inexplicable, tragic nature of reality moves the plot and forms a backdrop for the novel. The book opens with Macon and Sarah Leary returning from a truncated beach vacation and the sudden announcement by Sarah that she wants a divorce. Macon, the central character, is a forty-four-year-old writer of guidebooks for business-men who find themselves in foreign places but prefer the familiarity of home. The logo for the series, entitled Accidental Tourist, is a winged armchair, a motif suggesting Macon's attitude toward the disruptions of travel. In the opening pages of *The Accidental Tourist*, the reader learns of the death of Macon and Sarah's twelve-year-old son, Ethan, who was killed in a robbery at a burger stand. Besides their grief at the death of their son, Macon and Sarah must confront the permanent jarring of their world by the random nature of the crime: the robber shot Ethan as an afterthought; Ethan and his friend had impulsively stolen away from a summer camp. With Sarah's leav-ing, Macon's life tailspins, yet he strives desperately to maintain control, to reduce life to its simplest terms. He sleeps in one sheet sewn together like a body bag and showers in his shirt to save on laundry. In a spirit of fun, Tyler gives Macon an alter ego, a Welsh corgi, Edward, who becomes increasingly surly as Macon's life disintegrates. Through Edward, Tyler introduces the unpredictable Muriel Pritchett, a dog trainer set on finding a father for her sickly son, Alexander.

Told from a limited third-person point of view, *The Accidental Tourist* displays Tyler's art at its best: her eye for idiosyncratic behavior and the accidental quality of reality, her focus on family as the center of life's triumphs and tragedies. The family here is not only Macon and Sarah but also Macon's siblings: his sister Rose, whose romance with Julian Edge, Macon's publisher, forms a dual plot to Macon's romance with Muriel, and his two brothers, Charles and Porter. For part of the novel, Tyler centers on the Leary siblings, all marred by their mother's carefree abandonment of them. Both Charles and Porter are divorced, and Rose now maintains her grandparents' home for her brothers. What is striking about the house is its orderliness—every item in the kitchen is shelved in alphabetical order—and its changelessness. When Macon breaks a leg in a freak accident, he returns to his siblings and resumes life just as if he had never been married, had a child, and lived away for years. The characteristics of families, Tyler suggests, are permanently etched. It is the occurrences of life that constantly shift.

In *The Accidental Tourist*, Anne Tyler depicted the dissolution of a twenty-year marriage following the violent death of the Learys' son. In *Breathing Lessons*, she presents the opposite: the duration of Ira and Maggie Moran's marriage for twenty-eight years. Told primarily through flashbacks as the couple journeys to the funeral of a friend, the novel covers nearly thirty years in one September day and contrasts the Morans' courtship and marriage with the relationship of their son, Jesse, and his former wife, Fiona. From its beginning, *Breathing Lessons* concerns not only Ira and Maggie's bickering, love, and tolerance for each other but also Maggie's struggle to reconcile Jesse and Fiona.

Set in Pennsylvania and Baltimore, the novel has three principal divisions, each told from a restricted third-person point of view. The first and third sections focus on Maggie's consciousness, while the middle section, which constitutes something of an interlude, centers on Ira's thoughts. Somewhat reminiscent of the film *The Big Chill* (1983), the first section wittily depicts the music and mores of the 1950's. The second part depicts a side trip in which Ira and Maggie temporarily become involved with an elderly black man who has separated from his wife of more than fifty years. This section also provides Ira's family history and his response to his wife and children. Tyler reveals here a masterful handling of exposition through internal thought sequences and flashbacks. The novel's third section, which introduces the characters of Fiona and Leroy, her daughter, returns to Maggie's thoughts and her memories of Jesse and Fiona's relationship. A return to Baltimore with Fiona and Leroy completes the section, suggesting the cyclical nature of experience, a central theme in the novel.

From her earliest novels through *Breathing Lessons*, Tyler has skillfully balanced a lighthearted view of human nature with a depth of insight into the darker side of marriage. Maggie and Ira's marriage, while offering a sound balance of two contrasting personality types who can bicker and then reconcile, has its dark side also: a "helpless, angry, confined feeling" which

Maggie experiences "from time to time." Ira, too, realizes that marriage involves "the same old arguments, . . . the same old resentments dragged up year after year." The joyful side of Tyler's fiction is her fondness for zany characters, her keen eye for the bizarre in human behavior, which she observes with amused detachment, and her finely tuned ear for human speech. *Breathing Lessons* offers many examples, beginning with the zesty, lower-class names of her characters: Serena, Fiona, Duluth. Maggie herself belongs to a long line of lively, unpredictable Tyler heroines—most expert caretakers—beginning with Granny Hawkes in *If Morning Ever Comes*, Tyler's first novel. In fact, in both her acute observations of others and her repeated attempts "to alter people's lives," Maggie resembles her creator, the fiction writer who manipulates the lives of her characters to fill her plot.

Stella A. Nesanovich

Bibliography

Betts, Doris. "The Fiction of Anne Tyler." In *Women Writers of the Contemporary South*, edited by Peggy Prenshaw. Jackson: University Press of Mississippi, 1984. A brief essay on Tyler's adaptation of the short-story structure to her novels and a discussion of the theme of returning home in the first nine books.

Binding, Paul. *Separate Country: A Literary Journey Through the American South*. New York: Paddington Press, 1979. Contains a commentary by a British critic and writer, offering a non-American's view of traditional Southern characteristics of Tyler's work.

Gullette, Margaret M. *Safe at Last in the Middle Years—The Invention of the Midlife Progress Novel: Saul Bellow, Margaret Drabble, Anne Tyler, and John Updike*. Berkeley: University of California Press, 1988. Devotes a chapter, originally published as a separate essay in the *New England Review*, to Tyler's presentation of the conflicts of adulthood in her novels.

Robertson, Mary F. "Anne Tyler: Medusa Points and Contact Points." In *Contemporary American Women Writers: Narrative Strategies*, edited by Catherine Rainwater and William J. Scheick. Lexington: University Press of Kentucky, 1985. A discussion of the narrative form of Tyler's novels, focusing on her disruption of the conventional expectations of family novels.

Stephens, C. Ralph, ed. *The Fiction of Anne Tyler*. Jackson: University Press of Mississippi, 1990. A collection of essays selected from papers given in 1989 at the Anne Tyler Symposium in Baltimore and representing a range of interests and approaches.

Tyler, Anne. "Anne Tyler: A Sense of Reticence Balanced by 'Oh, Well, Why Not?'"Interview by Clifford Ridley. *National Observer* 11 (July 22, 1972): 23. An early interview with Tyler, useful for its discussion of her first four novels.

_____. "Anne Tyler, Writer 8:05 to 3:30." Interview by Marguerite Michaels. *The New York Times Book Review* 82 (May 8, 1977): 13, 42-43. An early interview in which Tyler discusses her writing interests and habits.

_____. "Because I Want More than One Life." *The Washington Post*, August 15, 1976, G1, 7. A statement of aesthetics by the author discussing her motivation and attitudes in writing fiction.

_____. "An Interview with Anne Tyler." Interview by Wendy Lamb. *Iowa Journal of Literary Studies* 3 (1981): 59-64. An interview held in Iowa City discussing, in part, Tyler's characters and her work through *Earthly Possessions*.

_____. "Olives Out of a Bottle." *Archive* 86 (Spring, 1975): 70-79. A partial transcript of a panel discussion with Tyler held at Duke University in November, 1974.

_____. "Still Just Writing." In *The Writer on Her Work: Contemporary Women Writers Reflect on Their Art and Situation*, edited by Janet Sternburg. New York: W. W. Norton, 1980. An essay on the balance required for writing fiction and rearing a family simultaneously, offering important background information on Tyler.

Voelker, Joseph C. *Art and the Accidental in Anne Tyler*. Columbia: University of Missouri Press, 1989. The first book-length study of Anne Tyler's fiction, this volume focuses on the development of Tyler's aesthetics and her treatment of character, particularly her view of selfhood as mystery and of experience as accidental.

JOHN UPDIKE

Born: Shillington, Pennsylvania; March 18, 1932

Principal long fiction

The Poorhouse Fair, 1959; *Rabbit, Run*, 1960; *The Centaur*, 1963; *Of the Farm*, 1965; *Couples*, 1968; *Bech: A Book*, 1970; *Rabbit Redux*, 1971; *A Month of Sundays*, 1975; *Marry Me: A Romance*, 1976; *The Coup*, 1978; *Rabbit Is Rich*, 1981; *Bech Is Back*, 1982; *The Witches of Eastwick*, 1984; *Roger's Version*, 1986; *S.*, 1988; *Rabbit at Rest*, 1990.

Other literary forms

Since publishing his first story in *The New Yorker* in 1954, Updike has truly become a man of letters, publishing in virtually every literary genre—poetry, short fiction, novel, essay, drama, art criticism, and autobiography.

Achievements

One of the major figures to emerge in American fiction after World War II, John Updike is widely acclaimed as one of the most accomplished stylists and prolific writers of his generation. Showing remarkable versatility and range, his fiction represents a penetrating chronicle in the realist mode of the changing morals and manners of American society. Updike's work has met both critical and popular success. His first novel, *The Poorhouse Fair*, was awarded the Rosenthal Award of the National Institute of Arts and Letters in 1960. In 1964, he received the National Book Award for *The Centaur*. He was elected in the same year to the National Institute of Arts and Letters. A number of his short stories have won the O. Henry Prize for best short story of the year and have been included in the yearly volumes of *Best American Short Stories*. In 1977, he was elected to the prestigious American Academy of Arts and Letters. In 1981, his novel *Rabbit Is Rich* won the Pulitzer Prize for Fiction and the American Book Award. In that same year, he was awarded the Edward MacDowell Medal for literature. While Updike's novels continue the long national debate on the American civilization and its discontents, perhaps what is most significant about them is their depiction of restless and aspiring spirits struggling within the constraints of flesh, of time and gravity—lovers and battlers all. For Updike (writing about the novel in an essay), "Not to be in love, the capital N novel whispers to capital W western man, is to be dying."

Biography

The only child of Wesley and Linda Grace (née Hoyer) Updike, John Updike spent the first thirteen years of his life living with his parents and grandparents in his maternal grandparents' home in Shillington, Pennsylvania, in rather strained economic conditions. In 1945, the Updikes had to move to the family farm in Plainville, ten miles away from Shillington. Updike's father supported the family on his meager salary as a mathematics teacher at the high school. His mother had literary aspirations of her own and later became a free-lance writer. A number of short stories, such as "Flight," and the novels *The Centaur* and *Of the Farm* drew upon this experience. As a youth, Updike dreamed of drawing cartoons and writing for *The New Yorker*, an ambition he fulfilled in 1955. Updike went to Harvard University in 1950 on a full scholarship, majoring in English. He was editor of the Harvard *Lampoon* and was graduated in 1954 with highest honors. In 1953, he married Radcliffe student Mary Pennington, the daughter of a Unitarian minister; they were to have four children.

After a year in Oxford, England, where Updike studied at the Ruskin School of Drawing and Fine Art, he returned to the United States to a job offered him by E. B. White as a staff writer with *The New Yorker*, for which he wrote the "Talk of the Town" column. In April of 1957, fearing the city scene would disturb his development as a writer, Updike and his family left New York for Ipswich, Massachusetts, where he would live for the next seventeen years and which would serve for the model for the settings of a number of stories and novels. During this time, Updike was active in Ipswich community life and regularly attended the Congregational Church. In 1974, the Updikes were divorced. In 1977, Updike remarried, to Martha Bernhard, and settled in Georgetown, Massachusetts.

During the late 1950's and early 1960's, Updike faced a crisis of faith prompted by his acute consciousness of death's inevitability. The works of such writers as Søren Kierkegaard and, especially, Karl Barth, the Swiss orthodox theologian, helped Updike come to grips with this fear and to find a basis for faith. Religious and theological concerns pervade Updike's fiction. In a real sense, like Nathaniel Hawthorne's more than one hundred years earlier, Updike's fiction explores for his time the great issues of sin, guilt, and grace—of spiritual yearnings amid the entanglements of the flesh.

Updike's success as a writer has enabled him to travel under government auspices. In 1964-1965, Updike traveled to Russia, Romania, Bulgaria, and Czechoslovakia as part of the U.S.S.R.-U.S. Cultural Exchange Program. In 1973, he traveled and lectured as a Fulbright lecturer to Ghana, Nigeria, Tanzania, Kenya, and Ethiopia. Updike's Bech novels and *The Coup* reflect those journeys.

Analysis

A writer with John Updike's versatility and range, whose fiction reveals a virtual symphonic richness and complexity, offers readers a variety of keys or themes with which to explore his work. The growing and already substantial body of criticism Updike's work has engendered, therefore, reflects a variety of approaches. Alice and Kenneth Hamilton were among the first critics to give extensive treatment to the religious and theological elements in Updike's fiction. Rachel Burchard explores Updike's fiction in terms of its presentations of authentic quests for meaning in our time, for answers to age-old questions about man and God, and of its affirmation of human worth and hope despite the social and natural forces threatening defeat of the human enterprise. Considering technique as well as theme, Larry Taylor treats the function of the pastoral and antipastoral in Updike's fiction and places that treatment within a long tradition in American literature. The British critic Tony Tanner discusses Updike's fiction as depicting the "compromised environment" of New England suburbia—the fear and dread of decay, of death and nothingness, and the dream of escaping from the complications of such a world. Edward Vargo focuses upon the recurrence of ritualistic patterns in Updike's fiction, the struggle to wrest something social from an increasingly secularized culture. Joyce Markle's thematic study of Updike's fiction sees a conflict between "Lovers," or Life-givers, and the embodied forces of convention, dehumanizing belief, and death.

In a 1962 memoir entitled "The Dogwood Tree: A Boyhood," Updike discusses his boyhood fascination with what he called the "Three Great Secret Things: Sex, Religion, and Art." The critic George W. Hunt contends that "these three secret things also characterize the predominant subject matter, thematic concerns, and central questions found throughout his adult fiction." Detailing Updike's reliance upon the ideas of Søren Kierkegaard and Karl Barth, Hunt's study is interested in the religious implications of Updike's work. A more sociological interest informs Philip Vaughan's study of Updike's fiction, which, to Vaughan, provides readers with valid depictions of the social conditions—loneliness, isolation, aging, and morality—of our time. David Galloway sees Updike's fiction in existential terms, seeing Updike's protagonists as "absurd heroes" seeking meaning in an inhospitable universe. More impressionistic but quite suggestive is Elizabeth Tallant's short study of the fate of Eros in several of Updike's novels. Believing that a thesis or thematic approach does not do full justice to Updike's work, Donald J. Greiner examines Updike's novels more formalistically in order to "discuss the qualities that make Updike a great writer."

Using a comparative approach, George Searles discusses Philip Roth and Updike as important social realists whose work gives a true sense of life in the last half of the twentieth century. To Searles, Updike's overriding theme is cultural disintegration—questing but alienated protagonists confronting crises caused by a breakdown of the established order. Jeff Campbell uses Updike's long poem *Midpoint* (1969) as a key to an analysis of Updike's fiction. Seeing Updike as an "ironist of the spiritual life," Ralph C. Wood discusses Updike's fiction—along with the fiction of Flannery O'Connor, Walker

Percy, and Peter De Vries—as depicting the "comedy of redemption," a study deeply indebted to the theology of Karl Barth.

In a compendious study of American fiction since 1940, Frederick R. Karl offers a useful overview of Updike: "Updike's fiction is founded on a vision of a compromised, tentative, teetering American, living in suburban New England or in rural Pennsylvania; an American who has broken with his more disciplined forebears and drifted free, seeking self-fulfillment but uncertain what it is and how to obtain it." While this rather global description fairly represents the recurring condition in most of Updike's novels, it does not do justice to the complex particularities of each work. Nevertheless, it does point to the basic predicament of nearly all of Updike's protagonists—that sense of doubleness, of the ironic discrepancy of the fallen creature who yet senses, or yearns for, something transcendent. Updike's people are spiritual amphibians—creatures in concert with two realms, yet not fully at home in either. Updike employs an analogous image in his novel *The Centaur*—here is a creature that embodies the godly with the bestial, a fitting image of the human predicament in Updike's fiction. His fiction depicts the ambiguity of the "yes-but" stance toward the world, similar to the paradox of the "already and the not-yet." In his fine story "The Bulgarian Poetess" (1966), Updike writes: "Actuality is a running impoverishment of possibility." Again there is a sense of duplicity, of incompleteness. In such a world, problems are not always solved; they are more often endured if not fully understood. Yet even the curtains of actuality occasionally part, unexpectedly, to offer gifts, as Updike avers in his preface to *Olinger Stories* (1964)—such gifts as keep alive a vision of wholeness in an often lost and fragmented world.

Updike's first novel, *The Poorhouse Fair*, may seem anomalous in comparison with the rest of his work. In fact, the novel depicts a collision of values that runs throughout Updike's work. As in so much of Updike's fiction, the novel is concerned with decay, disintegration, a loss or abandonment of vital traditions, of values, of connection to a nurturing past. This opposition is embodied in the two principal characters: ninety-four-year-old John Hook, former teacher and resident of the poorhouse, and Stephen Conner, the poorhouse's prefect. The novel is set in the future, sometime in the late 1970's, where want and misery have virtually been eliminated by a kind of humanistic socialism. Such progress has been made at a price: sterility, dehumanization, spiritual emptiness, regimentation. In a world totally run by the head, the heart dies. Hook tells Conner, in response to the prefect's avowed atheism: "There is no goodness, without belief." Conner's earthly paradise is a false one, destroying what it would save. The former prefect, Mendelssohn, sought, as his name would suggest, to fulfill the old people's spiritual needs in rituals and hymn singing.

Out of frustration with Conner's soulless administration, the old people break into a spontaneous "stoning" of Conner in the novel's climax. In effect, Conner is a corrupt or perverted martyr to the new "religion" of godless rationalism. The incident symbolizes the inherent desire and need for self-assertion and individualism. Conner's rationalized system is ultimately entropic. The annual fair is symbolic of an antientropic spirit in its celebration of the fruits of individual self-expression—patchwork quilts and peach-pit sculptures. In its depiction of an older America—its values of individuality, personal dignity, and pride—being swallowed up by material progress and bureaucratic efficiency, the novel is an "old" and somber book for a young author to write. In effect, Updike depicts an America become a spiritual "poorhouse," though materially rich. It is Hook, one of the last links to that lost America, who struggles at the end for some word to leave with Conner as a kind of testament, but he cannot find it.

In a number of stories and the novels *The Centaur* and *Of the Farm*, Updike draws heavily upon his experiences growing up in Shillington, Pennsylvania. Both novels—though very different from each other—concern the reckoning of a son with a parent, in the case of *The Centaur* with his father and in *Of the Farm* with his mother, before he can proceed with his life. This is emotional and spiritual "homework" necessary for the son's passage to maturity, to freedom from the past, yet also to a new sense of responsibility. As in all Updike's fiction, this passage is difficult, complex, and ambiguous in its resolution.

The Centaur is arguably Updike's most complex novel, involving as it does the complicated interweaving of the myth of Chiron the centaur with the story of an adolescent boy and his father one winter in 1947. While the novel won the National Book Award, its reception was quite mixed. A number of reviewers thought the use of myth to be pretentious and not fully realized, while others praised the author's achievement. The novel is part *Bildungsroman*, a novel of moral education, and part *Künstlerroman*, a novel of an artist seeking his identity in conflict with society and/or his past. Operating on different levels, temporally and spatially, the nine chapters of the novel are a virtual collage, quite appropriate for the painter-narrator, nearly thirty, self-described as a "second-rate abstract expressionist," who is trying to recover from his past some understanding that might clarify and motivate his artistic vocation. Peter Caldwell, the narrator, reminisces to his black mistress in a Manhattan loft about a three-day period in the winter of 1947, fourteen years earlier. On the realistic level, Peter tells the story of his self-conscious adolescence growing up an only child, living on a farm with his parents and Pop Kramer, his grandfather. His father is the high school biology teacher and swim coach, whose acts of compassion and charity embarrass the boy. On the mythic level, the father is depicted as Chiron the centaur, part man and part stallion, who serves as mentor to the youthful Greek heroes. As such, he suffers for his charges. By moving back and forth between the mythic and the realistic levels, Peter is able to move to an understanding of his father's life and death and to a clarification of his own vocation.

Just as Chiron sacrifices his immortality—he accepts death—so that Prometheus may be free to live, so too does George give his life for his son. While George is obsessed with death, it is doubtful that his sacrifice takes the form of death. Rather, his sacrifice is his willingness to go on fulfilling his obligations to his family. In reflecting upon this sacrifice by his father, Peter, feeling a failure in his art, asks: *"Was it for this that my father gave up his life?"* In the harsh reappraisal his memory provides, Peter is learning what he could not know as an adolescent. Love, guilt, and sacrifice are somehow inherent in the very structure of life. It is this that his mythicized father reveals to him in the very act of his narrating the story. For many critics, George Caldwell's sacrificial act frees the son to resume his artistic vocation with courage. For others, the novel is a mock epic showing in Peter the artist, the son of a scientist father and the grandson of a preacher, a loss of the metaphoric realm that makes great art possible and that leaves Peter diminished by his confinement to the earth alone. However the end is taken, the mythic element of the narrative richly captures the doubleness of human existence so pervasive in Updike's fictions.

The shortest of Updike's novels, *Of the Farm* is another tale of the intricacy of love, guilt, sacrifice, and betrayal. Stalled and failing in his artistic vocation, Peter Caldwell goes home through a creative act of the memory and imagination to recover his lost vision, a basis to continue his work. Peter can fulfill his Promethean charge because his father was Chiron. In contrast, *Of the Farm*'s Joey Robinson goes home to get his mother's blessing on his recent remarriage. Joey seeks forgiveness of the guilt he bears for the acts of betrayal that have constituted his life. He betrays his poetic aspirations by becoming an advertising executive and betrays his marriage to Joan and his three children through adultery and divorce. Bringing home for his domineering mother's approval his sensuous new wife, Peggy, sets the stage for more betrayals and recriminations. As the weekend progresses, Peggy and Joey's mother vie for Joey's soul. Joey cannot please both women or heal the wounds of his past betrayals. For Joey, Peggy is the "farm" he wishes to husband. At the end, failing to win his mother's blessing, Joey and Peggy return to their lives in the city, leaving Joey's mother to die amid the memorials of her own unrealized dreams. If the novel is an exploration of human freedom, as the epigraph from Jean-Paul Sartre would suggest, the reader sees that freedom escapes all the characters, bound as they are by conflicting desires, guilt, and obligation.

When Updike published *Rabbit, Run* in 1960, a story of an ex-basketball player and his floundering marriage set in the late 1950's, he had no intention of writing a sequel. Yet, Updike has returned to Harry "Rabbit" Angstrom once every ten years for four novels—*Rabbit Redux* (1971), *Rabbit Is Rich* (1981), and *Rabbit at Rest* (1990)—as a kind of gauge of the changes occuring in American culture. This series of novels is among the most popular of his work.

For *Rabbit, Run*, Updike uses a quote from Pascal for an epigraph: "The motions of Grace, the hardness of heart; external circumstances." Updike has commented that those three things describe our lives. In a real sense, those things also describe the basic movements and conflicts in the Rabbit novels. From *Rabbit, Run* to *Rabbit at Rest*, as the titles themselves suggest, Rabbit's life has been characterized by a series of zigzag movements and resistances and yearnings, colliding, often ineffectually, with the external circumstances of a fast-paced and changing world. *Rabbit, Run* takes place in the late 1950's, when Harry Angstrom, a former high school basketball great nicknamed Rabbit, at twenty-six finds himself in a dead-end life: with a job selling items in a dime store and a marriage to a careless and boozie woman. Wounded by the stifling boredom of everyday life and the cloying pressures of conforming and adapting to his environment, so characteristic of the 1950's, Harry wonders, confusingly, what has happened to his life. The disgust he feels about his present life is aggravated by his memories of when he was "first-rate at something" as a high school basketball great. Out of frustration, Rabbit bolts from his life-stifling existence, feeling that something out there wants him to find it. The novel is the study of this nonhero's quest for a nonexistent grail. Rabbit's zigzagging or boomeranging movements from wife Janice to mistress Ruth, the part-time prostitute, wreaks havoc: Janice accidentally drowns the baby; Ruth is impregnated and seeks an abortion. Pursued by the weak-faithed, do-gooder minister Eccles and failed by his old coach Tothero, Rabbit has no one to whom he can turn for help. Rabbit, like so many of Updike's protagonists, is enmeshed in the highly compromised environment of America, locked in the horizontal dimension yet yearning for something transcendent, the recovery of the vertical dimension. For Rabbit, the closest he can come to that missing feeling is sex, the deep mysteries of the woman's body replacing the old revelations of religion. Rabbit, though irresponsible, registers his refusal to succumb to such a world through movement, his running replacing the lost territories of innocent escape.

Ten years later, in *Rabbit Redux*, Rabbit has stopped running. He is back home with Janice and works as a typesetter. It is the end of the 1960's, and Rabbit watches the Moon landing on television as well as the upheavals of civil rights, campus demonstrations, and the Vietnam War. Rabbit feels that the whole country is doing what he did ten years earlier. As Janice moves out to live with her lover Stavros, Rabbit and his son Nelson end up as hosts to Jill, a runaway flower-child, and a bail-jumping Vietnam veteran and black radical named Skeeter. This unlikely combination allows Updike to explore the major cultural and political clashes of the 1960's. This time Rabbit is more a passive listener-observer than an activist searcher. Skeeter's charismatic critiques of the American way of life challenge Rabbit's unquestioning patriotism and mesmerize him. As a result, Rabbit is helpless when disaster comes—his house is set on fire and Jill dies inside. Rabbit helps Skeeter escape. Fearing for her lover's heart, Janice returns to Rabbit. Unlike the restless figure of the first novel, Rabbit now seems to have capitulated or resigned himself to those powerful "external circumstances" from which he once sought escape. Rabbit bears witness, numbingly, to a disintegrating America, even as it puts a man on the Moon. America's spiritual landscape is as barren as that on the Moon. The novel ends with Rabbit and Janice asleep together. Perhaps they can awake to a new maturity and sense of responsibility for what they do in the world.

In the first two Rabbit novels, Rabbit was out of step with the times— running in the placid 1950's, sitting in the frenetic 1960's. In *Rabbit Is Rich*, he is running again, but this time in tune with the rhythms of the 1970's. Rabbit now jogs, which is in keeping with the fitness craze that began in the 1970's. He and Janice are prospering during the decade of inflation and energy crises. They own a Toyota agency and are members of a country club. Rabbit plays golf and goes to Rotary Club lunches. Instead of newspapers, as in *Rabbit Redux*, he reads *Consumer Reports*, the bible of his new status. The ghosts of his past haunt him, however: the drowned baby, the child he did or did not have with Ruth, memories of Jill and Skeeter. The chief reminder of the sins of his past is his son Nelson, returning home, like something repressed, to wreak havoc on the family's new affluent complacency. Like his father of old but lacking Rabbit's conscience and vision, Nelson's quest for attention practically wrecks everything that he touches: his father's cars, his relationships. Rabbit can see himself in Nelson's behavior and tries to help him avoid recapitulating Rabbit's mistakes, but communication is difficult between them. With Skylab falling and America held hostage by Iranians, the present is uneasy and anxious, the future uncertain. Characteristically, Rabbit turns to sex to fill the spiritual void. He and Janice make love on top of their gold Krugerrands. Rabbit lusts for the lovely Cindy, but in the wife-swapping escapade during their Caribbean holiday, Rabbit gets Thelma Harrison instead and is introduced to anal sex—a fitting image of the sense of nothingness pervading American culture at the end of the "Me Decade." Updike does not end there. He leaves Rabbit holding his granddaughter, "another nail in his coffin," but also another chance for renewal, perhaps even a motion of grace, a richness unearned.

The sense of exhaustion—of a world "running out of gas" in so many ways—that pervades *Rabbit Is Rich* becomes more serious, even terminal, in *Rabbit at Rest*. The fuzzy emptiness and mindlessness of the 1980's pervade the novel, even as so much is described in such vivid detail. Rabbit and Janice now winter in Florida and Nelson runs the car dealership. Rabbit sustains himself on junk food and endless television viewing, images of the emptiness of American life under Ronald Reagan. He suffers a heart attack and undergoes an angioplasty procedure. His son's cocaine addiction and embezzle-ment of $200,000 from the business shock the family. Yet this often coarse and unsympathetic man continues to compel the reader's interest. He won-ders about the Dalai Lama then in the news. As the Cold War dissipates, Rabbit asks: "If there's no Cold War, what's the point of being an Ameri-can?" The man called "Mr. Death" in *Rabbit, Run* now must face death in his own overblown body and contemplate it in relation to a world he has always known but that now is no more. Can such a man find peace, an acceptance and understanding of a life lived in such struggle and perplexity? In *Rabbit Is Rich*, Harry confesses to Janice the paradox of their lives: "Too much of it and not enough. The fear that it will end some day, and the fear that tomor-row will be the same as yesterday." In intensive care in Florida, at the end of *Rabbit at Rest*, Rabbit says, "Enough." Is this the realization and acceptance of life's sufficiency or its surplus? A confession of his own excesses and indul-gences, or a command of sorts that he has had enough? These are only a few of the questions raised by the Rabbit novels.

Many critics praise Updike for being the premier American novelist of marriage. Nearly all of his fiction displays the mysterious as well as common-place but ineluctable complexities and conflicts of marriage. It is one of Up-dike's major concerns to explore the conditions of love in our time. His fiction is his updating and reworking of the Tristan and Isolde myth, about which Updike had commented in his review of Denis de Rougement's book *L'Amour et l'occident* (1956; *Love in the Western World*, 1983)—lovers whose passion is enhanced by the obstacles needed to be overcome to fulfill it; the quest for an ideal lover who will assuage the fear of death and the longing for the infinite; the confusions of *eros* and the death wish. Many of Updike's male protagonists are aspects of both Tristan and Don Juan in their quest for a life-enhancing or death-denying passion. Such are the ingredients in the novels *Couples*, *Marry Me: A Romance*, and *The Witches of Eastwick*. All the novels are set in the 1960's—the spring of 1962 to the spring of 1963 in *Marry Me*, the spring of 1963 to the spring of 1964 in *Couples*, and probably 1969 for *The Witches of Eastwick*. In their various ways, each novel tries to answer the question, "After Christianity, what?" Human sexuality is liturgy and sacra-ment of the new religion emerging in America in the 1960's—a new end of innocence in a "post-pill paradise." The three novels make an interesting grouping because all deal with marriages in various states of deterioration, and all explore the implications of "sex as the emergent religion, as the only thing left," Updike says. While not published until 1976, *Marry Me* was actually written before *Couples*. In fact, one story seems to lead right into the other. *The Witches of Eastwick* explores the theme from a woman's perspec-tive.

Both Jerry Conant of *Marry Me* and Piet Hanema of *Couples* are educated professionals, married with children, and live in upper-middle-class suburbs of great cities. They are both suffering spiritually, longing for an affirmation from outside their selves, for some sort of blessing and certainty. As Jerry says, "Maybe our trouble is that we live in the twilight of the old morality, and there's just enough to torment us, and not enough to hold us in." The mortal fear that such an insight inspires leads both men to desperate quests for a love that will mend or heal their spiritual brokenness or emptiness. *Marry Me* takes place during the second year of the Kennedy Administration, when the charm of the Camelot myth still captivated the country. Significantly, Updike calls *Marry Me* a "romance" rather than a novel, in order to suggest an attempt to use the freer form to explore the ambiguities of love, marriage, and adultery. The novel ends in ambiguity, with no clear resolution; in fact, there are three possible endings: Jerry with his lover Sally in Wyoming, Jerry with his wife Ruth in France, and Jerry in the Virgin Islands alone, on the island of St. Croix, symbolizing perhaps Jerry's self-immolation.

Couples takes place during the last year of the Kennedy presidency, including his assassination, and is thus a much more cynical book, harsher and darker than *Marry Me*. A certain light has gone out in the land; death and decay haunt the imagination. In contrast to *Marry Me*, choices are made and lives reconstitute themselves in a kind of cyclical way at the end of *Couples*. These two rather weak men fail at their quest to find in the flesh what they have lost in the spirit. Both men are believers and churchgoers, and both face a crisis in their faith. The church, committed to secularity and worldliness, fails them. Their respective wives are naturalistic and feel at home on earth and offer them little surcease to their anxiety. In *Marry Me*, Jerry must contend with Sally's husband Richard, an atheist with one blind eye, who insists on clear-cut decisions. For Jerry, however, every choice involves a loss that he cannot tolerate. In *Couples*, Piet is pitted against Freddy Thorne, the self-proclaimed priest of the new religion of sensuality. To Freddy, it is their fate to be "suspended in . . . one of those dark ages that visits mankind between millennia, between the death and rebirth of gods, when there is nothing to steer by but sex and stoicism and the stars." The many adulteries among the ten couples of *Couples* lead finally to divorce and disintegration of the secular paradise of Tarbox, the fictional suburb of the novel. Piet leaves his unattainable but earthbound wife, fittingly named Angela, for the sensuous Foxy Whitman, whose abortion of Piet's child Freddy arranges. When his church is destroyed by fire, Piet is freed from his old morality and guilt and the tension inherent in his sense of fallenness. Yet the satisfaction obtained with Foxy is a foreclosure of the vertical hope, and is a kind of death. Both novels depict the failure of sex as a religion as well as the profound disappointments with love in its romantic or secular forms. Such may be Updike's answer to the question he posed: "After Christianity, what?"

The setting of *The Witches of Eastwick* is a small town in Rhode Island during the first year or so of Richard Nixon's presidency, an era of protest and discontent. Three divorcees, Alexander Spofford, Jane Smart, and Sukie Rougemont, discover the power of sisterhood and femininity and become witchlike in their powers. The delicate balance of their friendship is upset by the entrance of the apparently demoniac Darryl Van Horne, who takes them all as his lovers. The novel's three parts, "The Coven," "Malefica," and "Guilt," suggest a progression from their newfound power and independence through an encounter with the demoniac to a rediscovery of responsibility through an awareness of guilt. Like Updike's many male protagonists, the three women must come to grips with death before they can reconstitute a meaningful life. Van Horne is a satanic figure whose machinations lead to a dissipation of the women's powers. When he chooses the young Jennifer Gabriel for his wife, the women employ their powers to create a curse to bring about Jennifer's death. When she does die, the women feel guilt, even though it is not clear that their curse caused the girl's cancer. Van Horne preaches a sermon on the evilness of a creation saturated with disease and leaves town with Jennifer's brother, Christopher. The three women disband and find their way into suitable marriages. Such use of witchcraft allows Updike to explore the nature of evil and its connections with nature, history, and technology. The ambiguities of feminism are examined in the context of the moral and social confusions of the late 1960's in an effort to break down the destructive and outmoded polarities of the patriarchical tradition.

The two Bech books—*Bech: A Book* and *Bech Is Back*—and *The Coup* are novels and stories resulting from Updike's travels to Eastern Europe and to Africa. Each work offers the author an opportunity to develop a very different persona from those of his domestic novels, as well as the chance to explore another aspect of "otherness" and "difference." *Bech: A Book* is a collection of seven stories about a middle-aged and very successful Jewish novelist, Henry Bech, and his various experiences both abroad and in America. The collection is framed by the fiction of Updike writing about an actual person contemporary with him. The book has a foreword by the putative author as well as two appendices. Such devices afford Updike an opportunity for humorous satire of the literary life in America. Bech emerges as a strong and believable character struggling with the failure of his success as a writer in a success-plagued culture. In *Bech Is Back*, Updike creates seven more stories about Bech's travels and his wrestling with the ambiguities of fame, fortune, and human worth, the protagonist's success with women an index of his success and worth as a writer. He must struggle with the question of whether he has sold out his talent for the marketplace, defiling both. Felix Ellellou, the protagonist of *The Coup*, is a bold creation for Updike, a black Islamic Marxist whose memoirs constitute the novel. Now in exile, the former president of the fictional sub-Saharan nation of Kush recounts the story of his rise and fall and of his perpetual struggle to avoid the ambiguous gifts of American aid. He fears not only the junk food but also the forces of secularity and

materialism that will ultimately make of his beloved Kush a spiritual wasteland. He virtually stands alone in his resistance to the so-called benefits of
American civilization, toward which he admits ambivalence. In Ellellou, one
can see an African version of Updike's body-spirit conflict so prevalent in his
fiction. For Ellellou, freedom must be freedom from material possessions, yet
he anguishes over his people's poverty-stricken plight. He believes that it is
better to die in poverty than from spiritual loss. In privation, he believes, the
spirit will soar. Despite Ellellou's stoicism, his faith is plagued by doubts. He
suspects that the new world religion will be godless and entropic. Updike's
African novel is a replay of the author's critical interrogation of the moral and
spiritual failures of the West.

Updike's concern with love, marriage, and adultery in so much of his
fiction links him to Nathaniel Hawthorne's great novel *The Scarlet Letter*
(1850), America's first great treatment of the complex social and religious
consequences of adulterous love. Three novels in particular treat different
dimensions of that adulterous triangle of Hawthorne's novel—*A Month of
Sundays*, *Roger's Version*, and *S.* Hawthorne's Dimmesdale is updated in the
figure of the Reverend Tom Marshfield, the exiled protagonist of *A Month of
Sundays*. Roger Lambert of *Roger's Version*, the professor of theology specializing in heresies, is Updike's treatment of Hawthorne's Roger Chillingworth.
Sarah Worth of *S.* is a contemporary depiction of Hawthorne's Hester, the
truly noble and strong character of *The Scarlet Letter*. Hawthorne's Dimmesdale is crushed by his inability to integrate the body-and-soul division. So,
too, does Updike's Marshfield suffer from this split in a novel with many
allusions to *The Scarlet Letter*. Marshfield marries the former Jane Chillingworth, whose father was Marshfield's ethics instructor. The retreat center is
managed by Ms. Prynne, who reads the diary entries of Marshfield and his
fellow clerical exiles. The novel traces Marshfield's integration of body and
spirit, a mending of Marshfield's fragmented self, enabling him to return to
his ministry as a true helper to the faithful. Roger Chillingworth in *The
Scarlet Letter* was the cockolded husband seeking revenge for his wife's
adultery. In *Roger's Version*, Roger Lambert imagines that his wife Esther is
having an affair with Dale, the computer science graduate student trying to
prove God's existence by computer. Dale is a kind of innocent, a fundamentalist seeking technological support for his faith. By the end, Dale's project
has failed, as Roger believed it would, and Dale returns to Ohio, his faith
demolished. Yet, Dale's project provoked Roger to revivify his own faith and
to engage his world more responsibly than he has. Updike's Sarah Worth of *S.*
is certainly one possible version of a late twentieth century Hester Prynne.
Sarah is a woman who has taken her life fully into her own hands without
shame or illusion. After bolting from her faithless but wealthy physician
husband, Sarah goes to an ashram in Arizona for spiritual renewal. That
proves to be a false endeavor, but Sarah survives intact (and with much of the

cult's money). Loving and compassionate yet willful and worldly, Sarah Worth dares to follow her own path.

With the astonishing variety and richness of his narratives, John Updike's fiction constitutes a serious exploration and probing of the spiritual conditions of American culture in the late twentieth century. The fate of American civilization is seen in the condition of love—its risks and dangers as well as its possibility for gracious transformation.

John G. Parks

Other major works

SHORT FICTION: *The Same Door*, 1959; *Pigeon Feathers and Other Stories*, 1962; *Olinger Stories: A Selection*, 1964; *The Music School*, 1966; *Museums and Women and Other Stories*, 1972; *Problems and Other Stories*, 1979; *Too Far to Go: The Maples Stories*, 1979; *Trust Me*, 1987.

PLAYS: *Three Texts from Early Ipswich: A Pageant*, 1968; *Buchanan Dying*, 1974.

POETRY: *The Carpentered Hen, and Other Tame Creatures*, 1958; *Telephone Poles and Other Poems*, 1963; *Midpoint and Other Poems*, 1969; *Tossing and Turning*, 1977; *Facing Nature*, 1985.

NONFICTION: *Assorted Prose*, 1965; *Picked-Up Pieces*, 1975; *Hugging the Shore: Essays and Criticism*, 1983; *Just Looking: Essays on Art*, 1989; *Self-Consciousness*, 1989.

Bibliography

Burchard, Rachel C. *John Updike: Yea Sayings*. Carbondale: Southern Illinois University Press, 1971. Seeing Updike as essentially an optimistic quester for answers to questions about life's meaning, this book covers Updike's fiction up through *Couples*. It contains notes, a selected bibliography, and an index.

Detweiler, Robert. *John Updike*. Boston: Twayne, 1984. This is an expanded and revised edition of Detweiler's 1972 study of Updike's fiction. It is an excellent introductory survey of Updike's work through 1983. It contains a chronology, biographical sketch, analysis of the fiction and its sources, a select bibliography, and an index. It provides a good discussion of religious and theological themes in the fiction.

Greiner, Donald J. *Adultery in the American Novel: Updike, James, and Hawthorne*. Columbia: University of South Carolina Press, 1985. An excellent comparative analysis and discussion of the treatment of adultery in three major American authors. Extensive discussion of *Couples*, *Marry Me*, *A Month of Sundays*, and *Rabbit, Run*, with brief mention of four other novels. Helpful index.

_____. *John Updike's Novels*. Athens: Ohio University Press, 1984. A close and thoughtful reading of Updike's novels through 1982 grouped topically, with notes and an index.

Hamilton, Alice, and Kenneth Hamilton. *The Elements of John Updike.* Grand Rapids, Mich.: Wm. B. Eerdman's, 1970. An early introductory study of Updike's fiction which focuses upon religious themes and issues, with index.

Hunt, George W. *John Updike and the Three Secret Things: Sex, Religion, and Art.* Grand Rapids, Mich.: Wm. B. Eerdman's, 1980. With discussions of the theologies of Søren Kierkegaard and Karl Barth and their relevance to Updike's fiction, the book is a critical study of Updike's novels through *The Coup* (1978) and a few short stories. It argues that Updike's fiction is preoccupied, in terms of subject and theme, with sex, religion, and art. The book contains a chronology, notes, and an index.

Markle, Joyce B. *Fighters and Lovers: Theme in the Novels of John Updike.* New York: New York University Press, 1973. An excellent thematic discussion of Updike's novels through *Rabbit Redux*, with notes, bibliography, and index. The book sees Updike's fiction in terms of a progressive conflict between lovers and life-givers and the forces of death and decay.

Uphaus, Suzanne Henning. *John Updike.* New York: Frederick Ungar Publishing Co., 1980. An introductory analysis of Updike's fiction through 1979. Biographical information, a chronology, notes, bibliography, and an index.

Vargo, Edward P. *Rainstorms and Fire: Ritual in the Novels of John Updike.* Port Washington, New York: Kennikat Press, 1973. This study discusses the centrality of rituals and celebrations in Updike's fiction. It contains notes, bibliography, and index.

Wood, Ralph C. *The Comedy of Redemption: Christian Faith and Comic Vision in Four American Novelists.* Notre Dame: University of Notre Dame Press, 1988. A sophisticated theological analysis of Updike's Rabbit novels as well as *The Centaur* and *Couples* along with a treatment of the fiction of Flannery O'Connor, Walker Percy, and Peter De Vries. The book contains notes and an index.

CARL VAN VECHTEN

Born: Cedar Rapids, Iowa; June 17, 1880
Died: New York, New York; December 21, 1964

Principal long fiction

Peter Whiffle: His Life and Works, 1922; *The Blind Bow-Boy*, 1923; *The Tattooed Countess*, 1924; *Firecrackers*, 1925; *Nigger Heaven*, 1926; *Spider Boy*, 1928; *Parties*, 1930.

Other literary forms

Carl Van Vechten had three major careers in the arts; he was a critic, a novelist, and a photographer. His music criticism includes *Music After the Great War* (1915), *Music and Bad Manners* (1916), and *The Music of Spain* (1918). His involvement with major American and European writers and artists of the 1920's and 1930's is chronicled in his autobiographies, *Sacred and Profane Memories* (1932) and *Fragments from an Unwritten Autobiography* (1955).

Achievements

The spirit of the "jazz age," the "roaring twenties," and the "lost generation" is nowhere better depicted than in the saucy and irreverent novels of Van Vechten. Van Vechten moved deftly through three careers: he began as a music, dance, and drama critic, producing several volumes of wide-ranging, urbane essays; then, he devoted himself to fiction, writing seven well-received novels in a decade which saw the first publications of Ernest Hemingway, F. Scott Fitzgerald, and John Dos Passos; finally, he became a noted photographer, specializing in portraits of writers and artists. In all his diverse endeavors, Van Vechten was witty, cosmopolitan, and above all, unconventional. He publicized the work of such writers as William Faulkner, Ronald Firbank, and especially Gertrude Stein, who remained his close friend until her death, and who assigned him as her literary executor. He was among the first critics to recognize the exciting cultural renaissance flourishing in Harlem and devoted much effort to helping establish the careers of Countée Cullen, Langston Hughes, James Weldon Johnson, Bessie Smith, Ethel Waters, and other black artists. He saw himself as a popularizer and supporter of avant-garde artists, and with a clear eye and self-assurance, he brought to the attention of the American public exotic figures ranging from Waslaw Nijinsky to Erik Satie, from Mary Garden to Igor Stravinsky.

Van Vechten, more than many of his contemporaries, lived the literary life with seemingly boundless enthusiasm. His verve animates all of his writing, including the essays he frequently contributed to such trend-setting journals as *Trend*, *The Smart Set*, and *Vanity Fair*, and this effervescent spirit informs his novels as well. His wide interests, diverse friendships, and tireless pursuit of the new, the brilliant, and the innovative make Van Vechten a fascinating guide to America's cultural life in the first decades of the twentieth century.

Biography

Carl Van Vechten was born in Cedar Rapids, Iowa, on June 17, 1880. His father was a banker turned insurance company executive; his mother was a college graduate, suffragette, and for her time, a political and social activist. Born when his parents were in their forties, Van Vechten had two siblings much older than he and so spent his childhood surrounded by four adults. Predictably, this atmosphere nurtured a precocious child. By the time he was an adolescent, Van Vechten had thoroughly immersed himself in whatever cultural offerings could be found in Cedar Rapids—opera, theater, concerts which stopped in the city on tour—and began to apply his own talents to amateur theatrical productions and family piano recitals. Physically he was an awkward youth—too tall too early, with large buck teeth—and his omnivorous appetite for culture made him feel socially awkward among his peers. Longing to escape from the complacent bourgeois existence of Cedar Rapids, he enrolled at the University of Chicago and, in 1899, took his first steps East, a direction which would eventually lead to New York and then to Paris.

At college, Van Vechten studied with Robert Morss Lovett and William Vaughn Moody. He also began writing passionately and composing music. After he was graduated, he took a job on the *Chicago American*; he was assigned to write short news pieces and collect photographs to illustrate news stories. He soon decided, however, that, for his purposes, Chicago was little better than Cedar Rapids. In 1906, he left for New York.

Van Vechten's first writing assignment there was an opera review for Theodore Dreiser, then editor of *Broadway Magazine*. Soon, Van Vechten joined the staff of *The New York Times* as assistant to the music critic. From 1908 to 1909, he served as Paris correspondent for the *Times*, a post which brought him into close contact with leading European dancers, sculptors, artists, and writers. When he returned to New York in the spring of 1909, he resumed his job as music critic, but he longed to return to Europe. He was back in Paris in 1914.

By then, Van Vechten had, in many ways, left his Cedar Rapids days behind him. In 1912, he was divorced from Anna Elizabeth Snyder, a childhood sweetheart he had married just five years before. Shortly after the divorce, he met the Russian-Jewish actress Fania Marinoff, an attractive and exotic-looking woman whom he would soon marry. In 1913, he met Mabel Dodge, the irrepressible center of her own vibrant salon; in 1914, at the second performance of Stravinsky's *Sacre du Printemps* in Paris, he met Gertrude Stein, at whose rue de Fleurus home he would soon encounter the leading figures of Parisian cultural life.

From 1915 to 1932, Van Vechten wrote an astonishing number of books—first several volumes of essays on music and the arts, then seven novels. He preferred the experimental, the daring, the works of young artists being performed, written, and conducted in America and on the Continent, and the enthusiasm with which he greeted such works helped earn their acceptance by his readers. He predicted the enduring greatness of Stravinsky at a time when some wondered if what they were hearing was, indeed, music. He approached his task as critic with "curiosity and energy," he said, and his tastes, idiosyncratic as they were, reflected his certainty in empathizing with the aims of modern artists.

In 1928, his brother died, leaving Van Vechten a substantial bequest which allowed him financial independence. This event coincided with, and perhaps made possible, Van Vechten's new career, that of photographer. He had his first show in 1934, and became a portrait photographer of such writers and artists as Gertrude Stein, Truman Capote, George Gershwin, Leontyne Price, and William Faulkner.

Van Vechten was the founder of several libraries and archives, including the James Weldon Johnson Memorial Collection (black art and literature) at Yale, the George Gershwin Memorial Collection (music) at Fisk University, the Rose McClendon Memorial Collection (photographs of famous blacks) at Howard University, and the Florine Stettheimer Memorial Collection (fine arts) at Fisk.

Analysis

In *Peter Whiffle*, Carl Van Vechten's hero expounds upon the art of criticism, Van Vechten's vocation in the decade before he wrote fiction. Recalling Remy de Gourmont, Whiffle asserts: "Criticism is perhaps the most suggestive of literary forms; it is a perpetual confession; believing to analyze the works of others, the critic unveils and exposes himself to the public." So, he continues, one learns more about the critic than about the object of his observations. "Criticism should open channels of thought and not close them; it should stimulate the soul and not revolt it. And criticism can only be wholesome and sane and spiritually stimulating when it is contradictory." Van Vechten, above all, believed that life itself was contradictory, that appearances often deceived, that absurdity ruled more often than logic. Nevertheless, he exulted in strong, creative, exciting personalities, and believed that such strength could overcome the inherent absurdity of life. If there were no Truth, no unalterable Facts, there could at least be Style, Anecdote, Spirit—those qualities which Whiffle said readers looked for in "the old critics"—and there also could be enthusiasm and joy.

Given Van Vechten's notions about literary criticism, it is no wonder that he gravitated toward fiction, where characters might easily express contradictory ideas and where the writer's style, spirit, and personality are expected to pervade the text. In his novels, Van Vechten emerges as an observant and perceptive critic of his own society and his particular time. His novels, as Donald Pizer notes, "Chronicle either in authorial asides or miniature essays the taste and interests of the decade from the conventional to the avant garde." His friends and acquaintances often made appearances, sometimes under pseudonyms, and current music, books, and paintings are evoked vividly. Aiming to analyze his world, Van Vechten also reveals his own particular point of view: that of the tolerant but wiser and older participant (he was nearly forty-two when he published his first novel), one who looks with bemused sympathy on the antics around him. He accepts—as his characters often do not—that the world is absurd; he is not shocked or dismayed by the suffering, unhappiness, and anguish beneath the glittering life of cosmopolitan high society because he knows that life offers joy and satisfaction, if only one knows where to look. He is aware of the conflict between the sensitive artist and a world which would deny him, but he believes that strength of personality and self-assertion can overcome many obstacles. In his acceptance of absurdity and his belief in the capacity of the artist to survive emotionally and psychologically, he stands apart from some of the younger men writing at the same time: Sherwood Anderson, Hemingway, Fitzgerald, Sinclair Lewis. Though he shares many of their artistic problems, he does not share their anger, and this ability to delight and be delighted distinguishes Van Vechten's fiction.

Peter Whiffle, in this novel about writing a novel, is a would-be writer, searching for self and inspiration in a troubling world. He encounters Van Vechten, who reappears in the novel to meet Peter at several stages of his artistic development; Peter confides his theories of life and art to the patient older man, and reveals the confusions faced by the artist as a young man. At first, Peter announces that he plans to write a book, and Van Vechten asks him what it will be about. About three hundred pages, Peter replies. "That is what it is to be about, about three hundred pages, three hundred pages of colour and style and lists, lists of objects, all jumbled artfully. There isn't a moral, or an idea, or a plot, or even a character. There's to be no propaganda or preaching, or violence, or emotion, or even humour." Art, Peter says, is necessarily abstract—never concrete; art is the pattern which emerges from artful juxtaposition. Some sixty pages later, Peter has discarded these notions and come to another conclusion: art "has nothing to do with style or form or manner. . . . The *matter* is what counts. . . . No style, no form, just *subject*."

Obsessed now with political and social revolution, Peter decides that he must opt for realism over expressionism; Theodore Dreiser—and not, for example, Georg Kaiser—must be his model. Again, some sixty pages later, Peter is thoroughly confused: "Never did I feel less sure of the meaning of art than I do here," he confesses. He has immersed himself in the world of literature, music, and painting, only to discover that no theory or formula will explain art. Finally, he decides that the personality of the artist and his ability to convey his impressions might yield a masterpiece of art. "I think a great book might be written if everything the hero thought and felt and observed could be put into it," he says. "These ideas, impressions, objects, should all be set down. Nothing should be omitted, nothing! One might write a whole book of two hundred thousand words about the events of an hour. And what a book! What a book!" That book will never be written by Peter Whiffle, however, nor would it be written by Van Vechten. Peter observes that one might be able to create a work of art from one's life, merely by living well. "I wanted to write a new Comedie Humaine," Peter says. "Instead, I have lived it. And now, I have come to the conclusion that that was all there was for me to do, just to live, as fully as possible. Sympathy and enthusiasm are something, after all. I must have communicated at least a shadow of these to the ideas and objects and people on whom I have bestowed them." He is disillusioned with the idea that the successful artist is a fulfilled human being. "All expression lifts us farther away from simplicity and causes unhappiness," he concludes. Of his own search for the meaning of art, he finds, "Everybody is striving to do something *new*, instead of writing or painting or composing what is natural. . . . The great secret is . . . to do what one *has* to do."

This paean to individuality and self-knowledge is the theme not only of *Peter Whiffle*, but also of many other Van Vechten novels. Indeed, *Peter Whiffle* is an example of what Van Vechten, in *Nigger Heaven*, calls a propaganda novel: his message is the celebration of self-awareness and a love of life.

Peter Whiffle leaves the provinciality of his native Toledo, Ohio, for the cultural capitals of the world. In *The Tattooed Countess*, Van Vechten reverses the process: Countess Ella Nattatorrini returns from an urbane European life to her childhood home, Maple Valley, Iowa. Maple Valley is as stifling as Carol Kennicott's Gopher Prairie, but unlike Carol, the Countess does not intend to enlighten the town. Instead, she decides to run from it, taking with her the only artist Maple Valley has spawned: Gareth Johns. Moreover, unlike Sinclair Lewis, Van Vechten does not depict small-town life with bitterness or rancor; instead, he is sympathetic toward the repressed characters of Maple Valley, just as he empathizes with the dreams of Ella and Gareth Johns.

The Countess, like Hester Prynne in *The Scarlet Letter* (1850), openly displays a symbol of nonconformity, of sexuality, of freedom: a tattoo on her arm. The "curious emblem" consists of a butterfly perched on a skull, with the phrase "*Que sais-je?*" beneath. Fragile, elusive beauty can distract humans from a preoccupation with their own mortality, but the butterfly must be taken for what it is, and not elevated into theories of art or into doctrines by which one decides to live. During a passionate love affair, Ella had the design tatooed on her arm, and it recalls for her not only her lost love—a sad reminder—but her ability to live fully, a notion she celebrates. Her sister is aghast: surely, even if one were foolhardy enough to be tattooed, one would do it in a discreet place. "That is the sort of thing we keep hidden here," she tells the Countess, but Ella Nattatorrini cannot live a hidden life. It is not Van Vechten's intention to flaunt Ella's quest for freedom and self-fulfillment, but only to allow her a world in which she, as well as the inhabitants of Maple Valley, can live as she must.

Nigger Heaven reflects Van Vechten's intense interest in black culture, an interest which went far beyond Pablo Picasso's fascination with African art or Gertrude Stein's interest in the Baltimore community upon which she drew for her story "Melanctha." Impressed with the vitality of the arts in Harlem, he befriended many black writers and musicians and brought them to the attention of important cultural leaders downtown. Without becoming politically or socially active in support of civil rights, Van Vechten managed to become a significant spokesman for an oppressed people through *Nigger Heaven*, a novel which, despite its blatant propaganda, is a vivid and sympathetic study of New York blacks of the 1920's.

The book centers on the relationship between Mary Love and yet another aspiring writer (surely Van Vechten had many models, black and white, from which to choose), Byron Kasson. Both are educated (Byron is a University of Pennsylvania graduate, Mary a librarian), articulate, sensitive young people, but their love and Byron's dreams are doomed to failure. Byron refuses to "see" Harlem and the real lives of blacks as suitable material for his stories; his insistence on his separateness leaves him isolated. Both the black and white communities look upon him as a misfit. Mary is willing to work within the limitations placed upon her and urges Byron to approach his own people with compassion and even humility. When he tells her he will use the prejudice against his people as a plot for a story, she cautions him against "becoming melodramatic, cheap even. Unless such a story is written with exquisite skill, it will read like a meretricious appeal to the emotions arising out of race prejudice." Ultimately Byron fails, not only in his story, but also in his effort to propel himself out of a culture which threatens to undermine all his hopes. Yet Van Vechten suggests that it is Byron himself—as Peter Whiffle had done before him—who causes his own downfall.

Van Vechten, like his writer-protagonist, faced the problem of seeming melodramatic in a novel which is in large part, as he put it, propaganda. He was, in 1926, anticipating the anger of James Baldwin and Richard Wright; for Van Vechten, "Nigger Heaven" (a black term, he explains, for the Harlem community) was ready to explode. Rarely is Van Vechten as sedate, controlled, and carefully paced as he is in this novel, and rarely is his authorial presence so discreet. *Nigger Heaven* is his most serious novel, his only attempt to deal with social issues in a culture and class different from his own; the book is a reflection of a deep commitment to social change.

Parties, Van Vechten's last novel, is an intense portrait of a dissolute and frenzied decade. David and Rilda Westlake, characters based on Van Vechten's friends Scott and Zelda Fitzgerald, move throughout the novel in a series of parties where they argue, drink, attempt seductions, gossip, toss off jaded remarks, and drink more, and still more. Vividly sketching his dissipated cast of characters, Van Vechten manages to portray their physical and emotional instability and the emptiness of their lives. Van Vechten's characters are often grotesque rather than enviably attractive. When the reader first meets David Westlake, he is a "distorted figure" with blood drying on his lips, crying "I've killed a man or a man has killed me." Rilda's entrance is by telephone: she claims to have committed suicide. An alleged murder victim appears alive, if not completely well, finally to be killed as the plot spirals. Among these living dead cavorts a sprightly seventy-year-old European aristocrat, the Grafin Adele von Pulmernl und Stilzernl, whose lively interest in parties places her in the company of the young Americans driven to drink and misery. She alone, unable to perceive the real meaning of the whirlwind social life, enjoys the parties and finds them amusing. "It is so funny," she tells David Westlake after he summarizes "the life of our times in words of two syllables. . . . We're here because we're here, and we should be extremely silly not to make the worst of it." The Grafin, delighted with David's pronouncement, has the last words of the book: "I love your country."

Though it was poorly received by critics, Van Vechten's novel succeeds in taking the prototypal Fitzgerald characters and spinning them in a mindless maelstrom. These are the damned, who spent a decade in drunken revelry, only to wake up, forced to confront a new decade and a new spirit. With *Parties*, Van Vechten's role as a social critic ended. He had chronicled an age, and written its epitaph.

Linda Simon

Other major works

NONFICTION: *Music After the Great War*, 1915; *Music and Bad Manners*, 1916; *Interpreters and Interpretations*, 1917; *The Merry-Go-Round*, 1918; *The Music of Spain*, 1918; *In the Garret*, 1920; *Interpreters*, 1920; *The Tiger in the House*, 1920; *Red*, 1925; *Excavations*, 1926; *Sacred and Profane Memories*, 1932; *Fragments from an Unwritten Autobiography*, 1955.

Bibliography

Churchill, Allen. *The Literary Decade*. Englewood Cliffs, N.J.: Prentice-Hall, 1971. Churchill examines the New York commercial publishing scene in the 1920's and attempts to recapture the excitements of this literary decade. Chapter 7, "Rocky Road to Immortality," sets aside several pages on Van Vechten and his contribution as an author and music and dance critic. Also contains some commentary on his first novel, *Peter Whiffle*, his personal life, and his persona of youthfulness.

Kellner, Bruce. *Carl Van Vechten and the Irreverent Decades*. Norman: University of Oklahoma Press, 1968. Essentially a biography on Van Vechten, emphasizing his interest and influence in the arts. Contains much valuable background information on Van Vechten and his relationships with fellow writers, artists, and dancers during the 1920's.

Lueders, Edward. *Carl Van Vechten*. New York: Twayne, 1965. A critical study on Van Vechten containing a brief biography, a discussion of his novels and other works, an afterword, a chronology, and a bibliography. A knowledgeable, sympathetic study by Leuders, who defends Van Vechten's work from critics' attacks on its superficiality and pointlessness.

_____. *Carl Van Vechten and the Twenties*. Albuquerque: University of New Mexico Press, 1955. Focuses on the period between World War I and 1932, when Van Vechten announced his retirement as an author of books. Lueders concedes that this study is neither a complete critical biography of Van Vechten nor an extensive social commentary of the times, but that it attempts to say something on both. Discusses Van Vechten's novels and volumes on music and art in the context of the hectic high life of the 1920's. Lueders, a personal friend of Van Vechten and notable critic of his work, has written an interesting study of this author and the decade during which he produced his novels.

Van Vechten, Carl. *Letters of Carl Van Vechten*. Edited by Bruce Kellner. New Haven, Conn.: Yale University Press, 1987. An intimate portrait of Van Vechten, as seen through his letters to friends, fellow authors, publishers, artists, biographers, and family members. The letters have been selected from private collections and private and public institutions. Incorporates some material from Kellner's book *Carl Van Vechten and the Irreverent Decades*.

GORE VIDAL

Born: West Point, New York; October 3, 1925

Principal long fiction

Williwaw, 1946; *In a Yellow Wood*, 1947; *The City and the Pillar*, 1948, revised 1965; *The Season of Comfort*, 1949; *A Search for the King: A Twelfth Century Legend*, 1950; *Dark Green, Bright Red*, 1950; *The Judgment of Paris*, 1952, revised 1965; *Death in the Fifth Position*, 1952 (as Edgar Box); *Death Before Bedtime*, 1953 (as Edgar Box); *Death Likes It Hot*, 1954 (as Edgar Box); *Messiah*, 1954, revised 1965; *Julian*, 1964; *Washington, D.C.*, 1967; *Myra Breckinridge*, 1968; *Two Sisters: A Memoir in the Form of a Novel*, 1970; *Burr*, 1973; *Myron*, 1974; *1876*, 1976; *Kalki*, 1978; *Creation*, 1981; *Duluth*, 1983; *Lincoln*, 1984; *Empire*, 1987; *Hollywood: A Novel of America in the 1920's*, 1990.

Other literary forms

Gore Vidal has written short stories, and he is considered a master essayist, having regularly published collections of essays. Vidal also wrote or adapted plays during the so-called golden age of television, and he wrote screenplays during the last days of the Hollywood studio system.

Achievements

Gore Vidal is a leading American literary figure. While primarily a novelist, he has mastered almost every genre, except poetry. He has won success in films, in television, and on Broadway. Many readers consider him a better essayist than novelist, though Vidal emphatically rejects that judgment.

While many of his contemporaries focused their writings on mundane details of everyday life, Vidal continued to write the novel of ideas. He maintained his focus on the largest questions: What is the nature of Western civilization? What flaws have prevented the United States from achieving its democratic promise? How does a free individual live an intellectually fulfilling and ethically proper life in a corrupt society?

Biography

Eugene Luther Vidal was born on October 3, 1925 (he took the name Gore when he was fourteen). He was born at West Point, where his father, Eugene, taught aeronautics at the military academy. Eugene Vidal helped establish civil aviation in the United States and later became the director of air commerce in the administration of Franklin D. Roosevelt. Gore's mother, Nina, was a beautiful socialite, the daughter of powerful Oklahoma senator Thomas P. Gore. Soon after Gore's birth, the family moved to Senator Gore's mansion in Washington, D.C. Gore Vidal, one of the most learned of contemporary writers, never went to college. His education began at the home of Senator Gore: the senator, who was blind, used his grandson as a reader and in return gave him free run of his huge library. In 1935, the Vidals were divorced, and Nina married Hugh D. Auchincloss, a member of a prominent family of bankers and lawyers. Gore Vidal then moved to the Auchincloss estate on the Potomac River in Virginia. Here his education included rubbing shoulders with the nation's political, economic, and journalistic elite.

Vidal was brought up removed from real life, he says, protected from such unpleasant realities as the effects of the Great Depression. He joined other patrician sons at St. Albans School, after which he toured Europe in 1939, then spent one year at Los Alamos School in New Mexico, before finishing his formal education with three years at Phillips Exeter Academy in New Hampshire.

In 1943, Vidal joined the army and served on a transport ship in the Aleutian Islands. His military service gave him subject matter and time to write his first novel, *Williwaw*. He finished his second book, *In a Yellow Wood*, before he left the army. In 1946, he went to work as an editor for E. P. Dutton and soon published *The City and the Pillar*. Good critical and popular response brought him recognition as one of the nation's best young authors. He used Guatemala as his home base from 1947 to 1949 and then bought an old estate, Edgewater, on the Hudson River in New York. He wrote five more novels before he was thirty years old.

Meanwhile, a controversy engulfed him and shifted his life and career. *The City and the Pillar* had dealt with homosexuality; because of this, the literary establishment removed him from its list of "approved" writers, and critics largely ignored his next few novels. To earn money in the 1950's, he wrote mysteries under the name Edgar Box and wrote scripts for the major live television dramatic series. He also became a successful screenwriter, with such films as *The Catered Affair* (1956) and *Suddenly Last Summer* (1959). In addition, he wrote plays. He achieved major Broadway successes with *Visit to a Small Planet: A Comedy Akin to a Vaudeville* (1957) and *The Best Man: A Play About Politics* (1960).

These were his years of "piracy," Vidal says, aimed at gaining enough financial security to allow him to return to his first love, novels. His years in Hollywood and on Broadway established Vidal's public reputation for sophisticated wit and intelligence. He ran for Congress in 1960, supported by such famous friends as Eleanor Roosevelt, Joanne Woodward, and Paul Newman. Although he was defeated, he ran better in his district than did the Democratic presidential candidate, John F. Kennedy. Vidal shared a stepfather with Jacqueline Kennedy and had become friends with the Kennedy family; this connection pulled him further into public affairs.

In 1964, Vidal published *Julian*, his first novel in ten years. It was a major critical and public success. Many best-sellers followed, including *Myra Breckinridge*, *Burr*, *Creation*, and *Lincoln*.

Conflict over civil rights, the Vietnam War, and the Watergate scandal made the 1960's and 1970's one of the most tumultuous periods in American political history. Vidal's essays, published in major journals, established his reputation as an astute and hard-hitting social critic. His acid-tongued social commentary brought him to many television guest shows, where he made many friends and enemies. He had spectacular public feuds with members of the Kennedy family and with such fellow celebrities and authors as William F. Buckley, Jr., Norman Mailer, and Truman Capote. In 1968 he was a cofounder of the New Party, and in 1970-1972 he was cochair of the People's Party. In 1982, he ran for the U.S. Senate in California, and, out of a field of eleven in the Democratic primary, came in second, behind Governor Jerry Brown.

While Vidal continues to participate in the tumult of Amerian public affairs, he lives quietly in Italy about half of each year. His longtime companion Howard Austen takes care of his business affairs and daily routines, leaving Vidal free to write. He has produced perhaps the most voluminous body of work of any major postwar literary figure.

Analysis

In an age and country that have little room for the traditional man of letters, Gore Vidal has established that role for himself by the force of his writing and intelligence and by his public prominence. He is a classicist in writing style, emphasizing plot, clarity, and order. Iconoclastic wit and cool, detached intelligence characterize his elegant style.

Since Vidal knows most contemporary public figures—including jet-setters, Wall Street insiders, and Washington wheeler-dealers—many readers comb his writing to glean intriguing bits of gossip. *Two Sisters: A Memoir in the Form of a Novel*, for example, is often read as an account of the lives and loves of Jacqueline Kennedy Onassis and her sister, Lee Bouvier. Some people search Vidal's writing for clues to his own life and sexuality.

Vidal draws from his own rich experience as he creates his fictional world. Yet he is a very private person, and he resists people's urge to reduce everyone to a known quantity. Vidal refracts real people and events through his delightfully perverse imagination. The unwary gossipmonger can easily fall into Vidal's many traps.

If one can with certainty learn little from Vidal's fiction about such famous people as the Kennedys, readers can learn much about his major concern, the nature of Western civilization and the individual's role within it. He is interested in politics—how people make society work—and religion, the proper perspective on life as one faces death.

In his early novels, one can see Vidal's interest in ideas. Vidal's young male protagonists find themselves entering a relativistic world in which all gods are dead. A "heterosexual dictatorship" and a life-numbing Christian establishment try to impose false moral absolutes. Society tempts the unwary by offering comfort and security and then removes the life-sustaining freedom of those who succumb to the temptation.

In writing his third novel, Vidal probed the boundaries of society's sexual tolerance. The result, *The City and the Pillar*, affected the rest of his career. To Vidal, the book is a study of obsession; to many guardians of moral purity, it seems to glorify homosexuality. In American fiction, either homosexuality had been barely implied or the homosexual characters had been presented as bizarre or doomed figures. In contrast, Vidal's protagonist is an average young American man, confused by his homosexual proclivities and obsessed with the memory of a weekend encounter with another young man, Bob Ford. While Bob regards the weekend as a diversion to be enjoyed and forgotten, Jim enters the homosexual world. If he is doomed, it is not because he prefers men to women, but because he is obsessed with the past. When he finally meets Bob again and tries to revive the affair, Bob rejects him. Enraged and humiliated, Jim kills Bob. Vidal later issued a revised edition in which Jim forces Bob to submit sexually; in the emotional backwash from the confrontation, Jim realizes the sterility of his obsession.

Vidal later said that he could have been president had it not been for the homosexual label applied to him. Readers assumed that Vidal must be the character he invented, but Vidal refuses to deny or confirm his alleged homosexuality. He is a sexual libertarian, who believes that sex in any form between consenting adults is a gift to be enjoyed. He believes, furthermore, that a "heterosexual dictatorship" has distorted human sexuality. "There is no such thing as a homosexual or a heterosexual person," Vidal says. "There are only homo- or heterosexual acts. Most people are a mixture of impulses if not practices, and what anyone does with a willing partner is of no social or cosmic significance." In 1948, people were not ready for that message. Although the book was a best-seller, such powerful establishment journals as *The New York Times* eliminated him from the list of "approved" writers. His next few books were failures, critically and financially.

Two of these books, *The Judgment of Paris* and *Messiah*, later found admirers. In these novels Vidal began to develop the style that is so recognizably his own. Moreover, it is in these two books that Vidal fully expresses his philosophy of life: "I have put nearly everything that I feel into *The Judgment of Paris*, a comedic version, and *Messiah*, a tragic version of my sense of man's curious estate."

In *The Judgment of Paris*, Vidal retells the ancient myth of Paris, who was asked by Zeus to choose the most beautiful of three goddesses: Hera (power), Athena (knowledge), and Aphrodite (love). In Vidal's novel, Philip Warren, an American innocent, meets Regina Durham (Hera) in Rome, Sophia Oliver

(Athena) in Egypt, and Anna Morris (Aphrodite) in Paris. Regina and Sophia offer him, respectively, political power and life of the intellect. To Philip, political power rests on manipulation of people, and intellectual life requires the seclusion of the scholar from humanity. He chooses love, but he also leaves Anna Morris. His choice implies that one must accept no absolutes; nothing is permanent, not even love. One must open oneself to love and friendship and prepare to accept change as one moves through life.

Many readers consider *Messiah* an undiscovered masterpiece. Religion, the human response to death and nothingness, has been a major concern in Vidal's fiction, especially in *Messiah*, *Kalki*, and *Creation*. *Messiah* is narrated by Eugene Luther, an old man secluded in Egypt. He is a founding member of a new religion that has displaced Christianity and is spreading over the world. Luther, who has broken with the church he helped build, scribbles his memoirs as he awaits death. The movement was built around John Cave, but Cave was killed by his disciples and Cave's word was spread by an organization using modern advertising techniques. One can readily find in *Messiah* characters representing Jesus Christ, Saint Paul, Mother Mary, and Martin Luther. The process by which religious movements are formed interests Vidal. *Messiah* shows, by analogy, how the early church fathers manipulated the Gospels and the Christ figure for their own selfish needs.

With *Julian*, Vidal again examines the formation of a religious movement, this time looking directly at Christianity. Julian the Apostate, Roman emperor from A.D. 361 to 363, had long been the object of hatred in the West, because he had tried to reverse the Christianization of the empire. In the nineteenth and twentieth centuries, Julian began to attract admirers who saw him as a symbol of wisdom and of religious toleration.

Julian, reared as a Christian, lived in an age when the modern Christian church was taking shape. Warring prelates conducted abstract debates that robbed religion of its mystery and engaged in persecutions that ignored Jesus' message of love and peace. Julian was trained as a philosopher. His study of ancient wisdom awakened in him love and respect for the gods of the ancient world and for the Eastern mystery religions then being suppressed by Christianity. When he became emperor, Julian proclaimed religious toleration and tried to revive "paganism."

Like Paris before him and Philip Warren after, Julian was offered the worlds of intellect, love, and power. Julian chose power, but he tempered the absolute authority of emperor with love and wisdom. He was also a military genius, who like Alexander the Great was tempted by the dream of world conquest. He was killed during an invasion of Persia.

Vidal bases his novel on a fictive memoir written by Julian and presenting Julian's own view of himself and his world. The novel opens in A.D. 380, seventeen years after Julian's death. Two friends of Julian, the philosophers Libanius of Antioch and Priscus of Athens, correspond as they prepare Julian's memoirs for publication. Their letters and comments on the manuscript provide two other views of the events described by Julian. Since they are writing as the Emperor Theodosius is moving to destroy the ancient religions, Julian's life takes on a special poignancy. Vidal's major point, says biographer Ray Lewis White, is that modern people of the West are the descendants of the barbarians who destroyed the classical world, and that the modern world has yet to be civilized. If Julian had lived, Vidal believes, Christianity might well have remained only one of several Western religions, and Western civilization might now be healthier and more tolerant than it is.

In 1981 Vidal took readers even further back into history in *Creation*. In 445 B.C., Cyrus Spitama, an elderly Persian diplomat to Athens and grandson of the Persian prophet Zoroaster, begins to dictate his memoirs to his nephew, the philosopher Democritus. Cyrus is angry after hearing the historian Herodotus give his account of the Persian-Greek war, and he decides to set down the truth.

Here Vidal traces the earliest foundations of Western civilization and the formation of major world religions. Cyrus, a diplomatic troubleshooter for the Persian court, takes the reader on a tour of the ancient world. He knows Persian emperors Darius and Xerxes; as a traveler to China and India, he meets the Buddha and Confucius, and he remembers his own grandfather, Zoroaster. In Athens he talks with such famous figures as Anaxagoras and Pericles and hires Socrates to repair his wall. In *Creation*, Vidal shows the global interaction of cultures that goes back to the ancient world. He rejects the provincialism that has allowed historians to wall Western civilization off from its Asian and African sources.

Next this master of historical fiction turned his attention to the United States. Starting with *Washington, D.C.*, Vidal began a sequence of novels covering United States history from its beginning to the post-World War II era. In chronological sequence, the novels are *Burr*, *Lincoln*, *1876*, *Empire*, *Hollywood*, and *Washington, D.C.* Vidal's iconoclastic view of the past may have shocked some readers, but in the turmoil of the Vietnam and Watergate era, many people were ready to reexamine United States history. At a time when many Americans held that the old truths had failed, Vidal said that those truths had been hollow from the start.

Burr is one of the most widely admired of Vidal's novels. Aaron Burr, the preeminent American maverick, appealed to Vidal personally. *Burr* is narrated by Charlie Schuyler, who in 1833 is a twenty-five-year-old clerk in Burr's law office. He is an aspiring author who writes for William Leggett and William Cullen Bryant, editors of the *New York Evening Post*. Disliking Martin Van Buren, President Andrew Jackson's heir apparent, Leggett and Bryant set Charlie to work running down the rumor that Van Buren is the illegitimate son of Burr; if the rumor is true, they can use the information to destroy Van Buren. The seventy-seven-year-old Burr responds warmly to

Charlie's overtures to write about his life. In the next few years, Burr gives the young writer copies of his journal and dictates to him his memories of the past.

Although Vidal's portrait of the Founding Fathers shocks some readers, his interpretation is in line with that of many of the nation's best historians. Vidal reminds the reader that Burr was one of the most able and intelligent of the Founding Fathers. Vidal allows Burr, from an insider's viewpoint, to demystify the founders of the republic. George Washington, Alexander Hamilton, Thomas Jefferson, and the other Founding Fathers created the republic, Burr says, because it satisfied their personal economic and political interests to do so.

Burr admires some of his contemporaries, especially James Madison and Andrew Jackson, but he detests Thomas Jefferson. Jefferson is a ruthless man who wants to create a nation "dominated by independent farmers each living on his own rich land, supported by slaves." What Burr cannot excuse is Jefferson's cant and hypocrisy:

> Had Jefferson not been a hypocrite I might have admired him. After all, he was the most successful empire-builder of our century, succeeding where Bonaparte failed. But then Bonaparte was always candid when it came to motive and Jefferson was always dishonest.

What are the motives of the Founding Fathers? Burr tells Alexander Hamilton: "I sense nothing more than the ordinary busy-ness of men wanting to make a place for themselves. . . . But it is no different here from what it is in London or what it was in Caesar's Rome." The Founding Fathers write the Constitution because it suits their purposes, and they subvert it when it suits their purposes.

Burr makes no secret of his opportunism, although he does regret his mistakes. He should have realized that the world is big enough for both Hamilton and himself, he says. Instead, Vice President Burr kills Hamilton in a duel and is then accused by Jefferson of heading a plot to break up the United States and establish himself as the king in a new Western empire.

Charlie does find evidence that Van Buren is Burr's son, but Charlie, having come to love the old man, refuses to use it. Van Buren rewards him with a government position overseas.

With *Lincoln*, Vidal surprised those who expected him to subject the Great Emancipator to the same ridicule he had directed at Washington and Jefferson. Vidal's Lincoln is a cold, remote, intelligent man who creates a unified, centralized republic that is far different from the one envisioned by the Founding Fathers. In *1876*, Charlie Schuyler returns to the United States from Europe, where he has lived since 1837. He left in the age of Jackson and returns in the age of Ulysses S. Grant to a booming industrializing, urbanizing nation. He watches, in the American centennial year, as the politicians steal the presidential election from Democrat Samuel J. Tilden. He sees members of the ruling class using the rhetoric of democracy but practicing it as little as they had in the days of Washington and Jefferson.

In *Empire*, Vidal paints wonderful word-portraits of Henry Adams, Henry James, William Randolph Hearst, John Hay, and Theodore Roosevelt, along with the fictional characters of newspaper publishers Caroline and Blaise Sanford and Congressman James Burden Day. The creation of the internal empire, begun by Jefferson's Louisiana Purchase, had already made shambles of the American democratic promise. Now Roosevelt and other American leaders begin to look overseas for new areas to dominate. Their creation of the overseas empire lays the groundwork for the increasingly militarized republic that emerges in the twentieth century.

Many of these same figures appear in *Hollywood*, set a few years later, in the administrations of Woodrow Wilson and Warren Harding. While the forging of the American empire continues, Vidal turns his gaze on a new force that is corrupting the democratic promise, the mass media. Newspaper publisher Hearst and the Sanfords have long understood the power of the press, but Hearst and Caroline Sanford see that the new medium of film has potential power beyond the printed page. Instead of reporting events, film could create a new reality, within which newspapers and politicians would have to work.

In *Washington, D.C.*, Blaise Sanford, his son Peter, Senator James Burden Day, and his assistant, Clay Overbury, are locked in a political and moral drama. Senator Day, a Southern conservative, much like Senator Gore, opposes the new republic being created by Franklin Delano Roosevelt, Harry Truman, and Dwight D. Eisenhower. He has a chance to be president but lacks money. Burden Day gives in to temptation and takes a bribe; his presidential bid fails, and later Clay Overbury, using his knowledge of the bribe, forces Day out of the Senate and takes his seat. Overbury is a young man who cares nothing for friends or ideas or issues. Winning personal power is the only thing that interests this politician, who is modeled on John F. Kennedy.

As Day is dying, he says to the spirit of his unreconstructed Southern father: "You were right. . . . It has all gone wrong." Aaron Burr would have understood what he meant.

If most scholars approved of Vidal's well-researched historical fiction, many staid readers were shocked at *Myra Breckinridge*. Myra opens her book with the proud proclamation: "I am Myra Breckinridge whom no man will ever possess." She maintains her verve as she takes readers on a romp through popular culture. Since the novel is dead, she says, there is no point in writing made-up stories; the film of the 1940's is the high point of Western artistic creation, although it is being superseded by a higher art form, the television commercial. Myra has arrived in Hollywood to fulfill her destiny of reconstructing the sexes. She has a lesson to teach young would-be stars such as Rusty Godowsky and old cowboy stars such as Buck Loner:

> To be a man in a society of machines is to be an expendable, soft auxiliary to what is useful and hard. Today there is nothing left for the old-fashioned male to do, . . . no physical struggle to survive or mate. . . . [O]nly in travesty can he act out the classic hero who was a law unto himself, moving at ease through a landscape filled with admiring women. Mercifully, that age is finished. . . . [W]e now live at the dawn of the age of Women Triumphant, of Myra Breckinridge!

Beneath the gaiety of Myra's campy narrative, a serious purpose emerges. Her dead homosexual husband, Myron, had been abused and humiliated by many males. Myra carries out her plan to avenge Myron, and to revive the Female Principle, by forcing Buck Loner to submit to her demands to take over his acting studio, and by raping with a dildo the macho, all-American stud Rusty.

Myra Triumphant is brought down by an automobile accident, which upsets her hormonal balance. Her breasts vanish, and she sprouts a beard; she is, in fact, Myron, after a sex-change operation. As the book ends, Rusty is a homosexual, and Myron/Myra is married and living happily with Rusty's former girlfriend. In a sequel, *Myron*, Myron and Myra struggle for domination of the single body and again have much to say about popular culture, the mass media, and human sexuality.

Some said that the audience Vidal had created for himself with *Burr* and other highly regarded books was destroyed by *Myra Breckinridge* and *Myron* and by his later campy fantasies *Kalki* and *Duluth*. Yet Vidal has written one best-seller after another, and his books have steadily gained critical admirers.

Vidal's books, essays, and television appearances stimulate, intrigue, and anger a large part of his audience. Yet his appeal as a writer and public figure has remained compelling. As long ago as 1948, with *The City and the Pillar*, Vidal made a decision to live his life and conduct his artistic career in his own way. To many admirers, he is a symbol of freedom. The turmoil of the modern age makes his civilized voice of reason seem more necessary than ever before. While he is often accused of cynicism, Vidal responds that he is a pessimist and a realist who also believes that people can, or must act as if they can, take action to make the world better. Daily headlines convince many readers, once shocked by Vidal's comments on contemporary society, that his vision hews fairly close to reality.

William E. Pemberton

Other major works

SHORT FICTION: *A Thirsty Evil: Seven Short Stories*, 1956.

PLAYS: *Visit to a Small Planet: A Comedy Akin to a Vaudeville*, 1957; *The*

Best Man: A Play about Politics, 1960; *Romulus: A New Comedy*, 1962; *An Evening with Richard Nixon*, 1972.

SCREENPLAYS: *The Catered Affair*, 1956; *Suddenly Last Summer*, 1959 (with Tennessee Williams); *The Best Man*, 1964.

NONFICTION: *Rocking the Boat*, 1962; *Reflections upon a Sinking Ship*, 1969; *Homage to Daniel Shays: Collected Essays, 1952-1972*, 1972; *Matters of Fact and of Fiction: Essays, 1973-1976*, 1977; *The Second American Revolution and Other Essays, 1976-1982*, 1982; *At Home: Essays, 1982-1988*, 1988.

Bibliography

Dick, Bernard F. *The Apostate Angel: A Critical Study of Gore Vidal*. New York: Random House, 1974. An entertaining and perceptive study, based on interviews with Vidal and on use of his papers at the University of Wisconsin—Madison. Dick focuses on Vidal's work rather than on his biography. The book contains footnotes and a bibliography.

Kiernan, Robert F. *Gore Vidal*. New York: Frederick Ungar, 1982. This study of Vidal's major writings tries to assess his place in American literature and gives astute descriptions of the Vidalian style and manner. The book, which uses Vidal's manuscript collection, contains a brief note and bibliography section.

Stanton, Robert J. *Gore Vidal: A Primary and Secondary Bibliography*. Boston: G. K. Hall, 1978. A well-researched 226-page annotated bibliography of Vidal's writings and writings about him. It is arranged chronologically by year and is indexed.

Stanton, Robert J., and Gore Vidal, eds. *Views from a Window: Conversations with Gore Vidal*. Secaucus, N.J.: Lyle Stuart, 1980. A compilation of interviews excerpted and arranged along themes. Vidal comments on his and other authors' works, on sexuality, and on politics. Vidal edited the manuscript and made corrections, with changes noted in the text.

White, Ray Lewis. *Gore Vidal*. New York: Twayne, 1968. A workmanlike short biography based on Vidal's manuscripts. To Vidal's delight, White did not try to guess at his motives or psychoanalyze him. Provides a straightforward survey of his life and a critical summary of his work.

Ziolkowski, Theodore. *Fictional Transfigurations of Jesus*. Princeton, N.J.: Princeton University Press, 1972. Features an intriguing analysis of *Messiah*, placing it in a long tradition of fictional transfigurations of Jesus, written by Thomas Mann, John Steinbeck, Nikos Kazantzakis, Graham Greene, and others.

KURT VONNEGUT, JR.

Born: Indianapolis, Indiana; November 11, 1922

Principal long fiction

Player Piano, 1952; *The Sirens of Titan*, 1959; *Mother Night*, 1961; *Cat's Cradle*, 1963; *God Bless You, Mr. Rosewater: Or, Pearls Before Swine*, 1965; *Slaughterhouse-Five: Or, The Children's Crusade, a Duty-Dance with Death*, 1969; *Breakfast of Champions: Or, Goodbye Blue Monday*, 1973; *Slapstick: Or, Lonesome No More!*, 1976; *Jailbird*, 1979; *Deadeye Dick*, 1982; *Galápagos*, 1985; *Bluebeard*, 1987; *Hocus Pocus*, 1990.

Other literary forms

Welcome to the Monkey House (1968) is a reprinting of all earlier short stories and twelve new ones. *Wampeters, Foma, and Granfalloons (Opinions)* (1974) is the first collection of essays. Kurt Vonnegut, Jr., has also written for Broadway and television and has published a children's book.

Achievements

Critical acclaim eluded Vonnegut until the publication of *Slaughterhouse-Five* in 1969. An immediate best-seller, it earned for Vonnegut respect from critics who had previously dismissed him as a mediocre science-fiction writer. Vonnegut has been honored as the Briggs-Copeland Lecturer at Harvard University, as a member of the National Institute of Arts and Letters, and as the Distinguished Professor of English Prose at the City University of New York. Through his insightful and sympathetic treatment of the psychologically and morally crippled victims of the modern world, Vonnegut has earned his reputation as one of the greatest humanist writers of his time.

Biography

Kurt Vonnegut, Jr., was born in Indianapolis, Indiana, in 1922. Both the location and the era of his birth helped shape his distinctive worldview, a worldview that informs all of his works. Growing up in the American heartland in the calm interval between the world wars, Vonnegut had a brief vision of a middle-class world that embraced the values of honesty, decency, and human dignity. For Vonnegut, this was the world as it should be, a world unravaged by violence and war, a world untouched by technology. This period of childhood happiness was, however, merely the calm before the storm in this life that would be rocked by a series of personal and national disasters: the death of his mother by suicide on Mother's Day; his prisoner-of-war experience in World War II; the deaths of his sister and brother-in-law; the dissolution of his first marriage; the bombing of Dresden and Hiroshima; and the Kennedy and King assassinations. All the heartaches of his family and his nation reverberate through Vonnegut's work, while the artist, through his fiction, strives to create a saner, calmer world.

During the Depression years, Vonnegut's family suffered emotional and financial setbacks. When Vonnegut entered Cornell University in 1940, his father forbade him to study the arts and chose instead for his son a career in science, a career with guaranteed job security. In 1943 Vonnegut left Cornell to enlist in the army, despite his own public opposition to the war. Less than one year later, he was captured by the Germans and, in 1945, survived one of the greatest massacres of the war, the Allied firebombing of Dresden. This horror pursued Vonnegut for twenty-three years, until he worked through the pain by writing *Slaughterhouse-Five*.

After the war, Vonnegut married and began studies in anthropology at the University of Chicago. After three years, he left college and took a job as a publicist with General Electric (GE), where his brother worked as a physicist. Vonnegut's background in science and his disillusionment at GE influenced his first two novels, *Player Piano* and *The Sirens of Titan*, both parables of dehumanization in a technological society.

Between 1952 and 1988, Vonnegut wrote more than a dozen novels, numerous essays, a Broadway play, and a musical work, *Requiem*, which was performed by the Buffalo Symphony. Despite his varied artistic talents, however, Vonnegut has always been known for his fiction. Vonnegut remarried in 1978; he and his wife, Jill, live in New York, where he continues to write.

Analysis

In his novels, Kurt Vonnegut, Jr., coaxes the reader toward greater sympathy for his fellowman and deeper understanding of the human condition. His genre is satire—sometimes biting, sometimes tender, always funny. His arena is as expansive as the whole universe and as tiny as a single human soul. Part philosopher, part poet, Vonnegut, in his fictive world, tackles the core problem of modern life: how can the individual maintain his dignity and exercise his free will in a world overrun by death and destruction, a world in which both science and religion are powerless to provide a solution? The reader will find no ready answers in Vonnegut, only a friendly guide along the questioning path.

Ilium, New York, sometime in the near future, provides the setting for Vonnegut's first dystopian novel, *Player Piano*. Ilium is a divided city. On one side of the river live the important people, the engineers and managers who program and run the computers and machines that run people's lives. On the other side of the river, Homestead, live the downtrodden inhabitants of the city, those locked into menial, dehumanizing jobs assigned to them by the central computer.

Paul Proteus, the protagonist, is the brilliant young manager of the Ilium

Works, a man being groomed for even greater success. Yet just as Ilium is a divided city, so is Paul divided about his life and his future. Paul suffers a growing discontent with his job at the Ilium Works, where people have been replaced by machines and machines are supervised by computers. Outwardly, Paul has no reason for worry or doubt. He has the best job and the most beautiful wife in Ilium; he is being considered for the highest post in his company; he is climbing the ladder of success. Nevertheless, Paul's uneasiness increases. At first he seeks escape, settling on a farm in an attempt to get back to nature and free himself from his automatic life. He finds, however, that he has become an automaton, completely out of touch with the natural world, and his attempt at escape fails.

Finally, Paul is drawn to the other side of the river. His sympathy for the dehumanized masses and his acknowledgment of complicity in their plight drive Paul to join the masses in armed revolution. The fighters take to the streets, frantically and indiscriminately destroying all machines. Yet the revolution fails, leaving Paul disillusioned and defeated, realizing that he has been manipulated by leaders on both sides of the conflict. Now he must surrender and face execution.

Paul's manipulation, first by those who would replace person with machine and then by those who would destroy the machines, is symbolized by the "player piano" of the title. The simplest of machines, the player piano creates its music without the aid of human beings, neatly rendering the skilled musician obsolete. Paul is entranced by the music of the player piano, in his fascination manipulated by the machine just as it manipulates its ivory keys.

The most striking symbol of the story, however, is the small black cat befriended by Paul as it wanders aimlessly through the Ilium Works. The cat, symbol of all that is natural and pure, despises the monstrous factory machines. The doomed animal is helplessly sucked into an automated sweeper, which spits it down a chute and ejects it outside the factory. Miraculously, it survives, but as Paul races to its rescue, the cat is roasted on the factory's electric fence, symbolizing humans' destruction by the forces of technology. With characteristic Vonnegut irony, however, *Player Piano* ends on an affirmative note. Although the price of escape is its life, the cat does escape the Ilium Works. Near the end of the novel, Paul sees beautiful flowers growing outside the factory—flowers rooted in cat excrement, signifying ultimate rebirth and a glimmer of hope for Paul and his world.

In his third novel, *Mother Night*, Vonnegut peers even more deeply into the human soul, exploring the roots of human alienation, probing the individual's search for his "real" identity, and uncovering the thin veil that separates reality from illusion. The story is told as the memoirs of Howard W. Campbell, Jr., a self-proclaimed "citizen of nowhere." A successful writer and producer of medieval romance plays, Campbell sees himself as a sensitive *artiste*. Nevertheless, he allows himself to be recruited by Major Frank Wirtanen to be an American double agent posing as a Nazi radio propagandist in Germany. Secretly, Campbell sends coded American messages in his propaganda broadcasts, but he does not understand the code and never comprehends the messages he transmits. Still unaware, he even transmits the news of his beloved wife's death.

Publicly, Campbell is reviled as a traitorous Nazi hatemonger, but he does not mind, because he enjoys being on the radio. Eventually, though, he begins to lose touch with his "real" self. Is he the sensitive artist, the cruel Nazi, or the American patriot? Like Paul Proteus, Campbell allows himself to be manipulated by those around him. With no will or identity of his own, Campbell is easy prey for those who would use him for their own ends.

Two of Campbell's manipulators are his postwar friend George Kraft and his sister-in-law Resi, who poses as Campbell's long-lost wife, Helga. George and Resi are actually Russian spies plotting to capture Campbell and transport him to Russia. They abandon this plan, however, when they realize their love for Campbell, and they finally attempt to escape to freedom with him. Before the three can flee together, however, the Russians are arrested by American agents. Campbell is arrested as well but is soon freed by his friend Frank Wirtanen.

Gripped by existential fear at finding himself a free man, Campbell appeals to a Jewish couple in his apartment building, a doctor and his mother, both survivors of Auschwitz. Campbell begs to be tried for his crimes against the Jews and soon finds himself awaiting trial in a Jerusalem prison. Before Campbell goes to trial, Frank Wirtanen sends a letter on his behalf, explaining how he had recruited Campbell and honoring him as an American patriot. Yet Campbell can never be a truly free man until he purges his conscience. Upon his release from prison, he is nauseated by the prospect of his freedom, knowing that he is one of the many people "who served evil too openly and good too secretly." In his failure to resist evil and his openness to manipulation by others, Campbell had given up his free will and lost his ability to choose. Coming to this realization, he finally asserts his will to choose and ironically chooses to die, vowing to hang himself "for crimes against himself."

Equally dark is Vonnegut's fourth novel, *Cat's Cradle*. In addition to its broad parody of science and religion, *Cat's Cradle* expands on Vonnegut's earlier themes of the dangerous misuse of science and technology, humans' moral responsibility in an immoral world, and the importance of distinguishing reality from illusion. The parodic tone is set in the very first line, "Call me Jonah," bringing to mind the Old Testament Book of Jonah. Like that Jonah, this protagonist (really named John) faithfully pursues God's directives but never truly comprehends the order behind God's plan. Continuing the parody, John encounters the Bokononist religion, whose bible, The Books of Bokonon, proclaims in its first line, "All of the true things I am about to tell you are shameless lies," an obvious inversion of the Johannine maxim "You will know the truth, and the truth will make you free" (John 8:32). In the world John inhabits, the only real freedom is the ultimate freedom—death.

John is writing a book, "The Day the World Ended," an account of the bombing of Hiroshima. His obsession with the destruction of Hiroshima foreshadows his involvement in the eventual destruction of the world by "ice-nine," a substance that converts liquid into frozen crystals. In *Cat's Cradle*, the atomic bomb and ice-nine are both the doomsday toys of an amoral scientist, Dr. Felix Hoenikker. Hoenikker pursues his work so intensely that he has little time for his three children, who grow up to be emotionally warped and twisted Products of Science. Hoenikker's only legacy to his children is the ice-nine he was brewing in the kitchen before his sudden death on Christmas Eve. After their father's death, the three children—Angela, Frank, and Newt—divide the ice-nine among themselves, knowing that it is their ticket to a better future. Newt, a midget, barters his ice-nine for an affair with a Russian ballerina. The homely Angela uses her portion to buy herself a husband. Frank gives his to Miguel "Papa" Monzano, dictator of the Caribbean Republic of San Lorenzo, in exchange for the title of general and the hand of Monzano's beautiful adopted daughter, Mona.

Pursuing information on the Hoenikker family, John finds himself in San Lorenzo, where he is introduced to Bokononism. The people of San Lorenzo are desperately poor, for the soil of the island is as unproductive as the Sahara. The island's teeming, malnourished masses find their only comfort in Bokononism, which urges them to love and console one another. John finds that, ironically, the religion started as a game by the island's founders. Knowing no way to lift the country from its destitution, they decided to give the people hope by inventing a religion based on *foma*, or comforting lies. The religion encouraged people to find strength in their *karass*, groups of people with whom they are joined to do God's mysterious will. To strengthen the faith of the people, Bokononism was outlawed, its founder banished on pain of death. As the people's faith grew, so did their happiness and their dependence on *foma*, until all the inhabitants of the island were "employed full time as actors in a play." For the inhabitants of San Lorenzo, illusion had become reality.

Soon after his arrival on the island, John finds that Papa Monzano is critically ill; it is expected that "General" Frank Hoenikker will succeed Papa and take the beautiful Mona as his bride. Secretly, though, Frank has no desire to rule the island or marry Mona. He is a simpering mass of insecurities, hiding behind his fake title. Frank's life, like everything around him, has been a lie: he has bought a false sense of dignity, which he wears like a military uniform, but inside he is gripped with fear, the same fear that pulses through the veins of the dying dictator. Papa and Frank become symbols for all people, running scared and grasping at false comforts as they confront brutal reality. Faced with the horror of an agonizing death, Papa clutches his vial of ice-nine, his last illusion of security and power. Uttering the desperate cry, "Now I will destroy the whole world," he swallows the poison and turns himself into an ice-blue popsicle. Papa's power proves illusory, however, as John and the Hoenikker children clean up the mess and seal off Papa's bedroom.

John, Frank, Angela, and Newt inform the staff that Papa is "feeling much better" and go downstairs to watch a military celebration. Yet, despite their success at covering up Papa's death and hiding their secret, they sense impending doom. As all the islanders watch the military air show, a bomber careens out of control and bursts into flame, setting off a massive explosion and landslide. As his castle disintegrates, Papa's body is propelled from the bedroom closet, plunging into the waiting sea, infecting all with ice-nine.

As the story ends, only John, Newt, and Bokonon remain, awaiting their imminent death. John recalls Angela's heroic end, remembering how she had clutched her clarinet bravely and played in the face of death, music mocking terror. John dreams of climbing the highest mountain and planting some magnificent symbol. Yet as John's heart swells with the vision of being the last man on the highest mountain, Newt mocks him and brings him back to earth. The story concludes with the last verse of The Books of Bokonon, in which Bokonon mourns human stupidity, thumbs his nose at God, and kills himself with ice-nine.

Like many of Vonnegut's satirical writings, *Cat's Cradle* functions as humanity's wake-up call. For Vonnegut, heroism is not a dream; dignity is not an illusion. Still, he understands all too well the fear that grips a man on the brink of action, the torpor that invades the soul. In his frustration, all the artist can do is plod on, calling out his warnings as he goes.

Vonnegut's efforts to touch the soul of humanity are most fully realized in his sixth novel, *Slaughterhouse-Five*, his most touching and brilliant work. Incorporating all Vonnegut's common themes—the nature of reality and illusion, the question of free will and determinism, the horror of man's inhumanity to man, the vision of life as an ironic construct—*Slaughterhouse-Five* produces "an image of life that is beautiful and surprising and deep." This often-misunderstood novel leads the reader on a time-warped journey, as popular films say, "to hell and back." Emotionally suffocated by his experience in World War II, Vonnegut waited twenty-three years to tell the story of his capture by the Germans and his survival of the Allied firebombing of Dresden, the calculated annihilation of a quarter of a million refugees and civilians in an unguarded city.

As befits a tale of such distorted experience, *Slaughterhouse-Five* breaks all novelistic conventions. The story is divided into ten sections, spanning the years from 1944 to 1968. Opening with a simple, first-person narrative,

Vonnegut describes his return to Dresden in 1967. He recounts his life after the war, discusses his wife and children, and relives a conversation with his old war buddy Bernard V. O'Hare, in which he reveals why *Slaughterhouse-Five* is subtitled *The Children's Crusade*. In the original Children's Crusade of 1213, Catholic monks raised a volunteer army of thirty thousand children who were intent on traveling to Palestine but instead were sent to North Africa to be sold as slaves. In the end, half the children drowned en route and the others were sold. For Vonnegut, this incident provides the perfect metaphor for all wars: hopeless ventures fought by deluded children. Thus Vonnegut prepares the reader for this personal statement about the tragedy of war. Nevertheless, the reader finds himself unprepared for the narrative shape of the tale.

Breaking from his reverie, Vonnegut reads from a Gideon Bible the story of Lot's wife, turned to a pillar of salt for looking back on Sodom and Gomorrah. To Vonnegut, her reaction was tender, instinctively human, looking back on all those lives that had touched hers, and he adopts Lot's wife as a metaphor for his narrative stance. *Slaughterhouse-Five* will be a tale told by a "pillar of salt." Vonnegut assumes the role of a masked narrator, a disinterested party, allowing himself the aesthetic distance he needs to continue his painful journey. Yet, when the reader turns to chapter 2, he finds another surprise, as chapter 2 begins, "Listen: Billy Pilgrim has come unstuck in time."

To increase his emotional distance from the story, Vonnegut, the masked narrator, tells not his own story but the story of pathetic Billy Pilgrim, Vonnegut's mythical fellow soldier. Through time travel over which he has no control, Billy is forced to relive the chapters of his life, in seemingly random order. For Billy, as for Vonnegut, his war chronology is too unsettling to confront head-on. Instead of assimilating his life experiences, Billy unconsciously tries to escape the memory of them by bouncing back and forth in time from one experience to another. Not until the end of the tale can he face the crucial moment, the horror of Dresden.

The reader first sees Billy as a forty-six-year-old retired optometrist living in Ilium, New York. Billy's daughter, Barbara, thinks that he has lost his mind. Billy has given up interest in business and devotes all of his energies to telling the world about his travels to the planet Tralfamadore. Two years earlier, Billy had been captured by aliens from Tralfamadore and had spent six months on their planet. Billy's belief in Tralfamadorian philosophy is the great comfort of his life, and he is eager to share this philosophy with the world. The aliens taught Billy, the optometrist, a better way to "see." On Tralfamadore, time is not linear; all moments are structured and permanent; death is merely one moment out of many moments in a person's life. The Tralfamadorians do not mourn the dead, for even though one may be dead in one moment, he is alive and happy in many others. The Tralfamadorians respond to life's temporary bad moments with a verbal shrug, "So it goes." Their world is a world without free will, without human responsibility, without human sorrow. On an intellectual level, Billy hungrily embraces their philosophy. Yet deep inside him (as inside Vonnegut) stirs the need to reconstruct his life, to reconcile his past. So, armed with Tralfamadorian detachment, Billy steps back in time to where it all began.

It is 1944, and Billy, a night student at the Ilium School of Optometry, is drafted into action in World War II. No soldier is more unsuited to war than is Billy. Timid and friendless, he is a chaplain's assistant, a hapless soul with a "meek faith in a loving Jesus which most soldiers found putrid." Billy's marching companion is Roland Weary, a savage young man, even by military standards. Weary's father collects ancient instruments of torture, and Weary regales Billy with gruesome tales of cruelty, giving the gentle boy an unwanted view of a monstrous world. Weary, a callous, stupid killing machine, is the natural result of man's inhumanity to man. Although physically robust, he is morally depleted, a symbol of the spiritually bankrupt world into which poor Billy has been thrust. Billy—kind, sensitive, tenderhearted—has no natural defenses against the barbarity which surrounds him. So he becomes unstuck in time.

After a brief respite of time travel, Billy returns to the war. He and Weary have been captured behind German lines, taken prisoner by two toothless old men and two young boys. The Germans are accompanied by a guard dog, a female German shepherd named Princess who had been stolen from a farmer. Princess and Billy are confused and shivering from the cold. Of the whole motley group, only the barbarous Weary belongs at war. Billy, Princess, the old men, and the young boys symbolize helpless humanity in the grip of military madness.

Billy and his fellow prisoners, including Vonnegut and Bernard V. O'Hare, are taken to a prisoner-of-war camp before their transport to Dresden. As Billy recalls these moments of his life, he is moved to time travel many times. He flashes forward to 1948, when, emotionally shattered by his war experience, he checks himself into a veterans' hospital for mental patients. Here the reader is introduced to Valencia Merble, Billy's unlovely fiancée, and Eliot Rosewater, his fellow mental patient. In the hospital, Eliot and Billy devour the science-fiction novels of Kilgore Trout. They are drawn to Trout's work for the same reason Billy is drawn to the philosophy of Tralfamadore: human experience on earth has been too disturbing; life seems meaningless. Escaping to the world of science fiction relieves the pressure, enabling Eliot and Billy to "reinvent" themselves in a kinder universe.

Before Billy returns to his war story, he again relives his adventures on the planet Tralfamadore, where he spends six months in the Tralfamadore Zoo, displayed in a glass cage. Here Billy learns of his own death in 1976. He will be murdered by Paul Lazarro, a former inmate in Billy's prisoner-of-war camp. The maniacal Lazarro, incorrectly blaming Billy for the death of Roland Weary, has plotted revenge since 1944. Naturally, Billy's innocence makes his meaningless death doubly absurd. At this time, Billy also learns of the eventual destruction of the world by the Tralfamadorians. While testing a new rocket fuel for their spacecraft, they accidentally blow up the universe. "So it goes."

When Billy returns to his war story, he and his fellow American soldiers are in Dresden, working in a factory producing vitamin syrup for pregnant women. Yet soon there will be no pregnant women in Dresden. The American soldiers are quartered underground in a former pig butchery—slaughterhouse number five. On the night of February 13, 1945, Billy (and Vonnegut) nestles safely in the shelter while the city is flattened by British and American firebombs. The next morning, the prisoners go aboveground, finding the city as lifeless as the surface of the moon. Only the one hundred American prisoners and their guards had survived.

In chapter 10, Vonnegut himself returns as narrator. It is 1968. In the intervening years, Billy has survived an airplane crash in which all of his fellow passengers have died. Valencia, frantically hurrying to see Billy in the hospital, has died of accidental carbon-monoxide poisoning. Robert Kennedy and Martin Luther King, Jr., have been assassinated. The Vietnam War is raging.

Finally, Vonnegut takes the reader back to Dresden. He and Billy are there, where the prisoners of war are digging for bodies, mining for corpses. Billy's digging companion dies of the dry heaves, unable to face the slaughter. Billy's friend Edgar Derby is executed for stealing a teapot. When the corpse mines are closed down, Billy, Vonnegut, and their companions are locked up in the suburbs to await the end of the war. When the war is over, the freed soldiers wander out into the street. The trees are blooming, and the birds are singing; springtime has finally arrived for Kurt Vonnegut.

Looking back on the novel, the reader realizes that Billy's time travels have been more than simply a coping device; they provide a learning tool as well. The jumble of events to which Vonnegut subjects Billy are not random and meaningless. Even if Billy remains blankly ignorant of the connections between events in his life, both the reader and the author learn about emotional survival in the modern world. For Vonnegut, who has called himself "the canary in the coal mine," Billy's story is a parable and a warning to all humankind: a warning that man must resist the temptation to abandon his free will, as Billy had, and an exhortation to keep one's dignity in the face of modern dehumanization.

That *Slaughterhouse-Five* is a story of survival may seem contradictory, ironic, but that is always Vonnegut's approach. It would be hard for the reader to imagine more death than he witnesses here—the slaughter in Dresden and the deaths of Billy, his wife, his father, and assorted soldiers, all culminating in the foretelling of the destruction of the universe by the Tralfamadorians. Yet the reader comes to understand that everything about Vonnegut's tale is ironic. Edgar Derby is executed, amid the Dresden corpse mines, for stealing a teapot; Billy, sitting in a slaughterhouse, is saved from destruction. No wonder Billy sees himself as the plaything of uncontrollable forces. Yet Vonnegut knows better. Billy, comfortably numbed by Tralfamadorian philosophy, never reinvents himself—but Vonnegut does. Writing this book enabled the author to face his past, his present, and his future. In fact, after writing *Slaughterhouse-Five*, Vonnegut proclaimed that he would never *need* to write another book. *Slaughterhouse-Five* embodied for Vonnegut the spirit of the phoenix: his soul, through his art, rising from the ashes.

After the spiritual and psychological rejuvenation wrought by *Slaughterhouse-Five*, Vonnegut became a totally unfettered artist in his next two books, *Breakfast of Champions* and *Slapstick*. In *Breakfast of Champions*, he sets all of his characters free, disdaining his role as puppeteer. Admitting that, in John Keat's words, he had been "half in love with easeful Death," he asserts that he has rid himself of this dangerous fascination. In *Slapstick*, he becomes frankly autobiographical, abandoning his aesthetic distance, eschewing all masks, facing his uncertain future and painful past with calm equanimity.

In his later works, Vonnegut's world has changed little: people are still cruel and false; living is still hard. Yet his fiction embodies a new harmony, a new personal courage, a renewed moral conviction and determination to make a difference in this world.

Karen Priest

Other major works

SHORT FICTION: *Canary in a Cat House*, 1961; *Welcome to the Monkey House*, 1968.

PLAYS: *Happy Birthday, Wanda June*, 1970; *Between Time and Timbuktu: Or, Prometheus-5, a Space Fantasy*, 1972 (teleplay).

NONFICTION: *Wampeters, Foma, and Granfalloons (Opinions)*, 1974; *Palm Sunday: An Autobiographical Collage*, 1981.

CHILDREN'S LITERATURE: *Sun Moon Star*, 1980 (with Ivan Chermayeff).

Bibliography

Broer, Lawrence R. *Sanity Plea: Schizophrenia in the Novels of Kurt Vonnegut*. Ann Arbor: University of Michigan Press, 1989. The comprehensive work covers all Vonnegut's major fiction from the perspective of psychology, viewing Vonnegut's characters as psychologically damaged by the traumas of the modern world. The book lacks a chronology, but has an excellent introduction, an index, and a thorough bibliography.

Giannone, Richard. *Vonnegut: A Preface to His Novels*. Port Washington,

N.Y.: Kennikat Press, 1977. This comprehensive work covers all Vonnegut's major fiction up to 1977. Giving special treatment to the unity of Vonnegut's themes, this book has an outstanding introduction, a brief chronology, a brief bibliography, and a brief index.

Klinkowitz, Jerome. *"Slaughterhouse-Five": Reforming the Novel and the World*. Boston: Twayne, 1990. This book contains the most thorough and most modern treatment available of *Slaughterhouse-Five*. With care and insight, Klinkowitz debunks earlier, fatalistic interpretations of the novel. Features a comprehensive chronology, a thorough bibliography, and an index.

_____, ed. *The Vonnegut Statement*. New York: Delacorte Press, 1973. Contains essays on Vonnegut "the public figure," Vonnegut "the literary figure," and Vonnegut's "literary art," including several articles by Klinkowitz himself. Although lacking an introduction and a chronology, the book has an extensive bibliography and an index.

Schatt, Stanley. *Kurt Vonnegut, Jr.* Boston: Twayne, 1976. This volume is notable for its discussion of Vonnegut's plays and short stories, as well as its retrospective of Vonnegut's life, entitled "The Public Man." It also offers a comprehensive treatment of the fiction, a brief chronology, a bibliography, and an index.

JOHN WAIN

Born: Stoke-on-Trent, England; March 14, 1925

Principal long fiction

Hurry on Down, 1953 (also known as *Born in Captivity*); *Living in the Present*, 1955; *The Contenders*, 1958; *A Travelling Woman*, 1959; *Strike the Father Dead*, 1962; *The Young Visitors*, 1965; *The Smaller Sky*, 1967; *A Winter in the Hills*, 1970; *The Pardoner's Tale*, 1979; *Young Shoulders*, 1982 (also known as *The Free Zone Starts Here*); *Where the Rivers Meet*, 1988.

Other literary forms

A complete man of letters, John Wain has published short stories, poetry, drama, many scholarly essays, and a highly respected biography in addition to his novels. Wain's writing reflects his determination to speak to a wider range of readers than that addressed by many of his modernist predecessors; it reflects his faith in the common reader to recognize and respond to abiding philosophical concerns. These concerns include his sense of the dignity of human beings in the midst of an oftentimes cruel, indifferent, cynical world. His concern is with a world caught up in time, desire, and disappointment.

Most significant among Wain's writings other than novels are several collections of short stories—including *Nuncle and Other Stories* (1960), *Death of the Hind Legs and Other Stories* (1966), *The Life Guard* (1971), and *King Caliban and Other Stories* (1978)—and volumes of poetry, such as *Mixed Feelings* (1951), *A Word Carved on a Sill* (1956), *Weep Before God: Poems* (1961), *Wildtrack: A Poem* (1965), *Letters to Five Artists* (1969), *The Shape of Feng* (1972), *Feng: A Poem* (1975), *Poems: 1949-1979* (1981), and *Open Country* (1987). Wain has also published criticism which communicates a sensitive and scholarly appreciation of good books. Readers should pay particular attention to *Preliminary Essays* (1957), *Essays on Literature and Ideas* (1963), *A House for the Truth: Critical Essays* (1972), *Professing Poetry* (1977), and his autobiography, *Sprightly Running: Part of an Autobiography* (1962). Of all his nonfiction, however, most readers believe that *Samuel Johnson* (1974) is his best and most lasting work. In this monumental biography, many of the commitments reflected in Wain's other writings come through clearly and forcefully.

Achievements

To understand something of Wain's uniqueness as a novelist, the reader must look back at least to the end of World War II. For about ten years after the war, established writers continued to produce successfully. Men such as Aldous Huxley, Graham Greene, Evelyn Waugh, C. P. Snow, and Anthony

Powell had made their reputations before the war and continued to be the major literary voices at that time. Most of them had been educated in "public" schools, then at Oxford or Cambridge, and were from upper- or upper-middle-class origins. Their novels were likely to center around fashionable London or some country estate. Often they confined their satire to the intellectual life and the cultural as well as social predicaments of the upper-middle class.

A combination of events in postwar England led to the appearance of another group of writers, soon referred to by literary journalists as the "Angry Young Men." Among these writers was John Wain, who, along with Kingsley Amis, John Braine, John Osborne, Angus Wilson, Alan Sillitoe, and others, turned away from technical innovations, complexity, and the sensitive, introspective protagonist to concentrate on concrete problems of current society. Thus, in the tradition of the eighteenth century novel, Wain fulfills most effectively the novelist's basic task of telling a good story. His novels move along at an even pace; he relies upon a simple, tightly constructed, and straightforward plot; clarity; good and bad characters; and a controlled point of view. The reader need only think of James Joyce and Franz Kafka, and the contrast is clear. What most of Wain's novels ask from the reader is not some feat of analysis, but a considered fullness of response, a readiness to acknowledge, even in disagreement, his vision of defeat.

Wain's typical protagonist is essentially an "antihero," a man at the mercy of life. Although sometimes capable of aspiration and thought, he is not strong enough to carve out his destiny in the way he wishes. Frequently, he is something of a dreamer, tossed about by life, and also pushed about, or at least overshadowed, by the threats in his life. Wain's Charles Lumley (*Hurry on Down*) and Edgar Banks (*Living in the Present*) bear the marks of this type. Often there is discernible in his characters a modern malaise, a vague discontent, and a yearning for some person or set of circumstances beyond their reach. Sometimes, this sense of disenchantment with life as it is becomes so great that the individual expresses a desire not to live at all, as Edgar Banks asserts in *Living in the Present* and as Gus Howkins declares in *The Pardoner's Tale*.

Wain is also accomplished in his creation of place and atmosphere. In *Strike the Father Dead*, he fully captures the grayness of a London day, the grayness of lives spent under its pall, the grayness of the people who wander its streets. When Wain describes an afternoon in which Giles Hermitage (*The Pardoner's Tale*) forces himself to work in the subdued light at home; when Arthur Geary (*The Smaller Sky*) walks the platforms at Paddington Station; when Charles Lumley walks in on a literary gathering; when Roger Furnivall (*A Winter in the Hills*) makes his way home through the Welsh countryside—at such moments the reader encounters Wain's mastery of setting and atmosphere.

The themes communicated through Wain's novels are, like his method, consistent. It is clear that he sees the eighteenth century as a time of dignity, pride, and self-sufficiency—qualities lacking in the twentieth century. Like Samuel Johnson, Wain defends the value of reason, moderation, common sense, moral courage, and intellectual self-respect. Moreover, his fictional themes of the dignity of the human being, the difficulty of survival in the modern world, and the perils of success have established him principally as a moralist concerned with ethical issues. In later works, the value of tradition, the notion of human understanding, and the ability to love and suffer become the chief moral values. In all his novels, he is primarily concerned with the problem of defining the moral worth of the individual. For all these reasons, Wain is recognized as a penetrating observer of the human scene.

One final point should be noted about Wain's capacities as a novelist. Clearly, the spiritual dimension is missing in the world he describes; and yet, there is frequently the hint or at least the possibility of renewal, which is the closest Wain comes to any sort of recognized affirmation. Charles Lumley, Joe Shaw, Jeremy Coleman, and Roger Furnivall are all characters who seem to be, by the end of their respective stories, on the verge of rebirth of a sort, on the threshold of reintegration and consequent regeneration. In each case, this renewal depends on the ability of the individual to come to terms with himself and his situation, to confront and accept at a stroke past, present, and future, and to accept and tolerate the contradictions inherent in all three. Wain's sensitive response to the tragic aspects of life is hardly novel, but his deep compassion for human suffering and his tenderness for the unfortunate are more needed than ever in an age when violence, brutality, and cynicism are all too prevalent.

Biography

Although his world is that of the twentieth century, John Wain is very much an eighteenth century man. He delights in pointing out that he and Samuel Johnson were born in the same district ("The Potteries") and in much the same social milieu; that he attended the same university as Johnson (Oxford, where he served from 1973 to 1978 as Professor of Poetry); that he has known, like Johnson, the Grub Street experiences and "the unremitting struggle to write enduring books against the background of an unstable existence." What chiefly interests the critic in surveying Wain's formative years are the reasons for his increasingly sober outlook. Wain's autobiography, *Sprightly Running*, remains the best account of his formative years as well as offering engaging statements of many of his opinions. In it, the reader finds some of the profound and lasting effects on Wain's writing of his childhood, his adolescence, and his years at Oxford.

John Barrington Wain was born on March 14, 1925, in Stoke-on-Trent, Staffordshire, an industrial city given over to pottery and coal mining. Here, as in other English cities, a move upward in social status is signaled by a move up in geographical terms. Therefore, the Wain family's move three years later to Penkhull—a manufacturing complex of kilns and factories and, incidentally, the setting for Wain's third novel, *The Contenders*—marked a step up into the middle-class district.

From infancy, Wain had a genuine fondness for the countryside. He immersed himself in the sights and sounds and colors of rural nature, all of which made an impression on him that was distinctive as well as deep. This impression developed into an "unargued reverence for all created life, almost a pantheism." On holidays, he and his family traveled to the coast and hills of North Wales—an association which carried over into his adult years, when, at thirty-four, he married a Welsh woman. His feeling for Wales—for the independent life of the people, the landscape and mountains, the sea, the special light of the sun—is recorded in *A Winter in the Hills*. Here and elsewhere is the idea that nature is the embodiment of order, permanence, and life. Indeed, the tension between the nightmare of repression in society and the dream of liberation in the natural world is an important unifying theme throughout Wain's work.

The experience of living in an industrial town also left an indelible imprint upon Wain's mind and art. His exposure to the lives of the working class and to the advance of industrialism gave him a profound knowledge of working people and their problems, which he depicts with sympathy and humanity in his fiction. Moreover, Wain's experiences at Froebel's Preparatory School and at Newcastle-under-Lyme High School impressed on him the idea that life was competitive and "a perpetual effort to survive." He found himself surrounded and outnumbered by people who resented him for being different from themselves. His contact with older children, schoolboy bullies, and authoritative schoolmasters taught Wain that the world is a dangerous place. These "lessons of life" were carried into his work. The reader finds in Wain's fiction a sense of the difficulty of survival in an intrusive and demanding world. The worst of characters is always the bully, and the worst of societies is always totalitarian. Beginning with *Hurry on Down*, each of Wain's published novels and stories is concerned in some way with the power and control that some people seek to exercise over others.

To cope with these injustices as well as with his own fears and inadequacies during his early years, Wain turned to humor, debate, and music. For Wain, the humorist is above all a moralist, in whose hands the ultimate weapon of laughter might conceivably become the means of liberating mankind from its enslavement to false ideals. Thus, his mimicry of both authorities and students was used as the quickest way to illustrate that something was horrible or boring or absurd. In both *Hurry on Down* and *The Contenders*, the heroes use mockery and ridicule to cope with their unjust world.

Wain's interest in jazz has also influenced his personal and literary development. He has spoken and written often of his lifelong enthusiasm for the trumpet playing of Bill Coleman; and he admits that Percy Brett, the black jazz musician in *Strike the Father Dead*, was created with Coleman in mind. Accompanying this interest was a growing interest in serious writing and reading. Unlike many youths, Wain did not have to endure the agonizing doubt and indecision of trying to decide what he wanted to do in life. By the age of nine, he knew: he wanted to be an author. He began as a critically conscious writer who delighted in "pastiche and parody for their own sake." Then, as now, he found most difficult the task of maintaining a steady plot line. Wain matched his writing with voracious reading. His early interest in the novels of Charles Dickens, Tobias Smollett, Daniel Defoe, and others in the tradition of the English novel influenced his later literary style. Like these predecessors, Wain approaches his characters through the conventional narration of the realist, and his concerns are social and moral.

The second major period in Wain's life occurred between 1943, when he entered St. John's College, Oxford, and 1955, when he resigned his post as lecturer in English at Reading University to become a full-time writer. Two friends made in his Oxford period especially influenced his writing. One was Philip Larkin, whose "rock-like determination" continues to be an inspiring example to Wain. The other friend was Kingsley Amis, whose work on a first novel inspired Wain to attempt writing a novel in his spare time. Wain wrote his first novel, not particularly because he wished to be a novelist, but to see if he could write one that would get into print. In 1953, Frederick Warburg accepted *Hurry on Down*, and its unexpected success quickly established Wain as one of Britain's promising new writers.

Wain's exhilarating experience with his first book was, however, poor preparation for the sobering slump that followed. Ill-health, divorce proceedings, and the drudgery of a scholar's life pushed him into a crisis of depression and discouragement. He tried to climb out of this crisis by leaving the university for a year and retreating to the Swiss Alps. There, he let his imagination loose on his own problems. The result was *Living in the Present*, a depressing book of manifest despair and disgust. Out of this period in his life, Wain developed a profound awareness of love and loneliness, union and estrangement. The essential loneliness of human beings, and their more or less successful attempts to overcome their loneliness by love, become major themes in his later fiction.

Analysis

As a novelist, John Wain has been described as a "painfully honest" writer who is always, to an unusual degree, writing autobiography. His own fortunes and his emotional reactions to these fortunes are, of course, transformed in various ways. His purpose is artistic, not confessional, and he shapes his material accordingly. As Wain himself states, this intention is both pure and simple: to express his own feelings honestly and to tell the truth about the world he knows. At his best—in *Hurry on Down*, *Strike the Father Dead*, *A Winter in the Hills*, and *The Pardoner's Tale*—Wain finds a great many ways to convey the message that life is ultimately tragic. Human beings suffer; life is difficult; the comic mask conceals anguish. Only occasionally is this grim picture relieved by some sort of idealism, some unexpected attitude of unselfishness or tenderness. What is more, in all of his writings Wain is a thoughtful, literate man coming to terms with these truths in a sincere and forthright manner.

In his first novel, *Hurry on Down*, Wain comically perceives the difficulties of surviving in a demanding, sometimes fearful world. Detached from political causes and progress of his own life, the hero is a drifter, seeking to compromise with or to escape from such "evils" as class lines, boredom, hypocrisy, and the conventional perils of success. Although the novel carries a serious moral interest, Wain's wit, sharp observations, and inventiveness keep the plot moving. His comedy exaggerates, reforms, and criticizes to advocate the reasonable in social behavior and to promote the value and dignity of the individual.

In *Strike the Father Dead*, Wain further extended himself with a work more penetrating than anything he had written before. Not only is it, as Walter Allen said, a "deeply pondered novel," but it is also a culmination of the promises inherent in Wain's earlier works. Plot, theme, character, and setting are integrated to tell the story of a son who breaks parental ties, thereby freeing himself to make his own way in life as a jazz pianist. Pointing to the foibles of his fellowman and probing the motives of an indignant parent, Wain's wit and sarcastic humor lighten this uncompromising study of the nonconformist's right to assert his nonconformity.

Two later Wain novels—*A Winter in the Hills* and *The Pardoner's Tale*—continue and elaborate upon many of the central themes of his fiction, but they surpass the earlier novels in richness and complexity. Both novels exhibit, far more than do his earlier writings, an interest in the tragic implications of romantic love; a greater complexity in character development allows Wain to portray convincingly men whose loneliness borders on self-destruction. Each novel is not simply another story of isolation or spiritual desolation, although it is that. Each hero is cast into a wasteland, and the novel in a sense is the story of his attempts to find the river of life again, or possibly for the first time. One of the themes that develops from this period in Wain's career is that personal relationships are the most important and yet most elusive forces in society.

Like Kingsley Amis's *Lucky Jim* (1954), John Braine's *Room at the Top* (1957), and Alan Sillitoe's *Saturday Night and Sunday Morning* (1958), Wain's first novel probes tellingly into a central problem of the 1950's. Its hero—Charles Lumley—is a creation of the postwar British Welfare State. As a disconnected youth on his own for the first time, he feels that neither his

upbringing nor his university education has prepared him for making a satisfactory living. Because he has a driving obsession to avoid the phony in life,
he detests the world he sees and rebels against whatever is bourgeois and
commonplace.

Hurry on Down has the characteristic features of the picaresque novel: a
series of short and often comic adventures loosely strung together; an opportunistic and pragmatic hero who seeks to make a living through his wits; and
satirical characterization of stock figures rather than individualized portraits.
Unlike the eighteenth century picaro, however, who is often hardhearted,
cruel, and selfish, Wain's central character is a well-intentioned drifter who
compromises enough to live comfortably. His standby and salvation is a strong
sense of humor that enables him to make light of much distress and disaster.
Lumley's character is revealed against the shifting setting of the picaresque
world and in his characteristic response to repeated assaults on his fundamental decency and sympathy for others. He remains substantially the same
throughout the novel; his many roles—as window cleaner, delivery driver,
chauffeur, and the like—place him firmly in the picaresque tradition. Lumley's
versatility and adaptability permit Wain to show his character under a variety
of circumstances and in a multiplicity of situations.

Lumley's character is established almost immediately with the description
of his conflict with the landlady in the first chapter. The reader sees him as
the adaptable antihero who tries to control his own fate, as a jack of all trades,
a skilled manipulator, an adept deceiver, an artist of disguises. Wain stresses
Lumley's ingenuity rather than his mere struggle for survival; at the same
time, he develops Lumley's individual personality, emphasizing the man and
his adventures. The role that Lumley plays in the very first scene is one in
which he will be cast throughout the story—that of a put-upon young man
engaged in an attempt to cope with and outwit the workaday world.

The satire is developed through the characterization. Those who commit
themselves to class—who judge others and define themselves by the class
structure—are satirized throughout the novel. Surrounding the hero is a host
of lightly sketched, "flat," stock figures, all of whom play their predictable
roles. These characters include the proletarian girl, the American, the landlady, the entrepreneur, the middle-class couple, and the artist. In this first
novel, Wain's resources in characterization are limited primarily to caricature.
The comedy functions to instruct and entertain. Beneath the horseplay and
high spirits, Wain rhetorically manipulates the reader's moral judgment so
that he sympathizes with the hero. In the tradition of Tobias Smollett and
Charles Dickens, Wain gives life to the grotesque by emphasizing details of
his eccentric characters and by indicating his attitude toward them through
the selection of specific bodily and facial characteristics.

Wain has also adopted another convention of eighteenth century fiction:
the intrusive author. The active role of this authorial impresario accounts for

the distance between the reader and the events of the novel; his exaggerations, his jokes, and his philosophizing prevent the reader from taking Lumley's fate too seriously. In later novels, Wain's authorial stance changes as his vision deepens.

Any discussion of comic technique in *Hurry on Down* leads inevitably to the novel's resolution. Ordinarily, a reader does not like to encounter "perfect" endings to novels; nevertheless, he is not put off by the unrealistic ending to this novel because he knows from the beginning that he is reading a comic novel which depends upon unrealistic exaggeration of various kinds. Elgin W. Mellown was correct when he called the novel "a pastiche: Walter Mitty's desire expressed through the actions of the Three Stooges—wish fulfillment carried out through outrageous actions and uncharacteristic behavior." The reader feels secure in the rightness of the ending as a conclusion to all of the comic wrongness that has gone on before.

The plot of Wain's fifth novel, *Strike the Father Dead*, is arranged in an elaborate, seven-part time-scheme. Parts 1 and 6 occur sometime late in 1957 or early in 1958; Part 2 takes place in the immediate prewar years; and the other divisions follow chronologically up to the last, which is set in 1958. The scene shifts back and forth between a provincial university town and the darker, black-market-and-jazz side of London, with a side trip to Paris.

Wain narrates the story from the points of view of four characters. The central figure, Jeremy Coleman, revolts against his father and the academic establishment in search of self-expression as a jazz pianist. Alfred Coleman, Jeremy's father and a professor of classics, is an atheist devoted to duty and hard work. Eleanor, Alfred's sister and foster mother to Jeremy, is devoted to Jeremy and finds comfort in innocent religiosity. Percy Brett, a black American jazz musician, offers Jeremy his first real parental leadership. Like Ernest Pontifex, in Samuel Butler's *The Way of All Flesh* (1903), Jeremy escapes from an oppressive existence; he has a passion for music, and once he has the opportunity to develop, his shrinking personality changes.

Strike the Father Dead marks a considerable advance over *Hurry on Down* in the thorough rendering of each character and each scene. By employing a succession of first-person narrators, Wain focuses attention more evenly on each of the figures. The result is that the reader comes away knowing Jeremy even better, because what he learns about him comes not only from his own narration but from other sources as well. Inasmuch as there are three central characters, *Strike the Father Dead* represents a larger range for Wain. Each interior monologue is a revelation; the language is personal, distinctive, and descriptive of character.

In the manner of a *Bildungsroman*, *Strike the Father Dead* is also a novel which recounts the youth and young manhood of a sensitive protagonist who is attempting to learn the nature of the world, discover its meaning and pattern, and acquire a philosophy of life. Setting plays a vital role in this odyssey. The provincial and London backgrounds and the accurate rendering of the language make the novel come alive. *Strike the Father Dead* moves between two contemporary worlds—a world of rigidity and repression, represented by Alfred, and a world of creativity, international and free, represented by London and Paris. The first world oppresses Jeremy; the second attracts and draws him. He dreams about it and invents fictions about it. Central to this new world is Jeremy's love of jazz. For him, the experience of jazz means beauty, love, life, growth, freedom, ecstasy—the very qualities he finds missing in the routine, disciplined life of Alfred.

Although *Strike the Father Dead* tells the story of a British young man who becomes successful, the success is to a certain extent bittersweet. In his triumphs over his home circumstances, Jeremy loses something as well. There are various names given to it: innocence; boyhood; nature; the secure, predictable life at home. The world beyond the academic life waits for Jeremy, and he, unknowingly, does his best to bring it onstage. With such a life comes a developing sense of injustice, deprivation, and suffering. These concerns become focal points in Wain's subsequent novels, as he turns toward the impulse to define character and dilemma much more objectively and with greater moral responsibility.

With its setting in Wales, *A Winter in the Hills* marked a departure from Wain's first six novels, all of which were centered in England. The story expresses, perhaps more comprehensively than any other, Wain's feelings for the provincial world, its cohesion and deep loyalties, and its resistance to innovation from outside. Furthermore, it is Wain's most ambitious presentation of the sadness of contemporary alienation. Here the reader finds Wain's sympathy for the underdog, his respect for decency and the dignity of man, his affirmation of life; here, too, is expressed Wain's deep interest in the causes and effects of loneliness and alienation.

The reader's first inclination is to approach the novel as primarily a novel of character, the major interest and emphasis of which is the constantly developing character of Roger Furnivall himself. Using third-person narration, Wain keeps the focus steadily on his main character as he progresses straight through several months that constitute a time of crisis in his life. Through most of the novel, Roger struggles doggedly against a combination of adverse circumstances, always in search of a purpose. Outwardly, he forces himself on Gareth, for example, as a way of improving his idiomatic Welsh. Inwardly, he "needed involvement, needed a human reason for being in the district." The guilt he carries because of his brother's suffering and death helps to propel him into a more active engagement with contemporary life. His conflict with Dic Sharp draws him out of his own private grief because he is helping not only Gareth, but also an entire community of people.

The reader learns about Roger in another way, too: Wain uses setting to reveal and reflect the protagonist's emotions and mental states. Roger's walk in the rain down the country roads, as he attempts to resolve his bitterness and disappointment at Beverley's rejection of him, is vividly depicted. It carries conviction because Roger's anxiety has been built up gradually and artistically. The pastoral world is a perpetually shifting landscape, and Wain depicts its shifts and contrasts with an acute eye for telling detail. Especially striking are the sketches of evening coming on in the Welsh hills, with their rocks and timber and vast expanses of green. Such descriptions help to convey Roger's yearning for happiness in a world which seems bent on denying it to him.

One major theme of the book is the invasion of the peaceful, conservative world of Wales by outsiders who have no roots in the region, and therefore no real concern for its inhabitants. These invaders are characterized by a sophisticated corruption that contrasts sharply with the unspoiled simplicity and honesty of the best of the natives. A related theme is the decline of the town: its economic insecurity, its struggle to resist the progressive and materialistic "cruelty, greed, tyranny, the power of the rich to drive the poor to the wall." Through Roger's point of view, Wain expresses his opposition to the pressures—economic, political, cultural—that seek to destroy the Welsh and, by implication, all minority enclaves. Thus, *A Winter in the Hills* is more than a novel about the growth of one human being from loneliness and alienation to mature and selfless love; it is also a powerful study of the quality of life in the contemporary world, threatened by the encroachments of bureaucracy, greed, and materialism.

The somewhat optimistic resolution of *A Winter in the Hills* stands in stark contrast to that of *The Pardoner's Tale*, Wain's most somber novel. In no other work by Wain are the characters so lonely, so frustrated, or so obsessed with thoughts of mutability, lost opportunities, and death. The novel is really two stories: a first-person tale about Gus Howkins, an aging Londoner contemplating divorce, and a third-person narrative (the framing narrative) about Giles Hermitage, an established novelist and bachelor living in an unnamed cathedral town, who gets involved with the Chichester-Redferns, a woman and her daughter, while he is working out the story of Howkins. It is the interplay between these two stories which constitutes the plot of *The Pardoner's Tale*.

Giles Hermitage is obviously the figure with whom Wain is the most intimately involved. He is a highly idiosyncratic figure with very recognizable weaknesses; he is easily discouraged (there is an early thought of suicide), and he resorts to excessive drinking. The root cause of his death wish and of his drinking is loneliness. Like Wain's earlier heroes, he is very much a modern man: vague in his religious and humanitarian aspirations; rootless and alienated from the social life of the community in which he lives; and initially weak and confused in his relationships with women. Plagued by anxiety, depression, vague discontent, and a sense of inner emptiness, he seeks peace of mind under conditions that increasingly militate against it. Add to his problems the ever-growing urge toward self-destruction, and the reader begins to recognize in this novel a truly contemporary pulsebeat. Hermitage is a stranger in a world that does not make sense.

Unlike Wain's earlier heroes, however, Hermitage tries to make sense of the world through the medium of his writing by stepping back into what he calls "the protecting circle of art." His approach to writing is autobiographical, personal, even subjective. The hero of his novel is a mask for himself. The author is creating a character who is in his own predicament, and the agonies he endures enable him to express his deepest feelings about life. In Hermitage, Wain presents a character who tries to create, as artists do, a new existence out of the chaos of his life.

The remaining major characters in *The Pardoner's Tale* bear family resemblances to those in other of Wain's novels. If the part of the lonely, alienated hero so effectively carried in *A Winter in the Hills* by Roger Furnivall is here assigned to Giles Hermitage, then the role of the manipulator is assigned in this novel to Mrs. Chichester-Redfern. Although a good deal less ruthless than Dic Sharp, she nevertheless seeks to exploit the hero.

The process by which Mrs. Chichester-Redfern is gradually revealed through the eyes of Hermitage is subtle and delicate. At first merely a stranger, she comes to seem in time a calculating and educated woman, the innocent victim of a man who deserted her, a seventy-year-old woman grasping for answers to some vital questions about her own life. She summons Hermitage under the pretense of wanting to gain insight into her life. From these conversations, the reader learns that she, like Hermitage, is confronted and dislocated by external reality in the form of a personal loss. Also like the hero, she desires to come to some understanding of her unhappy life through the medium of art. Her true motive is revenge, however, and she wants Hermitage to write a novel with her husband in it as a character who suffers pain. Then, she says, "there will be that much justice done in the world."

In addition to the alienated, lonely hero and the manipulator, most of Wain's fiction portrays a comforter. In his latest novel, the comforter is embodied in Diana Chichester-Redfern, but the happiness Diana offers is only temporary. In this novel, love is reduced to a meaningless mechanical act: Diana, also, is living in a wasteland.

The basic tension of this novel is a simple and classic one—the life-force confronting the death-force. As surely as Mrs. Chichester-Redfern is the death-force in the novel, Diana is the active and life-giving presence. She is depicted as an abrasive, liberated, sensual, innately selfish modern young woman who stands in positive contrast to the deathlike grayness of her mother. She is earthy and fulfilled, accepting and content with her music (playing the guitar satisfies her need for proficiency), her faith (which takes care of "all the moral issues") and her sexuality (which she enjoys because she has no choice). Diana goes from one affair to another, not in search of love (she claims she "can't love anybody") but out of a need for repetition. Diana defines love and meaning as the fulfillment of a man or woman's emotional requirements. To her, love does not mean self-sacrifice; rather, love is synonymous with need.

The world of *The Pardoner's Tale* is thus the archetypal world of all Wain's fiction: random, fragmented, lonely, contradictory. It is a world in which wasted lives, debased sexual encounters, and destroyed moral intelligences yield a tragic vision of futility and sterility, of isolation from the community, estrangement from those who used to be closest to one, and loneliness in the midst of the universe itself.

In retrospect, Wain's insistence on the contradictions of life is at the very center of his works, and is itself a tacit recommendation to the reader to look with honesty at the reality around him. For Wain, writing seems almost a test of his own honesty, reminding himself that, for the most part, he can look at things squarely, without flinching and without telling lies. This sense of stoic honesty is the single most dominant impression emerging from his work. Add to that a gentleness in his treatment of people, and there emerges the portrait of a man who from the 1950's has become more seriously, deeply, and intelligently the critic of contemporary English society. "I hope my work is taking on a deeper note," he commented once; "otherwise there's no point in going on."

Dale Salwak

Other major works

SHORT FICTION: *Nuncle and Other Stories*, 1960; *Death of the Hind Legs and Other Stories*, 1966; *Selected Shorter Stories of Thomas Hardy*, 1966 (edited); *The Life Guard*, 1971; *King Caliban and Other Stories*, 1978.

PLAY: *Harry in the Night: An Optimistic Comedy*, 1975.

TELEPLAY: *Young Shoulders*, 1984 (with Robert Smith).

RADIO PLAYS: *You Wouldn't Remember*, 1978; *A Winter in the Hills*, 1981; *Frank*, 1982.

POETRY: *Mixed Feelings*, 1951; *A Word Carved on a Sill*, 1956; *A Song About Major Eatherly*, 1961; *Weep Before God: Poems*, 1961; *Wildtrack: A Poem*, 1965; *Selected Shorter Poems of Thomas Hardy*, 1966 (edited); *Letters to Five Artists*, 1969; *The Shape of Feng*, 1972; *Feng: A Poem*, 1975; *Poems for the Zodiac*, 1980; *Thinking About Mr. Person*, 1980; *Poems, 1949-1979*, 1981; *Twofold*, 1981; *Open Country*, 1987.

NONFICTION: *Contemporary Reviews of Romantic Poetry*, 1953 (edited); *Interpretations: Essays on Twelve English Poems*, 1955 (edited); *Preliminary Essays*, 1957; *Gerard Manley Hopkins: An Idiom of Desperation*, 1959; *International Literary Annual*, 1959, 1960 (edited); *Fanny Burney's Diary*, 1960 (edited); *Sprightly Running: Part of an Autobiography*, 1962; *Essays on Literature and Ideas*, 1963; *The Living World of Shakespeare: A Playgoer's Guide*, 1964; *Arnold Bennett*, 1967; *Shakespeare: Macbeth, a Casebook*, 1968 (edited); *Shakespeare: Othello, a Casebook*, 1971 (edited); *A House for the Truth: Critical Essays*, 1972; *Johnson as Critic*, 1973 (edited); *Samuel Johnson*, 1974; *Professing Poetry*, 1977; *Samuel Johnson 1709-1784*, 1984 (with Kai Kin Yung); *Dear Shadows: Portraits from Memory*, 1986.

CHILDREN'S LITERATURE: *Lizzie's Floating Shop*, 1981.

ANTHOLOGY: *Anthology of Modern Poetry*, 1963.

MISCELLANEOUS: Thomas Hardy's *The Dynasts*, 1966 (edited).

Bibliography

Gindin, James. "The Moral Center of John Wain's Fiction." In *Postwar British Fiction: New Accents and Attitudes*. Berkeley: University of California Press, 1962. Gindin contends that Wain creates characters who always exhibit dignity and moral commitment. Considers Wain's first four novels and his stories in the volume *Nuncle and Other Stories*. In an introductory essay, Gindin evaluates Wain in the context of other authors from the 1950's.

Girard, David. *John Wain: A Bibliography*. London: Mansell, 1987. Contains a critical introduction to Wain's writings and a comprehensive list of his books and contributions to books and periodicals. Also includes other critical and biographical references and reviews of works by Wain.

Hague, Angela. "Picaresque Structure and the Angry Young Novel." *Twentieth Century Literature* 32 (Summer, 1986): 209-220. Hague views Wain's *Hurry On Down* as erroneously grouped with the "Angry Young Men" novels of the 1950's. She compares Wain's heroes with those in the novels of Kingsley Amis and Iris Murdoch; all are essentially loners who, like the picaresques of the eighteenth century, respond to tensions between traditional values and societal change.

Rabinovitz, Rubin. "The Novelists of the 1950's: A General Survey." In *The Reaction Against Experiment in the English Novel, 1950-1960*. New York: Columbia University Press, 1967. Rabinovitz places Wain in the context of novelists who embraced traditional values rather than those who experimented with unconventional ideas or forms, aligning Wain's novels with those of Arnold Bennett and eighteenth century picaresque novelists.

Salwak, Dale. *Interviews with Britain's Angry Young Men*. San Bernardino, Calif.: Borgo Press, 1984. This useful resource characterizes Wain as an "eighteenth century man." Engages Wain in a discussion of the role of criticism in the author's life, his goals as a writer, his response to the phenomenon of the Angry Young Men, and the sources and themes in several of his novels.

_____. *John Wain*. Boston: Twayne, 1981. After a chapter introducing Wain's life and art, the text contains four chapters on his novels, focusing on his early works, *Hurry on Down* and *Strike the Father Dead*, and two of his late works, *A Winter in the Hills and The Pardoner's Tale*. "Other Fiction, Other Prose" covers Wain's stories, poems, and biographical works. A selected bibliography completes the text.

ALICE WALKER

Born: Eatonton, Georgia; February 9, 1944

Principal long fiction
The Third Life of Grange Copeland, 1970; *Meridian*, 1976, *The Color Purple*, 1982; *The Temple of My Familiar*, 1989.

Other literary forms
Alice Walker has published several volumes of short fiction, poetry, and essays in addition to her novels. Walker was an early editor at *Ms.*, in which many of her essays first appeared. Her interest in the then little-known writer Zora Neale Hurston led to her pilgrimage to Florida to place a tombstone on Hurston's unmarked grave, to Walker's editing of *I Love Myself When I Am Laughing . . . And Then Again When I Am Looking Mean and Impressive: A Zora Neale Hurston Reader* (1979), and to her introduction to Robert Hemenway's *Zora Neale Hurston: A Literary Biography* (1977).

Achievements
Walker's literary reputation is based primarily on her fiction, although her second book of poetry, *Revolutionary Petunias and Other Poems* (1973), received the Lillian Smith Award and a nomination for a National Book Award. Her first short-story collection, *In Love and Trouble*, won the Rosenthal Award of the National Institute of Arts and Letters. In addition, she has received a Charles Merrill writing fellowship, an award for fiction from the National Endowment for the Arts, and a Guggenheim Fellowship. She has also been a Bread Loaf Scholar and a fellow at the Radcliffe Institute. *The Third Life of Grange Copeland* was widely and enthusiastically reviewed in journals as varied as *The New Yorker*, *The New Republic*, and *The New York Times Book Review*, although journals aimed primarily at a black readership were often silent or critical of the violence and graphic depiction of rural black life. With the publication of *Meridian*, Walker's second novel, her work as a poet, novelist, essayist, editor, teacher, scholar, and political activist came together. *Meridian* was universally praised in scholarly journals, literary magazines, popular magazines, and black-oriented journals. Some critics, mainly black male reviewers, objected again to the honest, straightforward portrayals of black life in the South and to Walker's growing feminism, which they saw in conflict with her commitment to her race. Walker's third novel, *The Color Purple*, was very widely acclaimed: Gloria Steinem wrote that this novel "could be the kind of popular and literary event that transforms an intense reputation into a national one," and Peter Prescott's review in *Newsweek* began by saying "I want to say at once that *The Color Purple* is an American

novel of permanent importance." These accolades were substantiated when Walker received the 1983 Pulitzer Prize for fiction.

Biography

Alice Walker was born in Eatonton, Georgia, on February 9, 1944, the last of eight children of Willie Lee and Minnie Lou Grant Walker, sharecroppers in rural Georgia. Her relationship with her father, at first strong and valuable, became strained as she became involved in the civil rights and feminist movements. A moving depiction of her estrangement from her father occurs in her essay "My Father's Country Is the Poor," which appeared in *The New York Times* in 1977. For Walker, a loving and healthy mother-daughter relationship has endured over the years. An account of that relationship is central to her essays "In Search of Our Mothers' Gardens" and "Lulls—A Native Daughter Returns to the Black South" and in Mary Helen Washington's article "Her Mother's Gifts," in which Walker acknowledges that she often writes with her mother's voice—"Just as you have certain physical characteristics of your mother . . . when you're compelled to write her stories, it's because you recognize and prize those qualities of her in yourself."

One of the central events in Walker's childhood was a BB gun accident which left her, at age eight, blind in one eye. Scar tissue from that wound, both physical and psychological, seems to have left her with a compensating acuteness of vision, despite the conviction that she was permanently disfigured. Walker was affected enough by the accident to say in a 1974 interview with John O'Brien, "I have always been a solitary person, and since I was eight years old (and the recipient of a disfiguring scar, since corrected, somewhat), I have daydreamed—not of fairytales—but of falling on swords, of putting guns to my heart or head, and of slashing my wrists with a razor." Walker's partial blindness allowed her to attend Spelman College in Atlanta on a scholarship for the handicapped, following her graduation from Butler-Baker High School in 1961. She left Spelman after two years—which included summer trips to the Soviet Union and to Africa as part of a group called Experiment in International Living—for Sarah Lawrence College, where she was graduated in 1965.

Walker's political activity controlled her movements during the years immediately following her college graduation: she spent the summer of 1965 in the Soviet Union and also worked for civil rights in Liberty County, Georgia. The next year she was a case worker for New York City's Department of Social Services, and then a voter-registration worker in Mississippi. In 1967, she married Melvyn Leventhal, a civil rights lawyer, and moved to Jackson, Mississippi, where she continued her civil rights work, lived in the heart of the South as part of an interracial couple, and taught at Jackson State University, while continuing to write stories, poems, and essays. She taught at

Tougaloo College in Mississippi for a year before returning to the East, where she was a lecturer in writing and literature at Wellesley College, an editor at *Ms.* magazine, and an instructor at the University of Massachusetts at Boston. By 1977, she had divorced her husband, accepted a position as Associate Professor of English at Yale University, and written six books.

Walker has continued to write, teach, edit, lecture, and read poetry across the nation from her base in rural Northern California.

Analysis

The story of Alice Walker's childhood scar provides the most basic metaphor of her novels: the idea that radical change is possible even under the worst conditions. Although she was never able to regain the sight in one eye, Walker's disfigurement was considerably lessened:

> I used to pray every night that I would wake up and somehow it would be gone. I couldn't look at people directly because I thought I was ugly. . . . Then when I was fourteen, I visited my brother Bill [who] took me to a hospital where they removed most of the scar tissue—and I was a *changed person*. I promptly went home, scooped up the best-looking guy, and by the time I graduated from high school, I was valedictorian, voted 'Most Popular,' and crowned queen!

That change and personal triumph is possible, despite the odds, is central to all of Walker's writing. Her work focuses directly or indirectly on the ways of survival adopted by black women, usually in the South, and is presented in a prose style characterized by a distinctive combination of lyricism and unflinching realism. Walker's women attempt not merely to survive, but to survive completely with some sense of stability, despite the constant thread of family violence, physical and mental abuse, and a lack of responsibility on the part of the men in their lives. Walker is simultaneously a feminist and a supporter of civil rights, not only for black Americans, but also for minorities everywhere.

Walker's vision has been shaped in part by a work from the first flowering of black writing in America: Jean Toomer's *Cane* (1923). She said in 1974 about Toomer's book, "it has been reverberating in me to an astonishing degree. *I love it passionately*; could not possibly exist without it." Like *Cane*, the first part of which centers mainly on women in the South, Walker's novels are made up of nearly equal parts of poetry, portraiture, and drama, broken up into a series of sections and subsections. Other important literary influences on Walker include Zora Neale Hurston, from whom she inherited a love of black folklore; Flannery O'Connor, who wrote of Southern violence and grotesqueries from her home in Milledgeville, Georgia, less than ten miles from Walker's childhood home; and Albert Camus, whose existentialism speaks to the struggle for survival and dignity in which Walker's characters are engaged. Walker herself has defined her "preoccupations" as a novelist:

"The survival, the survival *whole* of my people. But beyond that I am committed to exploring the oppressions, the insanities, the loyalties, and the triumphs of black women." *The Third Life of Grange Copeland*, on the surface a novel about the cycle of rage and violence torturing the lives of a father and his son, is as much about the recipients of that rage—the women and children whose lives are directly affected. Although the novel is unremitting in its picture of desperate poverty's legacy of hatred, hopelessness, and cruelty, it concludes optimistically with Ruth Copeland's hope for a release from sorrow through the redemption promised by the early days of the civil rights movement and by the knowledge and love inherited at the sacrificial death of her grandfather.

Walker's second novel, *Meridian*, picks up chronologically and thematically at the point where her first novel ended. *Meridian* describes the struggles of a young black woman, Meridian Hill, about the same age as Ruth Copeland, who comes to an awareness of power and feminism during the civil rights movement, and whose whole life's meaning is centered in the cycles of guilt, violence, hope, and change characteristic of that dramatic time. Thematically, *Meridian* picks up the first novel's theme of self-sacrificial murder as a way out of desperate political oppression in the form of the constant question that drives Meridian Hill—"Will you kill for the Revolution?" Meridian's lifelong attempt to answer that question affirmatively (as her college friends so easily do) while remaining true to her sense of responsibility to the past, her sense of ethics, and her sense of guilt of having given to her mother the child of her teenage pregnancy, constitutes the section of the novel entitled "Meridian." The second third of the novel, "Truman Held," is named for the major male character in the narrative. At one time, Meridian loves Truman, but his callous treatment of her and his desertion of her for Lynne Rabinowitz, a white civil rights volunteer from the North, causes their relationship to change. By the novel's end, Meridian has become teacher, confidante, and savior to both Truman and Lynne, whose eventual marriage is destroyed by the pressures of interracial tensions. The third major section of the novel, "Ending," looks back at the turmoil of the movement from the perspective of the 1970's. Long after others have given up intellectual arguments about the morality of killing for revolution, Meridian is still debating the question, still actively involved in voter registration, political activism, and civil rights organization, as though the movement had never lost momentum. Worrying that her actions, now seen as eccentric rather than revolutionary, will cause her "to be left, listening to the old music, beside the highway," Meridian achieves release and atonement through the realization that her role will be to "come forward and sing from memory songs they will need once more to hear. For it is the song of the people, transformed by the experiences of each generation, that holds them together."

Like her first two novels, *The Color Purple* has an unusual form. *The Color*

Purple presents the author's familiar and yet fresh themes—survival and redemption—in epistolary form. Most of the novel's letters are written by Celie, an uneducated, unloved, black woman living in rural Georgia in the 1920's; Celie's letters are written in what Walker calls "black folk English," a language of wit, strength, and natural humor. Ashamed of having been raped by her stepfather, a man whom Celie thinks at the time is her father, she begins to send letters to God, in the way that children send letters to Santa Claus, because her rapist told her to tell nobody but God. Although her early letters tell of rape, degradation, and pain, of her stepfather's getting rid of the two children born of his cruelty, the tone is nevertheless captivating, ironic, and even humorous. Soon the despair turns into acceptance, then into understanding, anger, rebellion, and finally triumph and loving forgiveness as the fourteen-year-old Celie continues to write until she reaches an audience, some thirty years later. Like the author, who began writing at the age of eight, and who has turned her childhood experience in rural Georgia into three novels of violence, hatred, understanding, love, and profound hope for the future, Celie is a writer, a listener, a thinker, and a promoter of Walker's constant theme: "Love redeems, meanness kills."

Writing in 1973, Walker observed that her first novel, *The Third Life of Grange Copeland*, "though sometimes humorous and celebrative of life, is a grave book in which the characters see the world as almost entirely menacing." This dark view of life is common to Grange Copeland, the patriarch of a family farming on shares in rural Georgia, his son Brownfield, and the wives and daughters of both men. For all these characters, the world is menacing because of the socioeconomic position they occupy at the bottom of the scale of the sharecropping system. Father and son menace each other in this novel because they are in turn menaced by rage born out of the frustration of the system. Although the white people of the book are nearly always vague, nameless, and impersonal, they and the system they represent have the ability to render both Grange and Brownfield powerless.

It is not accidental that these characters' names have agricultural connotations. "Grange" suggests a late nineteenth century association of farmers, a feudal farm and grain storage building, and a combination of graze and range, while "Brownfield" and "Cope*land*" are self-explanatory—for the inability to cope with the land is what leads both male characters along virtually parallel paths. For the father, the mere appearance of the white farm boss's truck is enough to turn his face "into a unnaturally bland mask, curious and unsettling to see." The appearance of the truck causes the son to be "filled with terror of this man who could, by his presence alone, turn his father into something that might as well have been a pebble or a post or a piece of dirt. . . ." Although Grange is, in this same image, literally a piece of land, he eventually returns to the South and learns to live self-sufficiently, farming a section of soil he tricked his second wife into giving to him. Brownfield, in contrast, is never able to escape from the sharecropping system, although he sees that, like his father, he is "destined to be no more than overseer, on the white man's plantation, of his own children." Brownfield is able to live obliviously on a farm in Georgia, content to blame all of his problems on others. The poor rural black workers of this novel are themselves little more than a crop, rotated from farm to farm, and producing a harvest of shame and hunger, cruelty and violence.

Unlike the men of the novel, the women are menaced by both blacks and whites, by both the agricultural system and the "strange fruit" it produces. Margaret, Grange's first wife, is both physically and mentally degraded by her husband and then sexually exploited by a white truck driver, resulting in her second pregnancy. Unable to cope with this situation, Grange deserts his family, after which his wife poisons both her child and herself. Following his father's pattern, Brownfield marries and begins to work the land, but after "a year when endless sunup to sundown work on fifty rich bottom acres of cotton land and a good crop brought them two diseased shoats for winter meat. . . ." he too begins to abuse his wife. Although Brownfield's wife, Mem, is a schoolteacher intelligent enough to try to break the cycle of raising others people's crops, her brief rebellion against her husband's malevolent beatings and mental tortures is a failure: he is able to subjugate her through repeated pregnancies that sap her rebellion as they turn her once rich and strong body into a virtual wasteland of emaciation. Because her body, which represents the land of the South, is still able to produce children despite its depleted condition, Brownfield is enraged enough to murder her in retaliation for her physical shape: "he had murdered his wife because she had become skinny and had not, with much irritation to him, reverted, even when well-fed, to her former plumpness. . . . Plumpness and freedom from the land, from cows and skinniness, went all together in his mind." Despite his irrational abuse of her, Mem is not ashamed "of being black though, no matter what he said. . . . Color was something the ground did to the flowers, and that was an end to it."

What the ground did to these generations of Southern black people is the subject of Walker's novel—the whole lurid history of violence, hatred, and guilt that she chronicles in this story of one family's griefs. By the book's end, Brownfield Copeland has murdered his wife and an unnamed albino baby, while Grange Copeland has murdered his son Brownfield—first spiritually, then physically—and indirectly has killed his first wife and her infant.

Walker's characters are allegorical representations of the classic modes of survival historically adopted by black Americans in dealing with their oppression. Brownfield identifies with whites by daydreaming of himself on a Southern plantation, sipping mint juleps, and then by bargaining for his freedom with the sexual favors of black women. Both of Grange's wives attempt to live up to the white stereotype of black women as promiscuous sexual beings, free of any moral restraints. Brownfield's wife, Mem, attempts the passive resistance advocated by Martin Luther King, but she is destroyed by what her husband calls "her weakness . . . forgiveness, a stupid belief that kindness can convert the enemy." Brownfield's daughter, Daphne, who calls herself the Copeland Family Secret Keeper, tries the strategy of inventing a falsely romantic history of the past, of the good old days when her father was kind, echoing those historical revisionists who try to argue that slavery was not that bad. Brownfield's other daughters try to stay away from their father altogether, regarding him "as a human devil" of whom they were afraid "in a more distant, impersonal way. He was like bad weather, a toothache, daily bad news," a description that suggests that traditional black view that white people are blue-eyed devils, impossible to understand, and to be avoided at all costs, rather than confronted.

Each of the title character's three lives (at home in the South as a sharecropper married to Margaret; in the North as a hustler of alcohol, drugs, and women; and finally back in the South as a farmer married to Josie and rearing his granddaughter Ruth) parallels a traditional survival strategy, which Grange summarizes as follows, "The white folks hated me and I hated myself until I started hating them in return and loving myself. Then I tried just loving me, and then you, and *ignoring* them much as I could." To put it another way, Grange tries at first to adapt to the system by believing what whites say about blacks; then he turns to the classic escape of the runaway slave—heading North to freedom; finally, he tries the technique of praising black life while ignoring whites altogether. A large part of the novel's devastation is caused by the repeated use of these techniques, not against whites, but against other members of the Copeland family. Only Ruth, the granddaughter through whom Grange seeks redemption, is able to deal with whites in an intelligent, balanced, nondestructive yet independent way. She has learned from her grandfather, and from her family history, that pure hatred becomes self-hatred, violence begets self-violence, and she therefore becomes the novel's symbol of the new black woman, ready to assume her place in black history as a courageous worker in the civil rights movement which the rest of her family has been groping to discover.

In 1978, Walker described her second novel, *Meridian*, as "a book 'about' the civil rights movement, feminism, socialism, the shakiness of revolutionaries and the radicalization of saints. . . ." Her word "about" is exact, for all of these topics revolve not chronologically but thematically around a central point—the protagonist, Meridian Hill. In some ways, Meridian *is* a saint; by the book's end she has sustained her belief in the civil rights movement without losing faith in feminism and socialism, despite family pressures, guilt, literally paralyzing self-doubts, the history of the movement, and the sexism of many of its leaders. In contrast, Truman Held represents those males who were reported to have said that "the only position for a woman in the movement

is prone." Although Truman Held is Meridian's initial teacher in the movement, she eventually leaves him behind because of his inability to sustain his
initial revolutionary fervor, and because of his misogyny. Unlike Brownfield
Copeland, Truman argues that women are of less value than they should be,
not because of skinniness, but because "Black women let themselves go . . .
they are so fat." Later in the novel, Truman marries a white civil rights worker,
whose rape by another black man produces disgust in him, as much at his
wife as at his friend. When Truman seeks Meridian out in a series of small
Southern hamlets where she continues to persuade black people to register
to vote and to struggle for civil rights, he tells her that the movement is ended
and that he grieves in a different way than she. Meridian answers, "I know
how you grieve by running away. By pretending you were never there." Like
Grange Copeland, Truman Held refuses to take responsibility for his own
problems, preferring to run away to the North.

Meridian's sacrificial dedication to the movement becomes a model for
atonement and release, words that once formed the working title of the book.
Meridian could also have been called "The Third Life of Meridian Hill"
because of similarities between Meridian's life and Grange Copeland's. Meridian leads three lives: as an uneducated child in rural Georgia who follows the
traditional pattern of early pregnancy and aimless marriage; as a college
student actively participating in political demonstrations; and as an eccentric
agitator—a performer, she calls herself—unaware that the movement is
ended. Like Grange Copeland in another sense, Meridian Hill is solid proof
of the ability of any human to change dramatically by sheer will and desire.

Meridian is always different from her friends, who, filled with angry rhetoric, ask her repeatedly if she is willing to kill for the revolution, the same
question that Grange asked himself when he lived in the North. This question
haunts Meridian, because she does not know if she can or if she should kill,
and because it reminds her of a similar request, posed in a similar way by
her mother: "Say it now, Meridian, and be saved. All He asks is that we
acknowledge Him as our Master. Say you believe in Him . . . don't go against
your heart." In neither case is Meridian able to answer yes without going
against her heart. Unlike her college friends and Truman Held, who see the
movement only in terms of future gains for themselves, Meridian is involved
with militancy because of her past: "But what none of them seemed to understand was that she felt herself to be, not holding on to something from the
past, but *held* by something in the past."

Part of the past's hold on her is the sense of guilt she feels about her
relationships with her parents. Although her father taught her the nature of
the oppression of minorities through his knowledge of American Indians, her
strongest source of guilt comes from her mother, who argues, like Brownfield
Copeland, that the responsibility for *all* problems stems from outside oneself:
"The answer to everything," said Meridian's mother, "is we live in America

and we're not rich." Meridian's strongest sense of past guilt comes from the knowledge she gains when she becomes pregnant: "it was for stealing her mother's serenity, for shattering her mother's emerging self, that Meridian felt guilty from the very first, though she was unable to understand how this could possibly be her fault."

Meridian takes the form of a series of nonchronological sections, some consisting of only a paragraph, some four or five pages long, that circle around the events of Meridian's life. The writing is clear, powerful, violent, lyrical, and often symbolic. Spelman College, for example, is here called Saxon College. The large magnolia tree in the center of the campus, described with specific folkloric detail, is destroyed by angry students during a demonstration: "Though Meridian begged them to dismantle the president's house instead, in a fury of confusion and frustration they worked all night, and chopped and sawed down, level to the ground, that mighty, ancient, sheltering music tree." This tree (named The Sojourner, perhaps for Sojourner Truth) expands symbolically to suggest both the senseless destruction of black ghettos by blacks during the turmoil of the 1960's, and also Meridian Hill herself, who receives a photograph years later of The Sojourner, now "a gigantic tree stump" with "a tiny branch, no larger than a finger, growing out of one side." That picture, suggesting as it does the rebirth of hope despite despair, also evokes the last vision of Meridian expressed by the now-shamed Truman Held: "He would never see 'his' Meridian again. The new part had grown out of the old, though, and that was reassuring. This part of her, new, sure and ready, even eager, for the world, he knew he must meet again and recognize for its true value at some future time."

Like Meridian Hill, Celie, the main character in Walker's third novel, *The Color Purple*, compares herself to a tree. Repeatedly raped by her stepfather, Celie is then sold into a virtual state of slavery to a man who beats her, a man she neither knows, loves, nor talks to, a man she can never call anything but Mr. _____ , an ironic throwback to the eighteenth century English epistolary novel. Celie tries to endure by withholding all emotion: "I make myself wood. I say to myself, Celie, you a tree. That's how come I know trees fear man." Like The Sojourner, or like the kudzu vine of the deep South that thrives despite repeated attempts to beat it back, Celie continues to express her fears and hopes in a series of letters written in a form of black English that is anything but wooden. The contrast between the richly eccentric prose of Celie's letters and the educated yet often lifeless sentences of her sister Nettie's return letters supports Walker's statement that "writing *The Color Purple* was writing in my first language. . . ." The language of the letters is at first awkward, but never difficult to follow. As Celie grows in experience, in contact with the outside world, and in confidence, her writing gradually becomes more sophisticated and more like standard written English, but it never loses its originality of rhythm and phrase.

Based on Walker's great grandmother, a slave who was raped at twelve by her owner, Celie works her way from ignorance about her body and her living situation all the way through to an awakening of her self-worth, as well as to an understanding of the existence of God, the relations between men and women, and the power of forgiveness in uniting family and friends. Much of this transformation is brought about through the magic of a blues singer named Shug Avery, who guides Celie in understanding sexuality, men, and religion without causing her to lose her own fresh insights, naïve though they are.

The letters that make up the novel are something like the missives that the protagonist of Saul Bellow's novel *Herzog* (1964) writes but never sends, in that they are often addressed to God and written in an ironic but not self-conscious manner. Because of the combination of dark humor and despair, the letters also evoke memories of the desperate letters from the physically and spiritually maimed addressed to the hero of Nathanael West's *Miss Lonelyhearts* (1933). Although Celie is unlettered in a traditional sense, her ability to carry the complicated plot forward and to continue to write—first without an earthly audience, and then to her sister, whom she has not seen for more than twenty years—testify to the human potential for self-transformation.

Discussing Celie's attempts to confirm her existence by writing to someone she is not certain exists, Gloria Steinem says "Clearly, the author is telling us something about the origin of Gods: about when we need to invent them and when we don't." In a sense, Shug Avery becomes a god for Celie because of her ability to control the evil in the world and her power to change the sordid conditions of Celie's life. Early in the book, when Celie is worrying about survival, about rape, incest, beatings, and the murder of her children, her only source of hope is the name "Shug Avery," a name with a magical power to control her husband. Not even aware that Shug is a person, Celie writes "I ast our new mammy bout Shug Avery. What it is?" Finding a picture of Shug, Celie transfers her prayers to what is at that point only an image: "I see her there in furs. Her face rouge. Her hair like somethin tail. She grinning with her foot up on somebody motocar. Her eyes serious tho. Sad some. . . . An all night long I stare at it. An now when I dream, I dream of Shug Avery. She be dress to kill, whirling an laughing." Shug Avery becomes a god to Celie not only because she is pictured in the first photograph Celie has ever seen, but also because she is dressed in a style that shows a sense of pride and freedom.

Once Celie's sister's letters begin to appear, mailed from Africa, where Nettie is a missionary, the ironic connection between the primitive animism of the Africans and Celie's equally primitive reaction to Shug's picture becomes clear. Although Nettie has crossed the ocean to minister to a tribe of primitive people, her own sister is living in inhuman conditions in Georgia: ignorance, disease, sexism, lack of control of the environment, and the ever-increasing march of white people. When Shug explains her own animistic religious beliefs—which include the notion that God is not a he or a she, but an it (just as Celie once thought Shug Avery was an it)—Celie is converted to a pantheistic worship that makes her early identification with trees seem less naïve.

When the narrator of Herman Melville's "Bartleby the Scrivener" tries to explain Bartleby's withdrawal from life, he thinks of the dead letter office in which the scrivener was rumored to have worked, and says, "On errands of life, these letters speed to death." In contrast, Celie's and Nettie's letters, ostensibly written to people long thought to be dead, speed across the ocean on errands of life, where they grow to sustain, not merely the sisters in the book, but all those lucky enough to read them. As the author says of *The Color Purple*, "It's my happiest book . . . I had to do all the other writing to get to this point." For the reader who has gotten to this point in Walker's career by reading all of her other books, there is no question that Alice Walker's name could be substituted for Celie's in the author's statement about her most recent novel: "Let's hope people can hear Celie's voice. There are so many people like Celie who make it, who come out of nothing. People who triumph."

Timothy Dow Adams

Other major works

SHORT FICTION: *In Love and Trouble: Stories of Black Women*, 1973; *You Can't Keep a Good Woman Down*, 1981.

POETRY: *Once: Poems*, 1968; *Five Poems*, 1972; *Revolutionary Petunias and Other Poems*, 1973; *Goodnight, Willie Lee, I'll See You in the Morning: Poems*, 1979; *Horses Make a Landscape Look More Beautiful*, 1984.

NONFICTION: *I Love Myself When I Am Laughing . . . And Then Again When I Am Looking Mean and Impressive: A Zora Neale Hurston Reader*, 1979 (edited); *In Search of Our Mothers' Gardens: Womanist Prose*, 1983; *Living by the Word: Selected Writings, 1973-1987*, 1988.

CHILDREN'S LITERATURE: *Langston Hughes: American Poet*, 1974; *To Hell with Dying*, 1988.

Bibliography

Bloom, Harold, ed. *Alice Walker: Modern Critical Views*. New York: Chelsea House, 1989. A book-length compilation of the best of criticism on Walker. Authors Diane F. Dadoff and Deborah E. McDowell explore the resonant Zora Neale Hurston/Alice Walker relationship. Naturally radical feminism is addressed in this study, and Bloom discusses the mother/daughter motif in Walker's works.

Christian, Barbara. *Black Feminist Criticism*. New York: Pergamon Press, 1985. Throughout the book there are references to the characters in Alice

Walker's novels. Chapters 2 and 6 focus entirely on Walker's women characters and the motifs in her work, in particular growth through pain. Chapter 17 discusses her novel *Meridian*, and chapter 15 her novel *The Color Purple*. The book is a valuable resource for black literature as well as for insights into Walker's characterization.

Davis, Thadious M., and Trudier Harris. *Dictionary of Literary Biography*. Vol. 33, *Afro-American Fiction Writers After 1955*. Detroit: Gale Research, 1984. Includes a short biography on Walker, criticism of her novels, and a list of interviews. A serviceable if uninspired introduction to Walker, with some discussion on feminist prose in the Afro-American context.

Fairbanks, Carol, and Eugene A. Engeldinger. *Black American Fiction: A Bibliography*. Metuchen, N.J.: Scarecrow Press, 1978. Lists Walker's novels and short fiction with selective entries and reviews of her writing.

Pratt, Louis H., and Darrell D. Pratt. *Alice Malsenior Walker: An Annotated Bibliography, 1968-1986*. Westport, Conn.: Meckler, 1988. A low-budget, typewritten volume, which nevertheless offers a wealth of information about primary sources on Walker. Includes lists of articles which refer to Walker only in a peripheral sense. Useful background information on Walker and excellent secondary sources.

Tate, Claudia. *Black Women Writers at Work*. New York: Continuum, 1983. A compilation of that most recent of literary genres: interviews with writers—in this instance, black writers. The interview with Alice Walker discusses *Meridian* and *The Third Life of Grange Copeland*.

EDWARD LEWIS WALLANT

Born: New Haven, Connecticut; October 19, 1926
Died: Norwalk, Connecticut; December 5, 1962

Principal long fiction

The Human Season, 1960; *The Pawnbroker*, 1961; *The Tenants of Moonbloom*, 1963; *The Children at the Gate*, 1964.

Other literary forms

The brevity of Edward Lewis Wallant's literary career did not allow for a long list of publications. He did contribute three short stories to the *New Voices* series: "I Held Back My Hand," appeared in *New Voices 2* (1955); "The Man Who Made a Nice Appearance," in *New Voices 3* (1958), and the posthumously published "When Ben Awakened," in *American Scene: New Voices* (1963). Wallant also wrote an essay on the art of fiction which was published posthumously in the *Teacher's Notebook in English* (1963). In addition, there is a sizable collection which includes unpublished manuscripts, the final drafts of his first two unpublished novels, some half-dozen short stories, various drafts of his published novels, the first act of a play, his journal and his notebooks, and miscellaneous loose notes and fragments. All of these papers are on deposit at the Beinecke Library at Yale University.

Achievements

Wallant's literary output was so small and his career so short that it is difficult to assess his place in postwar American fiction. Wallant's work is best seen in its relationship to kindred works in the late 1950's and early 1960's. Although he is still little known to the public, Wallant's four novels rank with J. D. Salinger's *Franny and Zooey* (1961), Saul Bellow's *Henderson the Rain King* (1959), Bernard Malamud's *A New Life* (1963), and Ken Kesey's *One Flew over the Cuckoo's Nest* (1962) as examples of what has been described as the "New Romanticism." Wallant's novels reflect an outlook on life that led him to write about the unfortunate, the outcast, and the common man, whom he portrayed with compassion and dignity. His unwaveringly realistic perception of life and its often painful demands leaven his general optimism. In each of his fictions, Wallant's central character is shocked out of a moral lethargy and into action on behalf of his fellow human beings. This shock is preceded by a submersion into the contemporary human condition, which provides Wallant the opportunity to explore the interconnections and disconnections of modern urban life. He was a committed writer whose commitment acknowledged the darker side of the lives of his characters. It is not surprising, then, that while some critics should emphasize the positive nature of Wallant's work, his "happy endings" and his optimism, there should also be those who find in his work a note of despair and a presentiment of his own early death. It was Wallant's achievement to fuse the qualities of an old-fashioned novelist with the perceptions of a modern urban realist. The combination resulted in novels which offer a particularly clear view of the 1960's.

Biography

Edward Lewis Wallant was born in New Haven, Connecticut, on October 19, 1926. His father, who was invalided by mustard gas during World War I, was almost continuously hospitalized during Wallant's early years, and he died when his son was six. Wallant, an only child, was reared in a shabby although respectable middle-class neighborhood by his mother, Anna, and two aunts. Except for his Russian-born grandfather, who told him stories of the old country, it was a household without males. During his years at New Haven High School, Wallant held a number of jobs including plumber's assistant, delivery boy for a drugstore across the street from a Catholic hospital, and hot-dog hawker at Yale football games. Although his academic career in high school was not remarkable, he did attend briefly the University of Connecticut. He soon left, however, to join the navy.

The final months of World War II found Wallant serving as a gunner's mate in the European Theater of Operations; after his discharge from the navy in 1946, he enrolled in Pratt Institute to prepare for a career as an artist. In 1947, he married Joyce Fromkin, a girl he had known since childhood; in 1948, they moved to Brooklyn. After his graduation from Pratt in 1950, he was hired by the L. W. Frohlich advertising agency, where he became art director for the Westinghouse account. In the same year, he also enrolled in creative writing courses at the New School for Social Research, where he studied with Harold Glicksberg and Don Wolfe. Under their guidance, Wallant wrote a group of short stories and a novel, *Tarzan's Cottage*, which was never published.

In 1953, Wallant moved to the advertising agency of Doyle, Kitchen, and McCormick. He also moved his family from New Rochelle, New York, where a son, Scott, had been born in 1952, to Norwalk, Connecticut, where, in 1954, his daughter Leslie was born. In 1955, his short story "I Held Back My Hand" appeared in *New Voices 2: American Writing Today*, edited by his writing instructor, Don Wolfe. It was his first publication. During the late 1950's, Wallant submitted to various publishers his early novels *Tarzan's Cottage* and *The Odyssey of a Middleman*, but neither met with any success. Wallant changed jobs a third time in 1957, moving to McCann Erikson as an art director, a position he was to hold until shortly before his death. His second daughter, Kim, was also born the same year. Another story, "The Man Who Made a Nice Appearance," was published in 1958 in *New Voices 3*, edited by Charles Glicksberg.

Wallant's third novel was accepted within twenty-four hours of its submission to Harcourt, Brace. Originally entitled *A Scattering in the Dark*, it appeared in 1960 retitled as *The Human Season*. Although it received few reviews, some were enthusiastic and helped to create a small, underground reputation for his work. In spite of its limited commercial success, the novel received the Harry and Ethel Daroff Memorial Fiction Award from the Jewish Book Council for the best novel on a Jewish theme. The publication of *The Pawnbroker* in 1961, also by Harcourt, Brace, established Wallant's reputation as a novelist. The book was nominated for a National Book Award, and the screen rights were sold to Sidney Lumet, who in 1965 made a critically acclaimed film starring Rod Steiger.

The modest success of *The Pawnbroker* came at a crucial period in Wallant's life. For years, he had balanced his work as an advertising art director with his after-hours vocation of writing, and he was having increasing difficulty in reconciling his two lives. A resolution of sorts seemed imminent when he received a Guggenheim fellowship in 1962, which allowed him to travel in Europe and to write full time. For three months, he traveled abroad. Joyce joined him briefly in Italy, and then Wallant went on to Spain. He returned home with the idea for a comic novel, to be called *Tannenbaum's Journey*, based on his travels. He also resolved to devote his life to full-time writing and resigned his position with McCann Erikson. He took a small room in New York to use as a retreat for his work. In spite of feeling tired, Wallant was excited by his prospects; the European trip had given him inspiration. Then, quite suddenly, he was stricken by a viral infection and lapsed into a coma. He died of an aneurysm of the brain a week later on December 5, 1962.

At the time of his death, Wallant had two novels, *The Tenants of Moonbloom* and *The Children at the Gate*, under consideration by Harcourt, Brace, and it fell to his editor, Dan Wickenden, to see these projects through the press. *The Tenants of Moonbloom* was published in 1963, as were two other pieces: a story, "When Ben Awakened," in *American Scene: New Voices*, again edited by Don Wolfe, and an essay, "The Artist's Eye," for the *Teacher's Notebook in English*. *The Children at the Gate*, although written before *The Tenants of Moonbloom*, was not published until 1964.

Analysis

Just before his death, Edward Lewis Wallant wrote: "I suggest that most people are nearsighted, myopic in their inability to perceive the details of human experience." It was a condition he found perfectly normal; there is simply too much energy used up in everyday life, having families, supporting oneself, and living in a community, for much insight into the lives of fellow human beings, except as they relate to one's own immediate needs. Yet there are times, Wallant noted, when people experience an unrecognized yearning to "know what lies in the hearts of others." "It is then," he wrote, "that we turn to the artist, because only he can reveal even the little corners of the things beyond bread alone." It is revealing that Wallant, first trained as a graphic artist, should title the one essay in which he set forth his artistic credo "The Artist's Eye." In this essay, Wallant explores the relationship between the observable, everyday world and the interpretation of that world through the writer's heightened sense of awareness.

In all four of Wallant's published novels, this theme of heightened perception is central. The protagonist, who has become emotionally insulated from life, experiences a reawakening of feelings and rejoins the world around him. This spiritual and emotional rebirth comes as the result of the death of someone who has become close to the protagonist. The impact of this death, which often happens in a shocking way and with suddenness, penetrates the emotional barriers Wallant's characters erect against the onslaught of modern, urban life: Joe Berman escapes the past, Sol Nazerman is rescued from both the past and the dim recesses of his pawnshop, Angelo DeMarco gets beyond his streetwise sassiness, and Norman Moonbloom overcomes his inertia and learns to act. In each case and with each novel, Wallant takes his readers into the lives of his characters and reveals the little corners of the human heart.

Wallant's first novel, *The Human Season*, is the story of a middle-aged, middle-class man who must come to grips with himself following the death of his wife. Joe Berman is recognizably a twentieth century Everyman who lives a life barely distinguishable from that of his neighbors. He is a Russian Jew who immigrated to America when he was a little boy, and he seemingly has attained the American dream, founding his own plumbing business, owning his own modest home, marrying, and fathering three children. His wife, Mary, of "obligatory blonde, American prettiness," as one critic has described her, dies prior to the beginning of the novel, leaving him alone to face life and his largely unrecognized emotions. The structure of the novel intensifies the tension between past and present by alternating scenes from the present, in which Wallant skillfully renders Berman's daily life through a series of highly detailed episodes, with incidents from the past, each of them exposing some traumatic memory. In their reverse progression into the earlier years of Berman's life, these dreams deepen one's understanding not only of Berman's character but also of the formation of his emotional paralysis. Beginning on April 30, 1956, the day of Mary's fatal stroke, they recede back to September, 1907, when Berman was a little boy of nine living in Russia. The dreams contrast sharply in their emotional vividness with the increasingly comatose quality of Berman's present life. He has become an automaton, living without connection in an environment increasingly alien to him. He lashes out at the objects which remind him of his wife's delicacy and sensitivity as he succumbs to his "numbing, disorienting grief." Finally, Berman tries to kill himself.

As he becomes more and more blind to the real world, the world of his dreams, his past, becomes more vivid until it begins to intrude into his present, waking life. Increasingly, Wallant returns to images of the natural sources of Berman's earlier feelings in his memories of his father and of his life in Russia. Although there is a pastoral quality to these memories, Wallant does not suggest a return to some agrarian ideal. Berman's dreams remind him of his human capacities and inaugurate his search for something which will approximate the bond with the nature of his youth. Among the dreams are recollections of his father and Judaism. Berman realizes how neglectful he was of his own son, who was killed in the war, and how estranged from the healing qualities of his Jewishness he had become. The death of his wife, after all, merely provides a catalyst for his sickness, causing his self-doubt and sense of alienation to surface. The initial moment of his illumination quite literally comes as a shock: in an attempt to fix a faulty television set, Berman is thrown across the room, and in his fear and astonishment, he begins to pray in a jumble of English, Yiddish, and Russian. In that moment, he discovers the meaning of all of the months of his suffering. He is alone.

It is from this revelation that he begins to reconstruct his life, one which will be authentic and will result in a new self. He discovers a craving for people; his dreams no longer haunt him but provide him with soothing images which strengthen his zest for self-renewal. In a scene that elevates the fiction to a mythical dimension, Berman is born again as he walks home in the rain after having "witnessed" the life around him. As the novel ends, Berman is waiting in his empty house for his son-in-law to take him home for a family dinner. In this final chapter, Wallant convincingly depicts a poignant example of man's infinite capacity for self-renewal.

Wallant abandoned work on a comic fiction, *Gimple the Beast*, to write his second novel, *The Pawnbroker*. As in his first novel, the central character is a middle-aged, Jewish immigrant. Sol Nazerman, however, did not arrive in America as a youth; instead, the forty-five-year-old ex-professor from the University of Krakow fled Europe and the death camps in which he had been a prisoner during World War II. Now he is the operator of a pawnshop in a black ghetto in New York City. The shop is owned by a minor underworld figure who uses it as a drop point for the transferral of illegal money. Nazerman is aware of the criminality of the operation but does not protest. He uses his income to support his sister and her family, who live in the suburbs. He also contributes to the support of his mistress, Tessie Rubin, who lives with her dying father. The novel brings together the nightmare world of the concentration camp as Nazerman remembers it with the corrupt urban world of the pawnshop.

As in *The Human Season*, the central character has walled himself off from the pain and suffering of the world around him. Amid the grotesques who visit his shop, Nazerman remains a private, isolated man. The novel is the story of his spiritual reawakening, which is largely brought about through the intervention of Jesus Ortiz, the black, Catholic assistant who works in the business, and whose energy and ambition awaken sympathy from Nazerman. The death of Ortiz during an attempted robbery of the shop, which occurs on the fifteenth anniversary of the destruction of Nazerman's family in the death camps, provides the shock that penetrates the insulation with which Nazerman has wrapped his feelings in order to maintain his delicate sense of survival. He recognizes the part he willingly plays in the chain of human exploitation of which his pawnshop is a microcosm, and he is forced to acknowledge the community of grief to which he belongs and from which he has so long isolated himself. The novel concludes with three acts of atonement for Nazerman as he rejoins the world. He telephones his nephew, Morton, and asks him to become his new assistant, thereby opening a father-son relationship with the young man who has been wanting it for so long. After the phone call, Nazerman sleeps and dreams, not a nightmare as he usually does, but a dream in which he is able to lay the dead past to rest. Finally, he, like Berman, learns to mourn and goes to Tessie to help her grieve over the death of her father. As in the previous novel, this act is an important sign of his rebirth.

The connections between Wallant's first two novels are more than superficial. The two protagonists, who have much in common, experience similar awakenings. Both novels interweave dreams with the narrative thread. Both men must expiate their guilt over the death of their sons. Berman never did respond to his son, who died in the war unaware of his father's love; Nazerman must seek forgiveness for the guilt he feels for the death of his son, who slipped out of his grasp and suffocated on the floor of a cattlecar on their way to the death camp. Both men are finally free from their past when they can fully and properly mourn the dead; then they can rebuild their lives again in the present. *The Pawnbroker* is the darkest of Wallant's books and seems to have provided a release for the marvelously comic voice of the last two novels.

During the summer of 1961 while he was awaiting the outcome of his Guggenheim application, Wallant underwent a radical shift in attitude concerning his vocation as a writer. In the little more than six months he took to complete the manuscript of *The Pawnbroker*, he drafted the first version of *The Children at the Gate*, a completed version of which was left with his editor before he began his European travels with the fellowship money.

The novel concerns the relationship between the literal-minded, nineteen-year-old Angelo DeMarco, who makes the rounds of a Catholic hospital to take orders among the patients for the pharmacy where he works, and Sammy Cahan, a clownish Jew who is an orderly in the hospital. DeMarco, who clings to a rationalism as a defense against the horrors of his life—his idiot sister, his fatherless home, his obsessively religious mother, and the dying patients among whom he must spend his days—is redeemed by the antics of Cahan, whose essentially emotional view of life provides DeMarco with his spiritual change. Unlike Berman and Nazerman, Cahan seems to have inherited his life-giving vision, which he is able to spread throughout the hospital. As with the pawnshop and later the apartment houses of *The Tenants of Moonbloom*, the hospital setting provides a microcosm for the world's suffering humanity against which the drama of the central character's spiritual growth can take place. Once again, it is a death, Cahan's, which shocks DeMarco awake to the final recognition of his stifling life and the possibility of rebirth, a recognition which is made concrete in DeMarco's ministrations to his retarded, childlike sister, who has been raped by their father. Like Berman and Nazerman before him, DeMarco reveals his growing humanity through his acts of kindness and tenderness.

The centrality of the dream-world which played so important a part in the previous novels is replaced here by a living world of dreams which DeMarco must shatter before abandoning his barricade of toughness. It is no coincidence that he first discovers Cahan in the children's ward at the hospital, for it is the childlike simplicity of the orderly, his trust and innocence, which DeMarco must rediscover in order to be reborn. *The Children at the Gate* reveals the intermingling of Christian and Jewish myths which Wallant used to such great effect in all of his novels. It is not only the accumulation of religious artifacts or references in the novel, but also Cahan's portrayal as the religious fool and his martyrdom in the Christlike crucifixion on the hospital gates which sets the tone. Just as the death of the assistant, Ortiz, in *The Pawnbroker*, precipitated Nazerman's rebirth, so here Cahan's death reveals to DeMarco the path he must follow. The roles of teacher and priest, the relationship between suffering and redemption, the confluence of death and rebirth form a religious nexus which gives this book its especially powerful message of commitment, community, and love.

Although there were comic elements in *The Children at the Gate*, it was only in *The Tenants of Moonbloom* that Wallant's comic genius flowered. His last novel exhibits a certainty of handling and a smoothness of execution which were the results of his growing confidence as a writer. Wallant had thrown over his job as an advertising man and had made a commitment to literature.

The Tenants of Moonbloom traces the emergence of Norman Moonbloom, an introverted rent collector who manages four decrepit apartment buildings for his brother, and who emerges from his passivity as the result of his contact with the urban flotsam and jetsam who inhabit his apartments. Moonbloom, who is thirty-three at the time of the story, has finally settled down after years of college and a number of majors. He is a rather average young man who has spent his life retreating from people, and although he would prefer to hide in the womblike security of his apartment, his tenants persistently intrude on his consciousness. Finally unable any longer to retreat from the world, Moonbloom plunges into his past, like Berman and Nazerman, to search for a base upon which he can build a relationship with life. Through a series of seemingly disconnected visions, Moonbloom awakens to an understanding of the humanity which he shares with even the most bizarre of his tenants. He launches a "holy war" of rehabilitation in order to try to respond to the needs of those human beings placed into his trust.

Through a series of jolts, not unlike the ones received by Wallant's other anti-heroes, delivered by the various inhabitants of Moonbloom's apartments, he is transformed. This is accomplished during three visits he makes to his tenants. Each successive visit further shocks him into responding. His reaction culminates in the frenzy of activity in which he engages to bring the buildings and by extension the lives of his tenants up to some sort of standard. Although Moonbloom, a former rabbinical student, is Wallant's final Christ-figure, this novel relies far less than its predecessors, most notably *The Children at the Gate*, on biblical imagery and allusions, despite Moonbloom's messianic zeal to convert his tenants into full-blown human beings. In his last novel, Wallant was to integrate the comic and the tragic. As one critic has written, Wallant moved from being a cautious optimist to become "the comic celebrant of man's capacity to live an energetic, courageous, and spiritually dedicated existence."

Wallant's reputation rests firmly on a small body of fiction which he wrote with much passion and energy. Necessarily, this reputation has been enhanced by the tragedy of his untimely death and the unfulfilled promise of his career. His prose reflects a joyful celebration of life, life in all of its manifest complexities. Although he has often been compared to two other Jewish writers, Bruce Jay Friedman and Nathanael West, Wallant did not succumb to the absurd fantasies of the first nor to the despair of the second. Perhaps his importance as a modern novelist is best summarized by a critic who wrote that it was his cautious refusal to accept "the existential despair and the universal isolation of modern man" which distinguished him from his contemporaries and led him to affirm quietly the worth and joy of life. Wallant's novels are a testament to the continuing resilience of the human spirit.

Charles L. P. Silet

Bibliography
Ayo, Nicholas. "The Secular Heart: The Achievement of Edward Lewis Wallant." *Critique: Studies in Modern Fiction* 12 (1970): 86-94. Compares Wallant to Dostoevski to convey his grim realism and emphasis of changes of heart, looking expressly at the religious element in Wallant's characters.
Baumbach, Jonathan. *The Landscape of Nightmare: Studies in the Contemporary Novel*. New York: New York University Press, 1965. Baumbach com-

pares *The Pawnbroker* and *The Tenants of Moonbloom* as examples of fictional structures in which characters must make a "truce with the nightmare of survival," a truce they achieve despite the brutality of the world.

Gurko, Leo. "Edward Lewis Wallant as Urban Novelist." *Twentieth Century Literature* 20 (October, 1974): 252-261. Examines Wallant's metaphoric use of the city, which is ugly, perverted, dangerous, and cruel. Gurko claims, however, that in its sprawling vitality, the city also contains "seeds of its own reconstruction."

Lewis, Robert W. "The Hung-Up Heroes of Edward Lewis Wallant." *Renascence* 24 (1972): 70-84. This substantial discussion examines all four of Wallant's novels, especially *The Pawnbroker*, paying particular attention to an analysis of Wallant's sensitive, intellectual characters and to his themes of suffering and rebirth. Lewis also looks at Wallant's use of myth.

Schulz, M. F. "Wallant and Friedman: The Glory and Agony of Love." *Critique: Studies in Modern Fiction* 10 (1968): 31-47. Offers a comparison of Wallant and Bruce Jay Friedman, particularly in their use of humor and the theme of love. Schulz finds Wallant's characters to be examples of growth in sensibility and his novels to be affirmations of order and rebirth.

Stanford, Raney. "The Novels of Edward Wallant." *Colorado Quarterly* 17 (1969): 393-405. Examines some of Wallant's characters and themes, concentrating especially on *The Tenants of Moonbloom* and *The Pawnbroker*. Wallant's characters tend to undergo rebellion which leads to their rebirth. Stanford includes a discussion of Wallant's realistic detail.

JOSEPH WAMBAUGH

Born: East Pittsburgh, Pennsylvania; January 22, 1937

Principal long fiction

The New Centurions, 1970; *The Blue Knight*, 1972; *The Choirboys*, 1975; *The Black Marble*, 1978; *The Glitter Dome*, 1981; *The Delta Star*, 1983; *The Secrets of Harry Bright*, 1985; *The Golden Orange*, 1990.

Other literary forms

In addition to several "nonfiction novels" (*The Onion Field*, 1973; *Lines and Shadows*, 1984; *Echoes in the Darkness*, 1987; *The Blooding*, 1989), Joseph Wambaugh wrote screenplays for the filming of *The Onion Field* (1979) and *The Black Marble* (1980). He also served as creative consultant for television productions of *The Blue Knight* and the series "Police Story."

Achievements

Wambaugh is widely regarded as an outstanding storyteller and the greatest novelist in the field of "police procedure" novels. All of his fiction and nonfiction works have been best-sellers, and he was awarded the Mystery Writers of America Special Award in 1973. Critics have praised Wambaugh's ability to combine objectivity and empathy in realistic depictions of life in a police force. No other novelist has so effectively conveyed the feelings of horror, isolation, despair, frustration, and helplessness experienced daily by police officers, as well as their reactions to these intense psychological pressures. The heroism and cowardice, anger and compassion, dedication and laziness, insight and ignorance of the average police officer on the beat have been brought vividly to life by Wambaugh. His believable portraits of policemen and policewomen are matched by cogent explorations of the sociopathic personalities of the criminals they battle, all of which draw the reader into a complete and compelling world of drugs, crime, alcoholism, and social and moral decay.

Biography

Joseph Aloysius Wambaugh, Jr., was born in 1937 in East Pittsburgh, Pennsylvania, the son of a small-town police chief. Following in his father's footsteps was not young Wambaugh's original intention. He entered the U.S. Marine Corps in 1954 and soon thereafter married his high school sweetheart, Dee Allsup. Discharged in 1957, Wambaugh settled in Ontario, California, where he became a steelworker and went to college part-time at night. He planned to be a teacher and eventually completed both a B.A. and an M.A. in English. In 1960, however, while in his senior year at California State College in Los Angeles, Wambaugh suddenly decided to become a policeman. For the next fourteen years, he worked as a detective in the Los Angeles Police Department (LAPD) and was eventually promoted to sergeant, despite several well-publicized run-ins with his superiors. These conflicts were occasioned by the publication of Wambaugh's first novel, *The New Centurions*, in which the hierarchy of the LAPD was irreverently satirized.

Wambaugh continued to be both detective and novelist until 1974. By this time, he had become so famous that his celebrity status had begun to limit his job effectiveness. He regretfully gave up police work for full-time writing, which he has continued, turning out a new best-seller about every other year. He lives in San Marino, California, with his wife and two children.

Analysis

All Joseph Wambaugh's novels deal with police officers, primarily in Southern California. Their environment is completely outside both the experience and the comprehension of most everyday, middle-class Americans, for it is populated with drug dealers, drifters, pimps, prostitutes, addicts, panhandlers, murderers, thieves, and other dregs of humanity. Supplementing the "bad guys" are the outcasts, outsiders, and victims: welfare mothers and their families, abused children, old and crippled pensioners, illegal immigrants, the mentally incompetent, and the chronically disaffected. Middle-class values have disappeared, and what are usually considered normal attitudes and behaviors seem nonexistent. In the cultures of the barrio, in the ghetto, and even among the wacky rich, police officers are charged with representing and upholding a legal system overwhelmed by the morass of modern society. Because Wambaugh himself was a veteran of the streets, the reader experiences his world through the mind of a policeman: it is full of darkness, desolation, and, above all, a sense of helplessness, for the fate of an individual, as well as the solution to a case, often turns upon trivial, capricious accidents.

This depressing background of urban decay sets the stage on which Wambaugh presents several themes. The most persistent is that real police work is very different from typical public perceptions influenced by television, motion pictures, and traditional police stories, which depict cops as superheroes who always get the bad guys and put them away. Again and again, Wambaugh's police officers express their frustration with juries who demand to know why it takes three officers with nightsticks to subdue a single, unarmed suspect, or why a police officer did not "wing" a fleeing felon rather than shoot him to death. Everyday people who have never had a real fistfight or attempted to aim a weapon at a moving target simply do not understand the realities of these situations. Police officers are not superhuman; they are normal people thrown into extremely abnormal situations.

Often, it seems as if the police are at war with a judicial system that elevates form over substance and technicalities over the determination of guilt or innocence. To the average patrol officer, vice-squad officer, or homicide detective, the courts are arenas where shifty, politically motivated defense lawyers and prosecutors conspire to overturn common sense, where judges and juries view police procedures and conduct with twenty-twenty hindsight, and where the rights of the defendant have triumphed over the suffering of victims. It is the average officer who most often encounters the anguish and suffering of those victims. These experiences alienate and isolate police officers from the rest of "normal" society.

Within the police force itself, the officers on the street are responsible to a hierarchy of "brass" who, for the most part, have never themselves worked a beat. In Wambaugh's view, the brass are primarily concerned with ensuring their own advancement and have little concern for the welfare of their men. He paints high-level officers, often with brutal humor, as buffoons who spend much of their time trying to seduce female officers, avoiding real responsibility, and protecting their reputations.

Given that he is a street veteran himself, Wambaugh's sympathies clearly lie with his former comrades. Yet what makes his novels extraordinary is his realistic appraisal of these officers, warts and all. Many of them are crude racists, and most resent the forced acceptance of women on the force, which began in the 1960's. Attempting to shield themselves from the sheer terror and pain intrinsic to their jobs, they exude cynicism and disgust with nearly everything and everybody, even themselves. They respond to the daily brutality they encounter, and which they must occasionally employ, with gallows humor, sexual promiscuity, alcoholism, and, far too often, "eating their pieces"— suicide.

Wambaugh's first novel, *The New Centurions*, follows the progress of three rookies from their training at the Los Angeles Police Academy in the summer of 1960 to their accidental reunion in the Watts riots of August, 1965. Serge Duran is a former athlete and former marine who has attempted to escape his Chicano heritage; Gus Plebesly is an undersized overachiever who is exceedingly afraid of failure; Roy Fehler thinks of himself as a liberal intellectual making merely a temporary detour from an academic career in criminology. In their development as police officers, all three face situations that force them to examine their beliefs about themselves. Initially assigned as a patrolman in a barrio precinct, Duran meets a Hispanic woman who teaches him not to be ashamed of his ethnic identity. Under the tutelage of a veteran patrolman, Kilvinsky, Plebesly gains the professional and personal assurance to become a competent officer. Fehler, however, fails to reconcile his intellectual views with the emotional realities of race relations on the street: he blinds himself to his own prejudices, tying himself into a psychological knot. His failure is dramatically symbolized at the end of the novel, when he is shot and dies.

The plot of *The New Centurions* develops chronologically and in episodes focusing on each of the rookies in turn. As Duran, Plebesly, and Fehler receive new assignments, Wambaugh takes the opportunity to display the operational peculiarities of the various divisions within the police force—street patrols, vice, homicide, juvenile, and narcotics—as well as to introduce a host of minor characters, both police and civilians, who reveal all the quirks and propensities of their world. Whenever a new character appears, Wambaugh adds believability and depth by interrupting the narrative to discuss some incident that has shaped this person's life and attitudes. These brief digressions are often darkly humorous and also allow Wambaugh to illustrate further the vicissitudes of life in the LAPD.

It is apparent that Wambaugh regards the Watts riots as a kind of watershed for civilized society and the rule of law. Until the summer of 1965, the police force generally dealt with specific crimes committed by and against individuals. The Watts riots, however, represented a fundamental rejection of the structures of lawful authority by almost the entire black community, and the department was astonished and overwhelmed by the senseless violence of mobs of ordinarily law-abiding citizens. At the end of the book, it is clear that, though a few officers seem to have guessed that some sort of qualitative change in social attitudes had occurred, most assumed that the situation would soon return to normal.

One of the main themes of *The Blue Knight*, Wambaugh's second novel, is that the situation did not, in fact, return to normal. Hostile media coverage of the riots focused upon the LAPD's lack of community-relations efforts, incompetence, and alleged brutality, while government investigations reported widespread racism and corruption throughout the department. Stung by criticism, department executives became increasingly image-conscious and ordered significant changes in training and operational procedures. One result was that the time-honored tradition of the individual policeman walking his beat was replaced by the two-person patrol-car unit. In the past, officers generally had been granted a large amount of latitude in dealing with situations on their beats and were usually trusted to keep order as they saw fit. The wise policeman developed a commonsense attitude, allowing certain kinds of violations to slide while others were dealt with immediately and often severely. The new breed of patrol officer, however, was supposed to stay close to his unit, maintain constant radio communication with his precinct, and limit his activities to those precisely within the law. The new policy was intended to ensure both the safety and the good behavior of officers, whose individual initiative was drastically curtailed.

The Blue Knight takes place in the midst of the transition from the old to the new; its main character is a traditional beat officer, William H. "Bumper" Morgan, a twenty-year veteran on the brink of retirement. Wambaugh examines Bumper's last three days on the police force, using the first-person viewpoint to help the reader perceive events directly through Bumper's eyes and ears. Though Bumper has been forced to trade walking his beat for driving a police unit, he insists on working alone and spends most of his shift out of his car and out of radio contact with his precinct.

Bumper's long experience has made him something of a sociologist and philosopher, and his observations represent Wambaugh's slightly irreverent tribute to the old police view of the world. As he makes his rounds, Bumper recalls for the reader many of the events of his twenty years on the force, as well as what he learned from them. Through these recollections, he reveals the essence of his approach to successful police work: never give or accept love, and always remain impersonal and uninvolved on the job. Unfortunately, Bumper's philosophy is a self-delusion. The excitement and danger of police work isolate him from everything and everyone outside of his beat, the only environment in which he is truly in control. In fact he is so completely involved that his life is nothing but his job. Thus, at the end of the story, despite postretirement plans for marriage and a cushy position as a corporate head of security, Bumper decides that he cannot give up his badge.

Though Bumper is clearly meant to be a sympathetic character, Wambaugh also endows him with flaws. He is overweight and indulges himself in vast feasts provided free by the restaurateurs on his beat. He is crude and flatulent, angry and vengeful, egotistic and very expansive in interpreting his powers as a representative of the law. Like many police officers, he imbibes copious amounts of liquor and is certainly no paragon of sexual morality. Sometimes, despite his experience, he even makes stupid mistakes, such as allowing himself to be drawn alone into a dangerous confrontation with student demonstrators. Bumper is softhearted but also tough, violent, and often frustrated. Ultimately, he appears as a tragic figure, unable to break with a career that casts him as a permanent outsider.

After leaving the LAPD in 1974, Wambaugh apparently felt the need to give free rein to some of the anguish and bitterness he felt about his career as a police officer. These emotions are expressed in his third novel, *The Choirboys*, which differs significantly from his previous works in both style and substance. In its structure, grim humor, and overall feeling of hopelessness, *The Choirboys* resembles Joseph Heller's *Catch-22* (1961), with the LAPD substituted for Heller's Army Air Corps. Like the military officers in *Catch-22*, the ten officers who make up the "choirboys" are losers and misfits: several alcoholics, a sadist, a masochist, a violent racist, and the like. Each chapter introduces a new character and relates a series of especially harrowing incidents that lead to the calling of a "choir practice," in which the group meets in a park to get drunk and vie for the sexual favors of two overweight waitresses. Choir practice allows the officers to let off steam and serves as a coping device against the horrifying realities they have faced. The sessions frequently get out of hand, however, and eventually lead to the unintended death of a civilian and the suspension of several of the group.

With its uninhibited street language, unrestrained cynicism, emotional violence, and unrelieved sense of futility, *The Choirboys* is saved only by the brutal hilarity of its bumbling protagonists and the ironies they suffer. The situations into which Wambaugh's policemen stumble are so outrageous that the reader cannot take them very seriously. Thus, even though Wambaugh's characters are incisive and believable, the world in which they operate is so impossibly awful that the reader maintains the objectivity necessary for laughter.

After *The Choirboys*, Wambaugh's novels became both more conventional in structure and more sentimental in tone. His main characters are still losers, and the sense of blind fate and the prominence of coincidence continue to dominate his plots, but, in the end, his protagonists seem to be at least somewhat redeemed; the climaxes always result in some kind of catharsis. Each of his succeeding books revolves around a single case, a kind of puzzle that is resolved, not through brilliant police work, but through dogged determination and serendipitous accidents. An excellent example is his next novel, *The Black Marble*, whose hero is Sergeant Andrei Mikhailovich Valnikov, an absentminded, brokendown alcoholic who is also a consummate and very touching gentleman. Valnikov was once a top homicide detective, but after he investigated a string of cases of sexually abused and brutally murdered children, he developed constant nightmares and started drinking to forget. Eventually, he suffered a breakdown and was reassigned to the robbery division.

Valnikov is paired with Natalie Zimmerman, an ambitious female detective who is bitter generally about the discriminatory attitude of the LAPD toward women and specifically about being stuck with Valnikov. She believes that her Russian-born partner is not only a drunk but crazy as well, especially when he begins to devote all of his still-considerable abilities to the solution of a case she regards as ridiculous: the theft of a prize schnauzer. Wambaugh follows their misadventures in discovering that the dog has been stolen by a trainer seeking to extort money from the owner, a formerly wealthy divorcée now unable to pay the ransom. As always in a Wambaugh novel, along the path to the solution of the case the reader becomes acquainted with a cast of wacky police officers and civilians, until Valnikov finally catches the criminal and wins the love and respect of his partner.

All Wambaugh's subsequent novels have followed the pattern established by *The Black Marble*: the often-coincidental solution of a crime by not-very-heroic police officers or former officers. Though he himself regards *The Choirboys* as his best work, it has not been representative of his style. Nevertheless, in all of his fiction, Wambaugh has explored essentially the same themes: the basic humanity of police officers and the pressures they face, the decline of traditional values in modern society, and the haphazard and accidental nature of fate.

Thomas C. Schunk

Other major works

SCREENPLAYS: *The Onion Field*, 1979; *The Black Marble*, 1980.

NONFICTION: *The Onion Field*, 1973; *Lines and Shadows*, 1984; *Echoes in the Darkness*, 1987; *The Blooding*, 1989.

Bibliography

Jeffrey, David K. "Joseph Wambaugh." In *American Novelists Since World War II*. Vol. 6 in *Dictionary of Literary Biography*, edited by James E. Kibler, Jr. 2d ser. Detroit: Gale Research, 1980. Jeffrey is the only scholar who has devoted much attention to Wambaugh. Here he has culled a brief biography from newspaper articles and offers some analysis and criticism of Wambaugh's works to 1978. Like many critics, Jeffrey admires Wambaugh's ability but does not like police officers. Thus, he is somewhat hostile to Wambaugh's more romantic novels such as *The Black Marble*, in which the hero is ultimately vindicated.

_____. "Joseph Wambaugh." In *Dictionary of Literary Biography Yearbook: 1983*, edited by Mary Bruccoli and Jean W. Ross. Detroit: Gale Research, 1984. Jeffrey updates his discussion of Wambaugh's works to 1983.

"Joseph Aloysius Wambaugh, Jr." In *Current Biography Yearbook: 1980*, edited by Charles Moritz. New York: H. H. Wilson, 1981. In addition to a brief biography, this article contains excerpts of press interviews with Wambaugh and critical evaluations of his works.

"Joseph Aloysius Wambaugh, Jr." In *World Authors, 1970-1975*, edited by John Wakeman. New York: H. H. Wilson, 1980. This brief analytical and critical summary is generally more favorable to Wambaugh than are others.

"Joseph Wambaugh." In *Contemporary Literary Criticism*. Vol. 3, edited by Carolyn Riley. Detroit: Gale Research, 1975. A good survey of longer excerpts from journal reviews of Wambaugh's early works.

"Joseph Wambaugh." In *Contemporary Literary Criticism*. Vol. 18, edited by Sharon R. Gunton. Detroit: Gale Research, 1981. More of the type of excerpts cited above, including reviews of *The Black Marble*.

"Wambaugh." In *Authors in the News*. Vol. 1, edited by Barbara Nykoruk. Detroit: Gale Research, 1979. A compilation of newspaper stories about Wambaugh. Includes two fairly substantial interviews with the writer while he was still a police officer.

ROBERT PENN WARREN

Born: Guthrie, Kentucky; April 24, 1905
Died: Stratton, Vermont; September 15, 1989

Principal long fiction

Night Rider, 1939; *At Heaven's Gate*, 1943; *All the King's Men*, 1946; *World Enough and Time*, 1950; *Band of Angels*, 1955; *The Cave*, 1959; *Wilderness: A Tale of the Civil War*, 1961; *Flood: A Romance of Our Times*, 1964; *Meet Me in the Green Glen*, 1971; *A Place to Come To*, 1977.

Other literary forms

Robert Penn Warren wrote successfully in so many genres that Charles Bohner called him "the pentathlon champion of American literature." In addition to his novels, he published short stories, numerous volumes of poetry, and a considerable amount of nonfiction. Warren's fiction and his poetry often consider the same philosophical themes: the meaning of history, the loss of innocence and the recognition of evil in the fallen world, and the difficulty of finding a moral balance in a world in which traditional Christian values seem to be faltering. For example, in his book-length poem *Brother to Dragons: A Tale in Verse and Voices* (1953), Warren begins with a historical event—a brutal murder of a slave by Thomas Jefferson's nephew, Lilburne Lewis—and creates a philosophical examination of man's fallen nature. Warren does something very similar in his novel *World Enough and Time*. The story is based on a murder which occurred in 1825, but the novel, like the poem, becomes an examination of man's fall from innocence and the difficulty of establishing moral ideals in a fallen world.

Warren's concerns over history and morality are also evident in his earliest, nonfiction works. In his first book, a biography, *John Brown: The Making of a Martyr* (1929), Warren contends that Brown did not tread the path of morality quite so righteously as Ralph Waldo Emerson had thought he had; in his fallen condition, Brown mistook his own egotism for pure idealism. Warren's neo-orthodox insistence on man's fallen nature and his skepticism about the possibilities of pure idealism, both of which are reflected in his novels, led him to accept the traditionalist attitudes of the Southern intellectuals who made up the "Fugitive Group," and he contributed to the Agrarian Manifesto, *I'll Take My Stand* (1930). Warren did, however, espouse a more liberal attitude toward racial matters in his later nonfiction works *Segregation: The Inner Conflict in the South* (1956) and *Who Speaks for the Negro?* (1965).

Warren's social criticism ultimately proved less influential than his literary criticism. His *Selected Essays* (1958) contains perceptive studies of Samuel Taylor Coleridge's *The Rime of the Ancient Mariner*, Joseph Conrad's *No-*

stromo (1904), William Faulkner, Ernest Hemingway, and Katherine Anne Porter. These essays are important not only for what they say about these authors but also for what they reveal about Warren's own work. Even more important than these essays, however, has been Warren's collaboration with Cleanth Brooks. Their textbooks, *Understanding Fiction* (1943, 1959) and *Understanding Poetry* (1938, 1950, 1960), helped to change substantially the way literature was taught in the United States.

Warren continued to publish literary criticism at intervals throughout his life; indeed, *New and Selected Essays* appeared in the year of his death, 1989. Yet with a poetry-writing career that spanned fifty years, he was at least equally well known as a craftsman in that genre. His poems have been widely anthologized, and he is recognized as one of the United States' foremost twentieth century poets.

Achievements

For most readers Warren's name is probably most associated with his novel *All the King's Men*, for which he won both the Pulitzer Prize for Fiction and the National Book Award. He also won the Robert Meltzer Award from the Screen Writer's Guild for the play based on that novel. Warren's short story "Blackberry Winter" has also been highly acclaimed and widely anthologized. Other readers think of Warren primarily as a poet, and with good reason; he has won the Pulitzer Prize for Poetry twice, first for *Promises: Poems 1954-1956* (1957), which also won the Edna St. Vincent Millay Prize and the National Book Award for Poetry, and a second time for *Now and Then: Poems 1976-1978* (1978). *Selected Poems: New and Old, 1923-1966* (1966) won the Bollingen Prize from Yale University, and *Audubon: A Vision* won the Van Wyck Brooks Award and the National Medal for Literature. Warren was elected to the American Philosophical Society in 1952 and to the American Academy of Arts and Sciences in 1959. He was named first poet laureate of the United States in 1986.

Biography

Robert Penn Warren's background and experience had a tremendous impact upon the thematic concerns of his fiction. He demonstrated the need, common to so many Southern writers, to cope with the burden of the past. He also wrote out of a scholar's familiarity with and devotion to certain prominent literary artists, past and present, particularly the Elizabethan and Jacobean dramatists, Joseph Conrad, William Faulkner, and T. S. Eliot. His academic studies, pursued in a long career as an English professor, may have had a great deal to do with the structure of his works and their typically tragic mode. His recurring subject, however, was the peculiar experience of the South; a love-hate relationship with a dying heritage runs throughout his work.

Born to Robert Franklin and Anna Ruth Penn Warren on April 24, 1905, in the tiny Kentucky town of Guthrie, Warren grew up in an almost classic Southern situation. His father, a banker and businessman struggling to support a large family, did not initially fire the young Warren's imagination as his grandfather did. The emotional bond between Warren and his maternal grandfather, Gabriel Thomas Penn, ripened during long summers spent on his grandfather's tobacco farm. Here, Warren experienced the pastoral charms of agrarian life, soaked up the nostalgic glow of the American Civil War from his grandfather, and absorbed the rhetoric and humor that permeates the Southern storytelling.

Gabriel Thomas Penn had been a cavalryman during the Civil War, and many an afternoon with his grandson was spent reliving the legendary time. It is not surprising that the boy looked upon the Civil War as America's great epic, as imbued with nobility and tragedy as Homer's *Iliad* (c. 800 B.C.). He was not blind, however, to the irony and ambiguity of his grandfather, as representative of the values of the aristocratic horse soldier. Warren has commemorated his realization that the romantic image of the Confederate cavalryman had its darker side in the poem "Court Martial" in *Promises: Poems 1954-1956*, which is about his grandfather's hanging of bushwhackers without benefit of legal trial. Since this poem was written much later, however, it is possible that the ambiguous view of the grandfather was partially constructed from a more mature understanding. The event, however, was a true one that evidently made a deep impression on the young Warren. In any case, Warren was absorbing background for a number of later novels, such as *Wilderness: A Tale of the Civil War* and *Band of Angels*. In neither of these does he write as an apologist for the Old South, but he does expose the moral shortcomings of Northerners, much as he does in his early biography of John Brown.

Warren was also absorbing the local tales of tobacco war, when the growers of dark-fired tobacco banded together to boycott the tobacco company that regulated prices. Warren's first novel, *Night Rider*, was written from childhood memories of such local stories. Warren's brother Thomas, who became a grain dealer, knew all the farmers of the region and was adept at repeating such tales.

The young Warren loved nature, collected butterflies, snakes, rocks, leaves, and aspired to paint animals (an interest reflected in his poem about John Audubon). Later, he hunted with his brother and learned taxidermy. These experiences were more important, perhaps, to the content of his poetry than to his fiction. In spite of his persistent affinity for nature, he usually recognized in his fiction its essential amorality: "The blank cup of nature," he calls it in *World Enough and Time*.

In spite of the contribution to his early imaginative development by his grandfather and his agrarian milieu, the influence of Warren's father was subtle and pervasive, perhaps more significant in the long run to the human relationships explored in his novels. Ambiguous father-son relationships appear over and over in such novels as *All the King's Men*, *The Cave*, *At Heaven's Gate*, and *A Place to Come To*. None is modeled after Warren's actual relationship to his own father, but they reflect a combination of admiration, guilt, and mystery that suggests some deep personal involvement in the issues they raise.

Warren has often admitted to an odd sense of guilt about "stealing his father's life." Robert Franklin Warren had wanted to be a lawyer and a poet, but had become a businessman instead, because of financial responsibilities not only to his own family but also to a family of half brothers and sisters left without a provider when his father died. One of Warren's favorite reminiscences was about finding a book with some poems written by his father in it and carrying it with delight to him. His father summarily confiscated the book, and his son never saw it again. Warren thought perhaps his father had been embarrassed or pained at this reminder of a goal long since set aside. According to Warren, his father never regretted the obligations that dictated the terms of his life. Indeed, he took joy in them. Warren speaks with an admiration bordering on awe of the seemingly effortless rectitude of his father, and the ideal relationship between his father and mother.

As the result of an accident when he was fifteen years old, Warren lost the sight of one eye and was thus prevented from pursuing a career as a naval officer, as he had planned. Warren went, instead, to Vanderbilt University and came under the influence of John Crowe Ransom and the Fugitives, a group of academics and townspeople who met regularly to discuss philosophy and poetry. Ransom soon recognized Warren's unusual ability and encouraged him to write poetry.

Warren was graduated summa cum laude from Vanderbilt in 1926 and pursued an M.A. at the University of California at Berkeley. While there, he became an ardent student of Elizabethan and Jacobean drama, which perhaps struck a responsive chord in an imagination already steeped in the violence and melodrama of Southern history. He started to work on a doctorate at Yale University, but left for Oxford, England, as a Rhodes scholar, where he received a Bachelor of Letters Degree in 1930.

During this period, Warren wrote his first book, *John Brown: The Making of a Martyr*. To some extent, this book grew out of an impulse shared with a number of his Vanderbilt friends and other writers of the so-called Southern Renaissance. They were concerned about the exclusively Northern bias of most historians dealing with events leading up to and during the Civil War and its aftermath. Certainly, Warren presents a jaundiced view of the radical abolitionist. Brown seems to have provided a nucleus for Warren's meditations about the effects of power and the misuses of altruism which were to be explored in a number of later novels, especially *Night Rider* and *All the King's*

Men. He also wrote his first fiction while at Oxford, a short story called "Prime Leaf," about the impact of the Kentucky tobacco war on an old man, his son, and his grandson. The old man has a role similar to that of the elder Todd in *Night Rider*, the wise man who bows out of the organization when it resorts to vigilante tactics.

Warren taught at a number of universities, including Louisiana State, where he lived in the legendary ambience of the Southern demagogue Huey Long, whose presence lies behind the fictional Willie Stark of *All the King's Men*. Warren later said that he knew nothing about the real Huey Long, but the mythical Huey was on everyone's lips. Even casual conversations often dwelt upon questions of power and ethics, of means and ends, of "historical costs." In an essay entitled "All the King's Men: The Matrix of Experience," in John Lewis Longley's *Robert Penn Warren: A Collection of Critical Essays* (1965), Warren writes:

> Melodrama was the breath of life. There had been melodrama in the life I had known in Tennessee, but with a difference; in Tennessee the melodrama seemed to be different from the stuff of life, something superimposed upon life, but in Louisiana people lived melodrama, seemed to live, in fact, for it, for this strange combination of philosophy, humor and violence. Life was a tale that you happened to be living—and that "Huey" happened to be living before your eyes.

These remarks demonstrate that Warren was not primarily a historical novelist, but rather a classicist, fascinated with the universal patterns in particular experience. Thus, he discouraged close comparisons between Willie Stark and Huey Long, pointing out that he wrote the first version of the story as a verse drama in Italy, as he watched Benito Mussolini, another man of the people, consolidate his power.

In Warren's writing career, the years from 1944 to 1950, though a dry period for poetry, were productive ones for fiction and literary criticism. Besides *All the King's Men*, he produced *At Heaven's Gate*, about the unscrupulous liaison between government and industry, and *World Enough and Time*, about a nineteenth century murder case. When Warren was poetry consultant for the Library of Congress in 1944-1945, Katherine Anne Porter, who was fiction consultant that year, threw on his desk the confession of Jeroboam Beauchamp, hanged for murder in Kentucky in 1826. Porter announced cryptically that she was giving him a novel. This was, indeed, the germ for his most complex novel, *World Enough and Time*.

Warren's dry period in poetry eventually ended after he divorced his first wife, Emma Brescia, married the writer Eleanor Clark, and fathered two children. He began writing excellent poetry and produced several more novels. A long association with Yale University began in 1950.

In 1986 Warren was named the United States' first poet laureate, a post he held for two years. He died of cancer in 1989, at his summer home in Stratton, Vermont.

Analysis

Often, what Robert Penn Warren said about other writers provides an important insight into his own works. This is especially true of Warren's perceptive essay "The Great Mirage: Conrad and *Nostromo*" in *Selected Essays*, in which he discusses the enigmatic speech of Stein in Joseph Conrad's *Lord Jim* (1900):

> A man that is born falls into a dream like a man who falls into the sea. If he tries to climb out into the air as inexperienced people endeavor to do, he drowns—*nicht wahr?* . . . No! I tell you! The way is to the destructive element submit yourself, and with the exertions of your hands and feet in the water make the deep, deep sea keep you up.

Warren interprets the dream here as "man's necessity to justify himself and his actions into moral significance of some order, to find sanctions." The destructiveness of the dream arises from man's nature as an egotistical animal with savage impulses, not completely adapted to the dream-sea of ideas. The one who learns to swim instead of drowning in the unnatural sea of ideas is he who realizes that the values he creates are illusion, but that "the illusion is necessary, is infinitely precious, is the mark of his human achievement, and is, in the end, his only truth." Warren calls *Nostromo* "a study in the definition and necessity of illusion." This phrase could also describe most of Warren's works of fiction.

Warren's classification of thematic elements in Conrad's stories could also be applied to his own. Warren writes that Conrad is concerned with the man who lacks imagination, but clings to fidelity and duty (like the old captain in *Youth*, 1902); the sinner against human solidarity and the human mission (like Kurtz in *Heart of Darkness*, 1902, and Decoud in *Nostromo*); and the redeemed man (Jim in *Lord Jim* and Dr. Monygham in *Nostromo*). Warren says that Conrad is most interested in the latter—"the crisis of this story comes when the hero recognizes the terms on which he may be saved, the moment, to take Morton Zabel's phrase, of the 'terror of the awakening.'"

One might note that in Warren's novel *At Heaven's Gate*, Jerry's dirt-farmer father fits the pattern of natural rectitude, while Slim Sarrett, the nihilistic, cynical artist, is certainly the sinner against human solidarity. No one seems to be redeemed in *At Heaven's Gate*, though Jerry might have a chance in a hypothetical future, since he has acquired considerable self-knowledge. Mr. Munn in *Night Rider* has also stripped away his own illusions, but he dies, like William Shakespeare's Macbeth, without redemption. In other novels of this period, however, Burden in *All the King's Men*, and perhaps even the murderer in *World Enough and Time*, achieve some kind of absolution. Warren and Conrad share this deep obsession with the need for redemption, and though the sentiment is religious and may be expressed in Christian imagery, it is consistently humanistic in emphasis. The world they both recognize is a naturalistic one, but man must live in two worlds, the world of facts and the world of ideas, which he creates himself. Warren's notion of submission to the realm of ideas is analogous, perhaps, to Ernest Hemingway's code of the hunter, the fisherman, the bullfighter, or the soldier, which provides existential meaning in a meaningless world.

Warren's early novels, particularly *Night Rider*, *All the King's Men*, and *World Enough and Time*, which critics generally agree are his best, trace a pattern of increasing complexity in the theme of man's vacillation between the fantasy of dreams and the reality of facts. After *World Enough and Time*, which is almost too densely packed and convoluted in theme, Warren relaxed his insistence that everything must be said on the subject of illusion and reality in one novel. Later works, such as *Meet Me in the Green Glen* and *Wilderness: A Tale of the Civil War*, though not conspicuously different in theme, concentrate on a particular manifestation of the problem—on the nature of love in *Meet Me in the Green Glen*, and on the nature of altruism in *Wilderness*.

Actually, Warren's examination of the apposition between the world of ideas and the world of facts begins in his first book, *John Brown: The Making of a Martyr*. Warren portrays the militant abolitionist as not so much obsessed with freeing slaves as with starring in his own myth. Brown is encouraged in this role by the unqualified praise of Ralph Waldo Emerson, whom Warren believed to be a writer of empty words, with little perception of the real world; Warren quotes Emerson as saying of Brown, "He is a man to make friends wherever on earth courage and integrity are esteemed—the rarest of heroes, a pure idealist, with no by-ends of his own." Warren did not for a moment believe that Brown was a "pure idealist"; moreover, Warren had a continuing distrust of "pure idealists," whoever they might be. In his fiction, Warren was inclined to show abstract idealists as lacking in self-knowledge, capable of self-righteous violence because they refuse to acknowledge their own irrational impulses. The best example of this personality-type in Warren's fiction is Adam Stanton, in *All the King's Men*, who assassinates Willie Stark because Willie, the man of fact, seduced Adam's sister.

John Brown, however, as a man who uses exalted ideas to inflate his own self-image, is more akin to Warren's Professor Ball, Dr. MacDonald, and Mr. Munn of *Night Rider*; Bogan Murdock, the industrialist, and Slim Sarett, of *At Heaven's Gate*; and Wilkie Barron, the manipulative false friend of Jeremiah Beaumont, in *World Enough and Time*. Willie Stark, though categorized by Jack Burden as the "man of fact," in contrast to Adam Stanton, the "man of idea," has his own idealistic dream of the people's hospital, free to anyone who needs it. Whether that dream was truly altruistic, however, or tinged by the secret need for a personal monument to his existence, is ambiguous.

Thus, Warren suggests that the self is itself part of the dream-sea of ideas. Warren's protagonists are often initially passive persons whose emptiness is filled by other more dynamic personalities. Having acquired a somewhat fictitious self under such influence, they proceed to act in the real world as though that dream were true—often with tragic results. Thus, Mr. Munn seems an innocuous, ordinary young lawyer when he first appears in *Night Rider*, but he is drawn irresistibly to his more dynamic friend, Mr. Christian, who has a legitimate concern for the plight of the tobacco growers at the mercy of the price-controlling tobacco company. Munn learns to savor his new role as labor leader. He is ripe, then, for indoctrination by more conniving, professional agitators, Professor Ball and Dr. MacDonald, who preach a secret society that will scrape the fields of uncooperative growers and punish backsliders who dare to violate the embargo. What begins as a lawful strike by the downtrodden majority becomes a lawless vigilante group that destroys crops, burns warehouses, and commits murder. In the case of Munn, the crisis of this psychic change in direction comes when he realizes that his assigned task to assassinate the tobacco farmer Bunk Trevelyon, whom he once defended in court on a murder charge, is not only his "duty" to the group; it satisfies something very personal in himself that he has not yet recognized. Trevelyon had committed the murder of which he was once accused, and the black who was hanged for that murder was innocent. Trevelyon thus becomes the symbol for Munn's half-conscious cooperation in framing the black, or, to use another favorite term of Warren, Munn's original sin. In this ritual of retribution, the shared myth of community justice fuses with Munn's private myth of killing the shadow-self, an act of both self-condemnation and deliberate concealment of a secret crime.

After this private confrontation and ritual killing of his shadow-self, Munn makes no more moral objections to anything Ball and MacDonald want to do. The three lead a concerted assault on the company warehouses, which results in a number of casualties. One person who dies is young Benton Todd, who had been an ardent admirer of Munn. Moreover, Todd hoped to marry Mr. Christian's daughter, Lucille, who has been having a secret affair with Munn. If Trevelyon symbolizes the murderous shadow-self that Munn has hated to acknowledge, Benton Todd suggests the lost idealism, the better dream that Munn has betrayed.

Munn's subsequent flight to the West to escape prosecution for a murder he did not commit might have resulted in redemption, but it does not. The pattern of redemption is presented to him obliquely by the story of Proudfit, the impoverished farmer who is sheltering Munn. Proudfit tells of his own checkered career in the West, as a buffalo hunter and hide-tanner, with companions as rough and wild as himself. Eventually, however, he lives in peace among Indians. When he becomes ill, the Indians care for him, using all their resources of natural healing and religious ritual. In his fever, he eventually has a vision of Kentucky, where he was reared, and a young woman waiting beside a stream. His strength then begins to return, so he leaves the Indian friends and goes back to find the very woman he saw in his vision, now his wife, and the very hill he saw, which is now his farm.

Proudfit's story is both an engrossing dialect narrative and a unique version of the underlying myth of death and resurrection. Proudfit's humble redemption contrasts with the myth of sin and damnation implied in Munn's career. Both Proudfit and Munn have a period of withdrawal (Proudfit, among the Indians; Munn, on Proudfit's remote farm), time to rethink their past lives and future goals. This experience is analogous, perhaps, to the withdrawal and contemplation that the mythic hero undergoes before he returns to his homeland as a new man. Munn, however, is not transformed. He does become mildly obsessed with the innocent black who died in Trevelyon's stead, but he cannot even remember the man's name. Perhaps his inability to name the scapegoat is intended to suggest Munn's distance from the redemption offered by Christ's sacrifice. This does not mean that Warren was advocating Christianity; he was admitting, at least, a moral vacuum where traditional values have been eliminated in a society concerned primarily with power and wealth.

The polarity of idea and fact receives more explicit development in *All the King's Men*. Again, an essentially passive person, Jack Burden, feeds emotionally on a more dynamic personality, Willie Stark. Burden calls himself— somewhat cynically—an idealist, but his idealism consists mostly of a fastidious preference for not getting his hands dirty with some of Stark's more questionable political maneuvers. Stark is good-naturedly tolerant of Burden's moral preferences, since he has Tiny Duffy to do his dirty work.

Burden considers himself a good judge of character and motives, but when a cherished image about the purity and goodness of his old girlfriend, Anne Stanton, is proven to be false, he is devastated and lost in self-doubt. Anne, who is quite a passive, unfulfilled person herself, has become Stark's mistress. Burden's first impulse is to flee, to escape, to drown, to fall into what he calls the Great Sleep. From this symbolic death, Burden is born again into a bleak but emotionally insulating belief in the Great Twitch—an understanding of the world as completely amoral and mechanistic, wherein no one has any responsibility for what happens. Here, indeed, Burden has stepped out of the fantasy of dreams into the reality of facts.

Burden can now consent to let Stark use the information he has uncovered concerning Judge Irwin's long-forgotten political crime. Burden soon discovers how brutal the world of fact can be, when Judge Irwin's suicide reveals that the judge was actually Burden's own father. Hardly recovered from this blow, Burden recognizes a measure of responsibility for the deaths of Willie Stark and his best friend, Adam Stanton, who is shot by Willie's bodyguard after the assassination. Through his passivity and noninvolvement, Jack Burden had virtually handed over Anne Stanton to his more dynamic boss, and thus set the stage for assassination.

The novel is a fascinating study of symbiotic relationships, of which the most striking is that between Willie Stark, the practical politician, and Adam Stanton, the puritanical idealist and perfectionist. Warren also suggests a politically symbiotic relationship between the demagogue and the people he represents. In social terms, the world of *All the King's Men* is more complex than that of *Night Rider*. Munn's career is essentially that of the tragic hero, the good but not exclusively good man who is corrupted by power. Willie Stark, however, is sustained not only by his own drive for power, but also by the concerted will of his constituency, who feel themselves to be socially and politically helpless. He is probably more significant as an antidote to their depression than as an answer to their physical needs. Even though Willie wants to change the world of facts for their benefit—build roads, bridges, a free hospital—it is for his psychological impact, exemplifying the triumph of the common man over the privileged elite, that he is beloved. Thus, even the man of facts floats in the symbolic sea of ideas.

If the relationship between dream and reality is complicated in *All the King's Men*, in *World Enough and Time* it becomes intricately complex. Seldom have human aspirations been so relentlessly exposed, one after another, as frail illusions. Though it might be termed a historical novel, since it is based loosely on an actual event, or a philosophical novel, since it comments repeatedly on the abstract meaning of human behavior and aspiration, *World Enough and Time* is better termed a psychological novel, or more precisely, perhaps, an examination of the psychological motivations for philosophizing. It is certainly not, like Andrew Marvell's poem "To His Coy Mistress," to which the title ironically alludes, a neat argument for seizing pleasures while one may. It is not a neat argument for any philosophical position, but it illuminates the sequential confusion of a reasonably thoughful, well-meaning person trying to identify himself and justify his actions.

Jeremiah Beaumont, the orphaned son of an unsuccessful Kentucky farmer in the early nineteenth century, becomes the loved protégé of Colonel Cassius Fort, a well-known lawyer and statesman of the region. Jerry's exalted view of Colonel Fort receives a cruel blow from his dashing friend Wilkie Barron, a popular man-about-town and dabbler in politics. Wilkie tells Jerry of a beautiful woman he once loved in vain, who was seduced by an older man who had come to console her when her father died. When the young woman, Rachel Jordan, had a stillborn child, the older man abandoned her. The knave who wronged her was the unimpeachable Colonel Fort.

The persuasive Wilkie succeeds in promoting in a somewhat passive Jerry a romantic vision of wronged womanhood. From this point on, Jerry creates his own drama of love and revenge, though Wilkie continues to manipulate him in ways he never understands until near the end of his life. Jerry repudiates Colonel Fort, his surrogate father, and woos and eventually wins the lovely Rachel, who is in a neurotic state of depression, not because of the supposed perfidy of Colonel Fort, but because of her baby's death. Jerry, blind to the real source of her despondency, hounds her into commanding him to defend her honor. Fort refuses a duel with Jerry, however, and the honorable vengeance seems destined to fizzle. Rachel is again pregnant, and Jerry is fitting into the comfortable role of country squire. An unknown messenger brings to Rachel a slanderous handbill in which Colonel Fort, presumably denying to his political opponents his affair with Rachel, claims that Rachel had slept with a slave. Fort had gallantly claimed paternity of the child as a chivalric gesture. This shocking document, which is actually a forgery written by Wilkie Barron, precipitates Rachel's labor, and Jerry's child is also born dead. Jerry, in remorse, kills Fort—not openly in a duel, as he had planned, but secretly, letting it appear to be a political assassination.

Jerry's trial is a bewildering process where deceit and truth become inextricably mixed. Wilkie Barron appears, however, and reveals Jerry's vow to kill Fort, the reaction Wilkie had himself orchestrated even before Jerry had met the wronged lady. All is lost, and Jerry is sentenced to hang. Rachel comes and stays with him in his basement jail cell, where they indulge in a passionate interlude—a veritable frenzy of love in the face of imminent death.

The unpredictable Wilkie appears at the last minute, after the lovers have unsuccessfully tried to commit suicide by drinking laudanum. Wilkie rescues them and sends them West to live in the desolate island refuge of a notorious bandit. This is a return to nature, but a nature devoid of its original innocence, incapable of healing the scars of "civilization." Jerry sinks into a bestial pattern and Rachel into insanity, eventually killing herself. Jerry, who finds out that the slanderous handbill came from Wilkie Barron, is himself murdered as he seeks to find his way back to the hangman, resigned now to the most austere prize of all—neither love nor honor, but simply knowledge.

The flight to the West seems an almost gratuitous extension of suffering, especially since the real Jereboam Beauchamp, who murdered Colonel Solomon Sharp in 1825, did hang for his crime. The real trial and death of Beauchamp and his wife, Ann Cook, were only slightly less miserable, however, than Warren's fictional account.

Warren's extension to allow further demoralization of the lovers does help to explore all possible approaches to the problem of reconciling the ideal and the real. At first, Jerry believes that the idea must redeem the world: the mental context defines the object. Unfortunately, this route leads to an idealism divorced from action and allows a further evil to develop in the world—the death of his child. Then he believes that the world will redeem the idea—that is, the act of killing Fort will vindicate the idea of honor. In his flight to the West, he commits a third error, the opposite to his first: to deny the idea completely and embrace the physical world—"to seek communion only in the blank cup of nature."

Perhaps this tortured journey through innocence and experience should arrive at some reconciliation of opposites, but, if so, that too seems more dream than reality. "There must be a way whereby the word becomes flesh," muses Jerry in his last days. Even so, "I no longer seek to justify. I seek only to suffer." If this is not a particularly lucid analysis of philosophical possibilities, it may nevertheless be true psychologically to the mental and moral confusion in which men live. Perhaps it is intended to represent that "terror of the awakening" which Warren remarks in Conrad's *Lord Jim* when the "hero recognizes the terms on which he may be saved. . . ."

In his later novels, Warren continued to deal with the tension between the ideal and the real. The central mystery is usually the self, which the protagonist does not know except through a painful dialectic between exalted idea and gross fact. The protagonist also suffers from an inability to identify his real father or the real home where he belongs. Jack Burden and Jeremiah Beaumont both have several surrogate fathers, but they are responsible for the deaths of those to whom they owe the greatest filial loyalty. In *At Heaven's Gate*, Jerry Calhoun rejects his real father, the man of natural rectitude and love, and gives his devotion to Bogan Murdock, who, in Conrad's phrase, is hollow at the core.

Even in Warren's last novel, *A Place to Come To*, the protagonist's first act is to despise his father and flee from his homeland; his last is to return to his hometown and make peace with the gentle stepfather he had never wanted to meet and the deaf father who had humiliated him as a child. As Warren wrote in "The Ballad of Billie Potts," the son must always return to the father, who often represents the flawed and fallen world which is our heritage.

The struggle between the ideal and the real in Warren's later novels is most explicit in *Wilderness: A Tale of the Civil War*, about an idealistic young Jew from Bavaria who comes to the United States to fight for the freedom of the slaves. When his father, a political prisoner in Berlin, dies, Adam Rosenzweig realizes that he has "lived only in the dream of his father's life, the father's manhood, the father's heroism." The trip to America is a way to star in his own heroic story. Adam's career in America is a progress in disillusionment; the telltale symbol of the compromising world of physical fact is his clubfoot, which he has desperately sought to hide in a specially constructed boot. If *World Enough and Time* is Warren's most complex treatment of idealism, *Wilderness* is his most direct treatment of this recurring subject, uncluttered by secondary themes or plots. Some critics prefer it for that reason, though it lacks the depth and humanity of Warren's earlier epic treatment of romantic idealism.

Meet Me in the Green Glen is a pastoral novel about the nature of love. The love of a homeless young Italian immigrant for a dowdy country wife begins with carnal passion devoid of any attempt to idealize sexual attraction. The ironically named Angelo has distinct similarities to Conrad's "natural man," Nostromo, who lives in the physical world with little thought of any other. In fact, Angelo protects himself from any really serious bond with Cassie, the frustrated wife of a paralyzed man, casting her in the more tawdry dream of "scarlet woman" with gifts of a tight red dress and cosmetics. Only at the last, when she pleads for his life in court by confessing to the murder of her husband, of which Angelo is accused, does he recognize a love that transcends the merely physical. Just as Adam in *Wilderness* becomes more human when he admits the strength of flawed reality, so Angelo becomes more human when he recognizes the strength of dreams. In spite of Cassie's confession, Angelo is condemned to die, because, in his ignorance of the racial situation, he violates the mores of the community. Cassie, unable to save her lover, drifts off in the dream-sea of ideas, forgetting the sordid elements of their affair and only retaining the dream that transcends the body's need.

In these and other episodes in his fiction, Warren showed his fascination with what he called, in his Conrad essay, "the Great Mirage." It is a dark vision which sees all human values as illusions, yet insists—with the passion which fueled six decades of creative work—that such illusions are necessary, and that man must continue to invent himself.

Katherine Snipes

Other major works

SHORT FICTION: *Blackberry Winter*, 1946; *The Circus in the Attic and Other Stories*, 1947.

PLAY: *All the King's Men*, 1958.

POETRY: *Thirty-Six Poems*, 1935; *Eleven Poems on the Same Theme*, 1942; *Selected Poems 1923-1943*, 1944; *Brother to Dragons: A Tale in Verse and Voices*, 1953; *Promises: Poems 1954-1956*, 1957; *You, Emperors, and Others: Poems 1957-1960*, 1960; *Selected Poems: New and Old, 1923-1966*, 1966; *Incarnations: Poems 1966-1968*, 1968; *Audubon: A Vision*, 1969; *Homage to Theodore Dreiser on the Centennial of His Birth*, 1971; *Or Else—Poem/Poems 1968-1974*, 1974; *Selected Poems: 1923-1975*, 1976; *Now and Then: Poems 1976-1978*, 1978; *Brother to Dragons: A New Version*, 1979; *Being Here: Poetry 1977-1980*, 1980; *Ballad of a Sweet Dream of Peace*, 1980 (with Bill Komodore); *Rumor Verified: Poems 1979-1980*, 1981; *Chief Joseph of the Nez Percé*, 1983; *New and Selected Poems, 1923-1985*, 1985.

NONFICTION: *John Brown: The Making of a Martyr*, 1929; *An Approach to Literature: A Collection of Prose and Verse with Analysis and Discussions*, 1936 (with Cleanth Brooks and John Thibaut Purser); *Understanding Poetry: An Anthology for College Students*, 1938, 1950, 1960 (with Cleanth Brooks); *Understanding Fiction*, 1943, 1959 (with Cleanth Brooks); *Modern Rhetoric*, 1949 (with Brooks; better known as *Fundamentals of Good Writing: A Handbook of Modern Rhetoric*); *Segregation: The Inner Conflict in the South*, 1956; *Selected Essays*, 1958; *The Legacy of the Civil War: Meditations on the Centennial*, 1961; *Who Speaks for the Negro?*, 1965; *Faulkner: A Collection of Critical Essays*, 1966; *Randall Jarrell, 1914-1965*, 1967 (with Robert Lowell and Peter Taylor); *American Literature: The Makers and the Making*, 1974 (with R. W. B. Lewis); *Democracy and Poetry*, 1975; *Portrait of a Father*, 1988; *New and Selected Essays*, 1989.

Bibliography

Bohner, Charles. *Robert Penn Warren*. 1964. Rev. ed. Boston: Twayne, 1981. An excellent all-purpose introduction, divided into thematic sections with subdivisions. Provides a chronology, notes, and an index. Also includes a bibliography in which secondary sources receive brief summaries regarding their merit and suitability.

Casper, Leonard. *Robert Penn Warren: The Dark and Bloody Ground*. Seattle: University of Washington Press, 1960. The first full-length study of Warren in English. Still valuable for Casper's effort to establish Warren's place in American letters credibly and with more reluctance than some successors to be effusively enthusiastic. Especially good in explicating Warren's novels. Contains an index identifying themes and a bibliography identifying much early Warren criticism.

Clark, William Bedford. *Critical Essays on Robert Penn Warren*. Boston: G. K. Hall, 1981. This study provides reviews from *John Brown* (1929) to Harold Bloom on *Brother to Dragons: A New Version* (1979). Separate essays include James Justus showing how Warren has created a myth out of the figure of Samuel Taylor Coleridge's Ancient Mariner, and Victor Strandberg demonstrating that Warren reconciles an awareness of evil with a Whitmanesque unity of being.

Gray, Richard, ed. *Robert Penn Warren: A Collection of Critical Essays*. Englewood Cliffs, N.J.: Prentice-Hall, 1980. Many of the essays in this collection date from the 1960's, and about two-thirds of them deal with Warren's novels. Represented in the volume are a number of recognized Warren specialists, among them James Justus, Leonard Casper, and Victor Strandberg. A competent and comprehensive essay prefaces the volume, which contains a short bibliography helpful to the general student.

Justus, James. *The Achievement of Robert Penn Warren*. Baton Rouge: Louisiana State University Press, 1981. Provides chapters on Warren's poetry, nonfiction prose, and novels. Develops the thesis that Warren's deepest conviction is that self-knowledge requires a diminution of the self, a capitulation to others: "His creatures, if they are lucky, can claim both individuality and brotherhood."

Strandberg, Victor. *The Poetic Vision of Robert Penn Warren*. Lexington: University Press of Kentucky, 1977. Strandberg attempts to treat Warren's poetry from three perspectives, "poems of passage, the undiscovered self, and mysticism." He admits that Warren's place as a poet is still very much in dispute and that Warren has exerted little influence on his contempo-

raries, but insists that his neglect is unjustified and largely attributable to
his success as a novelist.

Walker, Marshall. *Robert Penn Warren: A Vision Earned.* New York: Barnes
& Noble Books, 1979. Offers a comprehensive treatment of Warren's canon
well into the seventh decade of his life. Discussion and analysis are provided for major and minor works as Walker traces the development of
Warren's thought over a period of roughly fifty years, taking into consideration the contributions of a number of earlier critics. A chronology and a
bibliography are attached.

FRANK WATERS

Born: Colorado Springs, Colorado; July 25, 1902

Principal long fiction

Fever Pitch, 1930 (also known as *The Lizard Woman*); *The Wild Earth's Nobility*, 1935; *Below Grass Roots*, 1937; *The Dust Within the Rock*, 1940; *People of the Valley*, 1941; *River Lady*, 1942 (with Houston Branch); *The Man Who Killed the Deer*, 1942; *The Yogi of Cockroach Court*, 1947; *Diamond Head*, 1948 (with Houston Branch); *The Woman at Otowi Crossing*, 1966; *Pike's Peak: A Family Saga*, 1971 (completely rewritten, one-volume novel based on *The Wild Earth's Nobility*, *Below Grass Roots*, and *The Dust Within the Rock*); *Flight from Fiesta*, 1986.

Other literary forms

In addition to his long fiction, Frank Waters has written a number of books which combine history, ethnography, mythology, and speculative essay. All of these are centered in the American Southwest, and all deal, in whole or in part, with American Indian subjects. Of these, *Book of the Hopi* (1963) comes closest to ethnography in the strict sense, being the actual Hopi versions of their mythology, ritual, and belief, which Waters recorded from the words of tribal spokesmen. *Masked Gods: Navaho and Pueblo Ceremonialism* (1950) covers analogous material in relation to the Navaho and Pueblo tribes, and contains substantial sections in which these traditional beliefs are compared to the teachings of the Far East (particularly Tibetan Buddhism) and with the findings of nuclear scientists. *Pumpkin Seed Point: Being Within the Hopi* (1969) is a personal account of Waters' three-year residence among the Hopi, while he was compiling material for *Book of the Hopi*. *Mexico Mystique: The Coming Sixth World of Consciousness* (1975) treats the history, myth, and science (particularly calendrical) of Mexico. *Mountain Dialogues* (1981) is more eclectic in style, a series of essays ranging in subject matter from the relation of mind and matter to the bipolar symbolism reflected in the land around Waters' New Mexico home.

Waters' three biographies all deal with Western subjects: *Midas of the Rockies: The Story of Stratton and Cripple Creek* (1937) is the biography of Winfield Scott Stratton; *To Possess the Land* (1973) is the biography of Arthur Rochford Manby. *The Earp Brothers of Tombstone* (1960) is based on the recollections of Mrs. Virgil Earp and material from Waters' own research.

In 1946, Waters published *The Colorado* as part of the Rivers of America series (Farrar and Rinehart), and in 1964, an art monograph, *Leon Gaspard*. From 1950 to 1956, he was a regular contributor to the *Saturday Review* with reviews on books about the West. Numerous periodicals contain his essays on ethnography, history, and literary criticism, as well as a few short stories.

Achievements

Waters has given the American Southwest its finest and most complete literary rendering. In both his fiction and his nonfiction, he has sought to give literary vitality to the "spirit of place" imbuing that section of the American continent, and to show how this spirit variously affects the different races who live there, finding its expression in mythology, life-style, architecture, and ritual, all reflecting, in their different ways, the "vibratory quality of the land itself." Whether he portrays life by presenting the facts of history (as in his nonfiction), or in the symbols of his novels, or whether he writes about the mythological realm which occupies the zone between the two, his work captures the deep resonance of his locale, and thus the significance of place, per se, to man's development.

Waters is probably best known for his work on and about American Indians, and he is one of the few writers whose work has earned the respect of both the literary establishment and the American Indian communities. He is also one of the few writers who has worked successfully both in ethnography and in prose fiction. His firsthand knowledge of the Indian tribes of the Southwest and his deep respect for their traditions and their instinctual attunement to their locale have made it possible for Waters to write about these matters without romanticism, and thus to reveal not only the rugged dignity of their lives but also the value of their wisdom.

Thus, *The Man Who Killed the Deer*, Waters' most popular novel, has long been recognized as a classic in the literature on the American Indian, just as *Book of the Hopi* is a landmark in ethnography. In the late twentieth century, the relevance and quality of his other work resulted in a greater degree of recognition, made tangible by the republication of much of his fiction.

Biography

Frank Waters was born on July 25, 1902, and spent most of his childhood and youth in Colorado Springs. These years provided much of the material for his early novels *The Wild Earth's Nobility, Below Grass Roots*, and *The Dust Within the Rock* and consequently for their revised version, *Pike's Peak*. Waters' grandfather became the model for Joseph Rogier, the main character of these books, and Waters' boyhood experience in the Cripple Creek mining camps provided much of the background. His experiences as an engineering student at Colorado College (from 1922 to 1925) and as a day-laborer in the Salt Creek oil fields are also incorporated into these early novels.

After his work at Salt Creek, Waters traveled to California, where he was employed by the telephone company in the border town of Calexico-Mexicali. It was there, among imported Chinese laborers, opium dens, and general degradation, that he came across Tai Ling, who became the protagonist of *The Yogi of Cockroach Court*. This novel was actually drafted before the above-mentioned Colorado novels, but technical problems prevented its completion until some years later.

The move to California marks a dividing line in Waters' treatment of his material. The personal experiences from before the move went into novels of a semiautobiographical nature. Those which drew their material from after the move were not autobiographical, though they continued to draw their characters from people Waters knew, their settings from places he had lived, and even their incidents from actual events. (The ending of *The Yogi of Cockroach Court*, for example, was taken directly from newspaper accounts.)

From the Mexican-American border, Waters moved to the town of Mora in the Sangre de Cristo Mountains of New Mexico. There he wrote *The Dust Within the Rock* and planned *People of the Valley*, drawing again on his youth in Colorado. The latter novel takes its material from the Mora locale, an isolated valley that is inaccessible for most of the year and was settled by Spanish-speaking people from Mexico. It was in Mora, too, that Waters witnessed the rituals of the Penitente cult, which he incorporated into the novel.

After leaving Mora, Waters moved to Taos. From there, in the late 1930's, he drew the material (again, based on actual events) for *The Man Who Killed the Deer*, and later for two nonfiction works, *Masked Gods* and *Mountain Dialogues*. He continued to make Taos his home, returning there after the war and working as editor for *El Crepusculo*, a local Spanish-English newspaper; he also worked from 1953 to 1956 as an information consultant at the Los Alamos Scientific Laboratory. These latter two positions are reflected in *The Woman at Otowi Crossing*, though it is evident from *Masked Gods*, published sixteen years earlier, that Waters had long been concerned with the curious juxtaposition of atomic research facilities and Indian kivas in the Four Corners area. At present, Waters lives in the village of Arroyo Seco, near Taos in northern New Mexico.

In 1977 Waters was married to Barbara Hayes; thereafter the couple divided their time between homes in Taos and Tucson, Arizona. In his later years Waters has devoted his attention principally to the writing of nonfiction.

Analysis

The writing of Frank Waters is always concerned with the bipolar tensions which underlie human existence: male and female, reason and instinct, conscious and unconscious, progress and tradition, linear and nonlinear, matter and energy (or spirit). His fictional characters are involved in efforts to reconcile these polarities, either within themselves or in the world of events. The search for reconciliation is inseparable from what Waters has called "the spirit of place," for once one is able to embody the unconscious rhythms of one's locale, one may move more completely toward the reconciliation of bipolar tensions.

In another sense, his work is a continuing attempt to give literary expression to this spirit of place. Viewed sociologically, his novels show how this spirit imbues the various racial types of the Southwest. The spirit of place is found in the blood, is experienced as a "blood-power" from which one can never quite break free. Because of these instinctual or biological ramifications, the novels about "racial types" are not mere sociological studies, but expressions of a spiritual search.

Waters has said that the three novels *People of the Valley, The Man Who Killed the Deer*, and *The Yogi of Cockroach Court* express his interest in the racial types of the West: the Spanish or Mexican, the Indian, and the Mestizos, or those of mixed blood. *The Woman at Otowi Crossing*, which deals primarily with whites, completes this study of racial types. *Pike's Peak: A Family Saga* portrays the mingling of various racial types, but here, Pike's Peak itself is portrayed as an active agent.

Thus, this late novel makes graphic what in the previous novels was a subtle but powerful undercurrent: in all of Waters' work, the Earth itself plays a dominant role. It is the matrix which reconciles polarity. Fruitful and destructive by turns, benevolent or menacing, it resists man's efforts at domination or comprehension, yet demands of him that continuing process of individuation which is inseparable from the reconciliation of polarity. The Earth, the source of life, embodies a mystery which cannot be overcome but must be understood through faith. As the beginning and end of man's essential polarities (such as life and death, summer and winter), it is both a material fact and a rhythmic energy with which one must be in harmony.

Harmony, however, does not indicate a static equilibrium. Waters' novels end with reconciliation, yet the reconciliation leads to ongoing movement. As Waters points out in an explication of the Nahuatl hieroglyph "Ollin" ("Movement"), the tension between dualities results in movement. This movement is found not only in the processes of the natural world but also inside the heart of man. This ancient Nahuatl concept is reflected in all of Waters' novels. The central reconciliation is in the human heart, as the characters attempt to find that harmony in movement that enables them to be part of the great pattern of Creation.

People of the Valley was Waters' first nonautobiographical novel to be published. The most obvious social polarity—progress and tradition—is the main impetus of the plot. The government is going to build a dam which will uproot all the people of the Beautiful Blue Valley. The name is significant: the color blue symbolizes the abiding faith of the people in their traditional ways, and in the faithful fruitfulness of the valley itself. (This symbolic use of the color blue returns in other novels, most notably *The Man Who Killed the Deer*, where Dawn Lake, the center of the Pueblo religious life, is referred to as the "Blue Eye of Faith.") In this period, when their faith is threatened, the people of the valley look to Maria, a local bruja, for her reaction and her strength, her wisdom and her faith.

Maria has been in the Beautiful Blue Valley for as long as anyone can remember, and has become, in the minds of its inhabitants, synonymous with the valley itself. She knows its secrets and its cures and has lived through its periods of fruitfulness and flood. She is, then, an embodiment of the spirit of place; by turns, she is a goad and a comfort, a shrewd businesswoman and a prophet. As the story progresses (a chapter is devoted to each period of her life), it becomes clear why she is the repository of the implicit faith of the people: she is trusted because of her own implicit trust in the Earth, in the essential trustworthiness of its rhythms, even of its floods. Because she accepts the Earth in all of its many moods, she is the spokesperson for its wisdom. Like the Earth, she can be sharp and repelling, or healing and comforting. Like the Earth, she accepts all who come to her, whether as lovers, questioners, or even husbands. Within change, however, she abides in a faith that grows, year by year.

In addition, Maria makes the welfare of the Earth—of the valley—synonomous with her own welfare. She has reconciled the duality of self and other by making her own wealth inseparable from that of the valley, and hence of its people. The clearest example of this comes from her early life, when, destitute, she survived by gathering discarded wheat-seed from the local fields. This seed she divided into superior and inferior. The latter she used for food; the former she kept until spring, when she would trade it for a double measure to be collected at the next harvest. This process she repeated yearly. Because she kept the best seed for replanting, the wealth of the valley's wheat increased; because she received a double measure at harvest, her own wealth increased as well. Her wealth, however, was never monetary; rather, it was in the natural yield of the Earth, and in the faith that such a yield is sufficient for all purposes.

In the end, it is this faith that makes Maria significant. Faith, too, is the essence of the people of the valley, and of their traditions. Without such faith, life there is not possible. This faith, as she points out, is not a concept, but a baptism into life itself, into the rhythmic experience of harmony, which comes from giving oneself wholly to the spirit and energy of one's locale, the spirit of place. The significance of the dam is that it stops the flow of faith, which is likened to water. Faith refreshes life and gives it meaning; the dam causes stagnation, a break in natural rhythms. The example of Maria shows, however, that if one's faith is deep enough, it will not be disrupted by surface events. In the end, this faith is in the heart, and what one sees in the external world corresponds to one's inner nature.

The idea of faith carries over into Waters' next novel, *The Man Who Killed the Deer*. Whereas Maria had grown slowly into her faith, and had never been torn from it, Martiniano must find a faith within the exacerbated polarities of his nature. The disruptions of progress had not come to Maria until she was an old woman; they come to Martiniano during his formative years.

Because of this, his search is one of finding what he has lost, not simply deepening what he already knows.

Half Apache and half Pueblo, Martiniano's mixed blood indicates the duality of his nature, the spirit of independence and rebellion opposed to the spirit of acceptance and harmony. Sent away to a government school at an early age and thus deprived of his initiation into the kiva at the proper age, Martiniano must be taught to find harmony, not only with his world but also within himself, where the pole of masculine independence has not recognized the pole of the female imperative.

The story of the novel is, on the surface, a simple one. Martiniano has killed a deer out of season, against the regulations of the United States government as it is against those of the pueblo. The matter seems simple, but as the story unfolds, it becomes clear that the apparently simple event has many layers. It is not so much that Martiniano has broken the white man's law, but that his insistence on his own independence of action indicates an inner disharmony and a lack of wisdom. It indicates, finally, a lack of connection with the mystery of life itself. In place of this connection is a belief that a person can be free when alone, when cut off from society or the Earth, from the source of faith, symbolized by the lake in the mountains above the pueblo, "The Blue Eye of Faith," the center of pueblo's religious-ceremonial life.

The deer that Martiniano has killed becomes for him a totem, appearing to him in various places and guises to demonstrate that there is something in his situation that he cannot defeat by confrontation, something that he first must understand, to which he must submit. Eventually, the deer appears in his wife, Flowers Playing; as she grows with child, with the mystery of life, Martiniano begins to lose connection with her.

Martiniano learns, slowly, that even his own sense of manhood is held in bondage to the feminine part of his being, and that until he reconciles this polarity, he will never feel fully alive. This is best symbolized by the description of the Deer Dance (in a passage found in both *The Man Who Killed the Deer* and *Masked Gods: Navaho and Pueblo Ceremonialism*). Flower Playing is one of the Deer Mothers in the ceremony, the embodiment of the mystery of organic life. The Deer Dance symbolizes how the male force of independence and escape is held bondage, unwillingly but necessarily, by "the female imperative," the rhythms of Earth that are deeper than the ego. The dance offers another vantage on the spirit of place, here appearing as the "blood power" from which man can never break free, and upon which he is dependent for the development of wisdom.

There is another sense in which Martiniano's action was not done in isolation: his killing of the deer has repercussions that are felt in the wider sphere of politics. It has made more difficult the pueblo's case for restoration of Dawn Lake. As the pueblo elders point out again and again, one man's action is like a pebble dropped into a pool; the ripples extend far beyond the action itself. The effort of the elders enables Martiniano to see that much wider whole, of which he is an integral part, and without which he is an incomplete human being.

The pueblo elders embody a different way of knowing from that of the white race which has control of the lake. The polarity is rational-linear opposing nonrational, nonlinear. The method of the elders is intuitive, and, while it does not deny the validity of rational methods (any more than the female imperative denies the validity of the male drive for independence), it does indicate a deeper level of wisdom. The elders know the eventual result of their legal disputes over Dawn Lake far before these results come over the telegraph, even when all indications (relayed, of course, over the telegraph) point to the futility of their case.

To the elders—as, it seems, to Waters himself—linear or rational knowledge is not as encompassing or effective as the more intuitive method which comes so naturally to the Indians. The difference between these two methods of knowing is a duality to which Waters returns in later books, particularly *The Woman at Otowi Crossing*. It is interesting to note, in this context, that just as the pueblo elders correctly predicted that they would regain their Dawn Lake, so Waters himself, in his novel, predicted the actual political event; for just as in the novel the Indians regain rights to their lake, so, thirty years later, did they do so in fact, through a congressional decision in December of 1970.

Waters' next novel, *The Yogi of Cockroach Court*, takes the working of polarities one step further to juxtapose Eastern mysticism (particularly Buddhist) to life in a Mexican border town. Sociologically, Waters is here concerned with the Mestizo culture. Barby is an example of this type. Orphaned as a child, he is brought up by Tai Ling, who runs a small shop, The Lamp Awake, beside the prostitute district, Cockroach Court. The name of the shop itself introduces the duality of light and dark, associated respectively with the clarity of the mind and the darkness of the senses. Tai Ling is repeatedly pictured meditating by his lamp, amid the swirl of a violent, dark world.

Barby and Guadalupe (Barby's lover, and another person of mixed blood) cannot detach themselves from that dark world, which to Tai Ling is the result of blindness, the working out of karma. Their relationship is a tempestuous one, fueled by Barby's impotent desire for control. This impotence results from Barby's rootless feeling of inferiority, from his inner division. Where Barby is at the mercy of his internal division, Guadalupe is at the mercy of external ones. In the daytime, she is alive in the absorption in her own physical vitality; at night, she comes under the domination of Barby.

These complexities are interwoven with the life of Tai Ling, whose lamp illumines the darkness of the physical world in which he sits, even as his search for a way to transcend the play of polarities illumines the darkness of his mind. Inherent in Tai Ling's search for transcendence, however, is yet another polarity: The life of transcendence is itself polarized with life in a physical body. In this way, Tai Ling is still involved in duality, or karma, and in the end, just as Barby cannot dominate Guadalupe except in darkness, so Tai Ling cannot subdue the ongoing karma of the physical world until the darkness of death surrounds him.

Both Barby and Tai Ling bring about their own deaths by attempts to conquer the physical world. The difference between them is nevertheless a significant one: Barby dies while blinded by passion, aggression, and ignorance; Tai Ling, whose mind is clearer, finally sees and accepts his inner polarity, accepts his karma and his situation, and sees the folly of trying to transcend the world by separating oneself from it. Tai Ling, therefore, achieves a reconciliation, and though it comes at the moment of death, there is great hope in it, as Tai Ling finally comes to a unity with his world, comes to true knowledge.

Tai Ling's realization is not a rational one. He uses rationality to dissect his ego, but his realization is intuitive. He speaks of the difference between those who see that life's journey is a spiral and those whose vision is so limited that the curve of the spiral seems a straight line. To men of unconsidered action, whose vision is limited to the rational, horizontal plane, all seems linear, not cyclic. The man of contemplation, however, sees the nonlinear nature of things which underlies the linear but does not negate it. Thus, the treatment of two ways of knowing is here given an additional perspective.

The Yogi of Cockroach Court was published in 1947. *The Woman at Otowi Crossing*, Waters' next novel, was published in 1966. The intervening years saw the publication of *Masked Gods*, *The Earp Brothers of Tombstone: The Story of Mrs. Virgil Earp*, *Leon Gaspard*, and *Book of the Hopi*. In addition, Waters had worked as the editor of a local newspaper and at the Los Alamos Scientific Laboratory as a consultant. His deepening knowledge of and feeling for Pueblo traditions, as well as his firsthand knowledge of the activities at Los Alamos, are both brought to expression in the later novel.

The Woman at Otowi Crossing deals primarily with Anglos and thus completes the cycle of novels dealing with racial types. It also brings many of Waters' concerns into a contemporary focus. As in previous books, the action develops out of the tension between polarities. The developing, intuitive awareness of Helen Chalmers is juxtaposed to the development of the atomic bomb on the mesa above her. Both developments signal man's evolutionary potential, and both involve the unification of matter and energy.

Helen Chalmers has come from a broken marriage to operate a small teahouse at the edge of Pueblo Indian land. Coincident with the beginning of the Los Alamos Research Laboratory—called "The Project"—she discovers a growth on her breast. Her assumption that it is cancerous, and the resultant immediacy of death, triggers in her a chain reaction of explosively expanding awareness, an explosion which radically alters her view of the world around her and her relationship with it.

The scene of Helen's discovery ends with Facundo, a member of the pueblo kiva, tossing pebbles against her window. The moment is significant, for in the kiva, the Indians continue their attempt to understand and ensure the unity of matter with energy, or spirit. Facundo's response to Helen's condition is one of immediate comprehension, but his response is undramatic. He simply points to the sun, the source of life, empowered by the same unity of energy and matter that the men of the project seek to harness. Facundo's emphasis, however, is on the presence of that process, that reality, in each moment.

Thus, Helen's task becomes what will eventually become the task of everyone: to integrate her newfound knowledge with the tangible events of her life. The discovery of the bomb requires the same integration; the two discoveries together create a new world order in which one must learn to live. Again, the methods of the Indians point the way to reconciliation, for they have shown how the development of insight and the knowledge of the unity of matter and spirit can be integrated into, and are in fact a necessary part of, a stable, viable society.

Waters draws a number of additional parallels between the activities of the Pueblo kiva and those of the project. Both are shrouded in secrecy, and both have their selected initiates who take on new identities vis à vis the rest of their society. (Members of the kiva take on the identity of cosmic forces; men of the project take on new, common names: Niels Bohr becomes Nicholas Baker.) Both kiva and project exclude women, and in both there is an attempt to empower the mystery of life, to make use of the unity within duality represented by matter and energy, matter and spirit. (These parallels echo Waters' speculations in *Masked Gods*, where he writes of the common search of all people, whether in a Tibetan monastery, an Indian kiva, or an atomic research laboratory.)

Along with these parallels, however, the book demonstrates obvious differences as well. Primary among these is that the rituals of the Pueblo are to ensure the ongoing life of all creatures, whereas the activity of the project is directed toward death. The method of the kiva, being intuitive and nonrational, includes and embraces polarity, whereas the method of the project, being rational, divides one entity from another. Even this polarity, however, can result in a reconciliation, not in the external world, necessarily, but within the individual heart. The scientists involved in creating the bomb are presented in warm, human terms. Gaylord, a young scientist and the lover of Helen Chalmers' daughter, comes to a more intuitive, even mystical awareness as a result of his overexposure to radiation.

Pike's Peak is a kind of summing up of Waters' work. This may be understood literally, because the novel is a rewritten and shortened version of three early novels, the titles of which are retained as major divisions of the new novel. It may also be understood symbolically, because in its panoramic scope, *Pike's Peak* encompasses many of Waters' lifelong concerns.

Joseph Rogier, the protagonist, is largely a fictionalized version of Waters' grandfather; Waters himself, like the character March (grandson of Rogier, and part Indian), spent much of his youth in the mining camps of Cripple Creek, went to college as an engineering student, and worked in the Salt Creek oil fields. The novel transcends the category of autobiographical fiction, however, because of Waters' use of symbolism, in particular that of Pikes Peak itself, which stands as both tangible fact and intangible symbol. A mystery to be understood, an ungraspable meaning which one feels impelled to grasp, it stands at the borderline between the conscious and the unconscious, at once numinous and tangible.

The peak both draws and repels Rogier, who seeks within it for its golden heart. The pull is irresistible, and in his effort to plumb the peak, Rogier slowly lets go of all his social responsibilities. His building firm deteriorates; his family becomes near destitute; he loses the respect of the community and becomes an object of mockery. His search is an obsession, not for mere gold, and not for riches (though he is not above their temptation), but for the symbolic golden heart, within himself as it is within Pikes Peak, shining in the center of the dense granite, or in the center of the flesh.

The method of his search combines the rational and the irrational. The obsession is irrational, and at its service he places his considerable rational gifts and material wealth. Yet, despite his knowledge of engineering and geology, he cannot strike a significant vein, while men of lesser knowledge, and without his material resources, make seemingly lucky strikes, literally at the drop of a hat. Rogier's situation has parallels to that of Martiniano, for he, like Rogier, finds something in his search that he cannot conquer by rational means or external manipulation. Rogier's attempts to find gold—symbolic or literal—lead him increasingly deeper into darkness and isolation. Like the deer for Martiniano, the peak for Rogier becomes a sort of totem, appearing as a lure, as a guide, or as an obstacle—a truth he cannot grasp, but which is constantly within his sight.

The tragedy of Rogier is that his view of the world is linear. As a miner, he has literal and symbolic tunnel vision. By going straight ahead, mining a vertical shaft, he hopes to find the essence of the mystery symbolized by the mountain itself. Its apparent tangibility as real gold draws him irresistibly, but Rogier's linear viewpoint blinds him to the world around him, isolating him from the sympathies and understanding of his family. His search for truth takes place at the expense of human warmth and community, and he finds, as does Martiniano, that such obsessive pride—even if it seems to be a search for truth—is doomed to futility. Where Martiniano is finally able to understand his folly and arrange for his son to enter the kiva and so live in the harmony it had taken him so long to achieve, Rogier dies in psychological isolation, unable to release his passion into genuine human community.

For all that, however, the tragedy contains a triumph. March, Rogier's grandson, carries on a search encompassing many of Rogier's ideals. Of mixed blood, March shows promise of reconciling the intuitive ways of his Indian blood with the rational methods of his grandfather. Despite himself, Rogier has passed on to March a profound respect for depth and knowledge; one feels for him a deep sympathy, because for all his gruffness, even his selfishness, he has somehow managed to give March a profound respect for enduring value, and the determination to search for it, for the enduring gold within the dense rock of material being.

The search for eternal value in the midst of flux is a final polarity. Tai Ling sought it in his meditation, Maria found it in her inseparability from natural cycles; even Martiniano found it by acquiescing to the Pueblo's ways. For Helen Chalmers, the search was for a way to integrate eternal value into the apparently mundane particulars of everyday living. Thus, even the discovery of eternal verities is not a final resting point. The eternal is continually juxtaposed to and interwoven with the mundane, and just as the action of the novels is given impetus by this polarity, so the movement of the world both rises from it and expresses it. As each new layer is peeled off, new polarities emerge.

Waters' writing is a continuing attempt to penetrate and illuminate these symbolic and literal layers, and to find within movement the enduring values of human life. His characters seek these values within the temporal, within enduring change, the first cause and final truth. Thus, in Waters' novels, the Nahuatl hieroglyph "Ollin" comes to literary expression: that eternal movement comes from the tension between polarities. The reconciliation between polarities is found in the movement of tangible existence—in concrete substance, not abstract form; in the harmony within activity that expresses harmony with greater cycles, such as those of society, of one's locale, or of the Earth. In this sense, the expression of the spirit of place is an expression of the unity of mankind, for all are subject to the same enduring, cyclic existence. In a wider sense, Waters' writing is rightly considered mystical, concerned with the oneness of man with others, with the Earth, with all that exists.

Tim Lyons

Other major works

NONFICTION: *Midas of the Rockies: The Story of Stratton and Cripple Creek*, 1937; *The Colorado*, 1946; *Masked Gods: Navaho and Pueblo Ceremonialism*, 1950; *The Earp Brothers of Tombstone: The Story of Mrs. Virgil Earp*, 1960; *Book of the Hopi*, 1963; *Leon Gaspard*, 1964; *Pumpkin Seed Point: Being Within the Hopi*, 1969; *To Possess the Land: A Biography of Arthur*

Rochford Manby, 1973; *Mexico Mystique: The Coming Sixth World of Consciousness*, 1975; *Mountain Dialogues*, 1981.

Bibliography

Adams, Charles L. "Frank Waters." In *A Literary History of the American West*. Fort Worth: Texas Christian University Press, 1987. Waters' writing is analyzed as a product of his fascination with the power of place in human development. The challenge of his fiction was to master historical detail in the exploration of his themes, as in *The Man Who Killed the Deer*. His later books, beginning with *The Colorado*, expand on his theme of the relationship between land and people and deepen his analysis of the psyche. Claims that his study of Hopi culture strengthens his work in all genres and calls *Mexico Mystique* a synthesis of his themes, subjects, and symbols. Includes a selected primary bibliography and an annotated bibliography of secondary sources.

_____. "The Genesis of *Flight From Fiesta*." *Western American Literature* 22 (Fall, 1987): 195-200. The evolution of Waters' fiction prevents a simple explanation of the chronological development of his style and themes. For example, *Flight from Fiesta* was originally written in 1957 as a film called "The Flight" which was never made. Waters rewrote it much later, creating new characters to enrich the simple chase formula of the script. The expanded narrative shows Waters' deepening awareness of the allegorical potential of the relationship between White and Indian races, clearly reflected in the character of Inocencio.

Davis, Jack L. "The Whorf Hypothesis and Native American Literature." *South Dakota Review* 14 (Summer, 1976): 59-72. Benjamin Lee Whorf's notion of linguistic relativity, that perception is determined by the structure of language, is tested by analyzing Waters' *The Man Who Killed the Deer* in comparison to N. Scott Momaday's *House Made of Dawn*. Waters' plot represents the great gap between white and Native American cultures and parallels Whorf's conclusion drawn from a study of Hopi language. The difference between Whorf and Waters is Waters' emphasis on the nonverbal dimensions of pueblo consciousness which become mystical and communal. Like Momaday, Waters believes that great change is required for Western civilization to discover a fellowship through the nonverbal experience in pueblo culture.

Hoy, Christopher. "The Archetypal Transformation of Martiniano in *The Man Who Killed the Deer*." *South Dakota Review* 13 (Winter, 1975-1976): 43-56. The character Martiniano must undergo a fundamental psychological change to reconcile the conflict between his newly acquired white values and his native ones which occurs when he tries to return to his pueblo culture. This change can be explained in reference to the archetype of the Great Mother, as developed by Carl Jung and Erich Neumann.

Lyon, Thomas J. *Frank Waters*. New York: Twayne, 1973. Fills a critical vacuum by analyzing Waters' themes and artistic style. After sketching Waters' life, Lyon examines his nonfiction, showing him to be a writer of ideas with a sacred theory of the earth and Hopi mythic values. Focuses on seven novels as narrations of these ideas, from *Fever Pitch* to *Pike's Peak*, and also discusses his minor works, including the biography of *The Earp Brothers of Tombstone*, the children's biography of Robert Gilruth, his book reviews, and his essays on writing. The last chapter summarizes the book's thesis and calls for more study of Waters' work. Contains a chronology, notes and references, a selected annotated bibliography, and an index.

Malpezzi, Frances. "A Study of the Female Protagonist in Frank Waters' *People of the Valley* and Rudolfo Anaya's *Bless Me, Ultima*." *South Dakota Review* 14 (Summer, 1976): 102-110. These two novels portray stereotypical *machismo* cultures and also present positive images of women, such as Maria in *People of the Valley*. Maria is respected for her authority and power, grows stronger with age, and displays dignity in her acceptance of death. She arranges the migration of her people and prepares her own spiritual migration. A heroic and inspiring person, Maria is an example of an androgynous character liberated from stereotype.

South Dakota Review 15 (Autumn, 1977). A special Frank Waters issue, containing the essays: "The Sound of Space," by John Milton; "Frank Waters' *Mexico Mystique*: The Ontology of the Occult," by Jack L. Davis; "Frank Waters and the Visual Sense," by Robert Kostka; "Frank Waters and the Concept of 'Nothing Special,'" by Thomas J. Lyon; "Teaching *Yoga* in Las Vegas," by Charles L. Adams; "Frank Waters and the Mountain Spirit," by Quay Grigg; "The Conflict in *The Man Who Killed the Deer*," by Christopher Hoy; "Mysticism and Witchcraft," by Waters; and "Frank Waters," by John Manchester.

EVELYN WAUGH

Born: London, England; October 28, 1903
Died: Combe Florey, England; April 10, 1966

Principal long fiction

Decline and Fall, 1928; *Vile Bodies*, 1930; *Black Mischief*, 1932; *A Handful of Dust*, 1934; *Scoop*, 1938; *Put Out More Flags*, 1942; *Brideshead Revisited*, 1945, 1959; *Scott-King's Modern Europe*, 1947; *The Loved One*, 1948; *Helena*, 1950; *Men at Arms*, 1952; *Love Among the Ruins: A Romance of the Near Future*, 1953; *Officers and Gentlemen*, 1955; *The Ordeal of Gilbert Pinfold*, 1957; *The End of the Battle*, 1961 (also known as *Unconditional Surrender*); *Basil Seal Rides Again: Or, The Rake's Regress*, 1963; *Sword of Honour*, 1965 (includes *Men at Arms, Officers and Gentlemen*, and *The End of the Battle*).

Other literary forms

Evelyn Waugh wrote seven travel books, three biographies, an autobiography, and numerous articles and reviews. The only completed section of Waugh's planned three-volume autobiography, *A Little Learning* (1964), discusses his life at Oxford and his employment as a schoolmaster in Wales—subjects fictionalized in *Brideshead Revisited* and *Decline and Fall*. The autobiographical background for virtually all of Waugh's novels is evident in his travel books, his diaries, and his letters. His articles and reviews for English and American periodicals include a wide range of topics—politics, religion, and art—and contribute to his reputation as a literary snob, an attitude Waugh himself affected especially in the 1940's and 1950's.

Achievements

Waugh was esteemed primarily as a satirist, especially for his satires on the absurdly chaotic world of the 1920's and 1930's. His ability to make darkly humorous the activities of the British upper class, his comic distance, and his vivid, at times brutal satire made his early novels very popular among British and American literary circles. His shift to a more sentimental theme in *Brideshead Revisited* gave Waugh his first real taste of broad popular approval—especially in America—to which he reacted with sometime real, sometime exaggerated snobbishness. Waugh's conservative bias after the war, his preoccupation with religious themes, and his expressed distaste for the "age of the common man" suggested to a number of critics that he had lost his satiric touch. Although his postwar novels lack the anarchic spirit of his earliest works, he is still regarded, even by those who reject his political attitudes, as a first-rate craftsman of the comic novel.

Biography

Evelyn Arthur St. John Waugh was born in Hampstead, a suburb of London, in 1903 to Arthur and Catherine Waugh. He attended Lancing College from 1917 to 1924 and Hertford College, Oxford from 1921 to 1924, from which he left without taking a degree. Although Waugh turned to writing novels only after aborted careers as a draftsman, a schoolmaster, and a journalist, his family background was literary; his father directed Chapman and Hall publishers until 1929, and his older brother Alec published his first novel, *The Loom of Youth*, in 1917.

Waugh's years at Oxford and his restless search for employment during the 1920's brought him experiences which were later fictionalized in several of his novels. After leaving Oxford in 1924, he enrolled in the Heatherley School of Fine Art, where he aspired to be a draftsman; later in that year, he was apprenticed to a printer for a brief period. His employment as a schoolmaster in Wales in 1925 and in Buckinghamshire in 1926 formed the background for his first novel, *Decline and Fall*. His struggle to establish himself as a writer and his participation in the endless parties of London's aristocratic youth during the last years of the 1920's are fictionalized in his second novel, *Vile Bodies*.

In 1927, Waugh was engaged to Evelyn Gardner and, despite the objections of her family, married her in 1928 when his financial prospects seemed more secure after the publication of his life of Dante Gabriel Rossetti and his first novel. In 1929, while Waugh was working in seclusion on *Vile Bodies*, his wife announced that she was having an affair; the couple, temperamentally unsuited to each other, were divorced that year.

The next seven years of Waugh's life were a period of activity and travel. Two trips to Africa in 1930 and 1931 resulted in a travel book and provided Waugh with the background of *Black Mischief*. A journey through Brazil and British Guiana in 1932 resulted in another travel book and his fourth novel, *A Handful of Dust*. In addition, Waugh traveled to the Artic and once more to Africa; he was a correspondent for the London *Times*, reviewed books for *The Spectator*, and wrote a biography of Edmund Campion, a British-Catholic martyr. During this unsettled period, Waugh converted to Roman Catholicism in 1930, an event which provided much of the stability of his later life. In 1933, he met Laura Herbert, a Catholic, whom he married in 1937, after securing an annulment of his previous marriage from the Catholic Church.

Waugh's experiences during World War II are fictionalized in *Put Out More Flags* and the *Sword of Honour* trilogy. After several months unsuccessfully seeking military employment, Waugh joined the Royal Marines in 1939 and was part of an ineffectual assault on Dakar in 1940. Later in 1940, Waugh joined a commando unit with which he served in the Middle East, taking part in the battle of Crete in 1942. In 1943, after an injury in parachute training, Waugh was forced to resign from the commandos and, in 1944, he was granted military leave to write *Brideshead Revisited*. In the last year of the war, he served as a liaison officer with the British Military Mission in Yugoslavia, where he struggled against the persecution of Roman Catholics by the partisan government.

Waugh's life from 1945 to 1954 was relatively stable. The success of *Brideshead Revisited*, a Book-of-the-Month-Club selection in America, brought him moderate financial security and several offers from filmmakers. Although none of these film offers materialized, they resulted in the trip to Hollywood in 1947 that inspired *The Loved One*, and in several commissioned articles for *Life*. During this nine-year period, Waugh published four short novels and the first volume of the World War II trilogy. In the first three months of 1954, on a voyage to Ceylon, Waugh suffered the mental breakdown that he later fictionalized in *The Ordeal of Gilbert Pinfold*.

Waugh led a relatively reclusive life during the last ten years, avoiding the public contact that had made him notorious earlier. In this period, he finished the war trilogy, published a biography of Ronald Knox, another travel book on Africa, the first volume of his autobiography, a revision of *Brideshead Revisited*, and the recension of the war trilogy into a single volume; he also began several other projects which were never completed. Waugh died on Easter Day in 1966.

Analysis

Evelyn Waugh's novels are distinguished by the narrative detachment with which they survey the madness and chaos of the modern age. His characters participate in a hopeless, often brutal struggle for stability which hardens them to the absurdities of civilization and leads them, ultimately, to an unheroic retreat from the battle of life. Ironic detachment, thus, is Waugh's principal comic technique and his principal theme as well.

Because each of Waugh's novels reflects actual experiences, the nature of this detachment changes through the course of his career. In his early works, which satirize the havoc and instability of the 1920's and 1930's, he achieves comic detachment by splicing together the savage and the settled, the careless and the care-ridden, the comic and the tragic. Victims and victimizers alike are caught in the whirlwind of madness. Waugh's satiric method changes in his postwar novels: comically ineffectual characters still wage battle against the absurdities of life, but one is more aware of their struggle to maintain or recapture spiritual and moral values amid the absurdity. Waugh maintains comic distance in these novels by recommending a quiet sort of spiritual heroism as the only source of man's happiness in the uncertain postwar world.

Waugh's first novel, *Decline and Fall*, traces the misadventures of Paul Pennyfeather, a temperate, unassuming student of theology at Scone College, Oxford. He is "sent down" for indecent behavior when drunken members of the university's most riotous (and, ironically, most aristocratic) club assault him, forcing him to run the length of the quadrangle without his trousers. Like Voltaire's *Candide*, Pennyfeather is an innocent victim temperamentally ill-suited for the world into which he is thrust. Indeed, *Decline and Fall* owes much to *Candide* (1759): its Menippean satire, its cyclical "resurrection" of secondary characters, and the hero's ultimate resignation from life.

The action itself provides a thin framework for Waugh's satire on modern life. Pennyfeather finds employment, as Waugh himself did, as a schoolmaster in Wales—the only occupation, Pennyfeather is told, for a young man dismissed from the university for indecent behavior. At Llanabba Castle, he meets three characters with whose stories his own is interlaced: Grimes, a pederast and bigamist who pulls himself out of the continual "soup" he gets into by feigning suicide; Prendergast, a doubting cleric who becomes a "modern churchman" and is eventually murdered by a religious fanatic; and Philbrick, the school butler, a professed imposter, jewel-thief, and arsonist who manages to secure a continual life of luxury by his preposterous stories about his criminal life. At Llanabba, Pennyfeather also meets Margot Beste-Chetwynde, a rich socialite to whom he becomes engaged; he is arrested the afternoon of their wedding for unknowingly transporting girls to France for her international prostitution ring. His innocent association with Margot thus leads to his conviction for another act of "indecent behavior," this time leading to a prison sentence in Blackstone Gaol—a "modern" penal institution.

What strikes one about the novel is not the injustices served Pennyfeather, but the very madness of the world with which his innocence contrasts. Characters with criminal designs—Margot, Philbrick, and Grimes—are unaffected by changes in fortune; those in charge of social institutions—Dr. Fagan of Llanabba Castle, and Sir Lucas-Dockery of the experimental prison—are eccentrically out of touch with reality. Their absurdity, when contrasted with Pennyfeather's naïve struggle, defines Waugh's theme: the only sanity is to become cautiously indifferent to the chaos of modernism. At the end of the novel, when Pennyfeather returns to Oxford under a new identity and continues his study of the Early Church, he assumes the role of a spectator, not a participant, in the madness of life.

Although *Decline and Fall's* narrative structure is more derivative and its characters less fully rounded than those of Waugh's later novels, it displays techniques typical of his fiction at its best. The callous descriptions of the tragic—little Lord Tangent's death from Grimes's racing pistol or Prendergast's decapitation at Blackstone Gaol—and their fragmented interlacement into the plot are hallmarks of Waugh's comic detachment. Tangent's slow death from gangrene is presented through a series of casual offstage reports; the report of Prendergast's murder is incongruously worked into verses of a hymn sung in the prison chapel, "O God, our Help in Ages Past." The tragic and the savage are always sifted through an ironic filter in Waugh's novels, creating a brutal sort of pathos.

Waugh's fourth novel, *A Handful of Dust*, was his first to present a dynamically sympathetic protagonist. Pennyfeather, from *Decline and Fall*, and

Adam Symes, from *Vile Bodies*, attract one's interest largely because they provide a detached perspective from which one can observe the chaos of modern civilization. Basil Seal in *Black Mischief*, although a participating rogue, is amiable largely because of his comic disregard for the mischief he makes. Tony Last of *A Handful of Dust*, however, is a fully sympathetic character as well as a pathetic victim of the modern wasteland to which the title alludes. Unlike Paul Pennyfeather, Tony is not simply an observer of social chaos: his internal turmoil is set against the absurdity of external events, and in that respect, his quest for lost values anticipates that of Charles Ryder in *Brideshead Revisited* and of Guy Crouchback in *Sword of Honour*.

Waugh's theme is the decadence of tradition, emblematized, as it is in many of Waugh's novels, by the crumbling estates of the aristocracy. Tony's futile effort to maintain his Victorian Gothic estate, Hetton Abbey, thus symbolizes his struggle throughout the plot. He is wedded to the outmoded tradition of Victorian country gentlemen, while his wife, Brenda, embraces the social life of London. She eventually cuckolds Tony by having an affair with the parasitic John Beaver, whose mother, an interior decorator, sees in her son's affair an opportunity to "modernize" Hetton with chromium plating and sheepskin carpeting.

The pathos one feels for Tony is ultimately controlled by the absurd contexts into which Waugh sets the pathetic scenes. When his son, John Andrew, dies in a riding accident, Tony is left emotionally desolate, yet the cause of the accident is ironic; John Andrew's horse is startled by a backfiring motorcycle, a modern "horse." Later, one is made brutally aware of the irony of Tony's grief when one learns of Brenda's initial rection to the news of her son's death: she assumes it was John Beaver, her lover, not John Andrew, her son, who died. In the same way, Tony's later divorce from Brenda empties him of values he traditionally respected. He consents to the legal convention that he should give evidence of his infidelity, even if his wife has been the unfaithful partner. His evidence incongruously turns into an uncomfortable weekend with a prostitute and her daughter at Brighton, and the absurdity of this forced and inconsummate infidelity further defines Tony's loneliness. Ironically, it provides him with a means to deny an exorbitant divorce settlement that would force him to sell Hetton Abbey.

In the end, Tony searches for his Victorian Gothic City in the jungles of South America and suffers a delirium in which his civilized life at Hetton Abbey is distorted; these are made comically pathetic by interlaced scenes of Brenda in London trying to regain the civilized life she lost in her estrangement from Tony. Ultimately, she does not find in London the city she sought, nor does Tony in South America. Tony does find, instead, an aberration of his vision; he is held captive by an illiterate who forces him to read aloud from Charles Dickens's novels in perpetuity.

Perhaps Waugh's emotional reaction to his own divorce from Evelyn Gardner prior to the publication of the novel accounts for the increase of pathos in *A Handful of Dust*. Perhaps Waugh realized that thinness of characterization in his earlier novels could lead only to stylistic repetition without stylistic development. Whatever the reason, this novel depicts characters struggling for moral equilibrium in a way that no previous Waugh novel had done.

Brideshead Revisited is different from Waugh's earlier novels in two important ways. First, it is the only novel Waugh finished which employs the first-person point of view. (He had attempted the first person in *Work Suspended* in 1942, but either the story itself faltered, or Waugh could not achieve a sufficient narrative detachment to complete it.) Second, *Brideshead Revisited* was the first novel in which Waugh explicitly addressed a Roman Catholic theme: the mysterious workings of divine grace in a small aristocratic Catholic family. As a result, it is Waugh's most sentimental and least funny novel. Although it departed radically from his earlier satires, it was Waugh's most popular and financially successful work.

The narrative frame creates much of what is sentimental in the novel but also provides a built-in detachment. Charles Ryder's love for Sebastian Flyte during his years at Oxford in the 1920's and for Julia Mottram, Sebastian's sister, a decade later, live vividly in Ryder's memories when he revisits the Brideshead estate during a wartime bivouac. His memories tell the story of Sebastian's and Julia's search for happiness, but because they are remembered by an emotionally desolate Ryder, the novel is a study of his spiritual change as well.

Before he meets Sebastian, Ryder is a serious-minded Oxford undergraduate, not unlike Paul Pennyfeather at the end of *Decline and Fall*. Like Pennyfeather, he is drawn into a world for which he is unprepared, yet, unlike Waugh's earlier protagonist, Ryder is enthralled by a make-believe world of beauty and art. The Arcadian summer Ryder spends with Sebastian at Brideshead and in Venice are the most sumptuously written passages in any of Waugh's novels, reflecting—as Waugh admitted in his 1959 revision of the novel—the dearth of sensual pleasures available at the time of its composition. The change in style also reflects a change in theme. Sebastian's eccentricities about his stuffed bear, his coterie of homosexual "aesthetes," and his refusal to take anything seriously would have been the object of satire in Waugh's earlier novels. In *Brideshead Revisited*, however, the absurdities are sifted through the perspective of a narrator aware of his own desperate search for love. When Sebstian's make-believe turns to alcoholism, the narrator himself becomes cynically indifferent.

Ryder's love for Julia ten years after he has left Brideshead is an attempt to rediscover the happiness he lost with Sebastian. One is more aware, in this second half of the narration, of Ryder's cynicism and of the discontentment which that cynicism hides. When he and Julia fall in love on a transatlantic voyage back to England, they are both escaping marriages to spouses whose worldly ambitions offer no nourishment for the spiritual emptiness each feels. Julia's return to the Church after the deathbed repentance of her father causes Ryder to realize that he has fathomed as little about Julia's faith as he had about Sebastian's. The narration itself thus ends on a note of unhappiness which recalls the separtion of Ryder and Sebastian. In the epilogue following Ryder's memories, however, Waugh makes it clear that the narrator himself has converted to Catholicism in the intervening years. Ryder sees in the sanctuary light of the chapel at Brideshead the permanence he sought with Sebastian and Julia and finds contentment, if not hope for the future.

It is easy to overstress the religious implications of the novel. Indeed, many critics find Julia's hysteria about sin, Lord Marchmain's return to the Church, and Ryder's conversion strained. Some, such as Edmund Wilson, see the novel as an adulation of the British upper classes. *Brideshead Revisited*, however, is less a Roman Catholic novel than it is a lament for the past and a study in spiritual and artistic awakening. It was a turning point in Waugh's fiction: his novels after *Brideshead Revisited* dealt less with the absurdity of life and more with the spiritual values that have disappeared as a result of the war.

Perhaps the grimmest of Waugh's satires, *The Loved One* presents a sardonic vision of American culture. Its principal satiric target is Forest Lawn Memorial Park—a place that in many ways served for Waugh as the epitome of American pretensions to civilization. In "Half in Love with Easeful Death," an essay Waugh wrote for *Life* in 1947 after his visit to Hollywood, Waugh describes Forest Lawn as it would appear to archaeologists in the next millennium: a burlesque necropolis, like the tombs of the Pharoahs in its aspirations, but, in fact, the product of a borrowed, devalued culture. His version of Forest Lawn, Whispering Glades, is a distorted wonderland in which the cosmetic and the artifical substitute for beauty and in which banality is glorified and substitutes for the poetic vision.

It is fitting that the protagonist, Dennis Barlow, be a poet—even though an unproductive one who has been seduced to Hollywood by a consultantship with Megalo Studios. Like many of Waugh's other protagonists, he is the filter through whom one sees absurdities satirized. Like Basil Seal in *Black Mischief* and *Put Out More Flags*, he is an opportunist, flexible enough to engineer a profit for himself out of the chaotic world into which he is thrust. His vision is grimly sardonic, however, in a way that even Seal's is not.

When he first enters Whispering Glades, he is intrigued, as Seal would be, by its absurd glamour and by the potential of using that glamour to improve his own position at The Happier Hunting Grounds, a pet mortuary where he is employed. Whispering Glades, however, has a far deeper attraction; it would be the kind of place, if it were real, that would appeal to any poet, but Barlow is enchanted by its very fraudulence. At the man-made Lake Isle of Innisfree (complete with mechanized humming bees), Barlow falls in love with a mortuary cosmetician and enchants her by the very fact that he is a poet. The enchantment is false, just as everything is at Whispering Glades; he sends her plagarized verses from *The Oxford Book of English Verse* and pledges his troth to her by reciting a stanza from Robert Burns's "A Red, Red Rose" at The Lover's Nook near the Wee Kirk o' Auld Lang Syne.

If plagarism lies at the heart of Barlow's involvement at Whispering Glades, it also lies at the heart of Whispering Glades itself and the characters who work there—even though the place and the people are possessed by the utmost seriousness. The girl with whom Barlow falls in love is named Aimee Thanatogenos. Although she professes to be named after Aimee McPherson—the American huckster of religion whom Waugh satirized in *Vile Bodies*—her given name and her surname both translate into the euphemism that embodies all of Whispering Glades's false coating: "The loved one." Her enchantment with Barlow eventually takes the form of a burlesque tragedy. She is torn between Barlow and the head mortician, Mr. Joyboy—a poet of a different sort, whose special art is preparing infant corpses.

Aimee's tragedy results from a bizarre sequence of events, comic in its effects. When she discovers Joyboy's mother-fixation and Barlow's fraudulence, she seeks advice from her oracle, the Guru Brahmin, an advice columnist. When the Guru, Mr. Slump—fired from his job and in an alcoholic funk—advises Aimee to jump off a roof, she kills herself in the more poetic environment of Whispering Glades. Her suicide by drinking embalming fluid gives a doubly ironic force to her name and to the title of the novel. The tragedy ends with a darkly humorous catharsis. Joyboy, fearful that Aimee's death on his table might mar his lofty position at Whispering Glades, consents to Barlow's extortion and to Barlow's plan to cremate their beloved Aimee at The Happier Hunting Grounds. The novel's conclusion, thus, strikes the grimmest note of all: Barlow sits idly by, reading a cheap novel, while the heroine—a burlesque Dido—burns in the furnace.

In some ways, *The Loved One* is atypical of Waugh's postwar novels. In *Scott-King's Modern Europe*, and the *Sword of Honour* trilogy, Waugh turns his satiric eye on political issues. *The Loved One*, however much it satirizes American values, transcends topical satire. Barlow lacks the spiritual potential of Charles Ryder in *Brideshead Revisited*, even though he displays Ryder's callousness. Barlow is an artist in search of beauty, but he leaves California, ironically, with an artist's load far different from what he expected. It is the view of an ironist, like Waugh himself, who could hardly make a better travesty of Whispering Glades than it makes of itself.

The *Sword of Honour* trilogy, like *Brideshead Revisited*, is infused with a predominantly religious theme; it traces Guy Crouchback's awakening to spiritual honor—a more active form of spiritual growth than Charles Ryder experienced. Like *Brideshead Revisited*, *Sword of Honour* is more somber and more deliberately paced than Waugh's satires in the 1920's and 1930's, but it shares with his early works a detached satiric framework. Each volume is composed at a distance of ten or more years from its historical occurrence and, as a result, reflects a greater consciousness of the long-range implications of the absurdities presented.

Men at Arms concerns the chaos of Britain's first entry into the war, much like Waugh's wartime satire *Put Out More Flags*. One is immediately aware, however, of the difference in Waugh's detachment. *Put Out More Flags* was the product of a writer in his mid-thirties looking wryly at the days of peace from the middle of the war. Its protagonist, Basil Seal, is a mischief-making opportunist for whom greater chaos means greater fun and profit; the novel satirizes the madness of a world which leaves the characters trapped in the ever-changing insanity of war. *Men at Arms*, however, and, indeed, the entire trilogy, looks back from the perspective of the author's later middle age, with a sense of disappointment at the final results of the war. Appropriately enough, Guy is an innocent at the outset of the war, not a mischief-maker like Basil Seal. He is a middle-aged victim who is literally and figuratively cast into a battle for which he is ill-prepared.

Guy's heroic illusions are shattered in three successive stages through the separate volumes of the trilogy. *Men at Arms* concerns Guy's search for the self-esteem he lost eight years earlier after his divorce from his wife. As an officer-trainee in the Royal Corps of Halberdiers, Guy temporarily finds self-respect, but the elaborate traditions of the Halberdiers and his traineeship at commandeered prepatory schools causes Guy to revert to adolescence. His physical awkwardness, his jealousy of fellow trainees, his vanity about growing a mustache, his ineffectual attempt to seduce his former wife on Saint Valentine's Day, and the blot he receives on his military record at the end of the novel all seem more appropriate for a schoolboy than for an officer preparing to lead men into battle.

As in Waugh's earlier novels, the comedy of *Men at Arms* depends, not on the protagonist, but on the events and characters whom he encounters. Apthorpe, a middle-aged *miles gloriosus*, and Ben Ritchie-Hook, Guy's brigadier, represent two forms of the military insanity for which Guy trains. Apthorpe's preoccupation with boots, salutes, and his portable field latrine, the "Box," makes him an unlikely candidate for leading men into battle; Ritchie-Hook, whose only notion of military strategy is to attack, makes an elaborate game out of officer-training by booby-trapping Apthorpe's "Box"—a prank which causes Apthorpe to sink deeper into his madness. The confrontation between Apthorpe and Ritchie-Hook defines an absurd pattern which recurs later in the trilogy. Seeming madmen control the positions of power, and the protagonist is unwittingly drawn into their absurd worlds.

Officers and Gentlemen further trains Guy in the illogic of military life, this time focusing on the efforts of gentlemen soldiers to re-create the comforts of their London clubs during the war. The novel ends on a more somber note, however, than did *Men at Arms*. Guy finds temporary solace in the commando unit to which he is transferred after his disgrace as a Halberdier and believes again that he will find some honorable role to play in the war, but the British defeat at Crete at the end of this volume negates whatever notions of honor he entertained.

Even more than *Men at Arms*, *Officers and Gentlemen* relentlessly travesties espirit de corps and pretentions to heroism. Ian Kilbannock's gentlemanly service as a military journalist, for example, is to transform the ineffectual Trimmer into a propaganda hero for the common man. Julia Stitch's yacht, the *Cleopatra*, brings the comforts of the English social world to the Mediterranean war. The burrowing Grace-Groundling-Marchpole absurdly continues the secret file he began in *Men at Arms* about Guy's supposed counterintelligence activities. All of these events occur while England is suffering the first effects of German bombing and while the British disgrace at Crete looms ahead.

For a time, Guy imagines that the commandos are the "flower of England"; he even sees Ivor Claire as the ideal soldier, the kind of Englishman whom Hitler had not taken into account. The flower withers, however, in the chaotic retreat of British forces from Crete. Although Guy himself manages to maintain an even keel through most of the ordeal, the officers with whom he serves prove unheroic. His commander, "Fido" Hound, suffers a complete mental collapse in the face of the retreating troops; Ivor Claire, unable to face the prospect of surrendering, deserts his men and flees to India, where he is protected by his genteel birth. Eventually, Guy unheroically joins a boat escaping from the island and, exhausted, suffers a mental collapse. Guy initially resists Julia Stitch's efforts to cover up Claire's disgrace, but eventually destroys his own diary recording the orders to surrender when he learns that nothing will be done about Claire's desertion and when he learns of England's alliance with Russia. Unlike the first volume, the second volume ends with Guy's realization that he is an ineffectual player in a war that has lost a sense of honor.

It is curious to note that Waugh announced in the dust-jacket blurb for *Officers and Gentlemen* that, although he had planned the series for three volumes, he wanted his readers to regard it as finished with this second volume. The grimness of Guy's disillusionment thus sheds a somber light on Waugh's personal dilemma during the mid-1950's. After completing about a third of the draft of this second volume, Waugh suffered the mental collapse fictionalized in *The Ordeal of Gilbert Pinfold*. Guy's hallucination at the end of *Officers and Gentlemen* probably owes some of its vividness to the madness Waugh himself endured in 1954, and perhaps the numbness that affects Guy at the end of the novel reflects Waugh's own consciousness of his failing physical and mental powers.

Men at Arms and *Officers and Gentlemen* each deflate Guy's illusions about honor. *The End of the Battle* follows the same pattern in terms of wartime politics and in terms of Guy's military life, but in personal terms, Guy achieves a kind of unheroic, unselfish honor by the end of the novel. As a soldier, Guy accomplishes nothing heroic; even his efforts to liberate the Jewish refugees from partisan Yugoslavia is unsatisfying. Although most of the refugees are liberated, the leaders of the group—the Kanyis—are imprisoned and presumably executed. Guy's struggle with the Yugoslavian partisans and his disgust at Britain's alliance with the Communist-bloc countries further defines the dishonorable end that Guy and Waugh see in the war.

Unlike the two previous volumes, however, *The End of The Battle* ends on a note of tentative personal hopefulness, effected by Guy's renewed Roman Catholic faith. In the first two novels of the trilogy, Guy's religion lay dormant—a part of his life made purposeless since his divorce from Virginia. In *The End of The Battle*, the death of Guy's piously religious father causes Guy to realize that honor lies not in the "quantitative judgments" of military strategy, but in the spiritual salvation of individual souls. Guy's efforts to rescue the Yugoslavian Jews is selflessly honorable, even if ultimately futile. His remarriage to Virginia, who is pregnant with Trimmer's baby, is directed by the same sense of honor. Guy has little to gain emotionally from his remarriage; he does it for the preservation of the child's life and, implicitly, for the salvation of its soul. It is a different sort of heroism than he sought at the beginning of the war, possible only because Virginia has died.

Sword of Honour is, in many ways, a fitting climax to Waugh's literary career. It poignantly expresses his reverence for religious values yet recognizes the anomalous existence of those values in the modern world. It burlesques the eccentric and the absurd, yet moves beyond superficial satire to a more deeply rooted criticism of postwar politics. It displays Waugh's masterful ability to capture minor characters in brisk, economical strokes while working them thematically into the emotional composition of the protagonist. Waugh's importance as a novelist lay in his ability to achieve this kind of economy in a traditional form. He kept alive, in short, a tradition of the comic novel that reaches back to the eighteenth century.

James J. Lynch

Other major works

SHORT FICTION: *Mr. Loveday's Little Outing*, 1936; *Tactical Exercise*, 1954; *Charles Ryder's Schooldays and Other Stories*, 1982.

NONFICTION: *Rossetti: His Life and Works*, 1928; *Labels*, 1930; *Remote People*, 1931; *Ninety-Two Days*, 1934; *Edmund Campion: Jesuit and Martyr*, 1935; *Waugh in Abyssinia*, 1936; *Robbery Under the Law*, 1939; *The Holy Places*, 1952; *The Life of the Right Reverend Ronald Knox*, 1959; *Tourist in*

Africa, 1960; *A Little Learning*, 1964; *The Diaries of Evelyn Waugh*, 1976 (Christopher Sykes, editor); *The Letters of Evelyn Waugh*, 1980 (Mark Amory, editor).

Bibliography

Carens, James F., ed. *Critical Essays on Evelyn Waugh*. Boston: G. K. Hall, 1987. Contains twenty-six essays divided into three sections: general essays, essays on specific novels, and essays on Waugh's life and works. In his lengthy introduction, Carens provides a chronological overview of Waugh's literary work and a discussion of Waugh criticism. This well-indexed book also contains a bibliography of Waugh's writings and a selective list of secondary sources.

Cook, William J., Jr. *Masks, Modes, and Morals: The Art of Evelyn Waugh*. Rutherford, N.J.: Fairleigh Dickinson University Press, 1971. Considers Waugh's novels squarely in the ironic mode, tracing Waugh's development from satiric denunciation to comic realism to romantic optimism to ironic realism. Cook provides lengthy analyses of the novels, which he suggests move from fantasy to reality and from satire to resignation. Well-indexed and contains an excellent bibliograpy, which also lists articles.

Crabbe, Katharyn. *Evelyn Waugh*. New York: Continuum, 1988. Crabbe's book is most helpful: She provides a chronology of Waugh's life, a short biography, and five chapters of detailed criticism of Waugh's major novels. Crabbe reads *The Ordeal of Gilbert Pinfold* as an autobiographical novel. A concluding chapter on style is followed by a bibliography and a thorough index.

Davis, Robert Murray. *Evelyn Waugh: Writer*. Norman, Okla.: Pilgrim Books, 1981. Drawing from previously unavailable manuscript materials, Davis examines Waugh's fiction in terms of his artistic technique, his extensive revisions, and his reworking of his novels. After an opening chapter on Waugh's biography of Dante Gabriel Rossetti, Davis focuses exclusively on the novels, *Brideshead Revisited* and *Sword of Honour* in particular. Well-documented and well-indexed.

Lane, Calvin W. *Evelyn Waugh*. Boston: Twayne, 1981. Indispensable for Waugh scholars, Lane's relatively short volume contains a detailed chronology, a biography stressing the factors influencing his literary career, and lengthy treatments of Waugh's novels. Stresses Waugh's irony, satire, and conversion to Catholicism, which greatly influenced his fiction after 1930. Lane's selected bibliography contains articles, annotated book-length studies, and four interviews with Waugh.

Phillips, Gene D. *Evelyn Waugh's Officers, Gentlemen, and Rogues: The Fact Behind His Fiction*. Chicago: Nelson-Hall, 1975. Stresses the relationship between the real world and the world of Waugh's fiction. Drawing from Waugh's diaries, Phillips convincingly demonstrates the autobiographical content of Waugh's fiction. Each of Waugh's novels is analyzed in depth, with *Brideshead Revisited* considered his central novel. A selected bibliography lists many articles and books on Waugh.

Stannard, Martin. *Evelyn Waugh: The Early Years, 1903-1939.* New York: W. W. Norton, 1987. A scholarly, well-documented account of Waugh's early literary career, Stannard's biography provides valuable publication details about the novels and utilizes Waugh's diaries and letters. Also contains many photographs and illustrations, a genealogical chart of Waugh's ancestry, a selected bibliography, and an excellent index.